Philip Gould was polling and strategic adviser to Tony Blair and is now deputy chairman of Freud Communications. He is a visiting professor in media and politics at the London School of Economics and a member of the House of Lords. He lives with his wife Gail Rebuck in North London. They have two children.

THE UNFINISHED REVOLUTION

How New Labour Changed British Politics For Ever

PHILIP GOULD

ABACUS

ABACUS

First published in Great Britain as *The Unfinished Revolution:*
How the Modernisers Saved the Labour Party in 1998
by Little, Brown and Company
This edition published in 2011 by Abacus
Reprinted 2011, 2012

A CIP catalogue record for this book
is available from the British Library.

ISBN: 978-0-349-13857-2

Papers used by Abacus are from well-managed forests
and other responsible sources

MIX
Paper from
responsible sources
FSC
www.fsc.org   FSC® C104740

Typeset by
Palimpsest Book Production Limited
Falkirk, Stirlingshire
Printed and bound in Great Britain by
Clays Ltd, St Ives plc

Abacus
An imprint of
Little, Brown Book Group
100 Victoria Embankment
London EC4Y 0DY

An Hachette UK Company
www.hachette.co.uk

www.littlebrown.co.uk

For Georgia, Grace and Gail.

CONTENTS

FOREWORD

This new edition of *The Unfinished Revolution* has a brilliant analysis of aspects of our time in government that complements the earlier edition's description of the way we won power in 1997. In this foreword I focus on the fact that we are back in opposition again. However, Philip's reflections prompt some further ones of my own.

First, he rightly draws attention to the enormous creative force of the leading people, including Gordon Brown, in a way that is both typically generous of him and also serves to lighten what can sometimes seem an unalloyed story of tension and dysfunctionality. Actually more than that, there were times when the very tensions were themselves the product of deep policy issues over which it was right and natural there should be disagreement, and in respect of which out of the tension came solutions that kept the government together in the country's interests.

Secondly, there is something in the notion of the dialectical process of politics that Philip describes that illustrates where New Labour has to go today. The problems arising out of the financial crisis do raise critical questions about the relationship between, for example, the financial sector and the industrial base that will require a whole new engagement of inquiry and proposal. Likewise I think it clear that the issues of social exclusion – a segment of society set apart from the mainstream – remain largely unresolved. So there will be a set of new solutions and policy that arise as a result of the way in which the world is changing. My plea to my own party here is to make sure that these new solutions aren't old ones in disguise. But my own memo to myself is to recognise self-critically that there has to be change, and some recognition of what we got wrong as well as the pride in achievement.

Thirdly, one area where I completely agree with Philip, and which is a reproach to my leadership, is that in government I did not pay sufficient attention to continuing to build the party. There are a multitude of reasons for this – not least the enormous pressure of governing – but it was a fault. The truth is that building a modern party base is even more important in government. Also the way in which modern political parties need to function has to take account of the very different way people lead their lives today.

Finally, in the way Philip recounts the various crises and swings of government, there is an interesting reflection that occurs to me about those who govern and those who are governed. What those in government need is a constant replenishing of humility. It is hard, it is occasionally brutal, mistakes are made and there is a requirement perpetually to assess and to reassess and above all to listen. There is a risk that has to be guarded against that you feel people insufficiently appreciate the burden of governing. But often what it is, is really an attempt to make you better at doing it. That is the dialectic between state and citizen. So all the time you should be rediscovering that initial feeling of joy, hope and anxiety that accompanies winning power and produces a humility about exercising it. Experience gives greater confidence in making the decisions. But it should never excise that awareness of your own limitations and the uncertainty inherent in political judgement. As for the governed, they just need to remember one very simple thing: those that govern them are no better than them and no worse. In a democracy they don't come from outside the people but from within them. And in a modern democracy governing cannot be the responsibility of the government alone. They can't change a society that doesn't want to be changed. They can't improve, reform or take forward a situation against the people, only with them. The responsibility is shared. So just as the governing must listen,

so the governed – in this modern non-deferential society –
must be prepared to speak and to think before doing so. In
other words, people have to be willing not simply to make
demands but to make a contribution.

Now we are in opposition again and so is much of progressive politics in Europe. *The Unfinished Revolution* is an object
lesson in what to do and what to avoid in winning the struggle
to be elected. I would distil the following lessons.

*1. Start with an honest analysis of why you are in opposition,
not in government.*

I never had any serious doubt about where I stood politically.
I am a progressive not a conservative. When I analyse why,
I find that I think it is less about policy and is partly about
values. It is also about an attitude of mind. I am an idealist.
I still think that idealism motivates progress. It inspires people
to believe they can change the world. It leads them to create
in their minds a destination for that change. But it is not
always a reliable roadmap, still less an engine that gets you
there. It can lead you to believe that when people disagree,
it is because they have a problem with the destination rather
than with the map or motor. So we can end up thinking a
defeat is either about the people's failure to understand what
we are trying to do; or, as bad, about our leadership's failure
to understand what they should be prepared to do. As
someone said to me after 1992 and Labour's fourth consecutive election defeat: 'People have voted against us four times
in a row now; what on earth is wrong with them?' There is
a slight tendency on the left to believe that the people are
misguided when they reject us; a bit like the Gnostics of the
early Christian Church, who thought the path to salvation
was the attainment of a superior knowledge only to be grasped
by a select few. We can be exasperated with those who don't
share our view, rather than trying to understand, self-critically,
why they don't.

But another and equally potent delusion is contained in the various versions of 'the Leadership has sold us out' story. We then misdiagnose or over-complicate the reasons for defeat. We think that the gap between the enthusiasm with which parties are elected and the (at best) grudging respect for parties in government, was bridgeable with different leadership, or referable only to Labour's experience. No government is 'loved' in the way a party in the throes of a campaign, especially after years of opposition, can be. And, at some point, the country just wants change. So be incredibly careful in ascribing some vast philosophical crisis of identity to a defeat that can happen for the most prosaic of reasons. The danger with such ascribing is that in the shadow of defeat a whole series of highly disputable theses came to characterise the reasons for defeat, that usually have in common the belief the progressive party lost because it 'departed from its roots'.

So begin with a clear and frank examination of defeat. As *The Unfinished Revolution* shows, Labour spent the 1980s desperate to escape the true reasons for defeat, taking refuge first in the madness that the country voted for Margaret Thatcher in 1979 because Labour was insufficiently left-wing; and then making a series of tactical steps towards change that were almost always one election cycle behind necessity, and never added up to the strategic shift required. It is extraordinarily beguiling and comforting to think New Labour lost in 2010 because the brand became contaminated; we lost touch over Iraq and financial regulation. There is some truth in the Iraq part of this at least for some electors, but not enough truth to make it a comprehensive analysis of defeat. As I say later, when in government you are bound to 'lose touch' and time hurts all governments. But the notion we lost over Iraq and light financial regulation fits uneasily with the election of a Tory government committed to both. I know the Lib Dems are also important, but as the third party. I don't discount the impact of these issues, but I would hesitate before assigning them a central role.

The truth is Labour wasn't New Labour by 2010, at least not as I would recognise it. Our initial response to the financial crisis and the early plan for the banks was right. It was here Gordon acted at his best, intellectually rigorous, totally driven, sure in his touch. But in the end, we took an Old Labour way out of the financial crisis. We cut VAT and bought a traditional Keynesian analysis of how to stimulate the economy, then raised National Insurance and the top rate of tax to deal with the growing deficit. We slowed public service reform when we should have accelerated it. We highlighted the problem of immigration but ditched the one policy capable of controlling it – a system of identity checks. We moved from the crime agenda, not by a lot but by enough to lose the bite of earlier policies. We did 'lose touch', not with 'our roots' but with a public whose anxieties over tax, spending, immigration and crime were precisely the opposite of those on the left criticising New Labour. As a result, we did not seem like the party of the future.

2. The reason for defeat is nearly always because progressives don't 'own the future'.

This is a very difficult objective to achieve because predicting the future has never been tougher. Philip rightly identifies my preoccupation with modernisation. Put as baldly as that, it can seem rather technocratic and soulless. But for me it was always about meeting the challenge the future posed to the realisation of our values. The chief characteristic of the modern world is the scope and speed of change. It imposes on countries, corporations and people the need to adjust fast. The same is true of political parties. For progressives, this can often imply agonising choices over positions and institutions in which they are heavily invested. These too need to change. If they don't, then the left is vulnerable to the charge that they have avoided the need to change themselves and so can't win the trust to change the country.

Frequently, this is because we are public-sector orientated and the public sector is slower to change. So we end up defending antiquated systems and practices, especially if they are held dear by trade unions and pressure groups, when in the lives people lead, technology and modern lifestyles make those practices incompatible with the future. The right tends to do this on personal or social attitudes; we do it with public sector systems. Whenever I hear of a Conservative government proposing radical changes and a progressive opposition opposing them, I know we're in for a familiar old movie: the public don't like the changes, but kind of intuit that change is necessary; they sympathise and even show some support for those opposing change; but when it comes to the hard question of who leads them into the future, they heave a sigh and vote for those that know the future needs to change. It's never a movie with a happy ending, at least for us.

Labour opposed a series of changes in the 1980s that, when you analyse them in the broad sweep of history, were bound to come because they moved with the grain of the future. Customisation, adaptability, quality of personal service, all of this meant that privatising state-owned industries, opening up sectors to competition, was going to happen. Create more people with more income and more education, they are going to want to make more choices; hence the importance of tax as an issue for the aspiring working class as well as the middle class. The absolute key to understanding this and the emphasis of New Labour on 'globalisation' is to realise that globalisation is not driven by governments, but by people. It's people who are choosing to live and work differently. Stand against this and of course you will get the nostalgia vote. You just won't win an election.

So not just in vision and attitude but in policy and programme, ask one question: does this really fit the way the world is changing? Are we the ones who 'get' the future, or are we in our comfort zone?

3. Policy positions matter.

By this I don't mean detailed policy programmes such as only government can produce. I mean how your policy is strategically positioned. So for example, on law and order are you tough or liberal? Now if you put it like that, many progressives suck their teeth and feel uncomfortable. It's not as simple as that, they say. However, for the public it is. That's not to say you can't add to it – as indeed we did with 'tough on crime, tough on the causes of crime', the New Labour law and order slogan. The point is you can't fudge the basic position.

In the 1980s we went through unimaginable contortions trying to shift from a position of unilateral nuclear disarmament without explicitly saying so. To say so full-on was felt to be too unpalatable to the party; so we hedged. As a result, we just seemed incoherent; and therefore unsure; and therefore, on defence, not to be trusted. We did the same on industrial relations law. In fact, we did the same on the whole panoply of Thatcher reforms. We didn't want to say outright that we would keep a fair proportion of them. Once I became leader and said it, we got clarity on the basic policy position. Then, for example, on industrial relations law we were able to add things – a commitment to a minimum wage, to better maternity rights, to workplace equality for women and part-timers, the right to join a union. But we could only do that by making the first statement clearly.

4. The positions have to fit a strategic definition of your basic politics.

Politics is a far more intellectual exercise than people ever think. It's not expressed like that, seen like that and it's positively risky to communicate it like that. But it is quite cerebral in this sense. You will always end up with a strategic definition of your overall political position. The question is therefore: do you impose it on yourself or do your opponents do it for you? At its most basic, this positioning divides into right, centre and left. Now, I favour the centre for reasons I will give. But you can't escape fitting on that spectrum. Lots of progressive leaders try to. They don't like being bolted down. They want the freedom (and the loosening of the hard politics) to say: well I'm left on this, right on that, etc. In my experience, it rarely works. What is true is that, increasingly, successful leaders are positioning themselves in the centre and beyond the traditional left/right. But it's amazing how many progressives end up being positioned on the left (which is usually where Conservatives want them) without ever really meaning to. Or, even more common, they think using centrist language gets you round the problem of leftist policies. It never does, because in the end the policy positions matter and they will define the overall strategic position. They have to be intellectually coherent. You can proclaim that you have an attitude that likes business with as much fervour as you can (as Labour did constantly); if the policies don't match up, then forget it.

5. Good communications come from good policy.

One of the most common fallacies in politics is that you can have great communications and lousy policy and win. You can't. People may admire the campaign, but it won't prevent defeat. The 1987 election was a classic of this genre, as Philip relates. Owing to Peter Mandelson's brilliance, the campaign was stunning. We still lost by a landslide. By contrast, if you look at New Labour in 1997 or Bill Clinton in 1992 and 1996 and Barack Obama in 2008, all had a defined product; and then great communications worked brilliantly. Don't misunderstand me: strategy polling and communications are really important. Philip was a near genius at it. But in 2010, once Labour had lost its essential positioning and a cutting-edge programme about the future, nothing was going to salvage it.

6. Values are hugely important but they're not the challenge for progressives.

This is a really tough one and I am not sure Philip and I agree on it. Values matter. They are a badge of a party and

leader's identity. They rally and inspire. They are the reason
for the whole damn thing in the first place. But they're rarely
the reason for rejecting the progressive choice. It's nearly
always policy that defeats us.

This is in part because progressive values are popular.
Social justice, fairness, equality, community, solidarity – most
people subscribe to these values in societies like ours. So we
don't have to spend a lot of time persuading people to share
those values, though we sometimes have to persuade people
we represent them.

However, the perennial failure of progressive politics is
when values get muddled with policy proscriptions. The
latter change with the times; the former shouldn't. So the
way of achieving solidarity for the early twenty-first century
is bound to be radically different from that of the mid twentieth century. This is why the European social model so
urgently needs reform. The progressives should be the ones
leading that reform. Very often they defend the status quo
and oppose the reform. The only way that progressive politics will lead Europe right now is if we become the reformers.
By that I mean the reformers of the very ideas and institutions we created.

A party should be constantly in search of new ideas that
help translate the values into practical, relevant and attractive
policy. This is not about uprooting principles but about the
courage to think.

7. The best ideas today will often come from outside the party.

There's much more of an open market in ideas today. They
will cross party lines and traditions. Their author will often
come from outside the political inner circle. I found in government there was more creativity in business and the third sector
than in government; and in government itself and in the public
sector the creativity was often furthest away from the centre
or the top. Never once did I go on a visit to the grassroots of
a community or service and not come away with an idea.

In government, the time to search out and examine is much less. In opposition, use the space and time to engage with the real world, with its thinkers, the creators and originators of new ways of looking at things, or solving problems. Party structures and party policy-making should use the party organisation as a base to reach out from, not a laager to be contained in.

One of the most interesting things about today's world is the generation and exchange of ideas on a vastly greater scale than in the years before the internet. Make use of it.

8. People know that a leader is the leader of a party, but they distrust a leader who seems in thrall to it.

This doesn't mean picking fights with the party. It means simply this. The public always thinks of progressives as more party people. They think of them as more idealistic and sometimes more militant. They guess that if the party really had its way it might be much more radical. So they need the leader to be not just in charge, but with a concept of their interest that is larger and broader than that of the party. Put plainly, they want to know that they come first. This is why the recent decision of Ed Miliband to insist on choosing the shadow Cabinet is right.

In this book, Philip recounts the trouble Labour had with this notion and it is really instructive. There was always a sense that Labour leaders were transfixed between what they really wanted to do and what they could do. Of course, partly this is party management and all leaders including me have done it. But when it comes to the big-ticket stuff – defence, taxes, crime, foreign policy decisions of real moment to the national interest – you have to assert the position you believe in. What happens if you don't is very often not much noticed in opinion polls because you're in opposition and it doesn't impact people's lives directly. But when the real poll approaches, it is remembered and you are punished.

9. The maxim 'oppositions don't win elections, governments lose them' is wrong.

Actually the reverse can be true. Oppositions can lose elections. They lose if they think the government doing badly is enough for them to win. For progressives it usually isn't. The people need from us a positive programme and, as I said earlier, a core strategic definition. Even if the government programme is in difficulty they expect an alternative programme. Put it like this: without a decent programme, the opposition takes a huge risk. Also scandal on its own doesn't evict a government, unless it's vast.

Wherever I find opposition parties talking of how such and such a scandal will bring down the government, I'm nearly always looking at a party about to lose. Scandal can hurt; can help define a government; can, most of all, distract and discombobulate a government. But before the public change, especially if the alternative is a progressive party, they want to know what they're getting; and they will resist obstinately any idea that the 'scandal' of the government earns the opposition the right to govern in their stead. Sometimes it's true, Governments run into such difficulty that merely by playing it safe you can win. But in the case of progressives, even playing it safe requires a certain level of positioning and definition.

10. The centre or centre-left is where progressives do best.

There is a Holy Grail in progressive politics. It is that one day the people will decide that they've seen the light and been inspired to vote for radical left policies of a traditional sort. We just need to remember that all King Arthur's knights went after the Holy Grail and they all failed except one. You may be Sir Galahad, but it would be unwise to count on it. *The Unfinished Revolution* is a text about the perils of such a quest. I would argue that for all Labour's history it was only when it stood at the centre that it won. Some would argue Attlee's government was 'left', but in fact many of its policies were exactly where the centre of the day was located, especially following the 1930s and the war, when a coalition government was mapping out policies like the NHS before Labour enacted them (and, by the way, in 1951 we seemed to have moved from it and lost after only six years of government).

In the second decade of the twenty-first century, there are even more reasons why the centre is best suited to progressives and even to conservatives. People dislike ideology. They fear unaccountable power, whether of state or of market. They are less wedded to voting traditions. We won over two hundred seats in 1983 and were saved for the future, despite having a programme most of those voting for us disagreed with. It won't happen today.

The centre ground meets the prevailing mood of the governed towards their government, actual or protective. They put a high premium on competence and effectiveness. They want things done. So they will back radical change if they consider it necessary. But they want it conceived on the basis of what works, not what is politically correct.

The centre is also where the aspiring working class and the middle class tend to congregate and I believe that's where the elections are won. This can pose real challenges. If a progressive party moves to the centre it can find competition developing to its left or in new parties like the Greens or even single-issue parties. The question then is: do you sweep up to the left or aim for the centre, with the risk of losing some of that left? I think it's best to aim for the centre: if you take this ground, you corrode the right's support; some of that left will come with you anyway to win; and in any event, you have a mandate that allows you to govern sensibly. Tack to the left and you find you are never left enough; your programme becomes a risk; and some of that left vote flakes off.

None of this means that the centre is static, or that you cannot build out from the left towards the centre. For example, it could be argued that after the financial crisis, and in an era of the squeezed middle class, people are much more prepared to accept an analysis and politics that start from a position to the left of New Labour. If this position is articulated and chimes with the people, it then can be added to in order to bring more obvious centre-ground support, e.g. with the business community on board.

So I think in the post-2008 time it is possible to construct a different alliance of support. Of course, it has to meet in the place where people really are on issue, like tax and welfare, not where we might wish them to be. But the centre ground can shift, and if it does we can shift with it. That is where Labour is now heading. It will pick up the votes of disappointed Lib Dems in doing so.

The Lib Dems in the UK face a big problem. The old SDP/Liberal split is re-emerging in a modern fashion. What could stick together in opposition comes apart in government. The simple truth is you can't fight several elections to the left of Labour and then end up in coalition with a Conservative government pursuing Conservative policy. You try to pretend it all adds up, get a few scraps here and there, but its essential design flaw is blatant. After a time the people who voted Lib Dem regard the flaw as at best evidence of flakiness and at worst treachery.

So Labour has a strategic choice: do you go after voters on the left of the Lib Dems who believed in their manifesto, or those towards the centre who voted Lib Dem for all sorts of reasons to do with dislike of other parties, but who will happily trade policies?

11. In today's politics, issues of culture are important and progressives have to treat them with care.

As conventional highs of ideology over issues like state versus market have subsided to more flat proportions, so those of culture have risen. Take immigration. I'm in favour of immigration. I believe Britain and Europe have benefited from it. A portion of the concern about immigration is from people with dubious attitudes. But it's a big mistake to misunderstand the fact that for the largest portion it is a genuine worry about losing identity through losing control. It's not immigration per se that worries most people. It's immigration without proper controls and therefore without a say over it. If progressives get this issue wrong, they will pay a heavy price. The right sometimes plays such issues ruthlessly. We have to, as the lawyers say, 'confess and avoid', i.e. accept the problem, propose a solution and then get the permission to put the problem in context and defend lawful immigration. Law and order has similar ramifications.

In opposition, Labour is now faced with a very tricky balancing act. Again, a New Labour approach is the solution. What's the risk right now? It's simple. The Tories claim that 'multiculturalism' has failed (joining Conservative colleagues in France and Germany). This positions them well on the right. Labour then splits between its liberal and its working-class voters; and ends up in no-man's land.

In this context, the concept of Blue Labour is interesting. It's essentially an attempt to reposition Labour as the party of traditional values – as some put it, faith, flag and family (an inaccurate shorthand, but which kind of gets the general idea). This produces its dialectical reaction from the liberal or progressive wing that fears religion and nationalism as guiding sentiments.

How we deal with this goes back to what New Labour is about. It is traditional values in a modern setting, as John Prescott put it. Leave out either side of the equation and the sum is immediately imbalanced.

So, of course, we should be in favour of patriotism, and support the family and certainly not be dismissive or derisive about those with religious faith. But actually that's not the issue. The issue is: in a modern world what do you think those notions mean? What's the contemporary not traditional translation?

I would argue today that to be anti-Europe is not to be patriotic. In the modern world Britain needs Europe. I don't make that case because I think supporting the national interest is somehow out of date. I make it because, in the twenty-first century with the new emerging powers like China and India, with populations twenty times ours, it is not practical for the UK to wield power and influence without the weight of Europe behind us.

On immigration the issue is again simple: it is immigration we can't control. It's illegal immigration, asylum claims that are bogus and the legal rules that mean that even if someone is threatening us we have to keep them here. It is the putting of such people before those legitimately here in respect of things like housing and benefits. This is where we need strong, convincing policy.

But it would be utterly tragic and, by the way, useless politics to let this trend into 'immigration is a bad thing'. It isn't. Properly controlled, it's a good thing; in fact, an essential thing for a nation like Britain that needs constantly to replenish its intellectual capital. It is just that in the modern world, with its waves of economic migration vastly greater than ever before, you need to control it, to be in charge of it.

People forget that in 2005 the Tories sought to build the campaign explicitly around immigration. It failed because we took it head on. We agreed it was a problem, proposed a solution and accused them of exploiting the problem not dealing with it. The charge struck home.

Likewise with the family; we should support families and stand up for marriage – but point out always that we live in 2011 not 1911. We did a huge amount for families: Sure Start, childcare, better maternity and paternity rights, and I would also include civil partnerships. But we recognised that the traditional family unit is less common today. That's a fact. It won't be reversed. It's not only in Britain. The key thing is for us to be resolute in promoting responsibility. That's actually what people want. Parents accepting responsibility for looking after their children. Children taught respect and proper behaviour. People encouraged to look after their own parents with dignity. It's not white blokes with bowler hats or overalls, while Mrs busies herself as a dutiful housewife and knows her limits. I'm not saying there's not a market for this, just that it's not one that should interest us.

Dealing with these issues in a true New Labour 'Third Way' fashion is the only way to resolve what is otherwise an irresolvable conundrum: that Labour's working-class and middle-class voters often think different things. The approach set out here allows each to gain some recognition for their view and to find common ground. Most important of all, it is a position that is right in principle.

12. Being in power is the real politics.

The worst thing about opposition is its impotence. To begin with, opposition has a certain appeal. After you learn its tricks – especially how to clamber aboard bandwagons and accelerate them – it can even have the illusion of actual power. You can set the agenda, have the run of the media, put the government on the ropes – at least from time to time – and generally have quite a good time of it. But it always is an illusion of power, not the real thing. After a time it palls, and then, if you are serious about politics, grates and irritates.

Government is a hundred times tougher but a thousand times more satisfying. Look back at 1997–2010, and you may still only recall the end, with all its bitterness and defeat. Over time, however, the achievements are clear and they are real – real in their effects on people's lives, real in the change in the country, real politics. Think of the minimum wage; the huge cuts in hospital waiting times; the improvements in schools; the fall in crime; and a stack of things from a successful Olympic bid to civil partnerships to peace in Northern Ireland. Think of the relief of poverty of pensioners and how it used to dominate the news every winter and of the families who saw the support for children doubled. We can agree or disagree on Iraq or Afghanistan or Kosovo. But the country counted and in the creation of the Department for International Development and the trebling of its aid budget, we led the world in development policy. Most of all, by governing for twice as long as the previous longest Labour government, the Tories were forced to change and to pretend as much continuity as dislocation of policy. So, however beguiling, never forget what matters. Not passing resolutions or winning debates; but taking power and changing lives for the better.

13. The rhythm of government is a different rhythm from opposition.

We took too long to change rhythm on taking office in 1997. The rhythm of opposition is like permanent salsa; that of government an extended symphony, with a different pace for the different movements. In opposition, you wake up and ask: 'What shall I say today?' In government, you ask: 'What shall I do today?' The impact of the saying is immediate. The impact of the doing is only apparent over time. I learnt as government progressed that the day-to-day news coverage mattered much less than laying down deep themes of objectives and achievement. You think, when in the middle of it all, that the public is imbibing each drop of political soap opera, shenanigans and scandal. They're not. On occasion they will drink deeply. But most of the time they're taking the odd sip.

However, on the big picture – their lives, the country, its direction – they form a view that is surprisingly untouched by the transient and surprisingly registers what matters.

14. Optimism and hope inspire.

When you get on a plane, the last thing you want to see is a depressed pilot. You want someone upbeat, with something to live for! So even when attacking the government in charge, it's vital to give people a sense of lift, a sense that the future, whatever its challenges, is not without hope. The most brilliant example of this recently was of course Barack Obama. But actually, if you go through most successful campaigns, an appeal to optimism and the better self is part of it all.

This is especially important for progressives. Progressive folk don't get motivated just by the thought of being in power. For them, rightly, there has to be a higher purpose. That purpose is based on a world view that is essentially optimistic. We tend to believe in the best of human nature, our idealism makes us think all problems can be solved, our spirit is young not old. We are not world-weary or cynical. We are the preachers of possibility.

After thirteen years leading the Labour Party and ten years as Prime Minister, I still feel like that. I remain essentially optimistic. I believe in trying to change the world not manage it. I think there are no problems humanity cannot solve if it has the will and the belief. My experience of politics in opposition and government has altered; my policy proscriptions in 2011 are rather distant from those of 1981, but my disposition to hope rather than despair has, if anything, increased. I've seen politics work, in the poorest places of Africa and in the highest councils of global politics. Not always, not persistently; but enough for me to know politics can deliver, does deliver and is infinitely better than resignation to the blankness of indifference. In 2011, one million people will die of malaria in Africa. We can prevent it. I predict that in a decade we will. We should have done it sooner. But we will do it. Not by sitting there idle, but by acting in outrage and compassion at so many lives wasted. A decade ago, hundreds of thousands more were dying of HIV/AIDs. Many fewer now. It didn't happen by chance, but by choice.

So we can make those choices and we should. That is what politics is about. That is the true story behind *The Unfinished Revolution*. We made the choices to obtain power, we made the choices in power. In doing so we contributed, in ways large and small, to progress.

Tony Blair
London, August 2011

'We are communal histories; communal books.'

MICHAEL ONDAATJE, *The English Patient*

Volume I: 1985–1997

Introduction: The Land That Labour Forgot

Suburban dreams

As a boy I used to walk around my garden planning political campaigns. Some of the earliest books I can remember reading were David Butler's Nuffield election studies. Among the first thoughts I can remember were why Labour was on the left and the Conservatives on the right; why Labour was red, the Conservatives blue.

I knew that I was Labour, but I had little idea why. I never had any doubt that it was the right party. I was born with it. Equally, I had a visceral opposition to Conservatives and Conservatism. I am not sure where these feelings came from, but I know I had them at a very early age. My parents were Christians, and I drew my values from them: compassion; an instinctive support for the underdog; a sense that all people are born with equal intrinsic worth. But I was torn by contradiction: I wanted to protect the poor yet I wanted talent to soar; I wanted fairness yet I wanted aspiration to be uncapped.

I was not calm about all this, I was obsessed.

As time passed it did not get easier. I wanted to know why Labour supported a liberal society and the Conservatives supported a liberal economy. I wore the grass out on this one. I simply could not understand why liberalism was right in one place and wrong in another. I could not make sense of politics, but I knew that politics was at the heart of my life.

I can remember the shame that touched my family when Suez was invaded by the British in 1956, and the shadow of fear we felt when Hungary was invaded by the Russians.

I can remember being stunned when the Conservatives triumphed in the General Election of 1959.

I can remember the excitement of early television coverage of general elections flickering through on our black-and-white screens.

I can remember the words of John F. Kennedy at his inauguration, and thinking: how could anything so beautiful come to be written? Who did it? How was it done?

When Hugh Gaitskell died I worried about who would be the best leader for Labour. I backed Wilson because I was confident that he would win, but I was not sure about his politics.

When Labour won in 1964 I felt a thrill of excitement that has never left me. I remember the pride I felt at putting Labour stickers on my school bag, and in the windows of my home.

I remember joining the Labour Party in the spring of 1965, when I was fifteen; going to my first Labour Party meeting in the small detached modern home of Terry Molloy in Highclere Gardens in Knaphill; forgetting about my O-levels and doing nothing much for a year but canvass for the second Wilson election.

I remember my first contact with the 'Reading system' of canvassing, which I never understood then and still don't now. I remember knocking on door after door and trying to persuade people to vote Labour, all the time thinking: why are people so unsure, why don't they want to vote Labour?

Above all, I remember the night of 31 March 1966, when Labour won its majority of 96. I remember the exhilaration of the result, sitting high on the balcony watching the count below, but I also remember Cranley Onslow – the soon-to-be re-elected Conservative MP – telling me that if Wilson was given enough rope 'he will hang himself'. I privately thought he was silly, but he proved to be right. Labour would not form another majority government for thirty-one years, confounding Wilson's ambition and becoming the natural party of opposition.

The people Labour betrayed

I learned my politics where I grew up, around the small town of Woking in Surrey. Not in great northern cities, the Welsh valleys or crumbling urban estates. Not in places with great political traditions and dramatic folklore.

I learned my politics in an unexceptional suburban town where most people were neither privileged nor deprived, but nearly everybody was struggling to get by – which was not pretty, and grew uglier – where people lived in unassuming council estates or in tiny semi-detached houses, where university was out of the question for most and where nearly everyone went to secondary-modern schools.

I did not have a deprived upbringing. I had an ordinary upbringing, born and brought up in a twilight suburbia, where post-war council estates nestled alongside small, detached, red-brick Victorian villas.

The party I loved instinctively was to betray the people who lived here, its natural supporters: ordinary people with suburban dreams who worked hard to improve their homes and their lives; to get gradually better cars, washing machines and televisions; to go on holiday in Spain rather than Bournemouth. These people wanted sensible, moderate policies which conformed to their understanding and their daily lives.

Labour became a party enslaved by dogma: it supported unilateral disarmament, immediate withdrawal from the Common Market, nationalisation of the twenty-five largest companies, and marginal taxation rates at 93 per cent. It abandoned the centre ground of British politics and camped out on the margins, forlorn and useless, offering a miasma of extremism, dogmatism, intolerance and wilful elitism which put the hopes and dreams of ordinary people last.

I remember having dinner in 1983 with Michael Foot and his wife, Jill Craigie. They could not understand why the Labour Party had lost the election that June. Labour had offered education, choices and opportunities, but the people had turned on them. They read the *Sun* and abandoned the Labour Party. Yet it was not the people who had betrayed Labour, but Labour who had betrayed the people. The failures and convulsions of the late 1970s and early 1980s were so bitter as to disqualify Labour from power for a generation. Even in the 1997 General Election, an overseas observer of a focus group in Putney said to me, 'What did you do to these people that they fear you so much?'

Labour had failed to understand that the old working class was becoming a new middle class: aspiring, consuming, choosing what was best for themselves and their families. They had outgrown crude collectivism and left it behind in the supermarket car-park. I knew this, because they were my life.

The land meets the sea

I was born in 1950 in Beddington, south London, into a family with huge qualities but little ambition. This now seems derogatory; it was not then. My parents, both teachers, wanted to do what was right, not what was aspirational.

My father was not tall, about five foot nine, but he had a big voice and a strong presence. He could easily command a large audience, but was always nervous when he did it. As a child he was beautiful, and as a young man classically handsome, but he was never tidy and allowed his hair, first blond and then white, to flop carelessly around his forehead. It was always too long. His shoes were never quite clean, his suits dishevelled, and his glasses often held together with a paper-clip.

He favoured ingenious solutions to household problems: handles were attached to doors by unlikely combinations of matchsticks and rubber-bands, shelves would be fixed with a pencil stuck in a wall. These temporary solutions, apparently too unstable to survive the day, would last for years. He was like this not out of laziness or lack of aptitude, but simply because he did not care about the ordinary workings of physical things. All he cared about were his work, his family and his mission. And his mission was clear: to use his skills as a teacher to transform the lives of the children in his care.

He was born in 1913 in a large, detached Victorian house in the centre of Ringwood, near Bournemouth, the son of a mobile tailor who travelled the New Forest measuring and making clothes. I remember him with a tape-measure always around his neck. My father was in every respect a country boy, swimming in the fast, clear water of the Hampshire Avon and able to catch trout with his bare hands. In summer he played cricket among bemused New Forest ponies in Carvers, the great playing field that extended beyond the rambling garden of his house, and in winter he played football. A local newspaper headline of the day read: 'GOLDEN GOULD SCORES AGAIN'.

He went to high school in Brockenhurst and then to teacher-training college in Winchester. His life, and his father's life before him, were centred on the New Forest. His politics were non-conformist, individualist, Liberal. Although he later joined the Labour Party, he did so only out of pity, for I had become a rather hapless secretary of my local party; desperate for members, I begged him to help.

He was a fine and talented man who would have made a success of any career he chose. But he chose to serve people, and in particular children, whom he loved. For him, to be a teacher was the summit of his ambition. It was something to strive towards, something to become. He was totally committed to the concept of public service: he believed that you did things not to make money, but because they were right; you existed to make a contribution and to serve the public.

He started teaching on the Herbert Morrison estate in St Helier, Mitcham, which gave him his first taste of urban deprivation. Unable to serve in the war because he had lost all of one lung and a good part of the other to TB, he taught in makeshift air-raid shelters as enemy bombers raided south London. He met my mother during the war when he was bombed out of his digs and arrived, unannounced and home-less, to be a lodger at her mother's house. They were married as the war ended in 1945, and then went to Barnsley for his next teaching post before returning to Beddington, where he took up his first headship at the tiny Church of England primary school. They lived in a house attached to the school, where I was born.

My mother was Dutch. Her father, an artist and a Communist, lived on a houseboat in Amsterdam. They moved to England before the war and she went to school in south London, before training to be a teacher in Chichester. She was tall and gangling, but attractive, when young; her style was fresh, clean and windswept. She too put service first, always wanting to teach, to contribute, but if my father's watchword was duty, hers would have been compassion. She was softer than him, more romantic about life, more opti-mistic about the human condition – not an English pragma-tist, but a continental idealist. Her bookshelves were full of bright orange early editions of the Left Book Club. She liked ideas, she loved politics. She was a socialist.

Whatever the strange pull of destiny that brought together this odd mixture of Hampshire and Holland, it worked. He, rooted in the Hampshire countryside; she, by the waters of the Dutch canals. He, the land; she, the sea. It was not an easy marriage because both were so ill so often; she adored him and he loved her, but he was exasperated and eventually worn out by her constant sickness.

She was ill from an early age, with a degenerative condi-tion of the brain which we never fully understood. My father said that when I was a child she would wander off and leave me to cry. My first brutal encounter with her illness came when she stumbled into our kitchen, her face covered with blood, her left hand crushed after tripping on the gravel outside. This was the first stage in an odyssey of illness which hung over my childhood and a large part of my adult life.

Periodically she would have fits, when she would lose consciousness and her breathing would slow alarmingly. Gradually she spent longer periods in hospital, the longest being at the Atkinson Morley Hospital in Wimbledon, which specialised in diseases of the brain. There, she lay in bed next to a woman who for no apparent reason, and without warning, had lost the use of her mind. Her husband came to visit her each night, desperately upset that he could no longer speak to his wife, and she looked back, her eyes small seas of panic as the words no longer came. Overnight she had become a vegetable. This was my first contact with hidden tragedy; a subterranean world of blameless people whose lives had been wrecked without warning.

My mother died on 24 June 1972 at three o'clock in the morning. I saw her last the night before, when she was gasping for her final breath. She held my hand and I said the wrong thing, that I would always love her, for it added to her panic. Somehow she turned to me and managed to say, 'Whatever you do, look after your father.' I said I would, and I did. These were the last words she spoke to me, probably the last words she ever spoke. They came back to haunt me as he fought cancer during the General Election of 1992.

My father gave me duty, my mother idealism. They gave me both the land and the sea.

A New Labour childhood

In 1954 we moved to Byfleet and then in 1957 to Brookwood, part of the borough of Woking. My father was head teacher at the Knaphill primary school, which I attended and where I was happy, although a little in the shadow of my flame-haired, ferociously successful elder sister Jill. Our summers were spent in caravans at Highcliffe or Poole, or in my grandfather's house, playing in Carvers and sleeping in huge down beds, fishing in the same fast Avon waters which my father had swum in forty years before.

The only black cloud looming on the horizon was the 11-plus, which I had to take and was expected to pass. Every day, it seemed, the exam was mentioned, with assurances that I would do well. However, it was clear to me that my parents were bluffing and they were inwardly terrified I would fail. I was dyslexic and struggled at school. I was inundated with extra homework, old exam papers and tests to assess my intelligence. I refused to do any of it, resigned to my fate.

The day of the exam was awful. I walked into the room physically shaking, took one look at the paper and saw nothing but a blur. It was completely incomprehensible. I went home to lunch despondent but not desperate, determined to fight back in the afternoon, only to be greeted by my parents – my mother in tears, my father ashen – telling me I had failed already. I hated myself; I hated the system.

My father tried to persuade me to let him find a better school than the one I was now resigned to, but I stood by my emerging egalitarianism and insisted that I should go to the same secondary modern as all the other children. At the time this gesture seemed commendable; now it seems priggish. Either way, this was the school from hell.

First, everybody there knew they were a failure; already life had made its initial choices, and we were in the second division and not the first. Second, this was a secondary-modern school pretending to be a public school. The headmaster, a Mr Barnes, flounced around wearing his Oxford gown and addressed us daily as though we were at Eton. Life was playing a cruel trick on us: shunted into the bottom drawer, we were put into four houses – Raleigh, Langton, Grenville and Balfour – and were expected to conform to the conventions and prejudices of a genteel public school buried in the leafy lanes of Berkshire.

Third, there was the sadism. The extent of the corporal punishment is hard to exaggerate. It was like an epidemic. Boys were caned in classrooms, in rooms behind classrooms, in lockers, in the hallway. We were caned individually, in groups, outdoors, indoors, upstairs, downstairs. Whole classes were lined up in front of fences for a collective caning. And if the teachers were bad, the boys were worse. I still remember one boy in particular who acted like a young sociopath, beating me up on the bus on the way home from school each night.

Then there was metalwork. Metalwork was at the heart

of the school's rationale, preparing people for life not through using their minds, but through using their hands, and we spent two full mornings a week doing it. Mostly, we filed, but sometimes we were allowed to use the lathe. Always it was grindingly, gruesomely boring. One of my favourite lines of poetry remains Henry Reed's 'Japonica glistens like coral in all of the neighbouring gardens, / And today we have naming of parts.'[1] But that was about the waste and frustration of a few weeks' military training. For most people in our metalwork class, if the school had its way, this was a sentence for life. My friends and I endured the misery of these lessons thinking, 'So, this is it, then.' Whenever I hear people talk about vocational schools as opposed to academic schools I still shudder. Most of those who claim to believe in vocational education wouldn't send their own children anywhere near it.

When I was fourteen I was taken to the Royal Aircraft Establishment at Farnborough and shown a great open space that seemed to be just one vast metalwork lesson, full of people filing and lathing and assembling and measuring. The teacher with us looked around with pride and said, 'If you do really well in your O-levels, this will be your future.' And Farnborough was for the children who did well. God only knows what the school had in mind for the majority who would pass no exams. I was horrified: I was looking at the rest of my life. I decided then and there to fail my O-levels and escape, which I did.

I do not mean to disparage those who work in places like the Royal Aircraft metalworks, or their contemporary equivalents; quite the opposite: I admire them. The people I disparage are those who fail to respect the struggle and tedium of most people's lives, which are dominated by work that is boring, unfulfilling and increasingly insecure.

At school I learned to respect people's basic impulse to work hard and try to get on. I began to understand the common-sense responses of 'ordinary' people. I developed sympathy for hard-nosed attitudes on crime and defence. David Owen, in his book *Time to Declare*, describes how, as a student working on a building site, he came to respect the tough, uncompromising views on defence of his fellow workers.[2] This sounds condescending, but Owen was right. I developed a strong populist sense at a very early age that the opinions of the majority should be taken seriously.

Whenever I hear people being criticised for their blinkered and reactionary views on crime, or welfare, or aversion to paying taxes, I always ask silently: have you known the dreadful, repetitive tedium of manual work, not just for the long university holidays, but for life; lived in cramped houses, in communities where walking the streets late at night is not a safe option; known the cancerous insecurity of work as clerks or office administrators, not poor, but never safe, and always worrying about the cost of providing for your family?

I sat in the shadow Cabinet room as the self-interest and materialism that was gripping the electorate in the 1980s was described during a polling presentation. I heard the tut-tutting of disdain from the assembled advisers and officials and thought to myself: you all live in big, comfortable houses, have Tuscan holidays and drive large cars. What do you know about the way ordinary people live?

The secondary modern lacked any ambition for its children. I was told that I did not have the ability to take A-levels. I remember talking to my friends in what purported to be the school library and somebody started to talk about university, explaining that it was a place where people like us, who attended a school like ours, never went. I had no idea what university was, but I was determined to go. Eventually I managed it, but almost no one else did, although nearly everybody in the upper streams was quite capable of doing so. The potential that this school, and others like it, killed or maimed was nothing short of educational genocide. That is why I abhor selection at the age of eleven, but also why I abhor the potential that is still being wasted by a comprehensive system that was so badly flawed in design and execution.

The best thing about school was my friends. Most of them were tough kids: Thatcher's children, although they did not know it yet. John Huntley was sensitive and intelligent and wanted to become a vet; in fact, he became a scientist. He was my fishing and country friend. Most nights we would cycle off after school and find some hidden place to fish, hoping to forget the day. He had the misfortune to be the first in our class to be caned for something he did not do.

The rest of my friends were tough-minded and thick-skinned. Roger Gosden, the son of a carpenter; William Mitchell, a plumber's son; John Stuartson, whose father worked in a factory; Barry Williams, the son of a soldier. These were not privileged boys, not middle-class. They were what would now be called skilled working-class. They should automatically have been Labour supporters, but they were not, because their fathers all wanted to get on. Roger's dad was endlessly improving his house, adding odd bits and pieces to it that did not really work. They would buy and test the latest offerings of the emerging consumer society. They were beginning to take holidays abroad.

And they were tough about their politics. Every political judgement they made was rooted in hard, uncompromising common sense. With Brett Robinson, the son of a civil servant, I canvassed the whole of Woking, or so it felt, for the 1966 General Election. The tiny, grim, forbidding red-brick houses of Goldsworth; the bigger villas further from the centre of the town; the massive over-spill council estate of Sheerwater; the mishmash of suburban housing in Knaphill and Brook-wood. Housing that was not pleasing to the eye because each owner, like Roger Gosden's dad, had tried to put their own stamp on it: small porches erected incongruously over front doors; cheap modern windows clashing with Victorian red-brick walls; different shades of paint which owed no allegiance to the house next door; little extras stuck on to make the houses look better, but making them much worse.

Even then their owners were tough on crime, tough on welfare, tough on the Soviet Union. They were fiercely patri-otic, as was I. But in the course of their lives they had felt an almost tangible sense of British decline: the great post-war British confidence and achievements were ebbing away. They believed in fair reward for hard work; in responsibility; in standing on your own two feet. They wanted to get on, and they wanted a better life. Given the life they had, this was not surprising. They were early recruits to the new middle class. They might just have voted Labour in 1966, but it was easy to feel the aspirational appeal of the Conservatives. These were the voices, of my friends and their families, which the left stopped listening to. They were to become the new voice of Britain.

By this time I was enthralled by politics and would spend hours arguing with my friends: arguing for Labour, for fairness, for compassion, for society. This was grinding work – my compassionate values clashing uncomfortably with their hard-nosed ambition and unsentimental view of the world.

It was in this tension – between my soft, inner world of decency, fairness and compassion and my hard, outer world of tough-minded working-class aspiration – that my politics began to be formed. Tough and tender; strong but fair. Already I was becoming a New Labour child.

Competing trajectories

I left school at sixteen with one O-level in geography. The Friday flogger, Tom Lee, begged me to stay, but I was away, and never again – with one exception thirty years later – did I feel a breath of freedom like the one that night when I walked home from school.

Already I was obsessed with politics. I loved canvassing and telling, and attending tiny political meetings addressed by the local Labour candidate, Michael Downing, in deserted church halls. I loved the posters we used to put up, and the leaflets we put through doors. After Harold Wilson won in 1966, I attended the vast rally in the Royal Albert Hall which Wilson addressed and where Kevin McNamara was introduced after his stunning victory in Hull. But even though I loved it, I thought it could never be my life: that was for others, always on the other side of the television screen.

Instead, without any prospects, I decided to join the 1960s. I knew it was happening, and I wanted to be part of it. There was scarcely a political demonstration or rock concert I did not try to attend, a peripheral figure wanting to be part of the times. In Swansea I tried to disrupt the Springboks' rugby tour by running on to the pitch, but made it only to the perimeter fence; at demonstrations in Grosvenor Square I joined in enthusiastically, from the back; in Bath and on the Isle of Wight I sat in the mud and heard distant groans, and thought, 'Why am I here?' I joined Community Service Volunteers, working first in Pontefract with delinquent children, and then in Camberwell with recidivists recently released from long prison sentences. But the people at CSV thought I was using voluntary service as a substitute for life and threw me out. I was seventeen, with one O-level and no money.

I had no obvious prospects, but I still had a dream – a dream of going to university, that place the boys at school had talked about. It took me months of Saturdays poring over prospectuses in Guildford Library to find out that the new University of Sussex accepted students with no O-levels, as long as they had A-levels. I pounced, persuading the East London College that I needed a couple of A-levels to become a social worker. Three years later, with four A-levels and still only one O-level, I got into Sussex.

At a stroke, my life changed. The clouds parted and the sun came out. I studied politics, learned almost nothing, developed few new political ideas and refused to sit many of the exams, but this at last was the beginning of life. I dutifully attended *Das Kapital* reading classes but soon gave up. I knew that capitalism would not lead to revolution, and thought that this was a good thing. I rejected the diatribes of the student Marxists as mad nonsense, completely unconnected to the life I knew. Yet it was the International Socialists and the International Marxist Group who dominated student politics at university. In the face of their rantings I defended bourgeois democracy, even going on Sussex University television to defend the right of the Conservative MP Andrew Bowden to speak on campus. I thought free speech was indivisible and I did not believe that liberty should be so easily tossed away. I was still not fully sure what I believed in, but I knew it was not that. I managed a reasonable degree at Sussex, but I had learned little.

At the London School of Economics, where I completed my Master's degree in political theory, it was different. Here I was taught personally by Michael Oakeshott, the conservative philosopher. I studied Hegel, and for the first time found a system of ideas with which I felt comfortable. I liked Hegel for his concept of the dialectic. I was captivated by the idea of an identity evolving through contradiction and negation: 'To be what it *really* is, it must become what it is not.'[3]

Hegel helped me to resolve the paradox that had consumed my early life: the clash between the competing claims of the individual and the collective. I had explored the ideas of Hobhouse and liberal socialism, but I was unable to resolve the dilemma. Making sense of this relationship was central to Hegel: 'The human being finds his proper identity only in those relations that are in effect the negation of his isolated particularity – in his membership in a group or social class whose institutions, organisation and values determine his very individuality.'[4]

I loved Hegel's language, his ability to evoke a sense of the ebb and flow of ideas: 'When philosophy paints its grey on grey then has a form of life grown old, and with grey and grey it cannot be rejuvenated but only known.'[5] Hegel's idealism appealed to my imagination while Oakeshott's scepticism appealed to my common sense: 'Men sail a boundless and bottomless sea; there is neither harbour for shelter nor floor for anchorage, neither starting place nor appointed destination.'[6]

Hegel and Oakeshott are a good mix: the one seeing life as the unfolding of great ideas, the other as a struggle to get by in a world without meaning. In politics you need both these instincts.

Oakeshott also introduced me to the idea of 'intimation': of emerging change hinted at by early indicators, bringing to the surface deeper movements. 'Events that compose a pattern and at the same time intimate a sympathy for something which does not fully appear.'[7] This view of political change, of subtle intimations heralding the first emergence of deeper political shifts, has remained with me and I look constantly at public opinion for the first signs of subsequent, bigger change. God knows what Oakeshott would have to say about this, but it is one of the things I do in focus groups.

The London School of Economics helped me to formulate the ideas that have shaped my life, but I wanted to move on. I decided to try advertising. I did this to leave for a while the world of duty and responsibility I had come from, and to see another world: to experience capitalism in its rawest form. My father was horrified – to him it was a betrayal of my talent and a pact with the devil. But I learned to love advertising, and came to understand that, although the market is not perfect, for the most part it works reasonably well and often very well. This was the opposite of the conclusion I had expected to find. I went in sceptical of business, I came out a qualified supporter, and at least understood it first-hand.

In 1981 I started my own advertising agency with two friends, Brignull Lebas Gould Limited, which we sold after two years. I remained in advertising for a further twelve months, but I had already decided that I wanted to start working in politics. I went to the London Business School for a year as an escape route, and on 1 June 1985, two months after getting married, sat down at home in Notting Hill and declared my political consultancy open.

I had no money, no clients, no prospects, but one burning goal: to help transform the Labour Party so that it would win elections again. In all this I was spurred on by the words of the Tory PR adviser Tim Bell, who had told me just days before that there would never be another majority Labour government. I have never forgotten those words, never stopped being determined to prove him wrong.

A new Labour life

This, then, was my new Labour life.

A life begun in a land of suburban dreams, among

ordinary people asking nothing more than to edge slowly forward in their lives.

A life among working people with growing aspirations, gradually emerging as a new middle class, at that time forgotten by the Labour Party, but becoming the most powerful electoral force in British politics.

A life where I learned of the daily struggle of ordinary families – silent heroes making do, getting by.

It was a life that taught me that the children from my rather shabby, second-rate school, and their children after them, had voices which deserved to be heard, and that when Labour stopped listening to them it lost power and began its long slide into betrayal and extremism. I know the suburban sprawl I came from was an ordinary place full of ordinary people. But it was my place, and they were my people. I come from the land that Labour forgot.

This book is about the post-war journey of the hard-working majority as they moved from austerity to aspiration and demanded a new politics to match their new ambition. And it is about the parallel journey of the Labour Party as it moved, over almost a century, from representing the people, to ignoring the people, to betraying the people, until finally it became the people's party again.

And in a very small way it is about my own personal journey; a journey that began in a family and a community typical of the electorate that the Labour Party had ignored and mislaid, and ended as the voice of that electorate to a party struggling to win back trust.

Mine is a very small part – without me, Labour would still have won on 1 May 1997; Tony Blair would still be Prime Minister; the majority would still be huge – but it is a part that I am proud to have played. For twelve years I was lucky enough to be a voice within the Labour Party, for this new majority in Britain. Not disadvantaged, not privileged, not quite working-class, not really middle-class – they don't even have a name. I will call them the new middle class. I first met them on the streets of Woking thirty years ago. It would take that long for Labour to become their party again.

1

THE CENTURY THAT LABOUR LOST

The party of the night

On the night of 9 June 1983 I sat alone in my small flat just off the Portobello Road and saw the party I had supported for almost twenty years beaten into humiliating submission. Worse than that, I saw the final betrayal of the people I had grown up with, the people the Labour Party had been formed to serve but whom it had abandoned. Labour had not merely stopped listening or lost touch: it had declared political war on the values, instincts and ethics of the great majority of decent, hard-working voters. Where were the policies for my old school-friends – now with families and homes of their own – in a manifesto advocating increased taxes, immediate withdrawal from the EEC, unilateral disarmament, a massive extension of public ownership and exchange and import controls?

This assault on the hopes and aspirations of Labour's ordinary working-class supporters resulted in a massive electoral defeat. Labour lost a quarter of its 1979 vote. Its 9.3 per cent fall in the national vote was the sharpest collapse suffered by a major party at any election since 1945. At 27.6 per cent, its support was the lowest since 1918. It won only 3 of the 176 seats in the south outside London.[1] The land that Labour forgot had taken its revenge.

The result, described by Tony Benn as 'a remarkable development by any standards',[2] was in many respects the worst performance in Labour's history. Labour lost the young:

the largest swing to the Conservatives was among first-time voters,[3] who were to become Thatcher's Praetorian Guard, keeping her, and the Conservatives, in power for the next political generation. It lost the working class: the swing to the Conservatives was 4 per cent among unskilled manual workers; no other social class moved as far.[4] It even lost the trade unionists, where the swing to the Conservatives was 8 per cent.[5] The party of the working class and trade unionism had driven its traditional supporters into the arms of their historic enemy.

Labour had become so disconnected from the people it sought to serve that it appeared to inhabit a parallel universe. At a time when 90 per cent of working-class voters favoured a ban on secondary picketing, 79 per cent of manual workers wanted council houses to be sold off, and 56 per cent of working-class voters favoured cuts in both social security payments to strikers' families and income tax rates for people with large incomes,[6] Labour was seen to offer higher taxes, less freedom, less wealth, more strikes, less security.

Labour damaged itself almost beyond repair in 1983. Three images of the party were dominant in the election: division, extremism and weakness. Among defectors from Labour, a third gave 'extremism within the Labour Party' as one of their reasons for voting Conservative, a quarter said 'disunity'.[7] Only 13 per cent picked Michael Foot as the best potential Prime Minister. Nearly two-thirds picked him as the worst.[8] Little can be understood about subsequent Labour politics unless the full extent of the damage in 1983 is understood. To millions of voters Labour became a shiver of fear in the night, something unsafe, buried deep in the psyche, not just for the 1983 election campaign or the period immediately after it but for years to come. Like a freeze-frame in a video, Labour's negative identity became locked in time.

For the next fourteen years, indeed until the very last days of the 1997 election campaign, Labour became a party to be feared. One woman said to me just weeks before the 1997 election, 'When I was a child there was a wardrobe in my bedroom. I was always scared that one night, out of the blackness, a monster would emerge. That is how I think of the Labour Party."[9] This was typical. This woman was an ordinary working mother. And she was not alone in her fear. Labour had become the party of the shadows; of deep, irrational anxiety. Only modernisation would save it.

Labour's unique decline

The scale of Labour's collapse in 1983 was not only unprecedented in British terms, it was unique internationally. All around the world – from Australia to France, from Canada to West Germany – in the face of global recession in the early 1980s, incumbent governments were crashing to defeat. But in Britain the Conservatives were easily re-elected. In part this was due to the potency of the Thatcher government, recently strengthened by success in the Falklands. But the condition of the Labour Party in 1983 was just as important. The party had become an anachronism, a relic of the past trying to appeal to an electorate whose sights were set on the future. Although the post-war period had been dominated by the most extraordinary and unprecedented pace of change, other progressive parties had managed to adapt. From the 1940s to the mid-1980s, the world's leading twenty-two parties of the left lost only 2 per cent of their support. Within this, the social democrat and socialist vote fell by just 1.5 per cent.[10] Globally the left held up. It survived massive change with marginal loss of support.

The one exception was the British Labour Party. In the same forty-year period, Labour's average vote fell from 44.5 per cent to 31.8 per cent.[11] At every election between 1951 and 1983 – with the sole exception of 1966 – Labour's share of the total electorate fell. From a high point of 40.3 per cent in 1951, it had halved to 20.1 per cent by 1983.[12] The reality could hardly be starker: the British Labour Party declined faster and further than almost any other progressive party in the world.

Some of the erosion in Labour's support can be explained by the vast social and occupational changes confronting it in the post-war period. From the 1950s, the number of manual workers fell steadily while the non-manual classes grew. But the decline of Labour's working-class base does not fully explain the drop in its support. From 1951 to 1983, Labour's vote should have fallen by 11 percentage points as a result of the diminishing working class, but in fact it fell by a full 18 percentage points. Labour lost support dramatically *within* the working class: from 63 per cent in 1951 to 38 per cent in 1983.[13]

This decline reflected deeper changes in the working class: it was not only smaller, it was becoming upwardly mobile. In 1949, 21 per cent of men were in a higher occupational class than their fathers; by 1983 this figure had almost doubled.[14] And by 1983, 53 per cent of working-class fathers had sons in non-manual work.[15] The problem for Labour was that upwardly-mobile children were far less inclined to vote Labour; they felt they had moved on while Labour hadn't. The threat of occupational mobility was also linked to the challenge of geographic mobility, as people moved from the industrial north to service-based jobs in the south.[16]

The picture in 1983, then, was of a smaller, upwardly-mobile, more southern-based working class, with a vast increase in the number of routine non-manual workers. The point could not be plainer: there was a new majority in Britain – new working-class voters, new middle-class voters. And year on year Labour and this new majority were parting company. Labour was dragging behind; they were surging ahead. Labour had forgotten its purpose. As one voter in a focus group said in the early 1990s, 'Labour has left me, and I have left Labour.'[17] Most of the children I went to school with would no more have voted Labour in 1983 than flown to the Moon. Quite simply, they had too much common sense.

New times had come, but Labour was still the party of failed solutions, still the party of trade-union domination and state control. At the 1980 Labour conference Tony Benn was the authentic voice of a party trapped by its past:

I believe that we shall require three major pieces of legislation within the first month of the election of another Labour government, and I will tell conference what I believe those pieces of legislation are. First, an Industry Bill, which will give powers to extend public ownership as requested by the GMWU [National Union of General and Municipal Workers], to control capital movements as requested by the GMWU, to provide for industrial democracy as has been suggested and demanded by the GMWU, and that Industry Bill must be on the Statute Book within a matter of days after the election of a Labour government.

He went on to demand a Bill to transfer all powers back from the Common Market to the House of Commons, and the immediate abolition of the House of Lords.[18]

Labour's failure was doubly sad because it was neither inevitable nor replicated elsewhere. All over the world progressive parties were facing comparable demographic challenges, but only the British Labour Party lost support on such a scale over such an extended period of time. This stubborn refusal to modernise was unique to the British Labour Party, buried deep in its character, its ethos, implicit even in its founding moments.

A party born old

Labour was founded in 1900 at the dawn of a new century, in which Britain and much of the world became fully democratic, people gained increasing control over their lives and mass consumption of material goods became commonplace. In the twentieth century power shifted from the privileged to the people. Yet this was the century in which the people's party was marginalised. Labour has governed for just twenty of the last hundred years, the Conservatives for seventy. And Labour has never managed a full second term.

The Conservatives stole the people's century from the people's party because they modernised while Labour did not. As Anthony Seldon has written, 'In its constant quest to gain and hold on to power, the [Conservative] party regularly adapted itself to apparent changes in public preference. The Conservatives have been far more successful in capturing working-class support than the Labour Party has been in colonising the middle class.'[19]

This echoed Disraeli, who said in a speech in 1867, 'Change is inevitable in a progressive country. Change is constant.'[20] This is the central paradox of modernisation: the party of conservatism held power because of its ceaseless modernisation, the party of radical change lost power because of its conservatism.

The answer to this paradox lies deep in Labour's past, for the seeds of its decline were imbedded in its inception. Labour was born a conservative party: it was too close to trade unionism; too obsessive about public ownership; too tied to myth; too rooted in the past. David Marquand summarises this as 'the complex mix of assertiveness and defensiveness, of secular fragmentation and group loyalty, which has shaped Labour's tradition and contributed to the paradoxical conservatism of the labour movement'.[21] The paradox of Labour conservatism flows directly from the forces that helped create it.

The first force was Fabianism: a blend of gradualism, Marxism and utopianism which has been central in providing what has been called the 'ideology of "Labourism"'.[22] Fabianism didn't make Labour a statist party, but it helped. Influenced by newly translated editions of *Das Kapital* and the writings of William Morris, Fabianism helped to ensure that Labour's dominant intellectual tendency was collectivist, squeezing out more liberal and pluralist alternatives, and leaving a progressive legacy that was unbalanced in favour of the state. Marquand describes this as 'one of the main historical causes of the decline of social democracy'.[23] An understandable emphasis on collective action in the face of poverty exposed by the recession of the 1880s 'had in practice degenerated into a bureaucratic form of social engineering'.[24] Fabianism alone was not responsible for Labour's long obsession with nationalisation and public ownership, but it certainly helped.

The second creative force behind Labour was religion. Religious language and metaphor abounded in the party's founding years. Ben Pimlott writes: 'The Socialist Common-wealth was more than merely analogous to the second coming: in the imagination of speakers and audiences there was a blurring and a merging of the two.'[25] In the view of Shaw Desmond, an early Independent Labour Party orator, Labour had become a 'faith' rather than a 'politic' movement.[26] This fusing of religion and politics generated a sense of mythic destiny: victory will be ours if no compromise is made; if we are true to our principles we will reach the New Jerusalem, not *despite* suffering and setback but *because* of them. Out of this grew the preference for glorious defeat, the fear that victory can be won only at the price of compromise.

Trade unionism was the third inspirational force. Labour was essentially founded by the trade unions to represent their interests. Marquand writes: 'In a sense not true of its social democratic counterparts on the mainland of Europe, [Labour] has been a trade union party, created, financed and, in the last analysis, controlled by a highly decentralised trade union movement.'[27] Growing rapidly in numbers, attracting thousands of working-class people, trade unions had a robustness and common sense which the other Labour organisations lacked. But they were also the source of organisational rigidity and the block vote, and they were born of cautious, defensive progress. By nature more sectional and inward-looking than their continental cousins, British trade unions were rooted in crafts not industry, battered by hostile legislation in the 1890s and in 1906. They were not intrinsically modernising institutions.

Union influence was both organisational and financial. It has been estimated that the political levy raised £35 million at today's prices between 1914 and 1927.[28] In return for this money, the unions controlled the Labour Party machinery. A majority of National Executive members were elected nominally by conference, but in reality by the unions. From its inception, the Labour Party was 'an electoral machine based on the might of the trade union finance and its block vote at conference'.[29] This had advantages, but there was a high price to pay. Discipline was gained, but flexibility and the influence of ordinary party members was weakened. The capacity to modernise and adapt was to be the ultimate casualty.

The final element in the conservatism of the Labour Party is more human, rooted in the culture and psychology of the British working class. In H. M. Drucker's view, Labour's ethos as a party – its caution, its conservatism, 'its characteristic values and traditions' – derived directly from 'British working-class experience'. 'Labour's organisational and financial procedures, its attitude towards its leaders, even the personal style displayed by its politicians – all . . . are reflections of the party's distinctive working-class ethos.'[30] According to Drucker, the defining values of Labour 'arose from a collective experience of exploitation and from the gradual construction of defensive organisations'.[31] This made the party cautious, defensive and backward-looking. Drucker believes that Labour's sense of its past is 'so central to its ethos that it plays a crucial role in defining what the party is about to those in it'.[32]

All these forces – Fabianism, trade unionism, religion and a defensive working-class culture – blended to produce a party intrinsically resistant to change. This conservatism is the ultimate explanation for Labour's failure to dominate the century. It is the reason why Labour declined in the post-war period while progressive parties in other countries did not. Marquand makes this clear: 'In world terms Labourism is the exception, not the rule.'[33] Other possible options, which were still open at the start of the century, were closed down in 1918, when a new constitution, drafted by Sidney Webb and Arthur Henderson, was adopted. It had at its core Clause IV, with the commitment to public ownership:

> To secure for the workers by hand or by brain the full fruits of their industry, and the most equitable distribution thereof that may be possible, upon the basis of the common ownership of the means of production, distribution and exchange,

and the best obtainable system of popular administration and control of each industry or service.[34]

Later in 1918, at a second conference, the party accepted 'Labour and the New Social Order', the party's first extended declaration of its aims and values. This called for 'a genuinely scientific reorganisation of the nation's industry, no longer deflected by industrial profiteering, on the basis of the Common Ownership of the Means of Production'.[35] These documents, G. D. H. Cole wrote, 'unequivocally committed the Labour Party to socialist objectives'.[36] Egon Wertheimer claimed they marked Labour's transition from 'social reform to socialism'.[37]

In establishing itself as a socialist party immutably linked to trade unionism, Labour broke with Liberalism and cut itself off from the other great radical movement in British politics. The separation of Labourism and Liberalism stopped dead the possibility of building one united progressive party, similar to the broader coalitions in the United States and Scandinavia. The division of the left gave the Conservatives a dominance in government which their electoral support rarely justified. It also meant that the collectivist instincts dominating Labourism could not be ameliorated by the individualism and plurality of the Liberal tradition. Inevitably Labour's intellectual compass became unbalanced, tilting too far towards the state, away from the individual. This had always frustrated me: I wanted Liberalism and socialism to mesh, but it took me a very long time to see how it could be done.

One further nail in Labour's modernising coffin was added thirteen years later, in August 1931, when Ramsay MacDonald turned his back on his party and his Cabinet to form the National Government, which immediately destroyed Labour in a General Election. Described by Clement Attlee, then at the War Office, as the 'greatest betrayal in the political history of the country',[38] the National Government etched fear of betrayal deep into Labour's soul, heightening suspicion of change and adaptation.

Taken together, trade unionism, fundamentalism, utopianism and fear of betrayal were almost bound to make Labour resistant to modernisation, but they also, in another great paradox, left Labour prey to extremism. The comparative failure of Labour governments in the 1960s and 1970s was due in large measure to their inability or unwillingness to modernise either the party or the country. Yet their failure was seen by many in the party not as the failure of modernisation that it actually was but as yet another betrayal of party and principle by Labour's leadership. Their answer was not further modernisation, but yet more ideological purity, which resulted in extremism. It was perhaps inevitable that a party so infused with dogmatic certainty, so rooted in the myth of glorious defeat, would both precipitate the failure of Labour governments and then interpret that failure through the ideological prism that helped to bring failure about.

This is not to say that everything about Labour was ill-judged or reactionary – of course it was not. Labour was born from the quiet courage of generations of people who wanted the world to be a better, different place. It was born of idealism and vision and was to achieve an enormous amount. In 1945 it gave us probably the greatest reforming government of the century, which created a welfare state that gave life-changes and opportunity to millions of people. It is the party of decency, compassion, fairness and justice. But it is also a party created in a culture of caution and deference with an overbearing sense of its past: part political party, part religious movement, fuelled by a sense of destiny, accepting glorious defeat and fearing awful betrayal. For many, Michael Foot was not a leader who tried but failed woefully, but a martyr, a champion to 'the cause'. Too many saw him as Gwyn Williams did: 'There he stands, Member for Ebbw Vale, bone of our old bone, blood of our very blood, in his white hair and his cheekbones, his humanity, his generosity, his literacy and his stick, the only legitimate heir in the apostolic succession.'[39]

The circumstances of its birth made Labour a great and complicated party, earning and deserving of intense loyalty, brave in the face of adversity. But they also made it a party unlike other radical parties: conservative by instinct, destined to allow the people's century to slip through its fingers, betraying not its historic principles but the people who believed it was founded in their name.

Attlee's success

From 1918 until the fall of Clement Attlee's government in 1951 Labour's ideological consensus, which was rooted in public ownership and 'Labourism', held. The 1945 government was a massive achievement, reforming large parts of Britain's society and economy. It was able to do so because of the peculiar circumstances in which it was elected. Built on the foundations of war, national purpose, coalition and the alliance of both liberal and socialist intellectual and policy strands, it was less a Labour government than a progressive grouping which brought together not one intellectual tradition but several. Crucially, the success of the 1945 government was enhanced by its willingness to draw on the wider progressive agenda of the previous twenty years. As Tony Blair said in his speech to the Fabian Society on the fiftieth anniversary of the 1945 election victory, 'The reality . . . is that the Labour government's agenda grew out of the coalition government of the war.'[40] And it was a genuinely radical coalition that entered Downing Street. The liberal ideas of Beveridge and Keynes were the cornerstones of its reforms. The new liberal inheritance was as important as the Fabian, guild socialist or Marxist tradition. Despite the nationalisations, despite the instinct for planning, despite the singing of 'The Red Flag', the Attlee administration followed a progressive path which for a long time enjoyed the confidence of the liberal left. In many ways it was a one-nation government, utilising the patriotic fervour which had guided the war in the new campaign for social justice – 'Now Let Us Win the Peace'. For a time the Labour Party was truly the people's party, but this did not last. It was a successful government, but it survived for only six years and let in a

Conservative government which lasted for thirteen. In part this resulted from exhaustion and unavoidable circumstance. But there were deeper problems related to its failure to modernise. In his speech on the Attlee administration, Tony Blair listed three main weaknesses: 'First, a failure to recognise fully the realities of the new world order, manifested in the attitude of the government towards Europe; second, a reluctance to modernise the institutions of government itself – what Kenneth Morgan calls the Labour government's "stern centralism"; and third, a tendency to look back to the problems of the 1930s, not forward to the challenges of the 1950s.'[41] Even Labour's most successful government was undone, in part, because it looked backwards and not forwards. In 1951 the radical coalition collapsed. Nye Bevan's resignation over NHS charges and ideological struggle with Hugh Gaitskell amid the dying embers of the Attlee government set the stage for the revisionist battles of the 1950s.

The first voices of modernising dissent had been heard as early as the 1930s. In 1937 Douglas Jay wrote that socialists had been 'mistaken in making ownership of the means of production . . . the test of socialisation'.[42] He was joined by Hugh Gaitskell and Evan Durbin in a group of Oxford-educated and London-based intellectuals, who met under the auspices of the New Fabian Bureau which had been founded in 1931 by G. D. H. Cole.[43]

Defeat in 1951 strengthened revisionism, the first modernising tendency within the party. Revisionism has been defined as 'synonymous with some form of reinterpretation of doctrine so critical as to amount (in the eyes of orthodoxy) to heresy or deviation'.[44] This captures the essential flavour of revisionist dissent within the Labour Party: it is not disagreement, it is heresy – a challenge to the legitimacy of the myth.

W. H. Greenleaf describes the nature of this heresy: it is the 'tendency in the Labour Party to accept that the capitalist enemy is not what it was a couple of generations ago, that the economic and social state of affairs has been so altered since the beginning of the century that it is no good continuing to apply automatically perceptions based on the old analysis but necessary rather to think out a new programme relevant to the radically changed circumstances'.[45] In other words, to look at the world afresh and with true eyes. To break through the myth into reality.

Gaitskell's failure

Revisionism proper started in the Labour Party in 1952, with the publication of *New Fabian Essays*, and gathered pace in 1956 with Anthony Crosland's major work, *The Future of Socialism*. It only gained full political expression with Gaitskell's accession to the party leadership in 1955. This gave rise to what Lewis Minkin called Labour's 'revisionist metamorphosis'.[46]

Revisionism was based around two ideas. First, it disputed the fundamentalist conception that, in Samuel Beer's words, public ownership is 'an indispensable condition and a major expression of a radically transformed economy, society and culture',[47] replacing it with Crosland's view that 'the ownership of the means of production has ceased to be the key factor which imparts to a society its essential character'.[48] And, second, it defined socialism in what have become known as ethical terms: putting values and ideals above means. In emphasising 'personal liberty, social welfare and social equality' as the true essence of socialism, collectivist means and public ownership were relegated to secondary importance.[49]

The election defeat of 8 October 1959 persuaded many of the urgent need to modernise the Labour Party. In his diaries, Tony Benn describes seeing 'Roy Jenkins on *Panorama* advocating very modestly that you should drop nationalisation, watch out for the dangers of the union links and not rule out an association with the Liberals. He dropped in here on his way back home and we had a flaming row.'[50] But Benn discovered the next day that Richard Crossman, a leading intellectual on the left, agreed with Jenkins that nationalisation would have to be abandoned.

Revisionism soon came to mean, however, more than dissenting political voices. It was encapsulated in a defining political moment: the first, failed attempt to change Clause IV. On 28 November 1959 Gaitskell made a speech which foreshadowed Tony Blair's of 1994, thirty-five long years later. Gaitskell began in modernising terms: society and the economy were changing, and Labour had to change too. Labour, he said, had to adapt itself, 'to be in touch always with ordinary people to avoid becoming small cliques of isolated, doctrine-ridden fanatics, out of touch with the main stream of social life in our time'. He argued that nationalisation was a vote-losing issue, in terms of both performance and intention. Performance, he said, was central and the people would judge Labour by it: 'Our fellow citizens are more likely to judge the value of the public sector by their experience of it than from theoretical arguments in speeches or Labour Party pamphlets.'

Gaitskell argued that confusion over policy presentation had led to confusion over intention. Countless voters had been led 'to think that we intended to nationalise any and every private firm . . . simply out of a doctrinaire belief in public ownership'. And he went on to attack Clause IV: 'Standing as it does on its own, this cannot possibly be regarded as adequate. It lays us open to constant misrepresentation . . . It implies that we propose to nationalise everything, but do we? Everything? The whole of light industry, the whole of agriculture, all the shops – every little pub and garage? Of course not.' Finally, he insisted that Labour had to be a modern, forward-looking party: it was 'no use waving the banners of a bygone age'. He urged Labour's National Executive Committee to 'try to work out and state the fundamental principles of British democratic socialism as we see and as we feel it today, in 1959, not 1918'.[51]

Gaitskell was defeated and Clause IV stood. He was beaten by a combination of fundamentalism and the block vote. Harold Wilson said, 'We were being asked to take Genesis out of the Bible.'[52] Trade union leader Frank Cousins said,

'We can't have nationalisation without socialism, we can't have socialism without nationalisation.'[53] In the face of the conservative forces ranged against him, Gaitskell had no choice but to back down.

Failure to change Clause IV was symbolic, but much more important was the general failure of modernisation to break through in the late 1950s. At the time it was clear that significant sections of the party leadership knew what had to be done. Labour had to adapt, reconnect with ordinary people and drop its dogmatic attachment to nationalisation. This happened in Germany in 1959 at the Bad Godesberg Congress, where the German socialist party renounced Marxism in favour of social democracy. The language used by Gaitskell in public and others in private is uncannily similar to that used by Tony Blair and other modernisers a generation later. But it was to take a quarter of a century and the political collapse of Labour before these simple modernising truths could be accepted. Looking back now, I still feel a lingering sadness that the people and the party came so close to connecting but then were wrenched so inexorably apart.

Wilson's fudge

The early 1960s saw modernisation trying to break free, conservatism trying to restrain it. Harold Wilson's response was to choose neither tendency but to try to reconcile them both. Essentially he chose to fudge. Wilson was the first political leader I saw speak in public and he was tremendously exciting. Remembering him now, I see him in 1960s colour, while Gaitskell remains rooted in 1950s black and white. The irony of Wilson was that he appeared modern, but was in no sense a moderniser, which made him a frustrating and ultimately unsuccessful politician.

Wilson was always trying to bridge the gap between left and right, flitting from one to the other, persuading each that his loyalties lay with them. In April 1951, he tilted leftwards by resigning alongside Nye Bevan over the 'teeth and spectacles' issue, but then he moved to the right to replace Bevan when he resigned his shadow Cabinet seat in 1954. But the Gaitskellites were wrong to see Wilson as one of them, just as the Bevanites had been earlier.

Wilson's trimming to left and right was reflected in his first Cabinet in 1964. While senior positions went to former Gaitskellites such as Jim Callaghan and George Brown, the left was also rewarded. Senior left-wingers like Anthony Greenwood, Frank Cousins and Barbara Castle all came in from the cold. During his premiership, Wilson also fostered the next generation of left-wingers, including Michael Foot and Tony Benn.

In the face of continued tension between left and right, Wilson attempted to fuse the two wings of the party with a positioning of such brilliance that it would blind anyone caring to look for the join. His central insight was to link socialism to science. Britain was undergoing a scientific revolution, unleashing vast new technological and industrial forces. As he wrote in his preface to the Labour Party document 'Science and the Future of Britain', 'The central feature of our post-war capitalist society is the scientific revolution.'[54] And this revolution had to be planned. Planning meant public ownership.

At a stroke, Wilson transformed the debate. Public ownership was new, modern, scientific, state-of-the-art. It was part of the meritocratic, technocratic revolution which would regenerate Britain. But ultimately it was all a deceit, a compromise. As Keith Middlemas observed, 'What had really occurred . . . resembled the dosing of a malarial patient with quinine: the symptoms disappeared but the party was not really strengthened, nor were its ideological fevers cured.'[55] Ironically Wilson's one great modernising act – the attempt to reform the trade unions through 'In Place of Strife', published in January 1969 – failed because it united left and right against him. The conservatism of Jim Callaghan joined forces with the leftism of Tony Benn and the new trade-union radicalism of Jack Jones of the Transport and General Workers' Union; Hugh Scanlon of the Engineers' Union;

and Lawrence Daly, General Secretary of the National Union of Mineworkers.[56] Once again modernisation was smashed on the rocks. One commentator wrote of Wilson and Barbara Castle, the Secretary of State responsible for 'In Place of Strife', 'Like Gaitskell before them they underestimated both the entrenched interests of trade unions and their collective ethos of labourism which valued solidarity above everything else – even economic efficiency.'[57]

Wilson failed to modernise Labour, which put the genuine modernisation of Britain beyond his reach. His failure to resolve the competing claims of left and right, and to move beyond both to a new modernising solution, made civil war in the Labour Party inevitable.

The death march

From 1970 onwards, the left began their slow, inexorable assault. Labour's long death march had begun. The centre of gravity inside the party was shifting decisively to the left. In the following two years Labour committed itself to an enormous extension of public ownership, into areas such as banking, insurance and building societies and the construction and ship-building industries. The NEC (National Executive Committee) policy statement, 'Labour's Programme 1973', 'amounted to a clear repudiation of a revisionist social democratic approach', according to Tudor Jones, and called for 'a fundamental and irreversible shift in the balance of power and wealth in favour of working people and their families'.[58] The policy statement was described by Michael Foot as 'the finest socialist programme I have seen in my lifetime'.[59] Enthusiasm for public ownership flourished in the 1974 manifesto and by 1976 Labour's programme demanded 'the extension of public ownership into . . . leading companies in every key sector of industry'.[60]

Meanwhile, the Callaghan government – in office from 1976 to 1979 – struggled to stay on a pragmatic course, while impotent in the face of global economic forces and domestic union power. Labour's failure to modernise reached its nadir with the strikes of the winter of 1978–79, when the dead were left unburied, leading Jim Callaghan to note, eight years later: 'Even with the passage of time I find it painful to write about some of the excesses that took place.'[61]

As the left achieved a new ascendancy, the party began to split. The summer of 1980 was a turning-point, when a special conference at Wembley in May endorsed the fiercely left-wing policy document 'Peace, Jobs and Freedom' and booed David Owen off the podium for advocating multilateralism. In June of that year, John Silkin, Labour's industry spokesman, announced that he would propose a motion at the next party conference committing a future Labour government to British withdrawal from the EEC. After their joint, angry rebuttal of the idea, David Owen, Shirley Williams and Bill Rodgers became known as the 'Gang of Three'.

The final break came when Michael Foot was elected party leader in November 1980. 'We knew it was all over,' Shirley Williams has said.[62] David Hill, Labour's former chief media spokesperson and one of the few people to have worked closely with every Labour leader since Wilson, says it was an 'appalling' time. Labour politicians, he believes, didn't realise how serious it was: 'In the 1980–83 period everyone was at one another's throats, and everything was crisis management. It was all about Tony Benn fighting Denis Healey [for the deputy leadership of the party]. You got the most extraordinary period of conflict with a party that was unmanageable and a party which did not know how to change its ways, how to modernise itself, how to make itself unified. It needed the shock of the 1983 result to shake it up.'[63]

In January 1981 Roy Jenkins joined the Gang of Three in issuing the 'Limehouse Declaration', which established a Council for Social Democracy as a prelude to the new party, which was founded in March 1981. Within ten days the Social Democratic Party had gained over 40,000 members. 'We were pushing at an open door,' Bill Rodgers said.[64] In Brighton, in Liverpool and in Shipley, local Labour parties were taken over by Bennite apparatchiks. In Bermondsey, Peter Tatchell took over from Bob Mellish as the Labour candidate and turned a safe seat into a 9,000 majority for the Liberals. In London, Ken Livingstone ousted the moderate Andrew McIntosh from the Greater London Council. Four months after its foundation, the SDP came within 1,000 votes of stealing a seat in Warrington, a classic working-class constituency in Labour's heartland. Disenchantment with Labour had spread from the middle classes to the skilled working classes and lower middle classes. Labour's forgotten majority had had enough.

I was torn at this time, angry at the course the Labour Party had taken, understanding the frustrations of those who had left and agreeing with much of what they said. But never for a moment did I consider leaving Labour and deserting to the SDP. In part this was emotional: all my roots, all my instincts belonged to Labour. I was suspicious of the SDP, I sensed in it an elitism, the lack of a true populist politics. But most of all I believed that a new party was the easy solution, not the right one. However successful the SDP was, it could not destroy Labour but only rival it, leading to yet more fragmentation of the left. The one answer was to stay and fight, to change Labour completely and make it the fulcrum of a new progressive politics in Britain. As I sat in my flat on that awful election night of 9 June 1983, watching Labour put to the sword, I resolved that somehow I would make a difference. I would take my revenge. I knew that only modernisation could save the Labour Party – if it could only find a way.

2

Saving Labour

Meeting Mandelson

I first met Peter Mandelson at a dinner party at the flat of my future wife Gail Rebuck in 1984. He was then working for London Weekend Television; I was at the London Business School. Peter struck me as charming, confident and full of life, although even then he displayed the qualities for which he would later become infamous: when another guest made a remark at the dinner table which offended him, he blanked the man for the rest of the evening. And when someone said they were considering joining the SDP, Peter commented, with threatening charm, 'Oh, no, I don't think that would be a very good idea, would it?' His opponent made the mistake of trying to argue his case, but Peter cut him dead. 'The SDP is having its moment in the sun, but it will be Labour that wins in the end,' he said, before adding witheringly, 'In politics, it is best not to follow fashion.'

A year later, at my wedding party, a friend from university, LWT executive Robin Paxton, told me Peter had just been appointed director of campaigns and communications for the Labour Party, and he had hoped to bring him along. I had recently left business school and set up my political consultancy, which I was running from a small bedroom at home. I had no clients and really wanted only one: the Labour Party. Very excited, I told Robin I was desperate to meet Peter, so he arranged a dinner for us the following week.

I went alone to Robin's house in Islington. I was so petrified I cannot even remember who was there. The evening was a complete blur. Peter says now that I didn't look him in the eye once during the entire evening. We made small talk before he turned to me and asked why I wanted to work for the Labour Party. I talked much gibberish, but somehow explained my mission: to transform Labour's image and electability by using modern marketing and communications methods. I remember thinking at the end of the evening that I had completely blown it, but I gave him an eleven-page letter I had written earlier explaining fully what I wanted to do; it was, effectively, a job application. To Peter's eternal credit he ignored my nervousness and decided to back me. 'I was thirty-two. I'd just been appointed to a job about which I had absolutely no idea whatsoever and I had no capacity or ability or experience to do it,' he says.[1] Neither of us fully understood the challenge we were taking on.

Within a few weeks I had written, at Peter's request, another detailed letter outlining some of the problems he seemed to be facing. I thought Labour was failing to get across any clear messages: their objectives seemed muddled, their communications unfocused. They were running an economic campaign at the time called 'Jobs and Industry'. I told Peter they needed to find and repeat simpler messages based around clear objectives: 'Take for example your current major campaign, "Jobs and Industry",' I wrote. 'I know very little about the perceived effectiveness of the campaign, but I would think that there is a very good chance that it will prove much more effective in stimulating support at the grass roots and with party activists, than with projecting a message to the public at large. Does this constitute success or failure? Without a decent set of objectives it is very difficult to tell.' Labour seemed to have cut itself off from the modern communications techniques at its disposal. I added, 'I think I can best help you by doing what you simply haven't time for yourself; by conducting an objective and I hope exhaustive review of all relevant aspects of your communications operation.'[2]

I started work within days. In the next four weeks I interviewed over thirty people, from politicians to journalists to advertising executives, pollsters and direct-mail professionals, among them campaign co-ordinator Robin Cook, Mandelson himself and Labour's new General Secretary, Larry Whitty. I attended campaign meetings, research briefings and presentations, examined piles of documents and publicity material and finally wrote up the report in a fortnight.

Into the abyss

On the day Peter Mandelson arrived at Walworth Road, in October 1985, an employee in the post room tried to feed a colleague rat poison. It was symptomatic of the state of the party: completely demoralised and riven from top to bottom by hatred, rivalry and dissent. Neil Kinnock, who had fought Tony Benn to be elected leader two years earlier, had done his best to modernise Labour, but it had been a slow and painful process, carried out in the face of constant defiance from the left.

When he walked into the Leader of the Opposition's office at the House of Commons after his election in October 1983, he found 'absolutely nothing', according to Patricia Hewitt, his press secretary at the time. 'We didn't inherit any kind of procedures or knowledge or view of how things were done. Literally, there was nothing. The party was a shambles. Policy was not particularly high on the agenda. What we inherited was a situation in which the party had gone off in one direction, and the parliamentary party had gone off in a totally different direction.'[3] Neil Kinnock was a moderniser, but a moderniser rooted in the valleys of Wales. He was a man who, as a boy, wanted to be a miner, and now had a home in Wales, a lovely home in west London, and children who were going to go to university. He was a part of the Welsh working class who had made good thanks to the welfare state. From the very start he had fought extremism within the Labour Party, and his hatred of extremists was to be a consistent part of his modernising identity. Where his modernisation was ambivalent was in relation to the policies and values of the party, where he was torn between the need

for Labour to change and his instinctive and emotional attachment to the Labour Party of his youth.

Yet he was determined to reform Labour. In his leadership
campaign speech he had identified two areas – Europe and
the sale of council houses – where Labour policy had to be
changed. Seeing himself as a unifying leader, he set up joint
policy committees combining Parliamentary Labour Party
(PLP) and National Executive Committee (NEC) members
to try to make them work together. He created the Campaign
Strategy Committee (CSC), which he chaired, whose
membership included NEC, shadow Cabinet and PLP
members, as well as trade union general secretaries. He
brought in fresh, young faces to the leader's office, to create
a dynamism whose momentum would, he hoped, spread and
mobilise the entire party.

But before they could get to grips with anything, the miners'
strike began. Charles Clarke, Neil's chief of staff, remembers
Arthur Scargill coming to London to see Neil in the autumn
of 1983. 'Neil said to Arthur at that time, I remember the
meeting, "Have you got a strategy? Are you clear what you
are trying to do?" And it was clear from that point that Arthur
Scargill had no strategy to actually win the dispute, he simply
wanted the dispute.' The issue ran on through 1984, dominating, with 'one member, one vote' (OMOV), the Labour
Party conference that year, and only ending in March 1985.
'It made it very difficult to open up other ideological challenges in the way that we wished to do,' said Clarke. 'We were
forced on to the defensive against the leftists. There was a
very natural solidarity with the strike which people throughout
the Labour movement felt, and it made it very difficult to
promote other changes, both organisational and policy-based.'
Neil had wanted to deflect media attention away from division
in the Labour Party on to the policy issues themselves; the
strike cost him dear in terms of time. 'It played the old aspects
of the party back to their most recidivist approaches. On any
issue of proposed change you had a massive coalition around
the miners against that change, which in some cases threatened
victory on the issue itself,' said Clarke.[4]

The strike also hurt Kinnock personally. Coming from a mining community himself, his cousins, uncles and friends were all on the picket line. 'He couldn't do anything to undermine them,' said Hewitt, 'and politically he wasn't going to do anything that would enable Scargill and the left to blame him for the defeat of the strike, although his political judgement told him from the outset that this was a strike that was going to be lost. He couldn't say any of what he felt, and you can hear it in his voice. He sounds so strangulated in the interviews.'[5]

Kinnock's leadership took another huge step back when his attempt to introduce 'one member, one vote' for selecting parliamentary candidates was defeated at the 1984 conference. His failure to change the constitution and reduce the block-vote power of the unions set back modernisation by ten years. Clarke believes it was the key issue on which the Kinnock leadership went wrong:

> We lost really by two people in the T&G [TGWU] delegation and one person in UCAT. We were complacent because shortly before the Labour Party conference in 1984, in September, Ron Todd and Moss Evans, the then General Secretary and then incoming General Secretary of the T&G, came to Neil and said, 'You don't have to worry, the T&G vote is there.' They both said it, the outgoing and incoming general secretaries, they said you don't have to worry. And we did not work hard enough at getting that vote and so we lost the vote – and that was a terrible mistake which I bear a great deal of the responsibility for. We should have won. This was 1984 remember, and it was a long time, nearly ten years, before change finally went through. That was a terrible failure.[6]

By the time of the next party conference, in Bournemouth in 1985, the fight against Militant had exploded, and Kinnock turned on them: 'Implausible promises don't win victories. I'll tell you what happens with impossible promises. You start with far-fetched resolutions. They are then pickled into a rigid dogma, a code, and you go through the years sticking to that, outdated, misplaced, irrelevant to the real needs, and you end in the grotesque chaos of a Labour council – a *Labour* council – hiring taxis to scuttle round a city handing out redundancy notices to its own workers . . . You can't play politics with people's jobs.'[7]

The party was therefore at war when Peter Mandelson arrived to run an expanded communications department. 'You had party machinery and personnel without leadership, management or purpose, which needed to be professionalised. You had a communications operation which was wholly discredited and demoralised,' Mandelson remembers.

> There was almost a complete absence of interaction between the various elements – policy, organisation, communication. The physical arrangements summed up the situation, down to the unstable chair I had to sit on at a table which had three legs and was propped up against a filing cabinet, beside which was a decaying spider plant and a World War Two-style office telephone. You went in there and it was like being hit in the face by a cross between a blancmange and a brick wall. A blancmange in the sense that you couldn't really get hold of what it was that you were working in or for, and a brick wall because it was intractable, without dynamism or momentum. That was why in the first six months I was so anxious and sleepless.[8]

The interviews I did in the autumn of 1985 revealed an astonishing morass of communications networks within the party: committee upon group upon committee, leading to a chaos of indecisiveness, one-upmanship, hedging and ultimate stagnation. The situation, two years after Kinnock's election as leader and, as it turned out, barely eighteen months before the next General Election, was ludicrous. Apart from the NEC, the CSC and the leader's office, there was a Polling Committee, a Press and Publicity Committee, a Jobs and Industry Campaign Group, a Social Policy

Campaign Group, an NHS Campaign Group, the Breakfast Group – a media relations/advertising group, which did not exist officially because the NEC, in one member's words, 'does not admit of the need for advertising as yet and takes a dim view of advertising and related personnel'[9] – as well as the polling organisation MORI and the – *ad hoc* – General Election group, known as the GE Sherpas.

Advertising experts who worked with Labour at this time told me they were contacted by a variety of people from different departments, including Neil Kinnock's office, all asking them to produce unconnected advertisements with no apparent overall strategy. Mandelson had no idea Kinnock's office had been commissioning advertisements. 'Anarchy reigns,' he said resignedly when I told him. 'The leader's office thinks it's very special and over and above all forms of bureaucratic accountability and control. It is the leader's office.'[10]

'Organisational madness' was how MORI's Bob Worcester, who had worked with Labour for over ten years, described it. 'In my experience, I have had conflicting instructions from the head of press and publicity, the Prime Minister [Jim Callaghan] and the General Secretary, all of whom have told me to do something different. There are no clear lines of authority and responsibility.' The worst campaign strategically, he thought, was actually 1979, when there were two groups, one of which (the White Room group) was headed by Ivor Crewe:

> In the 1979 election, you had the White Room group who were doing some advertising [and] PR, research people, and you had the Transport House group, of which I was a part, and literally on the day before the election, this group working with the Campaign Strategy Committee, dealing with them every day, you had those guys being faced with an alternative final-day advertising strategy and set of ads. And in a room over at the St Ermin's Hotel I witnessed an industrial relations guy called Michael Callaghan being shown two alternative advertising executions and someone saying, 'Michael,

which one do you think your dad would prefer?' That was
forty-eight hours before the General Election.[11]

The 1983 campaign was also a shambles: Michael Foot's
driver used to wander in to the strategy meetings if he felt
like it.[12] Roy Hattersley went to see Foot ten days before the
election and told him he wasn't communicating for the
television age. Foot told him there was no way, in the final
ten days, after all these years, he could change his ways and
he was going to carry on as he was.[13] A small advertising
agency, Wright & Partners, was only appointed the day after
the election was called, giving it no time to prepare. The
election broadcasts were 'a disaster', thought Patricia Hewitt,
who had unsuccessfully fought the Leicester East seat during
the election. 'After Neil appointed me, I sat down and
watched them, and I thought if I had actually watched them
while I was a candidate, I probably would have resigned
halfway through the election. They were dreadful, dire.'[14]

The press office and the publishing and marketing division
were 'in mayhem', Mandelson said. The campaigns were
under-resourced, the staff over-stretched and demoralised.
Major speeches and policy statements were receiving little
or no coverage, drowned out by the noise from Arthur
Scargill, Derek Hatton and Bernie Grant, and Kinnock's
attempts to fight the left. The best publicity Labour received
in the whole of 1985 was Neil Kinnock's conference speech
attacking Hatton and the Militant Tendency in Liverpool.
But, powerful and effective though it was, it did not display
a positive agenda – a reason to vote Labour. 'Why are lunatics like Derek Hatton and Arthur Scargill continually
rampaging around?' Mandelson asked exasperatedly. 'They
have got to be rebuffed and neutralised.'[15]

Campaigns lacked clarity, force and impact; policies were
overshadowed by the actions of left-wingers. 'We've got to
get away from the idea that campaigning is just about an
NHS ambulance, a sticker saying "I Love the Welfare State"
and the launch of a charter,' Peter told me in 1985. 'Time,
political constraints, lack of intellectual rigour, distractions,

being embroiled in this, that and the other – who's got the time or the will or the energy to cut through and develop one or two key thoughts, statements, messages which we want to ram home by constant repetition? The idea of image-making comes hard to the Labour Party, because they're more interested in their product, they're more interested in getting over the nitty-gritty of their social welfare policy or their investment policy, or their exchange control policy.' Health, social services, housing, law and order and benefits were all very important issues for Labour, which needed to be addressed. 'In addressing them what we have got to do is: (a) have something relevant to say by way of policy which is attractive and not off-putting – which is very hard when it comes to law and order and Bernie Grant in one sentence eclipses everything that we have to say which is worthwhile about law and order. And (b) we have to say it loudly and repetitively. And we have to present an image of the party, or messages or use language or whatever, that chimes in with what people want to think. And that's what I think we've found very difficult to do.'

He pinpointed defence and the economy as easy issues for the Tories to use against Labour. 'We've got to acknowl-edge our vulnerabilities. It's not just a question of having a neat little formulation extracted from some document placed before the Home Policy Committee of the NEC, or some neat way of saying: "You're number one with Labour." People are not idiots. There's going to be a lot of biting on bullets.' Mandelson was already infuriated by his lack of control over the media. 'At the end of the day our communications vehi-cles are TV, radio and newspapers,' he told me. 'They are the uncontrolled media. The Tories are very good at control-ling them because a lot of them – newspapers – are politically committed to the Conservatives.'[16]

Although, through Steve Billcliffe at Walworth Road, the party was already doing some direct mailing, there was no targeting of marginal constituencies and the party had only just begun, reluctantly, to release money for qualitative research. Joyce Gould, the Labour Party's director of organisation, and Patricia Hewitt had asked MORI's Bob Worcester to conduct some focus group research for the 'Jobs and Industry' campaign. 'We decided we needed some focus groups on language to see if the voters were understanding a word of what we were saying,' Hewitt said.

> And Bob took out some prompt cards and stuff, and this came back with the wonderful finding that when you said 'public ownership' to the British people, they said, 'That's wonderful.' They were really in favour of public ownership. But when we asked what they thought public ownership meant, they said, 'It means privatisation – selling the shares to us, the public.' We asked what they thought about nationalisation, and they said, 'No, that's a bad idea. That's ownership by the government.' There was a wicked suggestion in one of the campaign strategy meetings that we should brief all our people to talk about public ownership rather than nationalisation.[17]

I was determined to scrap all the conflicting groups and committees and replace them with one central, integrated, professional group, which would run Labour Party communications using all the modern techniques at the disposal of the business world. Mandelson warned that we would face hostility: 'Don't forget that this is a political party. It's a democratic party. All the time in the Labour Party you are boxing with those people on the NEC – to whom at the end of the day we are all ultimately accountable below God – who do not know what we're doing, who, if they did, would oppose it, who are thoroughly ill-disposed towards all these methods and with whom you have to play it very carefully.'[18]

I also had to recommend who should head the committee. Robin Cook and Peter Mandelson had overlapping functions, and Larry Whitty was not yet confident of Mandelson, although he later backed him, quietly facilitating many of the changes Peter made. 'Larry doesn't trust Peter politically,' Whitty's political assistant Tony Manwaring told me.

Peter wasn't Larry's appointment. Larry's been increasingly impressed by Peter's managerial skills, but at a gut political level, he doesn't know whether if a real crunch issue came up – say, for example, the miners vote had gone the wrong way – there were circumstances in which Larry would have felt himself bound to argue for the party and that position against Neil. Larry does have very specific responsibilities to the party. Leaders come and go. The party doesn't, and Larry represents the party and the stability of the party. And there are a number of areas where you could criticise Neil's leadership, where things became issues and we didn't try to stamp them out before they became issues. Neil does do some pretty daft things from time to time.

Whitty should therefore chair the main communications group, Manwaring insisted, exerting some not very subtle pressure: 'I say this never to use it as a direct threat, but there is always the underlying thing: who pays the bills for an agency; who finances the whole thing; who's got to give it organisation and resources? The NEC does. And Larry is the person who will have to go to the NEC about it. I mean, you'd never actually say this, but it's an underlying truth that if it ever became an issue and Larry was against it, it would be extremely hard even for Neil to make progress.'[19]

If the interviews uncovered organisational chaos, focus group research was revealing Labour's disastrous electoral situation. On Saturday 23 November 1985, Leslie Butterfield and Paul Southgate from the advertising agency Abbott Mead Vickers, along with Roddy Glen from the Strategic Research Group Ltd, gave an all-day presentation at the offices of the advertising agency TBWA to Labour strategists, including myself, Mandelson, Cook, Hewitt, Chris Powell (managing director of BMP) and Tim Steel. Without a doubt, these research findings were the most important of any presented during the entire period I worked with the Labour Party. They displayed the fault-line between Labour and its potential supporters, the apparently unbridgeable gap between what Labour had become and what the British electorate now wanted. While Labour was still talking the language of nationalisation, unilateralism and high taxes, the British public was buying council houses and shares in the newly privatised British Telecom and British Petroleum, and revelling in the success of Britain's born-again military might. The presentation constructed a conceptual framework of Labour disqualifying itself from potential voters because it had adopted positions that were beyond what ordinary, decent voters considered reasonable and sensible. The minority agenda of the emerging metropolitan left, of militant rights in welfare, race and gender, was completely divorced from what the British people wanted from a government.

The first key group of voters represented at this meeting – women aged twenty-five to forty-four – delivered a devastating criticism of the Labour Party. These forty-eight women gave us the first definitive proof that Labour had moved beyond the pale for ordinary people. They were frightened: they saw society breaking down and their instinct was to retreat from it into their families. 'There's no morality any more,' they said. 'It's all about greed and hate.' 'You can't trust people if you don't know them. In the old days you could trust them.' 'We've regressed: violence, rapes, murders, riots. It seems to get worse. There's something every day now.' Their response was to look after themselves.

'Where people are feeling that society is threatening and hostile, there's a feeling that the one reliable, predictable thing within such a society is "me and my immediate family",' Butterfield explained. 'A feeling that society's greater hostility means that you've got to look after number one more than ever.' Self-interest was no longer a dirty word; they admitted openly that they looked after themselves first. 'You have to look after yourself these days – no one else will.' 'Your main ambition in life is to better yourself. You can't do that if everyone lives in the same house, gets paid the same, drives the same car.' 'If everyone votes for themselves, the party that gets in will be by far the best for the majority, won't it?' And finally, 'If by voting Tory I'll get a flat or a job then I'll do it. It may be selfish, but I'm not going to vote Labour to get a job for someone in Newcastle. I don't suppose he'd think about me.'

The issues they cared about were therefore those affecting their own personal and financial security: law and order, health, education, inflation, prices and taxation. Defence and the role of minorities within society, two of Labour's big pre-occupations, were at the bottom of the list. Composite motions at party conference on unilateral disarmament and rolling back Tory trade-union legislation were not going to win the electorate over. Even more worryingly, these voters proved to us that Labour had moved itself into the unacceptable left-field of politics. The researchers produced a chart showing an 'acceptable field' of politics where these voters thought debate was reasonable. Beyond this field were the unacceptable right and the unacceptable left. Nearly all Labour's policies were in the unacceptable left-field. Nearly all of the Tories' were in the acceptable centre. The researchers reported comments like: 'The Labour Party are lunatics when it comes to defence'; 'Whenever I think of Labour I think, "Oh no, Arthur Scargill"'; 'Labour waste money on useless things'; 'It's outrageous – they're spending a million pounds on parks for gays and lesbians in Camden'; and, 'What frightens me about the Labour Party is that they are so far to the left that you get union leaders with so many thousands of block votes deciding how the country should be run.' These voters did not even have the language to describe Tory extremism, as they did Labour's. 'When you talked about what was unacceptable on the left, people very quickly translated that into socialism, communism, "reds",' Roddy Glen said. 'When we talked about what was unacceptable on the right, that did not incorporate fascism; they did not have an equivalent terminology for the extreme right in the way that they did for the extreme left.'

The Conservatives were seen as selfish, single-minded, dogmatic and determined, but people said this was what they wanted from a government. Someone like Norman Tebbit – vulgar, aggressive yet fiercely successful, who branded Church of England bishops Marxists, told the unemployed to 'get on their bike', and attacked Kate Adie as biased

– connected with an aspirational electorate as the man to get the job done. This type of strong, uncompromising, harsh leadership was what the electorate would vote for in the secrecy of the polling booth. Most of them described Labour policies in negative terms and Tory policies in positive or neutral language. 'The majority feel that there is a lack of positive policies that come from the Labour Party that relate to ordinary, working people with their own homes,' Glen said. While Labour was seen as being good for the poor, unemployed and needy, the Tories were understood to be good for everyone else – including 'me'. These women – a combination of Tory and Labour voters – no longer believed Labour represented them. And what was more, although most of them had not decided who to vote for in the next election, they were certain of one thing: they would not vote Labour. Labour had disqualified itself from consideration. 'There are too many loonies,' they said; 'They are too militant'; 'I've always been brought up as Labour, but now I'd be frightened if they got back into power'; and, 'You can't vote Labour just because they've got a heart.'

The imagery they associated with us was appalling: word association threw up 'reds', 'commies', 'you will do what you are told', 'strikes', 'Scargill' and 'Militant'. For the Tories, the words were 'Surrey', 'mortgages', 'private pools', 'private hospitals'. When asked to draw the parties, they drew a small house, small car for Labour; big house, big car for the Conservatives. Many of them drew a series of uniform little houses to represent Labour; one added a steelworks and a job centre. There were pints of beer, and a general store with prices going up all the time. Perhaps the worst single illustration of the party showed no cars, people travelling to work on the bus, houses that looked the same, no O- or A-levels, and universities closed down. The Tories held champagne glasses, Labour people wore cloth caps. The things people associated with the Conservative Party were the things they themselves wanted; all the imagery associated with them was aspirational.[20] This was not surprising at a time when Tory privatisations were extending personal prosperity and

Chancellor Nigel Lawson was overseeing a mid-1980s economic boom. Meanwhile, Labour was debating welfare support for strikers' families, the imposition of wage restraints and union-brokered incomes policies.

That was only the first of the day's shocks. A second presentation on the same day, by advertising agency BBDO to outline the attitudes of 20- to 25-year-olds, introduced for the first time the concept of 'Thatcher's Children', those who started to think about politics in the mid-1970s. Thatcherism, we discovered, was the political norm for these people – not an aberration, but the basis for their political thought. They took for granted many of its principles and any political idea was considered within that framework. 'We call them Thatcher's Children because of this,' a BBDO researcher said. 'They approve of toughness; they agree with it. They know it's tough to get on. And they all want to get on; they've all got aspirations.' They liked their leaders to be tough, and associated weakness with the unions and the welfare state, in particular social security:

> People really want to distance themselves from unemployment. They feel like if they're in a job then they've made it; they don't want to talk about people who haven't made it. Collectivism breeds weakness in their view. They've got a very crude and brutalist view of how the world works. They see all the classic institutions of collectivism as being designed to protect the weak, but by doing that somehow we're all pulled down. It's not something they can justify on an analytical level, but the more they talk about it the more they feel that individualism is the way forward. It's like a disease.

This group of young people became increasingly Thatcherite as they relaxed and felt less restrained, and the subjects that really excited them were the Falklands – 'brilliant' – business, enterprise, achievement and individualism. They admired Thatcher even if they loathed her, liked aggression, and hated Militant and other left-wing groups, whom they believed were trying to pull the country back and stop growth and efficiency.

They saw tax cuts as a reward for working hard. Even unemployment came out as a Labour negative with these voters: it was a low priority, accepted as necessary, and anyway, they believed that 90 per cent of the unemployed were jobless through their own fault or choice. This, despite the fact that unemployment never dipped below 3.1 million between 1983 and 1987. 'The Labour Party they remember, in their pre-sixteen memories, is associated with inappropriateness, bad management,' the researchers reported. 'The only time the Labour Party was good was in history, what they've read at school – when the Labour Party were men in cloth caps, who spoke in funny accents, and were in Parliament getting things done for the people who voted for them. But that's not the case any more. Those images now are retrograde. Even the people we had who would be defined in demographic terms as DE, their aspirations were to be middle-class – everyone wants to be middle-class these days.'[21]

This, then, was the situation I found in 1985 – far worse than I could possibly have anticipated, far worse than many even now fully appreciate: a political party separated from its natural supporters by a chasm of fear, distrust, even anger; a campaigns and communications operation too pitiful even to begin the task of building a bridge across it; and a party not really understanding that it had to try.

My report, delivered in December 1985, ran to sixty-four pages. I criticised Labour's communications as badly co-ordinated, with unclear lines of responsibility and uncertain authority. The campaigns that Labour had run 'have not yet had any discernible effect in influencing the electorate', and the political communication from the party was overcomplicated. There was insufficient orchestration of the presentation of a policy, the press office was not proactive enough, selective targeting had been neglected and the potential of advertising under-exploited. My key recommendations included:

- The establishment of the Director of Communications as the central focus for all party communications, who would chair a weekly working group of key communicators and campaigners. A monthly Communications Co-ordination Committee with a broader membership which would co-ordinate the wider campaign effort.

- The formation of a Shadow Communications Agency (SCA), structured around the group at the Boase, Massimi, Pollitt (BMP) advertising agency which had run the campaign to save the Greater London Council. The SCA would focus and structure the professional communications expertise on offer to the party. 'Its role will be to draft strategy, conduct and interpret research, produce advertising and campaign themes, and provide other communications support as necessary.'
- Monthly qualitative research should be commissioned by the SCA, complemented by monthly MORI summaries, and both should be integrated more fully into campaign planning.
- Communications messages should be simplified, repeated and orchestrated around key themes.
- The SCA should commission a design company to examine all aspects of the 'corporate appearance' of the party, including the party logo.
- The establishment of a rapid-reactions unit to defend against 'own goals', attack those of the Tories, and exploit issues of the day.
- All campaigns should have the influence of electoral opinion as their first priority.

I also set out ten communications principles for the Labour Party, around which the communications structure and output of the party should be based:

- An agreed, early strategy
- Selectivity of target audience
- Simple message often repeated
- Orchestrated, cohesive presentation of the message
- Clear allocation of responsibility for tasks. Clear lines of authority and accountability. Adequate structures of co-ordination

- Positive, proactive press relations
- A shift in campaigning emphasis from 'grass roots'/opinion-forming to influencing electoral opinion through the mass media
- Proper use of outside expertise
- Less publicity material, used more often
- Highest-level political authority and support for the early and continuing implementation of these principles.[22]

Out of the shadows

Even as I wrote my report, a nascent Shadow Communications Agency was working on Labour's forthcoming social policy campaign. Chris Powell had offered to set up a shadow advertising agency using the same team – Alan Tilby and Paul Leeves – who produced the 'Save the GLC' campaign and who were seen as some of the best advertising people in London. I considered BMP to be the top London agency, and their best staff were Labour Party supporters at a time when advertising and PR were dominated by Tories. Peter Mandelson, aware that Labour did not have the money to employ an agency and that no agency at that time could afford to take on the Labour Party, which might have lost them business elsewhere, immediately appointed the BMP team and asked me to act as co-ordinator. Until the NEC formally approved the creation of a Shadow Communications Agency, however, we had to operate in secret.

We moved quickly from the social policy brief into all areas of Labour communications. At our very first meeting, on 19 December 1985, we decided to produce creative concepts not only for the social policy campaign but in economic areas as well, convinced that the next election would be won or lost on the question of economic management. Already we had volunteer planners and researchers working with us from the advertising agencies Abbott Mead Vickers, BMP and TBWA, as well as Chris Powell, Peter Herd and Ross Barr from BMP, Bob Worcester and Brian Gosschalk from MORI and Colin Fisher from SRU, a leading market research company. By mid-January, the SCA was effectively taking over Labour communications, although the Breakfast Group, set up by Robin Cook to bring together campaigning expertise, was still going. As well as creating the social policy campaign, we were preparing for the Fulham by-election on 10 April, working on the economic concepts, conducting focus groups and developing an overall communications strategy for the Labour Party. We had decided on our central objective for 1986: to get Labour from 35 per cent to 40 per cent in the polls. Although Neil Kinnock and Robin Cook knew we were working for Peter, only Mandelson knew the extent of our expanding communications empire.

If the first surrogate for the SCA was the Social Policy Group, set up at the end of the year to prepare Labour's 'Freedom and Fairness' campaign, the second was the Strategy Development Group, which we set up in February to cover strategic planning, design, public relations, direct mail and targeting. By the time we had moved on to creating sub-groups of journalists, PR experts and designers, the NEC finally caught up with us and officially approved the creation of a Shadow Communications Agency. Our first formal meeting was on 25 March 1986, at BMP's offices in Bishop's Bridge Road. Present were: Ross Barr, Leslie Butterfield, Robin Cook, Richard Faulkner, Colin Fisher, Brian Gosschalk, Peter Herd, Patricia Hewitt, Peter Mandelson, Deborah Mattinson, Chris Powell, Bob Worcester and myself. By June, there were seventeen projects in hand, from shadow Cabinet pairings to General Election planning, to a leaders campaign, a new corporate image and the development of a communications handbook. Twelve SCA sub-groups had been established, including a journalists' group; a writers' group chaired by Ken Follett and including Hanif Kureishi, Colin Welland and Melvyn Bragg; a broadcasting group; a target audience definition group and a conference group. We had established a week-by-week timetable for the entire period up to the next election. We were making monthly presentations to the Campaign Strategy Committee and almost weekly presentations to Labour's policy steering committees. Research into sensitive issues like defence and the standing of Neil Kinnock was in the field. The Shadow Communications Agency was now a fact of Labour Party political life.

Yet we had stepped into a morass, entering a party at war with itself at every level. The left-dominated NEC, which had shown little interest in campaigns and communications in the past, saw us as a direct threat. Shadow Cabinet members were at best suspicious, at worst openly hostile. Labour had become so distanced from the public that we were going to have to fight the party itself over every appeal to the voters.

This is not the party I joined

The first major challenge for the SCA was Labour's 'Freedom and Fairness' campaign, launched in April 1986. Peter Mandelson wanted a communications revolution and got it. We had played a part in the Fulham by-election, conducting qualitative research, developing a campaign theme around the line 'Nick Raynsford Lives Here', and executing it. It was the first time such professional marketing techniques had been used in a by-election. They contributed to an important victory, which helped counter the growing impression that the entire Labour Party in London was in the grip of the 'loony left'. Our win suggested a new dynamism in the party, while the Tories were still getting to grips with the aftermath of the Westland crisis and were about to become embroiled in the *Spycatcher* fiasco.

'Freedom and Fairness' – the name the party adopted for the social policy campaign – was our defining test. It was planned to complement the 1984–85 economic campaign 'Jobs and Industry', that indigestible glob of a campaign which was characterised by a huge output of paper and massive printing bills and which had had absolutely no effect on the public.

Mandelson used 'Freedom and Fairness' as a way of saying to the party, 'this is modern communications; this is how it works; this is how it succeeds'. It was like a controlled explosion: this is your future – like it or lump it. Mandelson said, 'It was absolutely essential for our modernisation project within the party to show (a) the relevance of communications; (b) how possible it would be to bring about changes if other sections of the party felt good about what we were doing at the top of the party; and (c) to get the public starting to come back towards us.'[23] We wanted to smash through the party's perceptions of how campaigning should be done. My final brief for the social policy campaign – the first complete strategy I ever wrote for the Labour Party – asked the creative team to undertake a political communications revolution. I demanded a campaign that was bright, modern and distinctive, a consumer not a political campaign, using normal consumer language and not 'political' terms. I wanted language that would be heard and understood in southern suburbs, with a visual identity that was so different it stunned people.[24]

We developed the idea of symbolic policies – minor initiatives like banning lead in petrol to symbolise Labour's concern for the environment. We commissioned Trevor Beattie, who would later become famous for creating the 'Hello Boys' Wonderbra advertisements, to create the campaign. We developed a slogan, 'Labour: Putting People First', which was later used by Bill Clinton as his 1992 campaign theme. For the Labour Party, the leaflets and posters were shockingly different. Mandelson loved it.

To many Labour politicians at the time, this was heresy. A campaign was a leaflet, a march, a speech, a cause and a defeat. Mandelson recalls showing the campaign material to Harriet Harman, then the shadow Social Services Minister: 'And Harriet said, are you sure that this slightly squashed-up black, grey and silver look and print-face is quite what we're looking for, given that it is so harsh and dark? And Trevor [Beattie] said, well yes, this is ballsy, and that's why it's going to succeed, and there was this drawing in of breath at the word "ballsy" in response to Harriet's question. But this did make people pipe down and listen to what we had to say.'[25]

The 'Freedom and Fairness' campaign was also to prove the first test of Kinnock's own commitment to professional communications. When we took the early drafts to him in the House of Commons on 4 February 1986, he was nothing if not enthusiastic. Barely before the presentation had got under way, he grabbed hold of the advertising concepts and started to present them to himself, excitedly issuing a torrent of creative judgements. Although a bit of a shock to the professional advertising people present, it showed he cared. But Neil himself was to balk at the end result. 'I don't think he quite saw it coming together in the cohesive, all-singing, all-dancing campaign that it was, with the impact that that had,' Mandelson said. 'And when he saw it coming together he was a bit worried by the radicalness of the new look.'[26] Kinnock thought 'Labour: Putting People First' was a poor substitute for the campaign title he had chosen originally, and he wanted to stick with 'Freedom and Fairness'. 'Labour's Campaign for Freedom and Fairness had more politics in it, and was therefore more likely to appeal to and carry the party,' Mandelson said. 'I think that his caution was right. But his counselling was wrong.'[27] In the end, Kinnock refused to shift, forcing Mandelson, who was determined to retain the more voter-friendly 'Putting People First', to go out on a limb, and not for the last time.

I had not realised how much guts Peter Mandelson had until Kinnock's office called him a week before the launch. 'They said he was very worried about this, and wanted to see me. They said he wanted the whole campaign to be recast, to be changed radically. I said that's not possible, because the launch is only a week away. And they protested and said that Neil hadn't passed these things, and I said no, he did. It was approved at the meeting. They said well, he's disapproving it, and I said well, he can't, it's too late.' Mandelson went to see Kinnock personally to explain, 'one of three occasions in my time there that I had to do that'. He took with him the photographs, mock-ups and other materials.

And Neil said, I just can't have this. He said the campaign name has to be 'Freedom and Fairness', because they are important concepts, important names and ideas that we have to own again. And I said I agreed with him, but that must come in the case we make, the argument we use and the language that supports that. But this is a piece of communication to the mass public, and whereas 'Labour's Campaign for Freedom and Fairness' is a party-oriented statement, 'Labour: Putting People First' is a public-oriented statement. We reached a compromise, by which I said I would overprint all our campaign materials with 'Freedom and Fairness', in addition to what was already there. We did it in very small print.[28]

The campaign was an unprecedented success – Militant called it an unnecessary facelift, and at its launch at the London International Press Centre the left-wing MP Eric Heffer stood, horrified, at the back and moaned, 'This is not the party I joined.' The Labour left had opposed political marketing for years. Jim Callaghan used to dread NEC election strategy meetings in the late 1970s, as Tony Benn and Heffer consistently attacked all opinion polling and most suggestions for advertising. But more enlightened commentators saw in 'Freedom and Fairness' the revival of the Labour Party. On 23 April, the day after its launch, the *Financial Times* hailed 'Mr Kinnock's new party', writing in a leader column: 'The British Labour Party is again beginning to look like a credible party of government.'[29] A *Daily Telegraph* story, picking up on the grey and silver, ran: 'Labour changes colour as it sheds its weary cloth-cap image.'[30] The tabloids hailed it as a victory for 'poster power'.[31] Even the morose *Guardian* called the campaign 'a really positive step forward in the political rehabilitation of a party which three years ago seemed to have lost the will to govern this country';[32] the *New Statesman* grudgingly conceded the new style might win votes.[33] And in a more generous leader column, *Tribune* commented, 'Freedom and Fairness could just be the campaign that wins Labour the next election.'[34] By today's standards, the campaign wasn't much: a few leaflets, a bold image, a memorable slogan. It was never going to win the election, but it did at least prove that we *wanted* to win it.

The rose and the thorns

It was Neil Kinnock who first asked for a complete redesign of the Labour Party. He had been impressed by the Swedish Social Democrats, who had developed a new corporate identity using a rose, and he called in Mandelson and me and asked us to do the same. Peter handed the project over to me and by March 1986, when the SCA was formally set up, we were already forming a design group to prepare the new corporate image, including a logo. In April, Mandelson wrote to Larry Whitty requesting his support – both financial and personal – for the redesign. The new, sharper look of the 'Freedom and Fairness' publicity material was 'vital to reinforce the impression of an innovative party shedding old associations and image', he wrote. 'This dimension will continue to be part of our communications strategy – a fresh party, new approach, on the move. As an important basis for this I am looking at our overall "corporate" image – everything that offers a visual impression of the party.' He wanted 'an entirely new visual facelift' to launch at conference, he said. 'This exercise is an integral part of our General Election preparations. Can I continue with your blessing?'[35] Whitty returned the letter to him with a scrawled note: 'Yes. But keep me informed on design and costs. We do not yet have a General Election fund . . . LW.'[36]

Lacking the money to run a vast creative campaign, I asked Michael Wolff, founder of Wolff Olins, who had designed the Bovis 'humming bird' logo, to see what he could come up with. When I first asked Wolff for his thoughts – without telling him what Kinnock had proposed – he spontaneously suggested using a rose. Peter, Michael and I spent hours and hours in the Battersea home of Philip Sutton, the artist, surrounded by dozens and dozens of roses – a whole roomful of them. We would wander around picking up one after the other, trying to choose which was the best.

'We picked out half a dozen, ones that spoke to me, or I liked, or I thought would say something to the public,' Peter remembers. 'I had no theory to apply. I had no idea what criteria to use.'[37] Michael, Philip and designer Clare Hamilton honed these down into various designs and illustrations, which we then took to Kinnock. I made notes of the meetings on two consecutive days:

25 June 1986
Went to Philip Sutton's home in Battersea – a real artist's home. Someone called it 'a bit of Provence in the middle of Battersea'. I was nervous because the designs were a bit too wishy-washy. Philip Sutton did the illustrations. I was a bit concerned that the corporate image would end up looking all wrong. There were two or three watercolours which, although they were much less powerful than some of the others, managed to combine humanity and sensitivity with clarity as a rose – and redness of the rose. They were clearly the basis of the right sort of approach. Clare presented the type and that was absolutely right. When Michael Wolff put together the rose and the type it was quite clear that he had developed a corporate image for the party which was in the same tradition of the other work he'd done.[38]

26 June 1986
At ten o'clock we left to pick up Michael Wolff, Philip Sutton and Clare Hamilton to present the corporate image to Neil Kinnock. As I suspected, we were left outside in a corridor somewhere waiting to get in to see Neil. Eventually we go in to see him. He is wearing a light suit, which doesn't suit him, and no jacket. But he's in a good, calm, affable mood. Michael is good with him, takes his jacket off. I take my jacket off. Peter Mandelson sits next to Philip Sutton; I sit on the other side of the room. Michael says how much he hates the grey (of 'Freedom and Fairness'), Neil agrees with him, they shake hands, a good rapport is created.

The meeting goes well. Michael presents the corporate image work, which I think Neil likes. They chat about the use of hands, how to use black hands, young hands, women's hands, etc. Talk about the colour of red the rose should be. Neil looks at a photo of his son playing rugby in a red strip. He says that this red is vermilion – compared to vermilion jobs Labour will create when they get into power! Neil also made a crack about how we'll be the best-dressed runners-up, but I don't think he meant it – or maybe just a little. The critical point of the discussion was really when Patricia mentioned that the rose would be shown at conference and Neil shook his head and looked like he didn't agree with it. He said, 'I don't want that to happen.' Patricia said, 'But you agreed to it.' Neil said abruptly, 'You might have mentioned it, but I never agreed to it.' It seemed like Neil had made his mind up. But then Peter came in, he looked Neil directly in the eye, and said calmly but with enormous authority, 'Are you sure, Neil? Are you sure we shouldn't have the rose at conference?' And gradually won him over. He said that the response to the grey was really only limited, a couple of letters opposing it, opposing what had been done with 'Freedom and Fairness'. He said people would like it. Neil looked down and said quite abruptly but with good humour, 'Let's see some designs for conference.' Peter had won him over. It was a good moment for Peter and for Neil. Later I talked to Michael Wolff, who said he thought the meeting had gone very well. He'd written a letter to Neil which said: 'Thank you for your time this morning, Neil. I was looking forward to meeting you, and listened carefully to your observations and suggestions about roses and hands, and different type-faces and colours. We will now concentrate on making the whole scheme practical. I'm very excited about what I think it can achieve.' He put a quote at the end from *A Midsummer Night's Dream*. Nice, but on the whole maybe a little over the top for Neil: 'The seasons alter: hoary-headed frosts fall in the fresh lap of the crimson rose.' I'll be inter-ested to hear how Neil responds to that.[39]

Eventually we had two drawings, which I took over to Peter Mandelson's house. Peter was in bed, ill. 'We disagreed over the length of stem,' he remembers. 'Neil wanted a short stem. I wanted a long stem. You wanted a long stem that would look softer, and in Lynne Franks' immortal words, "more Kleenex".'[40] In the end Peter decided on the long stem, against Neil's wishes. The rose was to become so unmistakably associated with Peter and the modernisation struggle that on meeting Mandelson for the first time, Prince Charles commented blithely, 'Ah, the red rose man.'[41]

Peter himself was still having to fight petty internal battles at Walworth Road while we were working on the rose. A note I made of a conversation with him at the time records: 'PM said that Geoff Bish, Research Director of the Labour Party, had attacked and assailed him at the Monday morning directors' meeting over the size of his office, which he said was a surrogate for an attack over the publicity (about campaigning) that Peter has been getting recently and the increase in his power. He said also that the publicity was not of his doing, and just evolved around him – as indeed did the size of his office.'[42] It was a minor issue at the time: at one NEC meeting, everyone laughed when Dennis Skinner, during a discussion about where to store the Labour Party archives, suggested they put them in Peter's office as 'he won't even notice they're there'.

We decided that in addition to the rose, we would give all the delegates peach-coloured wallets to carry their conference documents around in, imprinted with Labour's new rose, to match the conference backdrop designed by Michael Wolff. When the wallets were printed a week before the conference they came out, I think, more peachy than the backdrop itself, and when Peter and I took them to show Neil and Glenys Kinnock in Neil's office at the Commons, they retreated, horrified, into Neil's room and closed the door. 'Then Neil opened the door and said "Come in",' Peter remembers. 'I went in and Glenys said, "Oh, Peter, these will never do. You'll never persuade the NUM delegation to walk around with these under their arms." And Neil was looking ashen and really, really worried. So I said I'm sorry, it's too late. They've been printed, and we're going to have to use them.'[43] I nervously watched *Channel Four News* at 7.00 P.M. on the Monday of the 1986 conference. They were doing vox pops among party members, all of whom said the new image was fantastic. Even the peach wallets were a huge success. They were being stolen, begged, borrowed and bought by the end of conference week.

This was the conference at which the presentation of Labour entered the modern era, a defining moment in the modernisation of the Labour Party. By the time delegates arrived at conference it was a *fait accompli*. Even to the NEC it came as a shock – they hadn't really understood what we were up to. 'We never presented it to the NEC as a change in corporate identity,' Mandelson said.

> At the Press and Publicity Sub-committee of the NEC, chaired by Gwyneth Dunwoody, in the second week of September 1986, I went to the committee and as part of my director's report said that we were introducing a new campaigning logo for the party. We played it down, didn't say it was a change in corporate identity for the entire party, merely referred to it as a logo to use in our campaigns. They didn't know what a logo was or anything. I passed it round the committee. Gwyneth Dunwoody was really brilliant, really protected me and us throughout. She knew exactly what was going on and she just allowed them to be passed round the committee without any further discussion. It was all sort of 'yes, very good' and that was it and all agreed without anyone noticing. Then they got to conference two weeks later and came in to the conference hall and there was the rose, with 'Labour: Putting People First'. And it was everywhere, everywhere.[44]

Neil, too, had smartened up his image: with a short haircut, dark suits and white shirts. This was partly thanks to Joe Napolitan, a political consultant to Walter Mondale whom Patricia Hewitt had brought in to advise Labour. Napolitan had written a series of hard-hitting memos on Labour's vulnerabilities, and in his first direct note to Kinnock, in April 1986, he warned him that voters were not convinced

he would make a better Prime Minister than Margaret
Thatcher. 'You must do the things necessary to project yourself more effectively,' he wrote. He advised him to take a
television training seminar, dry-run his TV appearances,
critique them afterwards, and 'look like a Prime Minister . . .
You may truly be a man of the people – but you've got to
act just a little bit different than they do.'[45] Our SCA research
showed people wanted more authority, confidence and gravitas from Kinnock; although they liked him, he didn't yet
measure up as a leader.

In the summer of 1986 Labour reached 40 per cent in
the polls, with the Tories on 32 per cent and the Alliance
on 26 per cent. At conference, delegates voted to retain
nearly all the policies which had lost them the 1983 election
so dramatically. Most damagingly, defence dominated the
agenda as delegates and front-bench spokesmen argued over
unilateralism and US Defense Secretary Caspar Weinberger
argued that the party's unilateralist proposals would mean
the break-up of Nato. Neil Kinnock followed with a passionate
speech condemning nuclear weapons. 'I would die for my
country, but I tell you I would never let my country die for
me,' he told delegates.[46] At the Tory conference the next
week, stunningly stage-managed by Saatchi's, ministers
presented a series of new initiatives around the theme 'The
Next Moves Forward'. Labour's poll ratings started to slip.

Building on sand

The 1986 conference was Labour's most successful for twenty
years, but already the seeds of defeat had been sown. By the
end of the year, we knew how we wanted to fight the election. We wanted to focus on television; ensure brilliant,
memorable pictures; provide stories that fed into every stage
of the news cycle; concentrate on the leader and a small
group of key campaigners; plan the campaign around the
discipline of a tightly controlled daily grid. This is how the
1987 election was fought and it is essentially how Labour
has fought every national election since. 'We got ahead of

the game,' Hewitt, who was on maternity leave at the time, remembers.

> You [Gould] and sometimes Peter used to come down to my house, and that was when we worked on the grid for the election campaign proper. And we came up with this very simple device: we basically said, what is going to matter in this election campaign is television, and what's going to matter on television is the pictures, and we said, right, for each day there will be a theme and the pictures will be tied to the theme. And it was really simple, but nobody had ever done it.
>
> And so we created this grid, day by day by day, and I remember sitting around my dining-room table and you saying, 'On the Thursday before election day we've got to go really big, and it's got to be health because that's our big issue,' and so we wrote in Thursday minus six or whatever it is, 'health', and that was health and it was kind of written in stone. And it was very rigid and it caused all kinds of problems when we tried to repeat it in '92, but in '87 what it did was catch the media completely unprepared, and it was only about halfway through the election that they suddenly figured out that whatever they asked Neil about, the pictures were always the pictures we wanted. And so even when we had a very nasty defence wobble right in the middle of the campaign and they were chasing Neil around the hospital trying to ask him about defence, the pictures said 'health' – hospitals, nurses, caring. And it drove them up the wall, but it was too late for them to get out of it.[47]

This approach was a revolution, not just in Labour Party campaigning but in political campaigning by any party. It was the work of two people: Mandelson and Hewitt. Hewitt provided the logistical power. By early 1986 draft timetables were in place, each election day already taking tentative shape. The degree of early planning was extraordinary for the time. Mandelson provided the combination of organisational rigour and presentational brilliance which has become his hallmark. But Mandelson also understood the essential political imperatives that were the prerequisites for election success: the extreme left had to be smashed, at best, or sidelined at worst; the party had to appear electable; we had to stop the Alliance replacing us as the natural party of opposition. As he says, 'The plan for the election, after the conference in 1986, was to show that (a) we had beaten off the hard left who had taken control of the party in the years before; and (b) either to get rid of or to make as appealing as possible the policies that we had at the time. And to use Neil Kinnock as a symbol of sense returning, the hard left being seen off, the party changing and equipping itself for serious politics. We needed to reinstate ourselves as the serious challenger to the Conservatives, and to see off the Liberal–SDP Alliance.'[48]

But although the planning was extensive, the foundations were built on sand. To will an outcome was not to achieve it. Labour was developing a surface gloss and burgeoning campaigning competence, but below the surface it was riddled with flaws. Labour looked better, but it had not become better.

Joe Napolitan had written more memos to Kinnock's office over the summer, warning of Labour's problems, which included the perception of weak and incompetent leadership; extreme leftism; the undue influence of the trade unions; racial worries; and Labour's affinity for the perceived 'undesirables'.[49] He warned of likely Tory campaign themes: law and order; 'Kinnock can't even unite his own party – how can he expect to control the country'; control of the government by the trade unions; in a time of crisis, experience counts; 'Kinnock will open the door to a flood of new immigrants'; and, most dangerously in his opinion, defence – 'You can almost see their ads now: Labour's defence policy will leave Great Britain defenceless, naked to our enemies.'[50] After the fiasco at conference, he wrote a stinging note on the defence policy, warning that it put Labour at a serious disadvantage. 'The Labour Party today finds itself in the predictable position of being on the defensive in the forthcoming campaign, primarily because of its policy on defence,' he wrote. 'Deliberate adoption of a policy that puts a party or a candidate at serious liability even before the campaign begins raises doubts about the ability of that party or candidate to accept serious strategy recommendations that might overcome the self-inflicted wound. Labour's chances of victory in the next election were, in my opinion, tenuous even before the defence policy became official party doctrine; now those chances are even less.'[51] Accepting that it was impossible to change the policy, Labour needed to try to turn it into an asset, he said, by going on the offensive, attacking the Conservatives' running down of conventional forces and accusing them of 'putting all their eggs in a nuclear basket'.[52]

Our research over the summer into attitudes towards the party's defence policies confirmed everything that Napolitan had been saying. People had a simple, common-sense view of the issue – if you have a dog, no one will attack you; if someone else has a knife, you should have a knife also. There was some support for multilateral disarmament, but none for unilateralism. People thought Labour's defence policy was throwing in the towel. And in their essential, gut responses, they were right. It is difficult now to describe the folly of our defence policy at that time. It was incredible to anyone with any vestige of common sense. Once, at a meeting, it was suggested that Labour's policy was to repel a Soviet invasion with ditches. We all laughed. Peter Mandelson commented, 'Things may be bad, but they're not that bad.' But moments later Mike Gapes, the Labour Party researcher responsible for defence (and now Labour MP for Ilford South), came into the room, shamefaced: yes, it was true. Labour planned to counter the second most powerful armed empire in the world with ditches. 'But don't worry,' Gapes added, 'they are exploding ditches.' And this at a time of East–West tension. In October 1986 the Reykjavik summit between Gorbachev and Reagan broke up acrimoniously with no agreement on disarmament.

If our defence policy implied gradual surrender, our

presentational strategy for it was to go on the attack. Our proposition was not credible, but at least it was bold. It was the Tories, not us, who were weakening our defences, we argued – money spent on nuclear weapons was putting our security at risk by destroying our conventional forces. The Falklands War could not, for example, be fought today. Within two months of the end of conference we prepared a campaign, 'Modern Britain in the Modern World: The Power to Defend Our Country', which focused on making Britain stronger and better defended, by switching from nuclear to conventional weapons.

Unilateralism would come back to haunt us throughout the run-up to the election and during the campaign itself. A trip by Kinnock to see President Reagan in Washington at the end of March 1987 rebounded when Reagan gave Kinnock less than the allotted half an hour, and his press secretary Marlin Fitzwater told journalists afterwards, in direct contradiction to what Kinnock's staff had claimed, that the President had warned Kinnock his defence policy would threaten Nato. This contrasted badly with a successful trip by Thatcher to Moscow at the end of March, when she was mobbed by cheering crowds, enjoyed eleven hours of talks with an adulatory Mikhail Gorbachev, and cemented her international image as the 'Iron Lady'. The contrast could not have been more explicit.

Defence was bad, but there was worse to come. Labour was being damned by the insane extremism of its local councils.

The Tories had begun a campaign against Labour's 'loony left', headed by Environment Secretary Nicholas Ridley, who was ridiculing left-wing councils for intimidation and political correctness. This worked partly because of the brilliance of the Conservative attack; partly because of the relentless pounding of the tabloid press; but mostly because it was true. The Tories jumped on the GLC's Section 137 rule, which allowed council funding of every special-interest group from Chile Democratic GB through Brent Friends of the Earth to the Rastafarian Society. In Liverpool, Kinnock began moves to expel the Labour group leader Tony Byrne and the group secretary Tony Hood.

In the winter, qualitative research showed that Alliance supporters – the essential election battleground – were, not surprisingly, running scared. Fear of Labour massively outweighed dislike of the Tories. It was clear that our campaign had stalled, while the Tories had successfully grabbed the election agenda – they had shifted the emphasis off Thatcher, launched a series of successful policy initiatives from more acceptable ministers, introduced a sense that the economy might be turning the corner, and maintained a sustained attack on Labour over defence, the loony left, mortgages and social ownership.

Expecting an election in the summer, I wrote that we had to begin our campaign early in the new year and that 'the focus of the campaign should be a sharp, aggressive proposition, from which all communications would flow'.[53] We did not have one, and we were not to get one. What we had was 'Investing in People'. As I wrote at the time: 'This is a convincing logic but not an election-fighting proposition. We need one with a cutting edge, if only to act as a focus for all our creative work. All PPBs [party political broadcasts] and advertisements should flow from this proposition, the prime focus of the strategy should be to discredit the government's record, and the battleground of the campaign should be Kinnock against Thatcher.' And we should use fear. 'The only realistic hope we have got of overcoming the Tory campaign of fear is a counter-campaign based on dislike and hostility of the government, and in particular Thatcher. Like it or not, it is going to be a negative campaign. If we attempt to run a positive campaign within this context we will be swamped. Our positives will not be able to defeat their presentation of our negatives.' And if we were going to fight a negative campaign, I thought we needed at least one positive, which had to be Neil Kinnock. 'Presenting Labour in a positive light will be difficult, presenting Kinnock in a positive light much less so.'[54]

I was concerned, too, that the Tories were out-campaigning

us. In a note to Mandelson and Bryan Gould, who had taken over from Robin Cook as campaign co-ordinator, in December, I said we had to emulate the Tories' successful autumn offensive: 'They worked out a plan based on exploiting our greatest weaknesses, and defending their areas of vulnerability, which they then proceeded to systematically and ruthlessly implement. As Chris Powell said on Monday, when they pull the trigger the gun goes off. This is exactly what they did in 1983. In 1987 this is what we have to achieve.'[55]

But before we had a chance, we were torpedoed again. In January 1987 Deirdre Wood, a hard-left former councillor, was chosen as Labour's candidate for a by-election in Greenwich caused by the death of Labour MP Guy Barnett, against the SDP's Rosie Barnes. In the election in February we were slaughtered. Our 5,000-vote majority turned to a 6,000-vote lead for the Alliance. On the day of the defeat, Patricia Hewitt wrote a tough memo to Larry Whitty, Jack Cunningham and Frank Dobson, chair of London Labour MPs at the time. Explosively, it was leaked to the press. In it, she warned: 'It's obvious from our own polling, as well as from the doorstep, that the "London effect" is now very noticeable. The "loony Labour left" is taking its toll: the gays and lesbians issue is costing us dear among the pensioners, and fear of extremism and higher taxes/rates is particularly prominent in the GLC area.'[56] The memo caused outrage but was entirely accurate. 'It wasn't just coming up in London – it was all around the country,' Hewitt remembers. 'Charles [Clarke] and I had both tried but we couldn't get the London parties to start sorting it out. Finally, in a fury – it was a moment of ill-discipline – I wrote to Larry thinking I'll put this on paper and make it be taken seriously. And it was leaked. So that was another huge problem.'[57]

Colin Byrne began work as a press officer in Walworth Road just after the Greenwich by-election. He had read an article by Mandelson in the *Guardian* about the need for Labour to embrace modern communications and, impressed, contacted him. When he was taken on, he found the reality sadly distant from Peter's dream. 'The whole building was dismal,' he said. 'It was like starting work in a minor regional trade union headquarters in terms of morale, low quality of staff, lots of people round the place who seemed to have been there for thirty years. Literally guys in corners, smoking fags and drinking tea all day. It was very depressing, and not at all what I had expected from the rhetoric of Mandelson and modern mass communications.'[58] This was why they needed the SCA.

Kinnock made his disastrous trip to Washington in March, against the advice of Charles Clarke and Peter Mandelson, because he hated the thought of being accused of cowardice if he cancelled. He told me: 'If you fall off a bike you have to get straight back on it.' A Commons tea-room row between John Prescott, then the employment spokesman, and former Prime Minister Jim Callaghan, over defence, overshadowed the 'New Jobs for Britain' launch. And all this against a background of a country basking in four years of sustained economic growth. Inflation had not risen above 5 per cent; average weekly earnings had risen by 14 per cent in real terms; the FTSE 100 had quintupled in value; and the basic rate of tax was heading down from 33 per cent towards 25 per cent.[59]

On 10 March, I wrote to Mandelson with the latest focus group research, from lapsed Labour voters in Camden. This research was to lead to the big strategic decisions of the 1987 campaign. People were wary of us, but they did not like the Conservatives and felt a sense of inevitable despair at the prospect of their return. This despair was rooted in deep emotions and the big social issues: health; education; jobs; crime. This was the only ground we could fight on: emotional power based on social issues. The truth is that this was an election the Conservatives should have lost. People wanted them out, but did not trust us at all. As I wrote at the time, 'If we lose this election it will not be because they have done well, but because of the failure of the opposition parties to provide a convincing alternative. The election will, in effect, be lost by default.' The line we had worked out for the creative treatments, 'Isn't it time for a change of heart?' was 'too soft and insufficiently action-based for the current mood',[60] I warned, so we decided to settle on: 'The country's crying out for change. Vote Labour.' Strangely, although Peter and I agreed this strategy and built the campaign around it, Neil's thinking was a mystery to us. It turned out that by extraordinary coincidence his timing was the same as ours, so when the first Labour advertisement using this line, and his first campaign speech using the same deeply emotional theme, appeared on the same day, it was actually unplanned.

By the end of March, we were in third place, behind the Alliance, in the polls. Over April we recovered slightly, settling at around 30 per cent, with the Alliance on 27 and the Conservatives 41. In a review of the polls, I said the consequence of these shifts 'is the poll configuration the government has been looking for before calling an election'. Post-Greenwich damage to the party might have been so great, I said, that short-term recovery was impossible. Comparisons between April and January showed an even starker picture: government approval and satisfaction with Mrs Thatcher up, satisfaction with Mr Kinnock and Labour's policies down, satisfaction with Dr Owen and the SDP's policies up. The 7,000-plus PA/Marplan poll showed Labour losing 10 per cent in the north, 12 per cent in Scotland, 11 per cent in the East Midlands and 13 per cent in Wales compared to six months earlier. Victory, I concluded, looked likely for the government.[61]

Hewitt remembers the gloom around that time:

I remember talking to Neil a week before the election was called and we had had a poll which put us in third place, or in joint third place with the Liberals, and Neil and I were talking about this and we sort of looked at each other, and one of us said, we could go into third place, and we said, once we start sliding there's no bottom to this – there's no reason why we should bottom out at 25 per cent or whatever it was we got in '83 – we could just go into freefall. And I said to him, what we've got to stop happening is this becoming the story of who is going to be in third place. And that was I think the really crucial thing that our election campaign did. It just killed the Alliance.[62]

Kinnock showed great courage during this period, but he was prone to bouts of despair. I remember an SCA journalists' group meeting at which he spent most of the evening depressed about himself and the party's prospects. One journalist had the temerity to ask him, 'What would you do if you lose? Would you resign?' Neil smashed his fist into the table, sending cutlery flying, and said, 'I will stay. I will fight on. Because only I can change the party.'

Shortly before the election, Peter Mandelson organised a presentation and dinner with Neil Kinnock at BMP's offices. It was meant to be a relaxed, friendly, morale-boosting occasion, but that afternoon we were told Neil could not stay for dinner as Glenys had planned something different. However, he stayed for the presentation. Neil was very depressed that night, full of despair about our chances in the election and blaming himself, saying, 'Your work's great, but you can't change me.' This was typical of Neil: doubting himself; concerned about letting others down; but also psyching himself up for the General Election.

Glorious defeat

On 11 May, the day the 1987 General Election was called, Peter phoned. 'Have you heard?' he said. 'Let's get on with it.' We started the election more or less as we had finished in 1983, with a 28 per cent share of the vote in an average of the first three polls, the Alliance just behind with 26.6 per cent and the Conservatives in the mid-40s.[63] It was clear that this election was going to be a battle for second place. Perhaps even worse than our share of vote were perceptions of the party: 67 per cent thought we were too extreme; 69 per cent believed our leadership was poor; 73 per cent thought we were too divided and 55 per cent said the economy would be worse under Labour.[64] This was not at all the position in which we wanted to start the election. Eighteen months of communications modernisation and war on Militant had left us barely better placed than four years ago. This election was clearly the fight for the survival of Labour as the major opposition party in British politics.

We used to meet in Peter's small office in Walworth Road, where he would sit, feet on desk, outwardly calm, always apparently in control. In some ways we were perfectly prepared, but in others we were lost. We had the grid, honed to the minute; we had advertisements fused with the grid for almost every day of the campaign; we had a series of outstanding broadcasts culminating in Hugh Hudson's Kinnock party election broadcast, perhaps the greatest party political broadcast ever made. We had schedules for our key campaigners, television pictures meshed perfectly with our chosen storyline of the day, a new corporate identity, daily opinion polls and focus groups. The problem was that we also had glaring and potentially fatal deficiencies, policies basically unreformed since 1983 including a completely untenable defence policy, and a fearsomely hostile press. Margaret Scammell has estimated that 73 per cent of the *Sun*'s election coverage, 54 per cent of the *Daily Mail*'s and 46 per cent of the *Daily Star*'s was 'Labour-knocking' copy.[65] And we had two big enigmas: one was Neil Kinnock, the other was our central campaign strategy – what we were really saying to the nation. Neil's ratings were not good going into the election. He had been set back by two US trips, by defence, by the mishaps of the spring of 1987. But he approached the campaign with an energy and power that had been waiting to be released. He would storm around the office, ranting at the iniquity of his situation, saying, 'I may be written off now, but I will destroy Thatcher and Owen with the power of my words.' His anger and intensity were awesome. His strength came from his words, he believed his power was in his rhetoric. When his words flowed, his confidence soared. In the 1987 election, the power of Neil's words saved Labour.

Although we had all the apparatus of a campaign, we lacked a strategy. We knew that in order to win we had to focus on the economy. We needed a central, compelling argument. But the setbacks of 1987 smashed these possibilities on the rocks. We could not win on the economy. We could not develop a central campaign rationale plausible enough to grab victory from the Conservatives. All we could do was to fall back on our core strengths and produce a campaign so emotional, so intense, so rooted in our heartland social issues, that we could blast the Alliance away and ensure second place. Chris Powell remembers our strategy as 'basically damage limitation, both in the sense of the fears of the potential of the SDP to take over as the official opposition party and eclipse the Labour Party for ever more, but also in the knowledge that many of the policies that Labour then had would be extremely difficult to effectively sell to enough voters to get elected. In the election itself we used advertising to try and move the agenda about, combined with the press conferences, so that we would never get pinned on one subject and have great damage done to us and get the initiative on subjects that we wanted to talk about.'[66]

There was no certainty that Neil would rise to the occasion and the strategy would work – that these two crucial elements would fuse together. For the first few days of the campaign, it seemed they might not. The Alliance started strongly and slickly; one poll had Labour in third place. People started to write Labour off. And then, in a moment of extraordinary combustion, it all came together. Neil made his Llandudno speech – 'Why am I the first Kinnock in a thousand generations to go to university'[67] – and by the sheer force of his will, the extraordinary power of his words, the election tide was turned. Visibly, tangibly, the mood changed and confidence soared. Overnight, strategy, message and leader fused, producing an incredible energy. This moment, this speech, effectively ended the ambitions of the Alliance to be the second party in British politics. Although week one saw no change in the polls, the tide had turned.

Week two saw further Labour advances. The Alliance

campaign began to falter. Labour pinned the Conservatives back with a controversially worded advertisement: a broadcast remark by Norman Tebbit in 1983 saying, 'If unemployment is not below three million in five years then I'm not worth electing.'[68] Peter played this furore perfectly, constantly pouring petrol on the flames, culminating with a presentation of Tebbit's actual words on a cranky tape-recorder to the assembled journalists. Tebbit's words bore little relationship to the words on the advertisement, but it didn't matter. We had the tape, Tebbit was speaking, Peter was icily confident, the journalists were seduced.

Then came the Hudson party political broadcast, the moment, according to the Alliance strategists, when their campaign folded. The broadcast, an emotional biography of Neil Kinnock's life using romantic footage of Neil and Glenys walking along windswept cliffs, was brought to Peter by Hugh late in the night two days before transmission. It ended not with the word 'Labour', but with 'Kinnock'. This was an unprecedented development – fighting an election campaign under the name of the leader and not the party. It could hardly have been more daring or controversial. But Peter backed it without a murmur. As I watched, I marvelled at its power. Despite everything, the campaign had worked. The broadcast had the most sensational impact: Neil's ratings went up 16 per cent overnight. Some people say that the broadcast had no effect, that Labour still lost. They are wrong. Almost overnight Labour had shunted the Alliance to the sidelines. By the end of the second week the polls had begun to shift. Labour was on the move.

But at the start of the third week, Neil slipped up. Asked a fairly soft question by David Frost, Neil gave the impression that Labour's response to invasion would be civil resistance. Or, in David Owen's snide soundbite, 'He wants *Dad's Army* back.'[69] The answer was not entirely Neil's fault – the defence policy was indefensible – but it was an error and Neil blamed himself terribly for it. It gave the Conservatives an opening on defence and they pounded us mercilessly. From surging forward, we were now pinned to the ropes.

The Conservatives produced their one great advertisement of the campaign, 'Labour's Policy on Arms', with a hapless soldier holding his hands up. But we survived the week, Kinnock's ratings remained high, and the Alliance could not climb back. Defence was killed by a press conference devoted entirely to that subject, allowing the journalists to exhaust their interest in it and showing the wisdom of confronting serious political danger and not ducking it. Within days Labour was back on the attack, with the Conservative low point the famous wobbly Thursday, when a Gallup poll showed the lead narrowing to four points and Thatcher made a hash of health.

But this was the last good news for Labour. As we tired, the Conservatives moved into top gear. They attacked on taxation and Labour extremism, issues that were certain to hurt our vote. And they linked a massive tabloid attack with a huge advertising offensive on the classic 'Don't Let Labour Ruin It' theme. In response to this, Labour was running on empty. Peter was exhausted, drained by the awesome demands of the campaign. Roy Hattersley stumbled on taxation, which the Tory press jumped on. The *Daily Mail* denounced 'LABOUR'S LIES ON TAXATION'[70] while the *Daily Express* screamed: 'EXPOSED: LABOUR'S TAX FIASCO'.[71] Healey, put on the back foot over his wife's hip operation, fumbled on private health. We had no energy, no new ideas, no final-week burst. Meanwhile, Thatcher coolly went to Venice to meet world leaders.

The day of the election, 11 June 1987, we knew we had lost, but we couldn't predict how badly. I telephoned Peter and asked him what was the minimum acceptable result: the smallest share of the vote with which he and I could survive in Labour communications. He said 35 per cent. We got 31 per cent. I went in early that Thursday evening, and there was great optimism: a *Newsnight* poll was predicting a hung parliament. But at 9.30 P.M. a call came through from the BBC with their exit poll. Peter took the call in his office, watched in silence by myself, Deborah Mattinson, Richard Faulkner and the four Labour press officers. As he heard the poll result his face became ashen. 'It is bad,' he said, 'they're back with a majority of a hundred.' As the results rolled in, it became unbearable. I walked into the night and felt the awful pain of election defeat.

In fact, the campaign had been an extraordinary success. It had saved Labour. It need not have been so – a weaker campaign, any hint of the chaos and unprofessionalism of 1983, and Labour would have been smashed into third place, perhaps for ever. Labour's vote rose three points to 31 per cent. The Alliance vote fell almost four points to 23 per cent. A gap at the beginning of the campaign of less than 2 per cent had increased to 8 per cent: a massive shift in four weeks. Labour never looked back; the Alliance never recovered.

But it was still a crushing defeat, and on the issues that really mattered – tax, the economy, extremism – Labour had fallen back. It had modernised its communications, but not its policies or the party itself, and the best communications professionals in the world could not rescue it. 'In a way, we demonstrated the weakness of advertising and marketing,' said Chris Powell. 'It makes very little difference how well or how professionally you do the campaign if your leader and your policies are not likely to appeal to the broad mass of the population.'[72]

Yet we dragged Labour, in under two years, from a party which abhorred photo opportunities and still believed the way to address the public was to don a donkey jacket and harangue the party faithful at rallies into the glare of modern professional communications. We gave them a new identity, the red rose, the Hugh Hudson broadcast and the campaign grid. We ran a brilliant campaign and proved Labour was serious about winning and sufficiently self-disciplined to govern. It wasn't enough to win the votes we needed, but it was probably enough to secure the future of the party. Partial modernisation had saved Labour, but a basically unchanged party was still years away from earning the trust of the people.

3

THE LONG DECLINE

'Another load of bloody rubbish'

Immediately after the 1987 defeat I retired hurt to our house in Hampshire and hid, speaking to almost no one. Election defeat is like bereavement: a long, empty ache. It was not as bad in 1987 as it would be in 1992, but it was painful enough. For a couple of weeks I sat miserably alone, or took long walks around the Test Valley. I remember now only a cheerful call from Bob Worcester wishing me well.

But even as I sat and moped it became clear to me why we had lost and what we had to do next. We lost because we had not changed far enough, fast enough. The engine had been polished, but it was still a Victorian relic. I began gathering evidence for an election post-mortem which I completed in London in July and sent to Larry Whitty, Neil Kinnock and Peter Mandelson.

The strengths of the 1987 campaign were clear enough: apart from its professional organisation, it had developed a strong strategic focus – social, emotional, passionate. But there were weaknesses too. We were still fighting on our own ground, not taking back Conservative territory, or even reclaiming neutral ground. Effectively we gave up the economy, taxation and personal finance to the Conservatives, and in so doing forfeited any chance of winning the election. There was also no doubt that we tailed off in the last week. We were exhausted, we had no more strategic options. In the last, crucial few days, we lacked firepower.[1]

We had also been too vague, over-emphasising big, general themes while the Tories were precise, Exoceting the voters where it really mattered and linking the tangible benefits of voting Conservative (such as no strikes) alongside people's tangible fears (on defence, for example). On the economy we had been abstract and long-winded. I was honest about Neil, describing him as 'our greatest campaign asset', but criticising his decision to open the door on defence. His bearing had been 'oppositional rather than governmental', and misjudgements such as dancing at the final week's rally in Islington had undermined his stature.[2]

But the main conclusions of the evaluation were forward-looking and strategic. We needed to establish a planning group to examine demographic changes and how they would affect Labour; to look at changes in lifestyle, values and attitudes; to establish what the party needed to do to appeal beyond its normal demographic base.[3]

I followed the formal election review with a strategic note in late July, setting out more clearly what had to be done. Labour had been successful in regaining some heartland support, but had failed to win back key groups, particularly in the south and the Midlands. For Labour to form a government it would be crucial, I said, not only for it to appeal to its traditional support base – which came from a declining sector of the population – but also for it to attract new voters. In short, we had to reach out to the new middle classes. 'It is now essential that the party embarks on a major research project to identify why defecting groups have left Labour, and what must be done to win them back,' I argued.[4] This was the genesis of 'Labour and Britain in the 1990s',[5] the most comprehensive review of public opinion ever undertaken by Labour. It became the polling foundation upon which the party's modernisation was built.

Indications of the hostility my conclusions would face from some in the party came when Roy Hattersley, in stubbornly traditionalist mode on *A Week in Politics* in July, described equality and a freer society as the Labour Party's 'Sermon on the Mount', not to be abandoned because 'marketing men' found it wasn't attracting 'the trendy, upwardly-mobile middle classes'.[6] For me his argument encapsulated everything that had gone wrong with Labour. Fundamentalist in tone, imbuing political ideas with the power of immutable myth, resisting change, it seemed to sneer at people who wanted to get on and seek better lives for themselves and their children. For Roy, what has gone wrong for Labour is that it has capitulated to the middle classes. For me, what has gone right with the party is that it has now finally reached out to them.

We have different Labour dreams, and above all different conceptions of what and who the middle classes are: the difference between politics formed in the southern suburbs and in Sheffield's back streets. To Roy the middle classes are slick, southern, superficial. To me they are caring, hard-working, anxious, ambitious – ordinary people with dreams, living lives under the kind of pressure Roy left behind thirty years ago. They are, in one form or another, the great majority of our population and the great majority of the coalition Labour needed to build to win power. In 1987 they were Labour's future, as they are today. It infuriates Roy that Labour is obsessed with the middle classes. It infuriates me to hear progressive politicians with comfortable lifestyles pouring scorn on hard-working people who dare to aspire to a little of the same. But if Roy is resistant to middle-class politics he was kind to me: he was helpful in getting me established with the Labour Party in 1985 – something I hope he does not regret too much now.

But Hattersley was not alone. Rodney Bickerstaffe, General Secretary of NUPE, told the Labour Party conference in 1987: 'We cannot hand Labour over to marketing men to be packaged like breakfast cereal; our policies cannot be contracted out to the pick of the polls.'[7] Thankfully others, like Bryan Gould, campaign co-ordinator in the 1987 election, took a more enlightened view. He told *The World This Weekend* in July 1987: 'What we ought to be doing is looking at where policies ought to come from, what the demand is, what interests we ought to be serving. In that way we can make sure that the policy includes its popular appeal from the outset.'[8]

Mandelson himself didn't blink. Immediately he set in motion a polling and demographic review. It took four months and was chiefly carried out by Patricia Hewitt, who chaired the process; Roger Jowell of the Social and Community Planning Research; Paul Ormerod, an economist from the Henley Centre for Forecasting; Andrew (now Lord) McIntosh of IFF (a market research company); Andrew Shaw from Liverpool University and Deborah Mattinson, who had become my business partner, and was a crucial figure in Labour's communications revolution. The review was a huge undertaking; it was effectively an autopsy on the British electorate and its influence was enormous.

We presented it to the NEC and the shadow Cabinet on 20 November 1987. I introduced the meeting because no one else would. Peter and Patricia, as partisan party officials, watched from the back, not wishing to contaminate the objectivity of the findings. Speaking first was a terrifying ordeal because even at the time I was aware that this was a defining moment in the development of the Labour Party. We were about to tell the party that seventy years of history had been wrong: Labour had to take a different course; it had to modernise or wither away.

The atmosphere in the room at Transport House was tense. The room seemed vast, the audience massive. Somewhere sat Peter: insouciant and radiating a confidence I wished I could share. As I rose to speak, my knees trembled, my voice sounded hollow. I was saved by Dennis Skinner. 'Another load of bloody rubbish,' he growled. This broke the tension and lifted my nerve. At the time, I thought this was just Dennis being a Luddite; I suspect now that he was kindly rescuing me from my nerves.

I did not say much – I left that to others in a meeting which lasted three and a half hours. After it, no one who was present would feel quite the same about Labour and its future. The presentation was wide in scope and its findings were devastating: Labour's share of the vote had fallen by

17 per cent in twenty years, while the Conservative share had remained immutably solid. No single section of the population had left us more than any other. Labour had lost working-class votes as well as middle-class votes. All sections of society had deserted the party.[9]

The people who *were* voting Labour had done so out of habit: 27 per cent of its supporters voted Labour because it was the 'party of the working class'; 20 per cent because they had 'always voted Labour'. As one northern respondent said, 'I have always voted socialist. So have all my family.' But Conservative voters were more discriminating. They voted Tory because of Thatcher; because the government was doing a good job; because inflation was under control; because the Tories knew how to manage the economy. Only 7 per cent voted Conservative because they always had done.[10]

The reasons given for not voting Labour were particularly damning. Among lapsed Labour voters, extremism was the top factor; second was trade union domination and division; third, defence; and finally, weak leadership. People believed Labour would cut their standard of living and restrict their freedom to buy council houses and shares.[11]

One working-class ex-Labour voter said, 'I have changed basically because of my working position – what I want from life. I mean, eventually you want to buy a place. You want to get more out of what you earn.'[12] I wanted this voter back. Roy Hattersley was less sure.

These findings on their own were bleak. But worse was to come. The research had found that Labour's remaining support was habitual, its lapsed supporters visceral in their attitudes towards the party. But the underlying social and economic tide was making a bad situation worse. The numbers of manual workers were declining; home ownership was increasing; share-holding, private medicine and private schooling were becoming much more popular.[13]

There were some shafts of light among these damning social trends. Labour values continued to have strong support and, most important of all, less than half of the collapse in

Labour support in the previous twenty years could be ascribed to demographic changes alone: most of it was the result of the policies and image of the party. If Labour changed, so could its electoral fortunes.[14]

To some this was common sense; to others, heresy. At the end of the presentation there was silence, broken by Tony Benn, who apologised for criticising our research methods in advance. Most people in the room applauded. The SCA had let off a bomb in the heart of Labour.

The lion that didn't roar

The key figure in the initiation of the policy review which followed 'Labour and Britain in the 1990s' was Tom Sawyer, then Deputy General Secretary of NUPE and, from October 1994 to October 1998, General Secretary of the Labour Party. Tom has a quiet manner, but underneath it lies real toughness. He was and is one of the genuinely modernising figures in the Labour movement. He told the Fabian Society in June 1988, 'We want to win the next General Election. And to anyone who says this is crude or unprincipled, I say that to put Labour into government, into a position where we can put our principles into practice, is the most sophisticated and principled aim that the party could have.'[15] He is also loyal. After the defeat in 1992, Tom was one of the few who stood by those who had been responsible for the campaign. He did not turn in the wind. If you put together his contribution towards the policy review and his work as General Secretary, he is someone who can genuinely claim great credit for the election of a Labour government in 1997.

Not only did Tom have the idea for the review, he was also a key figure in its gestation and development, alongside Neil. 'After the election,' Patricia Hewitt remembers, 'Tom Sawyer came to see Neil and said, this is a much bigger task than we ever thought. We've got to go back to square one, look at aims and values, have a policy review. So it was Tom's idea. Neil bought it.'[16] They took the campaign strategy committee structure and adapted it to the policy review, with seven policy sub-committees each co-chaired by a member of the shadow Cabinet and a member of the NEC.

Neil Kinnock's two great modernising achievements were expunging Militant and ditching unpopular policies through the policy review. Many believed that Kinnock had decided at the outset the policies he wanted to emerge from the review, but he hadn't. He knew he wanted policies that would equip Labour for the future, but he was open-minded about their precise form. As Patricia Hewitt recalled:

Neil knew in advance the outcome he wanted only in the sense that he would recognise it when he saw it. What he wanted was something that would fit the 1990s. Right at the beginning, Hattersley said there had to be a philosophical framework for this, and Neil said okay – you write it. And he wrote 'Aims and Values', but no one took much notice of it.

With 'Labour and Britain in the 1990s' we were telling them why we lost the election, and how we had to change, to give a context to the policy review. And people were terrified by what we were telling them. So what Neil was saying – to the policy convenors, shadow Cabinet, NEC, party conference – was, don't worry about the old arguments, put yourself into the 1990s, the next chance we're going to have to fight an election. Stand in the future and then figure out what are the right policies for Labour to achieve its objectives. So he really gave the policy review committees a wonderful opportunity, a blank sheet of paper, and I think his overwhelming disappointment was that they didn't pick that up and run with it.[17]

The SCA was closely involved in the policy review process at all stages and undertook a research programme under Deborah Mattinson to complement the newly established policy review groups. Each group had a set of researchers assigned to it who conducted qualitative research. But polling cannot create policy, and the direct influence of the SCA on the content of the final review was less than is believed. If research had had more influence in 1988 and the people's voice had been heard more loudly, then the results would have been bolder, braver, more modern. Labour would have done better in 1992.

But in fact, with the exception of defence, where Gerald Kaufman brilliantly abandoned unilateralism, the polling evidence was largely ignored. Interesting themes and ideas that emerged through the review process tended to be blocked. We were stuck with 'functional intervention', 'social ownership' (a euphemism for back-door nationalisation), and a commitment to retake majority ownership of British Telecom and totally renationalise the water industry.[18] A highly interventionist supply-side strategy was still regarded as the only key to industrial recovery. 'I was very disappointed with the policy review,' said Charles Clarke. 'We should have been much more engaged from Neil's office. We were too respectful of the leading politicians.'[19] Most desperately, against the strongest SCA advice, John Smith was preparing benefits pledges which would trap us on tax for the next election. Although it took Labour forward, the policy review was fundamentally a missed opportunity for which we paid a heavy price in 1992.

Labour was changing too little and too slowly.

Despair

A general depression hung over the party by the end of 1987. In my diary, I wrote, 'Neil is in a malaise, which seems to be settling down over Labour Party advisers. There is exceptionally low morale at Walworth Road following re-organisation and staff cut-backs. Peter is talking about the difficulties of making progress at Walworth Road.'[20] Even some of Kinnock's closest supporters were beginning to question his leadership. Rumours that John Prescott might challenge Hattersley for the deputy leadership were rumbling on; the dispute tumbled into the beginning of the next year.

In January 1988 I wrote a private note to Mandelson warning of the dangers I felt we were facing: we lacked momentum; lacked confidence; lacked initiatives; lacked assertiveness. I warned that this could soon lead to a leadership crisis. We had to break clear of this and start looking like winners: 'At the moment I suspect that internally and externally people are sensing that Labour will not win the next election. This has to change.'[21]

But in fact things got worse. Tony Benn attacked Kinnock in a string of press releases and in March, as Nigel Lawson delivered his tax-cutting budget, slashing the top rate of income tax from 60 per cent to 40 per cent and reducing the standard rate to 25 per cent, Benn challenged Kinnock for the leadership. Defence flared up as an issue in June, after Kinnock appeared to hint first in a private lunch with the *Independent* and later in an interview on *This Week, Next Week* that he was considering a shift to multilateralism;[22] Denzil Davies, Labour's defence spokesman, resigned, accusing Kinnock of changing defence policy without consulting him. At the time, Kinnock's aides claimed he knew exactly what he was doing. Hewitt told the story of Neil's riposte when he came out of the *This Week, Next Week* studio and she said to him, 'You slayed a few sacred cows there.' Neil, she said, winked and replied, 'Just put them to sleep, lovey, just put them to sleep.'[23] But two weeks later, in an on-the-record briefing with executives of the *Independent*, he gave the impression that Labour defence policy was unchanged; unilateralism was still in.[24] Mandelson, who had no warning he was about to do this, was devastated. Shadow Cabinet members and MPs were briefing against Neil uncontrollably, and he was slated in the weekend press.

The truth is that Neil was exhausted and depressed. A fortnight later I had a meeting with two of those closest to him to discuss our Kinnock campaign. We were all concerned about him, he was under impossible pressure, much of it focused on supporting in public a defence policy he privately thought was madness. Neil had to carry within him the massive contradictions at the heart of the Labour Party, putting intolerable strains on him and his public voice.

'They mentioned two incidents,' I wrote in my diary, 'one of which was when he came out of the *Independent* interview where he did his U-turn back to unilateralism. He came out, his head spinning, apparently saying, "I don't know what I've said in there. It's all words to me. Words, just words." They also said that after the initial *This Week, Next Week* interview he came out saying exasperatedly, "What is our defence policy? I don't know what our defence policy is." In general, he appears to be in a very deep and melancholic depression and although he does seem to have come out of it now, these are exceptionally difficult times for him.'[25]

Neil was an extremely complex person, driven by a combination of courage and self-doubt. It was an essential part of his personality to express this doubt ocasionally; not a negative but a positive thing, letting rip his frustration at the confusion around him. Charles Clarke says Neil 'often became gloomy' about the state of affairs, but equally, he often became exhilarated: 'Neil was and is a very emotional politician. He felt very positively and very negatively.'[26] What happened in this period, he said, was that Neil dropped his guard a little and showed his true self to half a dozen people who hadn't seen it before. 'It started to become a talking point,' he said.

> While he may have been a bit gloomy, I don't think it was so different to what went on normally, and I think it got taken out of context. He always felt deep self-doubt about his own capacity to succeed – not for himself, I don't think he was a very personally ambitious person; I mean, obviously he has his share, as all politicians do – but he worried that he would betray the party and not bring it back to where it ought to be. He felt that he would be betraying his home, his parents, his background, his village, his constituency by not being up to it. This was his greatest fear.
>
> The academic snobbery which started running some time during this process was very, very damaging to him, because

people believed that he was stupid and so he started to wonder, was he stupid, which actually is the most awful untruth about him, he is one of the most intelligent men I have ever met. But he never believed it – if people said to him, 'actually you are very bright' he couldn't accept it.[27]

The loss of the 1987 election increased his insecurity: 'He felt that he had not done as well as he should have done in 1987 and therefore his self-questioning was greater. But I don't think it was qualitatively different to at other times.'[28]

The party looked ragged and divided. An *Observer* poll in late June put Labour 15 per cent behind the Conservatives.[29] The press turned on Neil, as did many of his colleagues. Joe Napolitan was emphatic: Kinnock has to go. You can't do this sort of thing and get away with it.[30] A *Sunday Times* MORI poll at the beginning of July had Kinnock seventeen points behind Thatcher, an 11 per cent fall – the largest ever in one month for a political leader.[31] Even Neil's closest supporters began to say he should step down. In my diary, I wrote, 'I begin to get a sense of Labour perhaps not being able to win power.'[32]

On 16 August 1988 Mandelson wrote a long and considered note to Charles Clarke, warning of the seriousness of the position in relation to Neil. In it he warned that the policy review, on which the chance of turning around the party's fortunes hinged, would fail unless Neil became fully engaged in the process and used it to project a new vision for himself, and for the Labour Party, and to restore his political authority. The note read, 'Returning from holiday I had expected the unfavourable media comment about us to abate in August. But it has not gone away. It has dug in rather seriously and the party, and Neil in particular, are going to have to project a strong sense of strategy at the conference and beyond if we are to recover fully our electoral credibility and his political authority.'[33]

He compared the party's pre-summer recess slump with the post-Greenwich period in 1987 – both occasions when Labour's fitness to govern became an issue:

In 1987 we had the election campaign to re-assert our positives, all combined giving very powerful and sustained projection, chiefly of Neil. This time, though, the negatives were
not countered effectively and that process of modernisation,
strong leadership and 'gathering strength' which has appealed
to the public, appeared to lose its impetus. Most critical of
all, we know, the architect of this process himself seemed to
falter, apparently becoming very indecisive on defence policy.

Why did this happen? Aside from the very damaging
defence imbroglio there were two other elements which could
have been approached differently. The first you have already
referred to is the policy review. Neil was personally not very
engaged in this and was clearly disappointed by its fruits (who
wouldn't be?). But I think his advocacy of the reports rather
reflected this. His subsequent speeches didn't pick up on the
reports in a stimulating way or with identifiable themes.

He felt also that Benn's leadership campaign had been rebutted
weakly: 'In sum, this lack of visibility and projection has had
an effect on the media, the public and the party. It has created
a loss of strength. It meant that when defence blew us off
course we were already vulnerable and didn't have strong
enough organisation or communications to fight back with.'[34]

Mandelson urged Clarke to involve Kinnock more in the
policy review process, and to stiffen his resolve to modernise
policies on tax and spending, industrial relations, law and
order and renationalisation. He wanted the national membership system to be implemented and one member, one vote
strengthened in order to offset the union tag: 'We have to
protect the party's constitution and rules from the ultra left.'[35]

His over-riding concern was about Kinnock himself, who
had lost his identity with the electorate. He needed to re-state,
clearly and repeatedly, his political goals and objectives, and
find fresh goals to refer to, to update and extend the 'Kinnock
agenda':

During the next year Neil's identity in the public's mind
needs to be associated not just with changing the party but

more directly with the country's future, the emerging economic, social and environmental issues of the 1990s and touching more politically on the 'me, my family, my hopes' concerns of the public. This, of course, is what the policy review is meant to be about. But it will not succeed unless we organise it, and Neil's involvement, differently . . . I think for Neil to be seen setting out the fresh thinking and the evolving ideas of the review is essential to restoring his political authority. For Neil personally (and in all senses he is the most important element in the strategy's success) it means re-establishing the strong identity he held previously and projecting himself more actively so that it's clear what he stands for and where he's going. In particular, it means overcoming those negative attributes which have been provided by the media since June that he is a nice person but a weak leader; that he talks too much and says too little; and that his social concern is not matched by his economic competence.[36]

Finally, Mandelson lamented the lack of a strong core message and vision for Labour, one that was about the 1990s and sparked thoughts of economic competence as well as social justice. He wanted modernisation of communications, of the image of the party leadership, and of party policy itself. This was a major note setting out Mandelson's way forward, his agenda for winning the election. In the event it was largely ignored.

The remainder of 1988 saw no improvement in Labour's fortunes. Neil made a strong speech at conference but it was overshadowed by Ron Todd, General Secretary of the TGWU, who spoke at a *Tribune* rally on the same day, mocking 'sharp-suited Filofax socialists with their cordless telephones'.[37] The conference also went on to back unilateralism, although by a smaller majority than in previous years. But the low point of the period was the loss of the Govan by-election to the SNP in November 1988, overturning one of the biggest Labour majorities in the country. It plunged Kinnock – and the party – further into despair.

New Labour's false dawn

In February 1989, confronting our parlous position two years before a probable General Election, and our predicted defeat in the forthcoming European elections, I suggested a concept to get Labour on its feet again. I called it 'New Labour'. It was an idea whose time was yet to come, but I was sure even then that the party had, in some way, to demonstrate real change by being uncompromisingly new. A line had to be drawn between the old Labour Party and the new, and 'New Labour' was a way to do it. However, only for the very briefest of periods did the reality of Neil Kinnock's Labour Party match the promise of New Labour. The idea died on the vine.

On 13 February I incorporated this concept of New Labour into a campaigning note, evaluating strategic considerations for the year ahead. Labour was 11 per cent behind the Conservatives despite high levels of economic pessimism; morale was low among Labour supporters; Labour was making no progress on the key issues vital in gaining trust: extremism, high taxes, nationalisation and opposition to council house sales. Labour had gone stale. It had lost the freshness of 1985–86, when voters saw Neil Kinnock's Labour as 'new' and full of potential. It was no longer Neil Kinnock's 'new model party'. 'New Labour has lost its zest and modernity,' I wrote.[38]

I set out what seemed at the time absurdly ambitious targets: a poll lead or poll parity by the end of June; net gains in the European elections; massive shifts in attitudes to the party. I wanted people's idea of Labour to reflect the following statements:

- 'Labour has changed. Neil Kinnock has delivered a New Labour party.'
- 'I trust Labour to form a government.'
- 'Labour has sensible economic policies and the team to run them.'
- 'Labour understands people like me.'[39]

In the months that followed, Labour met its opinion poll and European election targets. But it failed utterly to meet any of these attitudinal objectives.

Our short-term objective was to prepare for the European and local elections. I argued for a continuous five-month campaign, concentrated most intensely in the two-month election period from 8 April until 15 June. At its heart was a central strategic recommendation: do not trickle out the policy review; instead, make one, big-bang presentation. Crucially, bring it forward and make it the centrepiece of the European election campaign.[40] This was in complete defiance of the previous consensus about the presentation of the review, which had been to do it late, and do it gradually, in order to minimise the possibility of backlash and dissent. My view was the opposite: people would shift to Labour only if they were sure that it had changed, and only bold, demonstrable change would convince them of that. Dissent in these circumstances did not reduce our electoral appeal, but heightened it. It was evidence of change.

When I presented the note to the campaign team the response was incredulous. Everyone fell about laughing. We were behind in the polls. We were likely to lose seats in the European elections, not win them. But I insisted: I said we had no choice, we had to win them. We had to create a sense of momentum, bringing the policy review forward so that it was out in time for the elections. Peter was with me; he had no doubts. The policy review was to be brought forward and turned into a major event.

It was published in May, following a two-day NEC meeting to approve the seven policy documents. Its title, 'Meet the Challenge, Make the Change', was conceived by Barry Delaney, a leading advertising figure and one of Labour's most talented supporters. We chose it because we wanted a title that looked both ways – to the party and to the country as a whole – and said that what we were doing for the party we would do for Britain. But although it was a clever title, it was ultimately a fudge. It hinted at change, but didn't shout about it.

Despite its limitations, the review broke through as a news story. People began to recognise that Labour was changing. Within days of publication, we were two points ahead of the Conservatives in a MORI poll, our first lead since before the 1987 election.[41] In the European elections in June 1989 Labour won fourteen seats, the Conservatives lost fourteen. Those elections saw the first public signs of the fissures at the heart of the Conservative Party on Europe. Their fiercely anti-European campaign attacking 'Diets of Brussels' alienated many within the Tory mainstream. In May Margaret Thatcher had a decidedly lukewarm celebration of her decade in power, and in October she faced her first challenge for the leadership from the stalking-horse candidate, Sir Anthony Meyer. The Tories were beginning to look fractious and stale.

This was Neil Kinnock's finest hour, the peak of his electoral achievement. From then until the 1992 election the Kinnock project went into decline. That night Neil was happier than I have ever seen him. It seemed to be the start, the prelude to other and bigger victories. But it was not to be. The splash from the policy review was enough to win the European elections, but its content wasn't deep enough to win the General Election.

We were in political decline and had reached a strategic impasse. I continued to rattle out memos arguing for modernisation as the way to take us forward. 'No party has taken the modern ground and captured the new agenda of the 1990s,' I wrote.[42] I wanted us to generate appeal by creating a sense of a modern, forward-looking party with policies to match; Labour should be open to new, radical ideas, thinking creatively and side-stepping the constraints of traditional left-wing ideology. At conference, 'We must present emphatic demonstrable evidence that Labour has changed, and that the change is permanent. Labour is the modern party of the next decade, the Tories are the party of the past.'[43]

Although the 1989 conference, based on the policy review and using the same slogan, 'Meet the Challenge, Make the Change', was successful, with the party displaying unusual levels of discipline and unity, I was still uneasy. In October I wrote a post-conference strategy note. We were failing to move towards the new agenda with any confidence, I said. 'Labour has to move as far and as fast in the next eighteen months as it has in the last four years.' Labour was still not trusted, not safe. Above all, Labour was not yet New Labour. And the electorate wanted New Labour.[44]

Although 1989 was a turn-around year, the long decline that led to defeat in 1992 had already begun. In October 1989 Nigel Lawson resigned, setting in motion a chain of events that would produce Geoffrey Howe's resignation, Thatcher's toppling and the killer electoral blow of the parliament, her replacement in November 1990 by John Major. That year also saw the killer organisational blow for Labour's campaign, with the careless loss of Peter Mandelson.

To lose both looks like carelessness . . .

Labour's internal collapse began with the departure of Patricia Hewitt to the Institute for Public Policy Research at the beginning of 1989. Patricia has her detractors, but no one can doubt her talent. She was someone whom Neil could not afford to lose, and she believed she was forced out of the office following disagreements with Neil's chief of staff Charles Clarke, although Clarke insists he would have been 'very happy' for her to stay: 'There had been for a long time a kind of head-to-head rivalry between us, which wasn't easy, but I think we had found a *modus operandi* that was okay.'[45] She kept working for the party from the outside, cutting and reshaping the policy review to meet the rushed deadline before the European elections, and later playing a linchpin role in the 1992 election campaign.

Mandelson's departure was more complicated, more painful and more protracted than Patricia's. Peter first told me that he wanted to pursue a political career over lunch in the upstairs dining room at Braganza in Soho, just round the corner from my office in Old Compton Street, early in 1988. He believed that it was time for him to go his own way, to be his own person. He felt drained by the enormous exertions of his job, and was ready to move on. But he also felt, as Patricia did, a sense of rejection, of not being fully wanted by the leader's office or by senior party management. 'Everybody and his uncle is advising Mandelson to quit,' I wrote in my diary in January. 'He's done one good campaign, why should he try and do another which may not even be as good?'[46]

By the beginning of 1989, Mandelson's resolve had hardened. Some months after Patricia Hewitt had left, Kinnock asked him to be his press secretary. Mandelson said he would take the job but he wanted to have one chance of being selected for a seat. Kinnock refused, insisting he had to choose. He chose to stay on as Director of Campaigns and Communications and try for a seat, and Julie Hall – who eventually found the world of opposition politics frustrating and irrational – came in as Neil's press secretary.

During the European elections that June, there were rumblings against Mandelson from within Walworth Road. He gave all of his energy to that election, and delivered Labour's first major victory since 1974. But this still wasn't enough for those who were determined to undermine him. The European elections put Peter under almost intolerable strain. He had given everything. Yet a leading party official phoned him up afterwards and, instead of praising him, criticised him for his aloofness from the senior party staff during the campaign.

Although Peter wanted to leave, he could have been persuaded to stay had the will been there. After he was selected to stand for election in Hartlepool at the end of 1989, Mandelson wanted to stay on, overlapping with his successor. But Charles Clarke felt he should go immediately so that his replacement had time to get to grips with the job. 'I came to the view, which Peter didn't accept, but most other people that I speak to do think is right, that you can't have somebody who is a parliamentary candidate and is basically going to run their seat from the moment the election is called, doing the job of communications director right up until the campaign begins and then, as it were, stopping,' Clarke explained. 'Peter's view was that he could do both and that wasn't my view, and that may be a wrong view, I don't know.'[48] Colin Byrne, a senior Labour press officer at the time, believes it was a mistake. 'It was totally the wrong decision,' he said. 'Charles thought it was a betrayal of Neil for Peter to take his eye off the ball and go for a seat.' In the end Kinnock intervened, asking Peter to stay until October the following year. Clarke in turn insisted on advertising Peter's post in April, which was why Mandelson and the new Director of Campaigns and Communications, John Underwood, who was appointed by the NEC in June, ended up doing parallel jobs for four months.

And still the hostility worsened. Mandelson remembers Clarke telling him in March 1990 that if he stayed on in his job he would undermine the election effort. The bad feeling spread. In August 1990, Peter moved into a flat in north London with Julie Hall and Colin Byrne, whom Kinnock had voted for instead of Underwood to replace Mandelson. They were immediately accused of running an alternative communications base. When Julie let it be known she was going to share a flat with Colin and Peter, Charles Clarke sat her down in Kinnock's office and urged her not to. After Julie ignored him, Clarke's frustration boiled over. It looked like an act of blatant provocation by the three of them. Byrne recalls a row which occurred when Julie wanted to install a fax machine. 'Charles said if she bought the fax machine and put it into a flat where Peter was, he would refuse to pay her phone bills,' said Byrne.[48] It was out of character for Clarke, but such was the paranoia of the time that for Julie to live with Colin and share a flat with Peter was considered an act of open subversion. This sort of soul-destroying hostility nearly devastated Labour's 1992 campaign; at times we fought each other with more energy than we fought the Conservatives. Clarke felt he was in an impossible position, facing a campaign disintegrating, and a lack of loyalty in his closest team. He was a man of great intelligence and huge intensity: the driving force behind the Kinnock project. But as the campaign started to falter, his intensity sometimes turned to intolerance with the failings and shortcomings of others. Given the pressures of the time this was understandable – but not always helpful, as Charles admits now.

It was not as if our position was so strong we could afford to waste the talents we had. Although we were ahead in the polls, our position was tenuous and I continued to issue a series of stark warnings, still pleading for further modernisation. At the beginning of the year I warned in a memo that the campaign team was fragmented and did not work as a group: 'In short, Labour has stalled.'[49] In June, despite a ten-point lead in the polls, Nicholas Ridley's damaging resignation from the government, seething anger over the poll tax, and victory at the mid-Staffordshire by-election with a 21 per cent swing, I wrote, 'Labour has not changed enough . . . At the death, in the polling-booth, people may be more likely to vote for the devil they know and dislike rather than the devil they do not fully trust. As things stand the Conservatives are on course for an election victory.' I was also becoming desperate about our campaigning organisation. 'Without a campaign manager – one person in charge – Labour will find it hard to win,' I warned.[50]

Despite the poll tax and victories in the May council elections (which had been widely portrayed in the Tory press as a Conservative victory simply because Labour failed to gain Wandsworth and Westminster), we were not making any headway. I remember a meeting in Neil Kinnock's office at the House of Commons, at which Neil walked up and down talking, getting angrier and angrier as his frustration grew. Suddenly, by accident, he smashed a lamp to the floor. We all – myself, Julie Hall, Neil – tried to ignore it, embarrassed, and continued the meeting, transfixed nevertheless by the lamp on the floor. All except Peter. Without saying a word, and without looking at any of us, he crept across the room, picked up the lamp and put it back on the table, then slid back to his seat. Neil didn't pause for breath.

That summer Neil was exhausted, by constantly attempting to hold together a party threatening to fracture if he moved too far and too fast, and by the need to look restrained and 'respectable' for the press and the public – especially as the prospect of the war in the Gulf moved closer. Neil became so constrained that he began to struggle for words to express himself. He was concerned that he had lost his great power of oratory and became obsessed with the idea that he might have 'lost his words'. One of those closest to him remembers it: 'He didn't have it in him any more. After six years as leader he was emotionally and intellectually drained. The well was dry.'[51]

In fact, Neil had often struggled to find words when he was under pressure. Charles Clarke remembers when he went up to make his acceptance speech after he had been elected leader at the 1983 conference. 'He grabbed me by the shoulder, I'll never forget it, we were behind the podium and he grabbed me and said, "Charles – today of all days I haven't got a fucking speech, I haven't got a fucking speech, at this fucking conference." It was a classic illustration.'[52] Shakespeare and the Bible ran through many of Kinnock's speeches. Once, when they were looking for someone else to appoint in the office to help write them, Neil insisted on somebody who knew the Bible and Shakespeare. 'He believes that they are great texts for helping to illuminate things that go on, and he was constantly frustrated that other people were less committed to words than him,' said Clarke, who thinks Neil's attachment to words was born of his lack of self-confidence:

> They were very important to him, no question about it. Whereas I would give up after being sure I was 95 per cent there, he'd spend another five hours getting the last 5 per cent, which often made almost no difference to the way it went down. He was a perfectionist, he was a perfectionist more than anything else. He felt that people would make fun

of him if he simply repeated what he had said before, and therefore this stupidity thing comes up on the agenda again.

Neil's greatest virtue as a politician for me was that he believed politics was generally about argument. He didn't think it was just about emotions, he believed it was about argument, so he always tried to focus on an argument and then find the language to illustrate that argument. And his language was, of course, wonderful.[53]

Although the 1990 conference theme was 'Looking to the Future', I still didn't believe anyone meant it. 'The process of modernity and change within Labour should be unrelenting,' I wrote afterwards. On the most likely economic scenario, I warned, the Conservatives would get a winning 43 per cent of the vote.[54]

And then Peter left. 'Nobody even bothered to organise a leaving party for him,' said Colin Byrne. 'It was conference, we were in a hotel in Blackpool, and it was literally Peter's last day working for the party, on the staff. And no one had even organised a leaving card. Julie Hall and I had to go off with a couple of people from Peter's staff – people like Anna Healy – and put together a little leaving drinks party. Nobody at NEC level had even thought to do that. Peter, Julie and I drove in the streaming rain to his cottage in Ross-on-Wye and he just looked utterly disappointed that people he'd worked with for years hadn't even bothered to say goodbye. It was almost like an undue haste to get him out the door, and I just couldn't understand that.'[55]

Peter came to an agreement with the research company SRU, whose managing director Colin Fisher was a good friend of Labour, that he would work as a consultant for their company two days a week, leaving the rest of his time for Labour if it wanted him. His offer was never taken up and his talents were lost.

This was the position in October 1990: Hewitt gone; Mandelson going; a party not ready to govern; a leader not trusted to become Prime Minister; an organisation not fit to win.

Mandelson into exile

I first met John Underwood, Peter's replacement, for an informal interview over lunch when it was clear that Peter was leaving. He obviously wanted to be Director of Campaigns and Communications and I was quietly impressed, believing that he could act as a consolidating figure in a rapidly deteriorating situation. He seemed a nice man and a solid manager who could build a team with Colin Byrne, the other potential candidate for the job.

I was wrong. John took the job and immediately came under enormous pressure. He felt he had been appointed not because of Neil but despite him, which was true, and this put him on the defensive with the leader from the start. He believed Peter was running an alternative power base from the flat he shared with Byrne and Hall. Byrne insists this was untrue, although he admits Peter gave him and Julie advice: 'It was just Peter trying to help out from the sidelines.'[56]

By the time Underwood took over alone, after the 1990 conference, the battle lines had been drawn: Peter, Julie and Colin on one side; John Underwood on the other; Charles frustrated with them all, and me trying to hold the whole thing together.

But it was no use: John felt constantly undermined by Peter and by the SCA, and, I suspect, by me. I would often agree to meet him and he would be very late or not come at all. He was obsessed with the idea that there was a conspiracy against him. Gradually he unpicked the communications machine which Peter and I had built up. Barry Delaney, who had produced our party political broadcasts, was dropped and a more documentary style introduced. This was laudable but lacked style. I used long-suffering Hugh Hudson to fill the gap and he produced a string of broadcasts for us. John hated the job and became more and more depressed. Worst of all, he became increasingly suspicious of me, of Peter and of Neil.

But as we fought our battles inside Walworth Road, outside

in Westminster the most decisive event of the parliament was taking place: Margaret Thatcher's resignation on 22 November 1990, and her replacement by John Major. Even with Thatcher, Labour was set to lose. With Major it was almost impossible for us to win: he was the new, fresh, decent fellow people felt they could vote for. I remember hearing the result of the Conservative leadership election as I was driving back from a group discussion in Harlow. I listened to it and felt numb. I knew it was all over.

The opinion polls turned dramatically against us. There was a 9.5 per cent swing to the Tories, who shot into the lead. Even worse, there was a 24 per cent swing in perceptions of economic competence.[57] We kept fighting over the winter and spring, constantly distracted by the personal disputes in the communications team, which had started to spill into the press. Neil was becoming desperate. Colin Byrne had to remove himself to the south of France one week that spring simply to take himself off the scene for a while. Still, we did well in the May local elections and later that month we won the Monmouth by-election, orchestrated by Peter Mandelson at Charles Clarke's request, on a 12.6 per cent swing, with a majority of 2,406. Our winning claim in Monmouth, that trust hospitals would 'opt out' of the NHS, led to a massive row and Labour poll leads. The pressure we exerted stopped Major calling an election when the time was right for him: four years in, with a fresh leader, after a successful Gulf War which greatly boosted his ratings. He had his chance and he missed it.

That summer the Tories began their tax campaign, with promises to reduce the basic rate to 20p and costing Labour's plans at £35 billion, as John Smith, the shadow Chancellor, announced National Insurance increases for the middle classes. And John Underwood, who seemed to have aged about ten years in the previous twelve months, resigned. Although it was a blow to the party at such a crucial time, his departure was inevitable. He had been persuaded that too much media attention was being given to Tony Blair and Gordon Brown, whom he saw as Mandelson's protégés, and he insisted other members of the shadow Cabinet should have more exposure. I saw the end coming when he told me that he had beaten Neil once on the NEC and he would beat him again. He had the votes, he said. John was clearly walking through a minefield, and the end came soon.

His resignation in June 1991, after Kinnock refused to sack Colin Byrne, was sad but inevitable. It was also the final straw for Charles Clarke, who had spoken to many on the NEC and was frightened that resentment and mistrust was reaching an intolerable level. He angrily told us there could be no contact with Mandelson for the foreseeable future. Peter was effectively banished. Gripped by fear, loathing and paranoia, I think we were all going mad.

Beating adversity

In the centre of all this conflict I felt I just had to make things work. I knew this would be a thankless task which would almost certainly lead to ignominy. On New Year's Day 1991 I had sat down and discussed the situation with my wife. I was sure we would lose the election; I knew that I would be blamed; and that the period before and after it would be impossibly difficult. But I had no doubt about what I had to do – I had to keep going. I felt it was my duty.

But by the time John Underwood left in June, resentment against me was growing. Walworth Road was full of people who thought they should be making decisions but were incapable of doing so – they were all too busy fighting each other. David Hill, who took over Underwood's job in July, remembers inheriting a situation – with a General Election looming – where open warfare had been declared for the past year and where nothing was in place for the campaign: 'There was an enormous amount of mistrust. There was no sense of everybody running in the same direction. People didn't know who to trust. They had clearly in the previous year taken sides. There were three groups of people, really: people who had taken the side of John Underwood; people who'd taken the side of people who attacked John Underwood; and people who had wrung their hands and said, "What on earth do we do? We don't want to be on either of these sides.'"[58] Party staff at the Friday SCA meetings were also quietly seething about my influence. They resented me and what I was doing. I should have made more effort, perhaps spent more time making it work with them, but I did not. I was a man with a mission. I was going to make this campaign work and they could like it or lump it.

First, I tried meetings. The main meeting I suggested was a Thursday co-ordinating meeting, which became the Campaign Advisory Team (CAT). This was chaired by Jack Cunningham, the campaign co-ordinator, and its members included Julian Eccles, the secretary of the meeting; Larry Whitty, the Labour Party General Secretary; John Underwood (or David Hill, his replacement); Julie Hall and Neil Stewart from Kinnock's office; myself; and, later, Patricia Hewitt and Clive Hollick. The CAT met every Thursday at 9 A.M., first at the European Parliamentary Labour Party offices, then at the offices of Hollick's company, MAI, and eventually at the polling organisation NOP. It worked in the sense that it ensured the principals were in the same room and talking, and it covered all the serious planning ground. But it was based on a premise that was completely insane: it was secret. In the atmosphere of suspicion and hostility at the time, this seemed logical: we thought Walworth Road would object to our group, so we didn't tell them about it. 'There were strings of official people in the party who would have been furious,' said Charles Clarke, 'but you simply didn't have the calibre of people within the party you needed to run a major national election campaign.'[59] Now, as I write this, it seems clear that it was madness: the meeting that ran the campaign was to remain a secret to the campaign it was supposed to be running.

This was the first great flaw of Labour's strategy. Decisions were to appear as if by magic, coming from a source unknown to all but a very select few. 'We would have this secret meeting,' Hewitt remembers, 'then you would head down to Walworth Road for the official meeting. It was a joke. Parallel decision-making structures. You had a secret meeting structure with people brought in from the outside to compensate for the fact that the people on the inside couldn't do the job.'[60] Sally Morgan, now head of the political office at Number 10, who was then in charge of key seats at Walworth Road, says people 'half knew' what was going on: 'Everybody knew meetings were happening all over the place, but there was no guidance for us working at the sharp end. So some of us were just getting on and doing our own thing almost.'[61]

Gradually, I succeeded in widening the membership of the Thursday evening group. First I suggested bringing in Clive Hollick. I wanted him because he was sensible and knew about organisation; I felt that people would behave in front of him. In July 1990 he wrote a note, which was largely ignored, saying the campaign 'lacks (and needs) a unitary organisational structure'; that 'the Thursday group, by virtue of its secrecy, cannot give clear leadership'; and that it is 'vital that Neil Kinnock be involved in the process of settling the key ingredients of the campaign'.[62] None of his recommendations were implemented. The campaign never gained a unitary command structure; secrecy was maintained; senior politicians were never fully involved in the campaign; and neither, most fatally, was Neil Kinnock.

I then managed to get Patricia Hewitt involved because of her campaign skills and experience. It proved impossible, however, to get Peter in, although I mooted the idea from time to time. He had become a kind of non-person, never to darken the campaign's doors again.

The next meeting, also my idea, was a media briefing in Jack Cunningham's office at 8.30 each morning. This was attended by myself and the Director of Campaigns and Communications, and worked well enough. Jack made a big effort at this and all meetings. He did not want the job of campaign co-ordinator, but he made the best of an almost impossible situation and held together a campaign that was always close to disintegration.

On Fridays there was yet another meeting – the SCA

meeting – which effectively drove and organised huge parts of the campaign. If there was a focus for criticism that the SCA was too powerful, this meeting was it. I chaired it (it was attended by representatives from BMP, NOP, the Labour press office, Patricia Hewitt and someone from Jack Cunningham's office) not because I wanted to but because no one else would. Its power grew as the collapsing campaign structure thrust increasing amounts of responsibility on to Patricia Hewitt and me. On more than one occasion Larry Whitty asked me to take even more responsibility. By now I had developed a close relationship with Larry and did not want to turn him down – I felt I had a duty to keep the campaign functioning. As time went by the SCA became increasingly influential, and Patricia and I effectively took over the operational running of the 1992 campaign. It was this that caused the greatest post-election resentment. According to our critics, the campaign had been hijacked by outsiders – unaccountable, unelected, with their own modernising agenda. It was true that Patricia and I had power beyond our formal responsibilities, but we did not hijack the campaign, we rescued it from chaos and disintegration at the direct request of the General Secretary of the party.

The final meeting was David Hill's idea. As soon as he was appointed Director of Campaigns and Communications in June 1991, he said he wanted more politicians to be involved. So we started another Monday meeting with an open invitation to all politicians to attend. The only ones who came regularly were Roy Hattersley and Gerald Kaufman. Both were bastions of common sense, but they could only advise, they could not control. At almost every meeting they asked for access to Neil, for his greater involvement in the campaign. The request got nowhere. The meeting talked sense but influenced little. I, too, tried to involve Neil in it, but this was always blocked. Clive Hollick was also keen to involve Neil. On 4 December 1990 he wrote a memo that there should be 'regular, very short, meetings with NK on Monday at which the current state of research and strategy should be presented'. Charles Clarke believed that more meetings increased the burden on Neil. I can remember Gordon Brown and Tony Blair coming only once to the Monday meeting. They took one look at the chaos and indecision and decided their talents would be better employed elsewhere.

We were not helped by an atmosphere in which every move Gordon Brown made was considered to be jostling for the leadership. Although Gordon had made a pact with John Smith in which he wrote himself out of the running, Smith's supporters, foreseeing a fight for the leadership after the election, were already going into battle. 'The whole thing was so debilitating because every time Gordon appeared on TV, someone in John's camp would say, "Look, it's another bid for the leadership,"' Patricia remembers. 'It meant David Hill couldn't put anyone up without creating problems.'[63] Thus we were being deprived of one of our best campaigners.

Despite the frustrations and the organisational morass, we did get things done. In September the SCA produced a poster campaign on the NHS with sufficient impact to persuade Major to postpone the election again. We blew Major off course and he lost his last chance of a decent majority. If the SCA did nothing else in the 1992 election, it did that.

However, I was becoming hysterical about the management of the campaign. We had no political guidance. On 8 October I wrote a memo, identifying the following problems: weaknesses in political management; weaknesses in news management; poor teamwork; inexperience in the campaign team; poor co-ordination and integration; weaknesses with campaign leadership, political integration and political strategy; shadow Cabinet splits; lack of funds and a lack of a properly functioning opposition research operation. I suggested bolstering the Thursday Group; strengthening Kinnock's office; using experienced outside help, including Peter Mandelson; involving other senior politicians, including John Smith and Gordon Brown; and establishing a core organisational team.[64]

I also tried to draft in outside help directly. Mandelson

was beyond the pale and his re-entry would not be accepted. Patricia was back and the remaining big talent on the outside was Alastair Campbell, then political editor of the *Daily Mirror*. Alastair was and is a figure of immense power and ability. Peter Mandelson describes him as a 'genius'. I hardly knew him then; he had interviewed Neil for the Hudson broadcast and looked at me with the pity and contempt he reserves for people who come from professions like advertising. There was some talk he might join Neil as his press secretary, and I had lunch with him to discuss it. He wasn't keen, but he would have done it had he been asked. I didn't know it at the time, but this was another great missed opportunity – Robert Maxwell offered in 1991 to second Alastair to Neil Kinnock's office, but Kinnock and Clarke turned the offer down. More than anybody else Alastair could have helped Neil at this time, but the chance was passed over. This was a huge error, and Clarke admits it: 'We should have asked Alastair to come on board. The main reason that didn't happen was that it was a specific gift from Maxwell, and Neil didn't want to be beholden to Maxwell in any way.'[65]

Having rejected Mandelson and turned down Campbell, Labour was struggling to handle the media. Kinnock's relationship with the press was 'frozen', according to Clarke, who once went to Wapping, without telling Neil, to talk to the editor of the *Sun*. 'We simply did not tackle the media,' he said. 'I remember I went to see Kelvin MacKenzie at Wapping in January 1992. It's the only thing I ever did without telling Neil beforehand. And we had four hours at Wapping – me, Kelvin and a whole group of others going through things – and to his credit Kelvin never leaked it. And I told Neil the next day and he was furious that I had done it.'[66]

The final straw was Colin Byrne's departure that autumn. 'I saw it all fragmenting,' he said. 'I saw people starting to position themselves for jobs after an election which Labour was nowhere near actually winning, and putting more effort into that than actually keeping their eye on the ball. We should have been concentrating on big-picture politics and we were playing the sort of office politics you get in a small company.'[67] Byrne had enormous talent, experience and aggression – so much aggression, in fact, that he once tried to hit me in Westminster Hall because he felt Julie Hall, his girlfriend, was being badly treated and he blamed me. In fact Charles Clarke was letting it be known he was unhappy with her. Byrne left disillusioned and depressed. It was a terrible blow to the campaign.

On 12 December, I delivered the 1992 'War Book': the complete campaign plan for the election. I said our first weakness was tax, our second, lack of trust. The Tories' core message would be 'You can't trust Labour'. Their key attacks would be on tax, followed by Neil Kinnock, trade unions and extremism, and the core themes would be Kinnock against Major and high-tax Labour against low-tax Conservatives.[68]

By the end of 1991, the Labour campaign was in crisis. Planning for the election itself was in hand, but the pre-election period was empty of any content. There was no timetable; no day-by-day campaign grid; no strategic plan. I phoned Patricia at home and said we had to fix it. In her office in the attic of her house we planned a grid every week for the period from 1 January until a likely election in April or May. I then took this grid and forced it through the party machine, getting it approved in January. I was resented for this as well, and distrust of me increased. The seeds of campaign confusion were being sown.

Less than four weeks after I wrote the War Book the Conservatives hit us on tax, with the 'Tax Bombshell' campaign on 6 January 1992. I was out of the country and heard the news over the telephone. As the news went on and on – National Insurance, top rate of tax, £1,000 per family – I knew we were finished. And less than three months later the Tories launched their election campaign, with the slogan 'You Can't Trust Labour'.

We slogged on. The grid that Patricia and I had drawn up was pretty much implemented, and we did what we wanted to do, fighting long and hard through the spring. Gradually we crawled back to level-pegging with the

Conservatives and then nudged ahead. We were going to meet our first election objective, which was to go into the campaign ahead in the polls.

But by the start of the election a campaign machine that had been brilliant in 1987 and strong in 1990 had weakened almost to breaking-point. Peter had gone; Patricia had left her formal position; Alastair was not used properly. 'By the time we had moved into the period of the election campaign proper, we were exhausted and jaded,' says David Hill.[69] Charles Clarke agrees: 'Energy is very important, and we were lacking energy. Everybody was tired.'[70] The campaign team was riven with suspicion bordering on paranoia; lines of command were confused; and the leader of the party was isolated from his own campaign team.

But organisational collapse was the symptom, not the cause. The truth was that Neil's brave, necessary, crucial modernising project had been in political decline since 1989 and was now exhausted – physically, intellectually and emotionally. The policy review failed to be the modernising document the nation needed. Our defence policy was transformed but on trade unions, on public ownership and above all on tax and spending, essentially we were still stuck in the past.

For much of that year Neil's confidence was low and his colleagues were constantly at odds. Alastair Campbell, a close friend of his, remembers it: 'There wasn't much of a team effort going on. I think that made Neil quite angry and resentful. You never found the shadow Cabinet really pushing in the same direction at one time. They were pretty disparaging of Neil privately, which I think is unforgivable.'[71] Neil was in despair about this. At dinner during the 1991 conference I said to him, 'Why don't you talk to your colleagues and get them to act as a team?' He smashed the table and replied: 'If you're so bloody clever why don't you talk to them, and see how far you get?'

This was the state of Labour as it approached the election: falling apart together.

4

LOVE AND ANGER

Taxis

I spent hours and hours of the 1992 campaign in taxis, running between endless meetings at our three campaign headquarters – Walworth Road, Millbank, where we had a suite of rooms behind the main press conference venue, and Transport House, where the Shadow Communications Agency had its offices. The meetings started at 6.30 A.M. and recurred at what seemed like hourly intervals through the day, ending with a campaign strategy meeting on the top floor of Walworth Road at 7.00 P.M., when it seemed as if anyone who wanted to turned up. Notes of these meetings include strings of references to people who were missing, briefings lost in other offices, a driver being unable to find the shadow Cabinet member due at the press conference in half an hour's time. It was madness to separate us like this, but Neil's office decided at the last minute that it was a security risk to have us all at Millbank as planned. When the decision was announced by Charles Clarke at a Thursday CAT meeting, I lost my temper. I knew it would be a disaster, and the confusion it created led directly to our ignominious retreat from the battle of 'Jennifer's Ear'.

The SCA was housed in the room at Transport House in which press conferences had been held in 1987. I had a desk on one side with my assistant Kathryn Smith, who was brilliant beyond words. Patricia Hewitt's desk was on the opposite side of the hall. She was helped by Julian Priestley, now Secretary General of the European Parliament and a man of outstanding competence. The room between us was full of people: researchers, volunteers, helpers of all sorts. In an annexe Deborah Mattinson oversaw a complete polling operation. Our position in Smith Square, opposite Conservative Central Office, meant the Tories would regularly send in spies to see what we were up to: but as they wore tweed jackets and looked nervous it was easy to throw them out. The press, too, tried repeatedly to get in. The SCA, secluded in its own building, had an aura of quiet, mysterious power.

Without Peter, I felt personally accountable for the conduct of much of the campaign and I knew that our chances of reaching the finishing-post without major mishap were very slim. I had one simple objective: to be ahead in the polls on election day, and I did not think we would be able to achieve it. The responsibility felt overwhelming.

No election campaign has been more misunderstood than Labour's in 1992, and no account of it has been fully accurate. Our preparation had been extensive, but less effective and sharply honed than in 1987. I had in mind a campaign with three aspects: slickness, energy and fierce, relentless attack. In the event we only really achieved the first. For most of the time the campaign was slick and professional, but it lacked passion, anger, attack. Because the 1987 campaign lacked an overall theme and jumped from subject to subject on an almost daily basis, I had designed a campaign that unfolded in four phases: the economy; health, as our best attacking issue; education, to give Neil the chance to take off; a last week that recapitulated all three issues. The press conference sets, designed by Wolff Olins, were very beautiful. They were rosy pink at the bottom, merging into a soft blue at the top. The colours grew in intensity as the campaign developed. The campaign line was borrowed from the Australian Labor Party: 'It's time.' This line also unfolded as the campaign developed: 'It's time for health; it's time for education', and so on.

But when the election was called, at one o'clock on Wednesday 11 March, I sat alone in my office in Soho and felt a terrible sense of foreboding. I remembered the same moment in 1987, when I had thought we were facing certain defeat but I knew we were ready and would do our best. The atmosphere had been defiant and resigned, with a sense of camaraderie. In 1992, the mood was very different: the team was divided; the polls were extremely close, with Labour just ahead; people expected us to win; the press expected us to win. And I didn't think we would. What's more, I was alone. I telephoned Peter and we talked briefly about the fight in 1987, but I could tell that mentally he had already left London and was fighting Hartlepool. I picked up the phone and called David Hill, collected my papers, and hailed a taxi for Walworth Road.

Taxation

The first issue that dominated Labour's campaign in the 1992 election was tax. Maurice Saatchi told a friend after that election that the only issue the Tories had was tax, and that Labour gave it to them: 'If they'd dealt with it, we had nothing else.'[1] It is to my credit that the SCA tried to kill it, to my discredit that we failed.

In a brilliant move just before the campaign started, the Tories destroyed us in the Budget of Tuesday 10 March. This was partly our fault because we had already announced too many of our tax and spending plans: we were committed to raising taxes for the middle classes to pay for child benefit and pensions increases; we had said we would reverse any Tory income-tax cuts and we had only one surprise up our sleeves for our shadow Budget the following week – a fall in National Insurance. This was our sole escape route from accusations that we were hitting the middle classes. On Budget Day the Tories cut it off.

'I go to hear the Budget in the shadow Cabinet room,' I wrote in my diary.

> It was full of the economic advisers to the party, to the leader, to John Smith. It could hardly have been more tense. It was like walking into a Gold Seal battery, it was so charged. John

Eatwell [economic adviser to Kinnock since 1986] sat on his own table to the left, with a large sign saying 'reserved'. I crouched at the back out of the way, so tense I could hardly talk. By the time Lamont got to tax, David Hill and I were pacing nervously at the back of the shadow Cabinet room, waiting for the knockout blow. I was saying: '2p [tax cut]. It's got to be 2p.' David said: 'No way. They're not going to do it.' And then at the end, when there had been absolutely nothing, David said to me, 'You're right, it must be 2p.' But Lamont announced: 'There's going to be no cut in the basic rate of income tax. We're going to introduce a 20p band.'

John Eatwell, who had been glued to the screen in silence throughout, looked up, flung his papers over the table, and said: 'We can't respond to that. That's it. It's all over. We've got no money to spend. Neil's got no speech.'[2]

And he was right. The budget totally undermined our strategy. The Tories had looked at our figures and worked out that the way to kill us off on tax was a 20p band. No one had any idea how to respond. The room was in chaos. And I had an advertisement to produce – fast; it was going into the papers the next day and the concept I had prepared was based on the assumption that the government would cut income tax. The headline was, 'Georgina Norris died because the NHS is short of money. Meanwhile the Tories are cutting taxes to keep their election hopes alive.' The question was: was the new 20p band a tax cut? 'I asked David Hill: "Is it a tax cut or isn't it? Will we reverse it or not?" No one knew; it was pandemonium. Neil fudged the answer in his reply. By the time the politicians returned, John Smith storming through, Neil following looking drained, they had decided. They swept us into their office and told us they would reverse it.'[3]

When things had quietened down a little, I went in to see Neil alone. 'How was it?' he asked. I thought he was referring to the Budget, so I said, 'I thought it was a pretty poor Budget.' 'He looked nervous,' I wrote in my diary, 'and started to look at the floor. He said: "I didn't mean that; I meant how was my speech?" Well, I hadn't seen the speech because I was so wrapped up with this wretched advertisement, so I said lamely: "Very good." Then everybody else swarmed in and said: "Bloody good speech, Neil. Bloody good." Everybody was there. Roy was there. Everybody was drinking champagne. Everybody was happy. We thought that the Tories had messed up.'[4] That was our big mistake.

That was the last I heard about the Budget for a couple of days. On Thursday evening, the day after the election had been called, David Hill and I were discussing leaflets when a panic call came through for me to go immediately to Neil Kinnock's office in the House of Commons. As I passed the office of Jim Parish, the senior campaign officer, he gave me the front cover of the manifesto to look at. It was terrible, and since it was going to press the next day, I had to stay and fight the design company over the phone to get it changed – this was to be the mood throughout: chaotic and panic-stricken. I reached the House of Commons finally at 10.30 and made my way to the shadow Cabinet room, which was in half-darkness. Patricia Hewitt, John Eatwell and a few others were already there, shadowy figures in the half-light. You could almost touch the gloom.

The problem we faced was appalling and insoluble. The central premise on which the shadow Budget was based had been that the Tories would cut at least 1p off income tax. Our central proposal in response was to reverse the tax cut but drop National Insurance by 1 per cent, from 9 per cent to 8 per cent, which was the equivalent of an income-tax cut of 1p. The point of this was twofold: it would soften the blow of Labour's policy of lifting the National Insurance ceiling for those earning more than £22,000, and it would mean an effective tax cut for those earning less than £22,000. By introducing a 20p band, Lamont had presented us with an impossible dilemma. If we reversed the 20p band and cut National Insurance by 1 per cent, higher-income earners would be slightly better off, but around three or four million people earning between £3,000 and £10,000 would be worse off. On the other hand, if National Insurance was not cut and measures were taken instead to prevent lower-income earners being hurt (i.e. by increasing personal allowances), middle-income earners at £22,000-plus would be hit.

There had been almost non-stop meetings for the previous two days and no one had found an answer. Alastair Campbell, then still at the *Daily Mirror*, had been helping, and remembers it as the worst example of the chaos of the 1992 election. 'It just wasn't stacking up,' he said. 'I was helping them the night before the shadow Budget and you had a sense of this thing being put together at the last minute, which of course it was.'[5] In that dark, gloomy room, at eleven at night, we had to choose: hit the poor, or hit the middle classes. Patricia, David and myself argued strongly that Labour should cut National Insurance and take the risk with lower-income earners. But Neil believed Labour could not go into an election threatening to raise taxes for the poor. We shouldn't have had to do either, but the mess we had got ourselves into meant we had to choose. 'If we don't do something for the middle classes, we will lose the election,' I warned.[6] But Neil refused to hit the poor. We were trapped by the Tory strategy and by our own foolish pledge to raise the National Insurance ceiling to pay for child benefit and pensions. We were going to hit the middle classes.

The tragedy is that Neil had never wanted to raise taxes for middle-income earners and had tried to get the policy changed. By the time of the election, even John Smith, who was responsible for the policy, had reservations, but he would not or could not change it. They had left themselves only one escape from the tax trap – the National Insurance cut – and when the Tories closed that off they were snared. The meeting in the shadow Cabinet room went on until the early hours of the morning, but could find no escape.

These policies had never made sense and the SCA had consistently opposed them. They had their genesis in the policy review, which had failed to modernise Labour's tax and spend policies sufficiently and had also committed the party to publishing details of its tax policies in advance. In effect, it had committed Labour to the idea of a shadow Budget and to what its contents would be. I had tried to prevent it, and had repeatedly warned the policy review groups and John Smith of the consequences if Labour entered the election with a policy of raising taxes.

From November 1987 until April 1988, we had commissioned research on tax and benefits as the basis for the review of Labour's tax policy. The findings, which were presented to John Smith at the time, were emphatic. People were hostile to the principle of paying taxes which they felt did not benefit them directly. Recipients of benefits were often seen to be 'scroungers', with high levels of concern about fraud. There was intense anxiety about Labour and tax.[7] In April 1988 the SCA presented polling which said, 'Respondents thought Labour would increase taxes for everybody, with the result that the rich would be driven abroad, ordinary people would be worse off and there would be no incentive to work. Ultimately the country, in the words of one respondent, "would face ruin".'[8] This research should have persuaded John Smith of the extent to which Labour's loss of the lower-middle-class vote was related to its attitude to tax.

The research cut little ice in the policy review process. John Smith thought it inconceivable that we could go into an election without pledging to put a fixed amount on the basic benefits; any alternative wasn't even considered. 'He felt that by committing the party very soon after 1987 to the same level of increase as we'd promised in 1987 – not to have to put it up in line with inflation or anything – he'd pulled off an amazing piece of modernisation,' Hewitt said. 'It was just extraordinary – and that was the most you could possibly expect the party to agree to. It meant that as early as 1988 we were stuffed on tax for the next election.'[9]

At the beginning of July 1988 I wrote in my diary, 'We can see the last two and a half years as an oscillation between the social agenda, which is positive for us; defence, which is negative; and the economic agenda. We have to sort out the economic agenda because we lost the last election partly because of an economic failure on our part and partly because of the economic credentials of the government. We must sort out the economic policy as almost a discrete, separate product, sorted out and got right, and made into the bedrock of our credentials for government.'[10]

During the next four years the SCA had issued a series of increasingly urgent warnings on tax policies and the economic agenda. In December 1989 BMP had developed the concept of the 'aspirational classes'.[11] They argued that the key determinants of the next election would be 'financial well-being: spending power, taxation, interest rates'.[12] Qualitative research conducted at the time showed that despite the recession, Labour was seen as more likely to accentuate economic difficulties than the Conservatives.[13] The key target group was the aspirational classes – working-class achievers and the middle class under pressure. This is the group I came to call the new middle class. I define them as those people who call themselves middle- and upper-working-class, estimated by the British Social Attitudes survey to comprise 50 per cent of the population.[14] I came from this class and believe I understand it. It is the pivot around which progressive politics must revolve.

In January 1990 I had warned, 'Labour has had a successful year but is not on track to win an election. Labour lags behind on the key issue of economic competence; and while the Conservatives need a moderate performance to win, Labour needs an exceptional performance.'[15]

The council elections in May 1990, in which the Conservatives held Wandsworth and Westminster with very low poll tax rates, showed the importance of financial self-interest in determining voting intention. I wrote to Peter Mandelson: 'The Conservative device of comparing at all points the financial advantage of voting Conservative with the financial disadvantage of voting Labour was starkly effective. The most important lesson is that in the General Election financial comparisons will be used and will be effective. We must avoid any policy commitments that exacerbate such a comparison and maximise any financial incentives which alleviate it.'[16]

Two weeks later, on 24 May 1990, 'Looking to the Future', Labour's early manifesto, was launched (amid a row over whether the document was too glamorous because the woman on the cover, posing with my daughter Georgia, wore earrings). In it Labour said it would raise £2 billion in its first year of office by raising the top rate of tax to 50 per cent and removing the National Insurance ceiling to pay for pensions and child-benefit increases.[17] The die was cast.

A few days later I wrote another note to the CAT: 'The policy review has fallen short of expectations. In the key areas of trade unions and taxation Labour has not moved fast enough. A majority believe that Labour would raise tax for middle-income earners.'[18] The next month a survey of 1,200 people rammed home the same points: 'Tax was raised as a central problem for Labour'; 'Concerns about economic management magnify concerns about tax'.[19]

A few months before Mandelson left, at his request, Deborah Mattinson bravely presented to the shadow Cabinet in the summer of 1990 a presentation warning that a substantial majority of those polled – 70 per cent or so – believed they would pay more tax under Labour.[20] John Smith deeply resented it, saying he wouldn't be lectured to by 'admen and pollsters'. A period of estrangement between John Smith and the SCA resulted, although at the time I was urging Peter to give John a higher profile: 'The shadow Chancellor has high credibility in the economic area and this should be maximised.' But John was furious, both at the presentation and because I had recently discovered that the threshold for paying more tax was very low – about £16,000 – and was telling anyone who would listen that if this wasn't increased Labour would lose the election. 'John has got to hear about it and is very cross with me indeed,' I wrote in my diary. 'But I am trying to rebuild the relationship, although I keep telling him and David [Hill] that we will definitely lose with these tax policies.'[21]

Eventually John did realise that Labour was highly vulnerable on tax and that the recession made Labour's tax policies increasingly untenable. But he believed that his reputation for integrity was essential to our chances of re-election: that, given the other reforms Kinnock had introduced, Labour's standing would be destroyed if he, Smith, committed a U-turn on tax policy. 'All we have in politics is our integrity, and if we lose that we lose everything,' he told me. 'Neil's changed so much, I can't change at all.'[22] Although he understood the dangers of the policies and intended to use the shadow Budget to confound his critics and cut National Insurance, he was essentially committed to them and, in particular, believed as a matter of faith in the moral case for increasing benefits. His position was that the strategy should be amelioration of the policy, not abandonment of it.

Gordon Brown, then shadow Trade and Industry spokesman, took a wholly different view. He felt that the very idea of a shadow Budget was insane, and gave the Conservatives all the weapons they needed to attack us. He said, 'I think John's making a mistake, he shouldn't be giving any figures away at all. But we're stuck with it because we've committed ourselves to this pension and child-benefit rise.'[23] Neil also opposed the policy, but could find no way out of it. When he later floated the idea of phasing as a solution, it exploded in his face.

Tax was the key strategic and tactical issue in 1991. All through the year the SCA presented polling which warned of the dangers of tax. In an opinion poll on 24 April, tax was identified as the main reason not to vote Labour, with 54 per cent giving it as the primary reason.[24] This was fed into the campaign team and the appropriate politicians. Yet on 5 May, John Smith announced on *Frost on Sunday* that employees earning over £20,300 a year would pay extra National Insurance contributions to raise an extra £2.5 billion.[25] Three days later the Tories announced their aim of reducing basic-rate tax from 25p to 20p.[26] In June the Tories started their long tax campaign, with David Mellor costing Labour's tax plans at £35 billion.[27]

To make absolutely sure the politicians were getting the message, the SCA prepared a separate presentation for Labour's economic spokespeople – John Smith, Margaret Beckett, Tony Blair and Gordon Brown. The presentation, which was in the autumn, could not have been clearer or more emphatic. It was long and very forceful. It showed that tax was the top reason for not voting Labour, with 65 per cent agreeing with the statement that Labour will raise taxes for everyone. That figure increased to 72 per cent in the key C2 group: 'To the public, Labour is the party of high taxation. The fact that the lower end of the social spectrum feel that they will be taxed heavier is a matter of where they see themselves aspiring to as much as where they are currently.' We also told them Labour would have great difficulty winning the election with its current tax policies and urged them to broaden the argument on tax to include VAT, poll tax, interest rates and inflation.[28] The presentation made the politicians angry. Tony Blair and Gordon Brown were frustrated that we were in a position where our policy was both untenable and highly unpopular; John Smith, knowing what we said was all true, simply walked out.

Labour's senior figures were so divided, their truce so finely balanced, that it became almost impossible to get anyone even to listen to our pleas. Patricia Hewitt prepared a paper that autumn for the CAT on Labour, taxation and public spending, which once again spelled out the realities of the situation. 'The public,' she wrote, 'and especially target voters, believe that Labour will increase taxation for everyone. Fear of taxes is the single most important reason for not voting Labour.'[29] Qualitative research found that a threshold of £21,000 was not seen as particularly high – especially in the south east: 'Nobody wants to pay more tax.'[30] Charles Clarke saw the paper before it was presented and exploded. 'You don't fucking understand. We can't discuss it,' he shouted at Patricia.[31] It is difficult to describe how angry he was. Terrified of re-opening the issue and destabilising the careful truce reached between Neil and John, he insisted that all copies of the paper be returned and destroyed. 'I was very nervous about a dispute with John,' Charles explains, 'that's certainly true. I mean, I had a stand-up row with John at the shadow Cabinet away day in January, when he was not producing what Neil wanted him to produce. I felt very nervous about the relationship with John. I felt that that was a very flawed state of affairs. And it was a very febrile relationship.'[32] Neil considered sacking John. 'I think that he didn't feel strong enough, I mean we went through a whole series of processes, called emergency meetings of the shadow Cabinet and all the rest of it to instruct John. At the end of the day Neil had the decision to either sack John as shadow Chancellor or not. I think it was a straight stand-off, and John believed rightly that he was strong enough to resist Neil,' Clarke says.[33]

Despite this, tax wouldn't go away as an issue. Rational strategic planning dictated that if we couldn't change the policy, we should launch an initiative announcing our existing tax plans on our terms and before the Tories attacked us. The SCA produced scripts for a tax broadcast that would spearhead our economic broadcast and act as a pre-emptive tax attack. Neil didn't like them. I wrote in my diary, 'It was done in a way that was creative and intelligent, but nonetheless the policy was exposed, and Neil clearly didn't like the policy. You could feel it.'[34] Other politicians who were shown the script reacted with horror; they hated the policy, so they hated the broadcast. 'When they were shown the policy in the raw – that we were raising National Insurance by a very substantial amount for people earning over £21,000 to pay for child benefits and pensions – they realised that it didn't make political sense. Blair and Brown felt this most. They asked questions about who developed the policy; where had it come from, and so on,' I wrote. 'Neil's view was that these broadcasts were all very well and good but the key was that before we presented our economic case, the tax case was put, and put by John Smith, in December. This was absolutely Neil's view, that John had to do that.'[35]

However, John was unsure about announcing our tax plans early. He said to me: 'Why in politics do something that would make you unpopular? Why take the risk?'[36] His view was that tax for Labour was rather like the NHS for the Conservatives – if you raise the issue, it just gets worse. Patricia Hewitt said, 'We spoke to John about it, saying the tax attack would come, and we tried to work out a line – something like an early version of "eight out of ten people will be better off under Labour". But John wouldn't go for that because he kept saying, with some justification, until he saw the 1992 Budget, he wouldn't know what our figures would be.'[37]

I kept hammering away at John, trying to get him to address the tax issue properly. This tactic drove Charles Clarke to distraction and he eventually turned on me in the corridor outside the leader's office. 'You're getting a reputation for crying wolf,' he said. 'You're going on and on about this tax attack. It's never going to happen.'[38] To my eternal discredit, in the face of Smith's stubbornness and Clarke's antagonism, I lost heart and, temporarily at least, gave up. Four weeks later, in January 1992, the Tories launched their 'Tax Bombshell' campaign; our rebuttal, Norman Lamont as 'VAT-man', went up a lamentable four weeks later.

In the week after the tax bombshell dropped on us, Neil wrote a letter to John arguing the case for phasing in the higher National Insurance contributions, and then mentioned the option to journalists at a dinner at Luigi's restaurant in Soho. 'Neil's view was that we ought to make commitments about not raising tax,' said Clarke. 'That's what led to the Luigi's problem. All Neil's instincts led him to believe that we were going to raise taxes too much.'[39] Neil was anxious; an ICM poll had put Labour behind after the tax attack, and since the phasing idea had been floated already he decided to mention it. It leaked out the next day, just as Smith received Neil's letter proposing the idea. At our regular Thursday meeting the next morning, the atmosphere was explosive. 'Charles Clarke was emphatically of the view that we would make it clear that we were not deviating from policy. Julie [Hall] was of the view that we should say we are deviating from policy,' I wrote in my diary.[40] It was chaos. John Smith was furious and his confidence in Neil – never high – dropped further. Right up to the election he kept referring back to the Luigi's incident. When David Hill and I told John that Neil was going to attend the shadow Budget (this was very controversial at the time because of worries that Neil would be asked questions which were unanswerable), John was dismissive and came out with a typically sharp rejoinder: 'Dressed as a waiter from Luigi's?'[41]

After the election I wrote in my diary, 'This was a core disability at the heart of the Kinnock leadership, because the fact that he and Smith did not get on meant they never got to grips with the tax problem. If, before the election, they had been able to discuss it, they might have been able to solve it. But the relationship was not there and instead they accepted an uneasy compromise, their advisers kept them apart, and we were left with no big economic story to tell the voters.'[42]

After the election we were criticised for not using John Smith more, but there wasn't much he could say and he was occasionally unable to attend press conferences because of his health. However, this wasn't always the reason. In my diary, I recalled one press conference, on housing repossessions in London, which 'John refused to do because he wouldn't have been able to promise interest-rate cuts; Neil had pushed him to support entry to the ERM, which tied us to high interest rates'.[43] When I gave John the draft manifesto, the only comment he made was that he wanted a whole paragraph on an independent National Statistical Office – he was absolutely obsessed with having an honest system. Clarke believes Smith thought he could 'busk' it: 'John Smith fundamentally believed that the policy of "just leave it to him and he could busk it" would carry us through, and he believed everybody else was a combination of stupid or tactically inept in the way they handled things.'[44]

For all these reasons, the day after the 1992 General Election was called, John Eatwell, Patricia Hewitt, Neil Kinnock and I found ourselves late at night in the gloom of the shadow Cabinet room trying to decide whether to hit the poor or the middle classes in the shadow Budget in four days' time. And Neil insisted on protecting anyone earning under £22,000. The shadow Budget at the Institute of Civil Engineers the following Monday was an incredible political event. 'We arrived early and the atmosphere was extraordinary – tense, but exciting, electric,' I wrote in my diary. 'The whole place was packed full of journalists and hangers-on, business people who had been invited along. It was as though electric currents were being passed through everyone. I stood at the back. John Eatwell was behind me. He was so nervous he was rendered inarticulate. I have never known such an atmosphere, such a sense of occasion. Clearly, this was going to be the decisive moment in the election campaign.'[45]

Clive Hollick saw John Smith just days before the shadow Budget and asked him whether he was worried about the electoral impact of his proposals. 'No,' John said, 'we won't implement half of them anyway.'[46] It must have been the first occasion ever when a political party planned to break its pledges on tax the wrong way around, promising tax increases it never intended to deliver.

At first it seemed that the shadow Budget had killed off tax as an issue. Although the tabloids attacked it – and Anatole Kaletsky wrote in *The Times* the next day that it was the largest increase in tax for middle-income earners there had ever been[47] – initially it went down well with the broadcasters, who reported it favourably. But the Tories came back to hit us hard that weekend with a savage attack: having costed Labour's manifesto, they announced: 'The Price of Labour – £1,250 a Year for Every Family', to complement the notorious 'Labour's Double Whammy' posters.[48] The BBC's political correspondent John Sergeant reported that tax was the defining issue of the campaign and Bryan Gould, at a campaign strategy meeting, said the election was stuck on tax, tax, tax. I had a plan to get off it. It was called 'Jennifer's Ear'.

'Jennifer's Ear'

I accept full responsibility for 'Jennifer's Ear'. I was always hawkish on health, believing it was an election-winning issue which should be played very hard. The Conservatives' NHS reforms were a particularly explosive area. They led people to believe, and allowed Labour to claim, that the NHS as we knew it was under threat. But although fears about the NHS reforms simmered away, the issue flared up only if there was a specific controversy – for example, over the concept of 'privatisation' – or where real events demonstrating under-funding and chaos intruded. For the 1992 campaign, I wanted to produce a health broadcast so controversial, so shocking in its impact that it would turn the election for Labour. 'Jennifer's Ear' was not that broadcast, it was a softer version of the really shocking one. At the beginning of the campaign, we didn't even plan to use it. But I firmly believe it remains one of the most effective and successful party election broadcasts ever shown. The chaos around it was caused by organisational confusion and a communications breakdown for which I alone was not responsible. That party election broadcast forced the Tories out into the open on health. They stood there, exposed and vulnerable. And in an act of stunning feebleness, we walked away.

In the year before the election, powerful negative health campaigns by Labour had twice shaken the Tories, demonstrating its weight as an issue. The Tory counter-attack also shook Robin Cook, who was targeted by a relentless press campaign. The first decisive campaign was at Monmouth in May 1991, where Peter Mandelson had returned to mastermind the by-election fight. Going to visit Peter, who had reconstructed his old team and his old methods, was like seeing a campaigning king in exile – there was an energy, an organisation and sense of purpose that had been quite lost in Walworth Road. Peter had found an issue to fight the by-election on in a local hospital which was reported to be considering trust status. He invented the idea that trust hospitals had 'opted out' of the NHS and built the campaign around it. Labour won, health exploded as an issue and the Conservatives became convinced that Peter had black skills. Their defeat was instrumental in persuading the Tories not to go to the polls that autumn.

After the Monmouth by-election, qualitative research started to throw up the idea that the NHS was being made private. I turned this into privatisation, which seemed to me to be a killer concept. But privatisation was not a word that Labour's then shadow Health Secretary Robin Cook was happy to use. He was uneasy about it, often moving towards it but then pulling back. Harriet Harman, his deputy, had no such inhibitions and, displaying some guts, used the word with alacrity.

Labour's good spring turned into a bad summer. The Gorbachev coup of August 1991 gave John Major the chance to dominate the news, and the Conservatives edged ahead in the polls. We decided to run a ferocious health campaign to back the Tories off from an autumn election. During the summer, I developed, with BMP, the idea of exploiting voters' privatisation fears on a poster symbolising the horrors of a Tory fourth term. This was the second decisive negative health campaign. The poster was ghoulish, with four skeletons lined up against a black background. Around each skeleton was a sign: privatise the NHS; privatise the education system; raise VAT to 22 per cent; increase unemployment to three million. The headline read: 'How many more have the Tories got in their cupboard?' It was a brilliant poster, truly frightening. Unfortunately we only had the money to put one up. But one was enough. As it was being launched in September by Harriet and Robin, a journalist told me that John Major had made a comment about private insurance which poured petrol on the privatisation issue. The poster and the news joined to make NHS privatisation a massive issue. It dominated the news and Labour crawled back into the lead. This was a decisive moment because it finally persuaded the Tories not to call an election in the autumn, a fatal error as their lead in the marginal constituencies evaporated in a winter of recession. After the election, their pollster Robert Waller told me that an election called in September or October 1991 would have given them a lead of over 60 seats. Once again, health had turned the tide.

Although health worked well as an issue for us, it was always rough because the Tories had to fight so hard on it, and it was roughest on Robin Cook. He entered a period of campaigning purdah for four months because he was under constant attack for not having positive proposals. He decided to come back in February with plans for a new health offensive. In preparation for the campaign he phoned me up to say he wanted a graphic and a line. I arranged a meeting with Robin and Chris Powell, who was responsible for our advertising, but it went badly: Robin said he needed a proposal, Chris said he needed a brief, but eventually we got a graphic – a stethoscope in the shape of a £ sign – and a line: 'If you want to be well, you had better be well off'. Robin also approved a poster showing William Waldegrave as a highwayman with the line: 'Your money or your life'. A series of press conferences in February went well, but the newspapers were starting to dig into case histories we had given them. They found some flaws and went after Robin.

Gradually it became clear that the Conservative tabloids were seeking to destabilise him. Soon he came under further fire. A major document on under-funding had been leaked to us from the Department of Health, and the 'mole' had been found. His career was about to be destroyed and the tabloids were camping outside his home. The mounting tension erupted at the Park Lane Hotel on 13 February, where Labour was holding a gala dinner. David Hill, Gez Sagar, the Labour Party's chief press officer, and Robin went to a private room so David could explain to Robin what was happening. Robin had asked me to join them but Gez, who resented my influence, blocked the way. I barged past him and went to talk to Robin, who had just been told about the discovery of the mole. Understandably he was very upset, and felt responsibility for what had happened. The atmosphere was angry and emotional, typical of what was to follow.

The effect of the attacks was that Robin, who was now aware there seemed to be a tabloid offensive against him, felt undermined and keen to be more positive about health. However, I was unremitting in my insistence on attack. At a meeting with Robin I told him of my intention to produce a 'shock horror' broadcast on health, for use in the fourth of our five party election broadcast slots. BMP were developing two alternative concepts: one used real case histories, the other was based around a Ridley Scott reconstruction of a futuristic privatised hospital. Robin seemed nervous, but agreed.

BMP was also producing another broadcast, on privatisation – of health and education. It was about two children, one who used private health and education, the other who used state provision. We didn't know when or if we would use it. It was too complicated, not enough about privatisation and opting out. John Webster, the writer, went away and turned it into a straight health broadcast based around a girl with ear-ache, and linked it to a letter that had been written to Robin Cook by a man called John Bennett, who had a five-year-old daughter called Jennifer who had acute tonsillitis which was linked to grommets. The broadcast graphically showed the difference in treatment provided by the NHS and private healthcare.

I had also prepared the 'Georgina Norris' advertisement for use the day after the budget, about an eighteen-month-old girl with a serious heart condition who had died following several cancelled NHS operations. Thus, on 11 March, the day the election was called, we were already fighting on health. It was a very tough advertisement, one of the toughest ever to run in Britain. I phoned Mrs Norris many times to confirm that she was happy with it, and that the facts added up, and Cook agreed to go with it. But it was heavily attacked by the press, becoming known as the 'dead baby ad', and Robin was shaken again.

The following Tuesday, we held a meeting to discuss the main health campaign, which was being launched in a week's time. Robin came with his researcher Geoff Norris and Sam Etherington, a GP who had been advising Robin for some time and was also helping us with 'Jennifer's Ear'. We discussed the health launch and my proposed 'shock horror' broadcast for the fourth slot, in particular the one based on real cases. Robin was queasy about using real cases, but I presented qualitative research which showed that the public would support advertising based on case histories, providing the evidence stacked up.[49] We did not discuss 'Jennifer's Ear' because it was only one of many broadcasts floating around which I did not think we would use. We also assumed Robin knew about it, which was a huge error. BMP believed throughout that Cook had endorsed the 'Jennifer's Ear' broadcast because of Etherington's involvement in the shoot and because they had been given copies of Mr Bennett's letter to Cook. But, as it turned out, Robin knew little or nothing about it.

On Saturday 21 March, David Mellor launched the big Tory attack on Labour's tax and spending plans. The media loved it and it was clear we were going to be slaughtered in Sunday's papers. I began to think about upweighting the launch of our health campaign on Tuesday, as a way to turn the coverage. We had a PEB (party election broadcast) slot then, the second in the series, and we planned to show a 'switchers' broadcast in it: real people who had turned from the Tories to Labour over the previous four years. I considered scrapping this, or putting it on hold for later, and strengthening the health campaign launch with not just a poster, as we had planned, but backed up by the 'Jennifer's Ear' broadcast. We were still holding back the real 'shock horror' health broadcast until the last week of the campaign. I watched 'Jennifer's Ear' with David Hill and, in fact, thought it soft, and not controversial. We recorded Neil as a voice-over for the end of the broadcast and he saw and approved it. John Bennett came up to London on Saturday to record his letter to Robin Cook as a voice-over for the broadcast.

We weren't planning to use this; it was just an insurance policy. About this time, something about the broadcast began to make me nervous. Over the weekend I phoned John Bennett and all sorts of alarms went off. I did not find him convincing. I immediately made sure that his voice-over was not used and sent a note to the press office, insisting that no connection be made between the broadcast and the Bennett family. 'The idea for the broadcast came from a letter sent to Robin Cook by a worried father . . . [but] Philip is keen that Mr Bennett's case is not confused with our PEB,' Kathryn Smith wrote to Labour press officer Anna Healy.[50] The film stood alone without the Bennett family, and it had been developed independently of them. At that time it was actually called 'Mandy'; 'Jennifer's Ear' was a press description that came later.

On Sunday the press was terrible: 'Kinnock's middle-income massacre' – *Sunday Express*;[51] 'Gunning for Labour on tax' – *Sunday Telegraph*;[52] 'Labour's direct taxes give advantage to the Tories' – *Sunday Times*.[53] Even the cartoonists were at it: later in the campaign Jak in the *Mail on Sunday* drew a series of posters reading: 'More tax please we're British – Vote Labour'; 'Give more to the tax man with Labour'; '80 per cent tax under Labour – Glad to pay! Want to pay!'[54] And that afternoon, 22 March, I got a call from Robin saying he wanted to postpone the whole health initiative: he wanted to be positive. I didn't agree and said it was too late to postpone the launch.

The next morning, the day before the health launch, the tax attack was even worse. The Tories had launched the 'Double Whammy'/'Price of Labour – £1,250 a year' attack. The coverage in the mid-market press, whose readers we had to win over, was horrifying: 'Beware Labour's tax on ambition' and 'Lamont tots up Labour's incredible shopping list' – *Daily Mail*;[55] 'Why Labour have got it all wrong' – the *Sun*;[56] 'Labour's 50p tax shambles' – *Today*;[57] 'Labour's tax lies exposed' – *Daily Express*.58 I thought again about using 'Jennifer's Ear' instead of the 'switchers' broadcast to add weight to the health launch. Robin had still not seen the broadcast, and I planned to show it to him that Monday evening. But then fate intervened: I had a phone call from an old schoolteacher of mine, Mrs Hockley, to say that my father had been taken seriously ill and was in hospital in Weybridge. I went to Patricia, explained the situation, and effectively handed the whole campaign over to her. She just took it all on; she didn't flinch. Patricia was extraordinarily strong and brave during this period. It was a campaign of intense pressure, far more than the election campaigns that preceded and followed it. And for a while I was effectively disabled. But she just took the responsibility and soldiered on.

I was driven down to see my father. I had not seen him in six weeks and he was a changed man, wasted and neglected.

He was clearly dying. The hospital said that he had cancer. I was overwhelmed. I felt an immediate sadness but also a determination to go on, for him, for what he represented. But I also heard my mother's last words, 'Whatever you do, look after your father,' and so every day until polling day, late in the evening after the campaign had effectively gone to sleep, I visited him. I did not know if this affected my judgement or my energy. I did not know if it was the right thing to do or not, but I was determined to do it.

The following morning, Tuesday, I went to a research meeting at which there were conflicting views of how well 'Jennifer's Ear' had researched. Nick Moon from NOP said it was the worst broadcast he had ever tested. Deborah Mattinson said it was one of the best. But the 'switchers' broadcast had tested worse, so we finally decided to go with health. Robin had still not seen the broadcast and I tried to get him to watch it, but he didn't have time; he was frantic about the press conference. He agreed to go ahead with it nonetheless, and we decided we would take the line that it was not based on a real case. I thought we were safe.

The poster was unveiled in pouring rain and in front of a demonstration by Militant. It did not augur well. We had planned to show the broadcast at a special press conference, and the pre-conference briefing meeting was a mess; we had little time, everybody was tense. And then we had the phone call from hell. It was Lesley Smith, a press officer, who told Anna Healy that Julie Hall, who was travelling with Neil, had read out John Bennett's letter to journalists travelling with the Kinnock entourage. Lesley was shaken – she thought it was a mistake. Julie came to the phone and strongly defended what she had done. It was typical Julie – bold, gutsy and risky – but I knew we were in serious trouble. Somehow Julie had not been told by the press office that my office in Transport House had advised against making any connections between the Bennetts and the PEB.

We showed the broadcast at the press conference and it was as if a bomb had gone off. The effect was devastating. The press clamoured for details. Under pressure we started to offer them information about the case. We had a Campaign Management Team meeting that night, and afterwards Gez Sagar asked if the family concerned was the Bennetts. He said the *Independent* and the *Express* had details of the case and the consultant involved was saying our claims about the story were false. I remember frantically trying to contact Kathryn Smith to get the complete file on the broadcast, but I couldn't find her; she was still over in Transport House. I tried to track down the health team, but they had all disappeared. The press office was being overwhelmed with enquiries. In fact the BBC *Nine O'Clock News* and ITV's *News at Ten* were very positive – the best reports of the entire campaign. I phoned Mandelson in Hartlepool and told him we were besieged. He said whatever we did we must keep the details secret. But it was too late: we were leaking information.

The next day the *Daily Express* front page read: 'EXPOSED: LABOUR'S SICK NHS STUNTS'.[59] Their story was based on a claim by Jennifer Bennett's consultant that the delay in treatment had been due to an administrative breakdown and not, as we insisted, to under-funding. But the consultant, Mr Ardouin, had clearly blamed under-funding in a letter to the Bennetts a month earlier. He had said nothing at all about administrative failure. We still had the ground to fight on if we had the guts to do it.

As I thought controversy was necessary in order to move the agenda off tax and on to health, I was not unduly worried by the *Express* story. But I was about the only person who wasn't, and the campaign went on the defensive. The next day I was in a meeting with Hugh Hudson about the final campaign broadcast when I got a phone call saying that Jennifer's mother and grandfather had condemned 'Jennifer's Ear'. They were both Tories. I watched the news, Mr Bennett supporting the broadcast, Mrs Bennett denouncing it. By now I was hearing whispers, too, of a briefing against the SCA to some journalists, from someone within the Labour Party. Tension was mounting. Throughout all this Neil showed tremendous guts, spirit and loyalty, as did Charles Clarke, who said he thought the controversy was helpful.

That Wednesday, Peter Hitchens from the *Daily Express* jostled with Neil in the post-press conference scrum. The story moved on to Labour's campaign being knocked off balance, which unsettled the press office. They thought smooth campaigns won elections; I knew this wasn't necessarily true.

By the next day we had won the battle over under-funding, so the press moved its attention to finding out who had released the information identifying Jennifer Bennett. At our press conference in Nottingham Neil Kinnock denied it was Julie Hall. Then Julie put her hand up: she wanted to ask a question. Roy Hattersley, who was chairing the meeting, studiously and sensibly ignored her. Roy has a lot of experience, but a question from our own press staff was new to him. Robin Cook gave a very long answer to try to get past the situation. But Julie would not be stopped and marched up to the microphone to make a ten-minute outburst admitting she had released some information, but denying it was sufficient to identify Jennifer Bennett. It was a débâcle. This was our low point.

Later that day, at a Conservative press conference, we were offered a way out. William Waldegrave, the Tory Health Secretary, revealed that the consultant had contacted Conservative Central Office, who had put him in touch with the *Express*, before the broadcast had even been shown. So it was a stitch-up between the *Express* and Conservative Central Office – who had been warned by Jennifer Bennett's grandfather about the broadcast days earlier – and, more to the point, the Conservatives had been complicit in releasing confidential medical information to the press. Their culpability had been exposed, and we should have gone on to kill them. After the election I attended a seminar with Shaun Woodward, the Conservative Director of Communications at the time, who said the Tories knew about the release of information and were terrified about the consequences. He thought we should not have let up. At that moment we were ahead in the 'War of Jennifer's Ear'. But the ferocity of the attacks on us had unnerved too many people. We needed courage and we needed Mandelson, and we had neither.

Instead, we had another cock-up. On Thursday morning we released a health dossier of ten people who suffered from NHS under-funding out of the thousands who had contacted the party with similar stories. The tabloids examined them and claimed that most were inaccurate, and at the time the press seemed to be right. In fact, most of the cases stood up to scrutiny. Anyway, I didn't care; I still thought all the publicity was good. But other people were alarmed by it.

Robin came in at eleven for the briefing meeting. He was spitting blood, shouting at Patricia and me: why had we let out a dossier based on inaccurate cases? Why had we produced a broadcast based around a family, in which the mother and grandfather were Conservative? I talked to him later, quietly, about it all. I took responsibility for the broadcast, but not the dossier, which had nothing to do with me. We agreed to have a Health Service press conference the next morning, by which time the tabloids were in full flow disproving all the cases. I wrote about the morning in my diary:

6.45 A.M. – usual media meeting. Robin Cook storms in, face absolutely black, saying he has spoken to Neil Kinnock and he has agreed that whoever is responsible for the release of the dossiers must leave the campaign. There is silence: no one knows who is responsible. Then Neil storms in, equally angry. He is awesome, terrifying, shouting at the meeting. He wants to speak – now – to whoever is responsible for speaking to the consultant in the first place (which someone on the campaign did). At which point everyone starts to squirm under the table and hope that whatever it is that has been done, they didn't do it. The tension in the room is overwhelming. This is the most bloody and brutal meeting of my life. Patricia breaks into tears. Peter Herd, the account director, silently vows never to work in politics again. Gez, who I had not been getting on with during the campaign, has the balls to admit that it was him, he spoke to the consultant. He leaves the room with Neil, certain to die. It can't get any heavier or nastier than that. Throughout it all Charles Clarke is completely relaxed.[60]

We then gave up on health. I didn't want to, I thought we had the advantage, but the campaign was drained emotionally. It wanted to move on.

'Jennifer's Ear' was considered a disaster, and it was messy beyond words. I was attacked from all sides in the press that weekend (although not as heavily as I would be later), and an anonymous campaign colleague claimed in the *Sunday Express* that I was 'fighting for [my] political life'.[61] But it broke the stranglehold of tax, which never recovered as an issue in the rest of the campaign. Taxation increased by only 5 per cent as an issue of concern during the campaign. But health jumped from 32 per cent to 51 per cent, dwarfing all other issues.[62] Up and down the country, health and waiting lists dominated the local news. NOP polls showed 62 per cent claiming that health was the most important issue in deciding how to vote.[63] It is also true that tax and the economy were the most important unprompted issues in deciding the vote,[64] and of course they were fundamentally much more decisive. But in so far as it was possible to pull a campaign away from tax and on to health, that broadcast did it. Of course, the better way would have been to win the argument on tax, but that had to wait.

One final footnote. The polls throughout were very close, and obviously wrong, but the only time they showed big Labour leads was after the 'Jennifer's Ear' broadcast. I remember sitting in a café on the last but one Wednesday of the campaign, a week after the broadcast, waiting for the opinion polls. One put Labour ahead by 7 per cent, another 6 per cent, a third by 4 per cent.[65] For the first time in the campaign I felt a glimmer of happiness and vindication. It was a false dawn, but it indicated that whatever our true position 'Jennifer's Ear' had not hurt us – it might even have helped. Sometimes you have to go nuclear.

Kinnock

After tax and health, the third big issue of the campaign was Neil himself. There are two views of his electoral significance.

The first was put without sentiment by Joe Napolitan in a memo dated 8 March 1991, which said, 'The worst thing that happened to Labour was the ousting of Margaret Thatcher. With Kinnock as the candidate, Labour cannot win the next General Election.' He continued: 'Comparing the candidates directly is a lost cause. When the survey was taken in early January, Major's favourable/unfavourable balance was +55 per cent. Neil Kinnock's was −12 per cent. This gives a 65-point spread in Major's favour.'[66]

Anthony King and Ivor Crewe put a more considered view in *Labour's Last Chance*, in which they conclude Neil Kinnock's image and identity could only have lost the Labour Party under 0.5 per cent of the vote. One analytic model they developed of the 1992 election showed Neil adding 0.4 per cent to Labour's votes. Another contradictory model suggested that 'Major's net pulling power' in 1992 was in fact 0.5 per cent greater than Kinnock's. The latter is more likely to be right, but it is a very small amount which would still have left the Conservatives with a crushing lead. They made a telling point: 'It is worth emphasising again the importance of indirect leadership effects . . . Kinnock's importance to Labour almost certainly lay in his effect on the party's policies and image.' Furthermore, they argued, 'John Smith is a considerably more highly regarded Labour leader than his predecessor, Neil Kinnock, was; yet Labour's standing in the polls under Smith in the mid-1990s . . . was no higher than it had frequently been under Kinnock.' In summary, they thought Neil lost Labour votes because he lacked voter appeal, but added them because of the changes he made to the party and its policies.[67] And in the final analysis, Labour under John Smith was no more popular than it was frequently under Neil Kinnock.

I have enormous respect for Neil Kinnock. Without him, there would be no modern Labour Party, no huge Labour majority. He was and is a giant of a man who through the power of his personality lifted Labour into the modern era. He made the first great modernising breakthrough. He took Labour from the pathetic, unelectable shambles he inherited in 1983, with a Conservative majority of 144, to a party on the brink of government just 20 seats short of a hung parliament. Charles Clarke says of Kinnock:

> Neil was elected with one ambition in mind – to make Labour electable again and then hopefully get it elected. When he became leader after the 1983 defeat there was a real prospect of Labour never being electable again, of being a party which disappeared out of British politics. Certainly Neil felt that. His job, duty, responsibility was to make Labour electable again. And I think that's what he did. Not well enough to win the 1992 election, or to take, even, victory from the Tories in the 1992 election, which was a different thing, but well enough to lay the path for Labour to win the 1997 election in the way that it did. That is what I think Neil was about. But his achievement was fragile enough even after 1992 that we might not have won 1997. It needed the modernisation agenda to continue, which is what Tony did, to a fantastic triumph.[68]

Neil Kinnock did not change the Labour Party far enough, fast enough. This was his essential failure. He himself believes now that he should have moved more quickly, but the miners' strike, the one member, one vote defeat and Militant slowed him down right from the start. He became more cautious about taking on the party. 'There were some of us who thought that he could have moved faster,' said Charles Clarke. 'There were various organisational issues where he went for caution, and it is easy with hindsight to say we should not have done so. But it still remained the case that the main inhibition against moving more quickly was the fact that you immediately turn the party back to splits, with senior party people conducting battles in the media against the leadership. I myself thought we should have gone faster, as did Patricia, and we could have gone faster in certain ways, but to say absolutely categorically with the benefit of hindsight that going faster would necessarily have got us to where we were now a lot quicker is not absolutely convincing.' Those early errors fatally damaged Neil's leadership, he believes: 'The failures of the end were the failures of the beginning.'[69]

Alastair Campbell believes Neil was a little ambivalent about modernisation:

> I think there was a tension. Neil knew that the party had to be modernised and that modernisation was essential to any development of its electoral appeal. I think he knew that there were an awful lot of things in the Labour Party that were wrong, but he also had a sentimental attachment to some of the things that were wrong as well. He was deep-rooted in that sort of sentimentality, but nobody can say he didn't challenge it. He did challenge it, but time wasn't on his side to get the changes through. He did actually get an awful lot of changes through. It's hard to tell [if he could have moved faster] because you can't tell what he could have got through the party. I think he could probably have moved things more quickly on certain fronts, but you don't know. It's easy in hindsight to say that.[70]

Public perceptions of Neil Kinnock have been the basis of some of the most concerted attacks on the SCA, and also on me. After the defeat, and after John Prescott's attacks on the 'beautiful people'[71] who had hijacked the campaign, John and I had a reconciliation lunch at L'Amico in Westminster. John was very warm and for me it was a very moving occasion. His most consistent criticism was: why did you not present private polling about Neil Kinnock to the shadow Cabinet? There is still, today, a feeling that the SCA and I, in particular, represented the leader rather than the party; that by withholding information in some way we interrupted the democratic process. If they had had the full information, they could have acted against him.

On one level I can dismiss this attack lightly. As an election adviser it wasn't part of my brief to go to the shadow Cabinet and present polling information that undermined the party leader. It was not part of my role to get involved in internal party politics. It is also true that there is nothing in private polling that cannot be found in public polls.

But on another level my defence is weaker. It is true that I presented without compromise all negatives about all other aspects of Labour but not about its leader. I went pretty far, but not the whole way. I put loyalty to Neil first; but Neil knew from the start that the public didn't warm to him as a leader. There was no need for me to tell him. He agonised about it, he felt the pain of it constantly. Before the election, he considered standing down on more than one occasion. Patricia Hewitt believes he would have done so if he thought it would work. 'He talked about it,' she said. 'He was very down in the winter of 1991–92. He was demoralised by eight years of the press and most of his colleagues telling him he was as thick as two short planks. But he just couldn't see a way by which he could stand down.'[72] After the 1987 election he told me he felt that the better course might have been to have stood down.

On balance, I think he was right to remain party leader. Good leadership is not just how you appear on television, it is what you do. And while it is true that it would have been almost impossible to have won the election with Neil, it would have been little better with any other leader. It is easy to claim that a shift to John Smith would have significantly improved our position, but research carried out when he was leader showed he made little difference to Labour's image. The press were building Smith up as an alternative leader, but, if they had had their way, they would have turned on him before the election. 'I believe that Neil had decision-taking qualities,' said Charles Clarke:

> Neil was not a fudge leader. His sharpness could be wrong, of course. But he was about addressing issues, going in and getting things done. John believed you had to position things. He had a very good media image. And it's just conceivable that if you'd changed leader at the beginning of the campaign itself then it might have been okay, because by that stage the whole thing was so much in shape that his lack of leadership

qualities wouldn't have come through. But if you'd done it significantly before, even as late as January 1992, I think that his weaknesses would have been viciously exposed. It's the same reason that when people say today that John Smith could have won the 1997 General Election, I don't believe it. I believe that the capacity of leadership that is required to win these things is exceptional. And there are not many people who have that. And John was the classic consensual person, who could have become Prime Minister if he'd inherited the job from the previous Labour Prime Minister, à la Callaghan. He never had the leadership quality that was required to *grasp* leadership.[73]

Had Smith been leader, the media could have put him under enormous pressure on tax and Labour would not have changed its tax policies as much as it did under Kinnock. It would have been impossible to have formed a majority; the only likelihood would have been a hung parliament with Labour perhaps 6 per cent behind the Tories. Labour would have been forced to put up taxes, forced out of the ERM. It could easily have seen Labour defeated again in months rather than years. The process of history would have been cheated. We would not have won in 1997 with a majority of 179.

Neil Kinnock deserved that last chance and it was right that he had it. History was not short-changed, Labour advanced. The Conservatives took another course, dumping their leader to win short-term success. They won the election, but have lost power for a generation. The Conservatives still suffer from that one internecine act.

I asked John Smith after the defeat if he had considered trying to replace Neil before the election. He was appalled by the thought: it was Neil's right to be leader in 1992. Yet the British people never really took to him as leader, and there was nothing he could do about it. There was much talk after the election about how Neil was constrained by his advisers, that if he had been his natural self he would have done better. But this was not true. Nothing Neil could have done would have endeared him to the voters. We had a plan called Operation Liberation, in which Neil would cut loose, and become his real self. But it didn't work because his real self had changed, become older, wiser, different. In the run-up to the election, Alastair Campbell remembers the strain Kinnock seemed to be under: 'You got a sense of Neil trying to hold it together and you could feel the tension. He hadn't run out of steam, but there was a lack of cohesion, lack of drive. It wasn't a question of Neil – Neil had drive – there was just no sense that you'd got a machine on the march. It wasn't there.'[74]

Neil remained isolated from his campaign team. This, perhaps, is the greatest misunderstanding about the campaign. When I had lunch with John Prescott I explained, as best I could, what had happened in the campaign, much of which was new to him. But what he really couldn't understand was the estrangement between the campaign-team leadership and the party leader. He had thought that there was constant interaction between Neil and the campaign team, that the leader and key campaigning personnel were effectively oper- ating as one integral unit. John thought he had been shut out while we were locked in.

This wasn't true. John had little access to Neil, nor did we. For the last six months or so before the campaign started I hardly saw Neil and there was never, as far as I can recall, a time when he and his campaign team sat down and discussed the planning and operation of the election. The Thursday Group was in one place, Neil in another. We were all asking constantly for contact with the leader, but we never got it. The reason given was always the same: 'It would add to his burden, increase pressure on him, lead to endless demands that he would be unable to meet.' I don't know if Neil knew he was being protected in this way; I suspect not. Once I picked up a ringing phone in Neil's office and it was Neil. We started chatting and immediately it became clear that he was desperate to hear about what was happening on the campaign, of which he knew almost nothing. He wanted to know more and more. We talked for a very long time and could have talked longer. Neil was a man trapped in a glass prison. Whether he made the prison himself, or others made it for him, I do not know. Charles Clarke denies he was being over-protective: 'I think Neil was very focused on his own performance as he went up to the election, getting his own speeches right and so on. I think that time was very much at a premium. I certainly felt that a general run around the course in a rather vacuous way wouldn't help very much. Now, that certainly was not intended to be over-protective.'[75] I saw far more of John Smith in the period before the campaign. I worked with him closely and I hope warmly during this time, after he overcame his initial resentment at my criticism of his tax plans. But Neil was isolated from his campaign team, from the planning of his campaign, even from his senior colleagues.

However, although I saw little of Neil in the pre-election period, I saw a huge amount of him during the four-week election campaign itself. Still haunted by his hunt for elusive words, I remember him, head in hands, saying, 'Words: where can I get words? I must have words.' It is difficult to describe his courage and dignity during the campaign. He had a cold, he was very tired, but he fought and fought and fought. 'He had guts,' said Campbell. 'He's somebody who went into politics because he was genuinely motivated by a belief that politics was the way to get a better way of life for the sort of people he grew up with. And allied to that was a real sort of passion, temper – call it what you want – which had a good side and a bad side. The good side was that he actually got angry about things, but that also led to all sorts of problems for him as well, because a temper you can't control can become a problem. But he was properly motivated – he was, I think, a straightforwardly decent kind of bloke, soundly motivated throughout.'[76]

And he was always kind. He never blamed me for 'Jennifer's Ear'. Talking to him privately later in the campaign, I referred to the strain and trauma of that week. He said simply, 'That's what politics is about, Philip; love and anger.' Once when I brought my daughter Georgia into the campaign, he found the time to sing the whole of 'Georgia On My Mind' to her. He did every single thing expected of him, and just made one mistake when, at the Sheffield Rally, overwhelmed by the occasion, he was over-enthusiastic in greeting the crowd. And he still bitterly regrets that mistake. Nothing will have replaced for Neil the sense of loss he has about losing the 1992 election. He is the kind of man who will carry it with him always. But he need not and should not. He is the rock upon which the election triumph of 1997 was built. He is a modernising hero.

The Sheffield Rally and proportional representation

Of the many that have been given, the Sheffield Rally on 1 April 1992 is the least convincing reason for losing the election. Bob Worcester calls it the turning-point. That is nonsense. It was barely on the news and was hardly noticed. It did Labour little or no harm. The voters had bigger fish to fry. That said, it was a mistake – it looked over-confident, the politicians were over-exuberant and it was too American and glitzy – but this time it was not my mistake. It was a good idea which went wrong.

Charles Clarke had wanted a last-week rally to end all rallies. The idea floated around for some time and I went to various meetings before it floated off to Jim Parish, the senior campaign officer, who had the monumental task of organising it. Strategically, its point was to give Labour a major lift going into the last week, assuming we would be behind, or neck-and-neck. It was not designed for a situation in which Labour was 6–7 per cent ahead, when the rally would be useless. I still think the concept was sound; we couldn't have predicted the polls.

Parish's only instructions were to give it dignity and style, and for the shadow Cabinet not to walk with Neil across the stadium hallway because we did not want it to look triumphalist. On the day after the 'Jennifer's Ear' broadcast, at a meeting about the rally, I said it must have dignity and integrity throughout, and not look too much like an American convention. In the end the rally failed on all these counts and the walk happened, but I do not blame Jim. It was a great effort of organisation to have got it done at all.

Jim and I worked closely (at least I thought we did) through the election period. He was considered difficult, but he had real talent and I often defended him. But after the election he wrote a memo, which was leaked to the press, blaming the SCA for all the campaign's failings and me personally for the mishaps of Sheffield, simply because the rally started late, and that was my fault. I expect it did not matter very much. The later the better, probably.

The Sheffield Rally started late because I had reached an agreement with Robin Cook that 'Jennifer's Ear' would be expunged from the rest of the campaign; but I had forgotten about the video for the rally, which Hugh Hudson had produced and which contained an excerpt from 'Jennifer's Ear'. Somehow Anna Healy heard about this, and mentioned it to Robin. She was not being unkind, she was trying to be helpful. But Robin erupted – understandably – and I had to get 'Jennifer's Ear' out. I phoned Hugh, who was travelling to the rally, and begged him to take it out. He shouted at me, too – also understandably – but said he would try. As he was sitting next to Robin on the train, I don't expect much was said about me that was complimentary.

Meg Clark, Hugh's assistant, saved me, sending new pictures to Sheffield by satellite. I was panicking badly; this was the final straw. The video was due to introduce Neil and he was delayed waiting for it. When the video spluttered into life without 'Jennifer's Ear', I couldn't believe they had managed it. All I saw of the rest of the rally was a couple of clips on the news. And that's all the public saw.

Proportional representation is a more difficult issue. Peter Mandelson thinks it cost us dear in the last week, and so does Gordon Brown. There is little evidence that it did, but it was not the ideal way to end a campaign. Patricia has been blamed for this – unfairly, I think.

The drive towards proportional representation came from

a belief that it was the only certain way to make Labour safe. If you have PR, Labour can never govern alone. It will always be neutered, a consensus not an extreme government. Tony Blair had always opposed the idea of using PR to emasculate Labour. If you want to make Labour safe, change the party – don't duck out of the issue with PR. Blair believed that only when the party itself was safe would people vote for it. But that option was not available in 1991, and PR seemed a reasonable alternative; post-election research showed that the need to make Labour safe had been a key campaigning requirement. Neil supported the idea of a referendum on it, and this was included in the manifesto.

Post-election criticism focused less on the inclusion of a referendum on PR in the manifesto and more on the way it was raised at the end of the campaign. Patricia remembers: 'When we were planning the campaign, we knew that there was going to be this Charter 88 Democracy Day on the Thursday before polling, so David [Hill], Charles [Clarke] and myself agreed a form of words, which we cleared personally with Roy Hattersley.'[77] We knew the issue of PR would be raised and we had no power over it. It is almost certainly true that we should have tackled it earlier, but that said, there is no evidence that it harmed Labour in the end. Post-election qualitative research found people thought it made Labour safer, and Labour's lead gradually increased from 1 per cent to 3–4 per cent over the six days after the issue was raised (causing the Tory tabloids to turn viciously on Ashdown).[78]

The question was raised at the press conference on the Charter 88 Democracy Day. Neil read out the answer, which made people suspect the question had been planted, and also raised the profile of the issue. 'Neil was so determined and worried about saying the wrong thing, and because he pulled that piece of paper out, it looked like a plant and it absolutely wasn't,' said Hewitt. 'He pulled out a piece of paper and read the form of words so it looked as if Elinor [Goodman, political editor of *Channel Four News*] had been set up to ask the question, and it looked as if he was making

this great big initiative.'[79] Kinnock's answer was precisely
that agreed previously with Roy Hattersley, then Labour's
Home Affairs spokesman, and only pushed the boat out a
tiny way, inviting the Liberal Democrats to join a working
party to consider PR. It then took off as an issue, and Neil
was embarrassed on the *Granada 500* programme four days
later when he refused to say whether he was for it or against
it. He actually hadn't worked out what he would say if asked.
I had wanted us to concentrate in the last week on the recession and health, but we could not begin to break through
with the message. It was too late, the agenda had moved on,
PR had become the story. It became an issue less because
of its intrinsic merits, more because a hung parliament
seemed likely. I do not think it was wrong to open the debate
on it, given that it was bound to be raised, and indeed I
believe that if Labour had lost by 7 per cent and we had not
nodded towards some form of electoral reform the campaign
would genuinely have been open to criticism.

Into the night

Nineteen ninety-two was the toughest campaign I have ever
been involved in. It stretched all of us to breaking-point. It
was a campaign always close to cracking, conducted in an
atmosphere of tension and mistrust. The tension was eating
people up; personal relationships were sour. I said afterwards
that anyone who hadn't gone through that election couldn't
understand what it was like, and that was true. It was less
an election campaign, more a collective trauma. Yet, despite
all this, we all believed we could win. Not that we would,
but that we could. The polls – all of them – said we could
do it. But the polls were wrong.

At an SCA lunch on the Friday before polling I asked the
researchers who had been conducting the focus-group discussions if we would win. Yes, they said: we are absolutely
certain. I remembered this after the election and vowed I
would do the focus groups myself for the next election, which
I did. Even the cautious Roger Jowell predicted a hung

parliament. Some people have claimed that I said Labour could not lose the election, but this is wrong. What I said to the Campaign Strategy Meeting at the end of the campaign was: 'The Conservatives have lost the election. We have yet to win it.' This was true. People didn't want to vote Conservative, but they were not yet prepared to vote for us. The polls led me to believe we might win, but I could never actually see it: I couldn't imagine Neil Kinnock in Downing Street. Nor could the electorate.

Neil said later he became convinced he would lose over the last few days. I am not sure if this is true. I spoke to him often towards the end and he said: be cautious; play safe; avoid mistakes; we will just make it. I think he thought we were just ahead and the key requirement was not to blow it.

This illustrates the greatest mistake we made in the campaign. We allowed ourselves to become the incumbents: to take on the attributes of the government, rather than the opposition. This was largely the result of the polls, and the small leads they gave Labour throughout. We sat on our lead and acted with governmental caution; the Conservatives, a couple of points behind, fought like tigers and behaved like the opposition.

But that was only the first effect of the polls getting it wrong. The second was much more important: because Labour was ahead and assumed by much of the press to be the next government, thousands, perhaps millions, of voters were motivated to come out and stop us. This was partly because of the strength of our campaign; we persuaded voters we might win. If we had been behind in the polls the Conservative vote would have been lower. David Hill believes it was the polls and not Sheffield that seemed to turn the votes against us in the last few days: 'The day before Sheffield the opinion polls had shown us well ahead in three polls; they suddenly alerted the electorate to the fact that we might win. That was a problem.'[80]

My overwhelming feeling during that last week was complete exhaustion. I was aching with fatigue and nervous about the result, although on the evening of Tuesday 7 April

I walked up to John Major to try to cheer him up. It was quite late and Patricia and I were walking from Millbank back to the SCA headquarters in Smith Square. John Major's battle-bus was parked outside Tory Central Office and standing in front of it, looking sad, dejected and defeated, was Major himself. He appeared to have been abandoned. Patricia and I felt sorry for him, so we walked towards him and he brightened as we approached, putting on a smile. But as we got closer he recognised us and his smile became fixed, then disappeared altogether. We didn't know what to say, so we just shook his hand and walked away, leaving him as forlorn and lonely as when we had arrived.

But when I saw the newspaper headlines the next day I knew it was Labour that was in trouble. I arrived at the Millbank media centre at 6 A.M. and saw articles which were not so much negative as apocalyptic. The *Daily Express* headlines screamed of mortgage rises, race riots, chaos in the NHS and higher costs for six out of ten households if the 'shallow man' Kinnock was let in. 'Don't throw it all away,' it urged in a front-page opinion.[81] The *Sun* destroyed Neil and Labour with an eight-page attack entitled 'NIGHTMARE ON KINNOCK STREET', warning, 'He'll have a new home, you won't', 'A threat to proud history', 'My job will go', 'Prices set to jump', 'Do not trust his judgement or his promises', and 'Lest we forget – Hell caused by last Labour government'.[82] It delivered the final knock-out blow a day later with its front-page headline: 'IF KINNOCK WINS TODAY WILL THE LAST PERSON IN BRITAIN PLEASE TURN OUT THE LIGHTS'.[83] And on it went. The *Mail*, with 'Labour would have to raise loan rates' and 'Warning: a Labour government will lead to higher mortgage payments. There is no doubt about it. Interest rates will rise within days of Kinnock entering Number Ten.'[84] The *Express*: 'Can you really afford not to vote Tory?'[85]

I looked at those papers and silently wept. I could feel the fear of our voters: we would lose them in the ballot box, as I had predicted two years earlier – 'At the death, in the polling-booth, people may be more likely to vote for the devil they know and dislike rather than the devil they do not fully trust.'[86] I went home that Wednesday night and saw the polls reported on the *Channel Four News*, our lead melting away like snow. We had achieved our objective and got to polling day ahead in the polls, but only just. I knew that I had done my best in an almost impossible situation and helped to get the campaign through.

But I also knew that it wouldn't be enough, and I hardly slept that night. The next morning I voted very early and expected an empty polling station. I was shocked to find it packed – packed with hordes of elderly voters, one with a zimmer frame, all clearly come to stop us getting in. I knew then we had had it and phoned David Hill and others. We are, I told them, undone by the zimmer-frame vote. I was desperately sad. I had no doubt that we were finished. I stayed at home for the rest of the day, sleeping intermittently and fretting, getting the occasional hint of news about the exit polls, most of it good. David Hill phoned me just before nine o'clock and said the exit polls showed a hung parliament, but I was not convinced. I took a taxi to Walworth Road and, as I had done in 1987, made it drive by Downing Street, but I had the same certainty as then: we would not be in there tomorrow.

I went to the press office and the exit polls had worsened. Inside I felt numb; I knew what was coming. I went upstairs to Kinnock's office and they were convinced they were going into Downing Street. Neil Stewart, Kinnock's policy adviser, was certain: 'Tomorrow I will be in Number 10,' he said. Peter phoned, wanting to know if we had won this bloody election or not. No, I said. As the night progressed the polls got worse, and I knew it was all up. The Basildon defeat was clearly the end. For a brief period I went to the party at Millbank to show my face. I felt that was the least I could do. But the mood there was complete desolation. I returned quickly to Walworth Road. Peter phoned, distressed. You didn't deserve this, he said. Everything you did was better than 1987, and you deserved to win. It was not true, but he was being kind. After Basildon I said to my wife Gail, we are beaten, let's go home. I walked out of Walworth Road into the cold night, looking and feeling totally dejected. A lone reporter asked if I had any comment. I said, 'There will be another day.' I went home numb and defeated.

The next morning was worse. Major was triumphant. Labour had snatched defeat from the jaws of victory.

And then the recriminations began. People who had supported us, praised the campaign, worked alongside the SCA and agreed with everything we did, turned on us in defeat. I had seen this coming: I knew the reputation of the campaign was going to be torn to shreds. To lose once and receive credit for running a good campaign is possible; when you lose twice the knives come out.

It began with the press. *Tribune*, which had praised Labour's campaigners throughout and in its election-day editions, saying there was plenty of room for pride in a job 'done as well as it could be done',[87] turned immediately, taking revenge on the SCA and in particular Patricia Hewitt and me. Its former editor, Phil Kelly, who had fought and lost a seat in the election, took aim at the 'elitist and manipulative' techniques which Kinnock and his 'tight clique of supporters' had espoused. 'The glitz and gloss approach, far from enabling Labour to compete on equal terms with the Tories, positively obscured our message' and created 'alienated bewilderment' among voters, he wrote. 'At least the 1992 result means that Labour can dispense, lock, stock and barrel, with the well-meaning, metropolitan, middle-class ministrations of the Shadow Communications Agency and go back to real politics.'[88] In a vitriolic attack on Labour's 'image-makers' or 'party strategists' headlined 'LOOKING BACK IN ANGER', in *Tribune* in June, John Booth attacked Patricia and me personally ('Are we seriously expected to believe that we will win if Dennis Skinner has his humour honed by Patricia Hewitt . . . and should we all ask Philip Gould for the number of his hairdresser?'), demanded to know how much the SCA had been paid and for what, and concluded: 'Let us never again allow ourselves to be convinced that because some people get to the top they know what they are doing.'[89]

Vincent Hanna made a television programme claiming that the monitoring unit (a group of volunteers, including Glenys Thornton, who monitored grass-roots opinion) had been making constant protestations of disaster which the campaign leadership ignored. This was completely untrue. The last report of the group had said: 'With a little more effort this week, we may be able to win over the last 2 per cent we need to get a majority.'[90]

And then the big guns lined up: in an influential piece in the *Independent*, Anthony Bevins argued that Labour need not have lost, but had done so because of the arrogance of the campaign leadership, in particular the SCA. It quoted anonymous senior Labour politicians as claiming they hadn't even known we existed until they saw televised news clips of us working on the campaign, and effectively accused us of inventing Labour's manifesto behind the backs of the shadow Cabinet.[91] This broke the dam and open season was declared on the SCA. The conventional wisdom became that we, in particular Patricia and I, had hijacked the campaign while the politicians had been marginalised. And a lot of it came from the politicians themselves, who felt, understandably enough in the circumstances, that control of the campaign had been ceded to unelected advisers.

John Prescott was our most outspoken critic. In June, as the party prepared for an official post-mortem on the election, he demanded that the NEC reassert its authority over 'out-of-control' advisers, saying the campaign 'had a complete mess at the heart of it, particularly in the last week', with strategy made 'on the hoof' by unaccountable outsiders.[92] On *Frost on Sunday*, he added: 'For far too long [the party] has been controlled by a few people who abuse some of the authority given to them.'[93]

Clare Short said the campaign had relied too much on 'glitz' and opinion polling and claimed people had not voted for us because 'Labour was seen as having lost its soul, its identity, its integrity.'[94] A 'senior NEC member' attacked the SCA in the *Guardian*: 'Peter Mandelson invented this Frankenstein's Monster and it's out of control.'[95]

It became a fact. We lost because the SCA had ousted politicians and party officials. Then Jim Parish joined in the fray. Andy Grice of the *Sunday Times* phoned me the Saturday before the NEC's inquest into the election defeat and said he had bad news for me. Parish had written a report for the NEC inquest blaming the entire failure on the SCA and claiming we had mounted a 'wholesale takeover' of the campaign. His attack was bitter and personal: the SCA was 'a small team consisting of two [very] successful businessmen and another adviser, herself well-off . . . a group more remote from the people we had to convince it would be difficult to find'. He concluded: 'A future campaign must not be handed over to people who offer magic means of winning elections that ultimately ignore political realities.'[96]

People I barely knew even approached me in the street, insulting or blaming me. But a few offered encouragement. Tom Sawyer took me for coffee in Old Compton Street and showed me copies of the left-wing press that had been praising the campaign just hours before the defeat. 'You almost did it, son,' he said. He thought we were finished, our time had gone. I was deeply pessimistic. In July I wrote to Dennis Kavanagh (now Professor of Politics at Liverpool University, and the co-writer of the Nuffield election studies that had been my bible in my youth), reflecting that in 1987 I had said: 'You can't win a campaign in four weeks, but only in four years.' Now I was forced to admit: 'After four years' continuous campaigning, that excuse is no longer available.'[97]

But I did not stop, and I did not give up. I commissioned research immediately after the election to find out why we had really lost. And of course the normal reasons given – 'Jennifer's Ear', or the Sheffield Rally, or PR – disappeared under the weight of the evidence. The polling was clear: Labour lost because it was still the party of the winter of discontent; union influence; strikes and inflation; disarmament; Benn and Scargill. It lost because people thought they had left the party, and the party had left them. Labour and the voters were facing in different directions. The electorate looked 'onwards and upwards; they work hard; they want to do better for themselves and their families'. Labour looked downwards: 'Clawing back; turning the clock back; for Militant; anti-home ownership; strife; strikes; inflation. Not for me.'[98]

The conclusions were dramatic: if Labour was to have a chance of winning, it had to change completely. It should consider all options, including dumping the name. I had some sympathy with this view. I told the playwright David Hare a few months after the election: 'It is very hard for supporters to understand the word "Labour" belongs to the past.'[99] New Labour was eventually to provide a solution.

This research could not have been made clearer. The cleavage between people and party which opened twenty years before, and reached its peak in 1983, had still not closed. Labour was still not the people's party. It was still the prisoner of the past. Labour lost not because it had changed too much, but because it had changed too little. It lost because the process of modernisation had been too slow. I was asked by the General Secretary to present the research on why we lost to the NEC inquest on 18 June. Of all the presentations I have made, this was the worst. Bryan Gould, David Blunkett and John Prescott had said they would question me at the meeting. I was dreading it and asked Alastair Campbell to write an article in the *Daily Mirror* in my defence the day before the ordeal. 'It threatens to be one of the most explosive and nasty National Executive meetings since the days when they were all explosive and nasty,' he began. He printed the SCA's analysis of why Labour had lost the election, under the headline, 'Labour must look to the future – NOT for election scapegoats.' He criticised the politicians who were seeking to hide behind campaign officials, arguing: 'If politicians lost control of a political campaign, that is the fault of the politicians.' And most importantly, he argued for further modernisation, not retreat: 'Labour lost not because they changed, but because they didn't change enough.'[100]

Underlying all the criticism had been the basic political sentiment that we lost because we modernised, we lost because we sold out to the polls and the public. The next day I walked through the ranks of press and photographers and up the steps of Walworth Road like a condemned man. I told the NEC that campaign mistakes had not helped us, but that we had lost because we were still not trusted, still not changed enough. I presented the post-campaign research in its unvarnished form. Left-wingers including Joan Lestor and Tony Benn argued that modernisation had been tried and failed, and existing policies should be consolidated rather than dismissed as 'baggage', as some modernisers were suggesting. Paul Anderson wrote in *Tribune* that week: 'The whole approach adopted by Labour from 1987 to 1992, designed *precisely* to address lack of trust in the party and its perceived obsolescence, failed miserably to achieve its objectives.'[101]

The aftermath was almost over, but not quite. I spent the summer writing a series of campaign evaluation documents that took an endless time to prepare and compile. This was hell. All the time I was thinking: one percentage point. Just one. But I wanted to leave a legacy. I wanted the party to know what had really happened. I said that Labour must become the party 'of achievement and aspiration for ordinary working people'. Labour needed to become a mainstream, not a minority party. Labour should have the courage to say that it had changed.[102]

I spent much time with my father, who by now was staying with my sister. I fished in the local river, thinking of when he and I had fished the Avon all those years before. I felt remorse. I felt guilt. I did not answer the criticisms hurled at me because I felt I would have taken the credit if we had won, so I should accept the blame now we had lost.

I was with my father when he died. The last words I heard him say were, 'That is my son and I am proud of him.' I was determined to justify that pride. I would not stop fighting until Labour won.

5

A LINE IN THE SAND

Into the wilderness

The decline of the Kinnock project and the compromises that followed saw a split in the ranks of the modernisers. Peter Mandelson and I had become professionally estranged, impeding our mutual effectiveness. I had stayed at the centre of the campaign, close to Charles Clarke, who was the strongest figure in the team, its fulcrum. As Clarke and Mandelson fell out, this led to divided loyalties, and the distance between Peter and me had grown. But after the campaign, I decided that never again would I allow this to happen: good or bad, I would stick with Mandelson, stick with modernisation and never compromise. It was clear to me that Labour had to modernise completely or eventually it would die.

We were going to have to wait, however. John Smith wanted to heal the party, not reform it. His instinct was for consolidation, not modernisation. During the leadership campaign following Neil Kinnock's resignation after the 1992 election, fought between him and Bryan Gould, he expressed his reservations about the modernisation process: 'If radical change involves the Labour Party subverting its principles and aborting its mission, then I'm conservative in that very narrow sense.'[1] I knew my project wouldn't get far with him. He didn't want Mandelson either. Peter spent the two years of John's leadership kicking his heels in London and Hartlepool. On one occasion, he recalls saving a visit to the supermarket so that he would have something to do on a Sunday.

But there was no question that I would give up, or let the 1992 election defeat stand. I decided, instead, to leave Britain and learn more about campaigning; find out how other parties were modernising; discover how to win.

I was determined to remain privately and publicly loyal to John Smith. I believed modernisation was the only way forward, but I also believed it was time to be quiet. At a low level, behind the scenes, I helped John whenever he asked me to. From time to time I conducted focus groups for him, but I was clearly, and rightly, at the very fringes of the Smith leadership: out in the cold.

The SCA was closed down after six years. Its demise became public in October 1992 when party officials confirmed in *Campaign* magazine that they would 'wind up the team of volunteers who ran the last two election efforts'. A party official was quoted as saying: 'The relationships we had at the last election no longer exist, so we are in the process of seeing what else is on offer.'[2] We became non-people. A chapter was closed; it was time to move on.

Four weeks in Little Rock

I had begun to develop links with the Democratic Party in the United States in 1986, when its consultant Joe Napolitan started to help Neil Kinnock. Although Neil always refused to meet him, once deciding against seeing Joe when he was already halfway down the long corridor to Neil's office in the House of Commons, Joe was the doyen of political consultants, one of the first and one of the best.

After the defeat of Michael Dukakis in 1988, I visited the United States to talk to people who had been involved in the campaign, all of whom were feeling terribly the burden of defeat. It was quite clear where they had gone wrong: they had capitulated to the awesome Republican attack and they had failed to connect to the great American middle class. I visited the Democratic National Committee with Peter Mandelson the following year. In a long, rambling and not very successful meeting, Peter turned to me and said in his typical stage whisper: 'Do you know what the best thing about this meeting is, Philip? I will tell you. The best thing is the doughnuts.' I also organised and partly financed a trip with Jack Cunningham and Ken and Barbara Follett to learn about fundraising techniques.

Both Bob Shrum, a leading media consultant in the United States, and Mark Mellman, an American pollster, helped with the British election in 1992, although they were not paid. Bob wrote the final words of Neil's last conference speech in 1991: 'It is time to start transforming Britain from the country it has become, into the one we know it can be.'[3]

But I never met James Carville, who was later to manage Bill Clinton's election-winning campaign, and I met Stanley Greenberg, pollster to Clinton in 1992, only briefly, on a trip to garner polling advice in 1990. I am embarrassed to say that I neglected to take up Stan's offer of polling help at that time. But a connection was made, and one that obviously stuck in Stan's mind, because at the beginning of September 1992 I received a memo from his office which read: 'Stan is anxious to meet you here in Little Rock, Arkansas, at the Clinton Campaign Headquarters. We are anxious to have you observe the campaign, and to hear about your efforts.'[4] For me at that time – depleted, dejected, depressed – this fax was like water in the desert.

I took the first flight I could get to St Louis, then on to Little Rock. Before the flight, and at the stopover, I was being nagged by Bennett Freeman, a volunteer on the campaign: 'Get here faster, it's urgent, they want you to appear in a press conference.' The reason for their alarm was that the Bush campaign appeared to be trying to steal Conservative tactics and apply them in the States. An attack by Bush over a Russian trip of Clinton's seemed to echo the 'Kinnock: the Kremlin Connection' smear by the *Sunday Times*.[5] The Bush campaign had issued a press release saying: 'Back in the USSR. Six weeks after he organised a massive anti-war protest in London, then student Bill Clinton turned up at the Soviet Union for a visit during the dead of winter.'[6] The Republicans were also developing their own 'tax bombshell' attack.

The Clinton campaign's anxiety was partly rational, partly emotional. They had been following our campaign closely and felt dismayed and let down by our defeat. At a meeting the day after, someone from their campaign had said, 'We are on our own now.' There was a fear that somehow the same thing could happen there: the Labour jinx might cross the Atlantic.

I travelled to Little Rock with trepidation. I was the architect of a defeated and discredited campaign. My esteem was low, my confidence shot. What could I offer them? I expected them to be dismissive and arrogant, but I could not have been more wrong. Arriving at that campaign was like leaving the shadows and coming into the sunlight. I was greeted with more warmth than I imagined possible, certainly more than I deserved. I was told repeatedly, 'Everyone here has been defeated two or three times in presidential elections. Defeat is how you learn. We want to learn from you.' The campaign was not only friendly, it was also awesomely efficient: a great, co-ordinated, self-confident machine which was trampling Bush to defeat. It was like entering a different world. That campaign saved me professionally and, in a different way, personally. Their warmth that autumn began my recovery from defeat.

I wrote in my diary in early October:

Arrived at Little Rock. Two taxi-drivers playing dice under a tree. Flat, vast country. Small pink barns and farmhouses. Take a cab to the Capitol Hotel. Old Southern style: the best hotel in Little Rock. Am met immediately by Bennett and Tom Hagemann [another campaign volunteer]. Agree a memo on the Kremlin connection smear story. Arrange to have dinner at 9 P.M.. Oversleep and am woken by Bennett on the phone. James Carville and George Stephanopoulos are waiting downstairs and where are you? James is getting angry. I am in a blind panic, and am totally disorientated. I am naked; jet-lagged; half-asleep. All this way and I am blowing it. I rush downstairs and they have gone. Except for Bennett who takes me to a restaurant where they all wait. Half-asleep I give a rambling account of the UK campaign. Then Carville asks a *Washington Post* journalist what he is writing tomorrow, and the poor man says it is a story about Clinton being a KGB spy. Carville gets extremely angry. He shouts abuse at the reporter and gets up and leaves. George follows. The journalist sits there, ashen-faced. I have a drink at the bar and go to bed.

The next day I get up at 6 A.M. and go to the 7 A.M. meeting. This meeting happens every day, but is a little later on Sundays. I enter a large cluttered room where all the key operators and players are working. This is known as the 'war room'. At the centre of the room is a huge desk in front of a vast sofa. This is where Carville sits. It is the epicentre of the campaign. The room fills with young, bright, attractive campaign workers – Kennedy volunteers thirty years on. Eventually almost the entire campaign is jammed into that one room. No one is excluded, everyone is invited. At the stroke of 7 A.M. Carville walks in. Huge denim jacket with 'Clinton '92' written on the back. Denim jeans, white T-shirt. Hard eyes. Rugged face.[7]

In a campaign, Carville is a towering, raging man, breaking the back of his opponents by force of will: accepting no setback, no mistake, no retreat. In his book he quotes a Vietnamese battle cry: 'Follow me if I advance, kill me if I retreat, avenge me if I die.'[8] That sums up his view of how to conduct an election campaign.

I continue in my diary: 'George Stephanopoulos follows. Small. Smart. Bright-faced. Attractive. Cool. Confident. Their entry produces hush and awe.' George in an election campaign is deeply pessimistic. He predicts the worst, believing in some semi-religious way that this will somehow stop the worst happening. He charms while Carville cajoles. Despite, or perhaps because of, their dissimilarity, they function brilliantly as a team.

The meeting starts. What's Bush doing today? An aide reports, and so it goes on. I am billeted to the debate prep room to be near Bennett Freeman, but I have no desk. I spend the day preparing a dossier on the Tory campaign. We take it to George Stephanopoulos. He sits cool behind his desk, constantly on the phone. He uses a miniature headset phone that means he talks to you and his caller at the same time.

At the 6.45 P.M. meeting there is far more detailed coverage of the campaign. Suddenly and without warning Rick Steidman, the Press Director, announces that Philip Gould is going to make a short speech identifying the differences between the UK and the US situation. I do this pretty well and they applaud. I feel I am on the way back.[9]

The press release I had worked on was covered the next day by the *Washington Post*: 'Bush, according to Clinton aides, is borrowing almost all his campaign strategy from British Prime Minister John Major. In interviews and in internal analyses of the similarity between the two campaigns, Clinton aides noticed the close resemblance between Bush's television ads charging that Clinton would raise taxes and ads run by the Conservatives against Labour earlier this year. More pernicious, the Clinton camp say, is the Bush campaign's effort to put a dark spin on a trip Clinton took to the Soviet Union . . . They argue this was a smear modelled after a similar attack on Neil Kinnock.'[10]

The British connection became a cottage industry in the campaign. Bennett Freeman is a former Rhodes scholar and committed Anglophile. He wrote a series of brilliant memos exploring the Bush–Major connection and analysing Labour's campaign failures. And it was certainly true that Bush was drawing extensively on the Major campaign. There was much talk of meetings between Conservative officials, including Sir John Lacey, in Washington. Shaun Woodward, the Tories' Communications Director in the 1992 campaign, later told me that senior Bush officials visited him in London 'and left his office bare', they took away so much material.

Bennett Freeman and I called ourselves the 'British operation'. One week after my arrival I wrote a long memo developing the similarities between the two campaigns and the dangers for Clinton. I said, 'It is the last week that counts;

forget the plaudits, concentrate on the smears; fear builds slowly, and only shows in the vote; tax and trust are the only issues that matter.'[11] This note was the genesis of the defensive strategy used by the Blair campaign five years later.

But a week into the campaign my confidence was fading. 'I do not know how long I can stay, or how long I should stay,' I wrote in my diary.

> I have no desk, I sit in the cafeteria. But I am not giving up. Bob Boorstin takes pity on me: 'Get a desk. You are now part of the campaign.' I grab a desk in the debate room and try to feel at home.
>
> The whole campaign is preparing for the debate. Bennett is entrusted with the job of personally travelling to the debate headquarters with a copy of the *Penthouse* interview with Gennifer Flowers, which also includes many revealing photographs. After much deliberation he decides to carefully cut out the photos for reasons of delicacy. He flies to St Louis and delivers by hand this copy of *Penthouse* cut to ribbons. The Governor just grunts.[12]

The atmosphere changed on the day of the first television debate between Bush and Clinton:

> Enormous tension about the debate. The war room is cornered off. A large TV screen is moved to the rest room (the campaign headquarters café) and as the debate gets closer people get tenser. Preparation for the debate has been incredible. Twelve vast books contain every rebuttal fact about Clinton, every attacking fact about Bush. This is all also on the computer, but the computer is too slow. The books are faster. Every time any claim has to be rebutted the relevant page of one of the books is torn out, and given to Bob Boorstin, who types in the rebuttal note. This is all done incredibly fast, and at incredible pressure. The rebuttal note and a line to take on the debate is finished and sent out to 200,000 media and other outlets before the debate has even finished. It is clear that Clinton has won the debate and relief flows

though the campaign. George comes on to the speakerphone the next morning: 'You were great last night.'[13]

When the debate season finished, Carville and Stephano-poulos returned to the campaign. 'James carries in a bright orange basketball. George warns about complacency. Some words are barred: "mandate"; "transition"; "White House". James supports him: "They will not go gently into the good night."'[14] One week before polling day I have to leave, to meet my family in New York. 'James greets me warmly as I go: "We are going to win this one for you guys." Bob Boorstin takes me to the airport. I am very moved. In New York I see the polls are close and get nervous. CNN has the gap at only 2 per cent. I am fearful that there will be some terrible repeat of the British election.'[15]

Five days before polling day I wrote a last-week warning memo to Stan Greenberg and Bob Boorstin from my New York hotel. It said the Clinton campaign should 'reawaken anger about Bush's record and maximise fear about a Bush second term. Only fear of Bush will overcome anxiety about Clinton. You have to shift the question in the next few days back to Bush's record. This has to be done with all the aggression and toughness that is necessary. You will lose more by not being tough enough with Bush than you would gain by being above the fray. Clinton must fight back on character. Voters expect it. Advertising must be tougher and more aggressive.'[16] I got no response and assumed the memo had been buried somewhere.

On Saturday 31 October I returned to Little Rock. Bob Boorstin sought me out and congratulated me on my memo. 'It has determined last-week thinking,' he said. Michael Waldman, who was working in the press office before moving to the White House, said that Stephanopoulos told him the memo had 'provided the basis for the last-week strategy'. I simply could not believe he had said this. I stood there open-mouthed.

On Sunday I went to see George. He said the campaign team had been in a full-blooded argument with Clinton, who was on a plane. The campaign wanted to attack Bush, the Governor wanted to stay above the fray. 'As this argument was going on my memo arrived and they read it over the phone to him, and it won him over.'[17] I doubt my memo actually made much difference, and I am sure its influence on strategy was exaggerated, but I didn't care. I may have failed to win a majority for Labour in Britain, but I had made some slight difference in the greatest electoral contest there is. This was a turning-point for me in every way. It restored my faith and gave me the will to go on.

Later I talked more to George. He was very nervous and asked me if this was what it felt like on the last Sunday of the Labour campaign. I said it was a different world.

On the eve of polling there was one last war-room meeting. The room was so crushed people were standing on desks, clutching on to each other to avoid falling off. George spoke briefly, emotionally, and introduced James, who made a remarkable speech:

> I think we are going to win tomorrow, and I think that the Governor is going to fulfil his promise and change America, and I think many of you are going to go on and help him. I'm a political professional; that's what I do for a living. I'm proud of it. We changed the way campaigns are run. Used to be there was a hierarchy. If you were on one floor, you didn't go to another floor . . . Everyone was compartmental-ised. And you people showed that you could be trusted. Everybody in this room. Everybody. I was thirty-three years old before I ever went to Washington or New York. Forty-two before I won my first campaign. And I'm happy for you all. You have been part of something special in my life, and I'll never forget what you all have done. Thank you.

He broke down in tears, unable properly to finish his speech. As he sat down the whole room shouted: 'One more day. One more day.'[18] The room was hot with bodies and emotion.

On election day the exit polls came early and it was clear by eleven o'clock that Clinton was going to win a massive victory. That night I stood for hours in front of the Old State House waiting for Clinton's acceptance speech. It was freezing cold. I was waiting with Martha Kearney of the BBC, who was doing a programme about the election. She asked: 'When is this going to happen for Labour? When will a Labour leader be making an acceptance speech?' I answered: 'When Labour has got rid of high taxes and trade-union dominance. When we have changed as the Democrats have changed.' She smiled politely at me, as though I had gone temporarily insane. Eventually Clinton came out and made his speech, accepting the presidency on behalf of the people. I felt proud but determined that one day I would hear a Labour leader make a speech accepting victory and determined that I would be part of it.

The next night I attended the campaign dinner in the back room of Doe's Eat Place, the now legendary steak restaurant in Little Rock. Bob Boorstin rose and made a toast: 'To Philip Gould and the British Labour Party for all their help.' Those Little Rock days were relatively brief, perhaps five weeks in total, but they changed me, and I like to think they changed – in part, through me – the subsequent course of progressive politics. Nothing would ever be the same again. Progressive parties would stop being victims and start to be aggressive; they would regain contact with the values and hopes of middle-class and working-class people; they would develop campaigning techniques that meant the left started to win elections far more often than they would lose; above all, they would regain the confidence and self-belief which had drained away in two decades of defeat. That night – 3 November 1992 – was the moment the era of conservative electoral dominance ended. As John Major watched these scenes in Downing Street he was seeing his own future.

There would be other times when I would have the opportunity to help Bill Clinton. The most decisive came in November 1994, when the modernising project in the United States was set back by awful defeats in the mid-term elections. At the end of October, a week before election day, I took my family to meet the President at the White House, and each of my young daughters said, as they had practised, 'Good afternoon, Mr President.' He had just flown in from the Gulf and wanted only to know about the state of the election. His eyes looked distant and watery: he expected the worst. Later we saw Vice-President Al Gore, on crutches because of a torn ligament. He chatted to my daughter Grace and laughed that her second name was Atlanta, making a perfect pairing with my other daughter's name, Georgia. I discussed the elections with George Stephanopoulos in his office next to the Oval Office. George was always relaxed. He would sit there with his feet on the desk as if he had all the time in the world. His room was always untidy, and he had Greek icons on the wall. He is religious. We discussed the defeat and thought about examples of politicians who had turned defeat into victory. François Mitterrand came to mind, and George asked me to write a memo on this and to send him some books. I did both, and wrote a note called 'Winning from Cohabitation'.

In it, I suggested Mitterrand's cohabitation strategy should be the model for Clinton. 'Mitterrand carefully positioned himself as the arbiter President, above the political fray . . . He was careful to intervene only when he had the support of a majority of the electorate. He did this by effectively vetoing unpopular legislation. He always used the national interest as the basis of his intervention.'[19] Thus was born the cohabitation strategy, which many believed helped save Clinton's presidency.

Middle-class dreams

Bill Clinton's election in 1992 showed the world that the left could win, and it showed the left *how* it could win. It was the moment the tide of history and events tilted from right to left. It was a victory founded on the ideas and characters of the three principals.

George Stephanopoulos was in charge of rapid response for the 1988 Dukakis campaign, but realised that in the face of the remorseless negativity of the Republicans a response unit was pathetically inadequate and the whole campaign had to become one large rapid-response unit. George handled the press cleverly during the campaign. His charm and personality meshed the campaign together, fusing its members into a team. He is a rare example of someone in politics who has real integrity, and because of that he inspires enormous loyalty.

James Carville was the Democrat who drew a line in the sand and stopped the Republicans advancing one step beyond it. Until 1991 the Republican advance had appeared unstoppable. Walter Mondale was blitzed; Michael Dukakis was humiliated; Democrats appeared too liberal to get elected, too soft to fight. First with Senator Harris Wofford's campaign in 1991, and then with Governor Bill Clinton, Carville turned the Democratic Party from victim to aggressor. Almost through the sheer brute strength of his personality he stopped the Republican advance. He revolutionised campaigning methods. He developed the concept of the war room (all the key campaign players in one shared physical space); he created flat, faster, more flexible campaign management structures to replace the previous orthodoxy of campaign hierarchy; he involved all members of the campaign in planning meetings; he genuinely changed the way people campaigned.

But it was Stanley Greenberg who – with others – broke the new strategic ground. He was able fully to articulate what I had always instinctively felt and had begun only falteringly to describe: that the left could only win through modernised parties, reclaiming values believed by many to be owned by the right, and most important of all rooted in the hopes and aspirations of ordinary working people.

Greenberg began his career as an academic at Yale, and then set up his own polling company. From the start he sought to refashion a new progressive consensus rooted in the middle class. Like Stephanopoulos, Greenberg knew what Dukakis had to do, but was unable to get him to do it. In a memo to Governor Dukakis in September 1988, Greenberg wrote: 'The swing segments of the electorate, particularly the Reagan Democrats, are looking for Michael Dukakis to speak to them in terms that demonstrate a real identity with the middle class.'[20] Greenberg did not give up after Dukakis ignored his advice and crashed to defeat. He wrote repeatedly about a new politics of the middle class. The article I read most often – so frequently, in fact, it became a kind of defining text for me – was called: 'Reconstructing the Democratic Vision', written for *The American Prospect* in 1990. It was Greenberg's attempt to draw up a strategic manifesto for the 1992 presidential elections. It started with a harsh attack on Dukakis. He 'did not articulate any set of principles, offered no special perspective, and invoked no deeply resonant historical experience. The public was left by default with a savage caricature created by Lee Atwater, Republican campaign strategist: a Democratic Party short on patriotism, weak on defence, soft on criminals and minorities, indifferent to work, values and the family, and, inexplicably, infatuated with taxes.' Greenberg was describing Michael Dukakis and the Democratic Party, but he may as well have been describing Neil Kinnock and the Labour Party in 1992.

This was the right analysis, as insightful in relation to the UK as the US. The beneficiaries of progressive politics in America 'no longer appeared to be the broad working population, but rather the poor', and the poor alone. The answer to this, he went on, is 'the middle-class project'. This meant: 'The Democrats need to reassert their claim to represent the majority of working Americans. The working middle-class needs to figure at least as centrally in the party's identity as the traditional blue-collar imagery of the New Deal coalition, because in our time the working middle-class constitutes the broad majority. To reach the middle class today Democrats need to accommodate "middle-class consciousness", containing three primary and interconnected principles: work, reward for work, and restraint.' This brought together the values of opportunity and ambition with the values of responsibility.

But Greenberg's central insight was that reaching out to the middle class does not exclude the poor; in fact, it does the opposite: 'Most poor people also work, or want to work, and identify strongly with middle-class aspirations of security and upward mobility.'[21] By reaching out to the middle class it is possible to build a coalition that includes the poor and is able to help the poor by winning government. More than anyone else, Stanley Greenberg gave life to the idea of a middle-class politics, and the possibility of a new progressive coalition which had the middle class at its heart. In his book, *Middle-Class Dreams*, Greenberg developed his analysis: 'Democrats cannot aspire to dominate this period and lead the country unless they re-invent their links with and regain the confidence of downscale voters – working and middle-class voters – who want nothing more complicated than a better life. Democrats will never renew the bottom-up idea unless they begin with middle-class America as the centre of their discourse.'[22] Greenberg was not saying that the middle class are the end-point of progressive politics, but that they are its starting-point. If the left wants to build a coalition which can be sustained in power, and which can implement over time a progressive agenda that will really help the poor, it must begin with the middle class. That is true in the United States, and it is equally true in the United Kingdom.

It was Bill Clinton who gave public voice to the new politics of the middle class. In July 1992 he made a speech encapsulating all that I had always believed: 'In the name of all those who do the work and pay taxes, raise the kids and play by the rules – in the name of the hard-working Americans who make up our forgotten middle class, I proudly accept your nomination for the presidency of the United States. I am a product of that middle class, and when I am President you will be forgotten no more.'[23]

British politics are not American politics. The American middle class is not the British middle class. But when Clinton spoke in this way, he spoke also for me, and for the people I had come from. The land that Labour had forgotten, the forgotten middle class. Both casualties of progressive politics gone wrong.

Back to stagnation

As soon as I returned to London from the 1992 Democratic victory I wrote a long document summarising the Clinton campaign, and Labour's strategic position, and sent it to the party leadership. Party staff say that it went down 'like a lead balloon'. It argued that Labour was perceived to be looking 'downwards not upwards', and 'backwards not forwards'; it was for 'minorities and not the mainstream' and it was 'not trusted to run the economy properly'. Organisationally, Labour was slow to adapt and had divergent structures of accountability. In terms of campaigning it lacked 'executive capacity; message; a persuasive economic argument; an effective rapid response and attack capacity; flexibility; integration; resources'. Finally, there was a lack of 'mutual support, openness and honesty'. The document argued for 'an agreed, unified decision-making structure; a rapid-response capacity; the development of a war room where all key campaign functions are included; the establishment of task forces and task leaders; the use of outside expertise; a new culture that is honest; supportive; trusting'. It called for comprehensive change in the campaigning capacity of the party – 'sticking-plaster solutions are not adequate'. Politically I argued that 'Labour needs a proper connection with the aspirations of ordinary working people'. It needed to be 'associated with improving the life of ordinary voters, not penalising them'. The document called this a 'new populism'. Labour needed a new relevance, shifting from being a party associated with the past to being a party associated with the future. Above all Labour needed a fresh start: 'A changed Labour Party is the basis of a new relationship of trust with the British electorate.' And this change must be open: 'Labour has not changed until it announces that it has changed.'[24] This was exactly what the Democrats had done when they called themselves the 'New Democrats'. This document was private, but in public too I was beginning to put my case. Patricia Hewitt and I worked together on an article for *Renewal* magazine in January, which argued that Labour 'should emulate Clinton's success in discarding the Democrats' image "as the party of the poor and of the past" by forging "a populism of the centre rather than the left".[25]

I went further, and organised a one-day Clinton conference at the Queen Elizabeth II Conference Centre in Westminster, with two unlikely co-sponsors, the TGWU and the *Guardian*. This conference included most of Clinton's major personnel, and caused a few waves within Labour. John Prescott objected to the Clintonisation of the party, and John Smith sent me private messages asking me not to be disruptive. But the conference went ahead. Stan Greenberg talked of the need to broaden class appeal and of opposition to the term 'middle class', as it was thought by many Democrats to be disparaging to the working class and the poor. Carville's partner Paul Begala spoke of Clinton being willing and eager to use the media. Elaine Kamarck, an adviser on the Clinton campaign, talked of a new Democratic Party relevant to the twenty-first century, which had moved beyond the left–right divide and excessive political correctness. The conference was ahead of the mood of the party leadership, but it was influential. Peter Mandelson was there and sucked it all in. *Tribune* attacked the conference and those who sought to learn from it, warning: 'The self-styled modernisers having nothing more substantial to offer than making Labour even more bland in pursuit of elusive affluent working-class and centrist middle-class voters . . . have failed to see that the main reason for "lack of trust" in Labour is that people can see through politicians who appear to be all packaging and no substance.'[26]

I was not a lone voice for Clinton within Labour. Margaret McDonagh, John Braggins and Alan Barnard, who were to hold senior positions in the 1997 election campaign, were all working in one capacity or another for Clinton. Jonathan Powell, then working for the British Embassy in Washington, now Tony Blair's chief of staff, was observing the Clinton campaign at first hand and building links that were later to prove priceless. Out of all this was born Millbank Tower and the 'war room' it housed; rapid rebuttal and the Excalibur computer; an obsession with message; and a tough, unremitting focus on hard-working people and their concerns.

Clive Hollick had also visited the Clinton campaign, and upon his return wrote a memo called 'Campaign '96', in which he argued for a 'new Labour Party, new policies on tax and trade union links'.[27] He presented these findings at a meeting with John Smith, Murray Elder and David Ward – respectively Smith's chief of staff and policy adviser. Smith's reply was telling: 'This is all very interesting, but I think you will find that it will be our turn next time.'[28]

At the time the message of Little Rock was not heard, but it could not be silenced. The Clinton experience was seminal for the Labour Party. Within five years almost everything that was written in my document had been implemented. Modernisation of Labour did not depend on Clinton, it would have happened anyway, but his election did give modernisation a road map. Above all it offered hope.

But for the moment, Labour was stuck. In May 1993, just a few months after the Clinton conference, I wrote to Murray Elder to reiterate that 'qualitative research shows no real improvement in Labour's position. In fact it is possibly weakening through an increasing sense that Labour is losing its relevance to ordinary people.' Worse, 'Labour's core level of support is eroding through demographic and ideological changes. Most estimates put it at between 30 and 35 per cent and reducing on an annual basis. To win, Labour has to gain new support from new groups. Labour has to move forward just to stand still.'[29]

In June I wrote an even tougher memo: Labour was most associated with trade unions; least associated with successful businesses, a clear vision of the future, and getting ahead. It had not gained sufficiently from the demise of the Conservatives. Its share of the vote was too low: 'Labour is not trusted; it is not relevant.' John Smith had yet to break through. He was 'legal; decent; honest and truthful', but was an 'invisible man', not 'dynamic or charismatic'. He was 'less well-received now than as shadow Chancellor or as newly elected leader'. The explanations I gave included: 'Distrust of the Labour Party influences perceptions of the leader. Labour is believed to be difficult and unmanageable. This undermines all Labour leaders.'[30] Clearly, changing the leader was no substitute for changing the party. 'John was essentially a fudge leader,' said Charles Clarke. 'Tony Blair was the linear descendant of Neil Kinnock as a modernising Labour leader. John Smith was not.'[31]

I don't believe John Smith took any notice of the notes I wrote him, but although he did not move, others did. Gordon Brown and Tony Blair were changing the party. Brown, now shadow Chancellor, was ditching Labour's tax and spend policies, refusing to allow us to get boxed into any spending commitments or tax-raising proposals, later promising that 'a Labour government would not "tax for its own sake"'.[32] Blair, shadow Home Secretary, was modernising Labour's approach to law and order, producing a new emphasis on the balance between prevention and deterrent: 'Tough on crime, tough on the causes of crime.'[33] He also began the process of reconnecting Labour to its heartland values. In February 1993 he said, 'If we do not learn and then teach the value of what is right and what is wrong, then the result is simply moral chaos which engulfs us all . . .'[34] Later that year he told the Police Federation annual conference, 'If we dare not speak the language of punishment then we deny the real world.'[35]

I worked far more with Brown than Blair at this time, conducting focus groups and writing strategy notes for him, because I believed that modernising our tax and economic policies was the crucial task. In September I wrote a strategy note flowing from two group discussions. I was not optimistic: 'Those respondents with direct experience of economic uplift had already drifted back to the Conservatives.' Respondents preferred an improved performance by the Tories to the upheaval of a new government – 'Better the devil you know' still ruled their votes. 'Labour was the party of minorities; not those on welfare; not for ordinary working people.'[36]

In this note I recommended what Dan Clifton, the

broadcasting officer at Millbank during the 1997 election, calls the worst campaigning line ever written: 'Stop the rot, and start to build.' But I also argued for a focus on tax and a continuing theme, using the line: 'You can't trust the Tories on tax.'[37] I wanted revenge.

It was clear that, despite reasonable polling leads, Labour was not on course to win next time around. Tony Blair and Gordon Brown knew that and chafed at their constraints. They believed only modernisation would save Labour. Blair repeatedly pushed John Smith on the issue of one member, one vote and the trade union link, and John always pushed him back. Patricia Hewitt remembers Tony Blair saying, 'We have to make changes *now* and be vocal about it despite our leader, because otherwise there will be nothing to inherit.'[38] Gordon Brown also tried to push Smith hard on OMOV and was 'vehement' in his opposition to the compromise which Smith finally brokered.[39]

Labour had a new advertising agency, Butterfield Day Devito Hockney, which did a good job, but campaigning and polling had regressed. I was invited to attend a vast polling meeting stuffed with academic experts, who said that we had no gender problem and we could safely put taxes up. I couldn't stand it and left. Merely an observer, I couldn't bear to watch.

Fighting the fear factor

As there was still no place for me with Labour, I took my memos to Europe, where Julian Priestley asked me to co-ordinate the European election campaign for the member parties of the Socialist Group in the European Parliament. This was a great strain on my family. I was working in Brussels from Monday until Friday and living in a hotel. My children were young, but I was determined – it seemed the next logical step.

The first part of the project involved a review of the political situation of all the socialist and social democratic parties in the European Union, based on interviews in all member nations. This was a massive task and the findings were predictable: progressive parties were losing ground because the demographic tide was against them; if they did not change they would face further continual decline. The conclusions could not have been more gloomy and I presented them to a massive audience of MEPs at a conference in Aix-en-Provence.

It was also clear that the EU was out of touch with public opinion almost everywhere, and the campaign theme had to reflect that. I devised the notion of a 'People's Europe', which was used by all members of the Socialist Group except the British Labour Party, who thought it too populist. I developed a new corporate identity for the Party of European Socialists; set up a Europe-wide rapid-response unit; arranged for focus groups to be conducted in all European countries; and had a television commercial made by Jacques Seguéla, media adviser to President Mitterrand, which was applicable in all nations.

This was a lot of work, but it gave me an insight into European politics. I was not impressed. There was little evidence of fresh thinking, new ideas or a drive to modernise. European progressive politics had gone stale. People accuse me of looking to the United States rather than to Europe, and it is true, I did. But this was not because I wasn't interested in what progressive parties in Europe had to offer. I did look, but I found little there. All the new thinking was being done in the United States. I became increasingly certain that uncompromising modernisation was the only answer for the left. In this Julian Priestley was a wonderful ally. He has impeccable modernising credentials.

I got the chance to put my new campaigning ideas into practice in elections across Europe. In Sweden, Norway, Greece and Holland, progressive parties won elections using Clinton's ideas. My central premise was that the right's main technique was the use of fear, and progressive parties had to learn how to fight it. I wrote all this down in a document called 'Fighting the Fear Factor', which was my campaigning bible. It argued that modern electorates are insecure, uncertain and anxious. They 'are more afraid of things getting worse than they are hopeful of things getting better'. This mood of anxiety about the future allowed the right to use the tactics of fear, enabling them to dominate politics for the 1980s and early 1990s. To defend against attacks rooted in fear, progressive parties had to respond instantly when challenged; establish war rooms to co-ordinate the campaigns; fight hard and with conviction and concede no ground; win on tax and the economy; avoid being caricatured as the incumbent. Above all, they had to 'change and admit they had changed'; only modernised parties would be safe from attack.[40]

But although Europe was welcoming me – and winning – I was still trying hard to bring these ideas back home. I wrote a very long memo on 9 May 1994 called 'The Labour Party: Preliminary Campaign Observations'. It stated that, tactically, Labour must develop a completely new campaigning capability: it must gain confidence, conviction, attacking capacity, rebuttal, flexibility, speed, integration. Strategically, I said Labour must become modern and relevant; win the economic battle; reconnect with its voting base. 'Labour must become once again the political instrument through which ordinary working people achieve their ambitions and reflect their opinions. This means developing policies that will persuade ordinary working people that they will be financially better off under Labour; connecting with the populist instinct of voters through policies that are tough on crime; opposing welfare fraud; supporting individual responsibility.' I said Labour's message should be based on a series of choices: social cohesion versus social disintegration; democracy versus centralisation; the people versus privilege; New Labour versus old Conservatism.[41]

I took it to Tony Blair the day before John Smith died. He was impatient. He held the document in front of him. 'This is all very well,' he said, 'but as far as I can see Labour will only win when it is completely changed from top to bottom. That is the beginning and the end of it.'

Tragedy

On 12 May 1994, Peter called to tell me there was something wrong with John Smith. We didn't think it was serious. A few minutes later I heard on the TV that he had died. I phoned Peter. He was devastated, as was I.

John's death had a profound effect on the British electorate. Not really connecting with him when he was leader, they missed him greatly when he had gone, and they recognised him as a politician who commanded enormous, widespread respect. In death the public revered him and through his death they started to feel differently about the Labour Party. They saw once again its deeper, finer qualities, so long submerged by failure and strife. John Smith healed a party that had become ill at ease with itself. He widened democracy in the party. But most of all, through the extraordinary national response to his death, he gave back to Labour the confidence and pride it had lost for so long.

Peter and I did not speak for some time after we had heard of his death. It was a shattering moment, but in the unspeakable cruelty of politics it was clear that private grief would soon mix with the public reality of a world moving on, and that the battle for the succession would soon begin.

6

ELECTRIC SHOCK TREATMENT

Blair emerges

Alastair Campbell saw leadership potential in Tony Blair at their very first meeting in the Members' Lobby at the House of Commons in 1983, soon after Blair's election as an MP. 'He was bright, personable, clever, witty, with a sense of what he wanted to do. A very strong sense. If you had said to me then: is this the kind of guy whom you would consider could one day be leader of the Labour Party, I'd have said yes. When did I actively start to think that he would be leader? I suppose it was a slow process really, but it was somewhere in the back of my mind while Neil was still leader.'[1]

Campbell and Blair used each other's skills:

I was a journalist and he was one of the politicians I would go to for insights into politics. Where I found Tony useful, as a journalist, was actually he was very good at analysing the weaknesses of his opponents, the Tories. He was very good at setting a political context for things. I would construct whole columns and magazine features around the things he would articulate. So that is what he's always been good at. He had the ability to make sense of complicated situations, articulate them simply and do it in a way that made people feel reassured by him. For someone who was then quite young he was really quite a reassuring figure, and I think I saw him as the kind of rounded, full personality who has an innate understanding of what makes people tick. He's kind of plugged in to them.

He remembers Tony Blair and Gordon Brown working as a team: 'I was always struck by Tony and Gordon and their ability to have ideas that would then be seen through the media. They did it pretty well together.'[2]

I first met Blair and Brown during the 1987 election, but I recall them only as fleeting shadows. The faces who dominated that election were Kinnock, Hattersley, Healey and Bryan Gould. Blair and Brown were hardly on the radar.

Yet soon after the election they moved from peripheral to central positions. They immediately knocked Bryan Gould into the margins. Bryan feels very bitter about this, and blames Peter Mandelson, but this is wrong. Bryan lost his way after the 1987 election. He was the public face of that election, and as such was brilliant. I remember one occasion when we had organised a press conference to show Hugh Hudson's final broadcast for the campaign – the press had arrived, but the broadcast had not. It got later and later, but Bryan kept completely cool. About twenty minutes after the broadcast was due to be presented he turned to me and said, 'Well, Philip, what is this broadcast about?' I told him, and without any sense of panic he walked towards the press, prepared to re-enact the broadcast to them in full as if this were a giant game of charades. Fortunately the broadcast arrived at the very last minute, but he would have done it. That kind of pressure takes its toll. The 1987 election campaign knocked the stuffing out of Bryan and he never fully recovered.

Blair and Brown had ability; they were a breath of fresh air; they were attractive on television. In 1988 Blair appeared in two consecutive broadcasts and in 1990 he and Brown, interviewed by Fiona Millar, who is now Cherie Booth's press adviser, appeared in a ten-minute film directed by Hugh Hudson. Fiona Millar describes the interview: 'We started out at Tony's house in London with the kids running in and out. There was a huge dilemma about whether we'd use the kids in the film, and he was just warm and nice.'[3]

At this time we occasionally used 'people metering', a research technique in which groups of people use dials to respond instantly to politicians speaking on television. A line appears on the screen indicating immediately how warmly or coolly the group is responding to what is being said and to the person saying it. We tested almost all the shadow front bench and the person who scored highest was Tony Blair. Even when he was faltering or not at his best, the line would shoot up when he started to speak. I remember thinking that the public response was disproportionate: Blair was good, but not that good. He seemed to be able to connect with the public in a way that transcended rational explanation. It was a response qualitatively different from that to any other politician.

This quality, which is hard to pin down, was central to Blair's emergence as eventual leader of the Labour Party and to some of the frustrations resulting from the contest for the leadership. Its very elusiveness meant that several people close to him missed it completely; they did not understand how this young, unseasoned politician, who was utterly unlike any previous Labour politician, could have such an extraordinary impact. Consequently, while some were convinced from as early as 1989 – much earlier than conventional wisdom would have it – that Blair was emerging as the natural choice as next leader of the Labour Party, others missed it completely.

Also central to Blair's political personality is a feeling that he can leave politics; his existence does not depend upon it. Over the years he has said repeatedly that he does not need to be a politician, that if it doesn't work out, he can leave and turn to another career. His family and his faith give him a breadth of experience and vision which takes him outside politics. This makes him an unusual politician.

The first time that I really thought Tony Blair might become leader was during his speech to the 1990 Labour conference, as shadow Employment Secretary. His autocue stopped working, which he was furious about afterwards, revealing his ambition and his impatience. But the early part of the speech, before he lost his place, proved he had a natural command of an audience and showed oratorical strength. Already Brown and Blair were eager to get on. I went to Brown's room during the 1990 conference and they were both there, the carpet littered with speech drafts, the atmosphere charged, both almost frenzied in their desire to get things moving: 'Why aren't we doing more, faster?'

As the times began to favour Blair, Brown was entering choppier waters. He had been the next natural leader of the party for so long that a backlash was inevitable, and it came. Several of the politicians I worked closely with in the pre-1992 election period began to grumble about Brown behind his back. Resentment and jealousy grew. Blair, on the other hand, was being spoken about in a different light: his colleagues were describing him as a future leader. In 1991 I would sometimes talk to Jack Cunningham about the next leader and he was certain: it would be Smith, then Blair. And at a party to launch Robert Harris's book, *Fatherland*, in 1992, when Mandelson, Blair and Brown entered as a group, Roy Hattersley looked at Blair, nodded at him and said, 'That is the man who will save the Labour Party.'

Just after the 1992 election, as part of my ritual post-election-defeat humiliation, I had to speak to the 1,000 Club of big donors to Labour at Millbank. I mumbled my analysis of why we had lost, nervous and faltering, hating every minute. Philip Hughes, the painter (and now my neighbour), gave me a particularly hard time. But Blair, confident and inspired, electrified the meeting. We lost because we did not change enough, he said; we would only win again when Labour had changed completely. His speech convinced both my wife Gail and I that he would be leader one day. Gail had gone to the meeting depressed and despondent but left thinking anything was possible – Blair had totally changed her view of the future. And it was this mantra, of modernisation and renewal, which Blair would bravely take from studio to studio after the 1992 defeat. When I showed him the post-election polling in his Parliament Street office, which proved Labour had lost because the process of modernisation had been too slow, he became manic: you must get it out, he said, people must know. So, for the one and only time in my political career, I leaked research to a national paper; the *Sunday Times*.

After the US election in 1992, Blair was disappointed in me because I did not use my Clinton campaign experience to push the case for modernisation harder. I had written an article for the *Guardian*,[4] which he thought pulled its punches, failing to make explicit the importance of modernisation to Clinton's victory. However, I was still feeling responsible for the 1992 defeat and thought I owed John Smith loyalty.

Despite Blair's emergence as a leadership candidate by 1992, at that time Gordon Brown was still ahead of him. Brown was the senior figure, and his period deputising for John Smith during Smith's first heart attack in September 1988 had marked him out as a true star. Had one of the modernising candidates stood in 1992, it would have been Brown and not Blair. Blair had wanted this to happen. A close aide of Blair's at the time says, 'Tony's view was that Gordon could have beaten Smith and that they should have run against Smith: Gordon as leader, himself as deputy. Tony's view was that Gordon would have won. He would have run as an out-and-out moderniser, and said that Smith was a conservative. Tony's view was that the party wanted to be led, it didn't just want to be sleep-walking, and if you sold it an out-and-out modernising message it would take it.'[5] Yet Brown did not stand against Smith, out of loyalty to Smith, just as he would not stand two years later.

I saw more of Brown than Blair from 1992 to 1994 partly because of work, partly because of temperament. While Blair was clearly going to flourish as shadow Home Secretary, I thought all the pressure would fall on Brown, shadowing the Treasury. It was clear he would be under immense strain and that if he sank, all hope of modernising the party would sink with him. I went to see Blair and said that for the next two years what time I had would be concentrated on Brown. He agreed that this was right. He thought Brown's task was massive.

It was not only political imperatives which pushed me

towards Brown. I found it easy to connect with him. Whenever I saw him, and see him now, my heart warms to him. He came to my home occasionally and Gail was fond of him. She would feed him books, which he would devour. He was always demanding: more ideas; more input; more focus groups. I often phoned him at home in Scotland to discuss strategy.

I felt slightly less at ease with Blair. He was a different kind of politician. I felt he had about him a sense of destiny, and this unnerved me a little. I did not see him a great deal socially, and when we did meet he had no time for small talk. He wanted only to know: how are we doing? Why are we moving so slowly? His preoccupation with Labour's unfitness to govern was continuous and intense. He was demanding, but in a different way from Gordon: he had a habit of asking the most difficult question, the one you didn't want to hear. And he expected an incisive answer.

Although I did not work closely with him during this period, I watched his progress. He was repositioning Labour as a party that would be tough on crime, which connected directly with my suburban populist instincts. This repositioning was classic Blair. One of his close aides at the time describes the process: 'What was fascinating about the way he approached it is that he said nothing, read a lot, thought about what the strategy should be, and then hit it.'[6] Blair's speech in Wellingborough after the murder of James Bulger in February 1993 was the point at which this strategy broke through. It attacked directly the liberal individualist consensus that had developed over crime, using the language of punishment, and right and wrong. Perhaps more than anything, this change in perspective towards crime reconnected Labour with its electoral base. Most people believe in punishment, they believe in right and wrong, they believe in discipline and order. That for so long Labour denied this, that they sought to excuse the inexcusable on grounds of education, class or other disadvantages, was unacceptable to large numbers of the electorate who suffered the consequences of crime on a daily basis. Now, what Blair said seems common sense; then, it seemed, in the annals of many on the left, iconoclastic. Although Blair was certain of what he felt, he was concerned about making a public speech on such a great personal tragedy as James Bulger's killing. He agonised long and hard about the speech and in the end released only a one-and-a-half-page press release after making it; it had enormous public impact.

However, it was his work on one member, one vote which really made the difference to his leadership credentials. Shifting decision-making within the party away from union block votes towards individual party members had long been an aim of the modernisers. Kinnock had attempted to bring in OMOV at his first party conference in 1984, but he had failed to build up a big enough coalition of support and the motion was defeated. He had been able to push through a compromise after the 1987 election, under which individual party members could vote on the selection of parliamentary candidates, but two-fifths of votes remained in the hands of local trade union branches. This 'unsatisfactory hybrid'[7] had remained in place until after the 1992 General Election. During the leadership election which followed Labour's defeat, both John Smith and Bryan Gould made clear their support for OMOV, and the pressure for change was intensified by Kinnock. One of his last actions as leader was to ask the NEC to set up a sub-committee to look at replacing party decision-making at conference by block votes with OMOV.

Blair joined the sub-committee (the union links review group), in October 1992, but was endlessly frustrated with the pace of change. He was continually pushing forward, much to the annoyance of John Smith, who was trying to pull him back. Smith wanted progress, but he also wanted unity; he feared nothing more than a divided party. Smith was constantly telling Blair to slow down. He would say, 'Tony, you are being too intellectual about this,' when Blair started to talk about OMOV. Sometimes Blair would let his real feelings show. His *On the Record* interview in January 1993 on party modernisation was about as bold as it was possible for a Labour politician to be at that time,[8] and went too far for Smith, who asked Blair to rein in his modernising instincts. One of Blair's aides remembers, 'Blair was fantastically politically frustrated. He was banging his head against the table after coming back from shadow Cabinet meetings. He basically said to Smith: "You've got to give us a lead, you've got to tell us which way you are going." Margaret Beckett was chairing the OMOV committee, but nobody in the committee had any idea what the Smith line was, or where he was trying to get to.'[9] The union links review group made its final report in July 1993. At last Smith had taken a stance on OMOV and forced the union representatives on the group to accept a compromise, giving more power to individual members but allowing the union block vote one-third of the votes in the election of party leader. This compromise was passed at conference in 1993, although there was union opposition up to the last moment and Smith was forced to threaten to resign if his OMOV plans were defeated. Even so, the vote was won only by a margin of 3.1 per cent.

Blair thought the settlement was too timid. 'He thought talk about ending the block vote would disappear once people realised that the unions still had all these votes, that they could continue to vote as a block. He thought there was an opportunity after 1992 to have a real symbolic break with Labour's past, and that opportunity wasn't being grasped. His feeling about the 1992 election was that we were always going to lose, because we hadn't shown how different we were. He felt that we were about to make the same mistake.'[10]

Although his position was more extreme than his colleagues would have liked, and it irritated them, he won their respect, especially John Prescott's. He was also a member of the union links review group and appreciated Blair's determination to resolve the inconsistencies in the party's internal democracy.

Blair's frustrations with the slow pace of change were shared by Brown. According to one of Blair's aides, 'The two of them [Brown and Blair] were at the end of their tether at the inability of most of the people in the party, and most of the leadership, to see that the party needed to change and that it wasn't just the fact that we had got close and therefore would win next time. Blair's view of Kinnock was that Kinnock had done great things to reform policies, had taken on the left, but had done nothing to change the culture of the party.'[11]

Although both Blair and Brown were frustrated, Brown's frustrations went deeper. Brown was making extraordinary changes shadowing the Treasury, abandoning the shadow Budget and the old policies of high taxation and high spending. He had allowed one opportunity to be leader to pass him by, and must have felt the tide of events moving slowly against him. Blair sensed this too, says one of his advisers: 'Tony's view of Gordon was that people go up and down, and that at that time Gordon was going down just as he was coming up. His view of Gordon was that he just had to stick to changing the economic policy, take the flak and not be downhearted. Gordon was becoming a bit depressed because of the internal party flak he was taking, and was not being seen as a great performer in public.' The two men worked closely together. Their offices were next door to one another: if Norman Lamont (then Chancellor) was making a statement, Blair would help Brown. If the Home Secretary (Kenneth Clarke) was making a statement, Brown would help Blair. 'Blair was incredibly supportive about how to rebuild Gordon, but Gordon was getting himself into a very black mood.'[12]

Brown's frustration was understandable. He had been fighting to modernise the party for almost a decade. He was changing the crucial policy areas of taxation and the economy, despite fierce and consistent opposition, and yet he wasn't getting the political credit he felt he deserved. A political trajectory that had been upwards until 1992 had now stalled, while Blair's, which had been behind Brown's until 1992, was edging past him. And this was happening within a political relationship that was and is as close as a political relationship can be. Blair certainly understood what was happening, and it was impossible for Brown, with his extraordinary political insight, not to know that events were slipping away from him.

This reveals a basic truth about politics. It is not always fair. At any time before 1992, including the 1992 leadership election, Brown would have been the natural modernising candidate. Around the middle of 1993 the mantle passed to Blair. Succeeding to political leadership requires a conjunction of two events: you must have the talent to meet the moment, but you must also have the moment that meets your talent. For perhaps four years Brown was ready, but the moment was not there. In 1992 it might have been, but loyalty stopped him attempting to grasp what was probably only half a chance. When the modernising moment finally came, when the music stopped, the moment was Blair's and not Brown's.

Both Tony Blair and Gordon Brown have outstanding qualities, but they are different. Gordon Brown is a dynamic political strategist, surveying the political terrain, spotting every movement, anticipating every consequence. He is almost impossible to defeat in argument. He lives in a world of ideas and has constructed a complete political philosophy, nurtured in Scotland and Scottish universities. His values are anchored in a passion to end social injustice and to create equal opportunity. He has restless, impatient energy, and is never satisfied. He moves from great warmth with flashes of charm to dour introspection and a strength of character that can sometimes appear brutal. He has a dogged, enduring courage. He achieves his ambitions the hard way.

Tony Blair is a brilliant strategist also, but of a different sort. He sets contemporary politics into a vast sweep of history that goes back to the Liberal–Labour split and forward into the next century. He wants to remake the big picture but carefully, combining long-term radicalism with short-term common sense. He cuts immediately to the quick, seeing instantly the essence of a situation, of an idea, of a person. He will follow his instincts whatever the consequences, leading sometimes to stubbornness and inflexibility. His values are rooted in community and Christianity: he is not afraid to talk about compassion. He has a sense of the destiny of the nation, and of the pulse of the people. In this he is like Margaret Thatcher. He can move quickly from a caution that frustrates to a daring that alarms. He has a confident, winning quality which makes life appear easy. Both these men could have been leader, but in July 1994 it was Tony Blair's time. The moment and his abilities matched. In as cruel an outcome as could befall Gordon, for a second time he saw his chance of leadership slip through his grasp.

The music stops

There was a moment on 12 May, perhaps two hours after we had heard that John Smith had died, when I began to feel a sense of foreboding about the battle ahead. There was obviously going to be a fight for the succession. It was a time of crisis for the modernisers. Everybody was deeply shocked by John Smith's death, yet it was inevitable that the future would quickly intrude on the past and our thoughts would move to who the next leader would be.

For Brown and Blair, of course, the situation was even worse. With grief over the loss of a father-figure came the realisation that only one of them could succeed him. Time was a luxury they did not have: non-modernising candidates were understandably considering their position, and within hours of Smith's death the media were discussing the potential candidates for the leadership.

Alastair Campbell was in a car leaving the BBC, where he had been reviewing the papers, when a message came to call his office. They told him that there was a rumour John Smith had died. He phoned Hilary Coffman in the Labour press office and could tell from the way she was talking that something was terribly wrong. He recalls:

> I then went straight to the Commons and made a few phone calls and spoke to Jack Cunningham, who told me John was dead. At that time I was on my way to ITN at Millbank to do something on TV and I was in the extraordinary position

of knowing he was dead but not being able to say that because I was doing this thing on television. I then went off and spent most of the day just doing the rounds and doing obituaries about John and I think, like a lot of people, I was quite shocked by how upsetting I found it all. I don't even know if I spoke to Tony that day, I might have done, I can't remember. There was a general understanding that people would not talk about what would happen next. I did an interview on *Newsnight* and I think there was an understanding with Mark Mardell that he wouldn't ask me. Not an agreement, but just 'that's off-limits' kind of stuff. Right at the end of the interview he said: 'Who do you think is the next leader of the Labour Party?' and I said Tony Blair. I don't think there was a moment's doubt.[13]

Blair had doubts, however. On Friday Campbell travelled to north Wales for a funeral: Glenys Kinnock's mother had died. Campbell spent much of the long and difficult drive on the phone: 'I was getting all sorts of calls from people, friends of Tony's, saying you have got to speak to him because he is basically saying it's got to be Gordon. Now I don't know how much he was constantly testing the argument. I think parts of him did feel the fact that they had come up together, and it had generally been accepted that Gordon was, as it were, the senior of the two.'[14] But Blair soon came to the conclusion that he had to stand. When I spoke to him a few days later he was already clear that he had no choice, and I reinforced that view. I do not know how Gordon Brown saw those first few days. He has not discussed it with me. However, from conversations with his friends and colleagues, I am sure that he was confident he would become leader. Yet within a very short time Brown would see the massive momentum building up behind Blair and watch his own leadership ambitions evaporate.

Part of the problem for him was the suddenness: John Smith's death froze a moment in time. The music stopped and the political ether set solid. Intimations, moods, tendencies, trends which had been discernible but not yet irrevocable were suddenly set in concrete. Although it had been clear to some of us in the year or so before John Smith's death that Blair had replaced Brown as the natural choice for the next leader, it was not yet an accepted fact and was certainly not clear to everyone. But within hours of John Smith dying a new political reality emerged, and there was nothing anyone – not Tony Blair, not Gordon Brown, not Peter Mandelson, not Alastair Campbell – could do about it.

I never doubted that Blair was the right candidate, but I knew also the huge personal crisis this would pose for Gordon Brown. I phoned him on Sunday 15 May, three days after John's death. We talked for a while and then with great courage he asked me the question he must have dreaded: who should it be, who would have the best chance of winning? I said Tony, without hesitation. Gordon asked me why, and I replied that Tony not only met the mood of the nation, he exemplified it. He would create for Labour and for Britain a sense of change, of a new beginning, which Gordon could not do. When he asked me if he should stand down, I replied, only if he could live with the consequences of doing so. It was not a question of personal ambition, Gordon said, but of giving up the chance to implement his ideas – ideas he had spent a lifetime developing. He said this with sadness and resignation. It was clear to me that he would not, in the last resort, stand against Tony. That he did not, that he stood down and gave way, was the action of a brave man.

The truth at that time was simple: Blair had no option but to stand. On 18 May I wrote a memo to Mandelson: 'Post John Smith there is only one viable strategic opportunity for Labour, and that is to become a party of change, momentum and dynamism. This is most certainly the mood of the country, and probably of a majority of the party. At this time Tony exemplifies this mood more completely than any Labour leader since Wilson. Gordon has prodigious strengths, but will be seen as an interim leader, halfway between John Smith and Tony Blair. At this time all strategic decisions must be taken on the basis of this national and party mood.'[15]

I considered the possibility of Blair standing down, but said that if he did there would be enormous disappointment in the country and the party. There would be a backlash against Labour and a belief that Labour was only prepared to take half a step forward; then a backlash against Gordon as the candidate who stopped Tony. The backlash would harm Gordon immensely. 'It is possible for Tony to win both in the technical sense of winning the election, and also in the broader sense of creating Labour as a party of change. By this standard it is almost impossible for Gordon to win. Any win for Gordon in these circumstances would carry a huge cost. The relationship with Tony would be damaged. The modernisers' cause would be damaged. The public would be dismayed and Gordon's chances of winning a subsequent General Election would be greatly harmed.'[16]

Writing a memo like that is easy; giving up the ambition of a lifetime is very hard. I realise now that I – and others, I am sure – underestimated the difficulty of Gordon's decision. To me, Tony was the natural choice as the next leader. But for Gordon it was about ideas and the long haul, and the huge strength of support for Tony must have seemed unaccountable. Our certainty, our view of the world, was not his. He did not know until the very last moment that time and chance were not to favour him.

Anyone who doubts Gordon Brown's stoicism should have seen him late on the evening of 20 July 1994, the day before Blair was officially declared leader, but when it was certain that he would win. Tony's acceptance speech was not finished, and Gordon was working on it in his office in Millbank. If you want to know what real loyalty is, it is this: Gordon Brown late in the evening, cursing, muttering, arms flailing as he punched words into a computer, writing the speech that just a few weeks earlier he believed he would be making himself.

Although it was clear to me, and to Alastair, that Tony Blair should be the next leader of the party, others saw it differently – and not only Gordon Brown's supporters, but also Peter Mandelson. Mandelson had always seen Brown as the natural successor to Smith:

Anyone who had any contact with me in the years preceding John Smith's death knows how committed I was to Gordon Brown. I worked for him day in, day out. I was his adviser. When I was Director of Communications, and beyond that, when I stopped in 1990, right up through the General Election of 1992 and beyond, I made sure that the machine served Gordon Brown. But I also made sure that the machine served Tony Blair as well, because they were both leaders of the modernisers, manifestly the most competent and able, and they were both superb performers. But nobody who knew me and knew the situation could seriously argue that I didn't put Brown before Blair right up until 1994. It was always Brown one, and Blair two.[17]

I know this to be true from endless conversations I had with Mandelson over this period. When the election for leader came, he was torn: 'When John Smith died both their standings were incredibly high, but within hours of Smith dying, the whole world had gone to Blair. It wasn't something that could be organised, managed, manipulated, it just happened,' Mandelson says. 'It could have turned into the most awful mess, but I didn't let go of Gordon, and didn't let go of the possibility of Gordon, until well into the next week.'[18]

This is consistent with my dealings with Peter at this time. From the moment of John's death he was hopelessly divided between his loyalty to Gordon and friendship with Tony. Quite simply he did not know what to do. Every day we would talk; usually several times a day. He wanted to be loyal to them both. I told him constantly the candidate had to be Tony, but he would not have it: Gordon and Tony both had claims and he would respect both. He wrote to Gordon on the Monday, a week after John Smith's death. His letter started by praising Brown's abilities, making it clear that although he had the qualities needed to be leader of the party, that was not the issue. It had become a question of presentation and media and public acceptability and the need to win the south. Tony Blair was now so far ahead that he could not withdraw. The only option would be for Gordon to stand as well, which would weaken Tony and might open the door to a new non-modernising candidate. If Gordon stood, it would need a massively upweighted media campaign and outstanding media-management skills, which Mandelson said he would be prepared to provide. This letter lent itself to different interpretations, but I think the central thrust was pretty clear: Mandelson was saying to Brown, you could run, but it would damage Tony; I would help, but it would be better if you did not stand. I do not see this as duplicitous: it was Mandelson trying to square an impossible circle. He kept on repeating, 'There will only be one candidate,' but in the early days he refused to say who it should be. Soon, he came to realise it would be Tony, but the change was gradual.

When I went into Peter's office on Tuesday 17 May he said, 'It is time we got down to work.' For Tony, I assumed, but I was wrong. Peter asked me to write a briefing note on how best to present Gordon in the campaign. He was determined to keep Gordon's leadership chances afloat so that time could be bought to make a calm and rational decision. He wanted to be fair to both. He would not allow a word to be said against Gordon. When Harriet Harman came into his office and said, 'It has got to be Tony,' he barked at her, 'That is not decided yet.'

At the time Mandelson said that he thought the best course might be to leave the stage for a while, and adopt a neutral, disinterested position. But he admits that was never really an option: 'I knew I could not get out of it because I was both their best friends and I was looked to by the media the whole time to represent what was going on among the modernisers. I was the agent, the publicist, the spin-doctor of the modernisers' cause.'[19]

After it became clear that Tony was going to be the modernisers' candidate, Mandelson says, 'I worked with Gordon to devise the best possible exit strategy for him that I could, which I did, which I think I managed incredibly well right up until the last moment. Gordon's people never

wanted Gordon to exit, but Gordon knew he had to. I was
the constant intermediary between him [Brown] and Tony,
organising right down to the last word of the briefing statement that we put together for the day that Gordon with-
drew.'[20] I was not party to these discussions: Mandelson was
under huge strain, and would not talk openly about what he
was doing.

The leadership election produced a breakdown in the
previously very close relationship between Mandelson and
Brown, although not between Blair and Brown. The bitterness after the election focused on the followers, not the
leaders. Blair and Brown speak only warmly of each other
and their relationship retains its strength, but the campaign
did leave its mark. Part of the problem now is that there is
no shared consensus about what happened. The account
that I have given above is simply not believed by many who
were involved. And my perspective is limited: I only saw my
small part of the events. But I am certain of some things. I
know that Gordon Brown acted with great courage in
standing down; that Tony Blair had no option but to stand
and did everything he could to support Gordon; and that
Peter Mandelson was caught between two loyalties and tried
to make the best of a difficult situation. Not everyone sees
it this way. Bitterness remains, but not between the two
principals. Campbell says, 'I was struck by what Gordon
did. It was a difficult thing to do. It was a ballsy thing to
do. But I think they have managed to hold their relationship
together. It is a very powerful relationship and a very powerful
motor within government, and some people around them
find it very difficult to fathom how it works, but it does. I
think that's because they have been through quite a lot
together. They are both basically decent blokes.'[21]

The leadership campaign

On the Monday after John's death Anji Hunter, head of
Blair's office and an absolute linchpin in his political life,
contacted me to ask if I would help on Tony's leadership

Michael Foot as deputy leader of the Labour Party in 1980, addressing an anti-nuclear rally in Hyde Park.

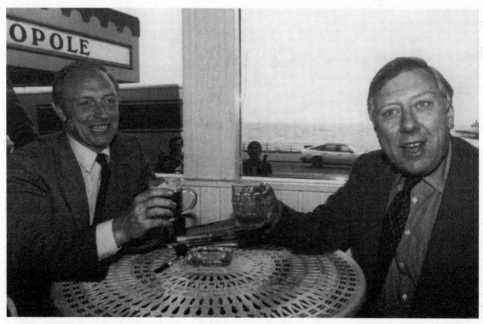

After the 1983 defeat: Neil Kinnock and Roy Hattersley, the new leadership of the party, in Brighton on the last day of the 1983 conference.

What a difference a year makes: the conference platform in 1985 (above)
and 1986 (below) – the first time the rose logo appeared at conference.

Roy Hattersley, Neil Kinnock, Denis Healey and Gerald Kaufman at the launch of the manifesto for the 1987 General Election campaign.

Patricia Hewitt (right), Neil Kinnock's press secretary from 1983 to 1989, with Harriet Harman.

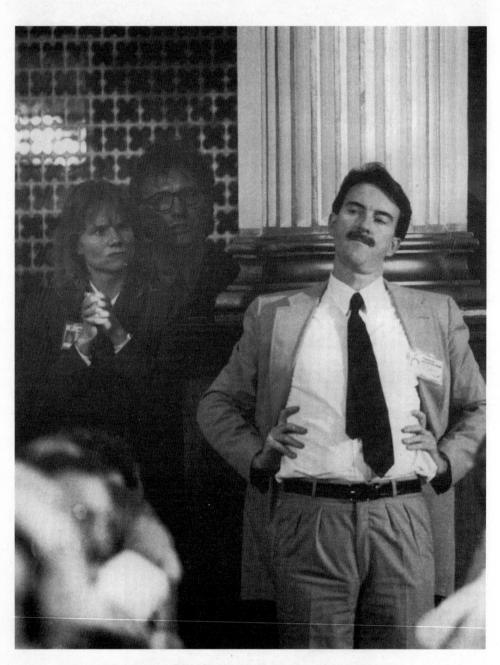

Peter Mandelson, Julie Hall and Philip Gould at the 1990 party
conference in Blackpool.

Popperfoto/Reuter

The 'skeletons in the cupboard' poster used during the 1992 General Election campaign.

Popperfoto/Reuter

A still from the infamous 'Jennifer's Ear' party election broadcast.

Neil Kinnock concedes defeat in the 1992 election. The Tories, this time under John Major, had won their fourth victory in a row.

John Smith, elected leader of the party after Neil Kinnock's resignation following the 1992 defeat.

Tony Blair and Gordon Brown at John Smith's funeral in May 1994.

The New Labour Party: Blair's first conference speech as leader, October 1994.

campaign. I phoned Tony at home. He was anxious, needing reassurance about whether or not he was right to stand. I said he had no choice, he had to do it. He invited me to his house and when we talked in his kitchen he had become more settled about standing. He was determined to go ahead, but was very worried about Gordon. Already, however, he was thinking about fighting the Tories in a new way. He did not want to get trapped on their ground: he said we should concede and move on – agree with the Conservatives where we could only lose, fight only where we could win.

Very early on I wrote a strategy note for the campaign, dated 17 May, called 'Strategy for the Leadership Election and Beyond', in which I identified a new political map and a new political mood. 'The electorate has lost hope, lost trust, and lost the confidence that things can improve. It has become sullen, resentful, unbelieving.' There was 'a lack of confidence in Britain, what is happening to it, and what is its place in the world. Britain in this mood is crying out for the right kind of leadership. This strategic opportunity can only be grasped by a shift from a strategy of consolidation to a strategy of change.' The strategy of consolidation was based around 'consensus and compromise' and 'would have produced a Labour vote of around 37–9 per cent: a low downside, a low upside'. This approach could not work now, I argued: we had to move to a strategy of change, based upon 'party unity through momentum', 'direction and dynamism'; 'electoral appeal through excitement, modernity and renewal'. 'The upside of this strategy is higher, perhaps 42–3 per cent of the vote. But so is the downside. A strategy of change is risky, but there is no other choice, and nor should there be.'[22]

The strategic components of this new approach were:

Change, which is a complete political project . . . a new approach to politics, and a political leader who embodies that approach. It is about radical ideas and fresh new solutions; it is about excitement and momentum . . . That is at the heart of the modernising project. For Labour, and for Britain.

Populism, which means Labour becoming once again the instrument through which ordinary people believe they can achieve their aspirations. We have to make it clear to working people that we understand their aspirations and that we want to make them better off; that we are against taxation for its own sake; that we are tough on crime; that we stress individual responsibility.

A new Labour Party: we must at some appropriate point say to the public – and to the party – that we are a new Labour Party. Radical in intent, driven by change, under-pinned by conviction, confident in our beliefs and ready to sweep the Conservatives away.[23]

I typed the note in my office in Brussels and began to shuttle between the two campaigns: the leadership campaign in London and the European election campaign in Brussels. Until Europe went to the polls on 9 June, I often had to commute between the two cities in one day: London in the morning, Brussels in the afternoon.

Once the European elections were over, the official leadership contest began. The ban on campaigning, which all candidates (Blair, Prescott and Beckett) had observed since Smith's death, ended. I attended Blair's campaign meetings, which were held at 8.30 A.M. in Jack Straw's office in Parliament Street, just along the corridor from Tony's. Anji Hunter had been keen for me to be at these meetings, but I was very cautious about re-entering British politics. I had been hit so hard after 1992. Anji insisted and gave me tremendous support and encouragement, so I arrived for my first meeting early. Jack Straw, an early opponent of Clause IV, welcomed me. Others then drifted in: Alun Michael (Tony's deputy on shadow Home Affairs); Peter Kilfoyle, a Liverpool MP with impeccable working-class credentials; Mo Mowlam, a politician who always spoke her mind regardless of the consequences; and Barry Cox, Tony's close friend and treasurer of the campaign. I said almost nothing, but I no longer felt a pariah, and from then on I attended the meetings every day.

I was uneasy about the way the as-yet undeclared campaign had started, and on 20 May spelled out my concerns: 'There is no sense as yet of the party falling in behind Blair; there is already a media backlash; and most dangerous of all there is already a media consensus on his weaknesses: that he is soft; that he may not be strong or tough enough to lead the party and the country . . . Only a campaign that is ruthless in maximising Tony's strengths will succeed.'[24]

When Gordon stood down for Tony on 1 June the atmosphere cleared. The next day I wrote a further memo: 'Last week was probably the most dangerous of the campaign, and TB came through it well. However, apart from the simple need to avoid complacency, there is progress to be made and the campaign must keep pushing ahead.' Blair's political identity had yet to be established: 'It can either be the agent of change and renewal or the combination of Bambi and Bimbo the media is trying to create . . . TB must make a speech that makes it clear that it is he, and not his opponents, who represents the real aspirations of working people. However, TB must go beyond this and build a broader coalition, including many of the middle class, because the desire for change, renewal and community does not stop at Birmingham or end at £35,000 a year.'[25]

In early June Blair wrote a memo summing up his themes for the campaign. It is astonishing, reading it now, how clear he was about his aims even then. This was, in effect, an early Blair testament. On the personal front, his first point was 'strong convictions based around Christian socialism; came to party through belief not background. Values at heart of his policies', followed by, 'family; more to life than politics'. He then highlighted guts, consistency and commitment to Labour, and an open and friendly style of leadership. Under a second heading, 'Strategic Principles', he wrote:

Change and Renewal: a new direction for the country; traditional principles but modern application; honouring the past but not living in it. Smith's legacy to us unity based around consensual and open style of leadership. This will be Blair's style. But without Smith we are going to have to be bold advocates of change rather than cautious . . . Excitement, inspiration, visionary: engendering new political mood . . . Ideas: a bold new agenda for the left. Breaking through old left/right barriers. Radical but modern, redefining what being left of centre means . . . Conviction: Blair believes in what he says; says what he believes.

Under a third category, 'Policy Framework', he outlined what he called a Basic Principle:

Socialism is not a set of rigid economic prescriptions but a set of values based around a belief in society and community: i.e. individuals prosper best within a strong and cohesive society, where opportunity and obligation go hand in hand. We have to renew Britain as a strong society – one-nation socialism – but do it for the modern world. This will mean a new direction for the country.

He then listed a series of new policy directions:

On society – to re-create terms of community and social cohesion, based on welfare whose purpose is not to create a set of dependants but to provide the opportunity for self-improvement; on the economy – economic regeneration through investment, and a revolution in skills; on the Constitution – a new settlement between society and individual, devolved power, individual rights; on Europe – Britain leading in Europe but re-shaping path of co-operation; on politics – change in style and manner: pluralist, open, inclusive; on party – transform party organisation towards campaigning and mass membership.[26]

This document underlines the constancy of Blair's ideas, and of his grounding principles. I added a section on message. These themes governed the leadership contest and dominated the next three years and beyond.

Blair's leadership campaign was anchored around a

manifesto and six major policy speeches. Peter Hyman, who has worked for Blair since the leadership campaign, spelled out the thinking behind it:

> There was a conscious decision by Tony that the campaign had to take Labour a strategic step forward; that we shouldn't just win, we should make use of the heightened exposure of the leadership campaign, which was unusual for a party in opposition. The cameras were on us rather than the Tories, so this was an opportunity to give out different messages about Labour. We did this not just through 'Change and Renewal' [the campaign document], which was a kind of surrogate manifesto, but also through five or six substantial speeches, which staked out a new territory for the Labour Party.[27]

On 6 June I conducted focus groups for Tony Blair, the first of many I was to do for the Labour Party in the period up to the 1997 election. Almost all of these were with one key group: 1992 Conservative voters who were considering switching to Labour. From them I constructed profiles for all the main political leaders. Major's negatives were terrible: he was considered 'weak, out of his depth, not up to the job'. The European election campaign had exposed the hollowness of his leadership and the growing ideological chasm at the heart of the Conservative Party. Clarke was disliked, Portillo seen as sinister. Only Heseltine had any kind of popularity. On Labour's side John Prescott was 'very popular', considered 'honest, blunt, straight-talking and no-nonsense'. Before television exposure Tony Blair was 'liked and considered a different sort of politician', although some – particularly men – thought he was too young. However, exposure to Blair on television transformed perceptions. They liked him, 'his charisma, his message of pulling together, and the sense of a new kind of politics. And a new politician.'[28]

Labour won a massive victory in the European elections on 9 June, and the Socialist Group retained their majority in the European Parliament. The next day I wrote a leadership election campaign document. I showed it to Tony, Peter and Mo, but Peter would not allow me to show it to the campaign team. He thought it would overwhelm them. It was long – fourteen pages – but I expect they could have coped with it. It brought together everything that had been written to date but included a new section on developing Blair's identity: 'The media want a beauty contest. Tony Blair must insist on a contest of ideas. The media want a nice, cuddly, telegenic family man. Tony Blair must give them an uncompromising champion of change.'[29] A day later, nervously, Tony announced his candidature to a packed meeting at Trimdon Labour Club in Sedgefield, the heart of his constituency.

On Thursday 23 June, Blair launched 'Change and National Renewal', his campaign manifesto. This was the first time he had pulled together his ideas into one coherent statement. It has been criticised for its 'thinness'[30] but that is harsh; it is better described as uneven, yet it laid the foundations for much of what was to come. David Miliband, now head of the Policy Unit at 10 Downing Street, says of it: 'I think that the first and last pages are very good. Where the Tories have gone wrong – economic and social failure, insecurity, which affects us all. You've then got New Labour's prescriptions. It's fairly basic, it's what appears in Clause IV, pretty much word for word. Then you have got the policy agenda which was stuffed in at the last minute. And then there is the Challenge for Labour, which is pretty good.'[31]

The document opens with a critique of the Conservatives: they failed because they 'saw all forms of social co-operation as inherently wrong, fit not for reform but for demolition. As a result the Conservatives consistently ignored the central importance to any successful country of ensuring that society works together to advance the interests of the individual'. The result of this was 'to tear apart the social fabric and encourage a narrow view of self-interest which was both selfish and ultimately self-defeating'. The document includes a paragraph which is a reasonable definition of Blairism:

'The simple case for democratic socialism is that individuals prosper best within a strong, active society, whose members acknowledge that they owe duties to each other as well as themselves, and in part at least, depend upon one another to succeed.' This was the basic sentiment behind the new Clause IV.

Although these principles were right and enduring, they had to be re-interpreted for a new age: 'The principles are timeless, but we should not merely accept as necessary, but advocate as desirable, the application of those principles to new circumstances.' This led to the need for renewal: 'economic renewal', 'social renewal', 'political renewal', 'international renewal' and 'party renewal'. The last was central to Blairism: reform of the nation required reform of the party; the one was dependent upon the other.

Blair ended with a re-statement of his basic approach to politics: Labour had to win at every level. 'To win the trust of the British people, we must do more than just defeat the Conservatives on grounds of competence, integrity and fitness to govern. We must change the tide of ideas.'[32] This was not simply rhetoric. It was central to Blair's beliefs, and he would repeat it often in the three years before the General Election.

To drive home his insistence that Labour had to win the battle of ideas, Blair followed his manifesto with a series of considered and fairly heavyweight speeches. David Miliband was chiefly responsible for drafting the education speech, delivered on 24 June; Derry Irvine, the constitution speech; Gordon Brown, Andrew Smith (a shadow Treasury minister) and David Miliband drafted the economy speech; and Peter Hyman worked hard on the welfare speech. All these speeches mapped out putative New Labour positions. They were tentative, but they began to set a new direction.

The leadership election was not free from anxiety. Blair did not perform at his best either in an interview with David Frost on Sunday 12 June, or in a *Panorama* televised debate on 13 June. On both he looked ill-at-ease and under-prepared.

By the end of June, however, the campaign feedback

reports were making it clear that Blair was going to win. In fact, they attacked him for appearing complacent: 'Two respondents said that Tony was not perceived to be campaigning hard enough. He is taking victory for granted.'[33] He wasn't, of course. In my meetings with him at his home he never took victory for granted. This was a continuing characteristic of Blair's, which resurfaced in the 1997 General Election campaign, when he would continually warn against complacency despite the poll leads.

Many people display a surface confidence that betrays inner insecurity. Blair is quite the opposite. He can often appear anxious about the outcome of events, but inwardly be absolutely confident, as in fact he was in 1994. It is this inner confidence that makes him so unusual as a Labour politician. When I visited him at home during the leadership campaign, he would appear outwardly nervous about winning, but when the point was pushed he would be unequivocal in his confidence that he was going to do it.

The leadership election was held during a sunny early summer, just as the election was three years later, and Blair liked to sit outside his house, lounging in a garden chair. He dislikes formality. I have never seen him work behind a desk. Usually, as Leader of the Opposition and as Prime Minister, he works from a sofa with his papers on a coffee table in front of him. But his casualness is deceptive. He moves suddenly from relaxed chat to a pointed question, and without warning will want to move on, often ending a conversation abruptly, as though you had suddenly said the wrong thing.

On 21 July 1994 Blair won a massive victory, with 57 per cent of the vote. John Prescott, always Tony's preferred choice, was elected his deputy. Once, when I suggested to him that the focus groups might favour another candidate, he brushed me aside, saying, 'I suggest you go away and refocus your focus groups.' Blair made a formal speech of acceptance at the Institute of Education, the speech which Gordon Brown had been working on so late at night. He then came to an upstairs room at Church House opposite Westminster Green and made a short, emotional speech of thanks. In it he thanked 'Bobby', a reference to Peter Mandelson, who had been his surrogate campaign manager. Mandelson's involvement had been kept secret because of supposed animosity towards him in the Parliamentary Labour Party. Mandelson says of this, 'Bobby was a sort of joke, but it was a private family joke. I was the sort of invisible linchpin of the campaign, and orchestrated it through Anji [Hunter], Tim [Allan] and Peter Hyman, without the campaign committee apparently realising it.'[34] This was not really true, because they knew Mandelson was the campaign's hidden guiding hand, but felt it best just to keep going as though he wasn't there. The secrecy was a hangover from the bitterness of Kinnock's years. It would have been better to have been open about it.

Blair's victory was the decisive moment in the 1992–97 parliament. Labour's lead in political identification, which is the key measure of electoral support, immediately increased from around 2 per cent under Smith to around 12 per cent under Blair, where it stayed until the 1997 election. Even more importantly, Blair's victory marked the point at which economic optimism and the Conservative share of the vote diverged.[35] For almost all the Conservatives' years in office they had been in tandem: the more optimistic people were about the economy, the higher the government's support. But Blair's election ended this connection. The public grew ever more optimistic about the economy, while support for the Conservatives remained static. Labour might have won under John Smith, but it was not a certainty and we would not have won by a landslide or anything like it: probably, we would have scraped home. But the majority would have been small, and a hung parliament not impossible. It was Blair who changed the political map.

Hitting the centre ground running

Blair wasted no time moving the party into the mainstream. Three days after his win he was interviewed by Brian Walden and, risking the wrath of the liberal consensus, made it absolutely clear that for most children he believed having two parents was better than having just one. Blair asked and answered his own question: 'Do I believe that it is best, it is easiest, that kids are brought up in a normal stable family? The answer is yes, I do believe that.' He then went further. When asked by Walden whether he thought it was wrong for women to choose to become mothers before they were in a stable relationship, he said, 'Yes. I disagree with what they have done.' He then made the essential populist point, the point that I had been waiting twenty years for a Labour leader to make: 'Can I tell you what is extraordinary, is the degree to which people have ended up associating the left with certain thoughts that are a million miles away from ordinary people.' 'Whose fault is that?' responded Walden. 'Maybe there is a bit of fault on both sides, but I tell you this: what is absolutely essential is this is the type of Labour Party that there really is today, where we know the importance of strong family community and family values.' He went on to say that the family was the 'essential, stable social unit'.[36]

Two days later Blair demonstrated a clear intent to persuade Conservative voters to switch to Labour. The heart of his General Election strategy was this: 'Many of those who voted Conservative are now asking serious questions about their quality of life and living standards and prospects for their children under the Conservatives. There is a great mood in this country for fresh thinking, for a new start.' He then made another decisive statement: 'There was a point in the 1980s when we went badly wrong and there is no harm in admitting that.'[37]

The *Daily Mail*, then the key influencer of middle Britain, ran an extraordinary editorial that day praising Blair. 'This paper is not in the habit of congratulating leaders of the Labour Party, but then few politicians recently have spoken with the courage and conviction of Mr Tony Blair.'[38]

Just two days later, on 28 July, and still only a week after his election as leader, Blair smashed more shibboleths, this time on education. The party was launching its education policy White Paper at the Institute of Civil Engineers. Blair had discussed this with David Miliband beforehand. He had made it clear to Miliband that he was going to make education a central priority of his leadership and that he intended to use this launch to refocus Labour's education policy away from vested interests and towards standards. He took over the press conference from then shadow Education Secretary Ann Taylor. When pressed hard on selection he denied that he would abolish it, a clear difference from the content of the policy document being launched at the same time, which stated, 'Labour rejects any system in which a few are selected at the expense of the vast majority.'[39] Pressed further about the content of the document, Blair replied with a smile, 'I think the document will repay very, very careful reading.' On the BBC *One O'Clock News*, when asked what the main points of the document were, he went even further, saying that his first point was that unfit teachers would be sacked.[40] Blair didn't like the party's policy document and was not afraid to say so.

On 29 July Blair went on holiday, but he had done his work. He had made it absolutely clear that he was setting the party on a new path. He had signalled a determination to ditch the old party and bring Labour back to the hopes and values of ordinary voters. But this was only a small step forward; Blair had a far bigger project in mind.

Building New Labour

On 22 July I wrote a 25-page memo – 'Consolidating the Blair Identity. Rebuilding Labour; Demolishing the Conservatives' – laying out the groundwork for a new Labour Party. This was a long and comprehensive document, which I wanted Blair to read on holiday.

First I spelled out the strengths and weaknesses of Blair's position. His strengths were 'freshness and a sense of change; confidence and self-assurance; that Tony Blair is a new kind of politician; that Blair changes what it means to be Labour.' His weaknesses were that he could be perceived as 'over-smooth', 'too soft and not tough enough', and 'inexperienced'. In response to this, 'Tony Blair should not be what he is not. This will not work and it will be counterproductive. He should not try to avoid the problem of youth by behaving with excessive gravitas. Nor try to avoid looking soft by behaving with excessive aggression. What he must do is build on his strengths, and build an identity as a politician that is of a piece with the political positions he adopts. He must be a complete, coherent politician who always rings true.'

The problem was that Labour lacked defining positions and in the rest of the document I attempted to remedy this. I argued that the real political agenda was a combination of right and left. It was right-wing on crime, welfare, immigration, discipline, tax and individualism, but left-wing on the NHS, investment, social integration, opposition to privatisation and unemployment. People wanted change, but they didn't yet want Labour. 'People have had enough of the Conservatives but they cannot understand why . . . whatever they think about the Tories they are not in love with Labour . . . There is still a lurking fear about unions and the loony left; there is potential concern about Labour because of its liberal social positions; there is anxiety about tax; there is almost no idea what Labour stands for.'

Worse still, there was a 'Conservative hegemony': 'Conducting these [focus] groups I am struck by the extent that the confidence and consistency of fifteen years of Conservative government . . . has established the framework through which these voters see the political world. Their scepticism of government action, their belief that everything has to be paid for, their social conservatism, their dismissal of so much that the left has to offer, shows the difficulties we will have in developing an alternative framework of ideas.'

Labour's only chance was to rebuild completely from the ground up. This meant: 'New foundations: a reason for its existence as a political party; a new structure, a central message to help change the political map; a new superstructure: defining positions supported by defining policies.' This reflected my belief that we would only win an election on the basis of a complete political project: starting with the foundations and then building upwards. Substance had to come first.

For me the foundations of the party were the people it was created to represent. Labour existed to be the party that must 'reflect the real interests and attitudes of working voters, not the left-wing myths about what working people want . . . it must reconnect with both "working-class" and "middle-class" voters'. I then wrote what I suppose is the heart of my political beliefs, a statement born explicitly of the politics of the suburbs I came from: Labour must recognise that 'what most voters want is, over time and without greed, to advance and improve their lives. In short, to become better off. This is absolutely critical. The progress and well-being of individuals and their families [should be] our central reference point in making sense of politics. It allows Labour to respect the value of work, which is, after all, the original reason for its existence.' The ultimate foundation of the Labour Party is not dogma, or even values, it is the hopes and aspirations of ordinary people. My instincts are populist: I put the people first.

Next I moved on to what I called New Labour's structure, the values and principles of the party. Labour had to be the party of 'change and renewal'; of 'the community advancing individuals'; and of 'a new Labour Party: beyond left and right . . . Labour must say that it is a new Labour Party, that is left-of-centre, but which has moved beyond old left–right boundaries. This means being tough on crime, welfare waste, standards and discipline, while also committed to the community, investment, and rebuilding the NHS.' Last was Labour's 'superstructure' – its defining positions – in which I started to lay out Labour's new dividing lines: welfare for independence not dependence; rebuilding the NHS but with modern application; influence, not isolation, in Europe.

This then was what I wanted New Labour to become, but that was only half the story. The other half was demolishing the Conservatives. 'Just as Labour has to be rebuilt, the Conservatives have to be demolished. It is clear that dissatisfaction with the Conservatives has not translated into enduring reasons for not voting Conservative. This has to change in an exercise in demolition that matches Labour's reconstruction.' The essence of the attack I laid out was this: 'The Conservatives are out of touch with ordinary voters and do not represent their interests. The Conservatives have made ordinary working people worse off. The Conservatives cannot be trusted. They have lied before, and will lie again.' I ended the document by saying that Blair must make 'a conference speech that should in effect rebuild the Labour Party'.[41]

These, then, were my strategic goals in the summer of 1994: the complete reconstruction of Labour and the total destruction of the Conservatives. I remember thinking as I wrote: this may be a trifle ambitious. But, more or less, it was achieved. I gave the document to Blair to read while he went on holiday in Italy and France. Out there he met up with Alastair Campbell and tried to persuade him to become his press secretary. Blair was staying at the house Alastair's family had rented in Flassan, with Cherie, their three children and, for a while also, Neil and Glenys Kinnock. The house was not large and the atmosphere was close and occasionally explosive. Blair had talked about the job of press secretary with Alastair just before the holiday, and Alastair had phoned me up to discuss it. He said he wasn't sure, but he seemed to want to do it. I told him it had to be his decision. He asked me what Labour's chances were of winning. I said I was certain Labour would win, a remark he threw back at me often in some of the dark days ahead. Campbell, who had by then been a political journalist for eight years, describes his uncertainty at the time:

Sometimes if you have been doing something for a long time you can't necessarily imagine yourself in a different role. What was good in a way was that I was driving down – Fiona was flying down with the kids – so I had a long time to think on my own. I had two impressions which came to me through the whole holiday – I literally took the whole holiday to think about it, which was a month. But two things came back to me the whole time. The first was that we lost the election and I was there thinking I could have made a difference. And the other was that we had won and I could have been part of it. Fiona was basically hostile, she felt it was too much. Neil was totally hostile and he was there on holiday for part of the time and was saying it will completely ruin your life. It will ruin your family's life, it will ruin your health. Life as you know it is over, forget it, don't do it. And then Tony appeared, stayed for a few days and we talked about all sorts of things, but in the end it was me thinking, you can't really say no to this, so I just had to go through the process of finding the rationale for it.

Central to his rationale was the importance of the media:

Tony was completely seized by the importance of how to get a better press than we'd had before. It was one of the things I used to argue with Neil about – and I completely understand why he found it difficult, because they were complete bastards to him – but I held the view that, however bad the press is, it can be worse, and it can be better, and you have got to work at it all the time. I think that was allied to a sense that I was thirty-six and that I'd pretty much done all I could do where I was and this new adventure could come up. There have been some absolutely awful moments along the way, but I haven't regretted it. There are all sorts of things I would have done differently and you do have to make sacrifices, but I don't regret it at all.

One of the other things Blair discussed with Campbell was Clause IV:

We had a long discussion, partly in the sitting-room, but we also went for a long walk and he was going through the kind of changes he wanted to bring in, and he said – he swore me to secrecy – for example, I am thinking about scrapping

Clause IV. And I said that would be pretty bold and it did have a certain appeal. Not because of any ideological bent. Although I have always been keen on the modernising thing, there has always been a heavy traditionalist streak in me. So I wasn't thinking great, let's smash up Clause IV. What appealed to me was the sheer boldness of it and the fact that this was someone who wasn't going to mess about.[42]

Over the summer Blair also spoke to Gordon Brown and Peter Mandelson about the abolition of Clause IV. Mandelson was keen, but typically cautious: 'I strongly supported it. It didn't take me long to make up my mind, but I did think about it. I always think about things. I never say yes immediately. I have my instincts but then I reflect.'[43] Campbell could not wait to get started. He wrestled with his decision all summer, but once he had made it he was impatient and he cut his holiday short. He phoned me on his return and told me of his decision. He sounded completely determined, as if nothing would stop him.

I went to see Tony Blair on 6 September and he asked me to work with him. He was in Neil's old office, having rejected John Smith's as too grand and detached from his staff. It was strange seeing Blair in Neil's old office: the same place, but a different era. For Blair, opposition was already a waste of time: something to be finished with as soon as possible. He paced around the room and wouldn't sit down. He could not have made his intentions more clear. 'Past Labour leaders lost because they compromised,' he said. 'I will never compromise. I would rather be beaten and leave politics than bend to the party. I am going to take the party on.' He was pleased Alastair had joined him, confident about the future, but tense, wired, impatient to get started. I wrote to him afterwards, confirming how much I wanted to help him. I started the letter plaintively (but I meant what I wrote and it was absolutely true): 'All I have wanted since I was a small boy was the chance to have a campaigning role in electing a Labour government, and this time I am sure I will get that chance.' Further on, I wrote (underlined to make the point): 'I am completely confident that Labour will win, but only if Labour is completely remade . . . Just as important as remaking Labour is the trust they place in you. Again, I am absolutely certain that if you are consistent, clear, tough and honest over the next two years, you will win their trust.'[44] On the same day Blair visited the TUC and briefed journalists that he would 'treat [the unions] in the same way that Labour treated business'.[45] This is typical Blair, boldly heightening the impact of a remark by cutting directly against the expectation of the context in which it is made. In America they call this 'counter-scheduling'.

The following day, Alastair Campbell was officially appointed Blair's press secretary. Two days later, on 9 September, Blair held his first extended 'brainstorming' session at the Chewton Glen Hotel in Hampshire, organised by Colin Fisher, managing director of the market research company SRU. There was the usual endless prevarication about who should attend. In the end, as well as Blair and Brown, there was Campbell, Mandelson, myself and Michael Wills, then a television producer, now an MP. I had written another huge document for this event, running to thirty-six pages. After receiving it, Tony told me tactfully that he preferred to have his memos on a single sheet of paper.

This document was grounded in a historical analysis of the double betrayal of the electorate by the two major parties. Post-war British politics had been dominated by two themes: the 'need for national renewal and modernisation; and the emerging individualism, consumerism and aspirations of working-class voters'. On both counts the Conservatives had done better than Labour. In the 1950s, 'the washing machines and welfare decade', the Conservatives had begun to identify themselves as the party of working-class aspiration. In the 1960s Labour had power, but Heath made the killer point in 1965: 'I would like to associate with a government which gives ordinary people the opportunity of leading fuller lives.' And, 'Labour are the true conservatives.' In the 1980s the Conservatives reached out and grabbed our territory and our voters. Thatcher started to renew Britain, and where the

Conservatives were succeeding in taking Labour's ground as the party of the people and the party of renewal, Labour was failing on both counts. The party had gained the unenviable position of being both extremist and at the same time timidly conservative. Labour had 'failed spectacularly in 1978–82, but these events were not an aberration in the development of the Labour Party, but the culmination of a long-standing failure of the Labour Party to either implement a consistent project for national renewal or represent the aspirations of its natural constituency.' The language is overblown, but the sentiments were right.

But in the 1990s the Conservatives had crashed too: 'They have lost their reputation for competence; their capacity for national renewal . . . and they are no longer the party of the aspirational working class or even the middle class.' It is extraordinary to contemplate just how incompetent John Major's administration was. By 1994 it had suffered a massive devaluation, the rebellion of forty-one MPs over the Maastricht Treaty and the loss to the Conservative Whip of a further eight, and the humiliating dismissal of the Chancellor of the Exchequer Norman Lamont, the man who had run Major's leadership campaign.

I continued: 'Deep-seated suspicion of Labour, which has yet to rebuild itself, and the crash of the Conservatives mean that the electorate has lost trust not only in the effectiveness of the two major parties, but in the process of politics and the effectiveness of politics itself.' Labour had 'not only to rebuild itself, but to rebuild the relationship between the electorate and the government. The issue is not just trust in Labour, but trust in government and politics itself.'[46]

Most of the Chewton Glen brainstorming session was dominated by Blair's insistence on arriving at new positions, new dividing lines, and working out what New Labour was. Brown's focus then, as now, was on opportunity. This has always been his guiding concept. Blair is anchored in community, Brown in opportunity for all. These are complementary concepts, but they are different; they give a different shade to their politics and their policies. Before lunch we walked in the sun, getting used to a new political reality. Neither Blair nor Brown looked fully comfortable in his role yet.

For me the day is memorable for one defining moment: in the queue with Tony, waiting for the buffet, we talked about the need for rapid change and Blair turned to me and made one of the most compelling political statements I have ever heard: 'Conference must build New Labour. It is time we gave the party some electric shock treatment.' Labour had to be made new. And Blair was going to do it.

In mid-September, when interest rates rose by 0.5 per cent to 5.75 per cent, Blair redirected Labour's approach to economic affairs. Instead of immediately condemning the rise in rates, as Labour politicians were expected to do, he indicated a shift towards fiscal conservatism by avoiding direct criticism of Kenneth Clarke's decision. In an interview in the *Financial Times* the next day he said 'inflation is the symptom not the disease'.[47] He went further on Radio 4's *Today* programme, claiming to James Naughtie that he could run the market economy better than the Conservatives. Naughtie was amazed: 'It is a long time since a Labour leader has said: "Vote for me because I know more about a market economy than the Tories."' Blair didn't flinch: 'But it is absolutely true,' he said.[48] Although he had been leader for just a matter of weeks, and spent a good part of that on holiday, Blair had already made huge strides in repositioning the party: bad teachers should be sacked; two parents were better than one; Labour had made grievous errors in the past; business was as important as unions; Labour could run a market economy better than the Tories.

By now, New Labour was an accepted figure of speech – at least among ourselves. On 1 September I had written a summary note with the heading: 'New Labour; Right as Well as Left'.[49] I do not claim the credit for inventing New Labour. I had first mentioned it as a concept in the spring of 1989, and it had stayed in the ether in the years to 1992. But it really became the natural next step in the modernisation of the party after the success of the New Democrats in the United States, when Blair grabbed the idea with both hands. He knew that only by contrasting 'new' Labour with 'old' Labour explicitly would the electorate believe that Labour had changed and could be trusted. But it was Alastair Campbell who turned the term 'New Labour' into an entirely new identity for the party. We wanted a slogan for conference. I favoured 'A New Approach from Labour', which I am the first to accept was a dreadful line. Alastair was working on some alternatives. We were in a meeting and Alastair, as is his way, scribbled down several lines, which he showed to me. One was: 'New Labour, New Britain'. He liked it best, but I thought it too crude. On 25 September, the Monday before conference, Jackie Stacey, who was in charge of presentation, including the platform set, was chasing Peter Mandelson for a decision about the slogan. We had both been cautious about the 'New Labour, New Britain' line. But Mandelson asked me, 'Which line will truly connect with the electorate?' In the course of a long, restless night worrying, I had decided 'New Labour, New Britain' was after all the right line, and so we agreed on it. Walworth Road stirred into mild rebellion: Karen Buck and Matthew Taylor from the campaigns unit, and others, were nervous. They were worried that the party would revolt, delegates might walk out of the conference hall. Alastair had to sit at the desk of Kate Garvey, Blair's able and effervescent diary secretary, and fight for his line. Putting New Labour in massive letters in front of hundreds of delegates was effectively renaming the party. It was a huge risk. But the slogan was used and there wasn't a murmur from the conference. This was the moment New Labour became a reality.

In late September I went to see John Prescott to present to him the results of focus-group research. He was in John Smith's old office. Wary at first, he asked me everything about New Labour. He wanted to know where it came from, what the voters thought of it, whether it was necessary. After half an hour he seemed convinced and his attitude became warmer. His main concern was that we were ditching what was good about our past, but he was persuaded that fear of Labour was so entrenched that a clear dividing-line was needed. That was typical of John: wary then warm; apparently traditional, but a force for change. However much he might hate it being said, John Prescott is at heart a moderniser. He is not frightened of reform, in fact he welcomes it, provided there is evidence to support the need for it. And most important, he is a genuinely populist politician who has the instincts and aspirations of working people close to his heart. He is also fair. He was the only one of my critics in 1992 who actually took the trouble to seek me out and ask me what had happened.

He was not so convinced by the plan to ditch Clause IV. He was troubled, but open to persuasion: if it was right he would support it. John may be a reluctant moderniser, but he is a moderniser nonetheless.

On 27 September Blair made his first important speech as leader, at the National Film Theatre, opening Labour's seminar on the global economy. It was an explicit attempt to redraw the dividing-lines in economics and an unambiguous rejection of 'tax and spend'. By now conference was upon us. One week before it, on 23 September, I had written to Tony begging for boldness. Not that I needed to. I said his speech should be 'so bold, so clear, so uncompromising, that [it] confounds the electorate, forcing them to change their minds . . . This is a risk, but it is the least risky course. If perceptions about Labour are not radically improved, Labour will lose.'[50] The days before the conference, when we had to take the final decision on whether or not to go for the reform of Clause IV, were confused and uncertain. Alastair Campbell recalls: 'In the days up to it [the conference] when we hadn't decided whether to do it or not, you were having different meetings with different people about the speech, some of whom knew, some of whom didn't, and sometimes you would forget.'

John Prescott's agreement was essential to the success of the Clause IV strategy. Campbell reflects:

There was no way we could have done it without John Prescott – not just John reluctantly agreeing, but John actually
giving his blessing to it. The night before I was practically
up all night, up and down the stairs to John's room, and
going through it. In the end it was John who said: if you are
going to do this, you have got to say it, you can't bugger
about. That was when we wrote in right at the last moment
to review our constitution for a new age. That actually came
from John – we were going to skirt around it. You can argue
that we skirted around it anyway, but the fact is that at one
point we were not going to mention the constitution at all.
I can remember there was a moment of extreme tension
because Tony had to broaden the circle of people who knew.

Early on Tuesday morning, around 1 A.M., Campbell called
all Labour's press officers into a hotel bedroom and
announced that the next day Tony Blair would ditch Clause
IV. People started to hyperventilate. Campbell recalls, 'I was
in this room – it was a difficult situation, I was still officially
a political journalist – and there were people there telling
Tony it was the end of the Labour Party and making it clear
it couldn't be supported.'

The period from then until the end of Blair's speech was
the most uncertain in his political career. He could have been
destroyed by the conference. Campbell says: 'I remember
Tony saying to me, what's the chance that by 5 P.M. tonight,
after the speech, that we are completely dead in the water?
I think I said 5 per cent. Yes, there's a chance, isn't there.'[51]
That morning saw a continual flow of shadow Cabinet
members coming to Tony's room to be informed of what he
intended to do. I had to be kept hidden; the change to Clause
IV was combustible enough without my involvement in it
being too apparent. Once, I hid in a wardrobe. Alastair left
out the last few pages of the speech when it was handed out
to the press to maximise impact and minimise risk.

Blair rose to the occasion, holding the audience so closely
with him that they did not fully realise what had happened
until the speech was over and the press office had begun to

give briefings. By then it was done: New Labour; new constitution. As Campbell says, 'Within five minutes of the speech
starting I knew it was going to work.' The change to Clause
IV 'was so overwhelmingly, blindingly obvious when you
think about it: one, that it had to be done; two, that it was
something that could be really useful in terms of the overall
message of what we are trying to do'.[52]

The speech was important for more than just Clause IV.
It saw Blair begin to articulate a new voice for Labour:

> To parents wanting their children to be taught in classrooms
> that are not crumbling, to students with qualifications but
> no university place, let us say, the Tories have failed you, we
> are on your side, your ambitions are our ambitions.
>
> To men and women who get up in the morning and find
> the kitchen door smashed in again . . . the video gone,
> again . . . to pensioners who fear to go out of their homes,
> let us say, the Tories have abused your trust, we are on your
> side – your concerns are our concerns.
>
> To middle- and lower-income Britain, suffering the biggest
> tax rises in peacetime history to pay the bills of economic
> failure, let us say, the Tories have betrayed you, again . . .
> Labour is on your side . . . your aspirations are our aspira-
> tions.
>
> We are back as the party of the majority in British politics,
> back to speak up for Britain, back as the people's party.[53]

This at last was the authentic voice of Labour: becoming
once again the party of aspiration for the working majority,
for the new middle class. But Blair wasn't stopping. On 8
November in a speech to the Per Cent Club – a group of
business people who pledge a percentage of their earnings
to charity – he said, 'Our country needs . . . enterprising
entrepreneurs.'[54] He promised that the basic elements of
Conservative trade union law would remain; that Labour
understood the disincentive effects of high marginal tax rates;
and that the minimum wage would be set at a level that
'avoids any adverse impact on jobs'.[55]

Six focus groups in November showed how far the party had moved. On 11 November I wrote, 'There is clear evidence of a real improvement in attitudes towards Labour in comparison with the Kinnock, Smith, and even the early Blair period . . . The most common response is, "I am going to give them a go." This may not sound much, but it is a lot. There is a definite sense that Labour may now be able to address the problems of Britain. Even the beginnings of hope. I have never before felt this in any previous period.'

The reasons for the change were, I wrote, a new Labour Party, the Blair leadership and the Blair–Prescott joint leadership. 'Tony Blair is a surprising choice as leader of Labour. He forces people to reassess their view of Labour. John Prescott is extraordinarily popular. Almost everybody likes him because of his honesty and directness . . . he and Tony Blair are considered a team that works, each mutually enhancing each other.' Finally, 'Blair and Prescott connect in a way John Smith never did. He was trusted but did not really impact on people in the way that the current leadership does.'[56]

Later that month the *Financial Times* published a leaked Conservative Central Office paper by John Maples, which was consistent with my own poll findings. 'If Tony Blair turns out to be as good as he looks, we have a problem,' he wrote.[57] Maples' analysis of the problems facing the Conservatives was accurate and insightful. The Tories were disliked because they were perceived as arrogant and out of touch. At least someone was telling the party leadership the truth, and at this stage it was still not too late for the Conservatives to change. Perhaps too late for them to win, but certainly not to avoid landslide defeat.

On 1 December the *Daily Mail* announced that the Blairs had chosen to send their son Euan to the London Oratory school. The headline said: 'Labour leader ignores party policy and puts family first.'[58] Blair was due to appear on *Good Morning With Anne and Nick*, where he was forced to defend his decision by saying that he wanted maximum choice for everyone. This was the point of most intense disagreement between Blair and Campbell. Tony and Cherie Blair believed that the London Oratory is a state school and a religious school and that it was the right choice for their son. As Blair had no intention of closing grant-maintained schools he did not believe he was being hypocritical. He also believed that this sent a signal out to parents everywhere that Labour was now on the side of those who wanted the best for their children.

Alastair Campbell saw it differently. He and Fiona are passionate believers in comprehensive education and felt that the decision to send Euan to the London Oratory would have a huge political fallout, as it did. The disagreement between Campbell and Blair was heated. But Blair would not be shifted. On grounds of principle, as a parent and politically, he was sure he was doing the right thing. His decision had a mixed political effect. Some of the electorate thought he was a hypocrite, others welcomed the clear signal that Labour wanted educational excellence, not educational mediocrity. In the event the decision was – just – more electorally helpful than not, but that didn't matter to Blair. He was convinced he was doing the right thing, in every sense, while Campbell remained unhappy about it.

On 12 December I wrote Blair a note confirming the improvement. Public opinion 'is now becoming settled in Labour's favour'.[59] On 15 December this poll report was given electoral substance by Labour's victory in the Dudley West by-election, in which the swing to Labour was 29 per cent – the largest since 1933. These polls proved Blair's decision on the Oratory had no effect on Labour's ratings.

In my last note of 1994 I wrote that at last we had a message: 'People versus privilege'.[60] Gordon had developed his 'fat cats' attack on the excessive salaries of the privatised utility bosses, and this gave substance to our message. It was not complete, but it was a start. The next twelve months would see us struggling to break through with a broader message encapsulating all that New Labour now stood for.

Winter doubts

In January 1995 the tide of public opinion turned a little. This happens sometimes almost by osmosis: as if one entity, the electorate changes its mind. I wrote a note warning, 'In comparison with pre-Christmas there was less enthusiasm for Labour . . . less anger with the government . . . Tony Blair is not connecting with the strength and immediacy of the pre-Christmas period.'[61] A series of policy confusions, over VAT on school fees, devolution and nuclear energy, had sapped momentum and fostered doubts. The first attack came from Ken Coates, Labour Euro MP, on 13 January: 'This young man [Blair] has not the faintest idea of how socialists think, and does not begin to understand the mentality of the party which he has been elected to lead.'[62] On 15 January Roy Hattersley argued for consensus: 'I have learned, during the forty years since Clement Attlee was Prime Minister, that the party does best when it is at peace with itself.'[63] On 21 January TGWU General Secretary Bill Morris said in a speech that he had seen nothing from Blair which would satisfy the wishes of the trade unions.[64] Blair was being attacked from left and right: different ideological perspectives linked only by conservatism. January also saw the arrival of Blair's new chief of staff, Jonathan Powell, who had been a diplomat in Washington. He added new skills to the operation: he understood government and how it worked and was vital in making Labour's transition to power so smooth.

On 15 February Blair took on the 'One Nation' mantle at a speech at the Newspaper Fund Lunch, and on 27 February Joy Johnson was appointed director of campaigns, media and elections. It was not to be a happy appointment.

By March 1995 the electoral situation had got worse. 'Support for Labour is highly fragile,' I wrote. 'It could collapse at any point . . . commitment to Labour is based on no real knowledge of the party or what it will do. No one has any idea of Labour's policies . . . [Support for Labour] is a leap of faith driven by desperation. This faith could be shattered at any time. It is vulnerable to attack from the Conservatives on the hard economic issues and the usual fears. It is certain that many of these switchers will return to the Conservatives . . . If Labour wins it will be on probation. With these voters Labour has come a long way, but it still has a long way to go . . . Labour is still definitely more of a risk than the Conservatives.'[65]

At an all-day meeting at Chris Powell's house at Fritham on 3 March, I brought all these concerns together. I listed Labour's weaknesses: 'Competence – can Labour really govern Britain? Labour is still feared and will be feared at the election . . . Labour is highly susceptible to negative campaigning . . . deep down people do not really trust Labour on the economy.' Labour will find it hard to win, I argued, because 'the British electorate is probably the most cautious in Western Europe . . . Labour's base is eroding; Labour carries massive historical baggage and deep-rooted fears; changing to Labour is a major upheaval. The Conservatives are nearly always the safer choice.'[66] The most noticeable policy insight of the day was that Gordon Brown and his team were keen, even at that early stage, for a degree of independence for the Bank of England. Ed Balls, Brown's economic adviser, presented these plans to the meeting at great length. John Prescott was not invited to Fritham, and when he found out about the meeting several weeks later he was furious that he had been excluded.

As the electorate started to get nervous about Labour, I became increasingly concerned about our campaigning capacity. Even the Clause IV campaign seemed to have ground to a halt. 'Our campaigning is a bit of a mess,' I wrote at the beginning of the year. 'What was working in 1994 has stopped working now.' This was because of 'policy uncertainty; defensiveness; campaigning gridlock; lack of preparation; a slow start to the Clause IV campaign'.[67] It seemed as if we were losing control of events. By this time – spring 1995 – I was attending Tuesday, Wednesday and Thursday meetings at 8.45 A.M. in Gordon Brown's office in Millbank. A large number of people went to them: Gordon

Brown, Labour chief whip Derek Foster, Jonathan Powell, Peter Mandelson, Brown's press secretary Charlie Whelan and policy aide Ed Miliband. The meetings started well, with Brown scouring the news, anticipating Tory intentions and generating an attack or response from Labour. But after a while they became bogged down and cracks started to appear.

Alastair was beginning to get nervous. 'I think we started to have a few problems – things started to get slightly ragged. I think some of the relationships became difficult. I've got to be honest, deep down I had doubts about whether we were going to win. Although I was always miserable and pessimistic, it was also part of my professionalism: thinking of all the things that could go wrong. I had a kind of sense that we were going to lose.' It was true that he could get gloomy. My family's nickname for this was 'the glums'. But he always had the capacity to come through it.

> I've always noticed that when things get slightly rocky, when they're starting to get out of control, I know that I can find it within me to get the towel around my head, to work out how to sort it out. On a grander scale that is what Tony can do. Whenever things have gone slightly wrong, when there have been a few days when we're feeling a bit off-balance and not quite so sure what to do, then – and it's often after a weekend, often after a holiday, often after something cataclysmic that brings everything to a head – he will just sit down and instead of him lounging back like he usually does, he sits forward with a bit of paper in front of him and goes through things, one, two, three, four, five. And he will have worked it out and it will be clear. Now I think that is leadership.[68]

Concern was growing, too, about Clause IV. The *Guardian* had reported on 30 December 1994 that Blair had become alarmed about the strength of opposition to its reform, which was true. Blair simply did not have the means to deliver the Clause IV vote in the party at large or even within the NEC.

Sally Morgan, head of Blair's political office in opposition and at Number 10, started to work for Blair at the beginning of 1995:

> From conference to Christmas nothing much happened. There was a general feeling that the thing was drifting and turning against us. Then we took a grip on it, a small group of us. But first of all we had to get the actual [Clause IV] position through the NEC. This took a lot of cajoling and talking. It took a lot of hours. Endless one-to-one discussions between me and them. Bringing them back on board. First of all I had to get them on board to support modernisation, because it had been bounced on them and they didn't know anything about it. They'd had no role in trying to convince the party of it, so we had to win a majority of them over to start being part of the solution, rather than being the opposition.[69]

Margaret McDonagh, General Election co-ordinator at Millbank and now General Secretary of the Labour Party, confirms this view: 'Between October and Christmas 1994, to be honest, everybody's eye was taken off the ball. Nothing happened. There was no campaign. I was rung at home over Christmas 1994–95 and asked to come into the office to organise the campaign, and there was just nothing there. There was no infrastructure. There was no reaching out, getting the message to all reaches of the party, and I suppose for me it was quite an eye-opener about how we all had to work together.'[70]

McDonagh and Morgan, with Anji Hunter and others, put together a highly effective campaign team that turned the tide. Derek Draper, formerly Mandelson's research assistant and founder of modernising magazine *Progress*, helped with the campaign in the constituencies. Blair began to meet party members in open forum. This type of interactive campaigning – direct contact between politician and voter – is an essential part of representative democracy. It enables politicians to be held to account, and the public or party members to be heard.

On 13 March 1995 the new Clause IV was presented to the party. Its development had been tortuous. Blair's policy unit worked on the first draft from October 1994 to January 1995. This was much shorter than the final version, and David Miliband thought it was pretty good. Most of the drafts were sent to me for comments. When the penultimate draft arrived I panned it, urging Blair to write it himself instead. Matters came to a head one Sunday afternoon with Tony Blair sitting on his bed, Alastair Campbell, Jonathan Powell and David Miliband perched around the room, while Blair's daughter Kathryn's party went on downstairs. In the end Blair wrote it himself, with one line – 'power, wealth and opportunity in the hands of the many not the few' – surviving from the policy unit draft. That was the work of Peter Hyman.

I liked the last and final draft and said so. The main sentence is long, but has power: 'The Labour Party is a democratic socialist party. It believes that by the strength of our common endeavour we achieve more than we achieve alone, so as to create for each of us the means to realise our true potential and for all of us a community in which power, wealth and opportunity are in the hands of the many not the few, where the rights we enjoy reflect the duties we owe, and where we live together, freely, in a spirit of solidarity, tolerance and respect.'[71] This is the essence of what Tony Blair has always believed: individuals should be advanced by strong communities, in which rights and responsibility are balanced.

Blair was also uncompromising on the economy: the new Clause IV calls for a 'dynamic market economy'; the 'enterprise of the market and the rigour of competition'.[72] It was a massive step forward.

The new Clause IV was adopted by a special conference at Westminster Central Hall on 29 April. The vote for the new clause was 65 per cent. But while 90 per cent of constituency parties had voted in favour, only 55 per cent of Labour's affiliated organisations, including the trade unions (most of whom had not balloted their members) had supported it.[73]

This incensed me: either we were a democratic party or we were not.

Despite the success of the Clause IV campaign I was still not happy. In April I wrote to Jonathan Powell that our campaigning needed 'dramatic improvement. Walworth Road is effectively useless as a decisive campaigning machine; there is a lack of follow-through; our opposition research/attack/rebuttal operation is not effective.'[74] During the winter and early spring I took a settled view: Labour was not yet ready. It had to change more. One week before the Clause IV triumph, to date modernisation's finest hour, I sat down and wrote a document. It was called 'The Unfinished Revolution'.

7

THE PROJECT

Winning the battle of ideas

If the period from 1994 until the Clause IV ballot in March 1995 was about electric shock treatment, jolting the party into the future, then that from May until the 'stakeholder' speeches early in 1996 was about giving substance to the New Labour concept.

This was partly a political project: making New Labour a party that could win elections and hold power, which was the focus of 'The Unfinished Revolution'. But principally it was an intellectual project to make choate the ideas, values and principles that comprised New Labour. We had lost two elections, partly because we changed the appearance of what we were without transforming Labour's substance. This time it would be different. New Labour would be a new party, built on firm intellectual foundations.

Tony Blair was obsessed with winning the battle of ideas. He believed New Labour would be nothing, could be nothing, without ideas at its heart. If a political party is not founded on ideas which have the power to dominate the political agenda, it is unlikely to win a convincing or sustainable electoral victory. Ideas matter in politics. Although it is claimed of New Labour that it won by adopting Conservative ideas, what was, in fact, central to Labour's success in 1997 was a belief among ordinary voters that something was profoundly wrong with the basic tenets of modern Conservatism. People felt society mattered and that society was deteriorating. They wanted to live in more decent, more caring, safer communities, but they needed to know that the price of a decent society was not an inefficient and cost-laden economy. This shift in public mood was as marked as the shift eighteen years earlier away from the state and towards the individual. In both years election results reflected changes in the intellectual *Zeitgeist*. Not just in the pages of the broadsheet papers, but in the homes of millions of ordinary citizens.

By the time of Blair's election as leader I could not claim to have anything approaching a coherent set of political ideas, but I had several guiding principles. I was passionately opposed to Conservatism. Instinctively rooted in the values of compassion and fairness, I was determined to help rebuild Labour as a new party, articulating the hopes and aspirations of a new middle class. I wanted a new, radical politics that would remove poverty but also encourage aspiration, respecting the individual while strengthening the community. Above all, I wanted to help develop a new progressive majority, holding power not just for one election, but for many. It was these principles that had given me the strength and desire to work with Labour for the past nine years and would keep me with it until its victory in 1997.

Blairism

Tony Blair arrived as party leader in July 1994 certain that Labour needed a new political identity. Even in 1992, after the election defeat, he had made this completely clear: 'Labour does need a clear identity, based on principle, not a series of adjustments with each successive election defeat. But the identity should be one for the modern world not a throwback to a romanticised view of the past.'[1]

He was also clear about the political identity he wanted Labour to have. As is well-known, it was deeply rooted in his Christian faith and his experience at Oxford. Here he had been introduced to Peter Thomson, an Australian mature student, by Geoff Gallop, another Australian and a Rhodes scholar. Blair once described Peter Thomson as 'the person who has most influenced me'.[2] Through Thomson Blair discovered the work of the Scottish philosopher John Macmurray, who was Grote Professor of Philosophy at London University in the 1930s. Thomson says of Macmurray: 'I was into this bloke called Macmurray. I think he was one of the most important British philosophers this century. And he was on to a concept of community. He used to say that the noblest form of human existence is friendship, and instead of being on a debt and credit ledger of "If you do this for me, then I'll do this for you," we ought to develop a sense of community where people were committed to the welfare of one another.'[3]

Macmurray's stress on the importance of the community grew out of the English idealist tradition. In the 1880s and 1890s the Oxford philosophers T. H. Green and Bernard Bosanquet inspired a generation of students to understand their experience through the spirit of community. Hegel's notion of civil society, combined with Plato's belief in the ethical nature of citizenship, helped produce a new philosophy which rejected the *laissez-faire* stance of Adam Smith and the individualism of the Utilitarians. In its place stood the concept of community through which the individual could realise himself. The concrete result was a series of Settlement Houses, where Oxford undergraduates taught and mentored deprived communities at the turn of the century. The most famous – Toynbee Hall – was where Clement Attlee's social conscience first emerged (and where I later went to college to study for A-levels in 1968).

The idea that individuals are defined by their relationship to the community, not in isolation from the community, is Blair's grounding idea, his core political insight. As he said at Wellingborough in 1993, 'We do not lose our identity in our relations with others, in part at least we achieve our identity through these relations.'[4]

The point is not that individuals are subsumed within a community and should be dominated by that community, but that individuals can exert an identity only through their relations with others, and that strong communities do not impede the development of the individual – rather, they assist it. This view connects back also to L. T. Hobhouse, the liberal socialist, himself influenced by T. H. Green, who wrote, 'The individual cannot stand alone, but that between him and the state there is a reciprocal obligation.'[5] The relationship between the individual and the community can never be fully resolved, because it is a relationship that by definition is always evolving. What is important to understand is that the relationship is intrinsic to people's existence, and that strong communities advance, rather than constrain, strong individuals. This was Tony Blair's intellectual heritage: not classically social democratic, but every bit as radical. Explicitly linking the individual to the community, implicitly connecting the Labour and Liberal intellectual traditions: a body of ideas destined to remake progressive politics in Britain.

Blair's commitment to the community found full voice during his time as shadow Home Secretary. He made a number of speeches analysing the condition of Britain, the most compelling of which came in the aftermath of James Bulger's murder:

> The importance of the notion of community is that it defines the relationship not only between us as individuals, but between people and the society in which they live, one that is based on responsibilities as well as rights, on obligations as well as entitlements. Self-respect is in part derived from respect for others, the notion that we are not just buyers and sellers in some market place, or individuals set in isolation, but that we are members of a community that owes obligation to others as well as ourselves and that depend on others to succeed and prosper. It is easy to deny the idea of community and some may feel unhappy with it. But call it community values, family values, or even spiritual values: what they all have in common is something bigger than me.[6]

Community was vital to Blair, but only part of his political project. The idea of national renewal was also central:

of a new national identity for a new era. From the start Blair had wanted to make Britain a renewed and modern country: 'Rebuilding Labour as a strong community, with a modern notion of citizenship at its heart, is the political objective for the new age. Labour must transform itself into a credible vehicle for achieving it. The project of renewal for Labour mirrors that for Britain. What the country wants is what Labour needs.'[7]

The 'Third Way' emerges

Community and national renewal were Blair's defining political ideas, the one being linked to the other. But Blair wanted to go beyond this, to create an entirely new approach to progressive politics, which he called 'new dividing-lines'. On 28 January 1993, he made explicit this new approach:

> This is a time when the fundamentals of political debate can move. There are new dividing-lines opening up in British politics. In them lie the opportunity for Labour, not just to punish the Conservatives for their mistakes but to establish its own credentials to govern. These new points of definition encompass both social and economic policy, from issues of economic management through to policies on family and crime . . . Let us be clear as to what divides Tory and Labour. It is not that they believe in personal responsibility and we do not, but that we recognise that personal responsibility is more likely to be furthered in a strong and cohesive society.[8]

This approach, which refused to accept the old Conservative dividing-lines and created new ones, metamorphosed in Blair's thinking into the 'Third Way'. It is possible the first use of the term 'Third Way' was by Pope Pius XII in the late nineteenth century, when he called for a third way between socialism and capitalism. But it was Tony Blair and Bill Clinton who re-invented the phrase, both separately developing a new politics that moved beyond left and right. Bill Clinton used the phrase in his State of the Union address in January 1998: 'My fellow Americans, we have found a Third Way. We have a smaller government, but a stronger nation.'[9]

Earlier, in an address to the Democratic Leadership Council in Cleveland on 6 May 1991, Clinton had said, 'People do not care about the rhetoric of left and right and liberal and conservative, and who is up and who is down and how we are positioned. They are real people, they have real problems, and they are crying desperately for someone who believes the purpose of government is to solve their problems and to make progress.' Although he did not use the term 'Third Way', he talked of a 'new choice' that 'plainly rejects the old categories and false alternatives'.[10] And he was not alone in thinking this. The Democratic Leadership Council, an organisation founded by Al From to make the Democratic Party more centrist and mainstream, was also trying to forge a new Democratic politics. In its 1990 New Orleans declaration the DLC continued to press for new, progressive direction: 'We believe the purpose of social welfare is to bring the poor into the nation's economic mainstream, not maintaining their dependence . . . We believe in preventing crime and punishing criminals, not explaining away their behaviour . . . We believe in the moral and cultural values that most Americans share: liberty of conscience; individual responsibility; tolerance of difference; the imperative of work; the need for faith; and the importance of the family.'[11] E. J. Dionne, the progressive political commentator, wrote, 'The "great American middle class felt cheated" by a liberal creed that "demeaned its values" and a conservative one that "short-changed its interests".'[12]

Tony Blair's thinking was entirely complementary to this. While Clinton was advocating a 'new way', Blair was talking about breaking the old left–right barriers. In his leadership campaign notes he made explicit a series of dividing-lines – 'breaking through old left–right barriers'.[13] In his speech to the National Film Theatre in 1994 he rejected the divisions set down by the Conservatives. 'The right were able to pose as the party of the market, enterprise, successful business, low inflation, low interest rates and prudent spending. The political dividing-lines were put in place entirely to suit them.' Blair was anxious to erect new political divides: 'The left-of-centre response should not therefore be to adopt Tory policies. That would be foolish because they have failed. But it should put in place the dividing-lines in better and more accurate places . . . The divide on the market is not that the right believes in it, and the left doesn't, but between the *laissez-faire* market approach of the right and the left's commitment to investment in industry and education . . . On tax the dividing-line is not between high and low taxes, but rather fair and unfair, coupled of course with the central tenet that "tax and spend" questions cannot be divorced from the state of the economy.'[14] A year later, on 30 November 1995, Blair reinforced the point: 'New Labour is neither old left nor new right. We understand and welcome the new global market. We reject go-it-alone policies on inflation and the macro-economy. We stand for a new partnership between government and industry.' He continued: 'We recognise, just as our founding fathers did, the need to pursue the common good, the belief that as individuals we do best in a fair and decent society where we look after others as well as ourselves. This does not represent a choice between self-interest and the interest of others. It is enlightened self-interest.'[15]

The 'Third Way' is a label, but it is also an approach that is rooted in the modernising tradition and in the themes of this book. I sensed in the playground of my secondary-modern school a clash between my soft compassionate values and the harder, common-sense attitudes of my friends. It has always been an intrinsic element of my approach to politics to connect my basic values of compassion and fairness with the understanding that people want to advance themselves with better houses, better holidays, better lives. As I grew older, I learned from direct experience the need to link my commitment to fairness with the imperatives of business and the market. Both were needed in the modern world.

The 'Third Way' appears to be an abstract idea, light years away from the hard lives of ordinary working people. But this is not so. Working people hold instincts that draw from both left and right, but move beyond them both. On a basic level people are tough on crime but supportive of a strong state role in education and health. They want a decent society but understand the need to compete and win in world markets. They want this now, but it is also what people were saying and thinking twenty or thirty years ago. People outgrew left and right long before the politicians did.

These new dividing-lines were a continuing obsession for Blair. His speeches from well before he became leader, his strategy notes, his conversation, were all infused with the need to remake the political map, to put new dividing-lines in place.

Blair had built the basis of a coherent intellectual approach based on three defining ideas – the community, national renewal linked to party renewal, and new dividing-lines, later to become the 'Third Way'. Each of these were eventually articulated in the new Clause IV. But despite this progress, the real work of rebuilding Labour had only just begun. Ideas were crucial, but so was building an election-winning and power-sustaining political machine.

The political project

The first pressing need of the project was therefore to turn new Labour from brilliant concept to concrete reality. This was the point of my document, 'The Unfinished Revolution', a graphic and sometimes raw account of the changes Labour had to make to become a party of government capable of winning not just one election but many, dominating the twenty-first century as the Conservatives had the twentieth. The document was a war-cry for total modernisation.

'The Unfinished Revolution' was written on 23 April 1995 and was sent to only a very few people. It was never leaked. What was leaked to the press was a shorter, summarised version, which also had a restricted circulation. Its full title was: 'The Unfinished Revolution: Winning Power, Sustaining Power, Transforming Britain'. It started with an introduction that is a modernising credo: 'Labour has not just to win the next election: it must win a working majority; it must have a project and policies that will transform Britain over an eight-year period; it must have a campaigning machine that will sustain Labour in power; it must become a party of sufficient structural and ideological coherence to support Labour in government, without splitting and without sabotaging. It must be aiming to achieve in the next century what the Conservatives have achieved in the last . . . New Labour is still a party in transition: midway through its revolution.'[16]

I had in mind Anthony Seldon's *The Conservative Century*: 'The Conservative Party's very pragmatism and adaptability will allow it to overcome the severe internal and support problems it faces in the 1990s and will in all probability ensure that the cycles of Conservative dominance will be repeated well into the twenty-first century.'[17] I was determined this would not happen – the next century would be Labour's.

I argued that the real tests for Labour lay ahead. 'Labour is always fighting the battle in hand, not the battle that is yet to come. For the great majority of the last ten years Labour has been comfortably ahead in opinion polls, but at decisive moments Labour has been found wanting. Labour wins the battle of the moment, but fails the ultimate test.' There were three measures by which to assess Labour's preparedness for the battle ahead: first, 'the state of the Conservative Party in 1979, the last time an opposition party won an election in the UK'; second, 'the state of the Clinton campaign in 1992, the last time a major progressive party won power from opposition'; and third, 'the likely state of the Conservative Party in 1997: the enemy that we will face when it matters, not the one we face when it doesn't'. Labour fell short on all these measures:

New Labour is not yet a cohesive, integrated political party sharing the same political ideology. In reality New Labour is a new party created within the structures of the old, like a butterfly trapped within its own chrysalis. This problem will become painfully apparent at the 29th April [Clause IV] conference, when the 30 per cent who were balloted will be for Blair, when around half the unions will be opposed. 30 per cent trapped within 70 per cent.

New Labour does not have the flexibility, adaptability, capacity for innovation . . . that is the hallmark of a successful political organisation . . . Labour does not yet have a political project that matches the Thatcher agenda of 1979, nor will be able to sustain Labour in government and transform Britain . . . New Labour is behind Clinton in almost all aspects of campaigning and campaign preparation. In addition, Labour must expect a Conservative recovery just before, or soon after, the next election.

Labour had to move on. It must complete its revolution. And to do so it needed a revolution in its structures: 'The new party must become the whole party. New Labour must escape from the 30 per cent/70 per cent trap. In the short run the union proportion of the conference vote should be reduced . . . In the long run Labour has to become a genuinely one member, one vote party. That is the only ultimate future for Labour.'

I added a recommendation which was to become highly controversial: 'Labour must replace competing existing structures with a single chain of command leading directly to the leader of the party. This is the only way that Labour can become a political organisation capable of matching the Conservatives. It will be more effective, and in a one member, one vote party, more democratic.' This offended everybody. It was in part a response to my short-term concerns about campaign organisation, but at root the point was much bigger than that: I felt then, as now, that only a unitary system of command could give Labour the clarity and flexibility it needed to adapt and change at the pace required by modern politics. This seemed to me to be a key element in the speed and success of Conservative adaptation in this century.

Conservative leaders had always had a powerful capacity to direct their party. Labour's structure had become too diffuse, with power shared between the NEC, the PLP, the conference, the unions and the constituency associations.

With that in mind, I believed all Labour's organisational structures should be transformed. 'Within the context of a new unitary command structure, the organisation must become flexible, responsive and innovative. It needs fewer people but better people; it needs flatter management structures; it needs a new culture rewarding risk and excellence; and it needs a new building.'

Labour had to revolutionise its policies: 'We must develop a Blair political project and a Blair policy agenda that is sufficiently bold, radical and robust to be capable of both sustaining Labour in government and transforming Britain.' This meant we needed a 'definitive Blair/New Labour document that matches and beats the "Right Approach" [Margaret Thatcher's policy paper of the mid-1970s] by spring 1996'. And we needed 'a policy agenda in place for conference 1996 that is more radical, more modern, more innovative than anything the Conservatives offer, and anything most of us currently envisage'.

Finally, Labour needed a revolution in its campaigning: 'The TB campaigning operation has been effective and successful. It has been well supported by the GB attack on tax and trust and excess pay. But the wider campaigning operation is simply not equipped to fight and win a competitive election in 1997. Walworth Road is effectively useless as a decisive campaigning machine at the national level; there are competing campaigning power bases; there is an enormous lack of trust; there is a lack of strategic preparation for initiatives, and when they are made there is a lack of follow-through: our rebuttal/opposition research operation is not working.' My solution was to focus all campaigning through the leader's office: 'There must be one ultimate source of campaigning authority, and it must be the leader . . . The operational heart of the campaign should be unambiguously established in the leader's office.'[18]

Other recommendations in the 26-page document included the suggestion that the daily media-management meeting be reconstituted and held in the leader's office, chaired by Jonathan Powell. This advice was wrong, and Blair rightly ignored it. Gordon Brown continued to chair the daily meetings throughout the campaign. I was being too purist: I wanted a unitary system of command, and that was the end of it. The system we developed was messier, but worked in part because of that. Blair was not interested in straight lines on organisation charts. He wanted the best talents at his disposal and he wanted those talents to work together, whatever the cost. This made the process more difficult but produced a better outcome, and his instincts were vindicated by the effectiveness of the campaign and the eventual result. In my quest for Leninist simplicity I had missed the bigger point.

With that one exception, I believe every word I wrote was correct and I would retract none of it. On 24 April I wrote to Blair, 'I have written a document called "The Unfinished Revolution", which spells out the challenges facing us and what we need to do to meet them. It is fairly bold and highly sensitive.'[19]

Peter Mandelson phoned me at home a few days later, wanting a summary to read. He needed it very quickly and I dashed off a two-page synopsis in less than an hour. For this summary, and only in this summary, I added the words: 'Labour is not ready for government: it needs to complete its revolution.' I sent the summary to Peter Mandelson, Jonathan Powell and Alastair Campbell. That was the last I heard of 'The Unfinished Revolution' for several months.

The intellectual project

'The Unfinished Revolution' was a private enterprise, written by me and me alone. It was the product of obsession, which explains its rawness, but sometimes in politics directness and obsession are essential to achieve change. I was determined not to dilute 'The Unfinished Revolution'; I wanted to write something with an explosive power capable of changing events. However, it was about structure and politics, and not ideas. And winning the battle of ideas was central to everyone, not just Tony Blair himself.

For the rest of 1995 this was my central preoccupation, as it was other people's. I spent much of my time talking to, and working with, David Miliband, Blair's head of policy. David is the son of Ralph Miliband, who wrote what proved to be an influential text for much of my generation: *The State in Capitalist Society*, which was one of the most widely read books among politics students when I was at Sussex.

Ralph Miliband must have been a wonderful father as well as a brilliant polemicist, because his sons Ed (who works for the Chancellor) and David are two of the most decent, kind and intelligent people you could wish to meet. David is always courteous and behaves with personal integrity; he does the right thing in all circumstances, public or private. He is fearsomely clever and easily grasps the post-war intellectual terrain, understanding in depth all the major current policy issues.

For much of the period – from the party's approval of changing Clause IV in April 1995 through Blair's stakeholding speech in January 1996, and until the launch of Labour's early manifesto, 'New Life for Britain', in July 1996 – David and I were engaged in constant dialogue. What is Blair's defining insight? How do we reconcile modernisation and community? Is it possible to conflate both concepts into one unifying idea? How do we reconcile populism which is for a majority of the people – most, but not all – with concepts of community and one-nation which appear to include everyone? David and I were obsessed with building a new, election-winning politics based on principle. Many of our conversations took place in a cafeteria in the House of Commons. We would sit and talk about New Labour and Blairism as the coffee machine hissed and gushed steam and we talked, I am sure, much hot air.

In this tortuous way we worked towards our new political project. Slowly Blair was giving substance to his ideas, fleshing them out. By the end of it, he would have five priorities for government based upon his analysis of the problems facing Britain: lack of a first-class education for the majority of children; community disintegration leading to crime and pressure on families; the poor performance of the economy, and the unstable relationship between government and business; a centralised and secretive political system; and isolation and lack of influence overseas.

Blair made several big speeches in the early part of 1995 that pushed the project forward, gradually making his dividing-lines clearer. On 22 March he gave his *Spectator* lecture, fleshing out his beliefs about the community, stressing the need for responsibilities as well as rights.[20] On 22 May he delivered his annual Mais lecture which set out how macro-economics dedicated to stability needed to be combined with an energetic and radical micro policy. The speech was suffused with new dividing-lines:

> As in the 1970s, we now need to recognise that a new approach is needed . . . a macro-economic framework to keep inflation low and stable is even more important now than was said in the 1980s. Far from being an alternative to Labour's long-term investment strategy, controlling inflation is an essential part of it . . . Too much reliance has been placed on deregulation alone to improve the supply side of the economy. There is an active role for government – particularly in, though not confined to, the improvement of human capital . . . Much of the current debate on taxation and spending is parochial and sterile . . . The key question therefore becomes not how much to spend, but what to spend it on, and how to improve the performance of the economy . . . I came into politics because I believe that a fair society and a more efficient one go hand-in-hand. By providing long-term economic strength and by raising the standard of education and opportunities of our citizens, we can achieve the stronger and more cohesive society I want to see. Social aims without economic means are empty wishes. By uniting the two we can build a better future for all our people.[21]

In each area of economic policy there was a new dividing-line, a new way forward. Here was another early 'Third Way' speech. Blair was rewarded with a *Financial Times* leading article, which said: 'There is now a coherent vision of what a left-of-centre government should do,' consisting of 'low inflation, fiscal prudence, increased competition, and long-term investment in education and infrastructure'.[22]

Later in the year, at the News Corp Leadership Conference on Hayman Island in Australia, Blair made even more explicit his new dividing-lines and commitment to a 'Third Way'.

> My case therefore is that neither old left nor conservative new right can provide the framework for the solution of the central question. If – and I accept this is the real challenge – the left can liberate itself from outdated preconceptions, strip its essential values out from the means of their application relevant to another part of their history, then a modern left-of-centre is the best able to provide security amid change. Let me make that case and in doing so demonstrate also why this new left-of-centre is not simply an accommodation of the right, but how it tries to move the political debate beyond the old boundaries between left and right altogether.[23]

Blair was feeling his way towards an explicit 'Third Way' philosophy.

The Conservatives blink

On 22 June 1995, John Major resigned as leader of the Conservative Party. I was in a meeting with Gordon Brown, Tony Blair and others when we heard. The moment it was announced, Blair asked us to leave so he could consider the new situation quietly. Gordon Brown and Alastair Campbell stayed, and later Peter Mandelson joined them. Blair hates big meetings at the best of times, certainly at moments of crisis. Joy Johnson – the party's communications director – was enraged at being ejected from the meeting: she wanted to be at the heart of things.

This was a moment of potential danger. Apart from economic recovery, the one anxiety I had about our election chances was that the Tories might ditch Major and elect a new leader. It seems that this was Major's feeling also, and so he embarked on the Doomsday scenario of seeking re-election. He challenged his chorus of internal opponents to 'put up or shut up'. To his amazement, Secretary of State for Wales John Redwood did 'put up'. Although losing Major could not have had the electoral impact of ditching Thatcher, Michael Heseltine as Tory leader would have posed a much more formidable threat. What Major did was the worst possible course of action for the Tories. When he announced the election the Conservatives' position strengthened – people welcomed the idea there was going to be a change. They couldn't believe that the Tories would re-elect Major. Their mood held throughout the campaign but the moment he *was* re-elected, it collapsed. The election had promised change but delivered the status quo, and the impact was almost all bad for the government. In a focus-group report of 6 July, I wrote, 'People felt used, and they felt manipulated . . . some thought the whole thing was a con, a charade, that Redwood had been put up to it . . . their resolve to vote Labour had been stiffened. One said: "I was nervous about voting Labour, but now a third of the Conservatives have voted against their own leader, so can I."'[24] What looked good in the short term, in the long run made things worse. It was a classic Major miscalculation.

It seemed that the Conservatives might be starting to crack. The night of Major's victory I had dinner with Maurice Saatchi, to celebrate the publication of a novel by his wife, Josephine Hart, which was being published by my wife, Gail. Maurice was cock-a-hoop about the leadership election and the result, which he had clearly been closely involved with. I told him he had just won the election for Labour. For a moment his confidence flickered and a trace of doubt crossed his face. This contrasted with his attitude the night Britain was forced out of the Exchange Rate Mechanism. Despite the appalling defeat this represented for his party and our country, he had been brimming with confidence. 'We will be able to keep Norman in for as long as we want,' he said, a comment which was probably as good an omen as any of the hubris that would be the Tories' undoing.

The project under pressure

August and early September saw the New Labour project come under pressure. On 11 August Richard Burden, MP for Birmingham Northfield, wrote in the *New Statesman* that he was 'ashamed' of the Littleborough and Saddleworth by-election (in which Chris Davies, the Liberal Democrat, won with less than a 2,000 majority over Phil Woolas, the Labour candidate). Peter Mandelson and I had both been heavily involved in this campaign and had hit Davies hard on his record, particularly on his attitude to the liberalisation of drug use. Burden went further, criticising the centralised power of the 'inner sanctum': 'I thought that kind of approach to political leadership went out of fashion when the Berlin Wall came down.'[25] His protest set off a period of carping about the style of Blair's leadership.

Then, on 12 September, a summary of my document 'The Unfinished Revolution' was leaked. The first indication I had that something was wrong came when my pager buzzed at 5.50 P.M. on 11 September: 'Call Alastair urgently.' This meant trouble. When I phoned him, he said, 'It's a bugger, this.' My heart sank. 'They have got one of my memos,' I said, thinking, 'Pray God may it not be "The Unfinished Revolution".' Alastair said, 'The *Guardian* has got the worst one. They've got "The Unfinished Revolution".' I just said: 'Oh, my God.'

When we had finished talking I got a copy of the memo out. The long document I had did not match the description Alastair had given to me. There was no reference in it to Labour not being 'ready for government', the phrase he had mentioned, and I assumed that the *Guardian* had not got a copy of the document but had been given a verbal briefing on its contents. I had momentarily forgotten the synopsis I had written. The BBC journalist Peter Kellner phoned from

Brighton, where the TUC was meeting. Blair was speaking to the conference the next day. The timing could not have been worse. Kellner was going to cover the leak for *Newsnight* that evening and wanted to confirm details of what was in the memo. Inadvertently I misled him because I had the long document and he was working from the summary.

The moment you are the centre of a bad news story, you become a person apart. Even though people are helpful, an invisible glass wall separates the person who has caused a problem from those who are trying to contain it. This has happened to me on three occasions: 'Jennifer's Ear', 'The Unfinished Revolution', and the leak of the 1997 election War Book, which I had largely written. Peter Mandelson phoned up and offered support. But I waited for *Newsnight* like a condemned man. Kellner came on in Brighton, being as supportive as possible but bursting with the excitement of a good news story. My picture popped up on screen, and then words from my memo appeared. I still thought it was a briefing, as the words Kellner was using didn't fit my document. I went to bed feeling sick, got up at five the next morning and bought the *Guardian*. 'LABOUR'S SECRET STRATEGY', read the splash. 'Party not ready for government. Call for central control by Blair.' The front-page lead by Seumas Milne read: 'A confidential strategic plan drawn up Tony Blair's closest advisers warns that New Labour is not ready for government and calls for a centralised command structure under the personal control of the leader . . . The report, passed to the *Guardian* by a senior Labour source, was written by Philip Gould, the Labour leader's campaigns and strategy consultant. It is understood that Peter Mandelson, the Hartlepool MP and Mr Blair's most trusted political confidant, collaborated in the report.' This was untrue, but the attempt to suck Peter into it indicated that he was possibly the target of the leak rather than me. Colour pictures of Campbell, Blair and Mandelson were splashed across the page.

Inside was the synopsis in full. I had forgotten I had written it, but the *Guardian* had it. The *Guardian*'s political correspondent Patrick Wintour detailed the damage the memo would do to Tony Blair: 'Disenchanted left-wing activists are likely to see it as confirmation that Mr Blair has a near-presidential agenda.' He described it as 'intemperate even for an extremely private document'.[26] I waited for the first news of the day on the BBC. Sure enough, the memo was the lead story. I watched, stunned, then went into work, knowing I would be doorstepped by television cameras. I did my best with them and went into my office to hide. Throughout the day the news coverage continued unabated. I received a stream of telephone calls with conflicting advice from various Labour officials: 'Do a doorstep' – David Hill; 'You shouldn't have done that' – Alastair Campbell. I was told that John Edmonds – General Secretary of the GMB trade union – was so rude about me in one interview that his comments could not be broadcast in full.

The next day was worse. The *Guardian* headline ran, 'SECRECY ROW SHAKES LABOUR'. Now I was getting really worried. For a moment it did look as though the New Labour project might be falling apart. Mandelson phoned and said, 'We are going to have to fight hard to get out of this one.' Inside the *Guardian* I was described as 'rumpled' and 'naïve', and not in it for personal publicity.[27] This was certainly true; I was hating it. The story was in all the papers and making headlines in some of them. *The Times* was sniffy about the memo,[28] but the *Independent* was supportive. Its leading article – 'From Molotov to Mandelson' – read, 'Mr Gould is right, of course. And not only is he right, but it is encouraging that the Blair entourage seems to recognise these problems.'[29] I don't know who wrote that article, but I thank them. I don't know either – and nor do I care very much – who was the senior Labour source who leaked the summary of the memo, although I have my strong suspicions. I know that it was not one of the small number I sent it to personally, and I suspect it was stolen off someone's desk. This was not something to be proud of.

Tony Blair went to Brighton and, typically, turned the

incident to his advantage. Campbell recalls, 'For a few hours it was a bit of a disaster, but all the media attention meant that by the time we got to Brighton people wanted to hear what Tony had to say. Tony always has a glint in his eye at these things – I am the same – I really like these big moments. The media think you are going to lose it and in fact you go there and stick it up them. Tony did a big, ballsy, barnstorming, off-the-cuff speech. We'd gone down to Brighton with people saying we were going to end up 5–0 down, and in fact we won 2–1.'[30]

Despite this, I sent a note of apology to Tony; he telephoned on Wednesday and was supportive: 'You said things that were true; it will work out in the long run.' But he was critical of my 'unfit to govern' comment. This is typical of Blair: I had just given him the worst two days since he was elected leader and he phoned me up to offer support. This quality isn't often found in politicians.

The affair hadn't quite blown over yet. I was told that the *Guardian* had a second memo, which they were going to leak before Tony's speech at conference. They didn't do it, but it made conference week uncomfortable.

The young country

Despite the summer turbulence, David Miliband and I, along with other people, were still trying to develop New Labour thinking, now focused on the 1995 conference speech.

On 18 August I wrote a note, 'Winning the Trust of the Centre Without Betraying the Left', in which I argued that we should reclaim the centre: 'Building a governing coalition does not just mean putting roots down on the left. It also means reclaiming the centre.' This meant being explicit about our centrist position: pushing the Conservatives to the right; pushing the Liberals to the margins and the left. But it also meant 'giving ourselves a real anchor on the left' by 'taking our "for the people" positioning and establishing it as the grounding principle that divides us from the Conservatives'. I summed it up in one phrase – 'Labour's new coalition:

anchored in the left, owning the centre, underpinned by a commitment to govern for all the people.'[31]

A week later I wrote another document, called 'What is New Labour?' I answered that it was the response to two challenges: the need to build a new Britain, and the need to build a new model of social democracy. Renewal was straightforward – we needed 'to build a new Britain with a new identity and a new self-confidence: our economy; our society; our politics all must be renewed'. The complicated part was rebuilding social democracy, which I argued was under threat because 'vast areas of our lives that were the traditional province of government are now being served by market solutions . . . global markets minimise the space for government intervention . . . demographic trends work against social democracy'. I asked, 'How far must modernisation go to meet these new conditions? Should it reform and modernise the existing model of social democracy, or should it reconstruct a completely new model?' Predictably, my answer was that New Labour must construct a completely new model of social democracy. 'Halfway solutions linking old models don't work,' I wrote. 'New Labour must be positioned in the centre.'[32]

However, we were still short of compelling concepts. It took Blair himself to provide them. Earlier in the year I had been chatting to him at a party Anji Hunter gave at her house in the country. It was a lovely summer's day and we were talking in the garden. As I spoke to Tony, my daughter Grace and Tony's young daughter Kathryn held hands and trailed behind us, talking about God knows what. After the normal niceties about how we needed to do more to win, Blair said he wanted to base his conference speech around the concept of 'one nation'. He had mentioned this as a theme in his leadership campaign notes, but I had forgotten. I did not like the idea much, nor did anyone else – it seemed too abstract – but he would not let go of it and as the conference speech came closer it became clear that this concept met the moment. It was centrist, and in origin it was a Conservative concept. Benjamin Disraeli first used the idea in his novel *Sybil, or, The Two Nations*: 'Two nations between

whom there is no intercourse and no sympathy . . . THE
RICH AND THE POOR.'[33] But the one-nation philosophy is as
relevant now as it was in the 1840s. It articulated Blair's
concept of community in a new way, which it linked to a
new patriotism. But it left unanswered the problem of
renewal. This had to wait longer and only in the final hours
before his conference speech that year did he develop the
idea of 'young country'. These two concepts, 'one nation'
and 'young country', were the pillars of his 1995 conference
speech. In my view, this was the strongest of Blair's pre-
election conference speeches. Certainly it meant the most to
me. It started with a passage linking Blair's political beliefs
to his Christian principles: 'The simple truths. I am worth
no more than anyone else. I am my brother's keeper. I will
not walk on the other side. We aren't simply people set in
isolation from each other, face to face with eternity, but
members of the same family, the same human race.'

These were also my most basic beliefs. He then talked
directly to his and my generation: 'Let me tell you about my
generation. We grew up after the Second World War. We
read about fascism, we saw the Soviet Union, and we learned
to fear extremes of left and right. We were born into the
welfare state and the NHS, and into the market economy of
bank accounts, supermarkets, jeans and cars. We had money
in our pockets never dreamed about by our parents . . . We
enjoy a thousand material advantages over any previous
generation, and yet we suffer a depth of insecurity and spiritual doubt they never knew.'

This too I found very moving. A final key passage linked
the values of community to the necessity for renewal:

Let's build a new and young country that can lay aside the
old prejudices that dominated our land for generations. A
nation for all the people, built by the people, where old divisions are cast out. A new spirit in the nation based on working
together, unity, solidarity, partnership. One Britain. That is
the patriotism of the future. Where never again do we fight
our politics by appealing to one section of the nation at the

expense of another. Where your child in distress is my child, your parent ill and in pain, is my parent, your friend unemployed or homeless is my friend; your neighbour my neighbour. That is the true patriotism of a nation.[34]

In a few sentences Blair brought together his core values, his commitment to community, his demand for renewal, and finally his patriotism. Although incomplete, these were the beginnings of a new progressive approach. The next day the press recognised that Blair was redefining social democracy – perhaps not quite the Bad Godesberg Congress, but potentially as seminal for British progressive politics.

Stakeholding: a first attempt at synthesis

New Labour was beginning to take real shape: a new constitution, big themes, positioned in the centre of British politics, pushing the other parties to the margins. But we still lacked one big, unifying concept.

I was determined to integrate Labour's one-nation message with its economic message. David Miliband and I spent weeks batting ideas back and forth on the theme of one-nation economics, and came up with a string of concepts. In a note on 12 November 1995 I proposed the theme: 'Efficiency and society are not mutually exclusive, but mutually dependent. For New Labour, society is a benefit, not a cost. The alternative view is put with brutal clarity by Maurice Saatchi when he says: "The choice is between the Conservatives, who are cruel but efficient, and Labour, which is caring but incompetent." We have to say that "cruel is efficient" is a fundamentally wrong view: "Efficiency needs society".'[35] I hardened this line on 9 December: 'The central insight of one-nation economics is that social capital and social cohesion enhance market efficiency and economic strength; social division and the depletion of social capital impair market efficiency, weaken economics.'[36] Here Miliband and I drew heavily on Francis Fukuyama's *Trust*, and the Harvard political scientist Robert Putnam's work on social capital and civic society. We needed a concept to unite the belief that efficiency and society are complementary. We needed to synthesise these apparent opposites and made some suggestions: 'One-nation economics; social capitalism; stakeholder capitalism; a cohesive market economy.' David Miliband wanted a 'stakeholder Britain that combines one-nation society with one-nation economics'.[37]

On 8 January 1996 Blair made his famous 'Stakeholder Economics' speech in Singapore. It burst through the media. I believed it pulled together many other themes and ideas that had been emerging not just over months, but years. Crucially, it linked the values of community to the imperative for efficiency: 'We need a new relationship of trust not just within a firm but within society. By trust I mean the recognition of a mutual purpose for which we work together and in which we all benefit. It is a stakeholder economy in which opportunity is available to all, advancement is through merit and from which no group or class is set apart or excluded. This is the economic justification for social cohesion, for a fair and strong society.'[38]

Alastair Campbell describes the circumstances of the speech:

The stakeholder speech was one of the most important. [Blair] was delivering it at the High Commissioner's Residence in Singapore. Jon Sopel from the BBC was the only journalist travelling with us. On the plane down we wrote the stakeholder speech and I had a real sense, as did Tony, that this speech would make a real impact. The night before I contacted two local stringers from the *Telegraph* and the *Guardian* who were there and I briefed them on the speech, telling them that this was the big idea. All I was trying to do was get the speech up overnight, to alert the London media to it. I then got Sopel in for a briefing, and it led the *Today* programme. But the trouble was that Tony was making the speech at a lunch to an audience of just forty local movers and shakers at the High Commission, which was meant to be private. This clearly could have been a problem, so in the end I persuaded

Sopel that he could film the event on the condition that the cutaways did not expose the smallness of the event. We had a backdrop made up, with Tony standing up on the podium with a lectern and microphone in a room no bigger than a kitchen.[39]

This speech immediately gave New Labour its defining idea, but unfortunately it ran into difficulty just as quickly: it was open to attack as being corporatist, just when corporatist solutions appeared to be failing in Europe and non-corporatist Asian tigers were starting to roar. Gordon Brown did not like stakeholding as an economic idea. He felt it was a hostage to fortune, exposing Labour to the risk of attack on grounds of social costs, and he queried the sense of adding to our strategic burden.

In its way it was a classic 'Third Way' speech, spelling out the need to mesh the impact of economic globalisation with the rights of social citizenship. The language of stakeholding may have withered, but the new approach underpinning it has prospered.

On 29 January Blair developed his political philosophy further, in a speech in Southwark Cathedral in which he gave full voice to his deepest beliefs, returning, without mentioning him, to the philosophy of John Macmurray. In a way this speech saw the closing of the intellectual circle – Tony Blair, the Labour leader, articulating the ideas of Tony Blair, the student:

I start from a simple belief that people are separate economic actors competing in the market place of life. They are citizens of a community. The identity of an individual comes through his relationship with others. We are social beings, nurtured in families and communities and human only because we develop the moral power of personal responsibility. Our relationships with and commitments to others are not add-ons to our personalities. They make us who we are. Notions of mutuality and interdependence are not abstract ideas: they are facts of life.[40]

In little more than a year, New Labour had moved decisively towards becoming a coherent political project. We had become the one-nation party: a party anchored in the centre, a modernising party determined to rejuvenate Britain, determined to fuse efficiency with community. We had set out new dividing-lines laying the basis for a 'Third Way', now arguably the dominant political approach throughout the world. Much had been done, and there was more still to do. But it was time to start winning the election.

8

REASSURANCE, REASSURANCE, REASSURANCE

Still unsafe

Nineteen ninety-six was the year we had to gain the voters' trust. Reassurance became the public face and strategic anchor of our campaigning as Blair, Brown, Campbell, Mandelson and I struggled privately in meeting after meeting to hammer out our campaign strategy and message, in what sometimes appeared to be an endless, frustrating process. And as we fought to reassure them, the public, faced with a steady drip of controversies from a series of shadow Cabinet members, including Clare Short on tax and Harriet Harman on education, began to lose faith. The year-long battle to keep their trust began with plans for the 'Road to the Manifesto', through its launch, the pledges, conference, and was only won when, finally, we reassured them that Labour would not raise income tax.

During 1995, while we modernised the party, we had still not persuaded the public that we had changed completely. Labour faced the same old problem: lack of trust. In the first memo he wrote to Tony Blair, on 8 June 1995, Stan Greenberg, who was helping Labour on a committed but unpaid basis, spelled out the need for reassurance. 'New Labour is defined for most voters by Tony Blair's willingness to take on and master the unions,' he wrote.

In the focus groups the switchers spoke of little else, because this is what qualifies Labour as a plausible electoral option. Blair and his party were seen to control the unions; the unions no longer seemed to control Labour. But voters need relentless reassurance. Almost a third of Conservative defectors to Labour worry about excessive union influence. The women defectors in the focus groups mostly shifted back to the Tories after a fairly moderate attack on Blair focusing on union influence. For the Liberal defectors, the reining-in of the unions allowed them to feel comfortable with a Labour vote.

'Change' voters are turning to Labour, not because of Labour, but because of their disaffection with the Tories. Our main task is to make sure that is as easy a choice as possible. This means reassuring these voters that Labour is 'safe', even though most of these voters are inclined to see Labour as 'dangerous'. The Labour leadership needs to reassure these voters again and again.

He listed a number of problems that needed to be addressed if Labour was to continue to be seen as 'new'. The major concern was taxation: 'Labour is not trusted on taxes: 42 per cent of the electorate believes they will raise taxes for everyone. 57 per cent of Conservative defectors believe Labour will betray them on taxes.' And also important, still, was what Greenberg called 'the basics': 'One of the preoccupations of Old Labour was a preoccupation with what the public often saw as "bizarre" issues: homosexuals, immigrants, feminists, lesbians, boroughs putting their money into peculiar things. Voters think that a serious party that represents the ordinary person focuses on things that matter to people in their lives, "addresses things that concern us".'[1] After ten years of reform and modernisation, and despite the great strides taken by Blair, Labour was still a prisoner of its past.

This is what many commentators never understood. They saw a big Labour lead, thought Labour was certain to win and therefore accused us of being too cautious. But the truth was more complicated. Conservative defectors and centrist, floating voters were always nervous about Labour, regarding it as potentially unsafe. This was true until the very last days of the 1997 election campaign. And it was only Labour's strategy of relentless reassurance that turned opinion-poll leads into a real majority.

Tony Blair had no illusions about the fragility of the electorate's trust in Labour. Polling towards the end of 1995 had shown voters shifting back towards the Conservatives and looking at us more critically. I reported on Conservative-to-Labour switchers in focus groups who were saying: 'Tony Blair is all right, but what about the rest of the party?'; 'They don't agree with him; they are biting their tongues, biding their time'. 'People want to be convinced that the party genuinely supports its leader,' I wrote. 'Many of these voters are now facing the real prospect of a Labour government, and this is scaring them.'[2] At one of our weekly campaign meetings at the beginning of January 1996 I asked Tony what the heart of his strategy was. His reply was emphatic: 'Reassurance, reassurance, reassurance.' From then until election day, we would fight to convince the country we could be trusted.

The endless grind of meetings

If 1996 was about trust, it was also about endless meetings. Early in the year we moved our daily media meetings to Millbank Tower, which was now creeping open for business. I was based there full-time from the beginning of January; Peter Mandelson started to move in gradually soon after.

But the weekly meetings with Tony Blair, Gordon Brown, Alastair Campbell, Peter Mandelson, Jonathan Powell and others, myself included, continued in Blair's office in the House of Commons. Blair had wisely ignored my advice in 'The Unfinished Revolution', and kept the same basic structure in place: Gordon Brown in overall charge of the campaign and of strategy, Peter Mandelson in charge of campaign management and Millbank.

These meetings and the campaigning process they

exemplified were never easy. For the entire pre-election period the process of strategy development and campaign management was frustrating, difficult and strained. This was partly because of relationships. The leadership election had led to a breakdown in trust between Brown and Mandelson, which sometimes improved, sometimes worsened. And from time to time other relationships suffered, which was inevitable given the pressures of the situation.

But there was a second, deeper reason why the process was so frustrating – the participants had different views of the campaigning process and all these had to be resolved.

Gordon Brown is constantly looking to anticipate the news and use it. He thinks that modern campaigning is news-driven or it is nothing; that the political landscape is constantly changing, always fluid – what is down now will be up soon. He thinks that you need permanent momentum. There is no end-point; you don't arrive; you are sailing constantly in a changing sea. Peter Mandelson can see the chaos, but wants to create order out of it. He wants defining landmarks, clearly delineated campaigns, events that can be planned and executed with consummate professionalism. He wants impeccable, perfect order. Alastair Campbell wants boldness: the audacious, unpredictable coup – the *Sun* coming out for Labour; Alan Howarth defecting.

Tony Blair combines intellect with instinct. He is forever seeking clarity: the single insight that explains a situation. He demands strategy constantly: his principal explanation for any failure is lack of strategy. But he also relies powerfully on his instincts, and he will back them in defiance of conventional argument. Once, after a long and convincing case against a controversial decision about funding the unions was put to him, and everyone in the room had agreed such a decision would be untenable, Blair looked at us all and said, 'But why can't we just do it?' He trusts his common sense and damns the consequences. Over the reform of the union 'closed shop', over Clause IV, over choosing his son's school – he knew what was right and did it, despite myriad conflicting voices.

I was seen as the voice of the electorate, and usually the voice of pessimism, and I was obsessive about the need to develop and repeat consistent messages. I wanted us to agree a campaign rationale and stick to it.

This makes a potent brew for any campaigning meeting: several different and often competing perspectives, and a time horizon that moved from the next day, or even the next hour, to the next year or longer. No wonder the meetings often seemed to go nowhere. But gradually, over time, a strategy and message were agreed and developed. It was tough, but we got there. I began to understand that good campaigning is, by definition, a struggle. There is no right way to do it, no one perspective that is always correct. Politics is so complicated you see from all sides of the mountain. You need conflicting views, different insights. And you need a process that is interactive, challenging, sometimes competing. This is easy to understand now, but it was hell at the time. Alastair Campbell describes the process:

> He [Blair] used to come in sometimes with a clear idea of what we were going to do that day, sometimes not. In terms of devising strategy I would say he relied, in terms of who he needed in the permanent orbit, on Gordon, Peter and myself. He relied upon you [Gould] for a strategic input which he valued for the fact that you were slightly outside, not in the maelstrom of activity the whole time. But we used to have these conversations that you just felt were going round and round in circles, because we were all saying different things, but we were pretending we were saying the same things. I think you were right, we did have different views. But in the end we were complementary. In the long build-up to the campaign I felt physically and mentally like a racehorse. I felt that we were testing the whole time, training, trying things out, building up stamina, finding out the things that could be rejected and working out the things that had to be developed, and by the time we got to the election – I feel we timed everything about right. Now you could argue about where all that came from, but I think probably it came from

all those hours. If you had a camera in there people wouldn't have dreamed of voting for us – it was ridiculous, circular conversations – and yet there was discipline in the end. We were honing all the time. But at times it was bloody grim, because you felt the election wasn't coming, because Tony and I were constantly telling each other that the Tories were doing well – partly it's a defensive thing, we had to build them up the whole time so we could get a proper sense of how we could do them in.[3]

If this pre-election process was grim for Campbell, it was worse for Mandelson, dealing with the tensions of the relationships. 'It was a nightmare, just a nightmare. It was a fruitless, demoralising, agonising, dreadful waste of energy – truly draining. It was like moving with a huge boulder dragging behind you.'[4] Nineteen ninety-six was exhausting. Progress was slow and often painful, but gradually we moved ahead. And we did address, in turn, all the big strategic issues. In the end it was Tony Blair who kept the show on the road. He trusted everyone in his team, and they all trusted him. The problem was that the electorate did not yet trust us.

'The Road to the Manifesto'

Lack of trust was not only a problem for Labour. The legacy of betrayal by both major parties meant politicians generally were not trusted by the public. The voters were reeling from Conservative U-turns on tax rises; the September 1992 devaluation of the pound; the 'Back to Basics' hypocrisy; Conservative misinformation over the length and depth of the recession. All were combining to induce an almost unshakeable contempt for the political process. This was one of John Major's most damaging legacies. Typical comments about the Conservatives from members of focus groups made this sense of betrayal vivid: 'cutting the throats of the home-owner'; 'fallen down on their promises'; 'I own a small business. They cut me off at the knees'; 'I opted to own my own council house. I ended up losing it'; 'They used working-class people'; 'They were always for the rich – we just fell for it'.[5] It was clear that the Tories had broken their contract with the British people. They had lost the people's trust, but in doing so had undermined public faith in politics and politicians generally.

I was becoming certain that the only way we could persuade the electorate that Labour as a political party had *really* changed was to take our manifesto to the party and ballot them on it. This would have two consequences. First, it would persuade the electorate that New Labour was real – that it was not just about Tony Blair, but a political project supported by the majority of the party. This would solve what Blair called the 'head and body' problem: that Labour's head, represented by him and other modernising leaders, believed one thing, but its body, represented by the party, appeared to believe another. And second, a ballot, as a real event and not just a rhetorical device, would help break through the wall of cynicism surrounding the voters. They were not impressed by words alone, they wanted actions and preferably actions involving conflict and opposition. Only then would they believe something had actually happened.

I first jotted down this idea in a note on 3 December 1995: 'We need a major new policy-based initiative in the spring. Words alone are not enough. They won't break though electoral scepticism and resistance. The best way of moving from words to action is to take our policy positions directly to the party, and win their support. It will kill the sense that the party and leadership are in a different place, and it will bring back the sense of crusade and mission we had with Clause IV.'[6] Three days later I wrote to Tony Blair directly: 'TB needs to go beyond rhetoric to action. This means, for example, taking a policy programme or statement directly to the party, overcoming opposition, winning their support.' Without conflict, I said, 'people are simply not convinced'.[7]

Later in the month I went to Blair's house for a polling meeting with Stan Greenberg. Blair at home is almost always the same: relaxed, friendly, casual. His children wander in and out of meetings. Once, at a weekend strategy meeting at his house, a series of loud and disconcerting noises emanated from a computer game which Euan was playing in the corner of the room. This was annoying other members of the meeting, but Blair didn't mind. He just ignored it. Sometimes Kathryn would wander in, asking for help with her homework. Cherie would often be there and would always be warm and supportive. Despite coping with the kids, coping with her job, coping with Tony, she still always finds time to be friendly. With Cherie there is no side: she is genuinely the person she appears to be.

On this occasion, Tony heard the polling and we discussed what we could do to bring the head and the body together. He had long been committed to direct consultation with the whole party membership and he decided – I think there and then – that balloting the early manifesto was the way forward. He had been searching for a mission for 1996, and this would be it.

On 19 December I wrote a longer end-of-year document – '1996: The Year Labour Changed Politics'. It was built on two premises: that the public still thought Labour a risk, and that Labour had 'to face and overcome a wall of cynicism'. I warned that Labour was not connecting with the electorate:

> In part this is because our positive messages in 1995 lacked the demons that give fire to our party reform messages: unions; nationalisation; old left. But it was mainly because our message now is not going beyond words to action as it did through [the abolition of] Clause IV. 'Modernisation of Labour' the message became 'modernisation of Labour' the fact. This illustrates a central truth of modern campaigning: that the scepticism of the electorate is now so advanced that words alone are not enough: message must be meshed with action.
>
> This means that we need a new approach to politics in which we actively engage the electorate, not talk to them as passive recipients of a message.

I called this new approach 'Partnership With the People'. Its centrepiece would be April–May onwards, 'when Labour takes its policies to the party and the people. The rhetoric of "partnership with the people" becomes reality. Labour takes its policy statement to the party and the country, not just listening but challenging and engaging. New Labour will achieve in 1996 with policy what it achieved with Clause IV in 1994.'[8]

'Partnership With the People' quickly became a central focus for our political strategy. In a note written in mid-January Tony Blair set out his strategy for 1996. He would write strategy notes every six weeks or so. This one said, 'We want to end by summer/autumn in the following position: a draft manifesto – "Partnership With the People" – which is effectively our contract with Britain. This should be a challenge to the party and to the country. It must be the campaign around which we hang policy, communication and maintain momentum. It should allow us to resolve any remaining policy positions; and be, in certain areas, both provocative and controversial. Besides "Partnership With the People", our attacking and positive messages should be honed, disseminated to the party and PLP and understood in the country.' He continued: 'We must definitely be New Labour, not old. A further raft of internal reform, if necessary, should be put together. Energy. Ideas. Vitality. The future not the past. We must be in the centre ground: the real one-nation party.' His note went on to outline New Labour's key themes and the 'attack on the Tories, depicting them as the party of the privileged few, not of ordinary people'. By hand Tony added: 'Most of all a complete and compelling dissection of their economic record. This is paramount.'[9]

It is difficult to believe the hours we spent discussing this note. Before we could move on to the plan we had to agree the note, and we never could. Sometimes we would get tantalisingly close, but we never quite made it. The note is not agreed even now, but it did contain two of the three defining themes of our election campaign – the future, not the past; the many, not the few – and the hours spent discussing strategy paid off in the end. We did – just about

– arrive at an agreed and tightly honed set of messages, but the process was endless, and is probably still not completed. At a meeting to discuss the referendum for an elected assembly in Wales after the election, the Prime Minister decided to give the participants a short seminar on the long and tortuous process of message development before the election campaign. 'It took hours and hours and hours of discussion to get it right,' he said. Long pause. 'And I am not sure we ever really finished it, or ever got it completely right.' I groaned. Alastair put his head in his hands, moaning, 'No more, no more.' This illustrates a central campaigning insight: the process is as important as the end-point. Often discussing a note is as important as the contents of the note itself.

The note also gave the green light to 'Partnership With the People', which Alastair turned into 'The Road to the Manifesto'. This was agreed by the NEC on 27 March 1996, and announced to a surprised press conference immediately afterwards. It was breaking new ground for a party to put its manifesto (even in early form) to a plebiscite of its members. But the idea had its roots in the very first note Tony wrote in his leadership campaign, when he called for ballots of the whole membership on policy issues. 'The Road to the Manifesto' was a series of policy statements and initiatives. Robin Cook was delegated to write it, and David Miliband used to meet him regularly to discuss its contents. Sometimes I would attend too. We met in Robin's Parliament Street office and went through a long and involved drafting process. I had no responsibility for policy, I dealt with message and thematic structure. In the end it was largely Blair who wrote it, working from Cook's draft.

The document, launched on 4 July 1996, was called 'New Life for Britain', a title invented by Alastair Campbell as he sat with me in a bar on a long beach in Majorca. As usual Alastair was sitting in the shade complaining about the sun. On holiday he is a creature of habit, liking to sit in the same place, wearing the same clothes, drinking a huge mug of tea. But he does write brilliant political lines – and very quickly.

The night before its launch Peter Mandelson, David

Miliband and I were up most of the night proof-checking 'New Life for Britain' in a design studio besides the Thames. We also did some last-minute rewriting. The most difficult decision was whether or not to include stakeholding as a section heading. Stakeholding had fallen out of fashion somewhat, but for reasons of continuity we felt it better to keep it in.

'New Life for Britain' was Labour's early manifesto, but it had another important element: after some struggle, it contained Labour's 'five pledges', later to become the centre-piece of our election campaign.

The pledges

The pledges had no single point of origin. They emerged over many months, following literally scores of meetings with politicians and dozens of focus groups. In one sense they emerged almost by accident. For about a year I had been taking out to focus groups rough summary copies of what I estimated rival manifestos would say. I anticipated the Conservative pledges would be: a referendum on the EU; no social chapter; no minimum wage; 'two strikes and you're out'; a grammar school in every town. Labour's, I guessed, would include more bobbies on the beat, cutting waiting lists and reducing class sizes. The Conservative one would be populist and right-wing; Labour's would contain very simple, very basic claims. After a while I noticed that the simpler the claim, the more powerful the communication. People wanted smaller promises that they could believe in, not larger ones which seemed incredible. I also found that if we said how the promise would be paid for, the power of the pledge was enhanced enormously. As our policy developed, we tested and re-tested it, with rival manifestos, until gradually the core promises began to emerge.

Although this was interesting, it was not taking us anywhere. The true parent of the pledge was Peter Hyman. Hyman had been a research assistant for Gordon Brown, then Donald Dewar, before working for Tony Blair. He was a communications zealot; obsessed with campaigning. He thought David Miliband and I lived in a world of abstract indulgence: stakeholding, one nation and renewal were all well and good, but they would butter no voting parsnips. We needed messages that were stark, clear and populist. Above all, we needed an offer: something concrete, tangible and desirable that we could hold out to the voter to match the Tories' promise of tax cuts. He was obsessed with this. For weeks he could talk about little but 'the offer'. Hyman says: 'Up against tax cuts it was not good enough to say merely your health and education may get better, you may have a more decent society. We needed to give people an offer. We needed to get people to say, "I want that; I will go out and vote for that," and "I can see what it is, and it is achievable, and it is costed".'[10] Hyman's relentless pursuit of populist communications paid off. In the election campaign it was us and not the Tories who had the simple messages and an offer people really wanted to hear.

Hyman and I both knew, therefore, that to break through the barriers of distrust we had to offer the electorate a simple contract: elect me and if, in five years' time, I have not delivered, then sack me. In developing the pledges there was constant interplay between Peter, myself, David Miliband and Matthew Taylor, head of policy for the Labour Party. The actual wording took weeks to agree, and Hyman spent hours developing alternatives. He recalls:

> First of all, there were many more than the five final pledges which we dropped either for good policy reasons or because the shadow Cabinet member wasn't happy defending them. Although the pledges seemed very simple, we needed to come at them from a hell of a lot of different angles: would outside experts think they were do-able? Were they do-able for the costs? Would the Tories attack them in the election campaign? Would they just fall apart? We had endless meetings in Tony's room, with Gordon and you [Gould] and Peter, going through exactly the arguments, what was feasible, could you get waiting lists down by more than that, was thirty and under exactly the right wording. There were a hell of a lot of considerations.[11]

The pledges were tested exhaustively. Four were agreed fairly early on: class sizes, jobs for the young, fast-track punishment, and cutting waiting times. The fifth was the problem. I tested several options: the university of industry, help for small businesses, cutting the starting rate of tax to 10p, a pledge that we would be tough on the economy, or just having four pledges instead of five.

I strongly favoured a pledge promising toughness on the economy. In a memo of 6 June 1996 I noted, 'The last ten groups have all shown a marked increase in economic optimism.' I also wrote that MORI had recorded a massive 19 per cent increase in economic optimism among switchers to Labour: 'There is no doubt that economic optimism among our core target is rising rapidly and is slowly affecting their vote.' I argued that 'The Road to the Manifesto' document should offer 'tough targets; financial discipline; no uncosted promises; prudence tax restraint . . . there is a case for a genuinely bold and startling manifesto commitment in the money area . . . a kind of mini-Clause IV for financial competence . . . Even if this is not done, the fifth pledge must be a money pledge. 10p [starting rate of tax] is our best offer but financial prudence is even more important.' Polling confirmed these instincts. 'The economic-prudence pledge provided massive reassurance, almost physical relief,' I wrote. 'Every respondent selected this as their first pledge.'[12] People wanted to be able to trust Labour on the economy.

I was pushing at an open door. Gordon Brown was obsessive about financial prudence and his adviser Ed Balls drafted the last pledge. This was not easy, and took dozens of drafts, but it was finally agreed: 'Labour will set tough rules for government spending and borrowing; ensure low inflation; strengthen the economy so that interest rates are as low as possible.'[13] Inelegant, possibly, but a quantum leap from where we had been in 1992, and a crucial building-block for election success. We also ensured that each of the pledges included details of how it would be paid for, which was as important in reassuring the public as the pledge itself. People took our promises much more seriously when they knew we could pay for them. Reassurance, reassurance, reassurance.

As early as June 1996 we were testing a pledge not to raise income tax, but Gordon did not want to show his hand until much later. For the later election pledge card we included our commitment not to increase income tax, and we inserted in the advertising a promise to hold a referendum on membership of the European single currency. This eliminated another attack the Tories were planning to use. An increasingly Euro-sceptical Tory party would no longer be able to accuse Labour of 'selling out' British sovereignty. Tony Blair was slowly reappropriating Labour's patriotic heritage.

The pledges worked better than anything else I have ever tested in politics. Nothing else came close. They worked because they connected immediately to people's lives; because they were relatively small, which gave them credibility; because they were costed; and because they were an explicit contract between the voter and Tony Blair. The fact that it was he who made the promise, he who offered the contract, added enormously to their power.

But although people loved them, politicians and media commentators did not take to them easily. The idea met with enormous resistance. Politicians just didn't see their point. They thought they were too small, too insignificant to base an election campaign on. But they missed the point: to the voters they represented substantial and real improvement in their lives. The fate of the pledges hung in the balance for weeks, until eventually it was decided to give them a go. Even then they were called 'early' pledges because the politicians wanted to make clear that other promises would be made later. They were finally turned into a credit-card-sized pledge card, with a picture of Tony Blair on one side and the pledges on the other. The card also included the crucial words: 'Keep this card, and see that we keep our promises.' Margaret McDonagh had first seen a card like this when she was working on the Clinton campaign in California. It was used to support 'Proposition 186' in a state referendum on health care. It had the four benefits of voting yes on the back. Peter Hyman went on to develop the card idea, and BMP made a mock-up. McDonagh still keeps the 'Proposition 186' card in her wallet.

The pledges survived months of relentless attack by the Conservatives, who were unable to break them down. Now they are central to government. They are being used by the people and the media to hold the government to account, which is how it should be. When Labour meets the pledges, a contract will have been kept, trust in politics restored a little.

Some people may be horrified that it required so much research to find out what people wanted, but they misunderstand. For election after election Labour has offered better hospitals, better schools, more jobs, but it has never been believed. The issue is not the promise, but *making the promise credible*. What research revealed was that the public wanted smaller, more concrete pledges, they wanted them costed and they wanted them presented in the form of an accountable contract. The result was more honesty, less fudge, more trust. Much of the media sneered, but it was the electorate who showed common sense and maturity, and I am glad they were consulted.

The pledges were included at the end of 'New Life for Britain'. Peter Hyman was furious. As far as he was concerned, they were the only real point of the document and they were buried at the back. He was right, and his fury continued unabated for some days. Peter was often furious, which is a good thing – good campaigners need passion and anger, and Peter is a very good campaigner. His desk was close to mine at Millbank. It was always surrounded by monstrous piles of discarded documents and memos. He would rush back and forth feverishly between my staff and the advertising executives with new ideas, new strap-lines, new visuals; that is, when he wasn't hurling derogatory comments at the latest Tory spokesman defending the indefensible on the news.

In its way 1996 was the year Labour changed British

politics. The pledges have established a new pattern which will not be broken: hard, concrete, accountable promises that are, effectively, a binding contract with the electorate; manifestos not just agreed by a few politicians in smoke-filled rooms but agreed by the party. This is the way of the future, it is the way trust in politics will be restored. But in 1996 trust in Labour was still not secured. Labour had had other problems on the home – and school – front.

'Why should we trust you?'

Harriet Harman's decision to send her son to the selective St Olave's school in Orpington, Kent came after Tony Blair had chosen to send his sons to the 'opted-out', grant-maintained London Oratory. That Blair sent his children to a grant-maintained school was an issue, but not as big a one as commentators made out. In any event the controversy missed the point. As Blair put it later, it was not an eleven-year-old boy who had destroyed our education system, but a seventeen-year-old government. Some people thought he was being hypocritical, but many, including – crucially – most of our core group of previously Conservative voters now considering voting Labour, thought it demonstrated a commitment to parental choice in education. What the public thought or said on this matter did not influence Blair. He and Cherie wanted their children to go to religious state schools, and the one they and their teachers thought would be best was the Oratory. Blair knew the choice would be unpopular, but he was determined to do it anyway. This is a vital part of his character as a politician: he follows his instincts, and damns the consequences. And his instincts are, by and large, the people's instincts. He connects to a rich vein of empirical common sense that has always been central to the British people. Once his mind is made up, almost nothing can change it. Alastair Campbell and others warned him that sending Euan to the Oratory could lead to media attack, but he would not be swayed. He thought it was the right thing to do.

Harriet Harman was in a different position. One of her children was already at the Oratory, which was just within the bounds of public and party acceptability, but sending her second son to a grammar school crossed a different line. Opposition to grammar schools was an act of faith for Labour, and the idea of selection at eleven was anathema to almost everyone in the party. Many, probably a majority of even Blair's office, thought she was wrong.

When the decision was announced on 19 January it led to a media firestorm. I was in Blair's outer office the evening that media and party baying was at its height. The atmosphere was all gloom. Enormous pressure was building for Harman to go. She had little support except from Peter Mandelson, myself and a few others who felt that if she went, New Labour lost. A signal would be sent to every voter in the land that Labour punishes parents who want the best for their kids. Blair asked me in to see him. We were alone. He sat on his sofa, tie loosened, feet on the table. Should she go or should she stay, he asked. It was a rhetorical question: he had already made up his mind. I said, 'She has to stay. We cannot allow old Labour to win.' This was his view too, and nothing, not the combined forces of every paper and every member of the PLP, would shift him from it. He had said he would not compromise and he meant it.

The focus groups were bad. In one meeting, on 22 January 1996, all eight members of the group thought Harriet Harman had done the right thing as a mother, but six out of the eight thought she had done the wrong thing as a politician. As Harriet remarked poignantly, 'It's easier to go through the eye of a needle than be a good mother and a good politician.'[14] I wrote, 'The damage to us is: honesty; trust; sincerity.' There was immediate damage to Blair: words like 'insincere' were being used to describe him, which had not happened for a long time.[15] I phoned Blair at home to tell him. He always insisted on getting bad news immediately. He was philosophical and said simply, 'Why can't people get a sense of perspective? This is just a mother sending her son to a state school.' The findings did not influence his course of action one jot. He had decided to stand by Harriet, he believed that to be right and that is what he did.

I thought we had been feeble in our response to the attacks. I wrote on 28 January to Blair and Brown, 'There are a lot of lessons to be learned from last week, but the most immediate was that once again, under real pressure, our message crumpled and we failed to retaliate effectively . . . If we do not fight [the continual Tory attacks], they will work and once again the electorate will awake blinking on a Friday morning not quite believing that they have elected them again . . . We are not tough enough, not hard enough, not brutal enough.' We had to fight back, accusing them of trying to hide their failure as a government behind spurious attacks on Labour front-benchers, I said, suggesting the following line of defence: 'As a parent Harriet Harman is making the best of a bad system; in government she will make sure all children get the best. What Britain needs is more politicians who face the real dilemmas of daily life, because they are best able to change the lives of ordinary people.'[16] But this was a week too late. I was too slow, we were all too slow. We failed to get our retaliation in first.

The spring continued to go badly for us. There was persistent sniping about Blair from disgruntled Labour MPs; growing resentment over the power of his office and 'spin-doctors'; some fierce and well-directed attacks by Major on whether New Labour would be 'tough on hypocrisy, tough on the causes of hypocrisy'.[17] Then, finally, came the resignation of Joy Johnson as Director of Campaigns and Communications. The only stories in the press were about splits and policy U-turns. By the beginning of March we were running into very choppy water. I wrote a note on 3 March called 'Fighting Back: Step by Step', trying to bolster confidence. Most of the campaign team were getting disheartened. Alastair Campbell was fed up. 'We are not in tailspin,' I said, 'we are not falling apart; we have taken a hit; and we are going to win.' And: 'Perseverance: we have to just battle this bad patch.'[18] The knock-on effects of Harriet Harman's decision had still not gone away a month later, when I broke the period down into two phases: 'Phase 1: Pre-Harman – very positive: mood almost matched Clause IV period. Stake-holding positively received. Phase 2: Post-Harman – breakdown in trust. TB not listened to with the same confidence. New Labour: just another party.'[19]

And while the voters continued to question whether they could trust us, we did even more to unsettle them. Clare Short was reported as saying on GMTV's *Sunday* programme on 14 April 1996 that 'under a fairer tax system people like her would pay a bit more tax'.[20] This shot through the elec-torate like a forest fire. On 1 May I summarised two groups conducted in Watford. 'These groups confirm the shift in mood against Labour since the Clare Short tax controversy,' I wrote. 'When prompted, everybody knows about the remarks of Clare Short. Several people believed that Clare Short had said that people earning £30,000 would be clobbered. The issue here is about trust as much as tax levels.'[21]

The voters were also confused by our announcement on 19 April that we were considering the abolition of child benefit for children over sixteen. I attended the meeting at which it was agreed that this was the correct thing to do: it sent out a tough, strong message. But it was a risk. I supported the decision completely and still do. Gordon Brown thought it essential to make and demonstrate tough choices. Unless we did this we would never be taken seriously on the economy. It was the right decision, but it was not popular.

By mid-May the voters were worried about splits within the Labour Party. In a note to Peter Mandelson I wrote: 'We are now in the most serious situation that we have faced since Tony became leader. If we continue to implode and disintegrate we can still lose.'[22] The first real evidence of economic improvement in June created a further increase in doubts about Labour: on 6 June I warned that these were two sides of the same coin – as things got better, people were more aware of the risk of Labour.[23] Opinion polling confirmed this trend. On 29 July Stan Greenberg wrote a report on a Labour Party poll conducted the month before: 'The survey does suggest some slippage in Labour's support over the last three months. On party identification Labour has lost 3 per cent of its net advantage . . . intense negative feelings about the Conservatives are down sharply: "cool" sentiments have dropped from 60 per cent to 53 per cent . . . There was also weakening of support within the Labour voting block, and that too is worth paying attention to. Intense support has fallen off somewhat.' The drop-off of Labour's vote and intense support was concentrated in 'volatile segments of the electorate', he said – voters under forty-five, and women. And central to the weakening in Labour's support was the strengthening economy: 'The changing perceptions of the economy are real, substantial and important strategically. An increasing number of people believe the economy is strong and a declining number describe it as weak.' This was a 'pretty dramatic change from April: an 18 per cent swing towards those thinking the economy is strong'.[24]

On the same day I reported on two focus groups among Conservative switchers to Labour, which confirmed a continuing trend back to the Tories:

> The economy has improved a little . . . people are frightened of losing the small gains they have made. In effect they are saying: 'Now that we are off the floor and things are a little better, we have something to lose, and Labour may put that at risk' . . . This small improvement colours their view of Labour. They are now far more likely to talk about Labour's past. They are convinced Labour failed economically in government. They think interest rates and taxes soared. That Britain under Labour was a bleak, strike-ridden place. Almost a kind of dark age for Britain. (This is not an exaggeration: a myth has developed about Labour in the past.) This makes a future Labour government a risk. Everybody in these groups thought taxes and interest rates would go up under Labour.[25]

The local election results on 3 May were good but not spectacular: Labour's share of the vote was actually down two to three points, the Conservatives up, and the Liberal

Democrats marginally up. But the changed political weather was not going to deter Blair. The next day, in an interview with the *Independent*'s Tony Bevins, he positioned Labour right on Conservative turf: 'Politics will alter dramatically in the next few years. But I cannot foresee exactly what shape it will take. There is no doubt that if we continue to occupy the centre ground, if we become the one-nation political party, if we attract support from the centre as well as the centre-left, then we will be able to benefit significantly. Many Conservatives have probably got a lot more in common with us than with those who have taken over their own party.'[26]

On 15 May Blair dismissed talk of splits as 'tittle-tattle'.[27] But it was clear that this was a period of potential danger for New Labour. The economy was improving, doubts about Labour growing, 'better the devil you know' was becoming almost a mantra in the groups. We were vulnerable in the spring and early summer, but the situation was to get worse. In high summer Labour came under massive internal attack and the Tories moved in for the kill. The battle was joined: would the New Labour line hold?

Demon eyes

'SHORT FLAYS BLAIR'S "DARK MEN"' ran the *Guardian* head-line on 8 August. 'Clare Short, the controversial shadow Cabinet minister, last night accused her leader's advisers of jeopardising Labour's chances of victory at the General Election and threatening its existence,' the article began.[28] Her accusations had been made in an interview with the *New Statesman*, in which she focused on 'Blair's misguided strategy'. She described his advisers as 'the people in the dark', whose 'obsession with media and focus groups is making us look as if we want power at any price'. She said, 'These people are making a terrible error. They think that Labour is unelectable, so they want to get something else elected, even though really it's still the Labour Party. This is a dangerous game which assumes people are stupid . . . They are saying, "Vote for Tony Blair's New Labour. We all agree that the old one was absolutely appalling and you all know that most of the people in Labour are really the old one, but we've got some who are nothing to do with that, vote for us!" One, it's a lie. And two, it's dangerous.'[29]

It wasn't an isolated attack. The week before, Joy Johnson had attacked Tony Blair in the *New Statesman* for his use of 'stilted language', like 'young country', 'the British dream', and 'stakeholding'. She continued, 'For New Labour it is time to drop the "new"' and start 'speaking the language of the people'.[30] On 28 July Ken Livingstone, writing in the *Mail on Sunday*, compared Labour under Blair to 'the old Soviet Union'.[31] Roy Hattersley joined in, writing in the *Observer* on Sunday 11 August that 'Miss Short's attack rightly or wrongly reflected what a lot of rank and file members are thinking . . . There are immense dangers in dismissing all that happened before the spring of 1994 as based on an outdated ideology which had nothing to do with New Labour.'[32]

The Conservatives reacted immediately with the most famous advertisement of the campaign. It appeared on the same Sunday in the *News of the World*, the *Mail on Sunday* and *Sunday Times*, and portrayed Tony Blair with red, demonic eyes, alongside the caption: 'One of Labour's leaders, Clare Short, says dark forces behind Tony Blair manipulate party policy in a sinister way.'

I heard about Clare Short's interview and the 'Demon Eyes' advertisement while I was on holiday in France. I thought the interview was a problem, but the Conservative advertisement an over-reaction. When Alastair Campbell came to visit us on holiday I put a copy of it outside so he could find the house. Alastair was not in good humour. He was having the holiday from hell, having given up his lovely house in Flassan for a cheaper one further north, which was noisy and had its entry barred by two dangerous dogs. On top of that, Fiona was ill. He was furious about everything. He thought the advertisement was effective, and said Tony was worried about it. He recalls, 'The holiday from hell was very difficult. It was the low point. I felt that you can do so much, but there are plenty of people out there who can undo it.'[33]

Back in London, Peter Mandelson was having to cope with it all. From France, I imagined him padding round his Millbank office, shoes off, phone glued to his ear, barking orders with his eyes fixed on the TV. His immediate instinct, which was the right one, was to react and not to ignore it. His strategy was to twist the advertisement from being a depiction of the dark and sinister forces behind Tony Blair, into portraying Tony Blair as satanic, which was incredible and would rebound on the Conservatives. For this he needed a bishop to condemn it. Peter Hyman discovered that the Bishop of Oxford was outraged by the advert and had put out a strong quote condemning the Tories for accusing Blair of being the devil. Hyman faxed it to Campbell, who said it was the one thing to make him smile that holiday. The advertisement was immediately rebranded on our terms. Not sinister forces manipulating Blair, but the desperate Tories labelling Blair as the devil. Ironically, Saatchi's now say that the eyes behind Blair were supposed to be Mandelson's, but he was too quick for them to be able to establish this.

Mandelson's strategy was high-risk. It made the advertisement famous, handing millions of pounds of free publicity to the Conservatives, and was considered internally and externally to be a mistake. Many in Millbank thought we should have kept quiet about it. It led *Campaign* magazine to give 'Demon Eyes' the award for advertisement of the year. But Peter was right and his critics wrong. Blair manipulated by sinister advisers ran the risk of being believed if the Tories were able to press it home; Blair as the devil did not. It positioned the advertisement to the British people in a way that was implausible and offensive. They felt a line had been crossed, and it began to make them angry: if all the Conservatives could offer the British people was an advertisement depicting Tony Blair as the devil, then they were not worth re-electing.

At the time, the advertisement appeared to be the highpoint for the Conservatives and Saatchi's in the campaign, but in fact it was the point at which their advertising and communications strategy was exposed as terminally flawed. They should never have conceded New Labour was a reality, they should have been apologising not attacking, and they should have claimed the credit for the economic recovery.

In France, Alastair, Fiona and his children moved in with us for a few days to escape the dogs. The mood was strange. Peter Mandelson was engaged in trench warfare with the Tories, but for us it was the final interlude before war began. We discussed the conference speech a little, but did not get very far. All Alastair wanted was to get back, to get into the fight. He was intensely frustrated about his aborted holiday and the situation at home. He spoke to Tony Blair once or twice and to Peter Mandelson every couple of days. I was calling Mandelson often, but when you are so far away it is hard to give useful advice. Peter felt under extraordinary pressure, dealing with a serious crisis while almost every other senior politician and campaign member was away. Once or twice his voice sounded strained, although he was clearly relishing the fight.

At our house in France that summer, though, the mood was glum. Alastair wanted to leave early and at five one morning he drove off with his family to start the journey home. There was a sadness about his departure, a sense that before us was the battle to decide all our futures. After years of waiting, it was upon us.

'Better the devil you know'

When I got back, posters were up spelling out New Labour's pledges. They were not inspired but they did what was required: they helped to brand us as the positive party, the Tories as negative and destructive. Mandelson had had a controversial summer, but he had been strategically skilful. The first twelve groups I did after the holiday showed 'a strong and probably strengthening resistance to the government'.[34] Labour had survived the assault. The conference that year was disciplined and brilliantly orchestrated. Margaret McDonagh did a superb job. Blair's speech received an extraordinary response. The theme of 'Labour's Coming Home' tapped cleverly into the feel-good mood engendered by England's soccer success in Euro '96 but, more to the point, fused directly with my sense that Labour had finally reconnected to the people it was created to represent. As in the previous year, the leadership was not defeated once. This was due to the extraordinary work of John Cruddas, assistant to Tom Sawyer, Pat McFadden, from Blair's political office, and Sally Morgan, who were in charge of political relations with trade unions and the party. They have a fixed way of working which is to say, perhaps three months before conference, that every vote will be lost, before gradually conceding that we have the chance with the odd one or two, before eventually winning every vote. John Cruddas is the master of this: he turns pessimism into an art form. The Conservatives also had a good conference, with John Major looking relaxed in a shirt-sleeved question-and-answer session, and the lead narrowed. In a post-conference evaluation document I wrote, 'The Conservatives are recovering on the back of the economy . . . but they will not recover to victory. There is a vast constituency of voters out there who are sick of the Conservatives, want change. They will see the Tories out.' I wanted to make people perceive the Tories as a risk: 'Transferring the burden of risk to them is the key to victory.' We had to build a 'devastating fifth-term campaign . . . A Major fifth term must not be allowed to become a comfortable option.'[35]

Late autumn saw doubts growing again about Labour, and also about Tony Blair. This may have been a consequence of the 'Demon Eyes' attack, but more probably it was just that he had now been leader for over two years and the electorate had got used to him. We had always been concerned about this. The long three-year period leading up to the election gave time for voters' normal cynicism to return. This was most pronounced among women: on 28 November I wrote, 'Women are far more nervous of Labour, appear to have less idea of what we will do, are more sceptical of our promises . . . The problem for us is that they see the election in terms of a single dimension: a contrast between the Tory record, and the threat of a Labour government.' I argued that the answer to this was to pose the threat of a Conservative fifth term, for when women were confronted with the prospect of a Conservative fifth term they were 'shocked or dismayed at the prospect of them getting back. The change in the dynamic produced by this shift to the Tory future is remarkable. Women who were drifting back to the Tories came straight back to us. This is not just a question of fifth-term fear, it is an issue of incumbency. As long as we allow the re-election of the Tories to be a gap in the voters' minds, we are allowing ourselves to be painted as incumbents once again, they escape as the challengers.'[36] Findings like this led to a series of meetings arranged by Sally Morgan and Anji Hunter, including Liz Lloyd from the policy unit, that focused specially on the concerns and anxieties of women. This linked to other initiatives including the 'Winning Words' campaign of Clare Short, Patricia Hewitt, Deborah Mattinson and Carmen Callil that tried to develop language that women could relate to. Women were always a central priority in the campaign. This paid off: the gender gap was closed.

Although I wanted to use fifth-term attacks, Tony Blair and Gordon Brown were uneasy: they wanted to fight the Tories on their record, what they had done, not what they might do in the future. Blair was also beginning to feel that we needed to become more positive and less negative in our campaigning. His speech to the Commonwealth Parliamentary Union in South Africa, fleshing out his conference speech idea of the 'decent society', was part of that positive programme.[37] Most of all, he was concerned about the tenor of our advertising, being prepared to accept the attacking posters of the forthcoming spring, but wanting to move ultimately to using positive advertising. His instincts told him the nation wanted it. We seasoned campaigners used to scoff at him for this, but in the end we came round to his point of view. Brown also held a fixed campaigning belief that every attack had to be balanced by a positive initiative

– otherwise the media would not use it and the voter would resist it. Negative messages needed positive messages to make them work. The Conservatives would have done well to heed this advice. In the end we compromised. We would start the year with the launch of a positive policy document and then move into a major fifth-term attack.

Thus the new year began with the launch of a new policy document, 'Leading Britain into the Future', and our fifth-term attack based around VAT on food, with a poster showing an egg being smashed. Both Blair and Brown disliked this poster and were relieved when it came down. Even Alastair Campbell lost faith in it. But it worked. It pushed the Tories on to the defensive on tax; Kenneth Clarke was forced to come out and rebut it. At the same time the Tories attacked us with a new advertising campaign, using a blood-red tear, and slogans like 'New Labour, New Mortgage Risk'. But it was lame – light-years away from the potency of 1992's 'Tax Bombshell'.

In the event none of this mattered to the electorate. It passed them by completely. On 9 January I wrote, 'There was almost no awareness of the campaigning initiatives of Monday, Tuesday, Wednesday. Even when shown coverage of these events people were unable to recall them.' However, a sense of '"Better the devil you know" was widespread. Typical comments were: "I am frightened about a leap in the dark"; "I feel comfortable now"; "Can I move to what I don't know?"'[38]

With less than four months to go before the most likely date of a General Election the voters were still nervous: it was time to deal with tax.

Winning the tax war

Tax was central to our strategy of reassurance. If the election campaign had one crucial battle, one defining fight, it was over tax. We lost the 1992 election and won the 1997 one in large part because of tax. Tony Blair and Gordon Brown both believed the shadow Budget in 1992 had been a mistake:

it revealed our hand and raised taxes for middle-income earners. Brown had thought the basic election strategy wrong: he believed we should have focused remorselessly on the recession – 'It's the economy, stupid'. For three years he had been arguing persistently that we shouldn't make public expenditure commitments which could only be met by increased taxation. Once he became shadow Chancellor under John Smith, there was never any doubt that Labour's tax and economic positions would change.

Reforming tax-and-spend was the central modernising task at the time. It was not simply a question of tactics or election strategy, but a matter of political principle: it was simply wrong. Brown and Blair thought the idea of solving problems by spending money raised through taxes was unsustainable in a modern global economy. It was impossible to compete and succeed if tax increased continually as a proportion of GNP. In the long run, sustainable additional resources for education and health had to come through reducing the cost of welfare, increasing investment to increase the rate of growth, through 'save and invest' not tax and spend. Blair had joined Brown in sounding the death-knell for old-style Labour economics in his 1995 Mais lecture when he said, 'No one wants a return to penal taxation, and of course the objective of any government is to lower rather than increase the tax burden on ordinary families.'[39] Blair and Brown had a gut feeling that hard-working families paid enough tax; why should they pay any more? Paul Keating, when he was Australian Prime Minister, once told Blair, 'Whatever you do, promise you will not go into the election promising to raise income tax.'[40] Stanley Greenberg explains why tax is so important:

Taxation was the symbol of an out-of-control Labour Party. When Labour was last in government a vast array of things were out of control. Public spending, strikes and taxes were symbols of that, and were the way people felt it most directly. And just for voters to hear Labour say that it would not raise taxes and – probably more importantly – hear Labour attack the Tories for their twenty-two tax rises, says to them that this is a Labour Party which understands the financial burdens of the ordinary citizens, this is a Labour Party that is able to rein in government spending and operate within limits. And therefore this is a Labour party that will not jeopardise the living standards of mainstream Britain.[41]

Soon after the 1992 election Brown scrapped the shadow Budget and began reassuring the public on Labour's economic competence and its tax plans. Helped by massive tax increases piled on to the electorate by the Tories in their first post-election budget, we slowly began to win the battle. For five years Brown largely took this upon himself; it was our most daunting task, our toughest issue. It put him under massive pressure: after the 1997 election he looked a different man, as if a weight had been lifted from his shoulders.

My first big meeting with Brown after the 1992 election was in spring 1993. He had publicly ditched Labour's election manifesto tax-and-spend plans in November, and the Tories' reputation for economic competence had been severely damaged by their forced withdrawal from the ERM and the tax increases they had introduced in Norman Lamont's March Budget of 1993, which had introduced the largest tax rise in peacetime history. Lamont also slapped VAT on fuel, something the Tories had explicitly ruled out during the 1992 election campaign. Brown had launched a series of withering attacks under the theme, 'You Can't Trust the Tories'. In a large conference room in 1 Parliament Street, where Brown used to have his office, next door to Tony Blair, I met with Brown's economic team and representatives from Butterfield Day Devito Hockney, Labour's advertising agency at the time.

Across a large table were sprawled dozens of advertisements and posters depicting various ways of attacking the Tories on tax. Our problem was that there was no consistency; we had no one way of describing the Tory tax increases. Some advertisements suggested income per family per week, others per year; some, total tax increase; one included a multitude of different designations. I remember saying angrily that we had to agree on one line of attack and one way of depicting the Conservative tax increase. I wanted revenge for 1992; I said we should take their 'Tax Bombshell' poster and ram it down their throats.

Our goal was to put the government on the defensive about tax increases as well as presenting an alternative to their policies, but throughout the summer and autumn we had trouble getting our message through. In June we were still considered untrustworthy and irrelevant; Labour's support was losing ground in the face of the Conservative betrayal, because of a feeling that we would do worse. We needed, I said in a note on 22 June, 'a complete party identity that suggests greater economic competence' and 'sensible, plausible, non-penalising policies, particularly in the area of tax'. I added, 'Nothing is as important as the message. Message development and delivery are Labour's greatest long-term failing, particularly in the economic area.'[42] The situation hadn't improved by September 1993: two focus groups in Northwood Hills, north London, showed women were angry, but believed a new Tory leader would rectify the situation. Men believed the economy was recovering. They showed no awareness of Labour's attacking arguments. 'Those respondents with direct experience of economic uplift had already drifted back to the Conservatives,' I wrote. 'Both groups preferred an improved performance by the Conservatives to the upheaval of a new government.' Our economic message was being impeded by cynicism about politicians in general and Labour in particular, 'a view that Labour is for the unemployed, the poor, and not for ordinary people in work'.[43] I wanted to develop a continuing theme – 'You Can't Trust the Tories' – with two specific examples to back it up: VAT on fuel and £8.50-a-week Tory tax increases. In October a group in Harlow insisted they had 'no choice' but to vote Conservative; they could not run the risk to their personal finances of a Labour vote. The ERM débâcle would have been handled 'much worse' by Labour, they believed. 'It would have been a disaster,' said one.[44]

During the winter of 1993–94 and the next spring, Brown took huge strides in transforming our position on tax, relentlessly attacking the Tories for breaking their election promises, accusing them of hypocrisy and beginning to position Labour as the sensible spending party. He had drawn up plans to cut VAT on domestic fuel to 5 per cent and proposed public–private partnership extending into hospitals and schools. Yet when I conducted focus group research in July 1994, I found not only resentment and anger at the Tory tax increases, but the belief: 'Still, after all this, Labour will raise taxes more.'[45] And at the beginning of the following year, despite Tony Blair's election as leader, quantitative research showed the position getting worse, not better: in February 1994 Gallup had 58 per cent believing taxes would rise under Labour; by early 1995 it had risen to 65 per cent.[46] We still had a long way to go.

Throughout the spring and summer of 1994, as Labour announced it would not reverse any tax cuts brought in by the Tories before the next election and Brown began to set himself up as the financially prudent 'Iron Chancellor', I worked on developing an economic message. The Tories had come to be seen as the party of the rich and privileged, and not of the working majority. But 'support for Labour remains soft', I wrote on 14 July; 'fear of reversion to old Labour remains strong; tax cuts and an expanding economy will pull significant numbers back to the Tories'.[47] I warned that the number of voters not trusting us on tax and the improving economy were forming the basis for both a Tory recovery and their future election campaign. We had to give ourselves economic credibility, I urged.

That autumn I warned Brown we still had taxation problems: 'Large numbers think that a higher-rate band, even when set at £100,000, is a tax on success. And there is a deep-seated unease with such a tax: to many it seems punitive rather than fair. Almost all voters think that although they believe Labour should oppose Tory tax cuts, if they do . . . they will lose the election.'[48] And 50 per cent of people still believed Labour would put up everyone's taxes. Economic optimism under the Tories was also beginning to rise.

We had been trying to undermine people's confidence in

the economy, using the device of Britain slipping to eighteenth place in the league table of national wealth. But as the economy appeared to strengthen, this claim lost credibility and Brown felt it impossible to communicate fundamental weakness in the face of the public's growing economic optimism. I wanted to continue to attack on the real economy, but Brown and his team felt they had to move on to a new strategy of making trust the key issue that divided the parties. If the public trusted Labour, then however economically confident they became they would still feel safe switching to us. Labour would float up with the economy.

Gradually a strategy began to take shape. For the last year before the election, almost all of our advertising and broadcasts featured tax in some form. In May 1996 we launched 'The Tories Hit You Where It Hurts', a poster featuring a twisted man with money falling out of his pocket and a PPB with a giant smashing up the country. The summer saw 'Same Old Tories, Same Old Lies' – posters carrying a red warning triangle. In September our first pledge posters went up. Just before we launched the 'Enough is Enough' campaign at the end of November, focus groups in Bury and Bolton showed deep mistrust of the Tories over tax, although it was still linked to anxiety about Labour on the same issue: we had moved on, but not enough. 'The improving economy is by far our largest problem,' I wrote. 'Better the devil you know' was still a common comment.[49]

In November 1996 the Conservatives attacked us with a new 'tax bombshell' campaign. Conservative Central Office re-ran their 1992 formula by producing a hundred-page document listing all Labour's alleged spending pledges and costing the total at £30 billion, which they translated into £1,200 a year in tax for the average family. The *Daily Telegraph* and *Newsnight* had warned the night before that it was to happen, and we were prepared. The document was rushed back from the Westminster launch to Millbank. There it was instantly distributed to all the relative policy personnel, who had facts and figures waiting to rebut it. 'When the Tories threw the tax bombshell at us, that showed Millbank at its best,' remembers Liam Byrne, a management consultant who had been seconded to Labour. 'All the politicians were there. People divided up the labour very quickly. Everyone processed a little bit. They brought it back together and rebutted it within three hours.'[50] The Tories launched their document in the morning, and by the time we called a press conference that afternoon the *Evening Standard* carried the headline: 'TORY TAX BOMB LANDS ON TORIES'.[51] 'That was when Central Office first faltered seriously,' says Byrne. 'They threw this stuff at us that had clearly been supported by the full mighty weight of the British Civil Service, and this small band at Millbank took it, caught it and turned it around within hours. They had the line ready for the early evening news. It was poetry in motion. It was tremendously exciting.'[52] We hit back again with '22 Tory Tax Rises Since 1992', a poster showing grabbing hands with the line, 'Enough is Enough', and, following the Budget at the end of the month, a poster proclaiming, 'Still £2,120 Worse Off Under the Tories – Enough is Enough.'

Our attacks were gaining ground, but we still had to deal with the problem of trust: the only way we were ever going to reassure the voters was to unveil our tax plans. There was never any question whether the basic rate should rise; it would have been political suicide. As far back as November 1995, Brown had announced proposals to drop the basic rate to 10p 'when affordable'.[53] That left only the top rate. Throughout 1995 and 1996 I conducted regular focus groups on this issue and the findings were always the same: people were wary of any increase in the top rate. When I suggested to respondents at a group in Watford on 1 May 1996 that the extra money from higher taxes on those earning over £100,000 could be spent on education, they were uneasy at what they saw as a tax on the rich. Suggestions that it could be used to fund a middle-income tax cut also met a wary response.[54] I never had any doubt: increasing the top rate put us at political risk. But there were other arguments: putting up the top rate of tax would make it clear where at least some of the money was coming from to pay for our spending plans. Blair was always instinctively against raising the top rate, Brown more inclined to keep the option open. In meetings they would discuss it as a matter of principle: did increasing the top rate reveal your instincts as a tax-raising party, or did it not? Blair thought it did, Brown thought it did not.

The Tories launched another attack on us on 6 January 1997, which we countered with a picture of John Major: 'Why trust him on the economy after 22 tax rises?' And two weeks later Brown, in an audacious coup, announced, first on the *Today* programme and then in a speech to Labour's Finance and Industry Group at the Queen Elizabeth II Centre in Westminster, that neither the basic nor the top rate of tax would go up under Labour. The Tories were pole-axed. It was as though a political mallet had been smashed through their heads.

It took some time for the tax pledge to break through, and it needed a national poster campaign, launched on 14 February, to do it, but our pledge turned the national mood and even by the beginning of February confidence was rising. 'These were the most encouraging female groups this year,' I wrote on 5 February. 'They did express worries about Labour: mainly interest rates, and fear of the unknown, but these doubts were containable.'[55] At the end of February I wrote, 'There is some evidence of a hardening of an anti-Conservative sentiment. The sense is of an electorate who spent the first six weeks of the year focusing (and worrying) about Labour, reshifting their focus on to the Conservatives and liking them even less.'[56] On 18 March, Stan Greenberg announced tax victory: 'Labour has won the tax issue and is making further gains. Labour is now trusted over the Tories on taxes by 11 per cent.'[57] This was an amazing victory and an extraordinary contrast to the tax débâcle of 1992. Labour had done what five years before had seemed impossible: it had beaten the Tories on tax. And without tax, as Maurice Saatchi said, they had nothing.

9

THE DARK ARTS

For the many not the few

I have once described political campaigns as acts of war, but they are acts of principle also. They are the way that progressive values can become progressive realities; they are the means by which progressive ideas can prevail and conservative ideas can be defeated; they are the instrument that can turn a compassionate instinct into lives made better.

For as long as I can remember I have believed that there is a continuing battle between progressive and conservative forces. For most of this century conservative forces have won in Britain, and for much of the 1980s they were winning across the world – winning (in part) because the right could campaign well, and the left could not. I felt humiliated by these defeats, but it wasn't me that was hurt: it was the millions of ordinary working people who deserved a better life, but who were repeatedly let down by progressive parties which campaigned poorly and did not seem to think that it mattered.

In 1985 I decided it was time to try to make a difference. I believed it was time that the progressive forces started to win. I was not alone: all over the world, but particularly in the United States, people were starting to say, 'We have to fight back.' So at the age of thirty-five I left a very well-paid career in advertising to set up a one-person consultancy with little money and no clients but with one aim: to use my communications skills to help the left beat the right; not just in Britain, but across the world. Two things were formative in my decision. One was Labour's appalling defeat in 1983. The other was a *Panorama* programme called 'The Marketing of Margaret',[1] showing the extraordinary, ruthless professionalism of the Conservatives and making it clear that unless Labour completely transformed its campaigning it could never hope to win.

I believe in the ascendancy of progressive ideas and progressive values. I believe in political parties that serve the people and advance their hopes. And I believe that it is the responsibility of all of us involved in progressive politics to advance our case with the greatest skill and professionalism. The people we seek to serve would expect nothing less, and our opponents will do nothing else. There is no reason why the interests of the rich and the powerful should be advanced by the ruthlessly professional techniques of campaigning, while these are denied to the poor, the disadvantaged, and the hard-working majority. We should be proud that in Britain, and increasingly across the world, progressive parties have now established themselves as the better campaigners. Political campaigning skills are not 'black arts', as they have been described, but a body of expertise that has every right, probably more right, to belong to the many, and not to the few.

This is a chapter about the entrails of campaigning. It is about the extraordinary preparations made by the Labour Party to secure victory in 1997 and about the skills and contribution of those who helped to make Labour's campaigning machine so formidable and so effective. It is also about my own personal view of campaigning – how I approach it, what I believe in. It is about those hundreds and thousands of campaign workers and helpers in the 1997 General Election who made sure that conservatism was beaten, and progressive principles could finally win.

Campaigning principles

There are few, if any, fixed rules of campaigning. My approach to political campaigning is dynamic and based on the need for constant change, continuous reassessment, and the resolution of contradictions, while always seeking to connect ideas to experience. I hope that this book as a whole is more able to articulate what I believe about campaigning than these few paragraphs can. But the following ten basic campaigning principles run through it.

1: Campaigning is holistic. It is a complete activity involving every element of the political experience. Successful campaigns must get not just a single element right, they have to get everything right. They have to be rooted in substance, in ideas, in values, in principles: these in turn have to connect to organisation and structure, which in turn must connect to message and to the delivery of the message, to every detail of every leaflet, to every performance on television. A campaign is like a vast, multi-dimensional structure moving forwards and backwards, upwards and downwards, meshing abstraction and concreteness, policy with presentation, future to past. The art of campaigning is to take this complication and make it compellingly simple.

2: Campaigning is dynamic. Campaigning is not static, it is the continuous unfolding of interconnecting events. A campaign is a fluid, interacting sequence stretching indefinitely into the distance. It is necessary to anticipate events and the consequences of those events; not just what will happen, but what will happen as result of it, and how this will influence us and what we should do next. It is essential in campaigning never to assume that the prevailing situation will continue, for it may not. It is also imperative to understand that what has worked before may not work again, what was successful in the last election may be stale or ineffective in the next. The soapbox was astoundingly effective for Major in 1992, laughable five years later.

3: Campaigning is about momentum. In politics either you have momentum or you are losing momentum, there is no middle way. Politics does not accept a condition of stasis, in which both parties are in equal and continuing balance. In a campaign you must always seek to gain and keep momentum, or it will pass immediately to your opponent.

Gaining momentum means dominating the news agenda, entering the news cycle at the earliest possible time, and repeatedly re-entering it, with stories and initiatives that ensure that subsequent news coverage is set on your terms. It means anticipating and pre-empting your opponent's likely manoeuvres, giving them no room to breathe, keeping them on the defensive. It means defining the political debate on your terms. Every political debate can be seen in two ways: one that will favour you, and one that will favour your opponents. It is essential that your definition prevails. Momentum is especially vital at the end of the campaign. Although it was clear that Labour would win the 1997 election, a week before polling day the size of the majority was uncertain. The last few days of the campaign, when Labour stormed to a crescendo and the Tories slunk away, lost the Conservatives dozens of seats.

4: Campaigning is about message. People think message just means a few words, often repeated, but message is much more: it is the rationale that underpins your campaign. It is your central argument, the reason you believe that the electorate should vote for you and not your opponents. This rationale is the most important thing to get right in a campaign. You must be clear about why you are seeking to form a government, or why you wish to be Prime Minister. A message can be formed in part by opinion polling and the attitudes and values of the electorate, but it must also come from the substance of what you represent: what is true about you, as a party or a politician. In the months leading up to the 1997 election, more time was spent developing the right message than doing anything else. The messages that emerged – enough is enough; Britain deserves better; people not privilege; future not the past; leadership not drift – appear very simple and uncomplicated, but they took years to develop. They were compelling to the electorate, but they were also true to New Labour.

5: Campaigning is about speed. The British electorate, like almost every electorate in the world, is subject to a continual assault by news. On radio and television news is broadcast every hour at the very least, often far more often. Almost everyone reads one or more newspapers which are competing in ferocious media markets and where the demand for news is insatiable. Any political assertion, however false, can spread through this media jungle with the speed of a panther. The world of politics is littered with assertions that are untrue, but are believed to be true because they were not effectively answered. An unrebutted lie becomes accepted as the truth. You must always rebut a political attack if leaving it unanswered will harm you. And you must do it instantly, within minutes at best, within hours at worst, and with a defence supported by facts. That is what the computer Excalibur and the Rapid Rebuttal Unit at Millbank were about. The first big Tory tax attack in November 1996 was smashed back within three hours with a convincing rebuttal document, and that effectively was the beginning of the end of the Tories' tax campaign.

6: *Campaigning is about endurance.* People who have not been involved in political campaigns do not understand the sheer physical toll they take. Campaigns now go on not just for weeks, but for years. Perpetual, continuous campaigning has become the norm, and this exacts an enormous physical and mental cost. In the 1997 election the Conservatives believed that by calling the election at the last possible moment and by having a long, six-week campaign, endurance would take its toll and Labour would slip up. There were moments when the election seemed an eternity away, but Labour absorbed the pressure better than the Conservatives and the long campaign simply heightened the demand for change. But the capacity for endurance – not just to keep going, but to make good, sensible, fast decisions when almost dropping with exhaustion – is an essential quality in campaigning.

7: *Campaigning is about trust.* Trust is the vital ingredient of modern politics, and it is also the most elusive: hard to win, almost impossible to get back once lost. People have stopped trusting politicians, they have become increasingly sceptical, they feel alienated and disconnected. To win trust we will need new and different ways of communicating and campaigning. The old ways will not do. This means moving from rhetoric to action. Not just saying things, but doing them. Changing Clause IV and balloting Labour's early manifesto are good examples of this. It also means entering into new and more accountable relationships. Increasingly politicians and parties will have to establish what are in effect contracts with the electorate. The pledges were the first example of this, but they will not be the last. The electorate will no longer accept the old rhetorical politics, it wants to hold politicians to account.

8: Campaigning is about beating fear. Almost always the electorate hovers between hope and fear. In the last election the electorate wavered continuously between a desire to get rid of the Conservatives and anxiety about a Labour government. In the referendum on the Good Friday agreement in Northern Ireland, on 22 May 1998, the Protestant electorate hovered tantalisingly between genuine fear of what the agreement might bring, and the hope that it might usher in a better future. In both cases hope won, but fear will not diminish as a factor in modern politics. Modern societies and modern economies mean more change, less continuity, and, inevitably, insecurity and anxiety will increase. Electorates will be less certain, more anxious, more fearful about the future.

In general, over the last two decades, the right has campaigned on a basis of fear, the left on hope. Almost invariably fear won. Fear is a more compelling emotion, more easily provoked. Reagan in 1984, Bush in 1988, Thatcher in 1987 and Major in 1992 all used fear shamelessly as a weapon: fear of taxation, fear of communism, fear of crime. But progressive parties have learned to defeat fear, through rebuttal, counter-attack, more aggressive, less passive campaigning, with an emphasis on message which connects directly with the insecurities of working families. Increasingly the electorate rejects purely negative attacks and demands more positive campaigning. It is now almost impossible to present a negative message without a positive message to complement it. The Conservative negativism of 1997 probably lost them scores of seats. Labour used only positive posters during the six-week campaign. But in an increasingly fast-changing world, insecurity is likely to grow, and with it the potential for fear-based campaigning. Progressive parties will have to fight harder to combat it.

9: Campaigning is about substance. However good your campaigning, you will not win, at least not comprehensively, if your campaign is not based on substance. Even brilliant presentation cannot sell a dud product. Labour lost in 1987 despite a brilliant campaign, and in 1992 with a creditable campaign, because it had not changed enough. The electorate knew this. It always does. It senses if politicians are not real, understands when policies or positions are bogus. Because voters get their information about politics largely from television, they search for clues to reveal the real character of politicians. They are always looking for indications of what is really true, what lies beneath the surface. They admire politicians who show courage, who do brave and unexpected things, who take tough and unexpected decisions, who do not back down under fire. Tony Blair was made as a politician by the courage he showed in ditching Clause IV. The electorate is now double- and treble-guessing politics and politicians all the time. Voters are desperate to get beneath the surface to the substance. The same is true of policy pronouncements. Media scrutiny of politics still concentrates on spin-doctors and sound-bites, while the electorate and most thoughtful politicians are moving on.

10: Campaigning is about a dialogue with the people. The most important thing a party must do in a campaign is listen to what the voters are saying. This does not mean doing what they say, it means knowing what they are thinking and feeling, and respecting it. In a media age new forms of dialogue must be created. Focus groups and market research are an essential part of this dialogue. So too are interactive party broadcasts, and 'Town Hall' meetings, at which politicians can be questioned and held to account. British Telecom logged 230,000 people who responded to an invitation to talk to Tony Blair following the broadcast that launched 'New Life for Britain' on 4 July 1994. The number gives some idea of the pent-up demand for involvement in the political process. People want to have their voices heard. This is not just about developing winning strategies or compelling messages, it is about paying proper respect to the opinions of the public and involving them in the political process. If this is not done, people will either switch off or start to reject the political process altogether. A political campaign should be a partnership between a political party and the people.

Millbank

Campaigning principles are one thing, but putting them into practice is quite another. Peter Mandelson's central preoccupation during the eighteen months before May 1997 was preparing the election campaign. He dedicated most of his energy and intellectual capital to this one task. He had found managing the 1987 election draining and he did not look forward to 1997. In the intervening ten years, campaigns had become incomparably more complex, the media more extensive and demanding: Sky has continuous twenty-four-hour news coverage which, although not watched by millions, spots errors and is monitored by journalists. The BBC and ITV have news bulletins throughout the day; news radio has become ubiquitous; the press are facing ever greater competitive pressures. This is why Millbank was such an essential innovation.

The idea of moving Labour campaigning to one modern, central space came from those of us who had worked on Clinton's campaign in 1992. The contrast between that integrated operation and our scattered campaign force in the British election began a drive for the creation of a similar 'war room' from where we could fight the next election. Tom Sawyer, General Secretary of the Labour Party, took the idea and pushed it through the NEC, which in September 1995 approved the £2 million budget to rent and refurbish a new

campaigns and media centre at Millbank Tower. After the
rabbit warren of Walworth Road, Millbank was like a breath
of fresh air. Instead of endless, scurrying corridors we now
had a single, open-plan office floor. People could talk to each
other and communicate effectively – a far cry from the ghastly
'meeting rooms' of John Smith House. It was bright and
professional, and had stunning views over the Thames. Its
openness promoted a sense of community. I believe it played
a significant part in reducing the wrangles and arguments
which had bedevilled Labour's previous campaigns. This was
a cultural revolution for many in the Labour Party: over the
next year the headquarters at Walworth Road were marginalised, and our entire campaigning operation expanded and
moved into the vast new office space, with a converted cinema
downstairs for press conferences. We set up rebuttal and
attack teams backed up by computerised research systems,
reporting to a unified command structure under the tight
control of Peter Mandelson. A lot of people's noses were put
out of joint, but many others were forced to embrace the
changes and admit that the way they had done things in the
past was wrong. The smoothness of the operation owed much
to work done quietly behind the scenes by Tom Sawyer, who
was unobtrusive, diplomatic and sensitive. He was supported
by Fraser Kemp, then General Election Co-ordinator and
now MP for Houghton and Washington East.

The press office was the first team to move in, at the
beginning of 1996, with Margaret McDonagh, then head of
the campaigns unit and later to become General Election
Co-ordinator when Kemp stepped down in October. Various
task forces and groups followed over the next few months.

I arrived in February 1996; Peter Mandelson spent the
mornings at Millbank from January but only moved in fully
in March. The atmosphere was depressed. Joy Johnson had
recently left her job as Director of Campaigns and Communications after a difficult twelve months. A former BBC
political reporter and a forceful proponent of news-driven,
story-led campaigning, she had been appointed to give our
campaigning drive and energy, which she did. She also

introduced some good initiatives like the daily brief sent out to all Labour MPs, candidates and councillors, but she was never at ease with Alastair Campbell and Peter Mandelson and she was never completely behind the modernisation project. She understood very well how to manage the news, but she was less comfortable organising a department. This was a difficult time. No one was in effective command. I used to hold regular weekly meetings in Walworth Road at which I invariably lost my temper. The atmosphere was too close to 1992 for my liking.

After Joy Johnson resigned nobody was appointed to replace her; Peter took over most of her responsibilities when he moved into Millbank Tower. 'It was like moving in as a liberating army,' he says. 'There were people cheering and waving flags, putting up the bunting and opening cheap red wine.'[2] Millbank was a mess: the campaigning team lacked cohesion and didn't work properly; the move from Walworth Road combined with the lack of leadership had created a sullen mood about the place. Peter was gloomy. Expected to take over the whole operation, he was unsure what to make of this vast space full of people he didn't know. I, on the other hand, loved it. After working for so long in small, isolated offices, I enjoyed working with so many people in such an unfettered environment.

The campaign headquarters was on two levels. The lower level was the main room, a vast space bordered on one side by huge windows which were covered by blinds for security reasons. There was no dedicated 'war room' in the Clinton manner, just one open space containing all the elements of the campaign. On the right immediately as you entered was Jackie Stacey, who was in charge of the presentation of the party: design, press conference sets, and so on. She has been working tirelessly as a communications moderniser since 1985, and is one of New Labour's true stars. She appears timid, but is fierce in her dealings with senior politicians, not afraid to tell them exactly how long they may speak at conference, for example, and is quite prepared to turn off the microphone if they overshoot their time limit.

At the centre of the floor was a collection of desks which became the campaign hub, where the chief media spokesman David Hill, Margaret McDonagh, Matthew Taylor (head of the policy task force), Peter Mandelson, Peter Hyman, Charlie Whelan (Gordon Brown's press secretary), Tim Allan (one of Tony Blair's press officers) and I sat during the election. But at the beginning we were scattered at different points around the vast floor. Immediately behind the central tables, so close that our chairs were always clashing, stood the Attack Task Force or Rapid Rebuttal Unit. Next door to them – in a separate, heavily locked room – the Excalibur database computer system whirred quietly. Beyond that lay media monitoring, who told us what the papers were going to say the next day, followed each nuance in the different editions, gave regular updates on all the news bulletins, and monitored every interview, story and speech on radio and on television.

Policy, led by Matthew Taylor, was to the side, by the river. With a policy officer covering every area of Labour's manifesto, they were crucial in putting out documents refuting the latest Tory allegations. Their phones never stopped ringing. One moment it could be a worried local agent from Bristol, the next Robin Cook about to go on *The World at One*, both demanding the last detail of Labour's programme. They rarely made mistakes; if they did, the fallout could be terrible. My area, which was a combination of strategy, polling and advertising, was in a corner on the opposite side from the river. My staff and the BMP team, when they arrived, huddled here.

Peter Mandelson had his own office, which he shared with Benjamin Wegg-Prosser, his able research assistant, who organised his life for him. There was a large conference room, which was too hot in the summer, too cold in winter, and in which the acoustics were so bad that discussion was impossible unless you shouted. Tom Sawyer and John Prescott had offices at the far end of the floor. The campaigns unit (responsible for co-ordinating the campaign from a national to a local level), led by Margaret McDonagh, was clustered around the conference room.

Above the main room was a smaller, second level, reserved for Tony Blair and his office. It was largely empty until the election, when it became very crushed. In one room, pressed together like battery hens, was the whole policy team, plus extras like Derry Irvine, who managed to find some space in between the head of policy, David Miliband, and policy adviser Liz Lloyd. Yet Blair's office didn't seem to mind their cramped accommodation. It created a new sense of camaraderie that had been lacking in the Leader of the Opposition's sprawling Westminster offices.

Peter Mandelson had been asked by Blair to get a grip on the campaign and he swiftly accepted an offer from Liam Byrne, from Andersen Consulting, to come and help. 'It was a mess,' Byrne, who arrived in April 1996 and was seconded to us until the election, remembers.[3] 'You had a random collection of people. They had what theoretically looked like a good organisational structure but no one really knew what they were doing and crucially it lacked leadership. There were lots of people in different units drifting along without anyone pulling them together. There didn't appear to be any strategy.'[4] Like an organisation after the chief executive has just left, it was spinning around and everybody knew it was a problem. We expected the election to be called in October, in six months' time.

First of all we got to work on Millbank's fabled rapid rebuttal system, in which we had invested £500,000 and which had become a complete shambles. At its centre was Excalibur, a computer with a huge capacity and the ability to read articles and documents and feed them directly into its memory like a photocopier. Unfortunately this capacity had been used indiscriminately, and it had collected a vast amount of data, including random pieces of MPs' correspondence, all of which were unfiled, unstructured and unprioritised like a massive electronic dustbin. Excalibur had to be emptied and the process of electronic gathering began again. During the heat of the campaign, the Attack Task Force often found it more convenient to use the paper files hanging on the wall than to trawl through the computer.

While we sorted out rapid rebuttal, which took several months, Mandelson attacked the campaign structure, which had been set up by Tom Sawyer, Fraser Kemp and Margaret McDonagh, and consisted of twelve task forces, ranging from logistics to attack, through the leader's tour, campaigns and message delivery. This in itself had been a small revolution for the Labour Party – the move from a directorate to a task-force structure. Mandelson used this as his way in, and worked punctiliously through each of the task forces. This is how Peter works: slowly; painstakingly; calmly; step by step. He likes to get the small things right. He thinks polit-ical success and failure rest on detail and planning.

'The building was great, like a great new toy,' he remem-bers, 'but I felt I had to be careful. I didn't want anyone to think I was moving in, sweeping up, hiring, firing, etc. I played it very slow, very long. The key thing I proposed to Tony was that in the whole political campaigning structure there had to be a General Election planning task force that we should ring-fence. That whatever messing around went on by anyone else in relation to any of the rest of what we were doing, the General Election planning should be sacro-sanct and protected and chaired by me.'5

When the work on Excalibur was finished, Mandelson asked Byrne to spend a month on a full-scale operational review of Millbank. Byrne reported in August that, although the infrastructure was good, Labour lacked the political management structure to run the operation effectively. The campaign needed underpinning with strong political support and a decision-making structure that was clear, agreed and unambiguous. Decisions were not being taken because there was no clear political command structure. This was a very difficult message for politicians to swallow. The lack of communication and co-ordination meant we were unable to sustain a coherent message. No matter how many initiatives we took, our message wasn't getting across.

'There was no chief operating officer,' said Byrne. 'We didn't have someone who pulled everyone together, who sat everyone down and said, right, you do this, you do that, what are the problems, let's sort them out, now go away and do it. We didn't have someone who could do that.'[6]

As a result, Margaret McDonagh was appointed General Election co-ordinator in October, and helped Mandelson enormously. Initially their chemistry was not ideal, but they were an excellent match: both were good at different things. McDonagh made things happen for Mandelson. 'There were sometimes complaints about Margaret from other senior managers,' Byrne said. 'People found her brusque, but I remember sitting in a meeting with Peter and Peter, as he often does, just sort of summed it up. He said the one thing about Margaret is at least she gets things done. And in a party which is short of finishers, which is short of implementers, Margaret stands out as someone who gets things done quickly, effectively and without fuss. She doesn't mind, she doesn't complain when she's been given a difficult job to do. She doesn't start grumbling or machinating. She just picks up the phone and gets on with it.'[7] Mandelson gave the whole place shape, coherence and direction, but McDonagh was crucial as his lieutenant. 'In an organisation as complicated as an election HQ, where speed is of the essence, you need someone who is going to act quickly and who is not going to second-guess you or question you or cause trouble or procrastinate,' Byrne said. 'When you give an order you need it executed. I mean, this was war.'[8]

The other major problem was the political leadership of the campaign, which was not cohesive and would not become so until the election period itself, when it did fuse. Gordon Brown was in political control of the campaign, Peter Mandelson in charge of Millbank. Relationships between them were not warm, often prickly, sometimes difficult. This was hard for both Mandelson and Brown, and difficult for the rest of us. Partly this was a matter of temperament and a once-close relationship which had been badly bruised, but it was also because of a difference in approach. The most telling example of this was the campaign grid. Peter had spent weeks working on this. Entire weekends were spent by him crafting a perfectly designed campaigning plan, replete with every detail for every day.

Finally he presented it to Brown, who resented and resisted it. He felt that news should dominate the election, and news by definition could not be foretold. It was fluid, unpredictable, impossible to pin down. It would escape from the constraints of any campaign grid. Peter understood the value of news, but felt deeply that without order and discipline there was chaos. His fear of disintegration and disorder in a campaign is almost visceral – it is an abyss we cannot slide into. The lessons of 1992 were engraved on everyone's mind. The truth is that both Brown and Mandelson are right: you need structures and you need flexibility. Labour's 1997 campaign was effective because these two impulses were married, but it was not an easy match and only happened after a long and difficult period of tension and disagreement.

That is how successful campaigns are built: on the synthesis of contrasting ideas and contrasting policies. One of Blair's great strengths as leader is that he understands this, and is able to make it work. He wants the best and he wants ideas and strategies to be tested and debated. He is only confident in an idea or a person if it has come through the fire. This is as true for himself as for others; he distrusts people who agree with him, he wants to be taken on. His view of the management of the campaign was simple. Brown and Mandelson are the best. They have brilliant but different campaigning skills, and he wanted both of them. In the short term it was difficult, but in the long run it paid off. He would not compromise on ability for the sake of harmony. In fact, the search for perfect team harmony is a fantasy in politics. Neil Kinnock's senior politicians were often at odds and this sometimes led him to despair. Throughout my twelve years working with the Labour Party, conflicts and tensions between senior politicians were a fact of life. The challenge of leadership is to accept this and to transcend it, and this Blair did brilliantly well.

Two other areas needed strengthening: message development and story development. Peter Hyman was moved from

Blair's office to work in Millbank full-time in order to strengthen the message, and Brian Wilson MP was moved across to work with the rebuttal team on a full-time basis. Brian enjoyed a warm friendship with Adrian McMenamin, who headed the team, which was staffed also by Richard Elson, Tristram Hunt, Adam Bowen and Will Parkes. The deputy political editor from the *Daily Mirror*, David Bradshaw, was recruited to develop material for the press office to send out. He also made sure that every important regional newspaper had at least one article a week from Tony Blair or a shadow Cabinet member.

Matthew Taylor was head of the policy task force, and a central figure. He used to exasperate me, primarily because he used to challenge everything I said. I find this annoying at the best of times, but with Matthew it was doubly irritating because he was so often right. He did the same with Mandelson, who took it better than I did. But he was always thinking, always protean. He had a new idea, fresh insights, almost daily, and would tell everyone about it. He was always trying to ridicule and humiliate me. He began to develop a tracking chart correlating my faith in opinion polls against the strength of Labour's lead. He would mimic my excessive delight if a poll was good, my manic despair if it was bad. I grew very fond of him.

Of equal importance was Labour's polling director, Greg Cook, with whom I worked closely. He transformed Labour Party polling, which had been in a mess before he took over. He took care to ensure that polling information came in from many sources and not just one. He assembled a complete picture. Tony Blair used to call on him often for polling information during the campaign.

Yet another hidden star was Alan Barnard, a big, fair-haired, often quiet but suddenly outspoken man, who is now in charge of campaigns. He combines nitty-gritty, street campaigning skills with an understanding of the needs of the modern media. Alan was the kind of man to drop everything to go and heckle John Major at an open-air press conference.

Slowly, very slowly, it all began to work. Margaret

McDonagh fought to bring everything together. 'Everything in the Labour Party's difficult,' she said. 'It's meant to be like that. You're talking about a hundred-year-old organisation that's very conservative and had to be changed root and branch.'[9] She adopted a holistic approach, integrating all the elements of the campaign. There were regular meetings between the task-force leaders, to communicate to them what was going on, and give them information on polling, message or whatever. These meetings were integrated with staff meetings, so the process was very open and people could contribute. Margaret introduced telephone conferencing to include constituencies and regions, assigned politicians to each of the regions, and gave each of the regional offices a politician to deal with to make everyone feel that they were part of the effort. McDonagh had learned the strength gained by integration at all levels when she worked on the Clause IV campaign – 'Ultimately, the party member knocking on the door would be saying the same as Tony Blair on *News at Ten*,' she said. 'I think that that is the one thing we did achieve in the election campaign.' Whatever was happening nationally would be mirrored locally:

> Generally now when you talk to people about the General Election, when you talk to anybody, whatever part of the party, whether they are a member, a member of staff in the regions or here, people always tell you about their contribution. They feel that they made one. They understood what their part was in the overall structure – they were a piece of the jigsaw and I think that that's just amazingly important for people. Also there was a realisation of the different roles between politicians and staff. Politicians behaved like politicians, they made political decisions, whereas in the past because the political decisions have been difficult to make they have concentrated on the detail or gone off into trying to run the organisation. This time they accepted the responsibility that they had to make political decisions. People like you, Philip, and me to some extent, kept throwing it back to them saying, no, you've got to make a decision on that; no,

you've got to make a decision on taxes; no, this is what is
happening on Europe. I think they were challenged. Yes, they
did deliver.[10]

It was a fraught twelve months. We all argued for much
of the time. At no point in 1996 did Peter Mandelson or I
believe Millbank was really working. Alastair Campbell never
had complete confidence in it either, and was always
complaining about it. For him, the progress being made was
too gradual and too slow. He thought the organisation was
poor and this made Blair anxious. Campbell often complained
that decisions were being made when he wasn't there, which
was true. It was particularly true of advertising, about which
he considered himself an expert. And in the final analysis,
the advertising owed as much to him as to anyone.

But in the first two months of 1997 things came together.
The daily meeting at 8.30 A.M. moved to Millbank from
Brown's office in Parliament Street, which was inconvenient
for him but made Millbank feel that it was the genuine centre
of the campaign. The place started to hum: the numbers
had swollen to 250 and the operation became bigger, noisier,
more exciting. Liam Byrne compared it to a City trading
floor. 'For a whole generation of comparatively young people
it was one of the most exciting things they'd ever done,' he
said. 'People were desperate to get in. It was a very young,
very vibrant place.'[11]

A system called Lotus Notes was introduced in the press
office – all the policy documents and press releases there at
the touch of a button. It provided a rolling agenda of breaking
news stories, a 'line to take' for all press staff, and a politician to call on. It was invaluable. Key campaigners out on
the road were linked by fax and pager to Millbank, where
each had their own political lieutenant so if there was a
problem their lieutenant could literally walk up to Peter
Mandelson and explain the confusion and clear a line within
seconds.

On the ground, workers overseen by the key campaigners
unit set up by Margaret McDonagh a year earlier had built

up detailed databases of switchers, so that Millbank had a
national database of key voters, largely people who were
Conservative or Liberal in 1992 and who were saying they
had now switched. They were our primary targets, together
with voters who were Labour but unlikely to vote – largely
young people. We meshed the information gathered on the
ground with the electoral register and census details and sent
out direct mail which was innovative and precisely targeted.
On the morning after the election was called, 3.2 million
items of direct mail were delivered.

Somehow, when the campaign started, Millbank swung
smoothly into action. 'I just feel very proud for the organisation staff and members and what they did,' said McDonagh.
'The organisation was completely transformed, and often we
brought people in here during the campaign, trade union
leaders or business people or whatever, and they were really
shocked about how it ran, really. During the election
campaign, in this space you had 310 people and they all
knew what they were doing and I think they knew at every
level in the party what they were doing. I think we reached
out much more. We were more confident. When you're not
very confident about what you're doing, it all becomes secretive.'[12] We had moved a long way since the days of the secret
campaign team in 1992.

The War Book

The strategic anchor of any campaign is the War Book, so
called because an election campaign is like a surrogate war.
In my interview with David Hare for his play *The Absence of
War*, I said, 'Political statements are not acts of sense, they
are acts of war,'[13] which sums up my feeling about a campaign:
it is a fight to the political death, with only one winner.
Central to the War Book and one of my core beliefs is that
you must be absolutely honest about your opponent's
strengths, and your own weaknesses, and that you should
put them in writing. It is a risk putting sensitive information
down on paper, but in my view unless you document hard

campaigning truths they will never be fully taken into account and will run the risk of being dodged or discounted.

In this I took my lead from Joe Napolitan, who told me: 'If a strategy is not in writing, it does not exist.' Unless strategy and the inputs into strategy are written down and agreed, they will not be there. They will be just an impression of a strategy: you will think you have it, but under the pressure of campaigning it will melt.

There are other views, of course. When Labour's 1997 War Book was released by the Tories in the middle of the campaign I was accused by them of naïveté in writing it all down. They were wrong. The truth may well be embarrassing, but in the long run, it is essential for the growth and development of any organisation that it is known, disseminated and can be read. Vital to political success is a complete understanding of your weaknesses. The odd leak is small change compared with that and, in any event, the leaked truth can not only help prod an organisation in the right direction, but also tell the world that it is still listening, it still cares.

The War Book is not just a matter of writing down party strengths and weakness and mapping out likely campaign manoeuvres. It is also about re-enacting or simulating the campaign with real voters. It is always essential to try to produce the most damaging campaign that your opponents are likely to come up with and then to expose it to the electorate, to gain their response, and to find the most effective defence against the likely attack.

I started to do this in the middle of 1995. In the beginning I used to focus on the likely Conservative manifesto at the time of the election, and see how it compared to the one I expected us to produce. But I also tested rough advertisements that simulated the Conservative campaign. By early 1996 I was testing 'New Labour, New Danger' in focus groups, because we had been informed that it was their probable campaign slogan. We also did quantitative polling on it. We would constantly be testing their best attacking arguments, and our best defences to them.

Although it had the potential to hurt, I was confident about the deficiencies of 'New Labour, New Danger' before a single member of the public had seen it. It legitimised New Labour, but more than that it was too negative. It was simply not possible to inject this message into the political bloodstream without it being preceded by a massive positive campaign.

Peter Mandelson asked me to start work on the War Book in early summer 1996, and I jotted down an outline summary on 10 June. In July, I booked a room at a hotel and spent the day with Peter Hyman and Liam Byrne attempting to predict the election. The first draft, dated 1 July, was flimsy. It had both Labour and Conservative strengths and weaknesses and predictions of how both major campaigns might unfold. But, as Peter Hyman says, 'It was just a first trawl over the campaign battlefield.'[14]

This was one of many drafts. We ended with version three, number two, which was the one that was leaked. It had a summary of our message at that time: 'Two futures: a future of hope with Labour, a future you cannot trust with the Conservatives.' It pulled absolutely no punches. It started with Labour and Conservative strengths and weaknesses. Our strengths were Blair, newness and the future, the many not the few. Our weaknesses were tax, interest rates, inflation, hidden left, fear of change. Conservative strengths were the strengthening economy, patriotism and security – 'better the devil you know'. Their weaknesses were 'in office too long', for the few not the many, betrayal and trust, drift and weak leadership, education and health.

I summed up the threats facing us: 'The economy; fear of Labour; Major; Europe.' The opportunities were: 'Blair/ New Labour; business; tax; education; fear of another Tory term.' I then spelled out in some detail the election battle-ground – staking out the competitive positions of both parties. For example, Labour would say, 'Major is weak', the Conservatives would say, 'Phoney Tony'; Labour would say, 'The Tories have been in power for too long', the Conservatives would say, 'Don't take the risk of change'.

The War Book then mapped out the Conservative campaign: a negative campaign based on the claim that Labour was dangerous; a positive campaign based on the proposition that this was the strongest economy in Europe. I assumed that the positive and the negative campaigns would be equally important in Tory tactics. In the event they fatally downplayed their positive campaigning. The likely Conservative campaign plan was mapped out too: each month we anticipated what they would do. This was not that difficult, as we had their advertising schedule and they almost never deviated from it.

Labour's campaign was also set out in detail. Blair wanted to structure our message around three anchors: Remind (about their record); Reassure (that Labour is new; that we have safe, common-sense policies); Reward (through the pledges). By November the War Book had our final dividing-lines in: leadership not drift; for the many not the few; the future not the past. These became a mantra. For the first time in perhaps thirty years Labour was getting a genuine message that would be used repeatedly by politicians. Eventually these were augmented by the culminating message of our campaign: 'Enough is Enough: Britain deserves better'. These messages appear very simple but they are the result of months of work, taking New Labour's big themes and making them completely accessible to the public.

At the cutting edge of our campaigning were what we called 'offers to the electorate': our positive offer – the pledges, and our articulation of what the Conservatives had to offer – the dark side of a Tory fifth term. Our offer was: 'Labour's pledge for a better future: cut waiting lists; cut class sizes; ban knives and guns; young people into work; strong economy, cut VAT on fuel'. We contrasted this with a Tory pledge for a future you could not trust: 'VAT on food; running down the NHS; continued decline in schools'. There was no mention of pensions in this: it was included only after Peter Lilley published his pension-plus proposals, and only after it became clear that the Conservatives were planning to end the state pension as we knew it. The pledges connected straight back to our need to build trust, to enter into a new and more accountable relationship with the electorate.

The War Book then went on to the target audience. We had five groups. The first were swing voters: switchers from Conservative to Labour were our key group and our primary focus by a long way. For example, almost all (over 90 per cent) of my focus groups were conducted within this group. But we also targeted women because of Labour's continuing gender gap in favour of men; first-time voters; the DE social grouping, our historic base; and the Pennine Belt, our key group of marginals. In the event we were successful among all groups. Over one and a half million voters made the direct journey from the Conservatives to Labour, a staggering figure. We closed the gender gap, we got 58 per cent of first-time voters, and we won every target seat in the Pennine Belt. The War Book also contained an extensive campaign grid, which was not filled in for security reasons, and a final section summarising our messages and pledges.[15]

Our War Book was comprehensive, but not yet decisive. Paul Begala, a senior consultant to Bill Clinton in 1992, wrote a penetrating critique of it, arguing for more focus, more attack. It is true that it was too long, but I believe that just as you must be honest about weaknesses, you must embrace complication before you can become simple and single-minded. Politics is complicated, multi-layered and dynamic. To make true sense of it you must respect its complexity, but then turn its complication into simple, sustainable, communicable truths. But this means a massive amount of work, and a huge process of distillation. If you just reach for the easy, shallow simplicity it will not last a week before it crumples under scrutiny. By the end of the campaign our message was five lines plus the pledges. It could all be written on the side of a match-box, but it took three years, several versions of the War Book and a small rainforest to get there.

Labour advertising

There is a myth about political advertising, largely spawned by the success of Saatchi's. The Conservatives won four elections in a row, and Saatchi's produced advertising for all the campaigns. Often it was very good, sometimes it was brilliant. Understandably, a winning election campaign and good advertising points intelligent minds to cause and effect: good advertising produces election victories. But this is nonsense. Advertising has an effect, but it is small and rarely decisive. For example, it is certain that in four of the last five elections advertising did not materially influence the result. The one possible exception is the 1992 election, where it can be argued that the 'Tax Bombshell' had some effect on the electorate. But even this is highly debatable. Labour lost that election because it was not yet electable. Its tax plans and tax reputation were the real issue, not the advertising attack. Almost always the role of advertising is marginal. How does one explain otherwise the fact that in 1997 the Conservatives spent millions more on advertising than in 1992, but won 171 fewer seats in the election? This marginality applies in Britain, where TV advertising is banned, but not, of course, in the United States and elsewhere, where unlimited campaign advertising is permitted. There, advertising can change the dynamics and the results of elections.

But advertising does have a role in Britain and it can be significant. It can help to set agendas. It can concentrate minds and force parties to agree on the one thing they want to say. It can capture the popular mood and express it in a single, memorable image or line: 'Labour Isn't Working' in 1979; 'Like Your Manifesto, Comrade' (comparing Labour and Communist Party programmes) in 1983; and 'Labour's Policies on Arms' in 1987 were good examples of this. Advertising is not vital, but it is important.

In the past Labour had produced successful campaigns, but not in the 1983 election where Johnny Wright, working in impossible circumstances, produced the lamentable 'Think Positive, Act Positive, Vote Positive' campaign.

In 1984 the left hit back with brilliant advertising developed by BMP for the 'Save the GLC' campaign. It focused on the one issue generated by the abolition of the GLC which could unite all groups: they were taking away your right to vote. Their 'Say No to No Say' campaign was outstanding (although it did not save the GLC). Because it was supported by Ken Livingstone (MP for Brent) it gave advertising credibility on the left, softening its pariah status.

I always wanted BMP to do Labour's advertising, but for commercial reasons they were unable to in the beginning. So in part I recommended setting up the Shadow Communications Agency as a front organisation for BMP. This worked, and in 1987 BMP produced some visible and intelligent advertising. The advertising in 1992 was not as good, and when the SCA died, so did BMP's involvement with the party. I then recommended that Leslie Butterfield of Butterfield Day Devito Hockney be appointed. Leslie is a brilliant advertising planner (advertising's word for a strategist). He produced what I consider to be the single most influential piece of research ever conducted for Labour during my period of involvement (the 'Beyond the Pale' research of November 1985).[16] They did well, but when Blair became leader Mandelson and I thought it was time for a change: Peter wanted someone bigger. He needed to have confidence in the capacity of Labour's agency.

In the late autumn of 1994 I bumped into Peter Gatley, who was head of art direction at BMP. He was taking his son to the sandpit next to the Serpentine as I was taking my two daughters. He was desperate to work with Labour and felt that after all this time BMP deserved another chance. I thought he was right, and gradually the idea of re-appointing BMP took shape. The core of BMP, as far as Labour is concerned, is Chris Powell, its chief executive. Powell goes back further than anyone. He first offered his advertising help in 1972, and replaced David Kingsley as the third man of the three wise men who advised Harold Wilson. The other two were Peter Lovell-Davis and Denis Lyons. Powell did not work in the 1979 election, but had some involvement in 1983. He was responsible for getting Johnny Wright selected: 'All I did was dump poor old Johnny Wright with it – poor sod.'[17]

In 1987 Powell and the SCA had a successful campaign with a series of clever advertisements. One was based on Margaret Thatcher's stone heart – Peter Gatley spent weeks getting the actual stone carving absolutely right. In a series of presentations to the economic team in 1992 he pressed home our acute vulnerability on tax and interest rates. He says: 'The frustration we all had in 1992 was the failure to take action against what was obviously going to hit us. Between us we put together a strategy for responding, but no action was taken for dealing with it.'[18]

But returning in 1995 was not easy. 'I think our role changed enormously between 1985–87 and 1997. In 1985 in a way we were showing Peter Mandelson how to do it because he was new to it, but by 1997 he knew how to do it in his sleep. So where we had a central role in 1987 we had a far less central role in 1997. On top of that, rather than being Bryan Gould, Peter Mandelson and Philip Gould, you had a complete army of people all with different opinions in a general mêlée without a particular command structure.'[19] A typical meeting would include Peter Mandelson, Alastair Campbell, Margaret McDonagh, Peter Hyman, broadcasting officer Dan Clifton, Jackie Stacey, any number of strange young helpers and myself from the Labour side, and from BMP's side, Chris Powell, John Webster, Daryl Fielding, occasionally Simon Buckby, Gail Nutney, and various researchers – anything up to twenty-five people. Simon Buckby, the producer of the broadcasts at BMP, describes a typical meeting: 'This meeting would sometimes consider the slogan on tax and a really big decision needed to be taken – would we go with twenty-two Tory tax rises? – and sometimes this very same gathering would be looking at whether or not the shade of a leaflet needed to be a slightly different magenta to that presented by the agency. So these meetings had sprawling and huge agendas and they would genuinely consider what time train people needed to get in order to be at a poster launch with Tony Blair three weeks away, while at other times they would be saying, should we or should we not spend x million pounds on this poster?'[20]

Relations between politicians and advertising agencies are never easy, and as well as the ridiculous rows there were some moments when the two cultures clashed exquisitely. One day the new director responsible for the Labour Party account wrote a memo introducing herself, which began: 'Now we've been talking the talk, it's time to walk the walk.' This was enthusiasm, which we desperately needed, but it was not language that the Labour Party easily understood.

There was continual internal controversy about our advertising right up to election day itself. The BMP team never clicked with the Labour campaigners at Millbank, as it had when it worked through the SCA in earlier years. Younger members of Labour's team wanted newer, more fashionable agencies. Peter Hyman thought BMP lacked the political nastiness and killer instinct we needed. Millbank wanted hard, ruthless professionalism. They wanted an agency that would do exactly what it was told. Alastair Campbell just felt he could do it better. The BMP people had a hard time and they battled on. And they did keep us focused on tax.

BMP was also under occasional predatory attack from other agencies who wanted to work with us. Ironically, the agency we used most other than BMP was the old Saatchi & Saatchi, which Maurice and Charles Saatchi had left. They developed the 'Enough is Enough' line, and pushed our thinking towards being more positive and less negative.

We struggled to make our advertising arrangements gel, in awe of the Conservative advertising power. They had a huge amount of money to spend and we were at first fearful of their reputation. Whenever they launched a new advertising initiative we waited for the explosion and the damage it would cause – like war-time families in air-raid shelters in the last days of the war, awaiting V1 and V2 rockets. But after a while it became clear that the Tories were firing blanks. Their adverts, as Blair said, were everywhere: every street in every town had a Tory poster in it, or near it. It was like being occupied by an invading propaganda army. But I didn't think it was working.

In contrast to the Conservatives, whose advertising flowed off the production line according to a carefully worked-out plan, we never had the same campaign twice. We were groping our way towards solutions. Our advertising chopped and changed in style, design and theme, although for the most part we had one central message: tax. Jackie Stacey used to put them all up on the wall next to her desk to humiliate me. We started with 'Tories Hit You Where It Hurts' in spring 1996; moved on to 'Same Old Tories, Same Old Lies' in the summer; moved again to the pledges, virtually unvarnished, in September 1996; and finally developed the device of John Major facing both ways, with one side of his face saying, '1992: Tax Cuts Year on Year' and the other side saying, '22 Tax Rises Since 1992'. This was the best single attacking advertisement of the campaign. It hurt the Conservatives without damaging us because it was factual and people did not think we were being unfair. We followed it up with the tax pledge poster which was the most effective advertisement of the campaign. It calmed the mood of the electorate, pouring reassurance on them.

Tony Blair was never really happy with our advertising. He was always tetchy about it and wanted to be more positive. In the spring he started to talk about dropping negative advertising. At first Peter Mandelson and I thought he was mad, but gradually, because of the complete failure of the Conservative campaign, we came round to the same view. The Conservatives had yielded all the political ground associated with hope and positivity, and it was ours to grab.

In the end, because the final advertising plans for the election campaign seemed to be stuck, I arranged a meeting with only Peter Gatley and Alastair Campbell. Peter and Alastair clicked, and gradually we came to the conclusion we should be positive not in a timid way, but an intrusive and dominating way. I suggested bright, bold colours. Peter Gatley came back with stunning posters using vivid, unusual colours and the single line: 'New Labour, New Britain'.

Gatley said this advertising would break new ground and he was right. It was positive, it was bright, it exuded hope. Internally, reaction to it was very mixed, but Alastair and I loved it.

I did not, however, want to use the line 'New Labour, New Britain', preferring our campaign line, 'Britain Deserves Better', which captured the national mood perfectly: everybody felt they deserved better. But Peter Gatley hated this, he thought there was an innate contradiction between using positive colourful posters and a slightly negative line. In fact, he hated it so much, he resigned from BMP when I insisted on using it – at least, this was the reason he gave. Such is election madness. The next stage of the advertising was planned to be the colours plus the pledges. Finally, we would have a picture of Blair with the line: 'Vote Today. Because Britain Deserves Better'. Peter Gatley hated this too, and tried dozens of alternatives based on various clever lines. But I wanted to close the campaign as it started, with 'Britain Deserves Better', and a reassuring picture of Tony Blair. I didn't want to be clever, I wanted to win.

The election advertising and the tax advertising which preceded it worked extremely well, and in the case of the 'colours' posters broke new ground. It may not have received the recognition it deserved or the plaudits given to Saatchi's in earlier years, which is unfair on BMP, but a majority of 179 is its own reward.

PPBs and PEBs

Party political broadcasts and party election broadcasts, often dismissed as silly, irrelevant, dull and ineffectual, are in fact both powerful and important. They are a democratic asset, giving all parties the chance to put their case fairly, and their demise would be a loss to democracy. We put enormous energy and care into our broadcasts in 1997, producing, I believe, the best series of election broadcasts ever made.

There are two major problems with PPBs. The first is the 'turn-off' factor. Viewing figures for PPBs, even outside election times, can reach between eight and ten million, and during elections this rises. They are shown at prime times on BBC1 and ITV just before the main evening news, as well as on BBC2. This assures them of a huge audience. However, although a lot of people start watching, often caught unawares, our minute-by-minute breakdowns taught us that they rarely watch the whole broadcast, especially on the BBC, where they are least expecting it. They watch the first forty-five seconds or minute, then they turn over and surf around, then they come back, thinking perhaps it has ended, and watch another forty-five seconds before surfing some more only to return again, maybe watching the last forty-five seconds while waiting for it to end so they can watch the news.

The research we did showed how crucial it was to ensure our broadcasts were entertaining and engaging as well as informative. It also persuaded us not to make a five-minute film which told one story as a complete narrative, but to segment it and tell the same story again and again, so that people got the whole story in their forty-five-second block. We applied this model to virtually all the PPBs that we made.

The second problem with PPBs is that although their budgets are tiny – we had £35,000 for each one during the election – the viewers see them as regular current affairs TV, and therefore expect the same production values. They should not appear cheaper, nor should they be too glossy, otherwise viewers become wary. Therefore we banned 'Film on 4'-style 'arty' broadcasts, because people are suspicious of this and feel it is elitist. We made them to the same production standards that people might expect when they were watching the news or *Panorama*, adding a commercial element by repeatedly re-stating our brand identity – either our message, or a visual slogan, or Labour's own mnemonic. This combines a TV programme with an advertisement, which is basically what a party political broadcast is.

For the 1997 election, for the first time, we also planned our broadcasts as an integral part of the overall campaign, so that when, for example, we were banging home the message about 'Tory Tax Lies' in autumn 1996, the PPBs did the same: same message, same concept, same slogan, even the same typeface. Simon Buckby at BMP, a former television reporter and adviser to John Prescott, was responsible for them:

> The first 'Tory Tax Lies' broadcast is a very good example of splitting the five minutes into four segments telling a very strong message but in a humorous way. We chose to use the *Spitting Image* characters. In one segment after another we basically said, here is the 'Tory Tax Lie' on health, education, crime and tax. You only needed to watch one of those four segments to get the whole message, which was that the Tories can't be trusted because they betrayed their promises. The message was really hard – they are lying – but because it was told through identifiable characters, with humour, you could get away with saying something so much harder than if you simply had a talking politician saying: 'The Tories are liars.' All the evidence suggests that this was the most-enjoyed PPB we've ever made, because people just laughed at it.[21]

For the next broadcast, '22 Tory Tax Lies', in November, which helped launch the '22 Tory Tax Rises' part of the campaign and went hand-in-glove with the 'Enough is Enough' posters, we went for an entirely different approach and produced a pastiche of a horror film, portraying five typical families in five different situations, with a hand stealing money from them. There was, for example, a pensioner sitting by her gas fire which was going off because her money was being stolen. It was very hard-hitting. And in January we had the 'Oxo Mum' broadcast – a female, a typical *Daily Mail* reader whom our target audience would be able to identify with – going through four different segments of the five minutes to reveal the hurt and damage she had felt over the previous five years: education, health, crime, and finally, of course, tax rises.

Probably the hardest-hitting tax broadcast we produced was the next, shown in the middle of March just before the election was announced. I had been concerned that John Major had developed 'Teflon' qualities over broken promises and I wanted to connect him to his record. We again portrayed him as two-faced, saying one thing before an election but doing another after it, promising lower taxes and then raising them twenty-two times. It was hard, but it was accurate and fair.

Going into the election campaign, viewing figures for the broadcasts started to rise, and the segmented approach became less important. The first of our five election broadcasts, on 10 April, was deliberately reassuring and positive, coinciding with the launch of the business manifesto. We had business people such as Anita Roddick, Terence Conran and Gerry Robinson endorsing us as 'a party that business can do business with'. Margaret McDonagh met the participants, and Simon Buckby interviewed them, with a friend of his holding the camera.

Our second PEB was the famous 'bulldog' broadcast, interspersing shots of Tony Blair talking about his hopes and ideas with pictures of him meeting world leaders, and clips of Fitz the bulldog. It was a bold stride across Tory territory – Labour re-awakening national pride to make Britain great again. It was centred on a line from Blair, 'The Tories say Britain's good enough. We say Britain can be better.' This broadcast was planned over a long time, about six months. I tested an animatic – a cartoon replica – of the broadcast in focus groups and it researched well. There had been fears that it might alienate women because it seemed so aggressive, but that didn't happen. There were endless discussions about whether it had to be a formal interview with Blair or with him on the move, and how you could cut between the dog and Blair. And before we actually got agreement to film Fitz, we commissioned what turned out to be two or three months' worth of intensive filming between the documentary-maker Molly Dineen and Tony Blair. By February we had spent a lot of money and had set up Ridley Scott Associates to shoot the dog (on film), but still had no agreement to go ahead with it. Simon Buckby and I were very keen, others wary.

BMP had to make a big presentation at Millbank before Mandelson and Campbell would agree to let them film the broadcast. Blair and Brown were nervous too, and Blair only agreed to proceed with it after seeing an animatic of the broadcast in his office.

Film of the dog was all cut and ready by the end of February. The problem then arose that the footage Molly Dineen had shot did not work with the film of Fitz: in black and white, lethargic and gloomy at first then rising and trotting happily away, symbolising the renewal of Britain. Molly had been filming for two months and had forty tapes of Tony Blair. She edited them down to 8–10 minutes of highlights, which were gritty and personal but which just wouldn't fit with film of the dog. We needed new film of Blair 'rousing' the dog as he spoke, and it was agreed that Alastair Campbell would interview Blair in his house in Islington. 'For some reason, possibly because Tony felt too comfortable with Alastair, it didn't work,' said Simon. 'It didn't look powerful or strong enough.'[22] By now it was the beginning of April, in the middle of the election campaign.

At a heated meeting that included Alastair Campbell, Peter Mandelson, Margaret McDonagh, Simon Buckby and Dan Clifton, it was agreed to make two separate films – to ask Molly Dineen to continue cutting her forty hours into ten minutes, and to try to get some different footage of Blair for the Fitz broadcast. 'Molly was left to go and shoot her own film,' Simon said, 'and we agreed that Tony needed to have somebody who maybe he knew but was a bit more distant from than Alastair to interview him, so I did it. And we went to somebody's house in Wandsworth and shot it and there was something wrong with the colour. It was too pink.' We had to get it shot yet again, on the Saturday morning, 12 April, three days before it was due to be broadcast. Buckby and Mark Lucas, Labour's head of film production, went to Blair's house in Islington, 'and we shot him really quickly this time because he had a bloody good idea what he wanted to say and how he wanted to say it. And it worked. And Mark and myself went to the editing suite and edited overnight and chucked the pictures against the dog, took it back to BMP who rejected it because they preferred the original pink version and Alastair's interviews.'[23]

John Webster, the long-suffering director, cut another version of the film, which was a combination of Buckby's interview and Campbell's interview, and both films were brought to Mandelson and me on Monday morning for us to choose. We watched the version combining the two interviews, and it looked terrible. One moment Blair was sitting in front of this brightly lit window in Islington, the next he was obviously somewhere completely different, back-dropped by pink curtains. We chose Buckby's version. It was a wonderful PEB. When the music by Michael Nyman, from the film *Carrington*, came in at the end, you got a soaring sense of opportunity, of hope and prospect in the future of a Labour government. It created a sense that Britain could be better. It had been hard work, but it was worth it.

Our third PEB, on 21 April, was another classic example of humour allowing you to say something on television that you simply couldn't do in print. We wanted to portray the Tories as so out of touch that they had done things – and would continue to do things – that hurt the target electorate. BMP came up with the idea of showing the Conservatives at the end of conference singing 'Land Of Hope And Glory', looking ecstatically happy and pleased with themselves, cut against pictures of real Britain – powerful images of people living in the real world, with captions explaining what the Tories had actually done. So at the beginning, as the Conservatives rose up to sing, you saw old people in homes, moving into the rundown NHS, overcrowded schools, people being mugged on the streets, women with families not being able to afford food because of VAT, all ending in an amazing crescendo as the sea washed away a sandcastle as if Britain were being destroyed by the Tories. It was powerful television, directed by Simon Kellen Jones, who also made *Our Friends in the North*.

Molly Dineen's film of Blair came next. I had been sceptical of it, but Alastair Campbell and Molly were keen, and they were right to be: its honest, glitz-free, fly-on-the-wall approach broke through the scepticism of the electorate, at a time when they were fed up with the whole campaign, making it probably our most effective broadcast.

Our final broadcast on the Monday before polling day summed up all our earlier messages. We returned to the traditional story-telling format, but again segmented into four sections. Directed by Stephen Frears, it starred Pete Postlethwaite as a taxi-driver picking up a father and his young daughter, who has been in casualty for six hours with a broken arm. The message of the film was blunt: vote, and vote Labour, or here's what the Tory fifth term will look like. In the film the taxi-driver picked the pair up after the polls had closed and explained to the father that he should have voted because of what was going to happen to his daughter's future, running through crime, education, tax and health. At the end the clock turned back, the taxi-driver told them they still had time to vote, dropped them off outside a polling station and drove off, showing a glimpse of his angel's wings. There was a lot of opposition to those wings: Campbell naturally hated them and wanted them cut out; I wanted them in. In the end Peter Mandelson took the video to Tom Sawyer, the General Secretary, who liked the wings, so they stayed. And these things stick. In January I was doing a focus group when someone said, 'I voted Labour because of the taxi-driver who had wings.'[24]

Reading all this, the rows, the pettiness, the trivia, it's easy to think: what is the point? It's all ridiculous, why does it matter so much? But that misses the point. Of course, when highly creative people meet highly political people the odd lapse into absurdity is inevitable, but the hours and hours spent getting every last detail right matter. Most obviously, if our communications are professional, then it reassures people that we will be professional and competent in government. More importantly, it means that we are taking the electorate seriously, not taking them for granted. This came through as an important difference between the two campaigns: Labour seemed to be making an effort to win support, the Conservatives hardly trying at all. Making an effort, being a perfectionist over small details gets through to the public. They need signals that tell them: this party cares about me. And in the end, if we believe we are right, and they are wrong, we have a responsibility to present that message with the greatest skill and professionalism we can muster. Saying the right thing but saying it badly is an indulgence. We have a duty to do the best we can.

Focus groups and opinion polling

With the exception of 'spin-doctors', no campaigning phrase has been imbued with a greater air of nonsensical mystique than 'focus groups'. Why focus groups should have gained this elevated position I cannot tell. Old-fashioned qualitative research, another name for the same thing, has not taken off in people's imaginations in the same way, nor has quantitative opinion polling, which is now incredibly sophisticated and potentially much more influential.

Focus groups are important to me. The mystique surrounding them is ridiculous: they are simply eight people in a room talking. Their importance in modern politics is that they enable politicians to hear directly the voters' voices.

I first came into contact with focus groups, or qualitative research, or group discussions as they were then known (and still are to many research practitioners) when I worked in advertising in the 1970s. In those days the moderator, the person who conducts the groups, would also prepare the evaluation and write the report. I was soon dissatisfied with this and wanted to attend. When I did I found it fascinating, gaining an understanding which immediately transcended that given by the moderator's report.

When I left advertising and started to work with the Labour Party they were already using qualitative research. In November 1985 some of the finest researchers in Britain presented ruthlessly damning findings on the unelectability of Labour.

At that time I did not conduct groups, but often sat in

on them and always found them the source of enormous insight. This worked well until the 1992 campaign, but then research failed Labour. Both our quantitative polling, and to an extent our qualitative polling, failed to gauge accurately the public mood. All, or certainly most, of our researchers believed that Labour was heading for a hung parliament at worst, a small majority at best. I attended no groups during the 1992 election and I bitterly regret it. I decided there and then that I would conduct all my own groups, and that if I ever had a chance to work in another election I would conduct group discussions every single night.

I took my courage in my hand and conducted my first group. No one trained me, I just did it. And I loved it. I loved the direct contact with the electorate, the way that I could put arguments, hear arguments, confront arguments, develop ideas, feel the intensity of a point of view and hear the opinions, attitudes and emotions of ordinary members of the public.

I nearly always conduct focus groups in unassuming front rooms in Watford, or Edgware or Milton Keynes or Huddersfield, in a typical family room stacked with the normal knick-knacks and photos. The eight or so members of a group will have been recruited by a research company according to a formal specification: who they voted for in a previous election, their age, their occupation. They often begin nervously but then relax and talk freely, and usually do not want to stop.

I never analyse a group in isolation. I see them in relation to the other groups I have conducted, to the direction and purpose of the campaign, to the concepts that I and others may be developing at the time. In no way is this a passive process. I do not just sit there and listen. I challenge, I argue back, I force them to confront issues. I confront issues myself. I like to use the group to develop and test ideas.

I nearly always learn something new and surprising. People do not think in predictable ways or conform to conventional prejudice. In a group it is possible to test out the strength and depth of feeling around an issue, which can be more difficult, although not impossible, in a conventional poll.

Above all, what I get from focus groups is a sense of people's dignity, of the hard and difficult lives they lead. Most people work very hard and usually both parents work. They often feel insecure about their jobs, and are always worried about crime, the NHS, and schools for their children. Most people lead lives under pressure. They are sceptical about politics, but pleased that someone is prepared to listen to their views. Such is their scepticism and alienation that they cannot believe that a political party is interested in what they have to say. Sometimes at a focus group I would say that I was conducting this group for Tony Blair and its members would be astonished. Tony Blair cares what I think? He does care, and so do I. Focus groups do not of necessity involve dilution of principle or compromise – to say that implies that the voters are fools, which they are not. They want politicians who are tough, honest and courageous, and who govern with principle. That is why they respected Margaret Thatcher and in the end lost faith in John Major. The public want leaders who lead, they want governments that tough it out. But they also want to be heard. Of course, governing with principle and yet in a continuous dialogue with the voters is complicated. But modern politics is complicated. The electorate is more demanding and is right to be so. It is up to us to meet the new challenge. I do not just see focus groups and market research as campaigning tools; increasingly I see them as an important part of the democratic process: part of a necessary dialogue between politicians and people, part of a new approach to politics.

Not all groups work as they should. On one occasion two strangers seduced each other as the group was going on. Everyone pretended not to notice. Sometimes people get too angry, but mostly they work well.

For the three years before the election I did focus groups about once a week. For the six and a half weeks of the election I conducted them six nights a week. Mostly I focused on 1992 Conservative voters who were considering switching to Labour, our prime target group.

Focus groups in London
To give the flavour of a typical focus group of switchers from
Conservative to Labour, here are some comments from
verbatim transcripts, literally picked at random from a huge
pile near my desk. These groups were conducted in Edgware:

April 1996: 'Why have you stopped supporting the Conservatives?'

- 'I've lost a lot of money. I have got severe negative equity
  on a flat that we bought about two years ago. I have lost
  about half the value of it so we had to go to the building
  society to ask to borrow more. It's upsetting to say the
  least. It did come quite close to losing our house at one
  stage, but we were lucky we could pull through.'
- 'Overall we have gone back to the dark ages here. The
  NHS system here is just a complete, total nightmare.'
- 'I just feel that we are going backwards – they certainly
  aren't taking us forwards. Crime is rising, the NHS is
  going to pot.'[25]

May 1996: 'What do you feel about voting Labour?'

- 'I have thought about it. But Labour has got to be very
  careful over the next few months. They are being careful,
  but they have got to continue being careful. I don't really
  trust Labour.'
- 'There has been a huge success in how Labour has
  improved their image and they've done a lot of work.
  About ten years ago I wouldn't have touched them with
  a barge-pole, but now I just might. You do hear how
  Labour MPs are sponsored by the unions and you do
  wonder, though, just how in their pockets they are and
  how extreme they are. You still would be a little bit scared.'
- 'After the last time they were in, everyone had a bad
  feeling – a bad taste in their mouth. They can't completely
  change all their policies. They were so extreme that they
  really did have to move towards the centre, and I'm just
  not convinced that they truly have.'[26]

These answers give a clear sense of the dilemma facing these switchers: disillusioned with the Conservatives but wary of Labour. This mood remained until the end of the campaign.

Focus groups in the United States

As a comparison between focus groups in the United Kingdom and the United States, below is a diary account of focus groups conducted in Los Angeles in February 1995 by Stanley Greenberg for the President, which I attended along with George Stephanopoulos:

23 February: Arrive LA mid-afternoon. Palm trees in the airport. Fast transfer. My driver waits. Tousled hair, jeans, bright shirt: 'Hi, I'm Mike.' Guided tour through the sprawl of outer LA. Long drive to focus groups. Long detailed questionnaire. Women college graduates. The respondents introduce themselves. 'Hi, I'm Karen. I'm an actress. I just had a part in *Murder Incorporated*' (low gasps of admiration). 'I've had silicone implants, but they have inflated, poisoned my body, gave me rheumatism, but I struggle on' (moans of condolence). 'Hi, I'm Carol. I think criminals should have their hands cut off' (general assent).

Strongly pro-choice. Tough on welfare, didn't like Gingrich, but he has made his mark. Dole: Boring. Bureaucratic. Warm to Clinton: for the middle class. Tries hard. Done a lot.

Response to Clinton not at all like Major. No sense of betrayal. Not for the privileged. No extremism.[27]

24 February: The female groups are the same as last night. Concerns about crime, violence, having to work too hard. Clinton liked: decent, on our side, understands us, for the middle class, tried to get health care through: but ineffective, has not done anything for us. The women, as yesterday, were more self-contained, more optimistic, less beaten down than many British women I have spoken to in groups.

The men looked like a six-pack platoon. Uncompromising.

Unattractive. They were everything you imagine US blue-collar voters to look like. They were concerned about the same things but again not as angry as in Britain. They liked Clinton, but less strongly.[28]

25 February: Black groups in downtown LA. These groups were extraordinary. The black males were initially hostile: 'Who are you, sister?' 'Is this a black research agency?' The start was very aggressive. But then they soften and occasionally dissolve into farce. Tony the aggressive Afro-American poet from New York trying to develop a relationship with the moderator. They are open about their lack of knowledge and impressively supportive of the less articulate members of the group. They are angry, clearly feeling themselves the victims of racism, which is often subtle. 'They told me I couldn't have a car-washing job because I didn't have the experience. Only afterwards did I realise you did not have to have experience to wash cars.'

They are polar opposites of the blue-collar males. They appear almost impossible to contain in the same coalition. George Stephanopoulos is witty about his boss, the President: when one of the women says Clinton procrastinates, George says, 'You got that one right.'

The women were very impressive. They were intelligent, warm, supportive, honest, informed. They liked Clinton, they thought he was trying, particularly on health care, but he changed his mind too often, has not delivered. They were optimistic, strong, and put the white groups to shame.[29]

Alastair Campbell did not believe in focus groups, but he does now: 'Well, before I went to them I thought you were a bit of a nutter, frankly. But I never went to a focus group where I didn't get some sort of insight that was useful. I think one of the great dangers of politics is the sort of level you are at, either in opposition or in government. It is very easy to lose track, and the people who were talking were the people who had to vote for us, so you had to listen to what they were saying. Sometimes it was depressing because there you were working your balls off trying to communicate what you were all about and they knew bugger-all about it and yet they had opinions about it. Very strong opinions.'[30] Bruce Grocott MP (Blair's Parliamentary Private Secretary) was another convert. He was against the whole idea, but attended a couple of groups and became an addict.

Focus groups are only part of the polling programme. Equally as important, probably more important, are quantified opinion polls with samples of over 1,000. Political polling is far more advanced in the United States than in the United Kingdom for obvious reasons: the USA has dozens and dozens of elections, with large budgets for polling and media.

For the election and pre-election period we were lucky to have the voluntary assistance of Stanley Greenberg. Greenberg has taken quantitative research to new heights. Polls are no longer snapshots of public opinion, they are incredibly perceptive measures of where public opinion is, using long questionnaires with subtle and intelligent questions. Greenberg likes quantitative research because the process of writing the questionnaire forces strategic choices to be taken. After the poll has been conducted it is subject to a level of statistical analysis that transforms your understanding of the data. This is strategic research at its best, and it is incredibly valuable to a political campaign. Greenberg says of the use of modern polling techniques in political campaigning:

> It doesn't need defending. It is part of the democratisation of modern elections. Just as governments have changed, just as parties have changed, campaigns have changed. Democracy has changed. The institutions that used to be effective in mediating popular sentiment have atrophied, and have lost their ability to articulate. So the trade unions, for example, just don't have the kind of base that they used to have. If you want to know what working people think, you can't turn to these organisations which can effectively represent their members and so there is no choice but to go to people directly through these means. Politicians have always used various instruments to try to judge where the public stood. And now polls and focus groups are the best available means.[31]

In Millbank Greg Cook co-ordinated the whole polling programme with great skill. He made sure that as well as the opinion polls and focus groups, vast party telephone banks were in constant contact with switchers to Labour. Deborah Mattinson also conducted intensive polling in the key area of the Pennine Belt. It was a highly sophisticated polling operation, and a great credit to Cook.

Spin-doctors

The only campaigning phrase more abused than focus groups is 'spin-doctor'. It is used by the media without thought or understanding. Initially, 'spin' was a term reserved for the practice of putting the best possible gloss on an event breaking in the news. Typically, after a US presidential debate, James Carville and George Stephanopolous for one side and Mary Matalin, now Carville's wife and a spokesperson for Bush, for the other would rush – literally, run – to the awaiting media corps to give their line on the debate.

This was called 'spinning': putting your perspective on what happened. In 1996 I was in the media area after a presidential debate. It had a huge sign over it saying SPIN CITY. The moment the debate started it was as though the floodgates opened and dozens of spokespeople from both Dole and Clinton rushed into the room. The place was in complete turmoil – crushed, heaving, shouting, maniacal. At points just yards apart campaign representatives were spinning, putting their views of the debate. Above each of Clinton's team an assistant carried a prominent sign with the name of the person doing the briefing: 'Leon Panetta' (Clinton's chief of staff), 'George Stephanopolous', and so on. By the next debate the Republicans had caught up: they had their signs, too.

From 'spinning' grew 'spin-doctors', which is just a fancy name for media spokespeople. But from there somehow the name came to include anyone or anything included in what are believed to be the 'black arts' of campaigning. This is just media nonsense. If a 'spin-doctor' exists at all, he or she is someone responsible for media relations for a political party. This is a longstanding and completely unexceptional activity. In a world in which political parties, and other high-profile organisations, are under twenty-four-hour media attack, it is common sense to employ people to put the view of the party or organisation and to do it to best effect. In a modern media environment, competence and good communications are inseparable: you cannot have one without the other.

Of course, some media spokespeople do this with greater skill than others. Because of his long background in the tabloids, Alastair Campbell understands the needs of the press. He knows that unless you constantly feed the media stories, they will gobble you up. He thinks it a point of professional pride that he has to make the best case for Tony Blair: after all, that is what he is there for. Campbell is more than just a media spokesperson. He is also an outstanding strategist, but above all he has the presence and qualities of endurance which made him, in effect, the rock of the campaign. He has received much credit for the 1997 victory but he is still in some ways underestimated. Campbell is hard to get to know, difficult to break down. He tends to be suspicious of people, and categorises them into either a very small group who are acceptable or a very large group who are not. But when he does accept someone he is loyal to them: particularly if they work with or for him.

David Hill, until recently chief media spokesperson for the Labour Party, and another highly skilled and highly rated 'spin-doctor', describes how he works:

> The first rule is you have to understand and know the people you are dealing with. You have to be robust. You have to never tell a lie – telling lies is disastrous, because one of the most effective elements in being a spin-doctor is that they believe what you are saying to them. Because if you kill a story and then they find out that you are lying and in fact the story is true, you've had it in the future. So you've got

to be robust, you've got to understand your journalists, you've got to never lie to them, and you have got to recognise what they want. You have got to have speed, because if you don't get your strike in first, or if you don't follow something up quickly, then you get left behind. You must provide words, because they always need words. What you have got to do to be an effective spin-doctor – someone who can really do the business on behalf of the party – is be someone who the media can go to and say: 'Although I have got a story, if I've spoken to you I know the status of an issue. I know where it is taking me, I know whether it is going to take off or not.' Then you will have created a relationship with the journalists which is pivotal.[32]

Putting the best progressive case to the media should not be a reason for criticism, but a cause for pride. The ability to handle the media is essential in opposition and government. It is one of the ways progressive parties advance their cause, and serve the public well.

The grid

The grid is the heart of an election campaign. It is the point at which strategy, message and logistics all gel on one single piece of paper. A grid is not just a timetable – where leading politicians will be on every day of the campaign – but outlines the strategic and message imperatives that connect with the planning logistics.

Most task forces in Millbank drew up their own election grids. Jackie Stacey's team had compiled a detailed day-by-day plan of Blair's and Prescott's nationwide tours. Dan Clifton spent a great deal of time filling in a schedule of all the radio and television programmes that were planned for the campaign. Faz Hakim and Ian Howarth in 'Key Campaigners' drew up campaign diaries for all the shadow Cabinet visits. However, these grids stood alone and often did not relate to each other. They needed an overall master-plan to defer to and into which they would slot, giving the campaign shape, cohesion and a central message. Following the launch of 'Leading Britain into the Future' in early January 1997, Mandelson knew that the clock was ticking and that he had to get something down on paper, both setting out the structure of the campaign day and drawing up an early grid. He went to Waheed Alli's house in Kent on the weekend of 25–26 January, armed with his laptop and a warm jumper.

Mandelson spent the whole weekend in the living-room by a log fire, with his computer on his lap, bashing out notes to Tony Blair on a proposed daily structure of meetings and, more importantly, drawing up the first draft of the 'message grid'. Each day was allotted a separate page, with simple sections typed into the margins, including details of the morning and afternoon press conferences, the whereabouts of Tony Blair, the main photo of the day and key broadcast appearances of shadow Cabinet members. Each page contained only eight or nine simple facts, but they provided the umbrella for all the logistical and media scheduling. When Peter returned from Kent, he and Alastair went over it together before distributing it to Tony Blair's office, Gordon Brown's office and key staff at Millbank. Over the next three months it was discussed at countless meetings and went through a dozen redrafts. It was finally taken to a series of early morning meetings with Tony Blair and Gordon Brown at Millbank.

There was never a final draft of the grid. It was refined throughout the campaign, with Mandelson clipping new sheets into the purple folder which accompanied him to every campaign meeting. It now sits on the top of his bookshelf in the study of his London home.

The grid was brought to life by a series of late-night meetings organised with great skill and gusto by Anji Hunter. These meetings showed Anji at her best: she powered through them, mowing down anyone who was slow or unco-operative. There was no chance of an early night: pizzas arrived at about midnight and the grid would be finished come what may. These meetings started in early

1997 and continued almost until the election. They were crucial in making the grid real: agreeing events, locations, opportunities for photographs. They key participants – in addition to Anji – were Margaret McDonagh; Jan Royall, veteran grid organiser and longstanding senior aide to Neil Kinnock; Peter Mandelson; Alastair Campbell; Peter Hyman; and Blair's official photographer for the campaign, Tom Stoddart.

The grid is the heart of the campaign, bringing together all elements of strategy on one sheet of paper. Without a grid, the campaign cannot really be said to exist.

The Conservative campaign

We believed we were up against the most formidable political fighting machine in the world. We were – at the start at least – in awe of Saatchi's and their destructive potential. Jonathan Powell employed Jon Mendelsohn – former adviser to Greville Janner MP – on what was effectively a Saatchi-watch, virtually full-time. We wanted to know everything the Tories were going to do, before they did it. Jon used to write long and vivid reports about how we would be bludgeoned into defeat. 'I was trying to get a full handle on the Tories' *modus operandi*, to analyse what they were doing, how we should respond to it, what we should or shouldn't take seriously,' he said. 'I found this a very, very interesting duty at the beginning. I took a long time studying a large part of the Tory organisation, the personalities, the key figures involved.'[33]

Very early on in 1996 their complete media plan was leaked to us, and this was genuinely scary. First of all, they had a plan; second, they kept to it; and third, they had huge amounts of money – upwards of £10 million. It was all there: the launch of 'New Labour, New Danger' in July; then 'New Labour, New Danger' versions one, two, three, four and five, and so on and so on. Their plan was so reliable you could set your watch by it.

However, although we were in awe of the Saatchi/Central Office machine at the beginning, our respect soon waned.

From the start the Conservatives had not known how to react to New Labour. Initially they had three positions: Labour hasn't changed, it's still old Labour; Labour has changed, but it's just a carbon copy of the Conservatives, so why not stick to the real thing; Labour has changed, but is still as dangerous as ever. Maurice Saatchi explained these options to me in 1995 and moaned about the failure of the Conservatives to make a decisive choice. Eventually they did choose, but they chose the wrong one. They decided to concede New Labour and try to link it to 'new dangers'. This was a mistake. Conceding New Labour as a fact gave it the credibility it needed to be believed by the electorate. It made New Labour real. And the 'new dangers' of New Labour were spurious. Nothing frightened the voters about New Labour at all – all that frightened them was old Labour: unions, taxes, extremism. There was no way that their strategy could work. What the Conservatives should have done was try to present New Labour as a sham, and maintain that old Labour and old dangers were still lurking. That they did not is amazing. Saatchi's now say they were influenced by a survey conducted by Richard Wirthin in 1995, which claimed that New Labour was accepted by the electorate as an irreversible fact and that Conservative strategy therefore had to be built on that. If this was so, then this poll must have been conducted in a parallel electoral universe because the electorate was nervous about old Labour right up to the end of the campaign, and it has taken a Labour government to dispel these fears finally and completely.

But the Tories' worst error was to launch an attacking strategy too early. For the Conservatives to have any chance of winning they had to follow a strategy of three A's: Apologise; Achievements; Attack. They did make some sort of apology – 'Yes it Hurt. Yes it Worked' – but it was too partial and too arrogant. Major should have looked the voter in the eye and said, 'Yes, we made mistakes. Yes, we caused you pain. And we are sorry.'

Next they had to take credit for the economic recovery,

as Clinton had in the United States. Throughout 1996 they should have been advertising positively on the economy: linking the economic upturn with their performance in government. That they did not do this was the biggest strategic error of the campaign. Sir Tim Bell wanted to, as did Saatchi's, but Brian Mawhinney panicked, believing the Conservatives needed an attacking campaign to build morale and stop infighting. The result was that they got no credit for the recovery and alienated the electorate by the negativism of their approach. The more negative they were, the more voters felt they had nothing to offer.

The irony for the Conservatives is that all the elements were in place for electoral recovery: the economy was strengthening, doubt about Labour growing. But they missed their chance. A positive campaign in 1996 followed by a 'Don't Let Labour Blow It' campaign focusing on old Labour would have reduced Labour's majority.

From the summer of 1996 it became clear that the Conservative strategy was not working. Although it was creating some doubt about Labour, it was causing greater resentment towards the Conservatives. In mid-1996 Jon Mendelsohn had reported huge strengths in their campaigning machine. 'It soon became quite apparent actually that I was pretty wrong in the analysis, and it started tailing back quite considerably from that period to looking at their weaknesses,' he remembers.[34] The Tories had given up any claim to exemplify the future or hope or any kind of positive value. This left a vast space in the political landscape for Labour to occupy. Labour could be positive; Labour could represent the future. Blair understood this instinctively. The rest of us had to catch up, but in the end we got it right. The Conservative advertising was a gigantic own goal.

As the campaigning months passed, Mendelsohn's notes became less frequent. He found it harder and harder to say constructive things about what the Tories were trying to achieve. They were also hindered by a largely ineffective media operation. Charles Lewington, Sheila Gunn and the others who made up their press corps were simply no match for Millbank. They tried hard, but they were doomed. By January Mendelsohn had decided that the Conservatives' only remaining strength was fund-raising; the rest was worthless. Then John Major talked about 'two futures' in his New Year address and I began to suspect that the Tories had a copy of my War Book, as indeed it later turned out they had. I noticed soon after that we were being attacked by Brian Mawhinney for scare-mongering on lines closely related to those in the War Book. I was sure they had it, and I phoned Peter from holiday to tell him. Jon Mendelsohn spent weeks trying to find out who leaked it, but he never succeeded. Yet despite having the War Book, with all the polling information about target voters it contained – and the Tories did not do much effective polling themselves – as well as the complete list of Labour's weaknesses as we ourselves perceived them, they had continued to produce advertising that influenced no one but their own hard-core supporters.

'By about February 1997 I had become the personal punching-bag of Philip Gould, and every time he kept on turning to me and saying, "What are they going to do now? They're stuffed. Tell me what they're going to do,"' Mendelsohn remembers. 'At which point I think I developed myriad pathetic excuses for the paucity of the Conservative position ranging from "structurally they're not so bad, it's just the politics really" to even more embarrassing conclusions. Essentially, from January we knew they had completely screwed it because they had no understanding whatsoever of the electorate, the polling, of us, of themselves. They had no understanding of where it all stood and they could not mount a credible attack on us.' In the end Jon was forced to admit it. 'They have blown it,' he wrote.[35]

The final phase

Just as the election was about to be called, everything started to come together. Alastair Campbell, always sceptical, admits that at the end it all worked: 'If you ask me now how it was all put together I could not tell you, but it was.'[36] Peter Mandelson had a grip on the task forces and on the structure and organisation of the campaign. Margaret McDonagh was in effective charge of the logistics, which meant things worked. We had our messages and a theme, and BMP produced advertising expressing the line and the pledges in the brightest of colours so that Labour became the positive party. The grid was finalised. The sets were agreed. Peter Mandelson joined us all to sit at the central table in the middle of Millbank. I used to sit directly opposite Margaret McDonagh. 'Will we still be friends by the end?' she asked at the beginning of the campaign. We are. Gordon Brown and his team moved in. We were ready to go.

And then there was a strange lull. 'My overwhelming sense was of waiting,' said Liam Byrne.

> There was a point in about January–February when things looked as if they were suddenly coming together and I felt for the first time that we were going to be okay. There were so many differences of opinion about who was going to be in charge and what everyone needed to be doing, but in January–February everything suddenly came together. Then my sense was of waiting, waiting for the Conservatives to really hit us hard – and we kept waiting. I remember there was a period of two days – the only time I ever came close to hitting a panic button – when they hit us on trade unions because this was a real business issue that we needed to win. I think it's true to say that we wobbled for a day – for about a period of twenty-four hours, we wobbled. We then fully expected them to come and hit us with a couple more good right hands, and it never came. I remember talking with the business unit – we were expecting the great adverts, you know, Tory battalions to charge into us, and it just never came. We had just cut the ground from under them.[37]

Every week, and perhaps twice a week as the election drew closer, I conducted focus groups in London and the north-west. Afterwards I would phone up Tony Blair and talk to him about the voters and their mood. The closer the election got, the more reflective he became. Often I would call and interrupt him gently strumming on his guitar, calm, focused, preparing himself. He was ready for the fight. So was Millbank.

10

LANDSLIDE COUNTRY

Week one: Losing the election campaign

Monday, 17 March

We knew Major would call the election that day. Of course people were excited, but it was actually very calm in Millbank as we watched Major's election announcement outside 10 Downing Street. Everyone knew exactly what to do. Tony Blair did some interviews at lunchtime from a school. He looked nervous, but carried it off. Alastair Campbell was with him and remembers a sense of victory: 'We had done an awful lot of preparatory work, that school had been set up for weeks and we always said the minute the election was called we'd go to a school. And we fixed up live – Tony did a storming interview, absolutely storming. He looked right. I could sense then we were going to do it.'[1]

In Millbank, Peter Mandelson and Gordon Brown called a staff meeting of everyone in the building. The room was packed. They outlined the seriousness of the task ahead, that this was the moment everyone had been working towards.

That night I went to do my first focus group of the election. I had decided to conduct them every night for the next six weeks, except Saturdays. I was afraid of exhaustion. I took Labour's election campaign with me to be tested – every advertisement, every poster, about twelve of them. I bought a coffee and a chicken burger at Euston Station, as I have done dozens of times before, and got on a train to Watford feeling a settled calm: we are off, it is going to be okay. I then sensed that something was missing, and realised I had left Labour's entire election campaign by the Burger King at Euston Station. Desperate panic overcame me. I had no phone. I was compounding idiocy with idiocy. The thought crossed my mind that, for me, 1997 could become some terrible replay of 1992. 'GOULD LEAVES ELECTION CAMPAIGN ON EUSTON STATION.' I reached Watford and phoned Margaret McDonagh, hyperventilating – 'I have made a terrible mistake' – and explained what had happened. She was calm, talked me down. 'It will be all right,' she said. But the moment she was off the phone she screamed at one of my assistants to 'get down to Euston now'.

My wife was at home with the children. I got her down to Euston as well. Then I rang directory enquiries to find the telephone number of the Burger King; the only one they had was at Paddington. I arrived at the house where the groups were being held and stumbled through the first minutes, semi-hysterical. Then my pager buzzed: 'Posters found'. I relaxed. This is an omen, I thought. This time the gods are with me.

The gods were not with John Major. He was mauled in the focus groups. I went home and did what I would do virtually every night of the campaign: I wrote two notes, one to the campaign team – Tony Blair, Gordon Brown, Peter Mandelson, Alastair Campbell, Jonathan Powell, Anji Hunter and Margaret McDonagh – and a second, personal one to Tony Blair. This took until quite late, perhaps one or two in the morning. I was up again at five. This was not exceptional: most of the other people involved in the campaign worked these kind of hours.

I frequently phoned Alastair Campbell with findings from the groups. That night he told me that the *Sun* had come out for Labour. Stuart Higgins had paged him while Blair was doing a question-and-answer session in Gloucester earlier that evening. 'I knew instinctively what it was,' he said.[2] This was a sickening blow to Tory morale so early in the campaign.

The night's findings were clear: 'On the basis of these

groups Labour won the day. Fourteen out of sixteen respondents thought TB was the most effective performer on the
basis of news coverage. Major did most badly with women,
who thought him arrogant and lacking in humility.' They
particularly disliked him describing the election as 'fun'.
'Major's problem as a campaigner is that he is soiled by his
record. In 1992 his approach was new and he had no baggage.
Now he has a record of failure. Last time the mood was:
"Give him a chance". Now the mood is: "He has had his
chance". The soapbox worked then, it does not work now.'
And Labour's message – that Britain could be better – 'over-
whelms the Tory message that Britain is good enough'. The
Conservative message – 'Eighteen years has transformed
Britain. Don't take the risk with Labour' – only reminded
people they wanted change.[3] I wrote to Blair, 'You beat Major
today.'[4]

Tuesday, 18 March
I went to have acupuncture at seven. In my taxi to the office
I got a call from Blair. 'How was I?' he asked. How was
what? I thought. It turned out that he had been interviewed
for the *Today* programme on Radio 4. He was full of nervous
excitement, desperate to get going. Unable to face the humiliation of saying I was having acupuncture at the moment
the leader of the Labour Party was giving his first major
interview of the campaign, I lied and said I was at the gym.
Blair groaned. I squirmed with embarrassment. 'You too?'
he said. He had phoned Peter Mandelson for his reaction
to the interview and Peter really *had* been at the gym. Blair
and Campbell both thought we were completely pathetic.

Blair was anxious about the result. I decided to suppress
my usual pessimism and said we should be aiming for a 10
per cent, hundred-seat win. I said it was certain we would
win comfortably. I phoned Peter. We both felt foolish.

I arrived at Millbank where we were still on the nine
o'clock morning meeting schedule. We did not move to seven
o'clock starts until after Easter. Millbank was starting to fill
up. Peter Hyman had moved on to the central table, along

with, occasionally, Alastair Campbell. Margaret, who had saved my life the night before, suggested possibly I needed more sleep. She thinks I am cracking up, I thought.

In an annexe to the main campaigning space, shadow Cabinet researchers were assembling. A 'Reflections' group had been formed to give dispassionate strategic advice.

Blair's office was moving in upstairs, including Derry Irvine (Lord Irvine of Lairg) who was a huge figure in the campaign and who formed a special bond with Stanley Greenberg and myself. He was especially fond of Stan, and consulted him often, like a doctor. Working with Derry was one of the pleasures of the campaign. He combined a boyish sense of humour with a rather grand manner that I found both endearing and entertaining in a long, gruelling campaign. He was in Millbank to offer his forensic legal mind and to make sure the relationships worked. He was soon in action helping to dig us out of trouble on the issue of union recognition.

Peter Mandelson was cooler and calmer than in 1987. He sat at his desk, feet on the table, listening to the radio through earphones, watching television, ready to pounce. He rarely lost his composure: he was controlled and measured throughout. This is only one side of Mandelson. He is a balance of outward control, genuine self-confidence, lurking vulnerability and a biting sense of humour, and he normally moves quickly between these mooods. His greatest quality is his courage – often when a situation looks parlous he will ratchet it up, take a few more risks. He likes to be on the edge. But he also wants to have fun, squeezing the irony out of people and situations. During this campaign, however, he stayed in one mood: clinical, detached, in control, pacing himself and the campaign.

For most of the weeks that followed, I hated the 1997 campaign. It was a dreadful ordeal from beginning to end. I wanted only one thing: to win, to win massively, and for no one, not one single person, to say, 'We could have done better.' I was going to exorcise the ghosts of 1992. I knew that this degree of focus, this obsession, verged on a kind of madness, but I believe that many campaigners are in their way slightly mad. Through the force of my will, I wanted to drive the Tories into the ground. But one day, as I was wandering off to a focus group clutching my art bag and wearing crumpled, dishevelled clothes, Tony Blair's Jaguar swept past me with Blair, Campbell and Anji Hunter laughing at my apparent eccentricity, and I thought perhaps I was going too far.

The *Sun* dominated the mood on Tuesday. Robin Oakley, political editor of the BBC, poignantly described the dismay of the Tories: 'Old friends are passing them by on the other side of the street.'[5] At the morning press conference, Gordon Brown came under pressure for refusing to name the companies that would be affected by windfall tax. After the conference the BBC filmed Charlie Whelan briefing frantically in the foyer of the media centre, leading Peter Mandelson to give an order that no one was to brief inside the centre, because of all the cameras. We had a better afternoon: the Liberal Democrat MP Simon Hughes asked a question about the Downey Report into alleged corruption by Neil Hamilton and others at Prime Minister's Questions, and we realised sleaze could be catapulted to the top of the agenda again. The Scottish MP Brian Wilson was sent off to tour the Press Gallery to talk up the story. David Hill immediately got on to John Prescott to get him to front our end of the attack. 'We didn't want the Liberals at the forefront of this anyway, but also it was a disadvantage because it wouldn't have the same impact,' he said. 'So I immediately contacted John Prescott and said, "You have got to front this tomorrow morning. You have got to go and kick the shit out of the Tories over the latest developments in Tatton and Hamilton." And he went on the *Today* programme the following morning, after I had told everybody it was going to happen, so the story ran overnight and built up massive momentum. Prescott was on at ten past eight and went for them very effectively. It just took off.'[6] It was classic Prescott – funny, bombastic, hammering the Tories again and again. Sleaze was up and running.

The focus groups that night were good: 'All these

respondents have hardened in their support since they were last interviewed (around a year ago). Their position going into the election is clear: the Conservatives are finished, Labour should be given a go. This does not mean the election is a formality: it is a test that Labour must pass.' Labour had won the day, 'but by a closer margin than yesterday. Respondents did not really understand the windfall tax. It did not break through today.'[7] To Blair I wrote: 'You are beating Major comfortably. Seven of the eight respondents say you are outscoring him.'[8]

Wednesday, 19 March
The windfall tax was extensively covered in the broadsheets, but the Downey Report dominated the news. We had been preparing for a Tory attack on the latest jobless figures, which showed a substantial reduction in unemployment, but they were completely overshadowed by sleaze. All anyone wanted to know was why they had not published the Downey Report before the election. Michael Heseltine called the BBC news agenda 'a scandal'.[9] Brian Mawhinney toured the TV studios accusing us of mischief-making and attempting to cover up the good unemployment figures. Millbank staffers stood around the TV screens cheering as Mawhinney got more and more irate. It was being claimed that the election was called early to avoid publication. I did not believe it. Our intelligence had always been that Major wanted a long campaign, which was another of his appalling errors. All the long campaign did was make people fed up and heighten their desire for change.

The focus groups showed this was another strong day for us. 'This group was very good for us indeed. We still face campaigning challenges, but they can be dealt with.' However, the voters were already beginning to get impatient with the campaign: 'Women all used the same word – "muddle" – to describe the campaign. Men think the campaign is still in its slow early stages: the first ten minutes of a football match.'[10] To Blair I wrote, 'Your own position is remarkably strong,' but at the moment, 'you are our campaign; nothing else is on the radar'. I was convinced that we should be positive; the electorate was screening out negative messages. There were some worries too: our campaign 'is liked and admired' but 'lacks content and definition'; 'Europe is mentioned a few times – people want reassurance on it. If the Tories got the right message they could make progress on the economy.'[11]

Thursday, 20 March

The focus was all on sleaze. At the daily eleven o'clock strategy meeting, which had a large cast but did not always make much progress, Gordon Brown had one of the most brilliant ideas of the campaign. He wanted the Labour candidate in Tatton to stand down and for an independent to stand against Hamilton. The first time he said it, he mumbled it a bit and no one really listened. He repeated it and this time they took some note. It seemed like a Brown long shot: it was not really going to happen. But Gordon was a man with a mission: if he could, he was going to keep sleaze running until polling day. The more Hamilton and his wife appeared on TV, the less chance the Conservatives had to campaign on their agenda. Prime Minister's Questions had Blair and Major face-to-face in combat. Blair was angry, Major vicious. An interim report into the sleaze allegations was published, leaving a question-mark hanging over ten Tory MPs.

But out in Northwood, where I did my focus groups that night, the election was already going off the boil. People were starting to lose interest: they were using words like 'boring' and 'bickering'. 'Day-one excitement has fizzled out,' I reported.[12] These groups did not warm to Blair either: 'Five of the eight did not like you.' But, 'The crucial point of this group is that they are natural Conservatives who have had enough . . . It would take a lot to get them back to the Tories.' The risk to us remained the same: 'The Tories have potential on the economy and Europe but are as yet unable to unpick it.'[13]

Friday, 21 March

More sleaze, more boredom in the focus groups. The *Guardian* front page – 'Sleaze: the evidence' – was dominated by revelations that Major knew of £25,000 bribes paid to Tim Smith MP, but allowed him to remain as Northern Ireland Minister. This story dominated the news bulletins all day. Gordon Brown was waiting impatiently to see if the Labour candidate, Jon Kelly, would stand down in Tatton. Kelly was considering it, but the Liberals had to stand down too. I was already getting exhausted. I had doubts about whether I could keep doing groups every night. Margaret said I should ease up, but I was determined to keep going. My exhaustion was matched by the voters' boredom. 'The election has become a bit of bore. People are starting to switch off. Most women have very little sense of anything happening at all. Most men think it has been a slow start. This is in marked contrast to the sense of excitement and anticipation that was felt on Monday.' Meanwhile things were getting worse for the Tories. 'It is clear that sleaze is really starting to hurt them. In the short run because they [the voters] are starting not to believe Major, but more crucially because it connects directly to their recent history of incompetence and dishonesty. They are branding themselves as a government you cannot trust.' In response we had to be 'a positive voice in a sea of sleaze and cynicism'.[14]

Weekend, 22–23 March

On Saturday I went into Millbank for a short time. Peter was there and we chatted for a while. He was calm, reflective. I simply felt intense relief that I had got through the first week. I went home and collapsed.

On Sunday evening I drove out to do a focus group in Carpenders Park, close to Watford. It was a beautiful sunny evening and I had a sense of elections past. This one felt calmer, almost serene. The woman hosting the groups was friendly and kind; she was certain we would win. But the group dispelled my confidence: 'This group was far more uncertain than earlier groups this week, and gave much better guidance on how the Conservatives could mount a strategy of recovery. The best way back for the Conservatives is the economy. The basic premise of their poster "Britain is Booming/Don't Let Labour Ruin It" has the power to connect. To be effective the strength of the economy has to be linked to fear of Labour. If they can make the economy a risk, they can make progress. Anxiety about Labour focuses on the unions, interest rates, inflation, tax, Europe, inexperience.'[15] This response was typical and showed the folly of the Conservatives' strategy. As the campaign developed, more and more people became convinced that Britain was booming. A positive strategy from the start would have put the Tories in a different and stronger position.

I wrote to Blair, 'We are in the right place but they are not dead yet. We must watch the economy like a hawk.'[16]

Week two: Field of dreams

Monday, 24 March

The Tories began to do the right thing and attack on the economy, using better-than-expected trade figures to support their 'Britain is Booming' claim. John Sergeant on the BBC lunchtime news accurately observed that 'Tory guns are pointing in the right direction on the economy.' The proposed televised debate between Blair, Major and Ashdown was heating up as an issue. Michael Dobbs, the Tories' negotiator, attacked us for 'hiding behind Liberal skirts on this one'.[17] Matthew Taylor was angry over a briefing someone had given to the *Independent* that we would save £2 billion by merging the management of NHS trusts. More seriously, the *Daily Telegraph* splashed with a story on Labour's plans for union recognition at the workplace. They had a leaked draft of our business manifesto and claimed we had duped the CBI over union recognition rights.

Two focus groups in Slough showed people losing ever more interest in the campaign: 'Every day that passes leaves people more and more disconnected from the campaign.' I wrote that, 'We easily won the news. Seven out of the eight thought Labour was most impressive. This was because Major looked tired and carping. TB was fresh, confident and positive. This contrast swamped the Tory message.'[18] This note has a trace of complacency. It was tempting fate: this was to be our last good day for a while.

Tuesday, 25 March
The Conservatives dropped their education press conference and started attacking us on unions instead. The *Daily Mail* followed up the previous day's *Telegraph* story on the unions with a classic piece on how Labour would return Britain to the 1970s – coupled with lots of gritty images of the Grunwick dispute. The paper produced a list of sixty-three firms which would, they claimed, be dragooned into recognising unions. The Tories had picked up on it. In response, Gordon Brown made a small mistake in answering a question on unions, suggesting that a judge be involved in the adjudication process. He was angry with himself, but anyone answering questions in a General Election press conference is massively exposed, and he was given the wrong information. I was concerned. Fear of trade-union domination was probably our greatest single vulnerability: if we lost ground there, we would lose ground everywhere. The later news bulletins were dominated by Labour's proposals to hold workplace ballots on union recognition, and we were unable to hold to a consistent line. We changed our position three times that day when asked who would define 'workplace': first we said a judge, then, after someone discovered we did actually have a policy on this which everyone had forgotten about, we said some sort of arbitration committee, and finally we put the two together, by saying the committee would be chaired by a judge. Within one 'clarifying' telephone call to a journalist, David Hill had to change his line of argument three times after the intervention of the employment policy officer, Nick Matthews. Derry Irvine immediately called for all the requisite papers. The situation was getting out of control, and the shadow Employment Minister, Stephen Byers, was dispatched to the studios to calm things down.

Tony Blair was wandering around Millbank that night and saw a BBC *Nine O'Clock News* bulletin implying that Labour would surrender to the unions in office. Blair went over to Dan Clifton and said: 'You've got to get a grip on this, this must stop.'[19]

Meanwhile, the negotiations over the leaders' TV debate continued. There was ambivalence in the campaign about it. We were confident Blair would win, but were uneasy about it becoming a distraction, in effect sidelining the rest of the campaign. The Tories shared this ambivalence, which is why in the end the debate didn't happen. We had more negotiating firepower than the Tories: Campbell, Mandelson and Irvine up against Michael Dobbs. In the end the Tories blinked.

In the focus groups that night, unions were hurting us: 'Labour's union recognition proposals are a problem for us, potentially a very serious problem. This is because: unions plus Labour equals danger. Union domination is people's core fear of Labour. The proposal [for union recognition], however sensible and rational it might be, means more union power.' They were scared it would be the thin end of the wedge: '"Will it lead to me being forced to join a trade union if one is recognised?" Will pressure be brought to bear on them? People do not like the element of compulsion: that they will be forced to join trade unions.'[20] I had no doubt at all about what we should do: 'We must close this down immediately. There is no point in trying to hide it, or evade it, we have to confront it and kill it off as an issue.'[21] It did not need me to tell Tony Blair that.

Wednesday, 26 March
At the morning press conference Blair bided his time before moving in for the kill, appearing to go through the motions of the conference but really waiting for his moment: 'Anyone who thinks Labour has made changes in the party to give it all away to the unions or anyone else does not know me.'[22] This was enough to reassure the voters, effectively killing the story stone dead. 'It was a very uncertain time for about twenty-four hours,' David Hill remembers:

Very uncertain. It was one where it was quite difficult to actually answer the questions. But Tony came back and did a press conference the day afterwards and was stunning. He put it to bed. This was one moment during the campaign when I thought all the theatre coupled with all the authority of the leader came together, when all the people in the campaign were working in unison. Tony arrived for the morning press conference, and I actually can't tell you whether what he said was 100 per cent accurate, I can't tell you whether he put it to bed because his forensic skills on the subject were so stunning that there was no answer to what he said – what I can tell you is that his demeanour, his arrival, the theatre of his performance, the authority of his performance that morning meant it was put to bed – and that's all that mattered.[23]

It showed in the groups: 'TB's words were enough to reassure them. These words certainly stopped or at least massively reduced damage today,' I wrote. But I was relentless: 'We must be emphatic that we will not in any way be pushed around by any union. Fairness not favours; no turning back. The bottom line is simple: provided people think that this proposal is the end of it, then we are – just – safe. If they think that this is the first of many, or even of any, concessions, then we are in very serious trouble.'[24]

But even as the Conservatives put us under pressure on unions, they crashed into sleaze again. Tim Smith – one of the MPs being investigated in the cash-for-questions affair – resigned after it was revealed that he had accepted several thousand pounds for asking parliamentary questions. Major was having no luck. Or as David Hill ironically put it, 'God is a switcher.'[25] After a nasty couple of days, the tide had turned again. Hamilton and Smith were having an impact – and we had yet to hear of Piers Merchant.

Thursday, 27 March
The Tory MP Piers Merchant dominated the news. The *Sun* had caught him kissing a seventeen-year-old nightclub

hostess. This was a terrible day for the Tories, made worse when Heseltine went on the radio and said Merchant should resign, which Merchant refused to do. It emphasised the weakness of the Tory leadership and also killed the unions as a story.

Late in the day Michael Dobbs miscalculated in the debate negotiations. Mandelson and Campbell had put him under intolerable pressure, and he over-reacted, toughening his negotiating stance. No sooner had he done this than the Press Association had our response: 'The debate is dead in the water.' Campbell was not unhappy. 'I felt that if we weren't careful, because the media is obsessed with itself, there would have been focus on nothing but the debate and we actually wouldn't get through to the public and it would become a barrier. So to be perfectly honest I was not disappointed when the whole thing collapsed. Next time though, things may be different.'[26]

Progress was being made with the anti-sleaze candidate in Tatton. The Liberals were coming on board, an announcement was imminent. But in Carpenders Park the voters had had enough: 'The overall mood is clear. People are getting fed up and frustrated with this election. Too much bickering, too much sleaze.' However, the Conservatives were 'getting credit for the economy' and our greatest danger remained 'interest rates and inflation'.[27]

Easter weekend
On Saturday Jon Kelly stood down as Labour candidate in Tatton. We were searching for someone to stand against Neil Hamilton, to force him to resign – none of us thought he would tough it out. We assumed that the Tories would push him if he didn't jump. I went away for the weekend with my family. On Saturday I watched the news and saw the chairman of the Scottish Conservatives, Sir Michael Hirst, being forced to resign because of an alleged homosexual relationship. However, it soon transpired that this had more to do with internal Tory party ructions in Scotland than sexual misconduct. For a moment I felt pity for

them, but only for a moment. They were dying, but not yet dead.

On Sunday I wrote my first long strategy note of the campaign. 'The electorate are not connecting with the election and do not understand most of the issues. They find news bulletins fragmented and confusing.'[28] This last point was important. Night after night I would show people the news, and they would not understand it. This was most true of the BBC, partly because their news is delivered at a level of abstraction that loses many people, but mostly because they insisted on editorialising continually. It was always over to Huw Edwards (or whoever it was) for his view of the election. Sky, who played it straight, were most easily understood, and connected best. The BBC let down their viewers.

I said we were vulnerable on 'taxes/interest rates/inflation, Europe, unions', any signs of 'cock-ups' or policy confusion: 'This election is a test of our competence.' I was certain we should remain positive for now: 'We must have a positive core to our campaign . . . we need positive policies, initiatives. Otherwise the electorate will turn away from us. They want us to take them seriously.'[29]

I also wrote to Alastair Campbell about the launch of our posters on Monday. It was his idea to have dozens of multi-coloured posters, all displaying our 'Britain Deserves Better' message, parked in a field in Kent. Tony Blair was to stand in front of them, making a speech. Alastair called it 'the field of dreams', the name he gives Turf Moor, home of Burnley Football Club, which he supports. I called him and talked about the campaign. I said we should try to turn a corner strategically by saying we were fed up with negative campaigning and were going to go positive. We needed to lift ourselves out of the sleaze quagmire which was tarring all the parties, and position ourselves as the positive force in the election. My note was in the same vein: if we needed to refer to sleaze we should do it in 'sadness and a non-partisan way . . . We must try at all times to be positive.'[30]

On Easter Monday, as Blair was launching the pledge posters, David Blunkett was facing down the unions, addressing the NUT annual conference where a year before he had been jostled by angry delegates. He warned them that New Labour would govern for the whole of Britain, and not 'those who threaten and bully'.[31]

That night I conducted a focus group among men in Merton. They were certain to switch to Labour: 'They have made up their mind, and there wasn't much point in following the election closely.'[32]

Week three: The nation switches off

Tuesday, 1 April

Although we had been slugging it out for two weeks and I had already endured fourteen focus groups, the real election had not begun. The public was starting to go mad with boredom. We began our meetings at 7 A.M., with a daily press conference at 8.30 A.M. Our first press conference of the campaign proper had Alan Howarth, Tony Blair and Gordon Brown. There was a live link to John Prescott in Cornwall, with a Cornish pasty, surrounded by people in the sunshine. It all looked very happy and breezy. The leader's tour began, with three coaches, one for Tony Blair and his team, the others for the press. Alastair had slogans painted on them which linked sequentially: 'Leading Britain . . .', 'Into the future . . .', '. . . with Tony Blair'. This showed our attention to detail. We spent hours discussing it, worrying about getting the buses in the right order. Alastair particularly liked the idea of journalists paying to be part of a gigantic moving advertisement.

I went to College Green in Westminster to see the buses off. There was some excitement, but only a little. I was rocking with tiredness, blinking in the sunlight.

The results of our first tracking poll came in. Our heavily adjusted lead had us stable at 20 per cent. But the economy was strengthening at an alarming rate: a net 41 per cent believed the economy was strong. This was up 8 per cent on our poll just two weeks earlier, and compared with a net minus 24 per cent just one year before. Agreement with 'the

Conservatives have messed up the economy' was a net zero; it was a net minus 50 per cent a year before. Improving perceptions of the economy were beginning to have a political effect. Increased numbers thought the economy would be worse under Labour, and Labour's advantage on offering the best standard of living had slipped.[33] Slowly but surely, the Conservatives were gaining an economic foothold. But Blair was moving further ahead of Major. Stan Greenberg in his polling summary wrote, 'Major is clearly being hurt by sleaze and the negative quality of his campaign, particularly among women.'[34] The Conservatives were moving ahead with real power on the economy but were crippled by sleaze. I discussed the research with Blair, who was concerned about the economy factor.

Focus groups in Watford showed sleaze was becoming an even more serious issue for the Conservatives: 'It has become trashy and tabloid. Dominated by sex and the *Sun*.' And there was a new shift in the mood: people had 'increasing fifth-term fears about the Tories. The view of these voters is that if the Tories can win after all their lies, their incompetence, their corruption, then they will not have learned their lesson and be capable of anything.'[35] This was one of those moments when the national mood changes: the Conservatives did not deserve to get back, and if they did, who would control them? It became a refrain for the rest of the election.

Wednesday, 2 April
The Conservatives launched their manifesto. I watched it on television in Millbank and thought it could hardly have seemed more stale. It looked as if Major, the only one who spoke, was barely trying. Meanwhile, Tim Bell, John Gummer and Maurice Saatchi stood on the sidelines of the press conference, looking over-pleased with the result. Their manifesto was a scatter-gun of uncosted proposals and contrasted badly with our far more specific five early pledges. We spent all day trying to push the Tories on how they would pay for the manifesto proposals, which worked to a limited extent,

but we kept coming up against the problem that everyone seemed to have written them off so no one really cared. I knew the manifesto launch would die in the groups that night, and so it did: 'The manifesto did not connect with any of the group. It lacked life, excitement, energy, impact. The two words used to describe the launch were "desperate" ("They dreamed up these ideas ten minutes before the press conference") and "apathetic" ("They weren't really trying").' It could not have been worse for the Tories, but it gave us a chance. I wrote, 'I think we have a real opportunity tomorrow. Tonight's group covered every age and class. They all voted Tory in 1992. Were not that keen on us, but today's [Conservative] manifesto launch convinced none of them . . . This masks a deeper dynamic that is beginning to dominate the campaign. Increasingly we are coming to represent hope, new ideas, a fresh approach, the future, while they are mired in the past. Tomorrow we must drive this contrast home: we are energy, verve, leadership, hope.'[36] To Blair I wrote: 'You are killing Major in this campaign.'[37]

Thursday, 3 April
There was no 8.30 A.M. press conference as everybody was preparing themselves for the manifesto launch. Margaret McDonagh, Jackie Stacey and Jocelyn Hillman, who was responsible for Labour Party publications, had spent weeks on the design of the manifesto, keeping it carefully under wraps. The manifesto was called 'Because Britain Deserves Better', and featured a cover photograph of Blair taken by Snowdon. The content was based largely on the earlier manifesto. Originally it was intended to base the chapters on the ten parts of the 'Contract' (a list of ten vows that Labour would uphold in government introduced by Tony Blair in his conference speech in 1996), but this idea was felt to be too restrictive and was dropped. In the event the contract was included at the beginning of the manifesto. On the Sunday before the launch, I read the draft introduction and did not like it. I noted that the first page included the words: 'anger, despair, appalled, distressed, ashamed, repelled'. This

was not the tone needed to reach out to wavering Conservatives. Blair rewrote the introduction himself and Alastair asked him to write out the ten-point contract in long-hand. This appeared – with corrections – over all the next day's press.

Peter Hyman had his way and the pledges were at the front. The manifesto did not contain many new ideas, but that didn't matter; the ideas it had were what the voters wanted and what New Labour stood for. It was launched at the Institute of Civil Engineers in Great George Street. Blair performed brilliantly, playing down expectations. He refused to smile when holding the manifesto for a photo-call, he talked about the need to make promises reliable rather than overblown, and he talked of the pledges: if at the end of five years Labour had not fulfilled them, it deserved to be voted out.

At the end of the launch Gore Vidal, who was making a film for *Newsnight*, held an impromptu press conference of his own in front of the stage, but he was quickly bundled away by Millbank Tower press officers and was pretty scathing about the way he had been treated.

Outside, the Conservative chicken (another failed and pathetic Conservative stunt, attacking us for not doing the TV debate with Major) was chased by a headless chicken from the *Mirror*. The actor who had to play the part of the Tory chicken was to suffer a great deal more abuse during the campaign. One particularly nasty moment occurred in Edinburgh when an ugly crowd ripped off his head and started chasing him along Princes Street. He soon acquired a personal bodyguard.

The manifesto was a complete success in the groups that night. Typical responses were 'not too radical, sensible, promising, common-sense, achievable'. 'It broke through their considerable barriers of scepticism, and it did not raise huge worries about: "Where's the money coming from?"' I wrote. But the voters were becoming increasingly fed up: 'People are tending to switch off political news.'[38] In a separate note, I wrote to Tony Blair and Alastair Campbell, 'We have to respond to the scepticism of the electorate, who seem increasingly to be switching off from the election. We are not yet being hurt, but we must find a way of connecting more effectively.'[39]

Friday, 4 April

The day after the manifesto launch, we entered our first real election storms. In an interview with the *Scotsman* newspaper, Blair made a comparison between the tax-raising powers of the proposed Scottish Parliament and a parish council, which was presented as a downgrading of the importance of the Parliament. Donald Dewar was in Millbank that day and was greatly agitated by this. The press jumped on it as a major 'gaffe', and the Scottish media in particular went into overdrive. A press conference the following day was like slow torture for Blair as the journalists harried him relentlessly over the comments.

The Tories were quick to attack. At an election rally at the Royal Albert Hall, Mawhinney held aloft the *Evening Standard* headline, 'BLAIR'S FIRST CLANGER', to the cheering audience. Some Labour staff felt deflated by this – the manifesto launch had put them on a high and now they crashed back to earth. I didn't mind the story so much, but it did blow up and for the first time in the election we were hurt by the news: 'Scotland was perceived as TB on the defensive, the party divided, the whole situation confused.'[40] I wrote to Blair: 'This was not a good day for us, probably the least successful day of the campaign. People felt you looked defensive and momentarily wrong-footed.' I continued, 'This one incident is not a problem for us, [but] if a pattern develops of Labour policy uncertainty . . . we will be harmed.'[41]

Weekend, 5–6 April

On Saturday we discovered that Charles Lewington, the Tories' director of communications, was briefing the Sunday press that Blair had to be told what to do by Peter Mandelson. Central Office was suggesting that he wore an earpiece at press conferences giving him answers down the line. They tried to suggest he was cracking under the strain. This truly was madness; if anyone was cracking up it was them.

But the *Sunday Telegraph* led with the headline, 'BLAIR: WE'LL PRIVATISE EVERYTHING'. The *Sunday Times* claimed that Blair had changed his mind not only on tax-raising powers for Scotland, but also on unions and privatisation. Privatising air-traffic control was raised as a possible Labour policy. This was the unfortunate result of some over-zealous briefing, an attempt to rebut the allegations that Labour had a 'black hole' in its spending plans. Unfortunately, the media soon found a clip of Andrew Smith at the 1996 party conference denouncing Tory plans for the sale of air-traffic control, saying repeatedly, 'Our air is not for sale.' Gordon Brown appeared on *The World This Weekend* to announce that in government Labour would compile a list of all public assets with a view to disposing of the 'inessential' elements.

Over the weekend Alastair Campbell told me that the BBC journalist Martin Bell was going to stand in Tatton. We assumed Hamilton would stand down; Gordon Brown did not believe the Tories could possibly be so stupid as to keep him in. But Central Office was not as tough as Christine Hamilton. Despite furious reports that Major wanted Hamilton to go, the Hamiltons stuck it out. The Tories then had to deny that they wanted to oust Hamilton, and instead had to support him as the official Tory candidate.

But John Major hit Blair hard on trust, and on *Breakfast With Frost* the Tories developed a 'Three U-turns' theme. Major accused Blair of 'slithering and sliding around' in a highly personal attack. We were now under pressure on three fronts: the unions, Scotland and privatisation.

But our second tracking poll showed us with a 22 per cent lead, a 2 per cent improvement on the last poll. Most importantly, our position on the economy was strengthening despite further improvements in economic optimism.[42] Greenberg explained this in his report on the poll:

On the key contested issues – particularly the economy – Labour is making gains, despite the still growing perceptions of a good economy. Labour has regained its lead on managing the economy (plus 5 points, up 5 points this week) and preserving the economic recovery (plus 3 points, a gain of 5 points). The worry that the economy could weaken under Labour has in fact dropped by 3 points this week. The Tories are failing to make gains on the economy because their posture is completely out of touch with the electorate. In the focus groups, the Tory defectors said with some passion the economy is doing better but not their 'standard of living'; the economy is 'lean and mean'; you now work 'under pressure'; more and more people have 'temporary contracts'; the economy is good because 'we're cheap'. In short, these voters are articulating our primary economic message: the economy is not working for the hard-working families of Britain.[43]

This poll exposed probably the most important dynamic of the election campaign: the Conservative failure to turn an improving economy into increased electoral support. But it also demonstrated why we could never for a moment relax: with the economy that strong, a Conservative breakthrough was always possible.

Week four: 'A horrible week'

Monday, 7 April
Blair made his big economic speech of the campaign in the City, which was well received, but we were entering what Mandelson believes was the worst week of the campaign. 'It was a horrible week,' he said, 'the only bad week, very difficult. We seemed to be on the run. The media felt they had got their teeth into something.'[44] The focus groups revealed the first real doubts about Labour: 'The U-turn attack, which was already a problem, now has real legs. U-turns are a trust problem, but also a competence problem.' The Tories, helped by the *Daily Mail* and the *Telegraph*, had us on the defensive for the first time. In response I argued that 'we must get our message right on privatisation. Our position

must be distinctive from the Tories. We must establish a clear dividing-line. It must be rooted in values and what works best for people. We must kill off the U-turns attack. Step by step we must get back our reputation for consistency and conviction. We must stand firm in the face of new attacks.'[45]

In my note to Blair I wrote, 'Somehow or other a combination of Scotland, the unions and now privatisation has got us into the wrong place on the campaign. We have allowed ourselves to be associated with the most unpopular policy of the government, while simultaneously getting a reputation for U-turns.'[46] I was concerned that we might be losing control of the campaign. Blair had to intervene that week to tighten things up at Millbank. Charlie Whelan was moved to the centre table, together with Tim Allan.

That night Blair appeared on *Panorama* and was put under intense pressure by David Dimbleby in an exceptionally aggressive interview.

Tuesday, 8 April.
Tatton dominated the news. Martin Bell was ambushed by Neil Hamilton and a huge media entourage, and when asked by Hamilton's wife whether he believed Hamilton was innocent, he replied, 'Yes.' The campaigners watching in Millbank threw up their hands in horror. After that we sent up a member of staff to try to sort things out for Bell. Adrian McMenamin, the head of rebuttal, produced a list, at Derry Irvine's request, of five or six things everyone knew Hamilton had done wrong. We quickly faxed it up to Bell's rather ramshackle operation in Tatton.

The group that night was a follow-up group of switchers from a year earlier. Six of the eight had stayed with us, but they were 'feeling increasingly disconnected from the election'. They felt 'Bell and Hamilton was a farce, but will seriously hurt the Tories because Hamilton and his wife are arrogant; because people believe they are guilty; because it makes Major look weak and pathetic'.[47] I wrote telling Blair that response to his *Panorama* interview was not positive. Half the group had seen it and tended to think he looked 'defensive' in an interview they conceded was aggressive and unfair.[48]

Wednesday, 9 April

Our ICM poll lead was down to twelve points, the Conservatives attacked us on air-traffic control, but Neil Hamilton was re-selected in Tatton. GMTV described this as 'Major's worst nightmare'. Millbank was jubilant, pictures of Neil and Christine were being pinned up across the office. Later in the day, an Institute for Fiscal Studies Report was published, showing that since the last election the tax burden under the Conservatives had increased by £11.5 billion.

I was spending more and more time with Derry Irvine; the more pressure we were under, the more you wanted someone like Derry around. He was constantly asking us how big the majority was going to be. Stan Greenberg always said massive – he thought 10 per cent was the minimum. Derry asked repeatedly, 'But is your track record any good?'

The groups that night clearly indicated a change of mood. 'Until last Friday the dynamic of the electorate was fixed and favoured us. People saw us as a beacon of positiveness in a sea of sleaze, and blamed negative, lacklustre campaigning from the Tories. The events of the last few days have changed this: people have lost some confidence in us; they are getting fed up with the campaign and disconnected from it. They see it as over-managed, over-packaged, and obsessed with point-scoring. People are thinking we are taking victory for granted . . . they want to see more fight and grit from us.' I added, 'People want to renew their faith in Tony Blair. They want to see him tested in real situations, facing real pressure.'[49]

Thursday, 10 April

Tempting fate, Blair took a question from the *Express*'s Peter Hitchens, who asked about the London Oratory and wouldn't shut up. Hitchens had been a problem for us in the 1992 campaign – a key player in the 'Jennifer's Ear' saga, making strong and repeated attacks on Labour. A talented columnist but fiercely right-wing, his question dominated the news until lunchtime.

Air-traffic control exploded as an issue when a trade union leader – Joe McGee, from the IPMS – said he had received written assurances from Labour as late as March that air-traffic control would not be privatised. The Tories were accusing us of U-turning. In fact they were right that we had altered our policy, but it hadn't happened that weekend, as they were alleging – it had been decided in January not to rule out privatisation. But it was a problem for us; we had floated the possibility of privatising it to plug a gap in our finances – the so-called 'black hole' which the Tories were shouting about, but which left us open to accusations of a U-turn. There was no way out.

'In a way, the air-traffic-control issue was the most difficult one for us throughout the campaign,' said David Hill. 'It was the most difficult one because there was no way we could just kill it, because if we killed it then the issue immediately came back to, well, how are you going to make good the gap in your accounting? If we didn't kill it, though, we were susceptible to accusations of a serious U-turn in the space of less than twelve months, and I am afraid that the tactics we used were the only tactics we could use. Which is that we complained and moaned and let it run and hoped that something would emerge that made it fizzle out.'[50] The BBC would not let the issue go and we went to war with *The World at One* for leading on the story. Hill accused them of setting themselves up as the official opposition to Labour.

That night the story broke that the junior Agriculture Minister, Tory MP Angela Browning, had announced she would be standing on an anti-single currency platform, in an attempt to blunt the appeal of the local Referendum Party candidate. We were going to be delivered from the air-traffic-control row. This was the moment Adrian McMenamin had been waiting for since the campaign began: anti-single currency election addresses had been a private obsession of his for months. It had been only a matter of time before one of the Euro-sceptic Tories came out of the woodwork and split from the carefully worked-out Central Office line. We had been monitoring all the constituencies thought likely to produce Euro-sceptic manifestos. No one had imagined Browning would be the straw to break the Tories' back.

The group that night suggested people were still unimpressed: 'Too much bickering and slagging off.'[51] The events of the last week had irritated them, but they hadn't moved from us.

Friday, 11 April
Friday saw the launch of our business manifesto, which was central to our strategy of reassurance. We had set up a business unit in Millbank the summer before to get the business community on-side. All Britain's top businessmen, and many in the small business community, had been invited to party events highlighting our issues – Europe, entrepreneurs, small business – and asked for their comments for our business manifesto. Even Alan Sugar and John Harvey-Jones gave us advice about what we should be doing. We followed it with the PEB that night.

The launch of our business strategy was overshadowed by the Tory implosion on Europe. We were scouring the country for Conservatives who would oppose the single currency in their election addresses. Whenever one was found, Adrian McMenamin would proudly parade their name around the office. Brian Wilson said Angela Browning 'came like a vision from the night' to help Labour.

The groups that night were mainly C2s and Ds – skilled and unskilled working class. 'The women were totally confused by the election and felt completely cut off from it. They find election news negative, complicated. It in no way speaks to them. And because they find the news incomprehensible and negative they assume that all politicians are lying.' I thought this gave us an opportunity: 'The Tories are now seen to offer nothing but negativism and scares; Labour is the party of hope. To capitalise on this we must find ways of breaking through the news with positive stories and positive messages.'[52]

Weekend, 12–13 April

Sunday saw Tony Blair launch the pledge posters in another of Alastair Campbell's 'field of dreams', near Milton Keynes. After the poster launch Alastair briefed that we were moving away from the current slanging match to a more positive campaign; Blair wanted to inject 'fresh vision, passion and conviction'. He was, Campbell declared, determined to grab the campaign by the scruff of the neck after the distractions of the previous week. The briefing got slightly out of hand, ending up with unwelcome 'LABOUR CAMPAIGN IN U-TURN' headlines. Unfortunately, John Prescott was alleged to have told a journalist, 'You can't tell the truth all the time. Nobody does,'[53] and the Tories tried to play it up. But Prescott's reputation as a man who always speaks his mind was too well-known and limited the story's potency. It wasn't going to run.

Research that night showed that the Liberal Democrats were capturing the change of mood better than us: 'The women's view of the campaign was that it was almost wholly negative, and both sides were to blame. This led to confusion, uncertainty, and made Paddy Ashdown a sensible, positive, appealing alternative.' The men thought similarly: 'They felt that Labour had wobbled on Scotland, *Panorama*, and privatisation, and that Paddy Ashdown was a strong, no-nonsense politician with a clear political message.'[54] This was the start of a long, good run for Ashdown in the campaign.

Week five: Don't bind my hands

Monday, 14 April

At the morning press conference Labour focused on education. At lunchtime Tony Blair said Labour was prepared to be isolated in Europe over fishing quotas. In the afternoon he returned to education, delivering a lecture at Birmingham University which led the evening news.

The day's most important development was yet another Tory flouting the 'wait and see' policy on the single currency.

This time it was the vice-chairman Dame Angela Rumbold. They were falling thick and fast now.

The groups were more settled: 'Four quiet days have calmed them down. No one mentioned privatisation or U-turns.' The dynamic of this group followed an increasingly familiar pattern: 'The group started with fairly strong commitment to Labour. It then went on to an exhaustive period of discussion about Labour and the risk associated with it, but finally decided that despite everything it was time for the Tories to go.'[55]

Tuesday, 15 April
The *Daily Mail*'s front page screamed: 'The battle for Britain. There is a deafening silence at the heart of this election and its name is Europe.' Angela Rumbold said, 'Integration has gone far enough.'[56] The Conservatives tried to say Labour was gagging its candidates, while they were allowing theirs to speak out. Two government ministers, John Horam and James Paice, became the most senior Conservatives to break ranks. Tony Blair and Alastair Campbell were in a hotel in Southampton, waiting to record a radio interview. They had just been to a pub. First, they heard a rumour that a government minister had resigned and then, later, they got the proper story. Blair, in his dressing-gown, said, 'They can't come back from this.'[57]

Peter Mandelson paraded around the green outside Millbank with Fitz the bulldog, the star of that night's broadcast. The dog had already caused some difficulty: Mandelson was at first under the impression it was called 'Fritz', and had been trying to work out how to present a German dog as a British symbol. Its genitals had had to be airbrushed out of the broadcast because of their excessive size. It was Peter's first formal election photo-call, the biggest public event he was involved in during the election. 'Peter was rather dreading it. It had all the ingredients for a disaster, but he pulled it off,' said Benjamin Wegg-Prosser, Mandelson's researcher.[58] I missed this, but was allowed to meet Fitz, who was temporarily kennelled in Blair's private office with a bowl of water and an air-conditioning unit to cool the dog down in case he over-heated. I rather took to him. His visit was planned by Mark Lucas with military precision. Mark had arranged a very sophisticated travel plan to make sure no one spotted the dog.

Fitz was a rare moment of light relief in a campaign that had to be suffered rather than enjoyed. It was not as hard, perhaps, as 1992, but was very tough in its way. It was about focus and endurance and never making a mistake. It takes courage to fight from behind, but it takes courage also to stay ahead. If we had slipped up, history would never have forgiven or forgotten. Everybody knew that. The price of failure would be unbearable. This feeling hung around Millbank like a dark cloud. I enjoyed almost none of the campaign, experiencing constant tiredness, and a ruthlessness that I had never known before. The Tories had to be finished off, battered to the ground. There could be no moment of weakness, no chance for them to come back from the dead. The journey had been too long for us to falter at the last. So I went through the campaign as a kind of living-dead person: emotionally numb, physically numb, spiritually numb, consumed completely by the will to win.

The groups that night were bad. The first was a set of Liberal and Conservatives voters who would not consider voting for us, but the second was a follow-up group of switchers to us, who had tended to move away from us: 'The election has been confusing, and confusion creates doubt; we have been under attack and look defensive.' Worse, Ashdown had moved on to our pitch: 'Ashdown and the Liberal Democrats are exacerbating our weaknesses and clouding our message. We claim to be the party of education, but they will spend more. We claim to be honest, but they say where the money is coming from. We are starting to lose some ground to the Liberals.'[59] Our mid-week tracking poll confirmed this trend. Greenberg wrote, 'Paddy Ashdown in particular, but also the Liberal Democrats, are making important gains. Their vote has climbed 2 points to 16 – up 4 points this last week. Warm feelings about Ashdown have gone up 5 points this survey.'[60]

Wednesday, 16 April
Europe was building up as a major issue. The papers were running stories saying that between 140 and 200 Tory candidates would come out against the single currency. The Conservatives were losing control. At their press conference, Major made his extraordinary 'Like me or loathe me, but don't bind my hands' speech, and the election burst into life. It was an incredible performance and I watched it in the media centre, transfixed. On the ITV news Michael Brunson described him as 'fighting like a tiger'. It made me nervous. I thought it could shift the dynamic of the campaign, and begin to unlock the hidden potential of the improving economy. Campbell, typically, thought him pathetic. Major cancelled his planned PEB that night and went straight to camera with the same argument.

Major's performance helped him and the Conservatives. For a few days it shifted the mood. The focus group that night liked him: 'Aggressive, confident, direct: a decent man, finally showing some spark. Trying to get control of his party.' And they were getting worried about Labour: 'There is uncertainty about us. People do not know what we stand for. We do not look confident enough.'[61] I was still arguing that we should be relentlessly positive for now, but the time was getting close when we should change direction and turn on the Tories. This was clearly a point of uncertainty and fluidity, a turning-point that would favour either them or us.

Thursday, 17 April
This was the day Blair reached full power. His team had been depressed since the *Panorama* interview, feeling they weren't connecting; the campaign was going well enough, but there was no feeling to it any more. 'Tony was basically in good shape throughout the campaign,' said Campbell. 'Nothing really went badly wrong during it. I thought generally we were in pretty good nick. There was a low point in the couple of days before the Edinburgh speech, when we weren't connecting, the media were bored and we weren't breaking through. We decided Tony should do

the speech in Edinburgh and completely let rip. That was important.'[62]

It was a turning point for us. As Major went back to Europe, holding out the promise of a free vote on the single currency, and again being undermined by stories that three more ministers had expressed their hostility to the single currency, Blair was in the Usher Hall, Edinburgh. He upped a gear and, in a mesmerising performance, threw away his notes and spoke off the cuff. Major might have had a good day yesterday, but Blair was closing in for the kill.

John Major's bubble of popularity was already beginning to burst: 'This was a much less good day for the Conservatives than yesterday,' I noted. 'They looked divided and confused. Major looked weak.'[63] Major's audacity had helped, but division was undoing them.

Friday, 18 April

The Conservatives, still convinced Europe was a winning issue, scored another spectacular own goal, producing an advertisement initially sketched by Michael Heseltine which depicted Blair as Helmut Kohl's puppet. In a reference to the forthcoming Amsterdam Summit negotiations, the caption ran, 'Don't send a boy to do a man's job.' I thought this was ridiculous and would rebound, but Blair was worried about it and came on the conference phone at the morning media meeting. We all tried to reassure him, but he remained concerned. Major came under pressure all day to apologise for it.

Major was also in trouble for hinting that any vote on a single currency would be a matter of conscience for MPs outside government. Unfortunately, he developed this policy on the hoof, without consulting Kenneth Clarke, who immediately distanced himself from the idea. The Tories were coming apart at the seams.

I was worried that I was missing out on some target voters, so I changed my recruitment criteria for the groups to people who were basically Tories. The results were extraordinary, and began to finally convince me that we were going to win.

For the previous ten days I had been talking to people who had started the campaign intending to vote Labour, but were now having doubts. This evening's groups, though, showed me there was another dynamic at play: 'Tories are leaving [the Conservatives] because of the negativity of their campaign. Almost all members of both groups believed that they would end up voting Conservative at the outset of the campaign. They had doubts but they felt the power of the campaign would persuade them to once more vote Tory.' In fact, the opposite had happened: the campaign had turned them off because the negativity and abuse of the campaign had persuaded them that the Conservatives had nothing new to offer.

'All this was eloquently summed up by one female respondent, who said, "I wanted to stay a Tory voter but I feel that in all conscience I cannot do so given the nature of the campaign they have fought."'[64] The Conservative campaign was losing them votes. Our voters might be getting nervous, but theirs were feeling completely alienated.

Weekend, 19–20 April
Our weekend tracking poll showed that my suspicions that Major's 'Don't bind my hands' speech would shake up the election were valid. Greenberg wrote:

> The dynamic of the race is changing – which will require a pointed response from Labour. Labour's lead has dropped from 21 points to 16 points in this survey. The Labour slippage was due entirely to the consolidation of the Conservative vote. There is considerable cause for alarm in these numbers. The bloc of solid Labour voters has dropped to 35 (down 6 points), when it should have been solidifying. Among women the rise in uncertainty is very dramatic, with solid support dropping 12 points. The explanation for this is the economy. Perceptions of a good economy have risen from 68 to 72 per cent. Voters now believe the economy will be *weaker*, not *stronger* under Labour (by 10 points). The cause of this shift to the Tories is an improvement in perceptions of John Major:

his job performance jumped 6 points; he gained 8 points on 'leadership' in comparison with Blair, and 7 points on strength.[65]

All this was a direct consequence of Major's speech, lifting perceptions of Major and allowing the Tories to start gaining credit for the strength of the economy. The Tories put this down to Europe. In fact, what mattered was that Major had finally shown some strength. Europe wasn't the issue; it was leadership.

On Saturday Kenneth Clarke waded into the Europe row, saying people who thought Europe was a threat – including, therefore, Michael Howard – were talking 'paranoid nonsense'.[66] The press office wanted to play this up, but Gordon Brown wasn't keen: Europe was closer to their agenda than ours. Focus groups on Sunday continued to show our female voters getting nervous. The men were all right, they saw the Conservatives falling apart, but 'the women were getting nervous about change as the election drew closer'.[67] This was inevitable. My view was that it was getting close to the time to attack, and that we had to be ready with fifth-term fears.

Week six: The War Book

Monday, 21 April
Jacques Santer, President of the European Commission, entered the fray with an attack on Euro-sceptics, for 'unjustified and misplaced' attacks on the EU.[68] This could have been a bigger problem for us had he done it earlier in the campaign; it gave the voters and the Tory Party a common enemy. The Tories could even have started to unite around it. Malcolm Rifkind, the Foreign Secretary, certainly tried to make the most of it. He attacked Blair for his 1996 conference speech, in which he had declared that he would 'never allow this country to get isolated' in Europe. But it was too late. Blair turned the issue around to leadership, flaying Major in an attack on his authority. Yet Millbank was wary

about the Tory return to Europe – we knew it was a potentially vulnerable area. We got the *Sun* to run an article by Blair the next day, promising that he would 'slay the Euro-dragon'.

The focus groups thought Blair was 'strong and sincere', Major weak. And at last Ashdown, whom we had been attacking for four days, was running into the ground: he was described as 'an old bore'. Ashdown had started well but had been unable to develop his message: he needed to move from 'a plague on both your houses' to a political offering of his own: this he was unable to do. Blair was back in the saddle.

It was now time to attack: 'We have got to confront the voters with the possibility of another Tory term. Our positive credentials are well-established. Ashdown is faltering. Attacks will get it up in the news. We must use our advantages: energy, strength, dynamism. We must power our way through the next ten days.'[69]

Tuesday, 22 April

All day there were rumours of a very bad poll for us and we were desperate to get hold of it. Strangely, Adrian McMenamin, who went to the Tory press conferences every day (as they sent someone to ours), had been approached by their research director, Danny Finkelstein, that morning. Finkelstein asked him, 'How are your plans to get Frank Dobson elected as a Cabinet minister going?' McMenamin replied, 'If the polls are to be believed, quite well I think, thank you.' Finkelstein said, 'You won't be saying that this evening.'[70] I don't know if he knew about the bad poll or not. There was a black shadow over the day, and at five in the afternoon the poll came in: ICM in the *Guardian* had us just 5 per cent ahead. Our leads on economic competence and Europe were slashed. Mandelson looked at me coolly and said, 'I thought we were supposed to be doing well in this election.' But people kept very calm; we suspected at once it was a rogue poll. Margaret said, 'I don't care what the poll says, I will fight them on the streets and get our

The War Room at Millbank Tower during the 1997 General Election campaign.

Fred Jarvis

Peter Mandelson in the War Room, April 1997.

Fred Jarvis

John Prescott on the hustings during the 1997 campaign.

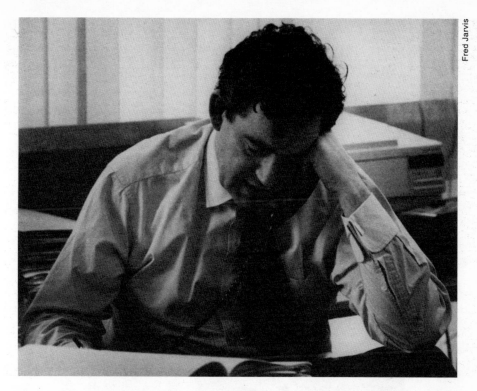

Gordon Brown as shadow Chancellor, in his office at Millbank.

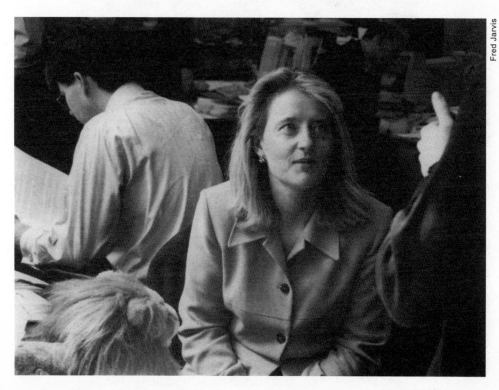

Margaret McDonagh, General Election Co-ordinator, at Millbank.

The final Sunday: Blair reviews the papers with David
Miliband (top), Anji Hunter (middle) and Alastair
Campbell (bottom).

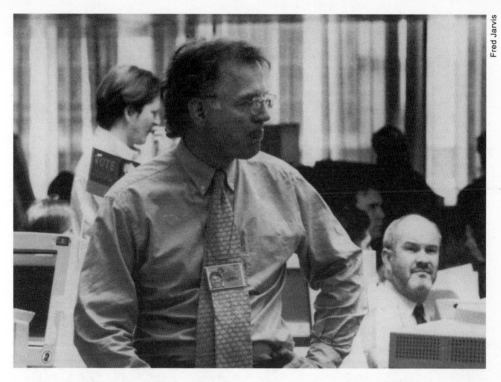

Philip Gould and David Bradshaw (right) in the War Room during the
1997 campaign.

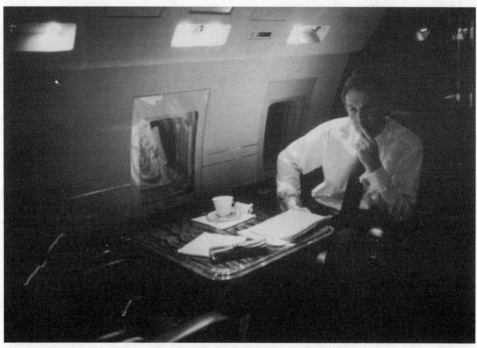

Tony Blair flying from Sedgefield to London after the polls had closed; during the
flight it became clear that Labour had won a massive majority.

Tony Blair and Cherie Booth at the Royal Festival Hall, 2 May 1997.

The new Prime Minister in Downing Street, 2 May 1997.

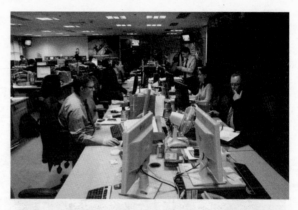

Clockwise from left, David Muir, Alastair Campbell, Douglas Alexander, Marianna Trian and Ray Collins at the 2010 campaign desk.

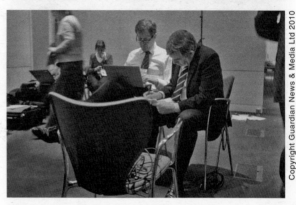

Philip Gould and Alastair Campbell.

Peter Mandelson in the campaign conference room.

Alastair Campbell and Gordon Brown working in a back room at Bloomberg, photographed by Martin Argles.

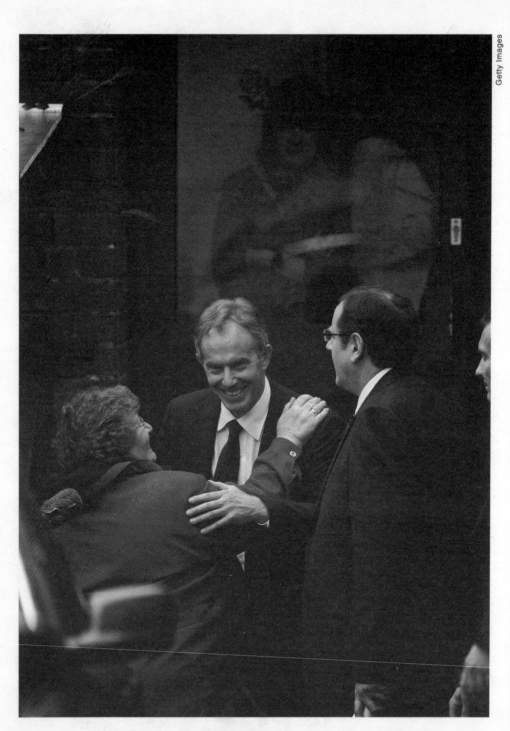

Tony Blair with Carol Linforth, director of events, in Sedgefield.

voters out one by one and door by door if I have to.' She was tough. Blair heard about the poll in a hotel in Luton. He suspected it was wrong, but decided to take it at face value in order to smash complacency and to remind the electorate that the Tories could still win. He went immediately on to the attack in a speech in Stevenage, and decided that soon we would need to focus on the risks of a Conservative fifth term.

That night we got the most important private poll of the campaign, saying Labour was up 1 per cent with a 17 per cent lead. This meant that the Tory advance had been checked. It also meant the ICM poll was wrong. But it showed, too, that the Tory gains revealed in our last poll had largely been held.[71] Greenberg reported: 'The survey sends mixed signals. On the one hand, the poll offers a sense of relief that the drop last weekend was really a movement to a lower plateau and not the first signs of a collapse. On the other hand, the race has changed in important ways. Major and the economy have both achieved a higher standing which lessens the desire for change and allows worries about Labour to matter more. This argues for a greatly increased focus on fifth-term worries.'[72]

I conducted two groups that night, and though there were some doubts, it was clear they were going to hold. The response to Blair on the news was very strong.

I wrote a note that night to Blair that exposed the ruthlessness and obsession that had consumed me during the campaign: 'You have spent five weeks building up your positive credentials and you are now able to go after him. You can hit him on Europe, you can hit him on education, health, crime. You have to hunt him down and finish him off.'[73]

I spoke to Blair and told him not to worry about the ICM poll. I said it was hopelessly wrong and should be discounted.

Wednesday, 23 April
Our lottery day. We held a special press conference to announce plans for a 'people's lottery'. It took off well, according to David Hill. 'It was a really big-impact story and

it went like a dream,' he said.[74] This was a proper, positive story, which was good because trench warfare recommenced only hours later. Early in the day Peter Hyman, who like me was obsessed with bringing home to voters the dangers of a Tory fifth term, jokingly suggested, 'Why don't you write a really lurid fifth-term memo and have it leaked so we can get the fifth term up as a story?' There was no need – the Tories were about to do it for us. Sitting in a strategy meeting in the late afternoon Alastair Campbell's pager went off. He made a call in the meeting room and gave me a quizzical 'you've done it again' look. The Tories had my War Book, and they were distributing copies of it outside Central Office.

I knew this was embarrassing, but didn't feel it was terminal. Gordon Brown was very concerned because it contained our weaknesses as well as our strengths, and these focused on the economy. His face blackened when he read what I had written. I felt a glass wall surround me once again. It was the lead story on Sky News and Radio 4's *PM* programme, and once again I watched myself at the centre of a storm. Judith Dawson, senior political correspondent on Sky News, said, 'I cannot for the life of me understand why these callow youths write this stuff down.' Alastair was angry on my behalf and stormed off to the lobby to do a briefing. He saw the leak as an opportunity rather than a threat:

I don't think you should advertise your enemy and what the War Book was, was our strategy. And one of the developments in modern media is that it is interested in strategy – it reports strategy. I felt that there was nothing for us to lose in this. Once you get over the fact that the media is obsessed with leaks and the fact that leaks happen, so what? I felt the document actually was a coherent case for the campaign strategy that we were doing. So while we were talking about it, I said get me enough copies and I'll go round to the press gallery and do a briefing on the basis that they've made a terrible mistake, because what they've done is drawn attention to our strategy. I'll say this is where we are, and you'll see that unlike them we've got a clear strategy, we've followed it all along the way, and we're now looking at an attack on the fifth term.[75]

By the time the briefing was over the press began to believe we had leaked it.

I had forgotten they had the War Book, and the leak surprised me. This time I wasn't named, but the media came hunting for me anyway. I slipped out to my focus group by the back entrance, feeling uncomfortable.

The groups that night showed increasing momentum towards us: 'TB is breaking through more strongly than ever. We are starting to surge, they are starting to sink. For the next few days we can attack as it gives us power, differentiates us from the Tories. But from about Monday we need to make a turn and move to a message of hope.'[76]

Thursday, 24 April
This was our final-week launch, again held at the Institute of Civil Engineers. The strategy was stark: five positive pledges versus five fifth-term fears, one of which was that the state pension would be abolished. This was true. Under the Tories' own proposals state pensions would in time be scrapped.

I had wanted to attack the Tories on fifth-term pension fears for two years, but neither Blair, Brown nor anyone else would have it. It was too incredible. When Peter Lilley announced what was, in effect, privatising pensioner care and introducing private pensions for young people, their resistance collapsed. The Tories were announcing what I had been blocked from predicting. On that Wednesday morning, Adrian McMenamin was sitting next to Baroness Blatch, one of Major's personal aides in the campaign, at the Tory press conference. Norma Major came in and sat behind him and began chatting with Blatch. Earlier Norma had been talking to Alastair Goodlad, the Tory chief whip, who had told her how he had been producing a whole load of leaflets on pensions because they were very worried we would attack them on it. Adrian heard all this, then reported it back to us at Millbank, and we thought it ought to be followed up.

Even so, pensions would not have taken off as they did had the Tories not leaked the War Book that afternoon; the issue was suddenly given currency and saliency. 'The War Book was very important,' said David Hill. 'They launched it, Mawhinney comes on the *PM* programme, says, "This shows how appalling they are," and then says, "We are launching this to reveal the gutter politics that the Labour Party is undertaking, the sort of things they are saying about pensions" – and I said, "Go for it." And I kept saying "Go for it" all the time – "Go for them on pensions, they are terrified on pensions." Then we went for it on Thursday morning and changed the press conference, and on the Friday I remember saying, "Go for it again." I was like a dog with a bone.'[77] Rather than let the issue die, the Tories kept attacking us, which poured petrol on the flames. They held a bizarre press conference, headed by Stephen Dorrell, with a picture of Tony Blair as a chameleon changing colour under the banner, 'You can't believe a word Blair says'. They attacked Blair for 'telling bare-faced, despicable lies' over pensions. They went into a tailspin. It was madness.

The groups that night were again typical: 'nervous about us' but unlikely to return to the Tories.[78] I wrote to Blair and told him our latest poll gave us a 19 per cent lead, but also noted that 'it is absolutely essential we do not slacken off in the face of this improvement but that we drive this dynamic home. Momentum is all in the closing days. You are already performing at a superb level but you still need to build more as polling day approaches.'[79]

Friday, 25 April
The *Independent* was conducting some focus groups of its own, which they claimed showed the election was going to be close. They were misreading the responses: doubts about Labour do not always turn into Tory votes.

Labour led on crime, and ITN's Michael Brunson

reported: 'Pensions has been fought to a draw.' The *Daily Telegraph* ran the headline: 'LIAR, LIAR, ELECTION'S ON FIRE'. Blair was unhappy about the way the pensions issue was portraying him. It was probably the first time in history Labour had fought so aggressively. Our claim that the Tories would abolish the state pension sooner rather than later was justified by what they had said in the past; we never actually said pensioners would lose their pensions, but that was how our attack was interpreted. When Blair was asked directly, 'Are you saying pensioners will lose their pensions?' he simply replied along the lines of, 'I would never tell anybody to trust the Tories about anything.' He refused to withdraw 'one iota' of Labour's allegations.

Both the Tories and the press were astounded at how hard we were fighting. Not content simply with winning, we were beating them to a pulp. 'This is all in the context of an election which is palpably won and comfortably so,' said Hill. 'It knocked the Tories all over the place. They were stunned at the strength of what we were doing. They were stunned that we stuck to it.' Even the journalists were shocked that morning. Hill recalls:

I had the most extraordinary exchanges with journalists and broadcasters on the Friday morning. Tony was very calm at the press conference and did a tremendous job, and I then came out and had Adam Boulton [Sky News political editor], Robin Oakley [BBC political editor] and various other people saying, 'What on earth is going on here? Why are you deliberately misleading the general public?' etc., etc. I said, 'What the hell's wrong with you lot? Why are you getting so steamed up about this?' And they said two things: 'One, you're so far in front you don't need to get rough like this. Secondly, we don't expect things like this from you. These are the sort of things that only the Tories do.' And I thought that was fascinating, having been around for so long that even given this steely leadership of Blair, the fact that there were people like Mandelson and Brown at the political helm, there were people like Alastair Campbell and myself who have got a

reputation in terms of the way we deal with the press – even
with that team in place in terms of the public image of the
party, there was still this perception among these journalists
that Labour played as the gentleman and the thugs were the
Tory party. That was still there right at the end of the
campaign.[80]

In the groups that night, the issue was finely balanced but
we were just ahead: 'Pensions mostly works for us. In terms
of who is believed, Major and Blair are about equal. However,
the gain for us is that it makes us look strong, rooted in
conviction, different from the Tories.' Our current attacking
strategy, I said, had strengths and weaknesses. 'The strengths
are many: it keeps the focus on them; it stops us being the
incumbent; it shows TB to be strong; it gives us momentum;
but it makes us vulnerable to Lib Dem erosion; and it means
that we are not offering a reason to vote for us. But on
balance it is working.'[81]

Maurice Saatchi has said that pensions turned the tide,
that the lead was falling to 5 per cent and pensions pulled
it back up.[82] This is nonsense – a post-election Tory myth.
Our lead fell a little after Major's 'Don't bind my hands'
press conference on Europe, but it picked up before pensions
were on the map. Pensions helped us a little, but made no
substantive difference to the result of the election.

I tried to keep the pressure on Blair: 'In general your
attacking stance of the last week has been effective. But soon
you must make the turn and focus on your positive message.
In general your position is very strong. But it is not yet
secure. This is for two reasons. There are millions of voters
out there who have yet to make up their minds. And the
election is not just about winning, it is about winning a big
majority. For both these reasons it is essential that we do
not slow down, but speed up. The party with momentum
at the end will make disproportionate gains. We must keep
momentum, we must stop the Tories getting it.'[83]

That afternoon, Neil Kinnock came into Millbank, at
Peter's invitation, to address us. It was an emotional moment

for Neil and the staff. He said he wished that he could have had this dedication, these skills in 1992. The battle was now between 'the desperate and the determined'. But there was no malice, no rancour, only the hope that we would finish the job that he had started in 1985.

That night we had the results of another tracking poll, which showed us rallying again. Greenberg wrote, 'The survey shows a strengthening of Labour's position at the current level and a weakening of the forces that destabilised the race a week ago. With exactly a week before the election, confidence in Major's leadership and the economy have fallen back. Labour is holding stable at 45 per cent. Labour has been tested, and has come through stronger.'[84]

Weekend, 26–27 April
Late on Saturday evening I went into Millbank. Peter Mandelson was there. We talked calmly about the prospects. After twelve years, we were close. We had almost done it.

The Sunday papers were excellent, with the *News of the World* coming out for Labour and the *Sunday Times* leading on an anti-Tory story. Even the *Observer* was at last being supportive. The polls were strong, with ICM giving us a fifteen-point lead. The news also had shots of Blair with Richard Branson, in contrast to Major ambling around Huntingdon like a retired gardener.

I wrote a 'last four days' note to Alastair Campbell. I said that our lead was down to 16 per cent and economic optimism was up. Major was up on his job approval. In focus groups there was absolutely no perception that there would be a landslide. 'Everybody believes the election will be close. Tony's tone was not right in some of the bulletins. It is absolutely essential that no impression is given that this election is won. We should never discuss Friday, even in terms of humility. TB must repudiate any sense that there is going to be a landslide. He must throw the idea out. Instead he should connect with the real feelings of the people: the election will be close; every vote needs to be won.'[85]

Final week: Into the sunlight

Monday, 28 April

Today the Conservatives started to die. Blair phoned me and was nervous about the last few days, getting the tone right. I told him that Stan Greenberg was confident of a landslide. Blair's message was now spot-on. 'This is not a landslide country,' he repeated throughout the day. I think it was Alastair's line, although he only remembers 'a blur' by then.

Major went on a meandering tour of parts of the country, his passion gone. He returned to College Green at Westminster to warn the assembled journalists that 'We only have seventy-two hours to save the Union.' The old 1992 attacks just weren't working. He was fading. Blair was brilliant in the East Midlands. The atmosphere in Millbank became almost relaxed; Major's flying tour looked ridiculous and desperate and Blair just kept improving. He was at the best he has ever been that week – he just got better and better.

The groups that night were the moment I had been waiting twelve years for: 'There was a definite sense tonight that the final mood is shifting to Labour. Taken as a whole, these women gave out a tangible sense that a collective decision was being taken to vote Labour. One said, "My friends are voting Labour, so I shall."'[86] The earth had moved, we were going to do it. I wrote to Blair, 'You got your message and tone absolutely right. Battling for every last vote in the country is absolutely the right message. There is a discernible sense of a deeper turn towards us. You could almost feel them tilting towards us as the election comes to an end. They still have doubts, but they are going to do it. For the next two days you must keep battling for every last vote.'[87]

Tuesday, 29 April

The final press conferences of the campaign. Labour returned to its ten-point contract. Major was limp, Blair fantastic in Bristol. Even Alastair Campbell began to feel optimistic:

You couldn't tell, the longer the campaign went on. You get all the data and things, but frankly, polls have been wrong before, you do have to rely on your gut sense of where things are. I can remember Glenys [Kinnock] coming back one night in the 1992 election campaign from Basildon and saying, 'They're just not looking me in the eye.' And I felt in those last few days that we were just connecting in a way that was extraordinary, really getting through to people. Everywhere you went people were warm, they had a sense that something was happening. These public meetings we were doing, you know normally you'd get a bit of aggro and there just was none of that those last few days. Very warm, big crowds. You could sense as well in terms of the media that things were moving. In terms of the message it was really important that we kept going, we kept saying it was close, we kept saying we were fighting for every vote.[88]

The media seemed to swing behind us in those last few days. No longer interested in making Blair look silly, they ran fantastic pictures, for example, on polling day, in the market in Stockton-on-Tees, standing above a sea of heads, pointing, looking like the next Prime Minister.

Campbell was increasingly disappointed at the lack of Tory fight. He recalled afterwards, 'I'll tell you what was interesting in terms of the campaign, it was like being a boxer and you've psyched yourself up to go the fifteen rounds and at the end of the thirteenth round your opponent, who you've battered into the canvas, just gets up and walks away. And for the last few days while we'd been keeping up this relentless pressure, they'd gone.'[89]

The groups confirmed the choice the nation was making: 'These groups offer more evidence of a tilt in mood towards Labour. There appears to be a growing consensus even among nervous Labour voters that Labour is going to win. This is giving comfort and support. The single biggest failure of the Tory campaign is that they have offered nothing to their lost supporters; no promise; no reward; no positive future; just relentless negativity.'[90] To Blair I wrote, 'You have been fantastic these last few days. Both days have been clear wins for us. We have exactly the contrast we want in the last few days: they are tired and sagging, we are urgent, surging.'[91]

Wednesday, 30 April
The final day. Stan Greenberg wrote a memo predicting Labour would get 43 per cent and the Conservatives 31 per cent.[92] He got it right to the point. Later he talked to me about the election campaign:

> There were two dynamics. One centred on the Tories, their time in power, the state of the economy. Very important to that was, I think, a public impatience, a public who were tired with the Thatcherite project of simply dismantling the state as the response to current challenges. The other side was Labour able to finally communicate through an election that it had settled the issues that had created so many doubts about the social democratic project in Britain. I think that most of the elections of the '70s, '80s and '90s were not about the Conservatives, not about Thatcher. It was the reputation of the Labour Party and its project that scared people. The country had moved on, the Labour Party had not. Labour had gone through perhaps two elections where it was trying to address these issues, but not with the drama that Tony Blair addressed these issues. There was a finality about the way he addressed them. In this election, I don't think the voters were constantly agonising over whether this was a tax-and-spend Labour Party which would drive the economy into the ground at the behest of the trade unions. I think these issues were largely resolved, and the voters were able to look forward.[93]

Millbank thinned out as staffers headed for the key marginals to work on the ground on polling day.

I knew we would win by a huge margin. Around midday I slowly packed up my papers and my personal belongings and left Millbank for the last time as a member of the campaign team. It was over for me. For a moment I felt pure, undiluted happiness. I knew we had won, I knew the long journey was over. I walked to my wife's office and arrived unannounced, carrying my bag and my belongings. I said to her, we have won, and it will be a landslide, before falling asleep on her sofa.

But I was not quite finished yet. That night I did the last focus group, a follow-up group of 1992 Conservative voters who had switched to Labour. They had remained 100 per cent solid for Labour, were certain to vote for us. The journey was finally coming to an end. The circle had closed. Those terrible focus groups when Labour was a pariah – unelectable, for the past, for extremism, for the minorities – had gone. This group was voting Labour. Adrian McMenamin went to canvass the next day. He panicked when he saw the kind of people going out to vote: 'When you've done this for fifteen years you think you know what a Labour voter looks like,' he said, '[and] I thought we were going to lose the election. I was leaving my daughter with my mother that night and said to her, "We're going to lose, it's a disaster." I was really convinced of it. But the truth was, these people were Labour voters; they just hadn't voted Labour in the last sixteen years so they looked different to me.'[94]

I wrote one last polling report:

People are going to vote Labour tomorrow. They have some doubts, but they are going to do it. The respondents have connected to almost all elements of our strategy: business reassurance, health, education, strong leadership, our positive approach. They saw the campaign as a test and Labour has passed it. The Tories are clearly in trouble. But in the last days the Libs have also started to fade. Ashdown looks tired, their message has become confused. There will be no last-minute panic rush back to the Tories. Some nervous switchers, undecideds will go back, but they will not affect the result to any material extent. But we must retain the right note throughout tomorrow. People are still deciding. We must take nothing for granted. The winning margin should be around 10 per cent. I cannot see any circumstances in which it will fall below the 5/6 per cent we need for a reasonable working majority.[95]

It was done. I wrote to Blair, saying he would win by at least 8/9 per cent. But still I pushed him: 'Even today you should not let up, people will be making their minds up. You are still taking nothing for granted, you are still dismissing the possibility of a landslide.' I talked of Labour in power. 'In government the cynicism will start working for you. People expect promises to be broken, so that if you keep any of your promises, let alone all of them, faith in politics will be restored. You must never deviate from your New Labour project. You should not shrink from unpopularity, you should not court it either.'

I closed on a personal note: 'It has been a great privilege to have had the opportunity of working with you during this period. You have been a great leader of the opposition, and will, I think, be a great Prime Minister. Today marks the end-point for me. The election of a Labour government has been the prime purpose of my life for the last twelve years. Best of luck today and in the coming years. You are going to win.'[96]

Much later, Sue Nye, Gordon's assistant and someone else who had worked for so many years to get Labour elected, called. She had Gordon on the phone. He was worried. The vote in Scotland seemed soft. Could it all go at the last? His voice was tired and warm. I reassured him: this time, the fates would not deny him. Tomorrow he too would win. I sat up late into the night, thinking of the past.

Thursday, 1 May
I voted and waited. At lunchtime I went to a local café and got the first exit polls at 2 P.M. – we would win by a landslide. I had dreamed of that exit poll showing us ten points ahead for ten years, but when it came, nothing happened. I couldn't feel anything. I spent most of the rest of the day in a state of shock, a kind of emotional paralysis. I phoned Jonathan Powell, who was at Tony's house in Sedgefield, and

told him the exit-poll result. He took it to Tony Blair and Peter Mandelson, who were talking in the garden. 'I felt relief, some excitement,' said Peter, who was expecting a majority of about seventy. 'Tony was quite elated but, you know, it's not over till the fat lady sings. He didn't yell or anything, but he went, "God, do you think it could be true?" I said I hadn't a clue and I will not presume or bank on anything until we get the votes.'[97] After I'd spoken to Jonathan I went home and called James Carville, who was waiting by the phone. 'For these few moments,' he said, 'you will breathe pure oxygen for the one time in your life.' I phoned George Stephanopoulos. 'Good news, I hope,' he said.

At 9.30 I drove into Millbank past Number 10, as I had in the last two elections. At Millbank I met up with Stan Greenberg and Paul Begala, who was here to observe Blair's victory. The later exit polls came out – we had won by a huge margin. When the results came in, it was like a dream. Blair and Campbell, in Sedgefield, had done little all day, waiting, people telephoning, friends coming in and out. They didn't watch the television, except for the exit poll. 'Everybody said, "Oh, isn't it great" and all that,' Alastair remembers, 'and I was miserable by then. Really miserable. And Tony was saying, "Is it real?" There was a wonderful moment when he made me phone Millbank and tell them to stop being so happy.' It only dawned on them that it was for real when they were at the count. 'That was the only time we watched the telly and a whole series of Tories just fell,' Alastair said. 'And I remember at one point Tony turning to me and saying, "What on earth have we done here?" It was when Forsyth went.'[98] Michael Forsyth, Secretary of State for Scotland, had just lost his Stirling seat with a swing to Labour of nearly 8 per cent.

In Millbank, Alastair's message had come through – you are being too triumphalist; the election is not won yet – and was met with the derision it deserved. We heard the Tories were briefing that we would get a majority of seventy. We drove to the Royal Festival Hall, where a victory party had been quietly organised by Margaret McDonagh, who sat within three feet of me, without me even knowing.

I walked in, and people started to clap me on the back and shake my hand in a way I could never have imagined happening. Less for what I had done, more because I had just stuck with it all these years. I was in tears. I can't actually remember very much; it was too much to take in. Peter arrived and immediately started to do interviews. I joined him. We both felt completely vindicated; the long fight was over. Blair was on his way down in the plane with Alastair Campbell. 'People find this odd, but it was quite subdued,' Campbell remembers. 'There's some pictures of this, where Tony and Cherie are sitting there, and Fiona and I are sitting here. And my pager was on the table and it was going, like, every five seconds, with another Labour gain. It was getting ridiculous. And we were just sort of talking away quietly.'[99] They scribbled some notes for Tony's speech, arrived at Stansted airport and drove into London.

We waited outside as the dawn gently broke. In front of the Festival Hall a huge stage was erected, waiting for Blair. On Waterloo Bridge the traffic stopped, buses were stationary, people waited. Every physical space was filled. For the first time I felt exalted. 'It did start to build up on the way from the airport,' said Campbell, 'but then we got stuck in a one-way street for about twenty minutes, listening to the radio saying, "and we hear that the Prime Minister is just a couple of minutes away" and we could hear "Things Can Only Get Better" [Labour's campaign song] and we were stuck in a one-way street.' Eventually they arrived. 'Tony and Cherie were in the car in front, Fiona and I were in the second car, and I had his notes in my inside pocket. So we get up the ramp and see all the crowds there and he jumps out of the car and is running off and I think, "Oh shit," so I jumped out of the car while it was moving and the wheel went over my ankle. I thought it was probably broken. For weeks I had this kind of bruise right across my foot, and I had to run up and get to him and give him the notes.'[100]

Blair made his speech: 'Truly it is a new dawn. I said that if we had the courage to change we would win, and we did.'[101] Neither Alastair Campbell nor Tony Blair enjoyed the party at the Royal Festival Hall much. Alastair says, 'We went upstairs somewhere quiet after Tony did his speech, and I said to him, what did you make of that? And he said, "God, I'm jealous. Weren't you?" And I said, "yeah", because I didn't feel any of it at all. I was in this mode where if anything infringed upon it, like people being happy or all this stuff, it just didn't get through. I feel really bad about it.'[102]

Later Blair made a speech to a smaller audience, thanking everybody. I saw Alastair, looking like a man possessed, still totally focused. He rushed towards me and we hugged. Then Cherie spotted me, pulled me across and I hugged her and Tony too. It was over, we had done it. I walked with Gail into the morning sunlight, this time, at last, a winner. I thought of my children waiting at home, still not really believing, still nervous that victory would somehow slip from our grasp as it always did. I thought of my father who had hoped for this moment, but doubted it would come. Most of all I thought of the quiet suburban street that I had come from, and felt pride that people from that street, and millions like them, had dared to vote Labour, and were forgotten no more.

AFTERWORD: THE PROGRESSIVE CENTURY

Winning in the suburbs

We took the newspapers home with us to persuade my daughters, Georgia and Grace, that Labour had finally done it. They had been up most of the night, worried, not really believing it. A few hours later, at half-past eleven on 2 May, I waited with the children and hundreds of others outside the gates of Downing Street. At first the police refused to let anyone in, which caused a bit of a row, but eventually the gates opened and the crowd rushed through, feeling like a small liberation army. At first most of us were Labour Party workers, who had fought for this moment for many years, but soon other people arrived and the atmosphere became carnival-like, euphoric. Anji Hunter was cheered as she arrived and went into Number 10. Then the Prime Minister and Cherie Booth began making their way up Downing Street, greeting the crowd, thanking people, to chants of 'Labour's coming home'. I was so exhausted I barely took it in. Alastair Campbell followed, looking proud but shattered. Tony Blair stopped in front of Number 10 and spoke: 'I say to the people of this country – we ran for office as New Labour, we will govern as New Labour . . . For eighteen long years my party has been in opposition. It could only say, it could not do. Today we are charged with the deep responsibility of government. Today, enough of talking. It is time now to do.'[1] I shook Alastair's hand but he hardly noticed, he was already gone, on to the next challenge. The door to Number 10 opened, and he slipped inside.

I went home and collapsed in a fog of exhaustion. The first dramatic days of the Blair government were a background blur. A few days later I went back to Woking to pay respect to my parents, who had missed this moment. At first much appeared to be the same: tiny red-brick Victorian villas still fighting with post-war semis, but now they had tiny conservatories and satellite dishes added on. The cars were better and newer, and the shops were full of microwaves and videos instead of black-and-white televisions and unwieldy tumble-dryers. The suburbs had changed, but this time Labour had changed with them. I went to the house that I had grown up in, and saw the large garden, now overgrown, in which I had first dreamed of working in political campaigns, first worried about what I really believed in. My journey was over.

Labour's journey was over too. It had won an extraordinary victory on 1 May. The statistics of success were a mirror image of the failure of 1983, the election that had finally persuaded me to get involved. In 1983 Labour had lost by 144 seats, in 1997 it won by 179 seats: a shift of 323 seats in fourteen years. In 1983 the swing to the Conservatives had been 6 per cent, in 1997 the swing to Labour was 10.3 per cent.[2] Tellingly, a Conservative lead of 8 per cent among skilled working-class voters had been turned into a Labour lead of 21 per cent.[3] And most satisfying for me, 1.8 million Conservative voters in 1992 were estimated to have switched to Labour in 1997.[4] This scale of direct switching had been deemed impossible by many commentators, but was at the heart of New Labour's election strategy. These were the voters I had spoken to weekly, then daily, for three long years. Labour, a party almost dead in 1983, was now reborn. Labour did not win in 1997; New Labour did. Only when Labour had been completely modernised – and signalled this change through what was effectively a new name for the party – could dissatisfaction with the Conservatives be turned into positive support for us. Those 1.8 million Conservative voters in 1992 would not have switched had Labour not modernised; nor would white-collar workers have moved to Labour in such huge numbers; nor would Labour have won back the great mass of working-class support which had switched to Margaret Thatcher in 1979 and 1983. In focus groups across England, Wales and Scotland, among all social classes, it was the fact that Labour had become New Labour that gave people the confidence to make the change. New Labour was the last line of defence against people's fears and memories, their images of extremism and failure. It was a line that held.

The progressive century

Although May 1997 was an end-point, it also marked the beginning of a new journey. Labour had won its greatest election victory, but it has never won a full second term. More than that, Labour has never been able to establish itself as the dominant party of government, or even as a consistent governing party. This is New Labour's next challenge: to hold power not just for one or two terms, but to build a progressive coalition which dominates the next century as the Conservatives have commanded this one. David Marquand calls this the progressive dilemma: 'How to transcend Labourism without betraying the labour interest; how to bridge the gap between the old Labour fortresses and the potentially anti-Conservative but non-Labour hinterland; how to construct a broad-based and enduring social coalition capable of not just giving it a temporary majority in the House of Commons, but of sustaining a reforming government thereafter.'[5] This is the test by which the New Labour government should be judged. When critics attack New Labour for caution, for failing to be radical enough, early enough, for making tough economic decisions, for trying to impose order and discipline, they are trapped in the conservative mind-set that kept Labour in opposition for so long. If a progressive coalition can govern Britain for a majority of the time then more poverty will be removed and more real change implemented than could ever be achieved by short, sharp, occasional spasms of radicalism. Lasting change can only happen over time, as part of a progressive project for government. The alternatives have failed Britain and its people. We lack schools that are good enough, hospitals that are modern enough, streets that are safe enough. The British people lack skills, opportunity and ambition. Our public infrastructure has been allowed to crumble, our national identity is uncertain. We have let people who do not use our schools run our education system, and people who do not use our health service run the NHS. This is the price Labour has paid for losing the last century. We need a new long-term radicalism, to ensure that progressive instincts become rooted in the institutions of the nation, just as conservative instincts were in the past. New Labour may have won an election, but now it has to win a century.

A new progressive politics

Labour lost the last century because it failed to modernise, and lost connection with the people it was founded to represent. It was a party trapped by its past, even at the moment of its birth. If Labour is to win the next century it needs a new progressive politics: welcoming change; reaching out to the new middle class; reshaping the political map.

Managing change: the progressive opportunity
In the twenty-first century the pace of change will be so fast, so all-embracing, that it will in effect be an age of permanent revolution. In the economy, increasing globalisation will mean that the whole concept of national businesses and national markets effectively disappears. Competition will intensify, information will flow so quickly that any new business development or insight will be known by competitors within minutes, possibly seconds. Technological advances are going to take our breath away.

This will have enormous social impact. The changes that have already happened have left most people in developed democracies feeling insecure. The idea of a job for life has gone, the hope of a job for a decade is fading. Families will face increasing strain as both parents work, the pressures on communities grow and traditional bonds and values further erode. The external environment will appear increasingly hostile. In 1985 people in focus groups described the world out there as dark and menacing, but a world that could be blocked out by shutting the front door. Eleven years later the viability of this form of defence had collapsed. One woman in a focus group in 1996 described the world outside 'like a black slime that could seep under your front door'. The menace of 'outside' could no longer be stopped by slamming the door in its face, it was too pervasive. Change is everywhere: always unsettling, sometimes threatening.

Labour failed in the twentieth century because it retreated from change. It can only win the next by embracing it. Working people and their families will choose parties of the left which seek to equip them to manage change, rather than parties of the right which expect them to cope with it alone. Tony Blair describes this process: 'Ordinary people see change happening at a pace and depth they find frightening. They seek security amidst the whirlwind. They try to regain some control over their lives as change hurls them this way and that. Our task as modern governments is to help them do it. But here is the dilemma. People know that change cannot be resisted. There is no comfort in isolation. It doesn't work. But neither do they want change to control them, to rule them. So: our task is to equip people for change, to shape its impact, to make sense of it, to embrace it in order that we make it work for us.'[6]

This is modernisation for the many. Modernisation which gives to hard-working families the tools and resources they need to advance and prosper. Modernisation which meshes the values of community with the imperative of efficiency in a way that understands the necessity of both as well as their mutual dependence. Modernisation which knows that we cannot enter the new world of change without the capacity to compete, but nor can we enter it without strong and decent societies, because if we do, the strain of change will be unbearable, the cost unacceptable. This is the progressive opportunity.

The new middle class: the heart of the new progressive coalition
Over 60 per cent of people now believe that they are, to one

degree or another, middle-class. This new middle class does not just include people in white-collar jobs: 50 per cent of people in skilled manual occupations consider themselves to be to some extent described by the term 'middle-class'.[7] The middle class can no longer be viewed as a small, privileged sub-sector of society. Mass politics is becoming middle-class politics. Winning the century means winning middle-class support.

The new middle classes are the aspirational working class in manual occupations, and the increasingly insecure white-collar workers with middle- to low-level incomes. These are the children I was brought up with, the people of the suburbs. They do not lead easy lives but lives of struggle and hard work: wanting little more than a better life for themselves and for their families. In the past Conservatism has claimed them with promises of individual freedom, lower taxes, a reduced role for the state, unfettered aspiration. But changing times have made middle-class voters wary of the ideology of the right; social breakdown has exposed the limits of individualism, emphasising the importance of the family and the community. Change is the basis of a new progressive coalition because it affects the old working class and the new middle class, both insecure in the face of change, both wanting an active government that will make change work for them, and not against them. Change is the lever that is increasingly pulling the new middle class away from the parties of the right as voters realise that only progressive governments can be trusted to manage it for them. Stanley Greenberg describes this new coalition: 'The new popular progressive majority will be built broadly among working middle-class families, shaped by the new task of helping people of ordinary luck to achieve a better life in a world of unimagined changes and of growing economic and family pressures.'[8] The new middle class is the key to the progressive century.

A new political alignment, a new progressive map
The progressive dilemma will only be resolved permanently when an enduring alliance is created, bringing together all

those with progressive instincts into one broad, pluralist political grouping – the party Labour could have been had it not split so fatally from the Liberals almost one hundred years ago. Only then will the left finally be completely trusted, only then will a progressive century be assured. It is time to heal the rift between the Liberal and Labourist traditions in British politics. Throughout the century the split in the progressive forces has impeded the left and assisted the right, and never more so than in the ten years after the formation of the SDP, when a divided left allowed Thatcherism to flourish long after it should have met its demise.

But the schism also cut Labour off from a body of ideas which would have broadened its base and widened its appeal. It is no coincidence that the most successful Labour government – 1945 to 1951 – owed much to the thinking and planning of two Liberals, Keynes and Beveridge, and to its one-nation characteristics drawn from wartime coalition experience. The split between the Liberal and Labour parties not only led to divided progressive forces, it led to divided intellectual traditions, separating Liberalism, with its emphasis on individualism and tolerance, from Labourism, which stressed solidarity and social justice. The result left Labour as a dogmatic, statist party, ignoring and marginalising the core liberal concepts of individual responsibility, self-reliance and civic rather than state action.

Tony Blair has done much to reconcile these two traditions; bringing together the ideas of community and the individual, and understanding their interdependent relationship, has always been central to his politics. Self-reliance, duty and responsibility are core Blair concepts. But in order to build a progressive alliance that lasts, either the Liberal Democrats and Labour will have to converge – effectively becoming one party – or New Labour modernisation will have to accelerate, broadening the party's appeal so that the Liberals are driven to the margins and New Labour alone becomes the broad progressive church of British politics. The better course would be for Liberalism and Labourism to unite.

But this will not be easy. It will require the Labour Party

to be generous, to reach out to a smaller party when in a position of great strength. It will require the Liberal Democrats to show the discipline and responsibility necessary to enable them to move from the margins to the mainstream of British politics.

The prize is great. If a new progressive politics can be realised, a new progressive century can be won: New Labour confirmed as a modernising party constantly adapting to change, and helping hardworking families to adapt too; providing a new way forward, linking the values of community to the exigencies of a modern age; building an enduring coalition of government centred on the new middle classes; reaching out to the liberal tradition which has long been its rival; and ending the debilitating split within the progressive forces in British politics – Labour reborn genuinely radical, almost one hundred years after its birth as a party rooted in conservatism.

The unfinished revolution

This is the boldest and most radical agenda in British politics today. It is the radicalism of the long term, of deep-rooted and enduring change.

It is a long way from the political settlement of 1918, and from Labour's terrible defeat in 1983. It is far removed from the days of the forgotten suburbs. It is the agenda of a modernising revolution not yet finished. But if this agenda can be achieved, the goal of a progressive century is within our grasp: a century in which progressive politics can take hold, and in which the great majority of working people are helped and supported by the Labour Party, not now and again, but again and again. This is why the Labour Party was formed. This is what it forgot for so long. We must win the next century as surely as we lost the last.

Volume II: 1997–2010

A LETTER TO THE NEXT GENERATION

Part 1

THEORY: THE FLOW OF STRATEGY

A Dance of Shadows

Governing is another country.

In opposition the map may be murky but the destination is assured. The campaign team are bound together by a glue of shared purpose that guides and exalts them as they strive to reach the summit and leave their pennant there. Once arrived, as President Clinton's campaign manager James Carville wrote, you breathe only for an instant the pure oxygen of victory, because at the very moment of campaigning success the journey of power begins.

Governing is different. The sense of shared purpose remains but is more opaque and disputed. Events and circumstances intervene, tiredness sets in, relationships unravel, the daily grind of responsibility becomes wearing. The public grow impatient, politicians frustrated, the media fractious. Slowly the glue of shared endeavour dissolves. You are in another place, no longer sharing the same map. The real question is: how much change can you achieve before your moment ends?

The preceding chapters of this book have been about the road to a New Labour victory, to the largest majority in modern times, to a time in May 1997 when all seemed possible. This new section is about the long grind that followed, the compromises it involved, the issues of integrity that constantly arose, the sometimes unendurable stress that government entailed, and of course, and most importantly, the extraordinary changes that are only possible if you gain and retain power.

At no point will the dust quietly settle over New Labour.

This was and always will be a controversial government. There will be endless revision and reinterpretation – about Iraq, about delivery and change and how much was or was not achieved, about Labour's economic record, equality, immigration, and the nature and success of public sector reform.

For a government criticised so often for its timidity and lack of boldness, the legacy of New Labour could hardly be more discordant. It has not, like so many other governments, slipped quietly into the long night; everyone has a view, angry and heartfelt. Some are passionately supportive, believing that New Labour is the only way to succeed; others believe just as passionately that we stood for nothing and achieved little. Few are neutral about New Labour.

There are many reasons for the feelings of anger: the huge and unrealisable hopes released by Labour's majority, the massive issues that New Labour confronted, the strength and power of so many of the leading characters. But at the heart of the government's capacity to unsettle is the potency of the New Labour idea, an idea that was subversive to both left and right. To the left because it appeared to be turning its back on a hundred years of Labour history and ideology, to the right because it demonstrated that Labour had discovered how to unlock the door to real, sustainable, repeatable power. New Labour threatened both the sanctity of Labour's past and the security of a conservative future.

What I have tried to do in the chapters that follow is to reach as much of the truth as I can beneath the fog of opinion and received wisdom that surrounds the New Labour government, the debate effectively a dance of shadows in which people take aim at non-existent targets. I am not neutral in this, I am a passionate participant. I am Labour, New Labour, and an unashamed supporter of Tony Blair. I am also by instinct a loyalist, and this is not a time in my life or career when I will turn my fire on friends and colleagues with whom I have worked for a generation.

But I do want to try to get to the truth. By truth I do not mean revelation or exposure, nor the apportionment of blame and recrimination. There is no future for Labour, or for Britain, in the politics of disparagement, in which to hold one point of view you need to denigrate the holder of another. Of course we need dispute, conflict, disagreement: that is the anvil of progress. But we must always be open and fearless, understanding not just our own truth but the truth in others. If you stop doing this, if you are blind to the merits of those you oppose or the arguments you disagree with, then you start to die intellectually, and if you are a political party you begin the long – or sometimes not so long – slide to electoral defeat. You only win power if you face up to the reality which has kept you from it, and you only sustain power if you renew. And renewal involves honesty, curiosity and courage. It is about being open to the uncomfortable. It is about compassion, forgiveness, and the humility to realise that none of us can be right all of the time, that we are all in our way flawed.

Any analysis of New Labour's success and failures must involve a discussion of the relationship between Gordon Brown and Tony Blair. I am open about this because I do not want it to be like a suspicious death in the family, which everyone knows has happened but is too embarrassed to discuss. I want to make sense of it, although I admit it was not always a pretty sight. When I started reading my diaries I thought what happened between them didn't seem too bad; but by the end there were some very black moments. I have tried to set this relationship in the round. It was not all dark, there was sunshine too. Like any serious endeavour, any meaningful relationship, it was complicated.

I have written this analysis now because I believe I have a responsibility to do so, and because this is a part of the story not yet told. It was written initially for the next generation of Labour (and not so Labour) supporters who grew up with New Labour but who may not feel they fully understand it, and may perhaps have lost faith in it. It is, I suppose, a letter from my generation to theirs. I want people to know what has been achieved, and what can be achieved again. The revolution is never finished.

The prism of strategy

The following chapters are essentially an account of New Labour through the prism of strategy: what that strategy was, how it was implemented, and how it must now change. I have written it in this way partly because I omitted serious consideration of strategy from my original book, deciding to focus on the 'what' of political campaigning rather than the 'why', but mainly because without a framework of this sort it is impossible to make sense of politics and political campaigning.

This framework provides a way of looking at New Labour, not as some zero-sum game, but as part of the constantly unfolding flow of ideas. New Labour emerged in reaction to the policy and politics that preceded it, and others will react to the changes that it was able to make. It is not meaningful within this framework to describe New Labour as dead, just as it will never be possible to describe nationalism, or liberal socialism, or equality, as dead. Ideas do not die, they connect to other ideas and move on, still there but changed. As Tony Blair rightly says, New Labour is not a time-limited concept. Nor, however, is it possible to say that New Labour can survive unchanged or unaltered. It must renew in reaction to the new conditions it has created: the core consistent, the application different. To understand the world, to understand politics, we must be able to understand the great sweep of history that helped create our moment, but also comprehend the future that will now shape it. We must read the past, but also the future.

I wrote The Unfinished Revolution fourteen years ago with this concept of renewal in mind. I knew that New Labour was on an upward curve and that one day its upward curve would end. I believed also that before its demise New Labour would have transformed itself into something different. But Labour in power renewed less than I hoped and the Conservatives held on to the original campaigning assumptions of New Labour much more tightly than I thought they would. This meant that we were an easier target than I would have liked, but it also meant that the Tories were using campaigning concepts that, although still valid, were not perfectly attuned to the demands of a new era. I think it is also fair to say that they may have missed what I hope is the central lesson of this book: that unless you base everything around a core political project then you will not achieve enduring success. New Labour was such a project; I am not sure the Conservatives truly had an equivalent in 2010, which is perhaps why they failed to gain a majority. In a way the Conservatives are trapped in New Labour's past. Learning the wrong lessons not the right ones.

What follows is broken down into a triad: theory, practice and the future. In the rest of Part 1 I shall deal with theory. Part 2 will be about the practice of New Labour in government, and Part 3 about its future. We start with theory.

No harbour of respite, no port of destination

Constant renewal is at the heart of my approach to political strategy. I have always seen the political landscape as in flux, continually moving as action begets reaction, change leads to change. In truth, 'landscape' isn't the right description, although it is the best that I can do. The political terrain is much more sea than land. As I mentioned earlier in the book, the conservative philosopher Michael Oakeshott uses water as his dominant metaphor for politics. He sees politics as an exercise in survival, a constant effort to survive on a hostile and dangerous sea. There is no extraneous purpose, no destination, no port of departure or arrival. All that matters is staying afloat: this is the skill and point of politics, and of life.

Oakeshott's metaphor was never enough for me. I see politics more as a river than the sea, politics not just about survival but going somewhere, achieving change. Much as I admired Oakeshott, I found Hegel and his idealism more satisfying, although more mystifying. Though I read him, I cannot claim I fully understood him, but he gave me a framework, and an intuitive guide.

Hegel's dialectic is normally characterised as a triad – thesis, antithesis and synthesis – but he rarely if ever used this specific terminology. The concept however is essentially the same: progression through contradiction in which the useful portion of an idea survives, although changed. History develops through the continuing flow of events, each a consequence of something that has happened before, and each in turn a cause of something that will happen later, a sequence of action and reaction that does not end. And Hegel had a particular view of change that later helped explain my view of public opinion. He wrote: 'The process of measure, which appears alternatively as a mere change in quantity and then as a sudden revulsion of quantity into quality, may be envisaged under the figure of a knotted line.'[1] This is how I came to see public opinion: small, incremental changes accumulate into bigger ones that lead in turn to a fundamental change. It follows that public opinion moves abruptly in stepped changes rather than in a continuous unbroken flow. A knotted line. One of the tasks of polling is to identify these small changes and anticipate when they are likely to accumulate to a point where a real shift in public opinion will occur: on migration, for example, or the fuel crisis, or confidence in a political leader. This is the early gestation of a contemporary theme described, for example, in the book *The Tipping Point*.[2]

Hegel, however, was not just a dialectician and philosopher of logic, he was also an idealist, in the German tradition. He saw the progression of the dialectic through contradiction, negation and unity not just as an abstract process, but as the gradual manifestation of mind or spirit, something he described as the Idea. It is this metaphysical interpretation of Hegel that is often so controversial and so distrusted. And it was, of course, this aspect of Hegel that Marx flipped on its head when he made the basis of history not the Ideal but the Material.

Although this kind of idealism is now unfashionable it has always been attractive to me, influencing my approach to politics. Not because I accept Hegel's deterministic assumptions of history but because I am sure that purpose should be at the heart of politics giving it meaning, shape and ethical foundation. Purpose helping us both in our conduct of politics and our understanding of it.

The process of dialectical progression is not linear, nor is it singular. It is happening continuously and concurrently in a vast cacophony of unfolding and dynamic movement. This is the reality that any political leader faces: the constant dynamic of changing trajectories, some short-term, some long-term, some arriving from the future, some flowing from the past, some big, some small – a 360-degree shifting panorama in which everything may matter, although not everything will. Always when I start thinking about a political problem I see it through this prism: a dynamic, flowing landscape moving forward in a continuous tide of events. It is not a mechanistic progression – events connect to events in ways that can be random and unpredictable, often chaotic – but there is, in the relentless political swirl, a pattern that can be found, a shape, a meaning, and out of that meaning strategy can grow.

The flow of strategy

For strategy to make sense of all this it must be fluid too, its flow matching the flow of events moving from simplistic cause and effect to chaos, pattern, interconnection and choice.[3] Strategies should never be static but always evolving: what worked once will not perfectly work again, a successful strategy once implemented inevitably starts to die as the conditions of its inception begin to disappear. As action leads to reaction, so the landscape changes, and so too must the strategy that seeks to change it. The purpose that should be at the heart of strategy must stay constant but the means of achieving it cannot. This is the central paradox of strategy: that it is both fluid and constant. Tony Blair would often say 'The strategy is as always New Labour', which was of course true. New Labour is a constant, but it is also changing. New Labour was recognisably the same concept in 2007 as in 1997, but also indisputably different. The core stays the same, but the form changes. 'Strategy emerging over time as intentions colliding with and accommodating to the changing reality.'[4]

These then are the components of strategy. Strategy is *holistic*, seeking to shape and understand the entire political landscape – from policy to personality, from short-term to long-term. It has to understand the world in all its rich, interconnected and constantly changing diversity. Strategy is not one box among many, it is making sense of all the boxes.

Strategy is about *fundamentals*. It is not what you see on the surface that matters but the underlying substance: not just what things are but what they may become. The world is a constellation of forces in motion, some emerging, some declining. You can't see these forces, only their manifestations, and one of the skills of strategy – and of polling – is to establish whether an event is significant in itself or the revelation of deeper and more important movement.

Strategy is about *trajectories*. Political forces can be short- or long-term, lasting weeks, months or decades. They are never static, there is no settled place in politics. Everyone or everything in politics is on a curve that is either rising or falling; in fact, you can see politics as a multitude of competing curves; some with the lifespan of months, others the lifespan of decades, perhaps much longer. Day by day, reputations are damaged or enhanced, and predictions made of triumph or demise. But short-term fluctuations mean little, what matters are the long-term real trajectories that underpin surface movements. New Labour was on such a curve, as was the Liberal Party of the nineteenth and earlier twentieth century. All of us, whether in politics or not, are on some form of trajectory, much as we may try to escape it.

Strategy is about *purpose and project*. It is not, or should not be, simply an empirical and mechanistic process; it has to be given meaning through values. A strategy without purpose is merely a piece of intellectual machinery; political campaigning without purpose becomes a hollow technocratic activity. This is why a strong and serious project is so vital: the ideas, values, beliefs and policy that give meaning even in chaos and that made New Labour such a potent and sustained political force. Project turning a desire to win into a sustainable force for change. In government clarity of purpose matters even more than in opposition, because there are so many distractions, events beyond the control of any government, continuous media, issues demanding instant action. In the turmoil of government, a project is both your shield and your guide.

As a strategist, Tony Blair constantly looked ahead, as though driving a car along a highway. His core strategic position was to drive quickly, hold the centre of the road, force other drivers to extreme and indefensible positions, leaving them marginalised and broken down by the side of the road. He looked forward and saw not solidity but movement, seeing quickly and clearly the power of emerging forces. But he had more than that, he had the power to illuminate, not merely to explain the future but add new insight to it. No politician I have ever spoken to has surprised me so often with the freshness of his insight. That is why he was able to beat the Conservatives three times, and why he would probably have beaten them for a fourth time if circumstances had not made it impossible.

Gordon Brown looked to the future too, but in a different way. He did not want to force other drivers off the road, he wanted to ensnare them, pushing them step by step into positions from which there was effectively no escape. He saw strategy more as a game of chess: you move, then your enemies move, but as you have thought five or ten moves ahead you eventually trap them. His chosen device of ensnarement was the creation of dividing lines, putting your opponent on the wrong side of a crucial argument by means of pressure and tactics. These two approaches were different but complementary, and made Labour very hard to beat. They take us from strategy and into practice.

Part 2

PRACTICE: THE LONG GRIND OF GOVERNMENT

THE FIRST PARLIAMENT: 1997–2001

FINDING HIS FEET

Re-engaging

After victory on 1 May 1997 I thought the journey was over. If I had a purpose, then New Labour's victory had realised it. I genuinely had no thoughts beyond this – election campaigns are what I do, their end is my end. After the Clinton campaign, people were hustling for coveted positions in the White House. During our campaign, too, people were scheming and planning for what would happen later. Good luck to them, but it was not for me. All I cared about was winning, helping to get Labour over the finishing line first. For me, working on a political campaign is a noble thing, complete in itself, not a pathway to something else.

For the next few weeks I mainly stayed at home exhausted, feeling much as I had in 1987 and 1992, aching and tired and living in a kind of no man's land between sleep and consciousness. The difference was that when I woke up this time I felt the elation of victory, not the dark sickness in the pit of my stomach that accompanied defeat. After a while I started to come round, and knew I needed to do something. But what? I did not want to work in Downing Street – and I hasten to add I had not been asked. I felt campaigning and governing were different activities. Later, even when I had meetings almost every day in Downing Street, I never got a pass, nor did I seek one – I wanted the line between me and government to be as clear and unambiguous as possible. It meant inconvenience, but it also meant I kept a degree of independence, but as the days wore on and the government's progress was leading every news broadcast, I thought I had to do something. I did not want to be fully in, but certainly did not want to be fully out.

So I phoned up Peter Hyman, who was working on strategy at Number 10, and arranged to meet him at Downing Street. This in itself was a big moment for me. For thirteen years I had walked and driven past Downing Street determined never to enter the place until we were in power, and now it was happening. When I got through police security and walked along Downing Street, it was like entering a secret garden, the focus of my thoughts and emotions over so many years, for me probably the most special place I could be. I remember talking to George Stephanopoulos, an adviser to President Clinton, about working in the White House; he said he rarely had time to smell the roses. I never had that problem; every time I went into Number 10 I considered it a privilege. That morning, as I approached the famous black door, which magically opened before me, I really did think, How did this happen? How can I be here? And I never lost that sense of wonder, nor the knowledge that we had a unique opportunity to serve the people who had put us there. Above all, perhaps, I knew that having spent so many years and such effort getting here, we should not be dispossessed of power without an almighty fight. This combination of awe at being there and a manic determination to help us stay there was to mark my every visit.

A landscape of power

On the other side of the black door is a small hallway, not particularly prepossessing. It has none of the glamour of the West Wing of the White House, which sparkles like a film set, none of the sense of history that I had expected to engulf me as I stepped inside. Instead it is cosy, comfortable and friendly, with a makeshift rack for mobile phones, a couple of period pictures and not much else. When arriving for an appointment, people tend to hang about here in a kind of limbo; American visitors in particular always seem very disappointed. I spent a long time waiting here over the years, but I never minded. I was just happy to be there.

Ahead was a long corridor that led to the Cabinet Room, which is impressive and does feel full of history. Next to the Cabinet Room, and leading directly into it, were a couple of offices. The first of these became Tony Blair's office; the second belonged to his principal civil servants, including Jonathan Powell, Tony's excellent chief of staff, all of them jostled together in a space far too small. None of this was remotely intimidating or impressive. Tony was not really concerned about the physical space he worked in, he just wanted to get on with the job in hand.

Further around were a series of offices that I could never really make sense of, although Fiona Millar worked there, which always cheered me up. Further still was the famous door to the Cabinet Office, where Michael Heseltine had the famous plastic key card that gave him access to Number 10.

As you stood in the waiting room just behind the black door, there was a small corridor, leading a few yards ahead to what was then the press office, where Alastair Campbell was based. Having been used by Bernard Ingham and Joe Haines, press secretaries to Margaret Thatcher and Harold Wilson, this had a certain sense of history, but it was too small for the task of modern communications and after a while Alastair moved his team to the former Whips' Office in Number 12.

Immediately to the left of the waiting room was the corridor to Numbers 11 and 12. At ground level Number 11 is just a small office, a waiting area and a conference room in which we spent many hours during those infamous meetings at which the handover of power from Tony Blair to Gordon Brown was discussed. Upstairs was a large reception room with a balcony overlooking the Downing Street gardens, and above that was the old Number 11 flat that

Tony and Cherie used in their time in Downing Street. It was comfortable but in no way ostentatious, the best thing about it the clutter and domesticity of a normal family home. After Leo was born you had to pick your way through children's toys to get to a meeting. Often Cherie would be there, welcoming, but determined to protect both Tony and their family from unnecessary outside intrusion. It was as if we were entering a private space, which we were.

At the end of this corridor was Number 12, which had been the Whips' Office until Alastair – quite rightly – turned it into a state-of-the art communications centre, with a new office off to the side where I spent many hours in meetings. When Gordon Brown became Prime Minister he worked here in a Millbank-style open-plan arrangement that was entirely utilitarian, rather like a souped-up war room.

On the second floor of Downing Street are the impressive State Rooms, along with yet more offices that seem to go on for ever, in an Alice in Wonderland kind of way.

A few hundred yards from Downing Street was the Treasury, which until it was modernised had the authentic feel of early twentieth-century government: seemingly endless identical corridors with identical offices. I always seemed to get lost in these corridors, and although I attended many meetings at the Treasury, I never quite got the hang of it. I would arrive early, fearful of getting lost. Gordon Brown's old office was vast, with a conference table at one end and some green leather chairs at the other. You could feel the past in the old Treasury, it had a 'Corridors of Power' feel about it, and I always imagined that it was these offices that inspired C.P. Snow's evocative phrase.[1]

But the truth is that nowhere in the maze of government offices that I visited did I feel the cold blast of history and power that I expected and that you feel in the White House. I believed that I would walk into the pages of Harold Nicolson's diaries,[2] or those of Chips Channon[3] or John Colville,[4] but it was not like that. It felt like a government machine designed for another era: buildings once inflated by the imperial power of Britain now feeling somewhat out of place. Even the Foreign

Office, though magnificent, draws its mystique from Victorian imagery of India and an imperial world now quite vanished. Impressive though a visit there was, the most powerful sense was of nostalgia and faded glory.

I have described these buildings not as a kind of history or geography lesson but to show how the context and the terrain had changed. We had been a small team focused on a single objective, with just a few offices in Westminster and Millbank. It was not simply our objective that would inevitably fragment in government, so too did the pre-election proximity and sense of community. Centres of power were scattered across Whitehall and inside Downing Street, in a sprawl of offices ill-suited to modern government. This was not the major source of the problems that were to follow, but it didn't help. A meeting with Tony Blair took place within one kingdom, a meeting with Gordon Brown within another.

If I look back at the pre-election years I have a sense that we were a guerrilla-like band of obsessive campaigners, driven forward and driven together, albeit often with divisions and difficulties along the way. If I look back at Labour's period of government I see meetings and meeting rooms, and incessant walking between them, people scattered across a vast Whitehall landscape, camaraderie inevitably undermined by distance. You campaign in poetry and govern in prose, but you also campaign together and govern apart. The irony is that, at the moment your mandate is strongest, your insight and understanding of how to make government work is necessarily at its weakest. Tony Blair often said after he left office that if only he had known then what he knows now, how much more he could have achieved. This is one paradox that it is hard for any synthesis to resolve: when you start you know least, and when you truly know enough it is time to finish.

May 1997: Starting again

But in late May 1997 Tony was just starting and by pure chance was bounding down the corridor towards me as I waited nervously by the front door. He looked happy, glowing, confident, obviously enjoying the job. Without a beat he said, 'Where have you been? Come to the Monday morning meet- ings – eight thirty.' And that was that. Ten years of meetings and polling and hundreds if not thousands of memos started there. The 8.30 Monday meeting was held in the Cabinet Room and chaired by the Prime Minister, with his inner team in attendance; they combined policy, strategy and a general overview of the week. Additionally I attended a raft of meetings with various members of Tony's team, which was a formidable and talented group including Alastair Campbell, Anji Hunter, Jonathan Powell, Sally Morgan, Peter Hyman and Liz Lloyd.

I like meetings – they are a way of bringing life and energy to a diffuse group of people. I enjoy the banter and the warmth. But there were a lot of meetings. For ten years this was my life, at least four or five meetings a week in Downing Street, meetings with Gordon Brown and countless focus groups, notes and memos, all the time trying to keep my company afloat to pay for most of this. I loved it, and it was as I wanted it: inside but also outside, committed and yet still independent. I was in my heart a political campaigner and strategist and that is what I wished to stay. I wanted above all to be the voice of the public in Downing Street.

1999: Conviction and consent

Although I loved my work I was never fully comfortable in this new landscape; I certainly never felt fully at ease in Downing Street. I liked going there, but it was not my home, not my place. I felt none of the sense of belonging that I felt at Millbank and later at Old Queen Street and Victoria Street, the headquarters of the Labour Party where I spent much of my time – and all of it during any kind of campaign. In many ways I felt most happy and fulfilled conducting focus groups, when I could leave Westminster behind and just talk to people. Much of what follows is not my account of the period but theirs. I want their voice to be fully heard, step by step as the narrative unfolds. I also conducted focus groups for this chapter to find out what people felt in retrospect about Labour, and how they saw their own, and Labour's, future. I have not cut politicians out of this story, in fact what I have written has its own kind of dialectic: public opinion reacting to politicians, politicians reacting to the public, and politicians reacting to each other.

The relationship between the public and politicians is complex. Modern government, probably all government, requires a balance between conviction and consent; you cannot lead effectively without both. The public want leadership with purpose, leadership that can be believed in, but they also want to be listened to and to be involved in the process of government. Without conviction, leadership meanders and does not inspire; without consent, leadership can hit roadblocks and sometimes even crash. But maintaining this balance is hard. Above all, the public want politics that delivers, that solves problems, that makes their lives easier. Often the public will oppose reforms in the short term but easily shift to supporting them in the longer term – or at least better understand them. You cannot achieve change without challenge, without making tough choices that often rub against the grain of popular opinion and received wisdom. If you stand your ground others will come. But it is also true that in the new world of interactive media, you need consent to achieve change in ways never before anticipated. This is why governing is difficult, always a kind of calculus, maintaining support but challenging that support in order to move ahead.

The story of Tony Blair as Prime Minister is in some ways the story of someone who moved the lodestar of his leadership from consent to conviction. This happened quite early, I think, in 1999. He wanted to be free of trying to please and accommodate, seeking instead to forge his own way ahead. But in the early days consent was crucial, because winning a second term was so vital. All of the key players in the campaign team were obsessed with the knowledge that Labour had never won two full terms and were convinced real and enduring change would not be delivered without it. Attlee's government achieved much in a single term but could have done so much more with two or three.

In maintaining this balance between conviction and consent, public opinion is vital and should never be underestimated. The electorate is wiser than you think. I can in all honesty say that I have never conducted a focus group in which I have not in some way been surprised and learnt something new. Many people hate the way that opinion polling and public opinion guides leaders but it is not wrong to listen to the electorate. It is they who live on the front line, under pressure, getting by, working hard, bringing up kids, living in challenging communities, and understanding more through their experience than many do through the vast ecosphere of received opinion and second-hand comment. New Labour was always about challenging the assumptions of elitism on both the right and the left, and for me talking to the public was the best way of making this possible.

My whole life has been spent listening to people and taking them seriously. That is not to say that I think polling and focus groups are the solution to democratic engagement, because clearly they aren't and can't be. My view has always been that connecting with the people through polling is an improvement on what went before, but is only a transitory stage before voters become fully involved in the political process. That is the next big step for campaigning and democracy, moving from polling to participation. In the meantime, it is better by far to listen to voters than to ignore them, or even to shout at them, although I quite understand how frustrating they can be. I have more than once lost my temper in a focus group, which is of course shockingly unprofessional but also makes these groups more a part of real politics. I argue, they argue back. I don't much believe in the absolute impartiality of political research: it is an art as much as a science, and perhaps above all it is a passion. Politics cannot be explained solely by the empirical reductionism of social science. Political consultancy is a cause more than a profession.

Despite the small numbers sampled, and the obvious lack of empirical rigour they entail, focus groups are the form of polling that I prefer. Although their scientific validity is less than that of an opinion poll, they are in a sense truer because you can talk to people as they really are, not as abstractions captured in a single moment. You gain access to real people with ideas and opinions that connect both to the past and to the future, who do not care much or at all about politics, and who think at one and the same time at many different levels. The complexity of public opinion reflects the complexity of politics; people have paradoxical views and opinions that cannot be reduced to easy choices or one-dimensional solutions. At its best a focus group is a place where you can dig beneath the surface and feel the forces gathering below.

There are many theories about public opinion and how it receives, accepts and digests political messages and infor-mation. Initially such theories were based on memory and immediate surface reactions, but now emotion and the deeper hidden connections of the brain are considered to have a greater role.[5] There is merit in both approaches, and the truth fuses a number of components, some on the surface, some in the depths, some midway between.

The metaphor I use is the flow of a river. The heavy sedi-ment at the depths represents the deeper values and emotional connections that guide so much of our thinking and which all of us hold. Nothing much will ever change this emotional base, and most of what we think and feel is seen through this filter. But higher up, the sediment is looser and attitudes and opinions, although still firmly held, can change over time or as the result of a dramatic incident. This is where the real battle for hearts and minds is fought. It takes a lot to change these mid-water attitudes but it can happen, with gradual, constant incremental changes suddenly leading to a qualita-tive leap forward. Most people will make an assumption, and will hold that assumption, despite countervailing evidence, until something tips or somehow snaps. It may take a long time for a politician to lose his reputation for competence, or for people to believe a recession really is coming. People hold on to what they know and believe as if lingering in an emotional and intellectual safe harbour, casting off to a new destination with great reluctance. They take a photograph of where they are and hold to it until the image is so discordant with reality that it has to be discarded. Sometimes they hold on to that original photograph and never desert it. In fact, research shows that the more countervailing information some people receive, the more partisan they can be.[6] Emotion is very powerful.

At the top of the river is the lightest sediment – fragments of opinion, unorganised and rootless, prey to the constant deluge of information that we are all now subjected to. So there is much turbulence near the surface of the river, which matters least, and little change at the bottom which matters most, but change will be happening, and change can be induced.

The crucial task of communications is to reach all levels: the depths, the middle and the surface; seeing them all as an interconnected whole. But first we need to be heard, because the public simply filters out messages it does not want to hear, and many of those messages are political. Before you can stir up the river sediment, you must find a way into the water. This is no easy task for today's politician, and depends much more on the electorate's interest in engaging than the politician's desire to get heard. The communications loop has been almost entirely reversed, information flowing from public to politician and not the other way round. But it is a mistake to think that the public ever completely switch off. They may not appear to care about politics, but they know when they are being ignored. That is why politicians must try and connect not now and again, but all the time. They are being watched even though they may not know it.

Perhaps what I like most about public opinion is the way that somehow or another when it does change, it changes collectively. Before every election there is a moment when the public seem to decide in unison not only what that election is about but what the words are that define it. In 1997 it was clear: Labour are safe enough to be trusted, we should give them a go – words, incidentally, that were rarely if ever uttered about the Conservatives in 2010. The decision then was: I want change, but can I trust the Tories?

The progress of public opinion: 1997–1999

The public certainly made a step change in 1997 and they were to hold that new mood for a very long time. New Labour effectively suspended the laws of political gravity for the best part of two years. In a Cabinet presentation in July 1999 I mapped out our position: 'Pre-election: disillusionment with the Conservatives, anxiety about Labour. Immediate post-election: euphoria. End of year one: settled confidence in the government.' Labour's polling showed a lead of 61 per cent against the Tories' 24 per cent in September 1997, which held to 53 per cent against 25 per cent in July 1998. And Tony Blair's net (positive minus negative) job performance was plus 89 per cent in September 1997 and plus 76 per cent in July 1998.[7]

Underneath the surface, however, Labour's position was not so assured. It is true that in the first year of government the public mood was positive and for the most part my only task was to warn against the danger of inflated expectations. But by 1998 the public started to grow more querulous, with issues about delivery gradually emerging. In the spring, focus groups held among switchers to Labour from the Conservatives were divided between the promise of hope and the pace of delivery: 'Blair has charisma'; 'more modern'; 'hope for the future' were some of the comments, but also: 'Maybe a slow start on some issues'; 'very slow on education, health service, seem to have ideas they do not follow through'; 'talk but do not deliver, not radical enough'.

In Putney in September 1998 this divide remained but the issue of immigration began to emerge, and the dissent became harsher and a little more bitter. The positive comments about Labour were: 'A message of hope, trying to put things right'; 'trying to get the country on the right road'; 'a lot of new policies for the young'; the negative ones were: 'They should try harder to make sure the country's not over-populated'; 'accepting too many refugees'. But mainly the issue was the pace of delivery: 'A lot of unfulfilled promises since 1997'; 'will always promise, promise, promise. Not sure they will fulfil their promises'.[8]

This mood continued till the end of the year, but by the start of 1999 the negatives were beginning to have more edge, and the mood of hope was starting to dissipate. Good things were: 'Stable on the economy'; 'not rushing into the Euro'; 'education – well done with literacy and numeracy', but the negative comments were building – 'very disappointed with health cuts'; 'closure of hospitals, sick people stuck on trolleys' – and spin and sleaze made their first appearance.[9] These comments were definitely in the shallow water of politics, reactive to media and not forming a coherent picture. Although fragments, however, they were interesting ones, because much of the later story of public opinion was contained in them. The knack, as ever, was in working out which were important and which not, and what was the underlying narrative that would ultimately link them all in the public mind. In those early days I knew immigration would be a major issue, though one I anticipated we would be able to contain, but the NHS seemed almost impossible to resolve. Now, however, the NHS is seen by the public as the greatest of New Labour's achievements, with record levels of satisfaction, while immigration has continuously grown as an issue and has become for some the central concern of our times.

The two trajectories: Blair and Brown

Meanwhile the process of government went on. While public opinion was cautiously making its way ahead, inside government the atmosphere was frenetic, pressured and often fractious, as Alastair Campbell's diaries make clear. Ironically the public was the swan serenely going about its business, the government the feet underneath desperately paddling to keep afloat. And the government was doing a lot: independence for the Bank of England, the minimum wage, devolution, peace in Northern Ireland, and much else besides. And although Gordon Brown and Tony Blair were two swans rather than one, they were at least in convoy.

The first term was probably Gordon's best in government. He had ideas, coupled with the relentless drive and stubborn determination needed to achieve them. A windfall tax on utilities, a new deal for the unemployed, Sure Start centres, tax credits – these are a strong legacy. He was the political equivalent of a Sherman tank: he simply would not be deflected. And he was New Labour, having a dynamic view of the relationship between private and public in which the old system of welfare would be transformed by a focus on work and independence, and the economy would be transformed by a focus on enterprise and opportunity. He seemed to owe more to the traditions of the Scottish Enlightenment than continental social democracy. Underpinning this was a commitment to financial responsibility which seemed to reflect the frugality of the manse. His great passions were the creation of employment and the elimination of poverty, but he saw these in a distinctive and modern New Labour way. Gordon was very focused and resented distraction from his plan; he didn't like events, he wanted constancy.

Tony Blair was in a different trajectory in government – he had to prove to himself and to the public that he was up to the job of being Prime Minister, which at forty-three, with no government experience, must have been daunting. Gradually, and then more rapidly, he realised he could fill the role, and he wanted to move step by step up to the next stage of leadership, welcoming the uncertainty of events and the challenge of the unexpected. At the same time he was learning how to be Prime Minister, finding his way to being a leader. Every new leader goes through the same process, some managing it more effectively than others, but all face the same basic challenge. Tony, though, never stopped learning; he was always rethinking what it meant to be a leader, effectively in a state of constant renewal. He was, and still is, uncompromising in his New Labour ideas but he is always restless and questioning, about himself, about policy, about the future.

Probably Tony's essential skill as a leader was his capacity not just to read the future, but to find a new way through it. This made him appear mercurial sometimes, and probably to some lacking sufficiently in long-term focus, but it also meant he never grew stale, and was always changing in his own way. His politics reflected his personality. Tony had a clear view of human nature and a deep understanding of what aspiration meant. He did not believe that the state could provide all the answers, and understood the complexity of motivation held by the electorate. And he had an instinctive understanding of the need to build a coalition of interests not just of middle and working class, but of entrepreneurs and the voluntary sector, south as well as north, young as well as old. And for him the pace and rhythm of politics was important. Momentum matters and Tony understood the fundamental truth that in a world moving at a frantic speed those that stand still will perish. For him permanent revolution was less of a risk than consolidation.

All this made him fascinating to work with, but I am sure from Gordon's point of view it also made him unsettling and disconcerting. I suspect Gordon equated Tony's speed and lightness of touch with a lack of substance and solidity. Tanks on one side of Whitehall, light infantry on the other.

Part of Tony Blair's process of leadership was inevitably a reconfiguration and hardening of his framework of ideas. It was not that he came to power without a clear conception of what he believed in – he was sure about his policy principles and the core assumptions of New Labour. He had a clear vision of the kind of modern, fair and tolerant country he wanted to help build, and understood the general principles that would form the foundations of national renewal, but what he did not have was a theory of reform that would make such renewal possible. He was clear about his aims and his basic values, but had not yet found a way of fusing his liberal instincts and communal values in a way that could create a liberating welfare state. The same was true of his foreign policy development. He began, through the crisis in Kosovo, when he led the campaign against Milosevic's policy of the ethnic cleansing of Kosovo Albanians, to fuse his commitment to universal liberal values with his collectivist sense of communal responsibility. In 1999 these ideas robustly came together, a process exemplified by two speeches: the Chicago speech on foreign affairs,[10] in which what became known as the Blair doctrine on liberal inter-ventionism was first expressed, and his speech to the party conference, in which he said New Labour's purpose was to take on the 'forces of conservatism' that held people back.[11] Together these constituted not only a development of New Labour but also an early summation of what might be called Blairism.

These two trajectories – Gordon Brown solid, consistent and unstoppable; Tony Blair learning, changing, renewing – had the potential to provide a perfect balance. But they also had the potential for instability, because the relationship was never in a steady state. With Tony you never knew quite what was going to happen, so Gordon could never feel confident that one day he would be leader. There are, of course, many reasons why their relationship broke down, but I did not believe those reasons were initially based on policy or values. I felt that both men started out as New Labour, and I saw in both their shared commitment to enterprise, the power of work, opportunity, the community and a new way of looking at political problems.

One was a Scottish Calvinist, a puritan in many ways, driven by the work ethic; the other a liberal socialist, driven by a passion for modernity. As in a Venn diagram, there were areas of disagreement but also areas of genuine overlap. Neither was a conventional social democrat, and both were absolutely determined to remake the Labour Party, and to remake Britain. When I look back at that time I feel a sense of energy, dynamism and change. There were differences but they could be lived with.

The gestation of the conflict between them came from

another place – it was an accident of fate and timing; two extraordinary individuals, each capable of becoming Labour leader in 1994, each without the other indisputably the dominant progressive politician of his age.

This mutual power was of course a great strength at times and enabled Labour and Britain to change, but there was always likely to be a reckoning. Both Blair and Brown were in different ways protean forces and both in their own ways were unstoppable. Only one could be Prime Minister, or at least Prime Minister in the first, decisive decade or so. Either of them could have been leader in 1994, but when the moment arrived it was bound to be Blair. He was the natural leader in waiting, he was the acclaimed choice of the party and the public. There was effectively no contest, Tony was going to win. I believed this for several years but never directly told Gordon (which I regret). I suspect few were really honest with him about the emerging truth of his position, fuelling a sense of betrayal and mistrust when the leadership moment came and passed him by. Gordon was always an angular and sometimes angry man, but he was also someone you did not want to hurt, and being completely honest with him was not easy. He was powerful and vulnerable at the same time.

This sense of betrayal was compounded by a view among some of Gordon's supporters that Tony was not really deserving of the job. Underestimating him both as potential threat to Gordon and as Prime Minister, they believed he was too insubstantial, too chimerical a figure to lead. Although Peter Mandelson adored Tony, his view for a long while was that Gordon's awesome strength and determination made him, not Tony, the natural leader. He used to say of Gordon that he had the colossal power needed to create but also to destroy. It is no bad thing to be such a force of creative destruction: many great leaders, from Churchill to Roosevelt, have been cast from this mould. In the early stages Mandelson underestimated Blair, seeing the dominant figure ahead rather than the fleeting figure overtaking him.

Mandelson's problem in this period was less that he was

disloyal, more that he was almost too loyal, holding on to assumptions that had been eroded by reality, and that the sudden death of John Smith forced into stark clarity. This was a real moment of dialectical revelation, when almost in a moment of epiphany he saw Blair's real qualities revealed, recognising that his friend was actually the natural leader.

This tendency among some in Gordon's group to under-estimate Tony, even to disparage him with a brutal crudeness that I did not really understand. This has largely changed, with most of my 'Brownite' friends coming to understand and appreciate Blair's leadership skills. Much of the poison has drained out of the system. But the perception that Tony was in some way undeserving harmed the relationship from the start, leading to an undervaluing not just of Tony himself but his achievements. Alastair Campbell constantly urged Gordon when he became leader to make a priority of defending Labour's record in government, and not to allow the turf wars of the past to undermine his fourth-term strategy and Labour's record of achievement. When two factions are fighting and it is perceived to be a win/lose battle, then strategy becomes flawed. In government we should have stood with greater unity and confidence about what we had achieved. On that, as on many other things, John Prescott was right.

The root cause of the tension and eventual conflict was simple: Gordon could never reconcile himself to the anguish and the horror of having the leadership taken from him by someone he considered a friend. This anguish turned into anger, and the anger burned. I described earlier in this book how Gordon asked me if he should stand down in the elec-tion against Tony in 1994. I said, 'Only if you could live with it,' and in truth he could not. He made a massive contribution to government and is a seminal post-war polit-ical figure, but he could never let this go, never break free of it. And I suspect what made it worse was the uncertainty over the future, his fear that once again the capriciousness of fate would take the leadership away from him.

It is easy to say Gordon should have moved on, controlled

his anger, given up on his resentfulness – not just because it was the right thing to do, but because it was the best thing for him. If he had adopted a different approach to Tony, been more conciliatory, more accommodating, more loving, he would have been happier and he would have been leader earlier. His strategy regarding Blair was flawed and counter-productive. But Gordon Brown is not Mother Teresa, he is a politician driven by passion, anger and insecurity, and the course he took was the natural course for him. I am sure he fought it, wanting a better way but never quite finding it. As in almost everything else in politics, however, he was divided, the constructive side of his personality fighting with the destructive side, something that his supporters described as good Gordon and bad Gordon. This conflict is not all negative: so many leaders have these internal contradictions. It is what powers them through, makes them creative, makes them protean. It is what made Gordon brilliant but impossible.

From Gordon's perspective Tony came through silently, moving from partnership to solo ascendancy with an ease and skill that would have surprised and destabilised him. Because of the intimacy of their relationship, because Tony is such a warm and engaging personality, Gordon must have felt a huge sense of shock and betrayal. That is completely understandable. They were, in a sense, brothers. One brother had to break clear and win, the other to live with the consequences, which for Gordon were very harsh. But Tony was right to do as he did, behaving with decency as well as ambition, although his feelings of responsibility and perhaps guilt never left him. In the end, despite his frustrations and his doubts, he believed he should honour the contract he originally made. This was like a blood relationship twisting and turning through time, as in a way it still does.

Even writing this I worry about what Gordon will think or feel when he reads it. I have tried to be as fair as possible but I have to make a judgement, it would be cowardly not to, and in the end the responsibility for the destructive saga that followed was much more Gordon's responsibility than

Tony's. It would be impossible to have observed these events over so many years and not believe this. I admire Gordon, I like him, he is an extraordinary political figure, but it would have been better for him to have done this another way. It is for the real brothers, one of whom leads the party, to do it differently, and I am sure they will.

But there is another side to this. In preparing these final chapters I read hundreds of focus group notes, and more strategy notes than I care to mention, coming to understand just how annoying the constant flood of memos must have been to Number 10. And I referred to hundreds of pages of diaries, covering almost the entire period; and the descriptions of the tension between Blair and Brown are vivid and sometimes shocking. But most of what I reread is not dramatic or sensational. Rather it shows the slow – and sometimes not so slow – development of public opinion, and the continuous process of strategic development. For much of the time this strategic process worked very well. Most of the time I worked effectively and closely with Gordon, finding him sometimes challenging but rarely truly impossible.

And this is just in my world, public opinion, strategy and campaigning. It omits both Tony's and Gordon's basic passion – in different ways it is true-for policy, and for implementing change. This was the day-to-day reality of what they did – policy on the NHS, on crime, on the economy, on education, on welfare, on immigration. Gordon was consumed by policy, but so too was Tony: one of his maxims was that the best policy was the best politics. This work, led in Downing Street by David Miliband, Geoff Mulgan and Andrew Adonis, went on continually. Even in the second term, dominated as it was in so many ways by Iraq, the establishment of Michael Barber's delivery unit maintained the focus on policy and its implementation.

And there were always points of connection as well as discontinuity. For example, before the 2001 election a few of us formed what we called a Sherpas group of campaign strategists, a couple of levels down from the bigger beasts.

The core of this group started in the late 1990s and comprised myself, Douglas Alexander, Ed Miliband, sometimes David Miliband, Spencer Livermore, Peter Hyman and, when necessary, Alastair Campbell. Week after week, month after month, this group did the grunt work of strategic planning – in 2001, in 2005, even in 2010, when I was too ill to attend meetings and we met occasionally at my house. The group just kept going, writing war book after war book, because they loved campaigning and they loved the Labour Party. They worked obsessively to keep Labour in power. Though there were always forces tearing apart the fabric of our relationships, others were there to mend them.

I do not want to romanticise all this, it is important to be honest. It is not the case that policy between Tony and Gordon went in unison, it clearly didn't. I am not saying that the relationship between them was anything other than dysfunctional – it was. But politics is never easy, never perfect. Most of us, in our relationships, know anger that can be destructive, and see only later what has been achieved, when the passion and the blame has subsided. And what was achieved was substantial.

1999: Public opinion and the politics of grievance

Meanwhile in the spring of 1999, the isolated fragments of public opinion were starting to form patterns that were more threatening for Labour. We were two years in from the election, effectively the halfway moment in the parliament. In April I wrote a long note called: 'Half-way there: Mid-term assessment', a wide-ranging appraisal of our position:

> In the last twenty years, probably in the last ten, the context in which governments operate has been completely transformed. The frustrations of the last few months, about the media; about follow through; about being under the constant pressure of unanticipated events; are partly the consequence of government, but they are also the consequence of this 'new

incumbency'. We govern within a totally new environment: a world of global markets and ceaseless technological change; a world where the transfer of information is instant and global; where the cynicism of the press is feeding the cynicism of the public and in turn exacerbating it.

This situation required new structures of government: 'Much of the existing structure of government is based on a model of the world that no longer exists, rooted in assumptions that are linear, hierarchical and compartmentalised. But the new world requires the opposite: speed, flexibility, creativity and integration.'

As a parallel to this, in June 1999 I wrote a note called 'Mid-term Disconnection: The new voter mood'. In this I said:

> We are still holding up in opinion polls and will continue to do so. Also the war [in Kosovo] is an exceptional moment in British politics and may have skewed perceptions. But with all these caveats I am sure that the mood has shifted. For the first time we can say that the honeymoon is over and that this Labour government is being hit by mid-term discontent. It is important to get a real feel for this new mood. The essential point is that it is emotional and not rational. People criticise the government but with literally almost no idea of what it has done. They say it has failed to deliver, but cannot say either what it has not delivered, or what it has achieved. The best way of describing this is disconnection: the government in one place, the public in another, in some way we have parted company, the mood is complaint, blame, dissatisfaction. People feel neglected and ignored.

By July 1999 I was focused on the central core of the electoral challenge facing us. In a note called 'Hard-working families: a new narrative for the government', I spelt out how the swirling fragments of public opinion were finally taking definite shape:

Most people feel their life chances are flat or somewhat upwards. They feel they work very hard, but that their work and contribution is not recognised. This personal narrative is important in itself. It reflects the pressures of more work, more global competition, less security. But people do not want to turn the clock back, they know change must be embraced, but they want help from the government: better schools; better health provision; low mortgages; fair taxes; the security of welfare without its abuses. This narrative of hard-working families must become absolutely central to Labour in the coming months and years. It is a narrative that we have tended to forget, leading to a sense of disconnection. It is a New Labour narrative, embracing change but enabling families to cope with it.

This note captured a gathering change in the electorate, and one that became perhaps the most important shift in public opinion during our period in government. The view was growing that those who worked hard and behaved responsibly were not being fairly rewarded, while others made gains they did not deserve, had not worked for, were not entitled to. An appropriate relationship between contribution and reward is, for most of the public, the core component of fairness, a kind of contributory fairness. The contrary view of fairness, the one traditionally associated with the left, is an equalitarian fairness: the view that equality and fairness are universally applicable values, intrinsic to the good society, and that society is morally better if it is more equal, more fair, more compassionate.

These two views – both valid – are at the centre of the modern political debate. There is little doubt however that in the UK and most Western democracies it is contributory fairness that has taken strongest hold. When people are asked what fairness means they invariably answer by one form or another of the same formulation: stop people abusing the system, give people who work hard a fair deal.

The problem, at least for the left, is not that the contributory concept of fairness is right wing but that many voters see it in those terms, a powerful idea intertwined with a series of political issues that are more naturally associated with the right: excessive immigration, welfare abuse, wasteful government spending, softness on crime. So a call for fairness has become a cry of grievance, resentment and anger, expressing the view that my life is bad because others are unfairly benefiting. Clearly this is fertile ground not just for the right but for the far right. Across Europe the social democratic state has become associated with a kind of unfairness; equality is seen not to be helping fair reward but hindering it. The emergence of this conception of fairness, the growing sense of grievance and the link to immigration developed almost inexorably in my research.

I had, and have, a typically New Labour response to all this. It was crucial to listen and to respect the opinions of the public, but also to respond in a progressive and empowering way. On the one hand I believe that every voice should be heard; we should listen to opinions that we may not like and with which we are uncomfortable. The politics of grievance can be harsh and it is never easy moderating a group where the sole focus is immigration. But immigration, like crime, like welfare abuse, is not an issue we can avoid; we must deal with it head on. Not just because of the sense of unfairness that people hold but also because it is for many an issue of democratic involvement. Immigration has changed Britain, culturally and ethnically, and in my view for the better, but this was not a process over which the electorate felt they had sufficient control or influence. It has left many who had little power in the first place feeling yet more disempowered. So much of this is about control, insecurity and fear. A start was made in dealing with the issue of immigration and almost alone on the left in the early days New Labour was prepared to make it: New Labour and Tony Blair did listen and did act. But rational progress alone could not hope to cope with this level of emotional concern. We did a lot but not enough, we faced up to the issue but did not confront it head on with argument, debate and involvement.

On the other hand, although it is right to listen it is wrong to believe that the politics of grievance can be solved by the policies of the right. I have moderated dozens of focus groups in which immigration was the dominant issue, and my political and instinctive sense has always been that the ultimate answer lay in more opportunity, stronger communities, better education and increased life chances, rather than simply blocking immigration and thinking all would be well. In the end conservative solutions will not work: they just move the anger to another place.

Perhaps most important, the politics of grievance is about control and empowerment and voice. If people are heard, if they have genuine influence over their communities and their lives, then they will feel less resentment. Paradoxically, the more people are empowered to act, the less extreme their opinions may be. The politics of identity and of empowerment must go hand in hand. We must hear the people on these issues, we must be tough where necessary and above all competent, but we must be confident that in the end progressive solutions will work, and conservative solutions will not. The answer to unfairness is not more unfairness; the left must win fairness back in all its various forms.

1999: Mid-term reflection

I was not alone in writing notes at this mid-point in our first term. There was a general sense that after two years we needed to take a long, deep look at ourselves. Alastair Campbell saw the problem as a failure of strategic communication, arguing for 'relentless, ruthless focus on key issues of domestic policy. It requires a strategy to explain what we have done so far, set it in the context of what comes next. Everyone who appears at conference should have it fixed in their minds, in each key policy area, *what we've done, why we have done it, what we are going to do next*. The public and the party do not know what we have achieved. The simple next aim is to have this coming at them from all directions.'

Jonathan Powell, as always, was fiercely New Labour:

'Our problem is not that we are too New Labour, but not nearly New Labour enough.' Peter Hyman took another course entirely and in a brilliant note, one of the best written in the government years, called for a 'Second Phase New Labour'. He argued that blame for our problems lay not just with a hostile media but in our own failure to shake ourselves out of a 1980s mindset. He believed that the key politicians – Blair, Brown, Mandelson – were trapped by the battles they had to fight in the 1980s: 'That mindset, once a laudable determination not to fall into the mistakes of the past, now prevents us from setting a more confident New Labour position that can galvanise party and public. [The answer is] a two-year transition from the first phase of New Labour to a more confident and better defined second phase.' He argued for a radical New Labour, based on a statement of mission that would force the political debate irreversibly to the left: He wanted 'Tony to be a conviction politician, linking Barrister Blair, Middle Class Blair and Moral Blair'. Always the most iconoclastic thinker in Downing Street, Hyman was the first person fully to articulate this particular view of the renewal of New Labour, which is now common currency. Tony Blair may not always have agreed with Peter, but he greatly respected him.

It is possible to argue that such intense internal strategic scrutiny was an indulgence, given our massive opinion poll lead and the apparent certainty that we would win the next election. Perhaps we were too nervous and panicky. However, it is also true that we only won elections because of this kind of obsessive self-scrutiny, winning in part because we kept convincing ourselves we could lose.

The outcome of this mid-term reflection was a change of mood and ideas from Tony Blair. He wanted to lead on his terms, to make clear what he believed in; he wanted another level of definition and purpose. He had already made a start on this in April in his speech 'The Doctrine of the International Community', in which he spelt out the implications of global interdependence, and the effects and consequences of globalisation:

If we can establish and spread the values of liberty, the rule of law, human rights and an open society, then it is in our national interests too. The spread of our values makes us safer. As John Kennedy put it: 'Freedom is indivisible and when one man is enslaved who is free?' The most pressing foreign policy problem we face is to identify the circumstances in which we should get involved in other people's conflicts. Non-interference has long been considered an important part of international order . . . but the principle of non-interference must be qualified in important respects. Acts of genocide can never be a purely internal matter.[12]

This doctrine of liberal interventionism is now accepted by many in the West; it is the basis of the NATO action in Libya. Of course, it is a doctrine now entangled with, and for many contaminated by, the war in Iraq, but its truth essentially holds: we are now a global community in which all of us have certain inalienable rights, and we have the responsibility on occasion to protect them. Once again Blair links the community to the individual, the liberal to the socialist tradition in progressive politics. And his understanding of globalisation and its domestic pressures parallels in many ways the anxiety and concern expressed in the focus groups. Globalisation was becoming the new terrain of politics, from Chicago to Croydon.

September 1999: The forces of conservatism

Back in the UK, Blair began to work on his conference address, and so began the gestation of the 'Forces of Conservatism' speech. In many ways it was in this particular speech that Tony really began to find his voice. A speech more subtle and nuanced than many remember, at one and the same time it was a defence of solidarity and community, modernisation and, above all, progressive politics. It was another step forward for the definition of New Labour and

Blairism. It was as always hell to help prepare the speech, a six-week period ending up with six nights in a hotel with almost no sleep. Tony basically wrote his speech but we all had to suffer.

His central argument echoed his Chicago speech:

> Global finance and communications and media. Electronic commerce. The internet. The science of genetics. Every year a new revolution scattering in its wake security and ways of living for millions of people. These forces of change driving the future. Don't stop at national boundaries. Don't respect tradition. They wait for no one and no nation. They are universal. We know what a twenty-first-century nation needs: a knowledge-based economy. A strong civic society. The challenge is how. The answer is people. The future is people. The liberation of human potential not just as workers but as citizens. Not power to the people, but power to each person to make the most of what is in them . . . The country run for far too long on the talents of the few when the genius of the many lies uncared for and ignored . . .
>
> To the child who goes to school hungry for food, but thirsting for knowledge, I know the talent you were born with, and the frustration you feel that is trapped inside you. We will set your potential free. And to those who have wealth, but who say that none of it means anything if my children can't play in the park, and my mother daren't go out at night, we share your belief in a strong community. We will set your potential free. The old order, those forces of conservatism, for all their language about promoting the individual, and freedom and liberty, they held people back. They stunted people's potential, they held people down. Year after year. Decade after decade.[13]

Tony saw this speech as the moment of breakout, in a way expressing a kind of UDI. Here is a brief excerpt from my diary describing what he said at the time:

29 October 1999

We spend about an hour with Tony saying that he feels that he's not connecting properly. He doesn't feel that he's breaking through as a politician and he's concerned and honest about it. He doesn't know quite what to do about it, he doesn't want to be a false 'politician of the people', just going around the place and shaking hands, and being 'out there'. It's not his style, it's not him; he wants to be honest, he wants to be real. He wanted to become himself and that's why he made the speech that he'd made, and he was happy with the forces of conservatism argument. He wanted to be an inclusive politician but a politician with conviction. A politician with urgency, a radical politician. A politician moving ahead the reform agenda.

This was a radical speech, out of kilter with the one-nation rhetoric that often preceded it, and Tony still claims it was his favourite. But the backlash was strong, misunderstanding I think his concept of conservatism. We pulled back, probably by too much, but in the longer term it was the engine of much of his thinking. In many ways it is a speech whose time has come.

2000: New millennium, renewed strategy

The year and the millennium ended with a burst of pessimism. On the one hand the polling was good and on the other hand the public were starting to become impatient, sceptical and disconnected. We had to consider how much of this was due to the character and policies of the Labour government, and how much to the immutable rule of politics that time in government leads to inevitable disconnection. And what of the bigger forces that surrounded our government: the rise of globalisation, the pressure on living standards in all Western democracies as new economies developed, the change in the amount and the quality of the media, the pervasive sense of long-term national decline, and the continuing cynicism about politics? We needed to decide whether to reach out to this mood and try to give it solace, or to rise above it and implement policies that, even if they were unpopular in the short term, might in the longer run make a difference.

It did not get dramatically better in the New Year. The Millennium Dome was not one of our greatest triumphs, although it is now a huge commercial success. On Millennium Eve I arrived at the Dome on the tube but got stuck behind a grated iron gate, squeezed into the tiniest of spots by the huge pressure of the crowds. Next to me were the editors of most of our national papers, similarly trapped. It was not going to be a good night. But afterwards I went back on the same boat as Tony Blair, and sitting on deck, seeing night-time London around me, feeling the hidden power of a new millennium, was moving and peaceful. Moments like that made it all worthwhile.

We ended the old century with the public unsettled but basically on side, Tony gaining an ever clearer sense of his own political identity. The next year was to be crucial. The imminence of the next election was informing everything, at least in my world. We were well into our normal eighteen-month planning cycle for an election campaign.

In January 2000 I conducted a set of groups. The government was perceived to be succeeding with the economy and education, but the NHS was 'too big to turn around', and the general mood disaffected. The Conservatives were 'weak, divided and useless' but their strength lay in their Euro-scepticism and patriotism and their tough line on crime and welfare. 'Britishness' featured regularly. People thought they were being taken over by Brussels, we were a soft touch, had lost our manufacturing industry. There was 'nothing to be proud of'.

At the root of the dissatisfaction was the continuing sense that hard-working families did not get a fair deal. 'And in a second note written at the same time, I argue that the enemy now was a corrosive, insidious cynicism: a belief that Labour couldn't deliver, Britain couldn't be changed. 'Let's not vote for them again.' For me the crucial thing was concerns about the breaking of the contract implicit in our election: 'New

Labour was built on the mainstream values of hard-working families. It won by offering a new contract with the people of Britain. The elements of this contract were clear enough: renewal of our public services; mainstream values that were tough on responsibility as well as rights; new leadership for Britain and the world.' Fairly or not, the electorate was starting to feel that this contract had been broken. I continued:

> The way forward is to make hard-working families the corner-stone of our project; make rebuilding the NHS a national project; becoming the patriotic party again; getting back to mainstream social values; rebuilding community; there is a public yearning for this. Crime, social disorder and civic disintegration are key to people's concerns and diagnosis about the state of Britain. We should be more ambitious, thinking in terms of transforming education: not just in primary schools but at every level and in every single way. We must give Britain the human capital it needs to fight and win in the next century of the knowledge economy.

Tony Blair and Gordon Brown both wrote notes at this time. Almost a year before an election, the pace was beginning to quicken. Blair argued in a note in May:

> I define our problems as not complex but simple. On policy the difficulties are: crime; asylum; the family; standing up for Britain. These are classic middle England worries. At present they wrongly think that either we are out of touch with them on these issues or we differ from them and they don't know why. There is no sense, outside of economic stability, of a big message. Big achievements – halving long-term unemployment; a million kids out of poverty; one million jobs; improvements in the NHS, falling welfare bills; big drops in burglary and car crime – are completely unknown or disbelieved. The answer? To correct the policy problems in so far as we can, and when we can't at least explain what we are doing, give reasons, put up an argument. On presentation it is to crunch the message down and put in place a system to get it across.

The message: we stand for traditional British values but have the courage to apply them in a new way for a new world. We need Britain to work not just for the top ten per cent, but for all our people.

Gordon's premise was that 'to sustain our support and give the government momentum, New Labour must speak directly to the material and social concerns of everyday working families, within the context of building a new Britain'. His key argument was:

'Working hard for hard-working families' is what binds together our constituencies in middle and lower income Britain (dealing with tensions growing within the coalition). It is what we believe the story of British values to be about: work, self-improvement, and fair play. Essential for the economic health of Britain – widening opportunity, hard work, self-improvement and long-term investment in work, education, and business. It is what gives us moral force as a crusade.

These notes share a joint focus on the challenge of globalisation, Blair and Brown agreeing that progressive parties had to find a way of offering both security and opportunity. Both focused on community fairness and a modern patriotism. Perhaps what is interesting is the Scottish Calvinism that shines through Gordon's note: he uses words like work ethic, self-improvement and hard work, a different kind of language from that of many progressive politicians. You feel the ghost of Adam Smith.

But there is a difference here, not just of political emphasis but of narrative: the means by which the electorate make sense of what we do and why we do it. We spent hours wrestling with what it should be. We had a narrative about the modernisation of Britain, which was Tony's home ground and which was exemplified by the slogan 'New Labour, New Britain'; a narrative about hard-working families which Gordon usually preferred; and a narrative about fairness and opportunity that underpinned everything else.

All of these represented core pillars of the New Labour project, so all were crucial, and you can see all of them in the notes of Tony and Gordon above. We were always trying to synthesise and blend them, but never totally succeeded and kept them as three narrative tracks that weaved together in different ways over the thirteen years. Perhaps this was the best way of doing it, they were all part of our story. One without the other two would be incomplete. 'New Labour, New Britain' was the core, but we were always building on it.

July 2000: Losing it, again

About this time I started losing my memos, or rather finding them plastered on the front page of the *Sunday Times*. It is bad enough forgetting the party's advertising at Euston Station as I did in 1997, worse to misplace some of the most uncompromising memos I have ever written.

It started with a phone call on Friday evening telling me a sports bag with some memos visible in it had been found at the Underground lost property office at Euston. I went there with a great sense of unease. The office did not exist and nor, of course, did the bag. Later I would spend a lot of time discussing the bag with Gordon, who was determined to find the culprit. He was obsessed with the bag, he thought the bag was key in some way to the mystery.

Sure enough, on Saturday I got a call from Downing Street saying the *Sunday Times* was in possession of a leaked memo written by me, one that was very negative about the Prime Minister. I felt sick, and immediately phoned Tony to apologise. This was a memo I had written attacking his speech to the Women's Institute. No one much liked the speech but I really took against it, saying: 'It makes you think less of him not more, partly it is a tone that tries to be conversational, but instead feels condescending, because it is a TB we do not know.' Even now, typing this, I cringe with embarrassment. Then another memo appeared in *The Times* and the *Sun*, the latter of which had the headline:

'Tony it's serious: they don't like us; They don't trust us; they may dump us'. By now I was feeling beyond embarrassment, I was feeling a kind of horror. This time Tony phoned me, and he was a little less friendly.

Then, perhaps worst of all, a short note of Tony's appeared, one that talked about eye-catching initiatives in response to the problems of crime and disorder. It was untypical of his notes, which are usually much more calm and reflective. I did not know if I was responsible for the leak, but everybody else thought I was. I attended the morning campaign meetings but I was a twitching wreck, trying to explain how the memos might have leaked. Everyone was searching for the person responsible, and because a note from the Prime Minister had been leaked the head of MI5 turned up in my office one day, unannounced. I was starting to panic. MI5's theory was that the au pair had done it. But one day a journalist phoned me, for which I will always be eternally grateful, and said it was probably Benji the Binman, an individual who goes around, or did once, taking notes and letters from people's rubbish – a kind of slow-mail equivalent to hacking. I immediately had security cameras installed, waiting up to try and spot him, but I never did. Of course I never threw another piece of paper away, with the result that my house became a kind of industrial waste unit. Later it was confirmed to me that the memo had indeed been taken from my rubbish.

It took a while for me to escape the trauma of the leaked memo period. That kind of scrutiny and intrusion, even on such a relatively unimportant matter, is horrible.

January 2001: The second resignation

Not long afterwards Peter Mandelson was to find himself at the centre of altogether more intense and politically difficult scrutiny, leading to his second resignation from the Cabinet. The incident exposed the fact that, however close they may be, teams can fracture under the pressure of government.

I had disagreed with most people on Peter's first

resignation, over a loan from his fellow minister Geoffrey Robinson. I was opposed to him going; I thought it would be a serious blow to people's perception of New Labour. But Tony Blair became fairly settled in the view that Mandelson had made an error of judgement, compounded by a failure to declare it when he became Trade Secretary running the department that was investigating Robinson. Tony phoned me that Christmas and asked abruptly, 'What do you think about Peter?' I said he should stay, that he embodied New Labour. Tony was having none of it; but I felt very sad. I was a regular visitor to Peter's house in Notting Hill, the one the controversial mortgage was raised for. He loved his home and his job and he was devastated.

The second resignation was different. Throughout the crisis Peter was low and lacking his usual fight, he was not himself – he is usually at his best in a crisis. The morning of his resignation he was upset, thinking he had let us all down. He seemed almost resigned to his fate, although later of course he challenged it. I consoled him but did not start fighting for him, which was a mistake. Had it been anyone but Peter we might have stood up for him, protected and supported him, but somehow he was required to live by different standards. We could have done more, and certainly I should have done more.

This second resignation drove Mandelson beyond despair; he fought back and did achieve retrospective vindication, but it was little recompense. A position in the Cabinet was so important to him – not so much a job, much more a way of life. The lineage that reached back to his grandfather Herbert Morrison was snapped when it should not have been.

We did not speak for a while after that, making it up on 11 September 2001, of all days. But later Peter told me that during his European Commission posting a day didn't pass when he did not wish to be back in British politics and in the Cabinet. When eventually he did come back for Gordon Brown, he deserved it.

If anyone had a dialectical career it was Peter. Starting with media management and fighting modernisation battles, he was defined as a 'master of the black arts'. And he was very good at it. But he wanted to be known not as a media expert but a capable politician in his own right. His early career kept him in the shadows for far too long, and perhaps we all colluded in that. It was only as Secretary of State for Trade and Industry and then Northern Ireland that he really found his feet, his true power and calling. He loved being a minister, loved the decisions, the atmosphere, the planning, the intrigue. In his later years in government he really seemed to be at one with himself and at ease in office.

There was always another 'knotted line' he had to travel, however, and that was his relationship to Gordon Brown. Although Peter adored and admired Gordon, he knew in 1994 that he had to choose Tony Blair, and that hurt Gordon. The pair became estranged, but Peter in his heart never gave up, and I suspect Gordon had similar feelings. So when Peter started having long conversations with Gordon in 2007 and 2008, I knew it was only a question of time before they reconciled.

It is not easy summing up a politician like Peter Mandelson in a few words. He has many strengths: his courage, his intelligence, his political judgement, his verve and sense of humour. But like all of us, he had his weaknesses as well, often the opposite of his strengths. He was brave but he could be reckless; his political judgement was good but his personal judgement was sometimes less astute; he was a consummate politician but sometimes so adroit that others became uneasy. He was like a cat who could squeeze through any opening, however small, however dangerous, and do so with an audacity that could be unnerving. There is no politician who is quite like Peter. He was, and is, a remarkable person who was a vital part of the New Labour journey.

May 2001: The General Election

Mandelson's resignation kept him out of the 2001 election, which was now upon us. The pre-election battlefield was clear: though the public were confident about the economy, they were concerned about the speed of delivery, worried we were stuck and lacked momentum. In contrast the Conservatives were extraordinarily weak: poorly led, divided, disorganised, and considered unfit to govern. At a deeper level people knew that the task of governing was huge, that some progress was being made, and the government was trying. There remained a basic desire for the government to succeed. This last sense – that the government was trying and had made some progress – turned almost by osmosis through the course of the campaign into: four years is not long enough, they deserve another go.

Many were saying that they had effectively voted Labour for an eight-year term in 1997. That had been a change election, but this was to be a continuity election: focused on the economy to provide the rock, a message of progress clothed in humility and striving, and with public services as the cutting edge of the campaign. The dividing lines were inevitable: stability versus boom and bust, and cuts versus investment. The Conservatives were narrow in their focus, effectively campaigning on Europe. Their big idea was 'ten days to save the pound', which the voters turned into 'ten years to get William Hague off television'. Politics can be very cruel.

This was our campaign in principle, and this was how it played out. But it was the most fractious campaign I had been involved in since 1992, although the most secure. It was almost as if the strength of our situation gave permission for the tensions of the campaign to emerge. The campaign was centred at Millbank, which I loved, and I sat opposite Margaret McDonagh, by then General Secretary, who did an amazing job: we only lost four seats, an achievement in which party organisation was crucial. The working situation was volatile to say the least but the campaign staff were as good as always.

This was a big step forward for us. A second election victory, at least one achieved with a majority, was unprecedented, and people were understandably nervous. I was certainly uneasy; winning an election was always an immense task. This was an election we were expected to win, but we still had to do it.

The topography in Millbank was the same as in 1997, but the character of the campaign was not. The Prime Minister still had his semi-separate group of offices at one end of Millbank, the Chancellor and his staff and supporting politicians at the other. Without Peter Mandelson, the balance of the campaign changed somewhat. In 1997 the centre of gravity had been the 'campaign desk' in the centre of Millbank, at which all the campaigning principals, including Peter, sat. In 2001 the campaign focus shifted to the small group of rooms around Gordon Brown, in which informal, but not really open, meetings took place almost continuously. It was a different way of working, and a different kind of campaign. Tony Blair never felt at home in Millbank during that campaign and it is not surprising. He was not always made greatly welcome.

The campaign was never bland. There were moments of high drama and moments of farce, but it was never for one moment relaxed. Here are a few selected entries from my 2001 campaign diary, which started with Gordon Brown's rueful pessimism:

14 May 2001
The polls good over the weekend, with leads of 17 points, 16 points, 20 points. When I went in with these polls to Gordon on Saturday during the first weekend of the campaign, he complained: 'They are too good, they are just too good.' I said, 'Why?' He said, 'They could only go down.' Gordon said he always saw a cloud in every silver lining.

17 May 2001
I went to a focus group and then discovered that John Prescott had punched someone called Craig in Wales and that all hell had been let loose. Phone calls from Anji certain that John had to apologise, long phone call from Tony who was supportive, believing John had acted instinctively and had to

be stood up. I was extremely concerned that if we got on the wrong side of this wave of public anger we could get a mini fuel protest in the middle of the campaign. I argued strongly that he should apologise and I did the same to Gordon in the morning. Tony had a different view, going out at the press conference the next morning to make light of it and turning it into a joke. And of course it worked, basically people came out supporting John. Tony said, 'Look, I had to do that, I had to make light of it because if I hadn't it would have turned it into a resignation issue and I didn't want that to happen.' And his judgement of the politics of it was as usual completely right.

23 May 2001

Throughout all of this there were real tensions. The atmosphere was completely fraught, not a great atmosphere in which to conduct a campaign. Much of the action was in constant huddled little meetings in Gordon's section, which you had to effectively break into; you just had to find the guts to go into them, you were rarely invited. The formal meetings happened but not at an absolutely fixed time. Something or other would happen and they would all just flow out from their offices as if by osmosis. Then I would have to text Alastair and he would try to get through on the conference phone and I would have to scramble under the table to get the thing to work. Tony was starting to lose faith.

24 May 2001

The bitterness and anger collapsed when we held a meeting to discuss the vast metal Trojan horse (to represent Tory health policies) that was being built almost entirely at Alastair's behest. Quietly he had designed and had constructed this massive metal horse, which towered menacingly in the courtyard outside. And then in the middle of a long, long meeting discussing this Trojan horse, involving about thirty people, the phone on the meeting table began to ring and Keith Vaz (who has absolutely nothing to do with the election campaign) came through on the conference link wanting to talk to Jim (whoever Jim was), providing I think the most surreal moment in politics I have known, except possibly for the terrible 1992 meeting with Neil Kinnock and Robin Cook. Everyone just burst into laughter, Keith is talking to everyone in the room, and Alastair kept the conversation going for a long while before Keith worked out what was going on. The paranoia disappeared for the moment.

7 June 2001: Election Day

I got up early, the sun was shining and I felt pretty optimistic. My phone wasn't working and I got hysterical about that. We went out to Harrow, did a bit of canvassing and it was good, people were positive about us. Labour voters, Labour women voters, were okay about us; they said they were going to vote. But I got to Millbank in a pretty tense state. Just as I got before security, Peter Kellner phoned me up and said that ITV were going to go on air with a majority of 175, and I knew we were okay and felt a huge burst of relief. Scrambled through security, got up into the War Room and told Alastair that ITV were going to go on air with 175. Of course he already knew it and it felt very good.

Gordon arrived and sat there fulminating about the seats we'd lost, how come we lost this seat, how come we lost that seat. If we had done this better, or that better, it would have been okay. I tried to reassure him, 'We have just won an historic victory and lost only four seats, so don't worry about it.'

This time victory felt so real compared to last time, which was just like a dream. I was with Rory (Alastair's son) and Georgia, Gail had arrived and fallen asleep in Tony's office. We went outside and John Prescott came through and then Ian McCartney, then Neil who shakes hands with Georgia. Then Alastair arrives and stands with Rory and Georgia; it is a very complete moment. Tony makes this wonderful speech and it feels better even than 1997. I said, 'Alastair, shall we go?' and he said 'Yes.' I get in the car with Alastair and we drive back almost too tired to talk. I drop him off at his house, after picking him up every morning for 18 months, day after day after day, 7.30 after 7.30 after 7.30, and he says, 'Thanks, I will see you in 2005.' And that's it. It's over.

People ask me why I love campaigning and that is the answer: it is impossible to have a better feeling than that. Of course there were tensions, and actually they were quite horrible, but there always are in great endeavours that involve genuine risk and reward. In the end it came together and for a few moments we became whole. Gordon Brown was a challenge in that campaign, but I wouldn't have missed a moment of it, and you can't have half of Gordon, it is all or nothing. It encapsulated the best, and the worst, of campaigning: drama, obsession, anger, chaos and farce – but also a majority of 175. But it was a victory that took eighteen months to build, during which there were literally hundreds of meetings, documents, and phone calls, focus groups and policy papers, and an extraordinary amount of energy, strain and exhaustion. Victory on that scale does not come easily, it requires huge resolution.

THE SECOND PARLIAMENT: 2001–2005

NEW FORCES

Reform and new forces

Once more we had won an election, the first time that Labour had ever won a full second term. I felt as exhausted as ever, and collapsed as normal, but I loved that post-election moment. Despite the tensions of the campaign things looked fairly well set. Gordon Brown was still pretty angry with Tony Blair, but we had a majority of 175, and the plan was always that the second term would be when we stepped up the pace. Perhaps most importantly, Tony had finally found his feet, with his political triangle now complete: progressive modernisation, liberal interventionism, and a new approach to the role of the state and public service reform.

Tony himself believes that it was in the year 2000 that he finally made sense of reform, evidenced by Alan Milburn's health plans of the same year. Tony's ideas had developed, and would develop again, but now they had a real sense of coherence, they felt like a kind of Blairism. Tony's agenda for the second parliament was public service reform and the Euro-referendum campaign, which Peter Hyman spent hours working on. Tony saw this as a significant move forward and was prepared to take on the Euro-sceptic media to do it. He strongly believed in the European ideal and still does, and saw this as a moment to break free from the press. But

– wisely – Gordon intervened, slowing and eventually stopping the process.

The forward picture did not look calm, although neither did government and change seem impossible to achieve. But, as always, events intervened, making the task different and probably harder. Events were starting to react to events. New forces were emerging that would change the political map.

First came growing signs of disagreement over Tony Blair's view of reform. This was exemplified in a post-manifesto discussion between himself and Gordon Brown in which Tony, frustrated by the pace of change in the public services, wanted to push harder for a new agenda based on choice and competition. Gordon resisted. I think it is fair to both sides to say that they started to pull away from each other on policy at this point.

I am not sure how much this disagreement was genuinely based on policy, and how much on a growing sense of estrangement between them. Steve Richards in his book *Whatever it Takes* argues that those around Gordon saw Tony moving from a social democratic position towards an increasingly liberal one, and saw dangers in that.[1] And it is true that the issue of public sector reform became the new prism through which distrust started to become apparent, because it exemplified all the various elements that would start to further weaken their relationship – disagreements about policy, positioning, electoral strategy and distrust over the leadership.

Although reform became the arena of the conflict, I do not believe it was the cause. The problem was more deep-rooted and long-standing than that. By this stage nothing that Tony did would have satisfied Gordon. I often used to sit in meetings and wonder: is this personal or is it political? I could never really disentangle the two.

From the very start choice had been an egalitarian issue for me: if the better off can enjoy choice, why can't the rest of the population? I see choice as a crucial expression of self-actualisation and empowerment. Alan Milburn often tells the story of the housing estate where he was brought up, where tenants could not choose the colour of their front door. This story strikes right to the heart of my politics: if some can choose, why not all? I did not want the NHS to be good enough, but the best that it could be. I wanted excellence for all and believed that choice and competition were essential in achieving it.

From my perspective the case for reform is proven. For all the controversy we had over the introduction of foundation hospitals and academies, nobody today is seriously talking about reversing these measures – the debate is how they should be taken forward. And that is because they worked. Research from the London School of Economics confirms this. A study examining the consequences of fixed-price competition brought in by the Labour government found that after reforms came into effect in 2006 there was a bigger drop in the death rate for patients suffering from heart attacks in areas where there was more competition. Competition based on quality worked, competition based on price did not, at least not fairly. But the coming years saw Blair and Brown drifting apart on public service reform. This lasted in its way until Tony left office; although sometimes more intense and sometimes less, it remained a tension at the heart of New Labour.[2]

The second emerging force was a rightward shift in American political leadership, with George Bush winning the election and taking office in January 2001. President Clinton's departure and the arrival of President Bush was a major turning point for Tony Blair. Clinton and Blair were more than friends, they were political soulmates. Clinton gave Tony advice and ideas but he also gave him support, he protected his Third Way, New Labour flank. When Bush was elected, however, Tony was determined to make the relationship successful. He believed it essential that a Labour Prime Minister be seen to be able to work well with a Republican President, part of our maturity as a political party. But much deeper than that, he believed profoundly in the Anglo-American alliance, born like me just after the war, and saw that relationship through a prism of noble and shared sacrifice.

The United States was crucial to Tony's strategic vision of the world: he saw the UK as the vital pivot between Europe and the USA, believing this to be Britain's historic role. Making this relationship successful was essential to Tony but there was a cost. Having lost the intellectual solace and support that Clinton had given him, for the rest of his time as Prime Minister Tony was to be flanked by a domestic rival increasingly to the left of him, and an international ally well to his right. It was not just Brown, but Brown and Bush. His job was to make that work.

The third emerging force, and the most important, was the terrorist attack on New York on 9/11. This event changed everything in the progress of the Labour government. Ironically I had been having lunch with Peter Mandelson when it happened. We were making up after the freeze produced by his second resignation, and the lunch was close. Then Peter got a message that one of the buildings in the World Trade Center had been attacked. We decided to call a halt and I went back to my office, which was crowded with people watching events unfold on television. It was clear what happened that day would produce a seismic change in global politics.

Tony Blair's instincts were to support the USA immediately and wholeheartedly. He saw this both as the right thing to do as our closest ally came under attack, and as an act of solidarity in the face of an assault on liberal values wherever they are held. Everything about Tony, every fibre of his being, strained not just to assist America, but to aid the world.

Tony did not expect this attack, but he had been thinking seriously about the potential threat of extremist Islam. He views religion as crucial to the unfolding story of modern politics. That very summer he had poured scorn on Alastair Campbell and myself for reading political books and our preoccupation with petty politics. Instead he had been reading the Koran. And at the last Labour conference I had had a long conversation with him about the growing influence of extremist Islam, the risks of religious fundamentalism. He was always positive and open about Islam but feared the dangers of extremism. Once again this revealed Blair's strength as a politician and a strategist: he could read the future in ways that others didn't and would so often surprise.

Even before the Iraq war, then, we had a changed political configuration. Tony was now a more coherent and confident Blairite, sure of the ground on which he stood and moving if anything to more explicit New Labour positions; Gordon settled now in his political trajectory and appearing to pull away from Tony's reform agenda; a Republican President in the White House, and the United States suffering the most grievous terrorist attack in its history. This was a very long way from the political landscape of 1997. New and powerful forces were emerging, some rooted in centuries-old conflicts.

Following 9/11 the mood darkened, and for a while overseas concerns eclipsed domestic worries. But not for long. The focus moved away from terror quite quickly. It was not that the events and consequences of 9/11 were forgotten, but they were submerged, incorporated into public opinion but not yet decisive in changing it. In this as in other terror attacks the British public had two core responses. One was stoicism, the belief that they would get through it all somehow, the other was tolerance. Although many in the electorate were resentful about levels of immigration which they saw as excessive and unfair, they refused for the most part to lapse into intolerance in the face of these attacks. They saw acts of terror not as the result of any religious or ideological dogma, but as the result of extremist individuals and groups, who were not representative of their wider religion.

This was most impressively evident when I conducted a group just two days after the London terror attacks of 7 July 2005. I expected anger and perhaps hate, but instead found a scrupulous call for tolerance and a strong desire not to blame or stigmatise any religious group. They saw the bigger picture, knowing that acts of terror were not isolated but part of a complex series of events, for which there were no easy answers. In part this is the result of a paradox of multiculturalism. Most people had first-hand experience of diverse religious and cultural groups, which may at some level have led to a sense of unease, but which also meant that different ethnic groups were not strangers, leading people to understand that those of different ethnicity were no more likely to be closet terrorists that anyone else. In any event the tolerance of that post-London attack period was extraordinary. Muslim voters felt beleaguered:

Focus group among Muslim C1/C2 (lower middle class/skilled working class), Southall, December 2001
Most feel the conflict as a war on Muslims not terrorism. Respondents pointed to both the language of media and the deaths of innocent Muslims in Afghanistan as evidence that this was a war targeted at the Muslim community rather than terrorists. Many respondents appeared to think that the 11th September attacks were perpetrated by non-Muslims determined to precipitate a war in Afghanistan.

But their feelings were also nuanced:

All respondents claimed to reject Bin Laden's call for a jihad. While neither condemning him or condoning him they refused his claims to be a Muslim leader. And TB was admired for his diplomacy and his defence of Muslims, but criticised for 'doing America's bidding'. He was generally seen as a moderating influence because of his diplomacy at home and abroad, and his categorical comment that this was a war on terror not Islam.

This focus on foreign affairs was necessary, but it did not mean that the domestic reform agenda was being forgotten. In fact the pace of change was increasing. Alan Milburn had published his health plans and was engaging in a serious programme of reform. And in Downing Street Michael Barber had developed his Delivery Unit, which he impressively describes in his book *Instruction to Deliver*, a masterclass in how government can achieve change. What is interesting in Michael's book is its focus on the idea of trajectory, almost his key concept of implementation: 'to predict, monitor and manage performance (at national and local level) rather than react, to know when you are on track'.[3] In effect the more diffuse political concept of trajectory had fused with the hard-edged trajectory of delivery. New Labour was getting there. Of course there are those that oppose targets and any kind of central intervention. But the truth is that reform must strike a balance between autonomy and intervention. You need empowerment and decentralisation for effective public services, but you also need mediating institutions, to ensure standards and to guarantee fairness. This is the difference in essence between New Labour reform and Conservative reform.

April 2002: The politics of patriotism

In the early spring of 2002 the public's attention had returned to domestic issues, and the position of the government improved somewhat. However I wrote a summary note based on four groups conducted in April which focused on patriotism, which was emerging as a serious issue: 'Concern about asylum seekers has extended into immigration, crime and civic disintegration. Britain is becoming a soft touch.' What was happening here was that feelings of personal grievance, emerging from a perception of unfairness, and a sense of national grievance, were starting to come together. Two of the big drivers of public opinion in this period were beginning to merge.

Of course patriotism has always been with us, but it was now emerging in a new form, more about grievance than pride. Britishness is probably the best possible example of politics as a dialectic. It is always seen as a point on a curve: the public simultaneously look backwards and forwards, seeing the nation either on an arc of decline or recovery. Mostly people see Britain as on a long-term journey downwards, from empire, to war, to post-war decline, and they struggle to make sense of this, having a much stronger image of Britain then than now. They are stuck with a photograph they know to be outdated and largely redundant. Sixty years ago, and possibly much more recently, people held a much stronger and shared view of national identity. It may largely have been a myth but it did exist. In Frank Newbold's wartime propaganda posters Britishness was always bucolic: carthorses returning home, lambs on the South Downs, a pub beneath an aged oak tree on a village green. George Orwell in the same period wrote:

> Yes, there is something distinctive and recognisable in English civilization [for Orwell English and British were pretty much interchangeable] . . . It is somehow bound up with solid breakfasts and gloomy Sundays, smoky towns and winding roads, green fields and red pillar-boxes. It has a flavour of its own. Moreover it is continuous, it stretches into the future and the past, there is something in it that persists, as in a living creature. What can the England of 1940 have in common with the England of 1840? But then, what have you in common with the child of five whose photograph your mother keeps on the mantelpiece? Nothing, except that you happen to be the same person.[4]

As well as being a far better description of my approach to politics and history than I could ever manage, this perfectly exemplifies the issue of our national identity: how do we build a conception of Britishness that is changed but still the same?

Many see this as the greatest problem facing modern politics, but I see it as one of politics' biggest opportunities. The British public are hungry for a new conception of Britishness, they crave a new sense of identity, and they know that this identity cannot be extracted from the past alone but needs to be built on current realities and a conception of what being British means in the future. The public want a new picture. I believe this is not an arduous task but an exciting one. The old bucolic Britain and the old industrial nation still retain mythical power but they are not Britain now, which is complex, multicultural, creative, sceptical, tolerant and fluid. Turning these fragments into a pattern is the Holy Grail of British politics, finding an enduring sense of national purpose is the fulcrum upon which lasting political fortune will turn.

This was why Tony Blair was so fixated with national renewal, because creating a modern patriotism is so central to our sense of meaning and identity. The task is to take the numerous fragments that comprise our contemporary nation, and to turn them into a new mosaic. Britain is an old country but also a new one. It needs a new photograph. This is not an abstract task. Concerns about Britishness and national identity fuse with concerns about community and fairness and with a sense of personal grievance. They are all part of the same flow. It was by now certain that the politics of hard-working families and the politics of an aggrieved patriotism were at the heart of the new political agenda.

2003: Iraq and its aftermath

Meanwhile the mood of the British public was darkening and concerns were growing about terror and Iraq, contorting the political landscape even more. The issue of whether or not Saddam Hussein possessed weapons of mass destruction (WMDs) had arisen. People were seriously worried.

> *Focus group, Bromley. 13 February*
> High level of fear and a feeling that the evidence is there for the early use of force against Saddam.
>
> Most respondents revealed very high levels of personal anxiety, insecurity and vulnerability. They felt a threat to Britain, to themselves and to their families was very real. They were scared, confused and anxious – almost impatient – for a resolution and victory in the war against terrorism.

By the end of February support for the war remained strong, but it was for many conditional upon a second UN resolution:

Focus group, Leamington Spa. 24 February
The men said they would support military action if the UN passed another resolution, but support was halved in the scenario where France used her veto.

The women were less supportive, only half saying they would support the war even in the event of a second resolution being passed.

By mid-March the public mood had become more supportive:

Focus group, Barnet. 18 March
Much higher levels of engagement with the issue were very noticeable. There is fear and trepidation but also relief that the uncertainty had come to an end. Many were taking real comfort in TB's strength and conviction.

Half the group supported military action without reservation, and the other half came round to that view by the end of the group: *'A few weeks ago I wanted to leave well alone, now I know we can't just sit back and do nothing.'*

The commencement of the war on 20 March led to a strong hardening of support towards the government, if also a sense of domestic neglect.

Focus group, North London. 20 March
In terms of the war support is increasingly strong, people believing that Saddam Hussein is evil and must be removed and that leaving him in power only makes things worse.

For the whole of the next month support for the war remained high. Almost at the moment of apparent victory, however, public opinion flipped. They wanted Tony Blair to come home:

Focus group switchers, Lewisham. 14 April
Military success in Iraq means that people are insistent that the PM refocus on domestic issues immediately.

Meanwhile the mood had changed, becoming darker and more fearful:

Fear of violent crime, lack of community and war in Iraq makes the world feel dangerous. People fear being cut off in a dangerous world. There is constant sense of threat on the streets and no trust between neighbours.

And later in North London, a sense of neglect was hardening feelings of unfairness and resentment:

Focus group, Muswell Hill. 28 April
The dominant mood in this group was frustration at a government that they do not feel is prioritising their needs. Iraq, asylum seekers and benefit cheats were felt to get preferential treatment at the expense of hard-working families. But still 'a high level of respect for the PM'.

But in June, when it was clear that Saddam's WMDs might not be found, the mood changed again:

Focus group, Wimbledon. 6 June
Respondents lacked trust in both the Government and TB. People are unsure whether or not WMDs exist but suspect that TB misled them to ensure the legitimacy of war. However at one and the same time respondents felt that TB was the 'best thing that had ever happened to Labour', but there is concern that he will imitate Thatcher's pattern of turning from a strong visionary leader to an out of touch dictator.

Underneath all this was a growing feeling of neglect and powerlessness, 'a sense that nothing I do or say makes any difference', and associated with it was an increased scepticism about politicians. This sense of powerlessness and cynicism links to increased concern about crime and security issues, immigration and, most strikingly, community disintegration. This was not just a finding of one group but many. Reading them again now it is striking how rapidly and starkly this new mood was starting to dominate the agenda. It was always there, but in black and white. Now it emerged in colour.

This is exactly how public opinion works, changing slowly then suddenly. There is no doubt that the political landscape after the war changed. The public were less trusting, more sceptical of politicians, and perhaps above all felt a sense of powerlessness in a world that was clearly subject to global forces that nation states could scarcely control.

The question is of course how much of this was the direct result of the Iraq war. My view is that the war acted as a catalyst for already emerging forces, speeding their development but not fundamentally bringing them into being. In any case it would be mistaken to see the Iraq war as an event in itself, something that happened independently of the global forces that were already changing the nature of the public mood. The attack on 9/11 happened, changing the context for the decade, and changing the context for Saddam Hussein. Although not responsible for the attacks, he immediately became more of a risk and more of a problem.

Public opinion is one thing, the substance of the issue is quite another. I was not part of the government that made these decisions, but I was able to observe from a close perspective and did have a series of conversations with the main protagonists. This may not help to explain the detail of policy but will I hope clarify the core issues of integrity and motivation.

On a personal note, I supported the invasion and still do. With reservation and qualification, it remains my view that it was the right thing to do. I am by instinct a liberal interventionist: I believe in the universality of human rights; I believe that we live in a global community and that the systematic abuse of human rights does sometimes require military action. And there is no question that Iraq under Saddam Hussein was a murderous and terrible place. The *New York Times* estimated that 'Saddam murdered as many as a million of his own people, many with poison gas. He tortured, maimed and imprisoned countless more. His unprovoked invasion of Iran is estimated to have left another million dead.'[5] Estimates of the number of Kurds alone he massacred vary from 700,000 to 300,000,[6] and estimates of the deaths resulting from the quelling of the 1991 rebellion vary from 60,000 to 200,000.[7]

These numbers may not be completely accurate, it is impossible for them to be so, but they do indicate a massive violation of human rights and loss of life vastly exceeding anything that happened for example in Libya, where Nato troops have rightly been involved. It has been argued that the difference is that in Libya there was evidence of armed resistance and conflict, making intervention legitimate in a way that was not possible in Iraq. The difficulty here is that the moral case for intervention rests less on the scale of the atrocities, more on the possibility of resistance to those atrocities, while in fact the greater the level of human rights abuse the harder it is to resist. This was the case in Iraq, where armed resistance was so brutally crushed. The true ethical dividing line is surely not the degree of resistance to an abusive government, but the level of human rights abuse that a government inflicts.

I always believed that there was a moral case for intervention in Iraq and agree with the journalist Nick Cohen that it was a progressive cause: Saddam was in the end a murderous and despicable dictator and it is the task of the left to help rid the world of such people.[8]

Equally, it is wrong to think that Saddam was a problem that suddenly emerged, without context or history. He had a long record not only of human rights abuse but of systematically breaking UN resolutions, and one way or another would ultimately have to be confronted. Tony Blair raised the problem of Iraq in his 1999 Chicago speech, and often in private conversation he would muse on the threat that the country's regime posed. I also believed the evidence that Saddam had significant WMDs. Although none were found the former weapons inspector and head of the Iraq Survey Group David Kay has said that Saddam could, and probably would have been, a threat in the future. As Kay said to the Senate Armed Services Committee, 'I think the world is far safer with the disappearance and the removal of Saddam Hussein. I have said I actually think this may be one of those cases where it was even more dangerous than we thought.'[9]

Perhaps above all, I believe in democracy, almost above everything, and I believed that democracy was and is possible in Iraq. And it may be, as Jack Straw has argued, that the imperfect democracy created in Iraq influenced in some way the democratic movement that is the Arab Spring.

Now I am definitely not saying that all this automatically justified intervention, because the consequences of that action were vast and resulted in a huge loss of human life. But it does mean that there was a case for intervention that was moral, legal and arguably progressive, and that to have done nothing would have been to take a different course of action, one with its own moral and geopolitical implications and consequences. I still believe the moral case for intervention to be right.

But my opinion is of little consequence here. What matters is the intentions and motivations of those involved in the war, and their capacity to turn those motivations into effective outcomes. On the ethical assumptions underpinning the intervention I have no doubt. I spoke to Tony Blair many, many times about Iraq, and he never doubted that WMDs existed and were a real and significant risk. There was no gap at all between what he said to me privately and what he said publicly. He was not late in appreciating the risk of Iraq but early, he was a longstanding believer that something, at some time, had to be done. The change in his judgement, the view that we needed action sooner rather than later, came from the changed context of risk resulting from 9/11. Of course he did not believe that Saddam was responsible for that atrocity, but the very fact of the attack happening made the threat of Saddam much less acceptable. On every level – morality, strategy, security – Tony Blair believed that the threat was real, and intervention was right.

It is also true that the implementation of the war – not so much the original campaign but the follow-up – was imperfectly done, and too much was left to the Americans.

It is undeniably true that the human cost was high, for many far too high, and there is no dodging or ducking that. But this was never a simple choice between the good and the bad, but an imperfect choice in which moral legitimacy rested on both sides. Tony believed that the better case was to intervene, so do I; others disagree and believe the war to be profoundly mistaken. I do not think we know yet who was right and who was wrong; we may not know for a very long time. Nothing that is written about the Iraq war should ignore the ethical complexity that infuses it, or assume that the balance of right falls all on one side. This applies both to supporters and opponents of the war, and certainly applies to me.

The war and the failure to find WMDs nevertheless had profound political and personal consequences. Public trust fell, as we have seen, though not yet dramatically. But in the Labour Party, and in Tony Blair's team, there were real human consequences. I remember going into Sally Morgan's office on the day in late April when photographs of the appalling treatment of prisoners in Abu Ghraib were released. She was virtually in tears, so shocked was she by it. 'What can we do, what can we do,' she asked. And on the day that Dr David Kelly tragically died I went straight round to Alastair Campbell's house as I was concerned for him, but he had yet to arrive back from a visit to the United States. A little later he rushed in utterly distraught, in no way responsible for Dr Kelly's death, about which he had learned on landing at Heathrow, but consumed by the pain of it.

There are, ironically given his unyielding public image, few people so touched by an event such as this as Alastair. I have never before seen him so affected, I knew it would not be long before he left his position. He had to be talked out of leaving that very day. And flying back from Scotland in the summer with the Prime Minister, each paper covered with bloody pictures from Iraq, you could see the pain he felt. They all – we all – believed it was the right thing to do, but a belief in the validity of a decision cannot hide any of us from the human costs, and nor should it. Tony and his team were human, they knew the consequences of war, and felt those consequences deeply.

And for Tony Blair this led to a crisis in his personal confidence and a feeling that perhaps he should depart. Polling in the autumn was miserable: there were doubts about trust and delivery, and an increased concern with asylum and immigration. War was not at the forefront of public concern but had clearly affected the mood. There was uncertainty about Blair's future but no consistent call for him to go. Mostly the sense one gets from reading these groups' comments is of an electorate that feels forgotten, wanting Tony Blair to re-engage.

This was an electorate feeling neglected by war, untrusting because of WMDs and lack of delivery, and moving on to a new agenda focused on community erosion, insecurity, migration, crime, and the futility and frustrations of modern politics. This was an extension of the previous mood, with still no substantial move away from the government. But an electorate edging towards hopelessness can quickly move towards anger. Tony was increasingly thinking he might be part of the problem rather than part of the solution. And it was about then, in November, that he attended the infamous dinner with Gordon in Admiralty Arch, at which he agreed to step down before the election if Gordon agreed to co-operate with him and with his agenda. (I concede there are different interpretations of this meeting but this is the one I believe to be true.) Tony did this out of a sense of responsibility and it was an act of integrity, but I am not sure it was wise. Prime Ministers cannot transfer their office from one to another; it is neither constitutional nor democratic, and is always likely to fall foul of events.

After that the mood changed. Tony did not mention any kind of agreement or even discussion. But he did ask me to reach out to Gordon's team, which I did with, I am afraid, too much enthusiasm for Tony's supporters. In the end my outreach mainly consisted of meeting Ed Miliband once a week on a Friday, to discuss the future, which I always enjoyed.

July 2003: The empty stadium and the politics of disengagement

Through all of this, the rise and fall of issues, the new forces and trends, one thing was becoming clearer and clearer: that people were losing faith in the way politics was normally conducted and were disengaging from the process. In any focus group, before talk about the economy, crime or the NHS, people almost always displayed a disdain for politics and politicians, not just switched off but often disillusioned and often angry too. I had written fragments about this in the last two years but brought them together for the first time in a presentation I made in July 2003, and afterwards in an article called 'The Empty Stadium'. This was an attempt to bring into focus all that was happening with public opinion: the issues, the concerns about globalisation, the effect of the media and ultimately the drift towards political disengagement. Dealing with this became a passion for me, as it did for Douglas Alexander who had been concerned about the matter for years.

The article started with a self-evident truth:

> Politics in the first years of the 21st century is becoming a minority sport. The institutions of politics, its culture, its procedures, its language and its rules, are turning away the public they seek to serve.

I then made a rather passionate plea for participation, which I will repeat here in part because it contains the essence of what I believe:

> For me, the starting point of progressive politics has always been the view that every voice, however powerless, however marginalised, sometimes however misguided, has the equal right to be heard. If equality starts anywhere it must start there, from the grounding assumption that a nation is nothing but its people, a democracy is nothing but its citizens and that every voice counts the same, has an equal right to be

heard. Sometimes the voice of the people can be uncomfortable, sometimes worse than that, but each of us has to make a profound and decisive choice: either we trust the people or we don't.

I next tried to explain the crisis facing politics:

> The current crisis of political disengagement has no one single cause, no easy solution. It flows from the whirlwind of change that has transformed the nature of our politics in recent years. Changes so vast and so sudden that the hidden assumptions of our current political paradigm have been shattered, although many were slow to see this, and some do not see it still. Central to this has been the onset of globalisation which has leapt over national boundaries and swept aside the traditional geography of politics. And as power becomes more global, and appears unaccountable, the citizen and the consumer demand more control, more accountability, and show less deference to the old institutions of authority. This is the ground on which the seeds of disengagement are grown.

Following that, I laid out the results of that crisis:

> This whirlwind of change has produced what I have called a three-sided revolution: a triangle of disengaged citizens more insecure than ever; consumers more empowered than ever; and communications more contaminated than ever. These are the three facets of political disengagement.

In defining the insecure citizen I drew on polling conducted across Europe, revealing three dominant forces 'leading to many Europeans exposed and vulnerable'. The first of these forces is *global schism*, in which 'people feel increasingly powerless in the face of these global tensions'. Crucially there is a perception of the decline of community within Western societies and the rise of the fractured society.

The second force is the growth of the *empowered consumer*.

I said that 'the empowered consumer wants self-actualisation, a world of connection, community and authenticity': citizen and consumer not artificially divided but individuals seeking the same outcomes in both public and private spaces.

The final element of the three-sided revolution is what I called the *contaminated transaction*. 'The growth of globalisation, the insecurity of the citizen, the empowerment of the consumer' leads to frustration, resentment and a loss of faith in politics. But, I said, it is the twisted and distorted nature of so much of the communication of politics that turns scepticism into resentment about politics, and ultimately to political disengagement. I cited Steve Barnett, Professor of Communications at Westminster University, who had laid out the four phases of media development: 'the age of deference; the age of debate; the age of journalistic disdain; and finally the age of contempt'.[10]

I made clear that 'the current dysfunctionality of political communication was a shared responsibility'; we had to escape from this 'dance of disengagement'. Politicians cannot change this on their own, I said; press and television must now accept they are part of the problem. If politicians have to stop spinning, then the press must stop abusing.

The media and how to deal with it was a central dialogue within the government for the whole of the period. New Labour believed that the media before 1997 had rendered the party all but unelectable and effectively destroyed the reputation of Neil Kinnock. Labour was like the skinny kid in the playground, bullied and harried and effectively defenceless. I know this because I was there, I saw the destructive power of the press, and saw too how it affected voters. And Tony Blair, Gordon Brown, Alastair Campbell and Peter Mandelson were determined that this should never, ever happen again. But the bigger issue was the challenge of governance in a frenzied and relentless media age. It is pointless arguing that this can be ignored: good government requires consent, communication and the capacity to act quickly and decisively in the face of continuous media and incredibly fast-moving events.

It was absolutely right for Alastair to modernise the communications operation in Downing Street, and right that Labour stopped being incessantly outmanoeuvred by the press and went on the offensive. It was true that Alastair fed the press, but he also fought it day after day. He was always conflicted about the media, needing to deal with it, to make it work, but relentless in his view that the press had too much power to damage both politics and culture, and should be confronted. From around the year 2000 he was like a broken record on this, and he is still going strong today.

Tony Blair had a different view. His first responsibility was to govern well, to make change possible, to avoid the shambolic media relations of Labour's past. His instinct was to make the current system function, not by capitulating to it but by manipulating it, making it work for the government. Dealing with the press, handling the press, keeping warm and positive relations with the press was part of the job. But privately he had a disdain for the press, which grew in time into a kind of bitterness; not so much because of the increasingly intrusive and destructive way it treated politicians, but more because he felt that the negativity of the press was holding Britain back.

And it is true that there was an 'optimism gap' between people's direct experience of their own local public services and communities, which was often good, and their view of these same issues seen nationally, which was often negative. It is entirely wrong to say, as some do, that we – and in particular I – simply played back the conservative *Daily Mail* opinions of middle England in an unthinking and reactive way. The task was not to play back *Daily Mail* opinions, but to try and disentangle the real and authentic attitudes of voters from the continuous drip of negative press coverage. The problem, however, is that although the press intensified and exaggerated many voter fears, these fears were often real and could not be discounted. If you step back and look at the growing forces of globalisation, the pressure on living standards, the erosion of communities, the problems caused by migration, it was clear these were serious issues that needed to be taken seriously. A negative press was feeding of the anxiety of the electorate.

Should we have acted earlier with the press? The answer is probably yes. But Alastair Campbell was almost a lone voice raging against the media; few others held the same view. The truth was that times were changing and we were slow, I think, to grasp this. Peter Hyman was right: we were trapped in a 1980s mindset, thinking the future an obvious continuation of the past. Our determination was never again to be defenceless media victims; we could not allow our government to be derailed by a hostile and destructive press. Our response was a combination of aggressive and pre-emptive press relations at the micro level and peaceful co-existence at the macro level. This worked and, for a long while, was a successful strategy, but by the halfway stage of the parliament it was becoming, as all successful strategies do, anachronistic. The need was for engagement and partici-pation, not persuasion and spin (something Alastair totally understood). We needed to rely much less on what the media thought.

It was not just that we were stronger than we believed at the time, but that traditional forms of media were weaker than we imagined, and getting weaker all the time. Tech-nology was dramatically changing the relationship between media and politics. This process is described brilliantly by Kavanagh and Blumler, who show how the post-war domin-ance of television gave way to increasing media fragmentation, and then to the growth of an entirely new electronic media.[11] At every stage, as competition increased and they came under more and more pressure from digitalised news and informa-tion, mainstream media were becoming less deferential and more aggressive and intrusive. But this was not a sign of increasing strength but the last hurrah of a declining and possibly dying industry. Competitive pressures drove news-papers to do things they should never have done, and for which they will not be forgiven for a long time.

British newspapers, already the least trusted in the devel-oped world, are now distrusted by 79 per cent of people in the UK.[12] Somewhere in the last decade two competing trajectories must have crossed: Labour stronger than it thought, newspapers weaker than they looked. But we did not see the moment and certainly did not seize it. It may be, however, that it always needed a new generation to make that change. This is a classic example of dialectical politics: Tony Blair right to build bridges of support with News International, Ed Miliband equally right to break them.

This then was my three-sided revolution: a conventional world of politics associated with insecurity, powerlessness and social disintegration; empowered self-actualising consumer citizens who felt increasingly alienated from the world of politics; and communication contaminated and distrusted. The only solution to the problem of the empty stadium: 'to effect a complete revolution, transforming our politics from passivity to participation. If we are to fill the stadium, we need a new kind of politics, and a new kind of campaigning that puts participation at its heart. I call this participatory democracy.' It is a form of politics I am still deeply committed to.

January 2004: Starting to plan the election campaign

By the end of 2003 we were just eighteen months from a General Election, and I attempted my first 'war book'. In reality this was just a summary of public opinion, but it is a good way to sum up where we were. Our lead was at 1 per cent among likely voters; we had lost voters to disengagement, to the Conservative Party and to the Liberal Democrats. The agenda had changed, with crime, asylum and the NHS pretty much tied as the leading reason people gave for Britain going in the wrong direction.

Labour was ahead on the economy, education and the NHS, but only by relatively small margins (5 to 8 per cent); the Conservatives were ahead on asylum (by 17 per cent),[13] crime and Europe. The Conservative lead on these traditional right-wing issues seduced them into fighting a right-wing, populist asylum campaign, which was a mistake. This got them heard but would never get them a victory – the British public don't vote like that. My view was that we had to fight the election on the economy, find a way of reconnecting with the electorate, achieve closure on Iraq and become once more the party of the future.

The new year began with the government scraping home by five votes with its legislation to introduce university tuition fees, which was a crucial step forward for Tony Blair's reform agenda. The next day the findings of the Hutton Inquiry into the death of Dr David Kelly were pre-released to Downing Street. It is difficult to imagine the stress this caused. Tony Blair was always calm, but most people were nervous. This, by the way, gives you an idea of the pressures of modern politics: winning a crucial division by the narrowest of margins one day, seeing the findings of a crucial report the next. It was clear from the tone of my conversations that the report would be largely positive for the government.

The next day I went to Downing Street and read Alastair Campbell's speech in a rush, wanting to see Lord Hutton's statement. This was a mistake and I definitely let Alastair down; the speech was too strong and I should have intervened. In politics you can never for a moment lose your focus. Tony Blair did well in the House of Commons, demolishing Michael Howard, but the report was so much in our favour the media turned it into a whitewash, and we gained little.

After Hutton Tony was reflective, facing up to his own position with honesty. A little later, I gave him the results of a new poll conducted in early February 2004 which gave us a 5 per cent lead, but he turned the conversation on to himself:

> We were talking about the poll for a long time and then he just said, 'What about me in all of this, what do they think of me, how much of a problem am I?' He said voters are right to say someone should take responsibility, and that someone should be accountable. Perhaps that should be me and perhaps I should resign, perhaps I am the problem. I say that is an

issue for him and he has to decide what is right and moral, and to try and make a distinction between his short-term and long-term popularity. I said wait until the late spring and the early summer and we will see where we are. He said he was already thinking about it a lot, look what happened to the BBC when Greg Dyke resigned, the public turned towards them and the same thing may happen if he resigned. It was a very reflective and moving conversation. I thought he was a remarkable person being so honest about all this, for under-standing that he may have to resign because of the failure to find WMDs and because he might become a liability rather than an asset. It was moving and commendable.

It was typical of Tony, who has the character and the courage to face up to issues that are unsettling and uncom-fortable.

Meanwhile, on 17 April I conducted a focus group among loyalist Labour voters. The outcome was very disturbing, showing how the deeper flows of politics were starting to stir: a harbinger of much that was to come.

Two focus groups, Doncaster, 22 April
The women felt optimistic about their lives. It was clear that this was driven in large measure by improving living standards. The men were also clearly better off, but their whole view of politics was dominated by asylum and immigration. This was expressed in very angry, bitter language with at least five of the group saying they would vote for the BNP. Labour's achievements were just swept away by what was effectively racism.

I wrote that politics was 'dividing between a rational choice based on a considered judgement of the economy and public services, which we are set to win, and a politics of emotion in which asylum, race and insecurity become the dominant issues'.

Of course politics is always divided between the rational and the emotional, but these groups greatly troubled me. The male group was not just intimidating but frightening, and the sense that both groups accepted an improvement in living standards and public services, but allowed it to be swept away by race, was disturbing. You could see how right-wing parties had gained such ground in continental Europe.

2004: Poster wars

The next campaigning stop for me was the European elections, which were led by Gordon Brown and Douglas Alexander. I attended a European campaign meeting on 17 May in which you could almost feel the political chemistry shifting, as a sense of Tony Blair's possible departure became gradually apparent. This diary entry encapsulates the new mood:

> There was an absolute bloodbath in the press over the weekend about the possibility of Tony leaving. I go into an extraordinary meeting with Gordon, who comes in looking completely confident, almost shining. In comes a whole gang of people, Peter sits next to me and doesn't say a word throughout the whole thing, slightly slumped. Sally and Pat representing Downing Street are marginalised at the end of the table. I sit right opposite Gordon because I want to show that I have got a grip on this situation. Then John Prescott arrived, this great glowering figure like something out of Shakespeare, huge energy with sort of self-generating anger, he has great presence. I go through the grid and Gordon handles it all extremely well; he's like the Godfather as they come bearing gifts to him, and afterwards there is a huge amount of energy in the room. He is a remarkable person (but on the other hand Sally says this is one of the worst organised meetings she has ever been to in her life), but you cannot deny the energy and the power.

But slowly over the summer it became apparent that Tony was rethinking. He dropped hints, he said he would not go without a fight. It was clear that he did not feel that he was getting co-operation from Gordon either in terms of their relationship or policy. This incensed Gordon, leaving their relationship at a new low. It had probably been ill-advised of Tony to make any kind of commitment in the first place; it was almost certain to end badly. When it came to the crunch Tony thought it was his responsibility and his obligation to stay. But Gordon was furious, and I knew that the future would now be tough. And so it proved, almost at once.

Tony wanted to organise the European campaign around Alan Milburn as party chair and Douglas Alexander as campaign co-ordinator. However, the politics of the situation stopped Alan becoming chair; instead he became campaign co-ordinator, usurping Douglas. The combination of Tony clearly staying and this reorganisation was too much for Gordon, who effectively disengaged from the campaign, declaring silent and not-so-silent war on it. This was a problem: we were planning to focus on the economy and it was difficult to get Gordon's agreement on anything, let alone posters. I got round this by a series of surrogate meetings in which Spencer Livermore, an adviser to Gordon and a brilliant campaign strategist, would with great courage approve the advertising on Gordon's behalf without Gordon knowing. The problem was that eventually Gordon was bound to find out, and this was what happened.

Tuesday, 14 December 2004
Meeting today with the political strategy group with Tony, Gordon, John Prescott, Ian McCartney, Matt Carter, Sally, Pat, and myself. Alan [Milburn] goes through the economic campaign and Tony says he wants Gordon's help. Gordon retorts by saying he has never seen the posters, which is true, and everybody looks at me: why haven't I shown him the posters? Of course I have not shown them to him because he refuses to see them. Spencer had quietly agreed them but I don't want to drop him in it. Matt (the General Secretary) had got a technical clearance from Alan Milburn, clearance from Tony, but he [Spencer] obviously had not, so I was just left to hold the baby. Tony looked at me like I was an idiot

for not showing them to Gordon but of course there was no possible chance to do so. But it was grim, and then John said 'Have you got the posters?' I said, 'Do you want them now?' He said, 'What do you mean . . .' He started to shout at me about the posters and it was ghastly. Anyway we all left. I left feeling like a complete wanker for not having shown the posters.

I felt very dejected but was determined to make it work with Gordon. I phoned him up at 10 p.m. and said sorry about the posters. He said, 'Why are you apologising? I don't want your apologies, what right have you got to suggest that I had seen the posters when I hadn't.' I said I hadn't said that I had. Then he starts this great tirade against me; he says that I am not honest about the polling. 'Why can't you just be honest with me, you just lie about the polling, you just don't give me the polling.' Whereas in fact we have been giving him the whole frequency questionnaire, he has been having all of it. But he goes on about the lying and then he said, 'You couldn't even save Douglas Alexander and you're useless now, you can't do anything now. You have just become Alan Milburn's bag carrier.' He had a burning sense of injustice and of anger. I just couldn't break it down, I said, 'I was just trying to make it work.' He said, 'You are not honest with me as far as our relationship is concerned.' On and on and on, and in the end he started to kind of make a speech and it ended. But fucking hell, it was tough. Anyway, I am going to see Spencer tomorrow with Alan and Ian and let's see what we can do to make it work.

I would not say that this was worse than much I'd experienced in many another election campaign, it goes with the territory. You can't just have the good bits. But it was the only time that Gordon was really angry with me and I understand why: he was just so frustrated with the situation. In any event he had a point, it was partly my fault: I had screwed up the posters and had tried and failed to protect Douglas Alexander. I thought the designation of me as Alan Milburn's bag carrier amusing, but not half as funny as Alan did; he still uses it today. In any event I took the posters around to

Gordon and he liked them and all was well. But I felt I had travelled back in time to 1992.

January 2005: Rebuilding the band

By January Alastair Campbell, who had left Downing Street in 2003, was back effectively running the campaign and thinking the whole thing an unsustainable shambles. Of course he thinks that about everything, but this time he had a point. He really thought we might lose. We also both thought strongly that Tony Blair had to be absolutely aware of his relative unpopularity; we hammered him on that, at one point effectively saying he should stand down. But total truth is what Tony always wanted, or anyway what he always got. My diary at the time rather sums this up:

> Tony was staying in this huge suite in a St Andrews hotel on Thursday when Alastair confronted him: 'If Gordon was to become leader and not you he would get more seats.' He did not hold back and when I turned up Tony said, 'Well, my pollster and my communications media strategist both think I should go, so thank you very much.'

But we were not trying to eject him but test him. That is our responsibility, and the responsibility of all advisers. Perhaps we went too far, but better that than not far enough.

It was clear to me, and to Alastair, that to run an election campaign with the two principal politicians estranged would be impossible. This had probably always been the case but in this instance, with a disgruntled electorate, the war a recent memory and the economy the key issue, some degree of harmony at the top was essential. It didn't really matter who was responsible, it had to be fixed. About this time, around a year before the 2005 election, I had predicted a 3 per cent Labour lead, believing, wrongly, that this would translate into a majority of 80-plus seats. But 3 per cent is a very small margin; you can add a point or two to it during a campaign but you can also lose a point or two, and if that happened our majority might be effectively wiped out. My view was that it was right for Tony to stand again, but that we had a responsibility to the Labour Party to maximise the lead that we might achieve, and absolutely not to allow our majority to reach parlous levels. This seemed to me totally non-negotiable.

So began a seemingly endless process, led by Alastair, to effectively reform the band. There was no doubt that Brown was more in favour with the public than Blair at this point: Tony's favourability was 39 per cent in December 2004, Gordon's was 57 per cent.[14] This does not mean, however, that Gordon would have done better in an election. At the time I thought it possible, but I now do not. If Tony had left at that time and in that way a significant amount of our coalition would have been lost, leaving the electorate anxious and uncertain. It is true that anti-Iraq voters would have returned to us, but in the end the negatives would have balanced out the positives.

And even more essentially, as became clear in the 2010 election, having the two of them campaign together was better than having only one. I lost count of the number of times that campaign staff – from all camps – would say in 2010: if only we had Tony. Not because they necessarily wanted him back as leader, but because the pairing of Tony and Gordon in an election campaign was so much stronger than one alone. I also believed that this was one of those win/lose games in politics. If the pair of them campaigned separately and at odds with each other it could potentially have been fatal. I had worked for much of the year in the campaign headquarters and the campaign simply was not working. Without shared economic data and shared resources, everything had stalled. But I knew also that if Tony and Gordon campaigned together it would outflank the Tories and give a focus and a power to the campaign that would substantially add to our strength.

That is why, as always, I went the extra mile, working with Mark Lucas (our outstanding film producer) to persuade the late, hugely talented Anthony Minghella to produce an election broadcast that featured both Tony and Gordon. I know many in the Blair camp did not like that broadcast, but I loved it, and as I type this I have a still from it on my wall. I thought it a brilliant demonstration of how to turn potential disaster into advantage, of constant strategic renewal. Probably the whole thing went too far with the two of them eating ice-creams together on the campaign trail – at which point Blair's team wanted to shoot me – but the strategy was right for Labour and for Tony.

When in the end they did come together and resolve their differences, it was like the cracking of an ice floe. I was with Tony when he made a very early post-rapprochement phone call; he just said how much happier he was that Gordon was on board, how relieved he felt. It was impossible at that moment for Tony to hide his basic affection for Gordon, and not to realise how complex their relationship was. Gordon was very difficult, but almost until the end, Tony never lost either his capacity for warmth towards him, or his apprecia-tion of his talents. This was why he was continually so ambivalent about him – as were Alastair Campbell and I, and as in the end was Peter Mandelson.

Once when I was particularly frustrated with Gordon I phoned Tony and ranted. He just listened and said, 'Philip, in the end with Gordon we always end in the place we started.' And that is true. Essentially, for some of us at least, that first bond held. Many people do not understand this and believe it a position lacking in basic integrity, but for me there was no escape. It was a band that could not in the end break up.

Polling wars: The 2005 election

The strategic imperatives going into the 2005 election were of course different from any that had come before. We were not just attempting to win a second term, but a third: totally new water for the Labour Party. Tony Blair laid out his broad prospectus for the election in a long note written in September 2004, starting with his vision:

A Britain where if you have the merit, you have the chance to succeed and be rewarded for your success. A Britain where access to quality public services does not depend on your wealth. A Britain where there's help and dignity for those unable or too poor to fend for themselves. A Britain where the respect you show for others is shown for you. A Britain whose leadership abroad secured the influence we need in an interdependent world to protect and enhance the interests of the country.

He went on to his policy agenda:

A stronger economy in which economic opportunity is enlarged and hard work well rewarded; an education system based on excellence and lifelong learning; an NHS that is no longer a monolithic service, but a commissioner of care that is accessible, flexible and consumer driven; a welfare system where we spend money where it is fair to spend it; a law and order policy in which crime is falling year on year, community policing is back; a housing policy that encourages the development of new houses; local democracy revived; a civil service changed so that it is an effective instrument of policy; House of Lords reform completed; Britain with the influence and power to defend its interests and promote its values.

You may not agree with all of this, you may feel it is incomplete, but it is a coherent and progressive way forward for Britain, much if not most of it still valid now. It is quintessentially New Labour.

The voters too saw this as a different election:

Focus groups, Croydon. Lapsed Labour. Skilled working class
1 This group, as other groups have done, revealed the key dynamic of the campaign. That this third term election is totally different from our second term election – it is much more about change.
2 People have a sense that after eight years it is at least time to consider something fresh.

3 The huge exception to this is the economy. The economy is the best way to get off the third term hook. It both gives a reason for not voting Tory – they would mess it up – but also for giving us a mandate for our third term – prosperity for all. We should stay on the economy for as long as it takes.

By the middle of 2004 I had a pretty good idea of the campaign I thought we should run. On the one hand I was desperate for this to be the first genuinely participatory campaign. But in this situation, campaigning for the first time into a real headwind of opposition, I knew such a campaign would not be possible. Therefore I was determined to do the next best thing, which was to engage the voters in new ways as often and fully as we could. This was not just for idealistic reasons. I knew that unless we addressed voters' growing feeling of domestic neglect and bitterness, we had no hope of winning. We, and in particular Tony Blair, had to engage with how voters felt.

Some excellent research done for us by a company called Promise claimed that Tony had to understand that, having effectively fallen in love with him in 1997, the nation had now fallen out of love with him, believing that he had in some way deserted them. In the first term he had been permeable and porous, but in the second term he had been impregnable; driven by conviction, but a conviction they found hard and unyielding. They explained this not as I would have done by a growth in confidence but by its opposite: in the first term Tony, they believed, had the confidence to listen to people, but in the second term, because of a slight sense of self-doubt, he had moved from listening to rebuttal. The moment these respondents saw Tony behave as they wanted him to behave, their view of him was dramatically and positively reassessed, and they all came back to him. This, by the way, is why conviction and consent have to be so closely balanced. By now Tony had become a conviction politician. There were gains in that, but also a price.

There was no doubt that we had to listen and to engage to turn things around. This was the genesis of the 'masochism' strategy, in which voters were engaged to say in all honesty what they thought about the Prime Minister and open a process of debate. Tony hated this with a vengeance, but he recognised he had to do it, and this form of interactive communication will be an enduring feature of future election campaigns. I also changed the system of polling so that it was more frequent and more fluid, using open-ended internet samples of one or two hundred to try and get the depth of a focus group with some of the statistical veracity of a larger poll. This worked well; I always felt I knew where the electorate was and where it was moving. I also had a rule that all polling, good, bad or indifferent, would be circulated to everyone on the campaign in an unedited and unmediated form. This worked too, none of it was leaked.

We had two pollsters that year: Stan Greenberg, who had served us so well for so many years, and Mark Penn, pollster to Bill Clinton in 1996, who Downing Street brought in to provide a fresh set of ideas. Although they respected Stan and wanted him to stay, Stan blamed me for this, although I had nothing to do with it, and in fact opposed it, but I took the fall. Stan and Mark loathed each other, although they were both good in different ways. It was not an easy situation, and not one I handled particularly well.

The other side of the strategy was almost the opposite. I had visited John Kerry's 2004 campaign in the USA and seen close up how chaotic and pressured it was. Most of all I was struck by the weakness of the message, and by its inconsistency compared with that of Bush, who started and ended with a message based on security. I was certain that elections fought in volatile, uncertain times required a totally focused message: the voters needed an anchor they could believe in, one that was constant.

My strategy therefore was open through participation but unyielding in our focus on the economy. I called this hard/soft campaigning. Not ideal, perhaps, but right for the times.

The last piece of the jigsaw was a strategy for immigration, developed in a typically counterintuitive way by Tony Blair. He argued that the public simply would not elect an opposition that was basically a single-issue party. At some point in the campaign they would be repelled by it, and that was our moment to strike – not with an anti-immigration speech, but with a liberal approach based on good management of the situation. Focusing on immigration management, not the rejection of immigration. And this is exactly what happened and how we killed the issue of immigration in the campaign.

Iraq however was to prove a more divisive and decisive issue and one that we were less successful at dealing with. The campaign was not marked by significant internal dissent (except for the sporadic outbreak of polling wars); we were working as one team, united in a sense through fighting against public opinion that was in so many ways hostile. Tony was not fully fit for the campaign, his back was out, but he battled on. Gordon was near his best, rising to the occasion, making me feel that he could well be leader.

Here are some excerpts from my election diary:

Wednesday, 6 April 2005
Tony and Gordon did about an hour and twenty minute press conference and they were just fantastic together. When they came back they kind of stood facing each other discussing the strategy, discussing how they were going to sort out various aspects of the campaign. It was quite the most amazing thing; people just watching them. They looked like two great elephants snorting and snuffling and slowly discovering they hated somebody else, that there were enemies out there other than each other; suddenly noticing the Conservatives and turning their venom on them and stamping their feet as if to attack.

Sunday, 10 April 2005
TB makes a really good Sedgefield speech. Peter phoned up and said he was worried about Tony being seen to be weak, and was the partnership strategy really necessary? I said it was, but I am not sure I convinced him.

The groups tonight absolutely dominated by immigration

and Tony and pretty grim stuff it was too; and the Tories are on immigration today.

Friday, 15 April 2005

The overnight poll is quite good. Everyone is totally exhausted, then we discover that they are doing immigration and Britishness again. His [Michael Howard's] campaign is pushing right to the edge of acceptability. Stan writes a note saying that we haven't got enough votes from anyone over 34. Penn gets cross with Stan's memos so there's a mini polling war going on. But there is a sense of things getting there, of just getting on top of it.

Friday, 22 April 2005

Tony made his immigration speech; it was magnificent. We finally got an advertising campaign together using 'forward not back' as a sign, which I wanted to do in the first place all that time ago. It would have been better if I'd got that done earlier; but never mind.

Sunday 24 April 2005

Huge Make Poverty History rally with Tony making a brilliant speech, Gordon also making a very good speech. Grace (my younger daughter) was there. Tony obsessed with this idea of framing the election as one that we can lose because the marginals will be close, which is a good idea. But I just want to get back to the economy and get on to risk.

A summary of the Attorney General's advice leaked, obviously the *Mail* had it and Channel 4 too, so God knows who else had it. The Tory liar posters seem to have had some effect; maybe we should have knocked back and responded harder. We have been stalled on Iraq all week but have got to keep going.

Wednesday, 4 May 2005

I do my last focus group that night which is just full of uncertainty. These people were drifting off to the Conservatives a bit, drifting back to us a bit on a better the devil you know basis. I write a note to Tony saying we will get from 36 to 38 per cent, the Conservatives will get 32 to 33 per cent, the Liberals 21 to 22 per cent. Based on this I predict a majority from 80 to 100.

Thursday, 5 May 2005: Election Day
Woke up terrified. Waited for Grace and we then went down to Mitcham and Morden where Georgia (my elder daughter) is an organiser for Siobhain McDonagh, and got lost on the way. First phone call from Peter Kellner, who said the over-night polls from last night were finishing at five or six on his panel, the same kind of thing this morning; nothing to worry about.

But later Peter Kellner called again at about 2.30 p.m. and said we are going to a 3 per cent lead in his new panel and I start to panic.

I go to Victoria Street. Andrew Marr comes on and says we are going to get a complete mauling in the marginals, it's going to be a slashed majority; I feel very grim indeed. There is this awful moment about midnight when Greg comes in, runs up and says it is going to be a hung parliament because we are losing Crawley and we are going to lose South Derby-shire; and then we are in panic mode. I think 'Shit', and Matt's face is white. But gradually the list of seats we are going to win gets longer and longer and the list of seats we are going to lose gets smaller and we kind of think we are going to get up to 80. And then it climbs back to 66 seats, which is what was predicted in the first place.

Tony phones and says what did us in was Iraq in the last week, which is true; and we have lost a lot of seats in London because people went to the Liberals.

Then I walk out into the early daylight to go to the National Portrait Gallery to hear Tony. Talked to Greg and he said we could have lost and we didn't and we are hugely relieved. The atmosphere in the party was amazing, the campaign staff just full of the fact that we had got a third term.

The next day I just felt happy that I wasn't trapped by a hung parliament or small majority for the rest of my life

and we had done it. Alastair felt depressed but I felt fantastically relieved and elated, in a way more free than after any
other election.

We had secured a third term with a substantial majority.
From our present perspective we almost take that victory for
granted, but it was a huge achievement – one that would
have seemed impossible just ten years earlier. And we had
won it because at the crucial moment the two principal
figures had come together, putting the party first. For a while,
when it mattered, they joined together again.

THE THIRD
PARLIAMENT:
2005–2010

GOING SOLO

The handover meetings

But this was to be a temporary truce, not a lasting peace. Almost immediately we started our dreaded handover meetings, which started badly and got worse and worse. There was by the way no sign of a coup at this time, just relentless pressure.

Just a couple of excerpts from my diary will illustrate what these meetings, and many more, were like:

11 November 2005
The first TB/GB dinner is on 11 November. At the dinner itself Tony makes a little speech during which I had a great coughing fit. He said, 'Look, do you want to join us?' and Gordon looks after me and I was coughing away, it was awful and embarrassing. Tony wanted to divide the parliament in two halves; the first half is reform and the second half Gordon takes over, making it absolutely clear that he was going to leave in the middle of the parliament. Gordon said it doesn't work like that, you can't divide the parliament in two. They are snapping away like a married couple about the disagreements of their past. Whereas in the next meeting they are talking about the future, and the big substantive issues, this is about clearing away history. Tony seems like someone who has had enough, something has snapped within him.

Monday, 12 December 2005

Extraordinary GB/TB meeting. We went in to see Tony before the meeting. Alastair said, 'We are going to be neutral.' Tony looked shocked in a fake kind of way and said, 'Will no one support me?' Gordon was there and Tony arrived and Gordon then gave me a hard time for a note I had written the previous night saying that Gordon represented old politics and traditional politics. Then they all turned on me for writing the note. Alastair started by saying, 'We have got problems with trust, problems with organisation, problems with strategy and we have got to sort them all out.' I said, 'The fundamentals are okay with the electorate but we have got division and instability and we have got to fix it or we are going to go to shit.' Alastair got fantastically heavy about it and shut them into silence, saying that if they didn't get together they would all fuck up. Then Gordon and Tony just went at it in an extremely raw and deep way – Gordon accusing Tony of never keeping his word, Tony accusing Gordon of wanting him out now. But then it got deeper, with Gordon getting so angry it was like he was going to explode with anger. I kept on saying, 'If we work together in partnership it will get better,' he kept on saying, 'No it won't.' But it got better, we agreed there had to be a process. It was so intense it was clear that at the end of it there had to be some kind of process.

I phoned Alastair afterwards and said, 'Christ, I needed a drink after that.' He said it was like a rollercoaster, an absolute rollercoaster. The emotion up and down and up and down, and Alastair said, 'God, it was draining.' But it was better, it was raw and it was honest and at one point I felt it was genuinely like a therapeutic session. They were getting there. But blimey, what a session.

That was pretty much what it was like, and gradually, inevitably, they went their separate ways: Gordon Brown preparing for the transition, Tony Blair effectively going solo and, I believe, entering the most innovative and in many ways productive period of his time in government. He was embattled and somewhat worn down, but in policy terms he was really starting to fly. His reform agenda for the NHS was working, and the academy programme was proving to be the right way forward for schools. And he had thought seriously and deeply about immigration, wanting to find a way to balance his essentially liberal belief in immigration with the need to control and manage it.

His answer was identity cards, which he believed made possible a tolerant and humane solution both to the issue of immigration and that of welfare abuse. It is a paradox that what many believe to be an illiberal measure – identity cards – was conceived by him as a liberal solution to social problems. This was combined with an Australian-style points system to provide an economic test for immigration. The other answer, excessively rigid immigration controls, he believed illiberal and economically damaging. But this is the way Tony thinks, his ideas do not fit into boxes. In this period he also pushed forward his respect and security agenda. But that too was right: there are few greater restrictions on freedom than the fear of crime, especially if you are old, or vulnerable or disadvantaged, and such people are the most likely victims of criminal behaviour.

I believe that Tony Blair's public service reform agenda was right on every level. First it produced real fairness, designed to achieve not just equality of access but equality of excellence. From my political standpoint it simply had to be the case that what was available to the few – choice, personalisation, and the best possible standard of care – should be available to the many. We had to smash the glass ceiling of elitism. That requires not only a more equal society, but also a more even distribution of excellence.

And it works. Here is a short excerpt from a 2011 London School of Economics report on academy schools: 'Our results suggest that moving to a more autonomous school structure through academy conversion generates a significant improvement in the quality of pupil intake and a significant improvement in pupil performance.'[1] In another report the LSE stated that NHS reform between 1997 and 2007 not only reduced waiting times across the board but reduced inequity: 'Between 1997 and 2007 waiting times for patients having elective hip replacement, knee replacement and cataract repair in England went down and the variation in NHS waiting times for these procedures across socioeconomic groups were reduced.'[2]

Secondly, public service reform meets the demand of our times for more empowerment, more autonomy and more control. This does not mean that community and fairness are somehow forgotten, in fact quite the opposite: the better the quality of health care, the better the community, and ultimately fairness, will be served. The best possible attack on entrenched elitism is the countervailing power of democratic excellence.

Finally, public service reforms make possible the maintenance of high-quality public services even in the face of inevitable public expenditure constraints in the West as the centre of economic gravity inexorably moves to the new economies. Public service reform opens up not only real opportunity, but also real efficiency.

I know there are people who think late Blairism equates with neo-liberalism, but I disagree. Tony Blair introduced a model of reform that was radical in its attack on elitism and in its desire to generate more real opportunity for more people. But increased autonomy and choice does not mean that we move to an unregulated market in public services. We must always ensure standards are maintained and improved, and that fairness is ensured. We need choice but we also need a core. That is the fundamental problem with the Conservative public service reforms, they remove the institutional pressure for both standards and fairness, and is why they are not New Labour.

Meanwhile the handover meetings went on. Splits were beginning to show and the public was beginning to notice. In a fast-moving and dangerous world they wanted Labour to put the nation first, not be preoccupied with itself. There was an increasing sense of uncertainty as global forces and pressures became more and more dominant. The role of government, people felt, was to protect Britain in the face of these pressures. Concerns about immigration continued to heighten, and it was increasingly seen as a primary cause of other problems. People saw Labour as out of touch, not listening and dogged by sleaze and infighting. But they still had not given up on the government.

In a note to both Brown and Blair on 20 August 2006 I wrote:

> The public suspect we are coming to the end of our time, but they still believe that we can recover. They will give the next leader a fair chance. Despite the problems we face it is clear that we are still in the game. People want change and a fresh start, and if they get that from a new leader, they will be as happy as if that comes from the Tories. The absolutely key period is the new leader's first few months. The window of opportunity for the next leader is huge.
>
> The next leader is a major event for people and they are likely to want a contest. A top-down handover will feel undemocratic and undermine the chance of renewal. There needs to be a rite of passage into the new leadership.

A week in September, 2006

But by then the whole political map was to change once more as a result of the Israel–Lebanon war. The Israeli government reacted to Hezbollah provocation with a fierce and constant counterattack in which many Lebanese were killed, as were others on the Israeli side. International and domestic sentiment came out largely against the Israelis, who it was believed were acting disproportionately. The USA was almost alone in unconditionally supporting Israel.

Tony Blair was uncompromising and inflexible, probably too inflexible, in his support for Israel: there was little nuance in his position, as he subsequently accepted. But Tony does not easily move from an unpopular position if he believes it to be right, particularly if he is facing a wave of sentiment not fully rooted in what he believes to be the facts. He has an instinctive sense that if a point of view is born of a shared and politically fashionable mindset then the best first instinct is to resist it. Be that as it may, this position cut him off not just from the international community but also from much of the Labour Party. It left him much weaker.

I saw Tony on 31 August at Chequers, driving down with Alastair Campbell and Sally Morgan for a meeting with Tony's last team in government, which included the highly competent deputy chief of staff Liz Lloyd, Ruth Turner, who was so harshly treated during the 'cash for honours' affair, and Benjamin Wegg-Prosser, a very talented young strategic adviser. Tony was sitting at a wooden table outside looking a bit sheepish, saying that he had done an interview with *The Times* about his departure and was not happy about it. But we moved swiftly on and assailed him in our normal fashion, saying that his position was terrible, that he had to sort out how to handle the announcement of his departure date, which by then had been settled for mid-2007.

This was incidentally the meeting in which we had our most explicit discussion of values, one in which I challenged him as usual to use values more in his rhetoric and language. But he was emphatic that it was not something the British people wanted to hear, and certainly not something he wanted to tell them. His view on this subject was essentially puritan: it is the job of politicians not to talk values all the time but to fix real problems. This was not a pragmatic issue for him but a point of integrity. Talking values can become a substitute for solving problems, at least in the Labour Party, a kind of solace and distraction that gets in the way of the real purpose of politics, which is to make people's lives better in concrete, measurable ways.

That does not mean values are unimportant to Tony: they are central to who he is. But for him they are a given: on the left we agree on what our values are, the task is convincing the electorate that we have the competence and capacity to turn those values into real change. This was at the heart of his politics. I didn't and don't take this view, but Tony will never change his opinion on it. I believe that the articulation of values is part of the process of change. I am committed to purpose in politics, and I believe that this purpose should be explicit: people are more likely to follow if they share a cause, and know what that cause is. Tony's view, sincerely held for reasons of principle, led I think to a hollowing out of his message and his premiership, allowing people to believe that he is a more means-driven and pragmatic politician than he actually is.

The Times' headline the next day was 'Blair defies his party over departure date', which was unhelpful coming on top of the Israel–Lebanon war. Tony was not trying to extend his period as leader, but to strengthen his position while still leader by not announcing a specific date for his departure. There was no real agreement as to whether he should make such an announcement. Some like Peter Mandelson were wary, others like Matthew Taylor, the exuberant head of political strategy at Downing Street, thought it was the best way forward. Most people thought that if it was to happen, his forthcoming conference speech was the place to do it.

What Tony had done, however, was light the fuse to a bomb, and the explosion came on 4 September when Benjamin Wegg-Prosser phoned saying: 'The game is up. They are sending us a letter signed by fifteen or sixteen members of the 2001 intake calling for Tony to go.' It would be followed in turn by letters from the 2005 and 1997 intakes. That the letter was signed by former Blairite MPs Tom Watson and Chris Bryant made it particularly hard. People were briefing that Tony would be out by the end of the week. If ever there was a dialectical moment in politics this was it: clashing forces all over the place. I phoned Tony and he had a coldness about him I had not heard before, and perhaps a hint of pessimism. The next morning Downing Street was like a morgue. I wandered in to see Jonathan Powell, whose usual optimism seemed to have deserted him. He was reading a copy of the *Daily Mirror*, which had a big front-page leak about Tony's plans for a 'farewell tour'.

The mood soon lifted but the pressure grew and by midweek it seemed unstoppable. But then the unpredictable happened: the *Sunday Times* got hold of a story that Tom Watson had met Gordon Brown at his house the day before the letter was leaked. This effectively turned the situation on its head, with Gordon now vulnerable. But Tony stopped all counter-briefing, believing it would make the situation worse. Douglas Alexander and Spencer Livermore both phoned me, clearly upset, and a day or so later Gordon Brown called me. He said, 'Philip, you must believe me, I had nothing to do with this plot at all, nothing at all,' assuring me that he was 'going to change'. He was distraught.

I said the polling would be bad. I accepted his word but said we now had to heal and show mutual loyalty, otherwise the destructive effects would not be containable. I spoke to him again a day or so later and he was so low that I began to feel both worried about him and sorry for him.

In a way the so-called 'coup' had a kind of success. Tony did announce that he was leaving, but I knew the collateral damage would be difficult to manage. I sent Gordon a note. So did Alastair Campbell, and his was very tough, warning that there was a danger Gordon might be sowing the seeds of his own destruction.

I wrote that the events of the last week had been hugely damaging to the party and to him, and that the public would think, fairly or unfairly, that he had crossed some kind of line. Negativity about Gordon, which had been 'rumbling along at a low level for several months', had now dramatically come to the surface. I said that his strategy had to change and that he had to 'move from a posture that appears closed, defensive, controlling and aggressive to one that appears open, inclusive, confident and healing'. He should transform his working relationship with Tony: 'Give him warmth, give him support, give him affection. The single thing that would most help you with the public would be a sense that you and Tony have finally ended your differences and healed your relationship . . . This has been a long hard journey for you and Tony. If you can bring your relationship together and heal it your project will be safe. If not it may be doomed.' I added 'I will not desert you and I did not start working with you twenty years ago to leave you now. But all of us have to change.'

I believed then, as I do now, in the politics of healing. So too does Tony Blair, who was understanding and generous about these events in his memoirs. And both Tom Watson and Chris Bryant have since emerged as effective opposition MPs. This is the way politics moves, dialectically.

But there was a price to be paid. I wrote a strategy note to Gordon based on focus groups I had conducted the previous day. I said that it was '"grim reading", that people are especially angry that we are fighting ourselves when we should be fighting for the nation. You have been damaged by the situation. The main problem is disloyalty with over 70 per cent wanting loyalty to TB.' I continued that 'at the heart of this is the strong view that TB should not be forced out against his will. People feel that there are powerful democratic issues involved here. They elected him, he should not be forced out; perceptions of TB have risen since he said that he was going; and perceptions of David Cameron fallen . . . The Tories should be doing better than they are.'

In response to this situation, I said, the public wanted us to 'stop appearing to care about us and start caring about them'. They wanted relationships at the top to be healed: 'I do not think that the public will repair its relationship with Labour until Labour repairs its own central relationships'; 'the public wants loyalty: this is not the same as blanket agreement but is a basic test of our fitness to govern'.

'And there has to be a proper contest. They want the next leader to be elected in a way that is as democratic as possible. I remain convinced that the best way to legitimise yourself as leader and PM is to act as a bridge between the TB era and the new era. What is certainly true is that without a proper contest the public will rebel. The public are setting us a test. We have to show that we can move on from the last couple of weeks and can genuinely heal relationships.'

This period did reveal how political trajectories ebb and flow and sometimes clash at many levels. Partly this is in the nature of British politics, in which the position of a Prime Minister is always dependent on the continued support of his or her parliamentary colleagues. It is in a way the responsibility of those in Parliament not just to show loyalty but also to test and sometimes to pressure. And it is the responsibility of the Prime Minister to show mettle and repel these advances. That is how our system works, conflict in the rub of our politics. And by this stage Tony's position was weak and he aggravated it by tactical mistakes that made him still more vulnerable.

These events also revealed the flow of public opinion. The public sense that Gordon Brown was in some way disloyal did not last, and at a surface level was soon forgotten. But I think the public remembered it and stored it, and when times got tough again for Gordon it was recalled. For the public it was a fragment of a larger picture. Conversely it showed how positive perceptions of Tony Blair had been buried, deep in the subterranean depths of public opinion. They too were not forgotten, coming to the surface at a crucial moment, reminding us how sceptical we should be of the shallow mood of political opinion.

The so-called 'coup' tested Tony's relationship with Gordon to the absolute limit. There are many who believe the strategy of constructive engagement in his relationship with Gordon was essentially flawed and based on a kind of false romantic loyalty. But I think it was the only plausible approach, because of Gordon's talents and because splitting from him would not end the problem, merely move it to a different arena. In the end Gordon and his relationship to Tony had somehow to be managed, there was no escaping it. And it also reflected Tony's character. His optimism, his openness, his continued determination to make things work were some of the qualities that made him such a successful Prime Minister. And the more he displayed these qualities the better it was for him. In those moments he lost them, he lost for a while some of his power. It was instinctive for Tony to try and engage with Gordon, and essentially right.

When I sit back and think of Gordon I do not focus only on the anger and the arguments, but on his kindness when I was ill and the many moments of connection and warmth that we had. I believe that it was right to try and heal this situation, I only wish I had been more successful. The anger and the pressure from Gordon were entirely counter-productive, making things worse on every level from the personal to the political. Although Tony was right to pursue the approach that he did, I am sure he sometimes regrets it, and that he thinks myself and Alastair Campbell were in some way responsible, devising as we did the joint strategy for the 2005 campaign and making clear to Tony that it meant a handover some time in the third term. But Tony should not regret it. He made the government work, he made his project work and he got most of his reforms through, although perhaps later than he would have hoped. These were two giant forces that either had to work together or fatally combust.

Conference 2006: You are the future now

The next stage was the Labour Party conference, at which Tony Blair made one of my favourite conference speeches. It ended with the words: 'Whatever you do, I'm always with you. Head and heart. You've given me all I have ever achieved, and all that we've achieved, together, for the country. Next year I won't be making this speech. But, in the years to come, wherever I am, whatever I do, I'm with you. Wishing you well. Wanting you to win. You're the future now. Make the most of it.'

Although Tony was soon to leave, he was not giving up. He produced a policy review, 'Pathways to the Future', that extended and deepened his late agenda. It highlighted the rapid changes that were affecting society – crime and community disintegration; the challenges that Britain faced in a globalised world; a new role for the state as a strategic enabler – and focused on climate change and energy. Supported by a series of speeches on subjects ranging from law and order, social exclusion, science and multiculturalism to the press, this built on his third-term agenda of academy schools, NHS reforms, identity cards, and new measures on anti-social behaviour and crime.

Blair was unable to get his Fundamental Savings Review agreed but he was determined to shift the emphasis from spending alone to spending plus reform and efficiency, linking this to smaller, more strategic government. He feared that the dividing line between investment and cuts would be turned into another, less helpful dividing line: big state and waste on the one hand and reform and efficiency on the other, with Labour in the wrong place, which is effectively what happened. I am not saying his agenda was complete, but it was far-reaching, it was coherent and it was New Labour, the next stage in a project that was the steely spine of the ten years of Blair government.

May 2007: Scottish elections and the changing of the guard

The spring brought elections to the Scottish Parliament, in which, to help secure Tony's legacy and to build a decent foundation for the next leader, I was determined that we do well. Douglas Alexander ran the campaign and did so ably. It was essentially a twin-track strategy: Douglas led on a message of positive engagement, while I focused on the broadcasts, which were some of the most negative things I have ever done in politics.

We were joined by Patrick Loughran, our attack and rebuttal specialist at party HQ, who came up for the last few weeks of the campaign, and by David Cairns, who was a joy to work with and died far too young in 2011. The General Secretary, Lesley Quinn, was also a powerhouse. Gordon Brown and Tony Blair came up often and collaborated in this last campaign.

And somehow or another, from a 14 per cent deficit, we came within one seat of victory; for a while we even thought we had won. I loved working in Scottish politics and this was my third election up there, but I was getting very, very tired and Douglas sent me home for a few days. I think these were the early days of my illness, but they were days I loved.

★   ★   ★

We were now getting very close to the handover of power from Blair to Brown. There was of course no Labour leadership election, which was in my view one of New Labour's seminal mistakes. For Gordon to win the public, gain legitimacy, regenerate the party, make the space and the opportunity to refresh and renew, there simply had to be an election. After Gordon became Prime Minister I lost count of the number of times voters said in focus groups that he was unelected, that he did not have the right to the job. It was a huge error. But it was not really Gordon's mistake, it was like asking a football team (for example, my own QPR) to leave the automatic promotion spot at the top of the league, and enter the play-offs because the team would thereby get a bit fitter. No way was anyone going to do that.

I asked Blair a little earlier in the year what he thought Brown's state of mind was: he said Gordon was terrified that at the very last it would all be snatched away from him. In this Gordon had reasonable grounds for suspicion. I wanted a contest for all sorts of reasons, but one was to test Gordon, to settle once and for all the question: is he the right person for the job? I assumed Gordon would win but there was always a chance that he would not. That was a big risk for Gordon, or rather a small risk with a big downside.

In reality, though, the people who were responsible for the absence of an election were those who did not stand. They assumed that Gordon would win and were wary of entering a contest they were sure to lose. But this was in my view a misjudgement. They could have come out stronger and so would the party.

I tried hard to get David Miliband to run, but he thought it virtually certain that he could not win, and that to fight a campaign against Gordon in which he would be forced to attack him on his vulnerabilities was a dangerous indulgence that merely helped the Tories. David also felt quite deeply that he was not ready, and that to run knowing he would lose lacked seriousness. There were also personal considerations: he was building his family, which obviously mattered more than anything else to both him and Louise, his wife.

I thought that despite all this he should give it a go and asked Tony what he thought, certain that he would agree with me. But he didn't, not because he doesn't admire David, but because he thought the gap between middle-ranking Cabinet minister and Prime Minister too big in government. It was possible to make the step in opposition, but not in power. In the event no one stood, and a critical opportunity for renewal was lost.

Gordon started, I think, to appreciate Tony more as the vortex of leadership approached. When the Scottish elections were over I flew back to London with Gordon and discussed the leadership. He obviously thought it had come too late. But he talked warmly about Tony, saying that at least you knew with him where you were going. He gave certainty. Talking about himself, he was reflective, saying he didn't really understand the Scottish electorate any more. He seemed detached and rather sad, believing it would be difficult taking over in the summer and it would be better in the autumn. It seemed like a sad end for Gordon when in fact it was such a huge beginning.

June 2007: The end and the beginning

Tony Blair resigned on 27 June. I went to the peers' gallery in the House of Commons and saw his last Prime Minister's Questions. It was an extraordinary experience. Tony started quietly, gradually building momentum. He gave a very emotional reply to a question by Ian Paisley and then finally made a short and moving speech, ending with the words, 'I wish everybody, friend or foe, well. That is it. The end.'

I left the chamber feeling proud: proud of Tony, proud of what we had achieved, proud of winning three elections. Within hours Gordon was the new Prime Minister, opening with a good line: 'Let the work of change begin.'

And I was off. This was no time to hang around, to be a ghost at the party. For all sorts of reasons, I wanted to move on. I did not think it appropriate to work with Gordon: he had his own team, his own priorities, and they needed their own space. I wanted to concentrate on the task of renewing New Labour and thinking afresh. But I was willing to help with the General Election when it came, which I hoped would be sooner rather than later.

I was always a strong advocate of an early election. It was, I thought, almost our last chance of renewal as a party, but it was a big chance. I wrote in September 2005 (a memo leaked to the *Daily Mirror*):

> We need a bold and ambitious election campaign strategically designed to dramatically drive our vote up. It is far too dangerous to be stuck in the mid-thirties with the Tories a point or two behind. We have to have a strategy of audacious advance. I believe that what we have to do is to hold an early election after a short period of intense and compelling activity. A kind of 'shock and awe' strategy blasting through the opposition and us to the mid-40s. It is inconceivable that you will not enjoy a significant honeymoon when you become leader.

And this is pretty much what happened. Brown started well, facing down crisis after crisis, looking strong and in many ways the father of the nation – the perfect position for him. He was 9 per cent ahead before many weeks were out. Come the summer, it seemed obvious to me that Gordon had to go to the polls as soon as possible, ideally in early September. He had no lack of rationale for this: David Cameron was calling for an election, the public wanted an election, or at the very least they wanted a Prime Minister who was elected and had a mandate. Gordon could call an election at any time.

But August drifted into September and the very first chatter about an early election started to appear. I was told that the plan was to go for an election, but in May next year. That was absolutely too late; there was no way public opinion could be sustained at that level for that long, not after ten years, with the hidden undercurrents of disillusionment. Gordon's lead could not possibly last the winter.

The mood in favour of an autumn General Election grew

and I was brought in to help with the campaign. I was stationed at Saatchi and Saatchi, our advertising agency. By the middle of September a whole advertising campaign had been prepared, based in many ways on Peter Hyman's strategy 'a serious man for serious times'. The poster that summed up this was: 'Not flash just Gordon', and the agency had a whole campaign based on this. There was a problem though when Douglas Alexander essentially said we had the campaign, but not yet the policy to support it. From his perspective at least, the policy offering was pretty weak, but I still believed we should press on.

On the other side of London, Peter Watt, General Secretary of the Labour Party, was in full campaign preparation mode, spending over £1 million on leaflets and campaign materials. But the election was not called before the Labour Party conference, nor in Gordon's conference speech, nor during the weekend following. Meanwhile the press was in early election overdrive. That weekend, unwisely, a briefing was given to the effect that Labour would see what the polls were like the next weekend and then make a decision.

This was wrong on every level. It signalled our strategy, and it gave the Conservatives space and time to escape. In politics, if your opponent is on the ground you have to strike decisively and quickly, not give him a few days' grace – particularly if these few days include the Tory Party conference. Predictably the Conservatives rose to the occasion, George Osborne wrong-footing us with an announcement on inheritance tax and David Cameron delivering a powerful and unscripted speech that he had, apparently, spent the whole summer working on.

For much of that week I was holed up with Douglas Alexander and Spencer Livermore, waiting for the signal to go. I was certain it would happen, all political logic pushed in that direction. Then on Friday Peter Watt called me and said that he was pulling his staff out and sending them home, it was effectively off. The polling was not bad but the marginals were close, there was no certainty about the size of the majority. I could not quite believe this and still hoped that on Saturday Brown would call an election. I remember talking to Margaret McDonagh on the phone while she was out canvassing and we both felt he had no option but to go. Not because the upside was assured, but because the downside was so certain to be disastrous.

My view on this was clear. The public had not yet made up their mind about Gordon as Prime Minister. They had stored much evidence in their collective memory, some good, some bad, and in effect two potential portraits of him existed, one negative and one positive. The negative was uncharismatic, lacking leadership skills: a good Chancellor but a bad Prime Minister. The positive was of a strong man, his own person, a leader who had started well as Prime Minister. Either of these might take hold, the public had the hidden evidence for both going back for years. This is why for example the public's attitude to the so-called 'coup' now mattered: they take from the past and use it to judge the present.

I knew that if Gordon did not take the decision to hold an election that day, the negative portrait would win. His situation was not that of an entirely new Prime Minister taking the job, who would be given far more latitude; he was a leader with a history that the public was striving to make sense of. When the election was not called, negative definition did take hold, something that Gordon never really escaped from. If he had called the election and won, even by a small majority, he would have been transformed, the survivor of a hugely difficult rite of leadership passage, the winner of a fourth term. The image of him, and the reality too, would have changed.

Stasis

But the election never happened. Instead Labour, and Gordon Brown, entered a low period, in which the public moved from an engaged – and sometimes angry – dissatisfaction with Tony Blair, to a kind of passive resignation, a defeatist acceptance of Labour and Gordon. They never lost their sympathy for him, the feeling that he was a decent man doing his best – and this sympathy was to prove vital in the last days of the 2010 election, when our support rallied somewhat. But they never really believed in him as Prime Minister. Of course it is unreasonable and wrong to blame all this on Gordon. It is hard to follow a ten-year period in government led by a charismatic Prime Minister, to become a figure of change and renewal when you have played such a major part in the events of the last decade.

Furthermore, the challenges of the period were epic and in some ways unprecedented. Gordon dealt with the financial crisis well, understanding the global nature of the issue and bringing nations together under a common strategy, something subsequently sorely missed. But he did not gain politically from his success. The public had fixed on a certain view of him and he was mostly unable to challenge that definition. The public's overall view of that period is of stasis and Gordon works best as a politician who is powering ahead. It was my view that he needed to be an energising reforming Prime Minister using his strength to achieve change, and he could best do this by imple- menting the existing agenda and adding to it. Redefining New Labour to meet the new global challenges and their domestic consequences, renewing both himself and the government. Gordon tried very hard, in fact no one could have tried harder, but he never achieved the momentum in government he was looking for. And in the end it was not a genuinely New Labour government, slowing too much on the reform and respect agenda, and not moving early enough to balance a focus on spending with efficiency, reducing waste, and a new conception of the state and how it serves people. Which in turn slowed down our drive going forward, and the clarity of our offer.

But however bad it got for Labour, the public never fully trusted David Cameron and the Conservatives either, proof if it was ever needed of the truism that it is not just govern- ments that lose elections, oppositions have to win them. The public now entered a dark place, a kind of Bermuda triangle of frustration and despair. They wanted change but could not find it: they had lost confidence in Labour, did not trust the Conservatives, and thought the Liberal Democrats irrelevant. The 2010 election was pivoted on change but without, in the public's view, a viable political instrument of change that they could really have confidence in. This was both our problem and our opportunity.

January 2009: Politics in the slow lane

At last I was forced to pull back, at least from active engaged politics, but not entirely by choice. I was due to make a presentation to Gordon Brown about his political identity but on the previous day I had been diagnosed with cancer and so I was forced to phone Downing Street and withdraw, to be replaced by Alice Cartner-Morley, an excellent researcher who worked for Freud Communications. Within a few minutes Gordon had phoned up to give me support, which he continued to do. Politics for the moment was over. I had started working with Matthew Freud and he gave me immense support at a tough time. It also broadened my working canvas, enabling me to view the world in different ways.

But after I pulled through the surgery, and as my chemotherapy was still continuing, I started to have informal meetings with Douglas Alexander, Spencer Livermore, Patrick Loughran and sometimes Ed Miliband to discuss election strategy and to develop an early war book. I loved these meetings, they were a distraction rather than a strain, and everyone was very kind. For me, politics – or at least political strategy – is not a burden but a complete delight.

Alastair Campbell, of course, was round all the time and we always talked politics. He was clearly burdened by the situation, torn between his loyalty to the party and to Gordon as leader and to his own health and family. What people do not fully realise, I think, is how often in situations like this people in politics are focused on ethical questions. Where does real loyalty lie? Which way forward has the greatest integrity? At the heart of most politics, even at its most combative and difficult, is the question: what is the right thing to do? Even now, as I write this, I ask myself: am I being honest, am I

being fair? This too is part of politics, and a far larger part
than anyone imagines or is willing to accept.

In the ghastly state induced by my chemotherapy I distracted
myself by thinking how we could move from our present
position and win the election, or at least achieve a hung parliament. It seemed to me that the key was change. This was a
change election, and if we could in some way prevent the
Conservatives being viewed as a credible and trusted party of
change, then we could stop them. That August, while still
being treated, I wrote a long note to my little group of
colleagues. In retrospect I have no idea how I was able to do
it, but it was one of several such notes. I think my wife Gail
is right, for me politics is a kind of madness, but also at this
time it was an enormous relief. In my note I argued that
'change is the key to this election and its dominant pivot. The
party that best represents change wins . . . At the moment
they are change, and we are tired . . . We need to attack them
and advance on change. Erode them here and they lose ground
exponentially, gain here and we win exponentially. We have
to attack our opponent at their strongest point. Change is the
only issue with the strategic power to win this election for us.'

It was of course a hard task to reconfigure Labour as the
party of change after almost thirteen years in power. But I
was looking only for marginal gains, enough momentum to
establish a meaningful contrast with the Tories. This was
more than possible if we developed a big reform agenda.
The real objective was to block the Conservatives as the
natural party of change, and this we could do. It was clear
even from the tiny amount of polling that I had been involved
with that the public did not trust the Tories. David Cameron
had not changed the party enough, although he still had time
he had yet to do it. The whole burden of his strategy had
to be to demonstrate that the Conservative Party had been
genuinely transformed and now could be trusted to change
Britain. For him little else mattered.

The issue for the Conservatives was not the size of the
gap between the parties, or Labour's vote, but their own
vote, which they just had to increase to over 40 per cent.

You can pound Gordon Brown every day of the week, put negative posters in every location in the country, and this will still not improve your own position. And it is the depth of commitment that matters; putting down deep, enduring pillars of support that will survive the test of an election campaign. You can't fool the electorate.

In a note written later in the year, after I conducted a focus group in October, I was better able to understand the real flow of the electorate. It was after the financial crisis had broken and blame was being allocated everywhere, but mostly to the banks and the culture of excessive credit they had fostered. Gordon Brown was felt to have done well in the crisis, surpassing expectations: 'It sounds like he is doing a good job, and every other country is following his lead . . .'; 'I am amazed that he is doing so well.' But Gordon was not able to turn this success into enduring popularity. He had been a strong Chancellor but was not yet seen to be a Prime Minister. A lot of this was emotional: 'People see that he has done well but are not yet willing to allow this success to change their view of him. They are held back from doing so by feelings of resentment and a lack of empathy.' In a sense Gordon was unable to escape from his past, good or bad.

There was also a fixed view 'that this crisis did not alter the basic position: Labour's time was up: they are not going to allow a good week or two to change this perception, they are too committed to it.' There was also a perception, although not yet widely held, that 'Labour had contributed to this crisis, particularly in relation to debt and credit'. The electorate was emotionally blocked from returning to Labour, and we had to provide pathways back.

I thought the fundamentals of the electorate remained the same: 'This is a change election unwinnable on a position restricted to incumbency and experience. Experience gets us on the pitch but will not secure us scoring goals. We have to be owners of the future to have any chance of winning.' Conversely the Conservatives were slipping back because people believed that 'David Cameron lacked substance and had failed to genuinely change his party'.

I then moved to tactics: 'It is an uncertain election because of the unpredictability of the electoral system and the possibility of a hung parliament. Unless the voters decide to vote us out in a landslide they will find it very difficult to turn their individual preferences into the result they want. They will find it very hard to calibrate a small Tory majority, for example. If Labour can achieve a sufficient degree of hope about itself, and a sufficient degree of doubt about the Tories, then the election result comes quickly into play.' Finally, 'People have to develop a new narrative about us if they are to come back. Partly this is emotional, but partly policy: we have to show renewal, regeneration and a new sense of purpose. This must be approached as a major exercise in renewing our political project, in effect looking at the world in 2010 and beyond just as was done in 1997. We need to dominate the political landscape with the power of our new policy. The core of response should be a focus on the issues of globalisation and a focus on the politics of empowerment, identity and security.'

Of course it is easy to sit on the sidelines and make suggestions, much harder to implement them in a full-blown economic crisis. But I was sure that policy-led renewal in that last phase was crucial: it was the one decisive way that Labour could gain momentum in government.

June 2009: Blairites hit the rocks

Things, though, just got worse. The low point was the European elections in June 2009, at which Labour received fewer votes than the UK Independence Party. The political atmosphere became febrile, with confidence in Gordon plummeting and a growing belief that he should stand down as leader. It was clear that a crisis was unavoidable. Blairites were divided about what to do. James Purnell spoke to me shortly before he resigned as Work and Pensions Secretary and asked me my opinion. I said, 'Do as your conscience and your integrity demands and it will work out for you,' which he did. Resigning was the right thing to do and showed great courage. David Miliband did not discuss his decision to stay with me but afterwards I spoke to him and there was no way he considered it honourable or appropriate for himself to resign. It could have brought the government down and might have led to schisms that could not be controlled. He was angry this situation had developed.

Purnell and Miliband made different but ethical decisions. It was almost inevitable that the Blairites would split on the rocks at this point. You could feel the pressure building, you could sense the different responses. There was no plot, no orchestrated activity, just individuals responding in different ways to a difficult decision. And this is yet another example of the dialectical progression of politics. The resignations in June 2009 linked back to the 'coup' of September 2006, with supporters of Tony Blair not only resentful and aggrieved, but also fearful and concerned about the potentially appalling consequences of unseating a second Prime Minister. None of these were easy choices, everyone concerned in both these events was looking to do what was best for Labour, with different conceptions of loyalty leading people to different conclusions.

The question I must answer is, would Labour have done better under a different leader going into the 2010 election? I think they would, because the public demand for renewal was so large and because distrust with the Conservatives lingered. What the public really wanted was change underpinned with Labour values, and only we could provide that. This was a real strategic opportunity for Labour, but it required us to renew. And if we did convincingly renew we could have won.

But I was completely opposed to any further 'coup'. I knew that the public would never forgive us if we forced another leader out, and the ramifications might linger for a generation. And I always thought that Gordon would not fight that last election. I had it in my head that Tony would give way to Gordon, who would in turn give way to the next generation. In fact this is what happened, but after the election rather than before it. But it is also true that I expected by then that Labour would lose by 10 to 12 per cent and perhaps 60 to 100 seats, and I was completely wrong about that (Alastair Campbell, by the way, was completely right, having predicted a hung parliament for a long while). I never told Gordon my view of the leadership issue, which largely makes my opinion redundant. It is little use to have opinions if you do not make them known to the appropriate person at the right time.

I was however able to tell Gordon Brown the full serious-ness of our position at a meeting of his inner political Cabinet in November 2009. I said there was negativity about Britain and about politicians (who were being described after the expenses scandal as 'shysters' and 'crooks'), and negativity about Labour and its leader. I also said that we were ten to twelve points behind in the polls and that historical evidence showed that an opinion poll lead established at this time was likely to last.

The dynamic of the election, though, was that the public were defaulting to the Conservatives rather than embracing them; it was possible to win voters back. We needed a strategy that overtly put across the national interest, because 'the public believe that we are not leading with resolution, nor are we putting the interests of Britain first. We need to put Britain first, make tough choices, start winning the big arguments.' We should show a decisive shift towards a less partisan politics and move beyond dividing lines – in particular that between investment and cuts – which seemed redundant in the current situation. My view was that this strategy was the one that suited both Gordon and the national situation best. I continued to argue for new 'ideas and energy', which according to our polling was the best way of winning voters back.

Both Gordon and Ed Balls disagreed with me. They both thought me too pessimistic (which I was in terms of the Tory vote, though not of ours), but also disagreed in terms of the fundamental strategy. Ed in particular was sure that driving through the dividing lines was the best way of knocking the Tories back, and Gordon's strategist David Muir showed his own polling that supported that view. Ed in argument is always tough and convincing and you have to defend yourself with vigour; you cannot just slide into an argument without having thought it through.

I enjoyed the debate, although I thought Ed and David Muir were wrong, and I still do. There is merit in the attacking ferocity that they wanted to unleash, but we also needed a bigger, more inclusive, more patriotic voice. In the past Tony and Gordon and their strategic teams would balance this out, but in this situation it was more difficult. The truth is that there was no way that Gordon, in approaching an election like this, would abandon either his dividing lines strategy or his commitment to investment rather than cuts. The Tory vote did fall, but our vote stayed low as well. But for the last week or so of the campaign Gordon did transcend the partisan and gained a bigger, more forceful voice.

June 2010: The General Election

Early in the new year election planning started in earnest. I conducted a focus group in Edgware, getting into a taxi after it had finished. The driver said, 'I remember you, I attended one of your groups in 1997 when the Tories were still in power.' He then explained how he had lost his business, got a job as an accountant, in turn lost that and become a taxi driver. All this was an implied rebuke to me: it was as if the focus group had been the tipping point that had led to his decline.

To move the conversation on I asked him how the group had been. 'All I can remember,' he said, 'was the incessant bloody moaning about how bad Britain was, and how everything just gets worse and worse.' So perhaps it was ever thus, and the wheel of change just moves on.

Peter Mandelson, who was in charge of the campaign, started regular meetings involving Gordon Brown's key communications and strategy team, plus Alastair Campbell and myself. These meetings were held either in his office or occasionally at my house. They were attended by about fourteen people in total, including Ed Miliband, Douglas Alexander, Justin Forsyth, Sue Nye and Ray Collins, the

General Secretary. For the most part the atmosphere was relaxed, and all Gordon's team showed exceptional warmth to me. The problem was how to get a campaign organised with very little time, very little money, almost no polling, and a real lack of campaigning staff and infrastructure.

Having conducted some groups, I had resurrected the line 'a future fair for all', because it combined the two essentials of future and fairness. 'Future' was an important message, because for us to have any chance we had to neutralise the Tories' claim to be the party of change, and 'fairness' because values were our greatest strength and the Tories' greatest weakness. This election was basically a fight between the public's desire for change and their nervousness that the Tories could not be trusted to deliver it. There was a large gap in the political terrain between the Conservatives, who represented unsafe change, and Labour, who represented failed continuity. This was the space either party had to fill to get a majority.

This campaign was different too in its focus on the first televised debates ever to be held between the three main party leaders, which gave it a totally new structure and character. This helped us too, because without them we lacked both the resources and the time to build a six-week campaign. What we did have was a formidable collective campaign brain, and a team that never gave up. Douglas had been involved in elections for over ten years; frustrated but steadfast, he was always trying to think of a new solution. Alastair of course hated it but was magnificent in preparing Gordon for the leaders' debates. And I enjoyed working with Peter again in this last campaign, just as we had worked together in the first.

I thought Peter chaired the meetings and the campaign well, but slowly it dawned on him that the levers he was pulling were just not working. The machine that had been there in 1997 simply no longer existed. He could not understand this, it was an affront to his campaigning dignity. But he, like everybody else, made the best of it.

The campaign itself was like fighting through fog. It was very tough and lacked energy, but we kept going through determination and grit. Its mood, its character were unlike any I had fought before. It felt flat, lacking the raw, exposed energy of previous campaigns. I was immensely tired and was in truth getting ill again, and I made a small difference but not a great one. Normally in a situation like that I would flood it with energy; this time I could not. But I loved working with party staff like Greg Cook, Carol Linforth, Mark Lucas and Jackie Stacey, people I had been campaigning with for years. And through them I could get some things done, they were my energy.

Gordon Brown too was exhausted and kept going through willpower alone. I can picture him now the first time I saw him at our campaign headquarters in Victoria Street; he looked tired and depleted as though carrying the whole weight of the campaign on his shoulders, which in a way he was. I felt immense warmth towards him, but I also asked myself, how did we get to this place? This was in many ways an extraordinary reunion: Gordon, Peter, Alastair and I had been involved in elections since 1987. We may have been tired but we had both experience and confidence. And our opponents were showing their nerves, they were predictable, cautious. I felt they underestimated us, I thought we would win the tactical and strategic battle if nothing else. You knew what they were going to do before they did it, and how they would respond if attacked. Clearly the task was to somehow stay standing and then counterattack at the very end.

In many ways the debates saved us, Gordon performing well enough. And in the final debate, when he had been up most of the night after the ghastly incident in which he was infamously recorded describing Gillian Duffy, a potential Labour voter, as a bigot, he showed real resolve.

To make matters worse for me, I had left the campaign to make a speech in the USA and was trapped there by the volcanic dust from Iceland that closed airspace around the world. This did give me time to rest, however frustrating it was, but I kept on manically writing notes. When I came back I commissioned three sets of focus groups to be held the same night. It was immediately clear what was happening.

Public sentiment was moving towards Gordon, who was being viewed with increasing sympathy, earning admiration for his courage in just keeping going. Equally the public were not moving across to the Conservatives; they still did not trust them. And they were nervous too of actually voting for Nick Clegg, regarded by many as the 'winner' of the televised debates, much as they liked the look of him.

This was a mere crack in the wall, but it gave us the chance at least of recovery. If Gordon could really come out fighting, then sympathy could translate into a degree of support. I stayed up very late and typed into my BlackBerry a shift of focus from 'a future fair for all' to a 'future to fight for', a phrase to be used everywhere for the last week of the campaign. I was certain that if we showed fight and passion in the last few days we could get somewhere, and to his credit this is what Gordon did, making the best speech of the campaign at Citizens UK. Tony Blair popped in one day to party headquarters and made a small speech of his own, which was perfectly judged. You could feel the energy pouring into the room, the mood lifting. He of course was sure that even at that late stage New Labour policy could save the day, undercutting and outflanking the Tories. He never relents.

Tony was right, but by then the campaign was drained, fighting to survive. On the worst days I would sit in the evening alone with Peter Mandelson and Alastair Campbell, seeing the prospect not just of defeat but terrible defeat. You could feel the ghosts of past election campaigns in the room. The fight was still there but the fear was gradually growing. In this quiet room, twenty years became one; we were different people, changed over time, but all still essentially the same.

On election day I went out canvassing for my daughter Georgia, who was seeking election as a councillor for Kentish Town in Camden. I thought she had no chance, that the Liberal Democrats who held the seat would just sweep her away. She kept on saying that she would win, 'Just believe,' but I grumbled on that it was impossible.

By this stage no one had the faintest idea how the election results would fall, and I felt more anxious than ever before in an election. I had two worries: that the Tories would win an overall majority, and that we might come third. I hated both prospects passionately. I kept on phoning Alicia Kennedy (head of field operations at the Labour Party) and her team, and she said there was no chance of us coming third and that she did not think the Tories would win an overall majority. I didn't believe her. I was so concerned that I went in early in the afternoon to check on how we were doing, and her message was the same. I still did not believe her.

That night, full of foreboding, I drove for the sixth successive time past Downing Street to campaign headquarters. I went in and sat next to David Muir, who had been my companion during the whole campaign. I did not always agree with him on strategy but I loved his sheer persistence. He was like a terrier for Gordon. The room was full of nerves.

And then at 10 p.m. the news announced a hung parliament, with the Tories 19 seats short of a majority and Labour in a clear second place. Frankly I could not believe it. How on earth could a campaign so under-resourced, a party so unpopular, get a result like that? I literally ran halfway around the campaign headquarters, so surprised and relieved was I. I only felt one thing, that we had stayed on the pitch and could fight another day. That was the best chance to nail us the Tories would have in a long time. In 1997, in roughly an equivalent situation, we had a majority of 179; tonight they were expected to be short by 19 seats.

The talented Andrew Cooper, who was polling for the Tories, texted me convinced that the exit poll was wrong. I was not so sure. In previous elections they'd had an uncanny way of being right. And sure enough, as the night wore on and I went to see Alicia and her team for the hundredth time, I started to believe it. We were winning just enough seats to stop them. They had on the wall a chart displaying the key seats, which showed the point at which the Tories would be clear and get their majority. All night the Tory gains came closer and closer, moving inexorably up the wall like water slowly creeping up a flooded building. And then they stopped, 20 short of an overall majority. I felt reprieved.

It is of course conventional wisdom to say this was a terrible result, and by implication a bad campaign, but that is untrue. The foundations of the campaign could not have been shakier, it was always bending and felt on the edge of collapse, but it stood and survived, setting back a Tory advance that could – and honestly should – have devastated us. Of course it is terrible to lose, and we could and should have won. But that was not the responsibility of those working on the campaign, but of others, including me, who months and years earlier made decisions and took actions which were too late to undo in the last frenzied weeks. Elections are won and lost not in months but in years.

This was true both for us and for the Tories. We lost because we failed to renew quickly and substantially enough, the Tories failed to win because they did not change profoundly enough. Labour should be proud of the fortitude and courage shown during that campaign. It is one thing to win when the wind is behind you, quite another to hold together and scratch out a result when facing a massive gale.

When it was clear that the Tories would not win outright, I went home in exhaustion and collapsed. I wanted no more of it. We were in truth beaten and the fight to hold on to power did not interest me.

The next afternoon I went to Georgia's count at Haverstock school, just around the corner from Alastair Campbell and Fiona Millar's home. I went in to see Georgia's pile of votes towering up, leaving her Liberal Democrat and Tory opponents in the shade. She had done it and so had her two Labour colleagues, and I could not have been more proud. Yesterday's election result belonged suddenly to the past, this one to the future. When Georgia went up on the stage as a Labour councillor I almost cried; in fact I probably did a little, but I would never let Georgia see that. Afterwards we went to the pub with Alastair and Fiona and the new councillors and it was a moment of triumph for Georgia and her generation.

But we were still defeated and I hated it. We kept fighting for a few days trying to construct a coalition but in the end could not put it together, and Gordon Brown left Downing Street. I watched his departure on television, feeling immensely sad. Within ten minutes of going he phoned to thank me for what I had done to help him. It was a kind and moving call, but I still hated losing.

September 2010: The leadership election

There was one last hurdle, the leadership election. This I found very hard, because in a way it was 1994 all over again. I supported David Miliband, had worked with him, believed he would be an outstanding leader of the Labour Party – and one day, I hoped, Prime Minister. He was no New Labour clone, he was always in a different place from Tony Blair: much more of a social democrat, more conventionally Labour. His instincts matched mine: open, modern, facing the future. But he was far more than that, he was a friend, and a key figure for me in the long journey of New Labour. We talked for hours, and still do, about what progressive politics means and how we can build a new modernising politics.

On the other hand was Ed, whom I had been campaigning with for the best part of thirteen years and to whom I'd talked almost nightly during the last campaign. I had first seen him speak perhaps in 1998 at a party organisers' meeting outside London, jacketless and speaking off the cuff. He seemed a totally natural politician, and I told him that on all accounts he had to enter politics. And of course he did – sorry, David!

I did not share Ed's politics in quite the same way as I did David's, but I was very fond of him, and he too was a friend. Ed's passion was equality. He believed somehow that New Labour was based on compromise, that in its essence was a kind of triangulation that he did not like. It is certainly true that in all the years I have known him he was never fully comfortable with New Labour; he wanted something more emphatic, more categorical, in a way more ideological. But he instinctively understood many of the core concepts of New Labour. He knew we had to win a majority that would include middle-class and southern voters, that we had to add responsibility to rights, that we had to reach out and include. He is forward-looking and one of his complaints about the campaign was that it simply lacked enough about the future, it lacked vision.

So there was an overlap, but it was incomplete. The best way of putting this is to look at his shared responsibility speech at Coin Street Neighbourhood Centre in June 2011. On one level this was a classic New Labour speech, asking for all of us – both those with power and advantage and those without it – to bear responsibility. The difference is that Tony Blair's starting place was a 1980s Labour Party that refused to confront the issue of responsibility, where asking for responsibility from those abusing welfare would be beyond the pale, and where business would be something to be discouraged, not supported. Conversely Ed grew up in a twenty-first-century Labour Party which was nervous of attacking business, and much more comfortable with attacking crime and welfare abuse.

For Tony the speech would have all been about the Labour Party confronting hard realities; for Ed it was all about attacking unhealthy concentrations of power, something he was to do directly with News International. The point here is that essentially the same speech, or at least the same concept, had different meanings to different politicians at different times, a perfect example of the dialectical progression of politics. Constant yet changed.

But I hated the conflict between the two, and it upset me, my illness leading me almost to a longing for healing and unity. I knew this would be difficult, in the short term at least. It had been obvious to me for a long time that both brothers would stand, so as far back as the autumn of 2009 I approached Ed (at a birthday party for Peter Mandelson) and told him directly that if there was a leadership campaign I would vote for David first and Ed second. It was awkward, but I was determined not to make the same mistake as in 1994 not saying explicitly whom I would support.

David declared his intention to stand on the Thursday after the General Election and I spoke to Ed on the phone that night. It was clear within seconds that he too was determined to stand and that nothing would stop him. In truth, so passionate was he about it, it was clear that nothing should. I felt that we simply could not have a repetition of 1994, when the lack of democratic process cramped and distorted the future paths of both candidates. I did not try to stop him, nor encourage him; it was entirely up to him. He felt that whoever won it would be okay. I doubted that, but again I was quiet about it. I felt the ghosts of the past hanging over that conversation, and I tried not to repeat the errors of history.

I helped David as much as I could during the campaign but with the recurrence of my cancer it was hard. I grew to admire him even more during that period; he showed extraordinary integrity, stopping anyone at any time from attacking his brother. I thought it very hard for David that Ed stood and I know how upset he and Louise were. That was no easy thing to deal with. Not easy for Ed either: you could sense afterwards the burden of it all.

I was upset when David lost, for him and for New Labour. David was completely devastated, trying to make sense of an impossible situation. He was angry and frustrated but determined not to let these feelings spill over into the Labour Party. Under no circumstances would he allow 2010 to turn into 1994. David does not get enough credit for this. He had taken an enormously hard situation and dealt with it; there would be no repeat of what had happened before. In time it will heal, and in the meantime there will be no recriminations. This is yet another example of dialectical movement, of moving on, behaving differently.

The moment Ed won it was clear we had to move on, that the political terrain had changed. New Labour was not dead, but the arc of New Labour that I had been trying so hard to renew had finally come to its end. A different trajectory was beginning; one that required a different strategy. New Labour would be part of it, but not all of it, and not its starting place. But the idea continues, even though the trajectory has changed. Ed's task is to hold to his progressive principles and his authenticity as a politician, while building and sustaining majoritarian positions that can form the basis of an election-winning coalition of support.

Tony Blair is totally right, in the introduction to his book, to say that elections are won when the centre is won, but he is right also when he says that the centre is not static but is always changing. Ed must win the centre in a different way, fusing principles that have worked in the past with the new political project he has embarked on, and the changing character of the electorate. This is not about compromise, it really is about progressing dialectically. If New Labour dies, so too Labour. But if New Labour lives on, albeit in a different world and from a different perspective, so does Labour. Ed is naturally suited to this; he sees the forward landscape fluidly and can bring apparently competing ideas together. I hope he succeeds, and I believe he can, but I hope also that the two brothers can transcend the fault-lines of the past and move ahead in a new and different way. That will be real evidence of the dialectic at work. I wish both of them well.

Part 3

FUTURE: THE REVOLUTION YET TO COME

FUTURE

Time and its consequences

I decided to write this during coffee with Brendan Foster, the Olympic athlete, BBC commentator and huge supporter of Labour and of the north-east. I was recovering from my second set of surgery at the superb Northern Oesophago-Gastric Unit in Newcastle. A couple of days earlier I had received my prognosis from the head of the unit, Professor Mike Griffin, and it was not positive. In fact, it was down-right negative: my chances, as the written report made clear, were 'slim'. I asked Brendan what to do. 'Write,' he said. 'Write it all down, what it was like, what you were thinking, what it all meant.' I had a responsibility to do this, otherwise any knowledge I had would be scattered to the wind.

So I started writing, first about my cancer story and then about my political journey. I started with cancer because I felt that was my first obligation, then moved on to politics, different journeys but of course always linked. The truth is that we are never one person but several, changing over time as one aspect of your character evolves, another subdues, only experience and adversity revealing who you really are.

This is one of the central themes of this new edition of *The Unfinished Revolution*: lives changing under pressure and circumstance, but in some ways always staying the same, as contradictions are revealed and resolved.

I think the central contradiction for Tony Blair is a tension between the world of values that ultimately drives him and the world of public politics he has chosen to inhabit. He prefers, if he possibly can, to keep these separate – this really is a church and state instinct for him. But his values are deeply held, perhaps more deeply held than any other politician that I have ever worked with, but it took the years of illness to allow me to discover this, and to learn the qualities that are his personal and spiritual core. There are really two Tony Blairs out there, the private and the public, connected but separate, and in many ways I would like to see them closer together, for the world to know the deeper power of Tony Blair.

Gordon Brown, too, has his contradictions, a huge protean and constructive force on the one hand, a more angry and sometimes negative force on the other. This tension is what gives him his huge power and makes him what he is, but it also impedes him, undermining his huge strength. Above all else Gordon wants to be good, to do good things in politics, which is both his goal and his justification, and when this task eludes him he can become frustrated. He is happiest when living closest to his conception of the good, least happy when furthest away from it. The best and warmest conversation I had with him was just prior to my first surgery, when he reassured me about what was to come. A conversation unencumbered by the complexities and exigencies of politics.

In all these years Alastair has been the rock around which events have swirled, steadfast in his support for every party leader from Neil Kinnock through to Ed Miliband, but mostly of course for Tony Blair. He is the ultimate loyalist, not just to Labour but to his causes and friends, always there when it matters. But for Alastair loyalty is not a halfway thing, it is 100 per cent or it is nothing. Giving all that he can, not just some of the time but all of the time, constantly pushing himself beyond reasonable boundaries and seeking perfection in all that he does. This level of commitment is indispensable to those around him, but daunting for him as he knows the burden and sacrifice of each new political challenge. Before starting to work on an election campaign he would circle it for ages like a swimmer nervous of the cold water, but in the end reluctantly dive in and swim relentlessly for as long as it took to get the job done.

He was obsessive about winning, success, teamwork and detail, but this obsession had a cost or, better put, it had its other side. For Alastair duty and perfectionism somehow find their opposite in the waves of depression that would sometimes sweep into his life. It is not clear to me what comes first, his sense of duty or the depression that somehow runs so close to it, but they are the continuing contradiction of his life, together becoming the driving force that enables him to achieve so much and with such extraordinary intensity. Alastair is the kind of person who would drive seven hundred miles in an evening to do a Labour Party fundraising event, cycle up Mont Ventoux in the midday heat just for the sake of it, or manically try to beat his ten-year-old son in push-up competition in a square in Provence. In other words, the kind of person you want on your side in an election campaign.

Peter Mandelson, of course, is a multitude of contradictions, with more dualism than a text by Descartes. In fact, I once did a personal presentation of all of them, which he describes in his memoirs. I will not repeat that here, but I think that at his core Peter is a private person leading a public life, more emotional and vulnerable than many realise. He really only trusts just a small group of people, and they stay with him through thick and thin, giving and receiving absolute loyalty. But beyond that the world is a less safe place and Peter, I think, seeks to protect himself from it, a world not deserving trust and perhaps best dealt with on that basis. But that is such an incomplete explanation of such a hugely complex person, who has such a rich variety of political skills. He could not just understand the political flow, but was able to reduce it to its political essence, making the complicated simple. No one was better at explaining a political situation. And he was relentlessly modernising, always the New Labour voice in the room, immensely proud of what it was and what it was able to achieve.

The curve of modernisation

These lives changed so much in the last twenty-five years, but all are essentially the same. As individuals complicated, as a group more complex still, seeming certain to break apart but always, somehow or other, pulling together at the key campaigning moments. There was never a steady state, the group was always in a kind of disharmonious flux, changing shape and alignments as the years went by, but in the end a kind of residual loyalty always won through, all returned in one way or another to the 2010 election campaign. As Tony said, all of us returning in the end to the same place.

This balance of change and constancy is certainly true of my life. This book starts with me as a teenager, wandering around my garden thinking manically about politics. Forty or more years later I am still doing the same thing. In that respect nothing has changed. I don't think a day passes without me thinking about politics or attempting to solve a political problem. This is a both obsession and therapy, the mind a kind of safe house that allows me to leave the discomfort of my illness behind. These days I am somewhat changed and much, much older than the boy who starts the book; a different photograph, as Orwell writes, but essentially, I hope, the same: living and breathing politics and still, basically, believing the similar things.

In those early days I developed a kind of embryonic New Labour position, which is still the core of what I believe today. That every voice had an equal worth, with an equal right to be heard; that aspiration should be applauded; that a binary left against right politics would not work, and would not be representative of the people of Britain; that compassion and responsibility can co-exist; that our progressive obligation is to try to change the world for the better; and that the future is what really matters in politics.

I am aware that these instincts were born of a particular time and place. The photograph that I have in my head of those days is of a boy talking to a group of friends in the playground of my local secondary modern school, a picture now in many ways out of date. That moment in the early and mid-1960s was a place on the curve of post-war realignment, part of the emergence of a new consumer class. I thought I was caught in a universal moment of time. In fact, I was living a life that could have come straight from a political sociology textbook. I was on two trajectories: the curve of post-war materialism and the much longer curve of modernisation that started in the mid-nineteenth century and still remains so central to my politics and to the world. But as kids in the playground we knew nothing of that, we were just living our own lives. My best friend from those school days, John Huntley, contacted me after he had read this book. He had made a similar journey to me, leaving school at sixteen and attempting to get into the dreaded Royal Aircraft Establishment factory (which I simply could not face). He was rejected as he failed a very basic mechanical test, but managed to get a job at an electronics company, which he hated and left after a year. But then he got a start as a laboratory technician while working part-time for a degree, then a Ph.D., and he eventually became a renowned scientist in his field of animal vaccine, with over a hundred publications. Like me, he disliked the ethos of our school and only thrived when he left and made his own way. This summed up my view of politics. The loss of potential in that school and at that time was huge, but John did it: he got out and in the end soared, showing how the liberation of potential is perhaps the most important thing in politics. But there is also a responsibility for all of us to take the chances that we have. We should not be glib about this: both really matter. Without responsibility, opportunity can be wasted or distorted; without opportunity all the responsibility in the world is meaningless. We need the ladders to climb, the courage and responsibility to climb them, and the support of others to help us on our way.

Of course, the world of the mid-1960s is not our world:

there has been a transformation in Britain and the world in the last fifty years. We stand on a different place on the curve of modernisation, seeing its advantages but also its pitfalls, and realising that the epicentre of aspiration and consumer fulfillment has slowly – and not so slowly – shifted from the quiet suburbs where I conceived my early ideas to China, India, Mexico and beyond. In many ways this is their time, their place on the curve more secure than ours.

The pace of change does not slacken. Rather, it increases: the velocity of change and how we deal with it now the central issue in our politics. We stand in the glare of change, sometimes blinded by it, but always aware that it is there. The issue is not just the speed of change but its character and consequent effects. Changes in quantity becoming changes in quality. I first became aware of this sitting watching excessive amounts of politics and news on television while convalescing from my first surgery in New York and then London. Increasingly what I could see was not just the normal flow of events and news items but a deeper sense of growing disorder and even chaos. And so in October 2008 I wrote a speech, 'Order out of chaos', arguing that the world had become so fast-moving, so complex, so fragmented that events would emerge which would be hard to predict, destructive in their impact and sometimes irreversible in their consequences. I was thinking mostly about issues of climate change and security, but the financial crisis that happened the next month was a perfect example of what I meant. Not, of course, that I predicted it in any way, but it was clear from the condition of this new world that events like that were going to happen. It also became apparent that the David Held view, Cosmopolitan Democracy,[1] was right: that as well as participating in our local communities we need new democratic institutions at the global level, controlling the stateless power of globalisation. We need a continuing chain of democracy and values linking our smallest and most intimate of communities to our global world. The local and the global are now inexorably intermeshed.

The forces of globalisation

In many ways these chapters read like a private history of globalisation, seen through the individuals and their families that it directly affects. Global forces touch almost every concern discussed on these pages, from squeezed living standards to community erosion, to migration, patriotism and political disengagement. It did not cause all these issues, but is a part of most of them. Globalisation is not, however, a static thing and has changed again, a process well spelled out by Stephen D. King in his book *Losing Control*.[2] King explains the shifting parameters of globalisation in the context not just of the last decade, or even the last century, but well beyond, showing how China rose then fell and now rises again; how the West was at first hesitant then dominant and then started to fade; and how Islam led, then retreated and then re-emerged in different and new ways. These events are not independent but interconnected, part of the long evolution of the world economy. And now globalisation mutates again, with economic power, wealth and consumer opportunity shifting away from the West as growth rates accelerate in developing economies and gradually slow in the developed world. The consequences of this are that inequalities between nations are decreasing as the new economies catch up at the expense of the West, but inequality within nations is increasing as lower and middle income groups feel pressured. This shift in power had other implications: an imbalance of capital flows between developed and emerging sectors, leading to an excess of savings in one and of debt in another; the search for high-yield unsustainable non-equity assets, leading to a shadow banking system and, in turn, to excessive and unwarranted lending and ultimately to global financial crisis. Excessive credit and borrowing were the responsibility not just of financial institutions but governments and consumers too. As the growth rate slowed and returns fell at every level, credit and borrowing filled the consequent gap.

If ever there was an example of a major event explainable only by an understanding of the underlying forces that helped create it, then this is it. This does not mean that what happened was inevitable, or justifiable, simply that what happened can be understood only when the deeper pattern is revealed. A pattern revealed not just by abstract analysis but by hundreds of conversations in dozens of focus groups all over Britain, in which I was not just talking to individuals but having a conversation with the world beyond. The world is connected: concern about unfairness and squeezed living standards expressed by a voter in Doncaster is matched by a sense of growing financial opportunity for a voter in Mumbai. Two sides of the world, two faces of globalisation, two conceptions of fairness – huge global trends articulated by families who may never meet but who will always in some way be joined. In a way, the forces described in this book finally revealed.

We are not trapped or powerless in all this; we can act to shape our political future. The question less what can we do, more what should we do? The dilemma facing us is vividly put by King, who says: 'The developed world needs to decide whether it wants the emerging nations to enjoy the economic opportunities that for so long have been enjoyed by the privileged and Western few, or instead whether it wants to retreat into a bunker that will only leave the economy as a whole facing political and economic catastrophe.'[3] This is too stark and simple a choice, but it makes clear the new political terrain: we do not enter a time of abundance as we go forward, but of constraint. This constraint is the result of a systematic shift in the structure of the global economy, leading in turn to new issues of fairness. King's dilemma – open or closed, relative decline or disengagement, have what we hold or try to share it – is a central question in modern politics, and one that we all have to face.

There are difficulties with King's concept of relative decline, one pragmatic, the other fundamental. The pragmatic point is clear. It is very hard for a politician to stand up and say that he or she wants relative decline: this is not immediately obvious as a vote-winning message. I suspect that this is what, at some level, President Obama believes, not so much in the decline of America but in an acceptance that the power and wealth of the United States has its limitations, and that others are entitled to their share of global gains. His problem is that the US electorate senses this and do not like it, and nor do his right-wing opponents, who are sometimes not entirely rational in their arguments. Obama is rational; his problem not in being honest about the limitations facing the US, but a difficulty in articulating a re-invented future in which American exceptionalism has new meaning and in which the next American century is redefined. This is a challenge that every Western leader now faces: to be honest about the future but creative, imaginative and optimistic about how we navigate our way through it.

The second difficulty is more fundamental: the real issue is not the conflict between slow-growth Western economies and high-growth developing economies – although that is important – but between a global economy that can be sustained and one that is unsustainable. Nothing ever lasts, and China, India, Brazil and the others will one day find themselves in a different place on the arc of progress and their growth rate, too, will start to slow. Constrained ultimately not by the competitive power of other nations but the inevitable limitations of a finite world. Imagination, creativity and the force of enterprise are limitless; the natural resources at our disposal are not. In the end our future has to be sustainable, because it is right and because it is the only way that capitalism can ultimately endure. As Will Hutton repeatedly asserts, 'the more capitalism adopts fair process, the better it works'.[4] Fairness is not only a conceptual necessity in this new world, it is a real and growing economic and social aspiration that will not be abated. Ironically, the sense of unfairness now driving through post-industrial and suburban communities in Britain will not rest here but will infuse the entire global community. It is not just economic opportunity that moves from British suburbia to the streets of Shanghai, but a commitment to fairness, linked to contribution, which in the end will mean that only fair economies and societies will be genuinely sustainable.

This is the battleground for the next great struggle in politics: how to balance optimism with constraint, openness with fairness, growth with sustainability. This is a challenge for the left, but also a progressive opportunity, and one of the reasons why New Labour remains so vital, based as it is on a politics that believes enterprise and fairness should mutually co-exist.

Of course, some of our critics will say that dealing with globalisation and rising inequality were at the heart of New Labour's failure, but there is a counter case. On equality, New Labour's record is much better than many assume. Not only did the rate of inequality fall – in marked contrast to the years that preceded New Labour – but income growth was distributed much more fairly, as the Institute for Fiscal Studies' survey of poverty and inequality under Labour makes clear: 'Taking the period 1996–97 to 2009–10 as a whole, all quintile groups have experienced income growth in the region of 1.5–2.0 per cent on an annualised basis ... this is very different from the experience under the preceding period of Conservative government, when income growth was stronger the richer the quintile group, a pattern consistent with strongly rising inequality.'[5]

The same pattern is true of education. A 2009 Department for Children, Schools and Families report[6] shows that Labour – modestly – narrowed the gap between disadvantaged and other pupils; deprived schools showed the most improvement, as did disadvantaged pupils. These were not huge reductions in inequality but a marked change from the pattern that preceded New Labour, revealing a basic direction of travel in favour of fairness in the face of countervailing forces. Nor is it true that New Labour left communities to fend for themselves in the face of these new global pressures. It is not just the investment in schools, hospitals and the crucial catalysts of community like the three thousand children's centres, it is the construction of a renewed community fabric, a hidden infrastructure of shared support. Polly Toynbee a serious (and often critical) observer of Labour's record in office, wrote in 2011: 'look at the New Deal for

Communities, the boldest initiative ever tried. This week I visited Aston Pride, the NDC that topped the 39 schemes Labour created in the nation's worst areas. Each was given about £50m to spend as local people chose over 10 years. That committed funding drew together communities weary of half-hearted previous attempts, always abandoned when money ran out. The 17,000 inhabitants of this multi-ethnic, high-unemployment patch of Birmingham had 17 often fractious mosques and six diverse churches, but slowly and with difficulty they came together and transformed the place.'[7] That kind of change was happening all over Britain, a complex web of community support that is now wrongly dismantled, the result of a clash between the government's one-nation positioning and its small-state instincts. David Cameron wishes to hold the centre, but some of his policies, almost under their own momentum, are pushing him to the right. A strong society and an empowering, facilitating state should not been see as in opposition to each other, but rather as complementary and mutually supportive. Not win-lose but win-win. Strong communities need effective local institutions that can act as catalysts for change and arbiters of fairness. This was New Labour's approach and much was achieved but there was, and is, much more still to do.

The age of discovery

Pivotal although globalisation is, it is just one of the many forces that shape our new world. Technology is in some ways as influential, and of course is completely connected to it. Although we often talk about digitalisation, I am not sure we always quite appreciate how fast it is moving, and just how dramatic and far reaching are its effects. Google, for example, was founded in 1998, the year this book was first published; Facebook in 2004; Twitter in 2006. When I initially wrote *The Unfinished Revolution* social media, now the toppler of governments and the occasional instrument of riot co-ordination, did not exist. Now 1.97 billion people use a computer and 664 million are on Facebook.[8] This has transformed industries, what we read and how we read it, and, crucially, what we know and how we know it. Information is instant, news not just immediate but democratic, opening up issue after issue that would otherwise never be discovered; transparency is now real; everything that can be known will be known. The internet has empowered those who are powerless and sometimes in parlous positions; it has changed the conduct of politics and the character of communications.

The last decade has seen what amounts to a latter-day Copernican revolution in the way that politics, and indeed all organisations, relate to and communicate with people. The old model was clear: commercial and civic institutions held both power and knowledge while the public was trusting and effectively deferential. Institutional knowledge and information were at the centre of our universe; they were our sun. The new model has changed this completely. Now it is the public who are the sun and politicians and corporations the orbiting planets, seeking to gain attention and win trust. The implications of this are immense. It means that old ways of conducting communications are no longer relevant, that the old models of politics are effectively obsolete and that companies are increasingly answerable not just to shareholders but to a world in which both citizens and consumers have a voice. We are moving into a world in which everyone can be a stakeholder, and democratised knowledge is moving us from an age of deference to an age of discovery. The truth is not received from authority like tablets of stone, but is something to be discovered by all of us through investigation, experience and verification.

In this new world of discovery it is clear that citizens and consumers are not driven solely by self-interest, but by motivations rooted in values and a demand for ethical disinterested decisions. Talk to any focus group about politics – or business – and it is immediately clear what people want. They seek truth and they crave honesty; they strive for authenticity, trusting leaders and institutions they believe to be driven by a higher sense of purpose. And who are prepared to take tough unpopular decisions and who are determined to put the long-term first. This sounds idealistic, but it is not. It is a hard fact of modern public life, and the modern conduct of business. Without a core of integrity, values and ultimately fairness, it is hard to gain and sustain success in this new world. Both consumers and citizens demand higher ethical standards and are quite prepared to veto any product or politician who transgresses these standards. Democratic citizens will discover the truth about the real character of politics and politicians. Democratic consumers will find what is really true of any brand or business, and will have the power to act on it.

In this new world boundaries are falling, individuals and institutions remaking themselves, held together not by the glue of the past but the shared purpose of the future. Individuals are no longer just consumers or citizens but both: consumers wanting the values of public life, citizens the creativity and efficiency of the private realm. And it is no longer as relevant if an institution is public, or private, or voluntary. What is critical is the purpose that drives it, and a structure flexible enough to be inclusive and pluralistic. We are at our best when working together, not caught in separate realms.

This is the landscape we now face, much changed from 1997: global economic power shifting; incomes squeezed for low- and middle-income families; rising inequality in Western economies; the politics of belonging and community more vital; feelings of unfairness hardening; concerns about migration increasing; but empowerment accelerating; democracy expanding; transparency a given; the importance of values increasing; the pace of technological change exploding: consumers, citizens and the institutions that serve them moving forward in new and less separate ways. You can look at this and feel awed and pessimistic, or you can feel optimism and hope. These are not reactions, they are decisions: optimism involves one course of action, pessimism another. I am certainly optimistic that there is more here to celebrate than to fear. But we have to be confident and assertive in the way that we face the future: we must have the courage to be open to the world, and the determination to make that future fair and socially just. If we decide on the opposite, if we chose retreat and isolation, then in the end we will be more vulnerable and our communities less secure. If we engage with the future and with globalisation, and do so on our terms, not only will we be financially stronger, we will become more empowered and in the end more powerful, influencing the course of events not reacting to them. To shape this future we need strategies that can accept contradictions and resolve them; to know that our purpose in politics is to turn values into change; to understand that the sustainable creation of wealth requires fairness; and that hope and aspiration are at the heart of progressive politics. The instinctive desire to look at the world not as it is, but as it can be. This, I believe, is the essence of New Labour.

The politics of purpose

But New Labour must move on, not just incrementally but substantially, meeting the need not just for new policies but a new approach to politics based on a renewed and deepened sense of our unifying mission. Purpose and synthesis have always been at the core of my conception of our political project. New Labour was never about cutting the difference between two alternative points of view, or a crude and unthinking triangulation. It is about the synthesis of contradictory trajectories guided by purpose, although I am not sure that New Labour in government had a sufficiently explicit purpose and a clear enough sense of the synthesis that guided it. It was there, but hidden, as Matthew Taylor once said, 'like a sex toy in the bedroom'. We all knew what we were for, but no one would talk about it.

For me there is no doubt what our purpose and our synthesis is, and it is best articulated by the idea of mutuality. This is the value most able to drive our politics and our lives. It contains within it the concepts of interaction and dialectic; it is reciprocal and implies contract; it makes explicit one of my grounding assumptions: that if we work together, and live together, in relationships of shared and fair contribution, then our success and our future will be sustained. At every point it brings us to inclusion and synthesis, and should always be the New Labour lodestar. Mutuality has such power because it derives ultimately from the concept that is at the heart of at least three religions, including my own: that we should treat others as we ourselves seek to be treated. Mutuality should be the basis of our progressive politics as it moves forward, linking rights to responsibilities, forming the basis of a new social contract that will provide the glue that our society needs, inclusive not exclusive, pulling together not driving apart; the basis of the economics of sustainability and the foundation of a new politics of mutual respect and civility. And it provides, for me at least, a synthesis within politics and between politics and faith.

In 1996 Tony Blair made his 'Stakeholder speech' in Singapore, in which he said that we need to recognise 'a mutual purpose for which we all work, and in which we all benefit. It is a stakeholder economy. In which opportunity is available to all, advancement is through merit, and no group or class is excluded. That is the economic justification of social cohesion, for a fair and strong society, a traditional commitment to a left of centre politics but with relevance today as it applies to a new world.' That was true then, it is true now.

This, then, has been my story of New Labour. Six elections, twenty-six years, an extraordinary journey by an extraordinary group of people, who through an almost unprecedented combination of talent, ideas, energy, determination and courage managed to win three elections, to change Britain and, in turn, changed the course of politics. I am aware that it is only a partial account, a sliver of the truth, but I hope it illuminates rather than obscures. There is far too much about me, and not enough about all the others who shared this journey and made far more significant contributions than mine. Looking back now, what I mostly I feel is a sense of awe, amazement and above all gratitude that I had the chance to be involved in this remarkable journey. It was for all of us a privilege.

These last chapters have been called 'A letter to the next generation', and that is what I have tried to write. Although this is the end of that letter, it is not I hope the end of my personal revolution. I believe that there is never a time when the revolution is finished, never a time to stop thinking, to stop renewing, to stop trying to change the world if only by a little. This is the last day of my holiday and Gail looks at me with a kind of despair: why will I never stop? But I was determined to complete this, partly of course for myself, but mainly for those who follow. I wanted all of you to know what it was really like, and to understand the effort and integrity that created this remarkable New Labour government. I want you to be proud of what we did, but impatient about what we did not do. Believing in our past so that you can be confident about our future. The future that is now yours to build, the revolution yours to finish.

NOTES

Further publication details can be found in the Bibliography.

Volume I: 1985–1997

Introduction
1. Henry Reed, 'Lessons of the War: 1. Naming of Parts', *The Oxford Book of Twentieth-Century Verse*, p. 478.
2. David Owen, *Time to Declare*, p. 39.
3. Herbert Marcuse, *Reason and Revolution*, p. 124.
4. Ibid.
5. G. W. F. Hegel, *Elements of the Philosophy of Right*, p. 23.
6. Michael Oakeshott, *Rationalism in Politics*, p. 129.
7. Ibid, p. 124.

1: The Century That Labour Lost
1. Ivor Crewe, 'How to Win a Landslide Without Really Trying', p. 2.
2. *Guardian*, 20 June 1983.
3. Crewe, op. cit., p. 14.
4. Ibid., p. 15.
5. Ibid.
6. Crewe, 'The Labour Party and the Electorate' in Dennis Kavanagh (ed.), *The Politics of the Labour Party*, p. 27.
7. Crewe, op. cit., p. 25.
8. Ibid., p. 23.
9. Focus group, verbatim transcript, 17 February 1997.
10. Crewe, 'Labour Force Changes, Working-Class Decline and the Labour Vote: Social and Electoral Trends in Postwar Britain' in Frances Fox Piven (ed.), *Labour Parties in Post-Industrial Societies*, p. 23.
11. Ibid.

12. Ibid., p. 26.
13. Ibid., pp. 36–7.
14. Ibid., p. 38.
15. Ibid.
16. Ibid.
17. Focus group, verbatim transcript, 12 September 1991.
18. Michael Cox, *Labour and the Benn Factor*, pp. 74–5.
19. Anthony Seldon, *The Conservative Century*, pp. 13, 18.
20. Benjamin Disraeli, speech in Edinburgh, 29 October 1867, quoted in *The Times*, 30 October 1867.
21. David Marquand, *The Progressive Dilemma*, p. ix.
22. A. J. Davies, *To Build a New Jerusalem*, p. 49.
23. Tudor Jones, *Remaking the Labour Party*, p. 109.
24. Ibid.
25. Ben Pimlott, 'The Labour Left', in Cook and Taylor (eds), *The Labour Party*, p. 180 (quoted in Jones, *Remaking the Labour Party*, p. 15).
26. Shaw Desmond, *Labour: The Giant With the Feet of Clay*, p. 197 (quoted in Jones, *Remaking the Labour Party*, p. 15).
27. Marquand, op. cit., p. 17.
28. Davies, op. cit., p. 119.
29. Ibid., p. 120.
30. Jones, op. cit., p. 9.
31. Ibid.
32. H. M. Drucker, *Doctrine and Ethos in the Labour Party*, p. 25 (quoted in Jones, *Remaking the Labour Party*, p. 9).
33. Marquand, op. cit., p. 17.
34. Labour Party Annual Conference Report, January and February 1918, Appendix I, Constitution of the Labour Party, Section 3 (d).
35. *Labour and the New Social Order* (quoted in Jones, *Remaking the Labour Party*, p. 5).
36. G. D. H. Cole, *A History of the Labour Party from 1914*, p. 56 (quoted in Jones, *Remaking the Labour Party*, p. 5).
37. Egon Wertheimer, *Portrait of the Labour Party*, p. 50 (quoted in Jones, *Remaking the Labour Party*, p. 5).
38. Davies, op. cit., p. 213.
39. Hilary Wainwright, *Labour: A Tale of Two Parties*, p. 82.
40. Tony Blair, speech to the Fabian Society commemoration of the 1945 General Election, 5 July 1995.
41. Ibid.

42. Douglas Jay, *The Socialist Case*, p. 195 (quoted in Jones, *Remaking the Labour Party*, p. 27).
43. Jones, op. cit., p. 26.
44. W. H. Greenleaf, *The British Political Tradition, Vol. 2*, p. 475 (quoted in Jones, *Remaking the Labour Party*, p. 25).
45. Ibid., p. 476.
46. Lewis Minkin, *The Labour Party Conference*, p. 125 (quoted in Jones, *Remaking the Labour Party*, p. 26).
47. S. H. Beer, *Modern British Politics*, p. 237 (quoted in Jones, *Remaking the Labour Party*, p. 27).
48. Anthony Crosland, *The Future of Socialism*, p. 41 (quoted in Jones, *Remaking the Labour Party*, p. 27).
49. Jones, op. cit., p. 27.
50. Tony Benn, *Years of Hope: Diaries, Papers and Letters, 1940–1962*, p. 318.
51. Labour Party Conference Report, 1959, pp. 109–13 (quoted in Jones, *Remaking the Labour Party*, pp. 46–8).
52. Davies, op. cit., p. 294.
53. Ibid.
54. Ibid., p. 302.
55. Keith Middlemas, *The Politics of Industrial Society*, p. 417 (quoted in Jones, *Remaking the Labour Party*, p. 86).
56. Crewe, op. cit., p. 28.
57. Davies, op. cit., p. 330.
58. Jones, op. cit., p. 91.
59. *Guardian*, 3 October 1973 (quoted in Jones, *Remaking the Labour Party*, p. 92).
60. Jones, op. cit., p. 102.
61. Davies, op. cit., p. 365.
62. Patricia Sykes, *Losing from the Inside*, p. 37.
63. Interview with David Hill, 13 March 1998.
64. G. L. Williams and A. L. Williams, *Labour's Decline and the Social Democrats' Fall*, p. 113.

2: Saving Labour

1. Interview with Peter Mandelson, 18 March 1998.
2. Letter to Peter Mandelson, 1 November 1985.
3. Interview with Patricia Hewitt, 13 October 1997.
4. Interview with Charles Clarke, 23 March 1998.
5. Interview with Patricia Hewitt, 13 October 1997.
6. Interview with Charles Clarke, 23 March 1998.

7. Neil Kinnock, speech to the Labour Party conference, 1 October 1985.

8. Interview with Peter Mandelson, 16 October 1997.

9. Private information.

10. Interview with Peter Mandelson, 9 November 1985.

11. Interview with Robert Worcester, 12 November 1985.

12. Interview with Patricia Hewitt, 13 October 1997.

13. Interview with David Hill, 13 March 1998.

14. Interview with Patricia Hewitt, 13 October 1997.

15. Interview with Peter Mandelson, 9 November 1985.

16. Ibid.

17. Interview with Patricia Hewitt, 13 October 1997.

18. Interview with Peter Mandelson, 9 November 1985.

19. Interview with Tony Manwaring, 10 November 1985.

20. Transcript of presentation by Leslie Butterfield, Paul Southgate and Roddy Glen, 25 November 1985.

21. Transcript of presentation by BBDO, 25 November 1985.

22. Philip Gould, 'Report on Labour Party Communications', 18 November 1985, p. 16.

23. Interview with Peter Mandelson, 16 October 1997.

24. Gould, 'Social Policy Campaign – Final Brief', 4 February 1986.

25. Interview with Peter Mandelson, 16 October 1997.

26. Ibid.

27. Ibid.

28. Ibid.

29. *Financial Times*, 23 April 1986.

30. *Daily Telegraph*, 23 April 1986.

31. *Sunday Mirror*, 27 April 1986.

32. *Guardian*, 23 April 1986.

33. *New Statesman*, 25 April 1986.

34. *Tribune*, 23 April 1986.

35. Letter from Peter Mandelson to Larry Whitty, 7 April 1986.

36. Ibid. (response from Larry Whitty handwritten at bottom of letter).

37. Interview with Peter Mandelson, 16 October 1997.

38. Author's diary, 25 June 1986.

39. Ibid., 26 June 1986.

40. Interview with Peter Mandelson, 16 October 1997.

41. Ibid.

42. Author's diary, 23 June 1986.

43. Interview with Peter Mandelson, 16 October 1997.
44. Ibid.
45. Memo from Joe Napolitan to Neil Kinnock, 15 April 1986.
46. Kinnock, speech to the Labour Party conference, 30 September 1986.
47. Interview with Patricia Hewitt, 13 October 1997.
48. Interview with Peter Mandelson, 16 October 1997.
49. Memo from Joe Napolitan to Neil Kinnock, 3 August 1986.
50. Ibid., 27 June 1986.
51. Ibid., 13 October 1986.
52. Ibid.
53. Gould, memo to the SCA Management Group, 17 November 1986.
54. Ibid.
55. Letter to Peter Mandelson and Bryan Gould, 12 December 1986.
56. Memo from Patricia Hewitt, 26 February 1987.
57. Interview with Patricia Hewitt, 13 October 1997.
58. Interview with Colin Byrne, 20 March 1998.
59. Gould, memo to Jeremy Kane, 3 March 1987.
60. Letter to Peter Mandelson, 10 March 1987.
61. Gould, memo to Jeremy Kane, 25 April 1987.
62. Interview with Patricia Hewitt, 13 October 1997.
63. Gould, memo to Jeremy Kane, 2 May 1987.
64. Ibid.
65. Margaret Scammell, *Designer Politics*, p. 140.
66. Interview with Chris Powell, 19 March 1998.
67. Kinnock, speech to the Llandudno Labour conference, 15 May 1987.
68. David Butler and Dennis Kavanagh, *The British General Election of 1987*, p. 114.
69. David Owen, *Time to Declare*, p. 693.
70. *Daily Mail*, 5 June 1987.
71. *Daily Express*, 6 June 1987.
72. Interview with Chris Powell, 19 March 1998.

3: The Long Decline
1. Philip Gould, 'SCA Campaign Appraisal and Next Action', 12 July 1987.
2. Ibid.
3. Ibid.

4. Gould, 'Research Note', 29 July 1987.
5. Labour Party NEC, 'Labour and Britain in 1990s', May 1988.
6. Colin Hughes and Patrick Wintour, *Labour Rebuilt*, p. 39.
7. *Campaign*, 2 October 1987.
8. Quoted in Hughes and Wintour, op. cit., p. 38.
9. Labour Party NEC, 'Labour and Britain in 1990s', p. 5.
10. Ibid., p. 9.
11. Ibid., p. 10.
12. Ibid.
13. Ibid., pp. 16–21.
14. Ibid., p. 24.
15. Quoted in Hughes and Wintour, op. cit., p. 103.
16. Interview with Patricia Hewitt, 13 October 1997.
17. Ibid.
18. Interview with Patricia Hewitt, 13 October 1997.
19. Interview with Charles Clarke, 23 March 1998.
20. Author's diary, 24 January 1988.
21. Letter to Peter Mandelson, 12 January 1988.
22. Hughes and Wintour, op. cit., pp. 84–6.
23. Interview with Patricia Hewitt, 13 October 1997.
24. Hughes and Wintour, op. cit., p. 90.
25. Author's diary, 17 July 1988.
26. Interview with Charles Clarke, 23 March 1998.
27. Ibid.
28. Ibid.
29. Author's diary, 28 June 1988.
30. Ibid., 30 June 1988.
31. Ibid., 3 July 1988.
32. Ibid., 5 July 1988.
33. Letter from Peter Mandelson to Charles Clarke, 16 August 1988.
34. Ibid.
35. Ibid.
36. Ibid.
37. Hughes and Wintour, op. cit., p. 97.
38. Gould, '1989 Campaigning Strategy Considerations', 13 February 1989.
39. Ibid.
40. Ibid.
41. MORI political polling, 18–22 May 1989.

42. Gould, memo, 12 September 1989.
43. Ibid.
44. Gould, memo, 14 October 1989.
45. Interview with Charles Clarke, 23 March 1998.
46. Author's diary, 24 January 1988.
47. Interview with Charles Clarke, 23 March 1998.
48. Interview with Colin Byrne, 20 March 1998.
49. Gould, 'Current Strategic Position', 10 January 1990.
50. Gould, 'Winning the Election', 13 June 1990.
51. Interview with Patricia Hewitt, 13 November 1997.
52. Interview with Charles Clarke, 23 March 1998.
53. Ibid.
54. Gould, 'Post Conference Note', 8 October 1990.
55. Interview with Colin Byrne, 20 March 1998.
56. Ibid.
57. Gould, 'Summary of Research and Strategic Implications', 20 December 1990.
58. Interview with David Hill, 13 March 1998.
59. Interview with Charles Clarke, 23 March 1998.
60. Interview with Patricia Hewitt, 13 October 1997.
61. Interview with Sally Morgan, 19 March 1998.
62. Clive Hollick, memo to Thursday Meeting, 30 July 1990.
63. Interview with Patricia Hewitt, 13 October 1997.
64. Gould, memo, 8 October 1991.
65. Interview with Charles Clarke, 23 March 1998.
66. Ibid.
67. Interview with Colin Byrne, 20 March 1998.
68. Gould, 'War Book', 12 December 1991.
69. Interview with David Hill, 13 March 1998.
70. Interview with Charles Clarke, 23 March 1998.
71. Interview with Alastair Campbell, 17 March 1998.

4: Love and Anger
1. Private information.
2. Author's diary, 20 April 1992.
3. Ibid.
4. Ibid.
5. Interview with Alastair Campbell, 17 March 1998.
6. Author's diary, 20 April 1992.
7. SCA, research into attitudes to taxation, 12 April 1988.
8. Ibid.

9. Interview with Patricia Hewitt, 13 October 1997.

10. Author's diary, 5 July 1988.

11. BMP research for the SCA, December 1989.

12. Ibid.

13. Ibid.

14. SCPR, 'British Social Attitudes' survey, 1996.

15. Gould, 'Current Strategic Position', 10 January 1990.

16. Letter to Peter Mandelson, 10 May 1990.

17. Labour Party, 'Looking to the Future', 1990.

18. Gould, 'Presentation of the Policy Review', 23 May 1990.

19. SCA, 'Campaigning Until the General Election', 26 July 1990.

20. Deborah Mattinson, presentation of SCA research findings on taxation, 25 June 1990.

21. Author's diary, 20 April 1992.

22. Ibid.

23. Ibid.

24. SCA, 'Campaigning in London', 24 April 1991.

25. ITV, *Frost on Sunday*, 5 May 1991.

26. *Guardian*, 9 May 1991.

27. David Butler and Dennis Kavanagh, *The British General Election of 1992*, p. 36.

28. SCA presentation, 12 November 1991.

29. Patricia Hewitt, memo to the Campaign Advisory Team, 29 October 1991.

30. Ibid.

31. Interview with Patricia Hewitt, 13 October 1997.

32. Interview with Charles Clarke, 23 March 1998.

33. Ibid.

34. Author's diary, 20 April 1992.

35. Ibid.

36. Ibid.

37. Interview with Patricia Hewitt, 13 October 1997.

38. Author's diary, 20 April 1992.

39. Interview with Charles Clarke, 23 March 1998.

40. Author's diary, 20 April 1992.

41. Ibid.

42. Ibid.

43. Ibid.

44. Interview with Charles Clarke, 23 March 1998.

45. Author's diary, 20 April 1992.

46. Interview with Clive Hollick, 2 July 1998.

47. *The Times*, 17 April 1992.

48. Butler and Kavanagh, op. cit., p. 105.

49. SCA, 'Summary Qualitative Research', 21 February 1992.

50. Letter from Kathryn Smith to Anna Healey, 24 March 1992.

51. *Sunday Express*, 22 March 1992.

52. *Sunday Telegraph*, 22 March 1992.

53. *Sunday Times*, 22 March 1992.

54. *Mail on Sunday*, 5 April 1992.

55. *Daily Mail*, 23 March 1992.

56. *Sun*, 23 March 1992.

57. *Today*, 23 March 1992.

58. *Daily Express*, 23 March 1992.

59. *Daily Express*, 25 March 1992.

60. Author's diary, 27 March 1992.

61. *Sunday Express*, 29 March 1992.

62. Gould, '1992 General Election: Evaluation and Implications', 22 September 1992.

63. Ibid.

64. Ibid.

65. Gould, 'Post-Election Evaluation of Party Election Broadcasts', April 1992.

66. Memo from Joe Napolitan, 8 March 1991.

67. Heath, Jowell and Curtice, *Labour's Last Chance*, p. 139.

68. Interview with Charles Clarke, 23 March 1998.

69. Ibid.

70. Interview with Alastair Campbell, 17 March 1998.

71. *Independent*, 25 May 1992.

72. Interview with Patricia Hewitt, 13 October 1997.

73. Interview with Charles Clarke, 23 March 1998.

74. Interview with Alastair Campbell, 17 March 1998.

75. Interview with Charles Clarke, 23 March 1998.

76. Interview with Alastair Campbell, 17 March 1998.

77. Interview with Patricia Hewitt, 13 October 1997.

78. Gould, '1992 General Election: Evaluation and Implications', 22 September 1992.

79. Interview with Patricia Hewitt, 13 October 1997.

80. Interview with David Hill, 13 March 1998.

81. *Daily Express*, 7 April 1992.

82. *Sun*, 7 April 1992.

83. *Sun*, 8 April 1992.

84. *Daily Mail*, 8 April 1992.

85. *Daily Express*, 8 April 1992.

86. Gould, 'Winning the Election', 13 June 1990.

87. *Tribune*, 9 April 1992.

88. *Tribune*, 17 April 1992.

89. *Tribune*, 26 June 1992.

90. Memo from Glenys Thornton to Patricia Hewitt and Philip Gould, 6 April 1992.

91. *Independent*, 25 April 1992.

92. *Independent*, 18 June 1992.

93. *Independent*, 22 June 1992.

94. *Tribune*, 3 July 1992.

95. *Guardian*, 18 June 1992.

96. *Sunday Times*, 21 June 1992.

97. Letter to Dennis Kavanagh, 7 July 1992.

98. Gould, '1992 General Election: Evaluation and Implications', 22 September 1992.

99. Interview with David Hare, 15 July 1992.

100. *Daily Mirror*, 17 June 1992.

101. *Tribune*, 26 June 1992.

102. Gould, '1992 General Election: Evaluation and Implications', 22 September 1992.

5: A Line in the Sand

1. Jon Sopel, *Tony Blair: The Moderniser*, p. 135.

2. *Campaign*, 16 October 1992.

3. Neil Kinnock, speech to the Labour Party conference, 1 October 1991.

4. Letter from Dianna Wentz, Greenberg–Lake Analysis Group Inc., 25 September 1992.

5. *Sunday Times*, 2 February 1992.

6. News release, Bush–Quayle campaign, 5 October 1992.

7. Author's diary, 6 October 1992.

8. Mary Matalin and James Carville, *All's Fair*, frontispiece.

9. Author's diary, 7 October 1992.

10. *Washington Post*, 8 October 1992.

11. Gould, 'British Parallels', 10 October 1992.

12. Author's diary, 11 October 1992.

13. Ibid.

14. Ibid., 20 October 1992.

15. Ibid., 21 October 1992.

16. Gould, 'The Final Week', 29 October 1992.
17. Author's diary, 1 November 1992.
18. Matalin and Carville, op. cit., pp. 461–2.
19. Gould, 'Mitterrand: Winning from Cohabitation', 13 December 1994.
20. Stanley Greenberg, 'The Dukakis Message, Speaking Middle Class', 20 September 1988.
21. Greenberg, 'Reconstructing the Democratic Vision', *The American Prospect*, No. 1, Spring 1990.
22. Greenberg, *Middle-Class Dreams*, p. 305.
23. Bill Clinton, speech to the Democratic Convention, New York, 16 July 1992.
24. Gould, '1992 Campaign Evaluation and Implications', 9 December 1992.
25. Philip Gould and Patricia Hewitt, 'Lessons from America', *Renewal*, January 1993 (quoted in Sopel, op. cit., p. 145).
26. *Tribune*, 8 January 1993.
27. Clive Hollick, 'Campaign '96', 28 July 1992.
28. Interview with Clive Hollick, 2 July 1998.
29. Gould, 'Assessment of Current Position', 20 May 1993.
30. Ibid.
31. Ibid.
32. John Rentoul, *Tony Blair*, p. 274.
33. Tony Blair on BBC Radio, *The World This Weekend*, 10 January 1993.
34. Rentoul, op. cit., p. 290.
35. Ibid., p. 160.
36. Gould, 'Strategy Note', 10 September 1993.
37. Ibid.
38. Interview with Patricia Hewitt, 19 March 1998.
39. Rentoul, op. cit., p. 327.
40. Gould, 'Fighting the Fear Factor', 8 February 1994.
41. Gould, 'The Labour Party: Preliminary Campaign Observations', 9 May 1994.

6: *Electric Shock Treatment*

1. Interview with Alastair Campbell, 17 March 1998.
2. Ibid.
3. Interview with Fiona Millar, 17 March 1998.
4. *Guardian*, 13 November 1992.
5. Private information.

6. Ibid.
7. John Rentoul, *Tony Blair*, p. 313.
8. BBC TV, *On the Record*, 17 January 1993.
9. Private information.
10. Ibid.
11. Ibid.
12. Ibid.
13. Interview with Alastair Campbell, 17 March 1998.
14. Ibid.
15. Philip Gould, 'Negative Consequences of a Two Horse Race', 18 May 1994.
16. Ibid.
17. Interview with Peter Mandelson, 18 March 1998.
18. Ibid.
19. Ibid.
20. Ibid.
21. Interview with Alastair Campbell, 17 March 1998.
22. Gould, 'Strategy for the Leadership Election and Beyond', 17 May 1994.
23. Ibid.
24. Gould, 'Leadership Election: Tony Blair Campaign', 20 May 1994.
25. Gould, 'Blair Campaign: Moving Forward', 2 June 1994.
26. Tony Blair, 'Themes', 2 June 1994.
27. Interview with Peter Hyman, 24 March 1995.
28. Gould, 'Focus Group Debrief', 6 June 1994.
29. Gould, 'Leadership Election, Blair Campaign, Campaign Strategy Document', 10 June 1994.
30. Rentoul, op. cit., p. 394.
31. Interview with David Miliband, 24 March 1998.
32. Blair, 'Change and Renewal – Leadership Election Statement', 1994.
33. Feedback Report, 28 June 1994.
34. Interview with Peter Mandelson, 18 March 1998.
35. I am indebted to Peter Kellner for this analysis.
36. Blair, interview with Brian Walden, 24 July 1994.
37. *Daily Telegraph*, 26 July 1994.
38. *Daily Mail*, 26 July 1994.
39. Labour Party, 'Opening Doors to a Learning Society', 28 July 1994.
40. BBC TV, *One O'Clock News*, 28 July 1994.

41. Gould, 'Consolidating the Blair Identity: Rebuilding Labour; Demolishing the Conservatives', 22 July 1994.
42. Interview with Alastair Campbell, 17 March 1998.
43. Interview with Peter Mandelson, 18 March 1998.
44. Letter to Tony Blair, 14 September 1994.
45. Jon Sopel, *Tony Blair: The Moderniser*, p. 267.
46. Gould, 'Destroying the Conservatives, Rebuilding Labour', 9 September 1994.
47. *Financial Times*, 13 September 1994.
48. BBC Radio 4, *Today*, 13 September 1994.
49. Gould, 'New Labour; Right as Well as Left', 1 September 1994.
50. Gould, 'Next Two Weeks', 23 September 1994.
51. Interview with Alastair Campbell, 17 March 1994.
52. Ibid.
53. Blair, speech to the Labour Party conference, 4 October 1994.
54. Blair, speech to the Per Cent Club, 8 November 1994.
55. Ibid.
56. Gould, 'Where Labour Stands', 11 November 1994.
57. *Financial Times*, 21 November 1998.
58. *Daily Mail*, 1 December 1994.
59. Gould, memo to Tony Blair, 12 December 1994.
60. Gould, memo to Tony Blair, 19 December 1994.
61. Gould, 'Urgent Action Resulting from Focus Groups', 20 January 1995.
62. *Daily Telegraph*, 13 January 1995.
63. *Observer*, 15 January 1995.
64. *Sunday Telegraph*, 22 January 1995.
65. Gould, memo to Tony Blair, 21 March 1995.
66. Gould, 'Where We Are, Where We Should Be Going', 3 March 1995.
67. Gould, 'Where Our Campaigning is Going Wrong; What We Must Do About It', 12 January 1995.
68. Interview with Alastair Campbell, 17 March 1998.
69. Interview with Sally Morgan, 19 March 1998.
70. Interview with Margaret McDonagh, 13 March 1998.
71. See the Appendix in Rentoul, op. cit., p. 495.
72. Ibid.
73. Tudor Jones, *Remaking the Labour Party*, p. 146.
74. Gould, 'Draft Notes on the Next Steps', 20 April 1995.

7: The Project
 1. Tony Blair, 'Why Modernisation Matters', *Renewal*, 4 October 1993.
 2. John Rentoul, *Tony Blair*, p. 38.
 3. Ibid, p. 42.
 4. Blair, speech to the Wellingborough Constituency Labour Party, 19 February 1993.
 5. L. T. Hobhouse, *Liberalism* (quoted in Blair's speech, 'Faith in the City: Ten Years On', 29 January 1996).
 6. Blair, speech to the Wellingborough Constituency Labour Party, 19 February 1993.
 7. Blair, 'Why Modernisation Matters', *Renewal*, 4 October 1993.
 8. Blair, speech at Durham University, 28 January 1993.
 9. Bill Clinton, 'State of the Union' address, 27 January 1998.
10. Clinton, Address to the Democratic Leadership Council, Cleveland, 6 May 1991 (quoted in Stanley Greenberg, *Middle-Class Dreams*, p. 276).
11. Democratic Leadership Council, 'The New Orleans Declaration: A Democratic Agenda for the 1990s', New Orleans, 24 May 1990.
12. E. J. Dionne, Jr., *Why Americans Hate Politics*, pp. 11–12 (quoted in Greenberg, op. cit., p. 277).
13. Blair, 'Themes', 2 June 1994.
14. Blair, 'New Policies for a Global Economy', 27 September 1994.
15. Blair, 'Time', 30 November 1995.
16. Philip Gould, 'The Unfinished Revolution', 23 April 1995.
17. Anthony Seldon, 'The Conservative Century' in Seldon and Ball (eds), *Conservative Century: The Conservative Party Since 1900*, p. 65.
18. Gould, 'The Unfinished Revolution', 23 April 1995.
19. Gould, memo to Tony Blair, 24 April 1995.
20. Blair, *Spectator* lecture, 22 March 1995.
21. Blair, Mais lecture, 22 May 1995.
22. *Financial Times*, 23 May 1995.
23. Blair, speech to the News Corp Leadership Conference, Hayman Island, Australia, 17 July 1995.
24. Gould, 'Focus Group Report', 6 July 1995.
25. *New Statesman*, 11 August 1995.
26. *Guardian*, 12 September 1995.

27. *Guardian*, 13 September 1995.
28. *The Times*, 13 September 1995.
29. *Independent*, 13 September 1995.
30. Interview with Alastair Campbell, 17 March 1998.
31. Gould, 'Winning the Trust of the Centre Without Betraying the Left', 18 August 1995.
32. Gould, 'What is New Labour?', 25 August 1995.
33. Benjamin Disraeli, *Sybil, or, The Two Nations*, pp. 65–6.
34. Blair, speech to the Labour Party conference, 3 October 1995.
35. Gould, 'How Can We Expect the People to Understand What We Stand For, If We Don't Agree Among Ourselves', 12 November 1995.
36. Gould, 'One-Nation Economics', 9 December 1995.
37. David Miliband, notes on stakeholding, 13 January 1996.
38. Blair, speech to the Singapore Business Community, 8 January 1996.
39. Interview with Alastair Campbell, 17 March 1998.
40. Blair, speech, 'Faith in the City: Ten Years On', 29 January 1996.

8: Reassurance, Reassurance, Reassurance
1. Stanley Greenberg, 'Strategic Observations on the British Elections', 8 June 1995.
2. Philip Gould, 'The Tony Blair Problem', 6 December 1996.
3. Interview with Alastair Campbell, 17 March 1998.
4. Interview with Peter Mandelson, 18 March 1997.
5. Focus group comments, May-October 1996.
6. Gould, 'Campaigning Note: The Budget and After', 3 December 1995.
7. Gould, 'The Tony Blair Problem', 6 December 1995.
8. Gould, '1996: The Year Labour Changed Politics', 19 December 1995.
9. Tony Blair, 'Forward Strategy', 16 January 1996.
10. Interview with Peter Hyman, 24 March 1998.
11. Ibid.
12. Gould, 'Strategic Findings', 6 June 1996.
13. Labour Party, 'New Life for Britain', 4 July 1996.
14. John Rentoul, *Tony Blair*, p. 430.
15. Gould, 'Focus Group Report', 22 January 1996.
16. Gould, 'Fight Back Now', 28 January 1996.

17. John Major, Prime Minister's Questions, 23 January 1996.

18. Gould, 'Fighting Back, Step by Step', 3 March 1996.

19. Gould, 'Strategic Appraisal and Next Steps', 4 April 1996.

20. GMTV, *The Sunday Programme*, 14 April 1996.

21. Gould, 'Focus Group Report', 1 May 1996.

22. Gould, 'How You Can Get Out of This Mess and Start Enjoying Your Life Again', 14 May 1996.

23. Gould, 'Strategic Findings', 6 June 1996.

24. Report by Stanley Greenberg, 29 July 1996.

25. Gould, 'Focus Group Report', 29 July 1996.

26. *Observer*, 4 May 1996.

27. *The Times*, 16 May 1996.

28. *Guardian*, 8 August 1996.

29. *New Statesman*, 9 August 1996.

30. Ibid., 2 August 1996.

31. *Mail on Sunday*, 28 July 1996.

32. *Observer*, 11 August 1996.

33. Interview with Alastair Campbell, 17 March 1998.

34. Gould, 'Focus Group Report', 6 September 1996.

35. Gould, 'Conference Evaluation', 17 October 1996.

36. Gould, 'Beating Fear of Labour', 28 November 1996.

37. Blair, speech to the Commonwealth Parliamentary Union, Cape Town, South Africa, 14 October 1996.

38. Gould, 'Top-Line Findings', 9 January 1997.

39. Blair, Mais lecture, 22 May 1995.

40. Interview with Alastair Campbell, 17 March 1998.

41. Interview with Stanley Greenberg, 2 July 1998.

42. Gould, 'General', 22 June 1993.

43. Gould, 'Economic Campaigning', 14 September 1993.

44. Gould, 'Focus Group Report', 17 October 1993.

45. Gould, 'Taxation and the Economy', 10 July 1994.

46. Gould, 'Economic Campaigning – Key Facts', 12 March 1995.

47. Gould, 'Developing an Economic Message', 14 July 1994.

48. Gould, memo to Gordon Brown, 12 October 1994.

49. Gould, 'Focus Group Report', 17 November 1996.

50. Interview with Liam Byrne, 13 March 1998.

51. *Evening Standard*, 20 November 1996.

52. Interview with Liam Byrne, 13 March 1998.

53. *Independent on Sunday*, 19 November 1995.

54. Gould, 'Focus Group Report', 1 May 1996.

55. Gould, 'Focus Group Report', 5 February 1997.
56. Gould, 'Voter Mood, Election Strategy', 27 February 1997.
57. Greenberg, 'The Pre-Election Survey', 18 March 1997.

9: The Dark Arts
1. BBC TV, *Panorama*, 'The Marketing of Margaret', 13 June 1983.
2. Interview with Peter Mandelson, 18 March 1998.
3. Interview with Liam Byrne, 13 March 1998.
4. Ibid.
5. Interview with Peter Mandelson, 18 March 1998.
6. Interview with Liam Byrne, 13 March 1998.
7. Ibid.
8. Ibid.
9. Interview with Margaret McDonagh, 13 March 1998.
10. Ibid.
11. Interview with Liam Byrne, 13 March 1998.
12. Interview with Margaret McDonagh, 13 March 1998.
13. Interview with David Hare, 15 July 1992.
14. Interview with Peter Hyman, 24 March 1998.
15. War Book, version 3.2, 13 December 1996.
16. Leslie Butterfield, Paul Southgate and Roddy Glen, 'Towards a Communications Strategy for the Labour Party', November 1985.
17. Interview with Chris Powell, 19 March 1998.
18. Ibid.
19. Ibid.
20. Interview with Simon Buckby, 19 March 1998.
21. Ibid.
22. Ibid.
23. Ibid.
24. Focus group, verbatim transcript, 24 January 1998.
25. Ibid., 18 April 1996.
26. Ibid., 5 May 1996.
27. Author's diary, 23 February 1995.
28. Ibid., 24 February 1995.
29. Ibid., 25 February 1995.
30. Interview with Alastair Campbell, 17 March 1998.
31. Interview with Stanley Greenberg, 2 July 1998.
32. Interview with David Hill, 13 March 1998.
33. Interview with Jon Mendelsohn, 17 March 1998.

34. Ibid.
35. Ibid.
36. Interview with Alastair Campbell, 17 March 1998.
37. Interview with Liam Byrne, 13 March 1998.

10: Landslide Country
1. Interview with Alastair Campbell, 17 March 1998.
2. Ibid.
3. Philip Gould, 'Focus Group Report', 17 March 1997.
4. Gould, note to Tony Blair, 17 March 1997.
5. BBC Radio 4, *Today*, 18 March 1997.
6. Interview with David Hill, 13 March 1998.
7. Gould, 'Focus Group Report', 18 March 1997.
8. Gould, note to Tony Blair, 18 March 1997.
9. BBC Radio 4, *Today*, 20 March 1997.
10. Gould, 'Focus Group Report', 19 March 1997.
11. Gould, note to Tony Blair, 19 March 1997.
12. Gould, 'Focus Group Report', 20 March 1997.
13. Gould, note to Tony Blair, 20 March 1997.
14. Gould, 'Focus Group Report', 21 March 1997.
15. Gould, 'Focus Group Report', 23 March 1997.
16. Gould, note to Tony Blair, 23 March 1997.
17. BBC Radio 4, *Today*, 24 March 1997.
18. Gould, 'Focus Group Report', 24 March 1997.
19. Private information.
20. Gould, 'Focus Group Report', 25 March 1997.
21. Gould, note to Tony Blair, 25 March 1997.
22. Tony Blair, Labour Party press conference, 26 March 1997.
23. Interview with David Hill, 13 March 1998.
24. Gould, 'Focus Group Report', 26 March 1997.
25. Interview with David Hill, 13 March 1998.
26. Interview with Alastair Campbell, 17 March 1998.
27. Gould, 'Focus Group Report', 27 March 1997.
28. Gould, strategy note, 30 March 1997.
29. Ibid.
30. Gould, note to Alastair Campbell, 30 March 1997.
31. BBC Radio 4, *The World at One*, 31 March 1997.
32. Gould, 'Focus Group Report', 31 March 1997.
33. Labour Party, Campaign Poll 1, 1 April 1997.
34. Stanley Greenberg, 'The First Campaign Survey', 31 March 1997.

35. Gould, 'Focus Group Report', 1 April 1997.

36. Gould, 'Focus Group Report', 2 April 1997.

37. Gould, note to Tony Blair, 2 April 1997.

38. Gould, 'Focus Group Report', 3 April 1997.

39. Gould, note to Tony Blair and Alastair Campbell, 3 April 1997.

40. Gould, 'Focus Group Report', 4 April 1997.

41. Gould, note to Tony Blair, 4 April 1997.

42. Labour Party, Campaign Poll 2, 6 April 1997.

43. Greenberg, 'The Latest Tracking and Other Matters', 5 April 1997.

44. Interview with Peter Mandelson, 18 March 1998.

45. Gould, 'Focus Group Report', 7 April 1997.

46. Gould, note to Tony Blair, 7 April 1997.

47. Gould, 'Focus Group Report', 8 April 1997.

48. Gould, note to Tony Blair, 8 April 1997.

49. Gould, 'Focus Group Report', 9 April 1997.

50. Interview with David Hill, 13 March 1998.

51. Gould, 'Focus Group Report', 10 April 1997.

52. Gould, 'Focus Group Report', 11 April 1997.

53. *Sunday Times*, 13 April 1997.

54. Gould, 'Focus Group Report', 13 April 1997.

55. Gould, 'Focus Group Report', 14 April 1997.

56. BBC TV, *Newsnight*, 14 April 1997.

57. Interview with Alastair Campbell, 17 March 1998.

58. Interview with Benjamin Wegg-Prosser, 20 March 1998.

59. Gould, 'Focus Group Report', 15 April 1997.

60. Greenberg, 'Tracking Two Weeks Out', 15 April 1997.

61. Gould, 'Focus Group Report', 16 April 1997.

62. Interview with Alastair Campbell, 17 March 1998.

63. Gould, 'Focus Group Report', 17 April 1997.

64. Ibid., 18 April 1997.

65. Greenberg, 'The Changing Campaign', 21 April 1997.

66. *Independent on Sunday*, 20 April 1997.

67. Gould, 'Focus Group Report', 20 April 1997.

68. Nicholas Jones, *Campaign 1997*, p. 232.

69. Gould, 'Focus Group Report', 21 April 1997.

70. Interview with Adrian McMenamin, 16 March 1998.

71. Labour Party, Campaign Poll 7, 22 April 1997.

72. Greenberg, 'The New Plateau', 23 April 1997.

73. Gould, note to Tony Blair, 22 April 1997.

74. Interview with David Hill, 13 March 1998.
75. Interview with Alastair Campbell, 17 March 1998.
76. Gould, 'Focus Group Report', 23 April 1997.
77. Interview with David Hill, 13 March 1998.
78. Gould, 'Focus Group Report', 24 April 1997.
79. Gould, note to Tony Blair, 24 April 1997.
80. Interview with David Hill, 13 March 1998.
81. Gould, 'Focus Group Report', 25 April 1997.
82. *Spectator*, 22 November 1997.
83. Gould, note to Tony Blair, 25 April 1997.
84. Greenberg, 'An Increasingly Stable Labour Vote', 25 April 1997.
85. Gould, note to Alastair Campbell, 27 April 1997.
86. Gould, 'Focus Group Report', 28 April 1997.
87. Gould, note to Tony Blair, 28 April 1997.
88. Interview with Alastair Campbell, 17 March 1998.
89. Ibid.
90. Gould, 'Focus Group Report', 29 April 1997.
91. Gould, note to Tony Blair, 29 April 1997.
92. Greenberg, 'A Stable Close to the Campaign With Some Chipping', 28 April 1997.
93. Interview with Stanley Greenberg, 2 July 1998.
94. Interview with Adrian McMenamin, 16 March 1998.
95. Gould, 'Focus Group Report', 30 April 1997.
96. Gould, note to Tony Blair, 30 April 1997.
97. Interview with Peter Mandelson, 18 March 1998.
98. Interview with Alastair Campbell, 17 March 1998.
99. Ibid.
100. Ibid.
101. Blair, speech at the Royal Festival Hall, 2 May 1997.
102. Interview with Alastair Campbell, 17 March 1998.

Afterword
1. *The Times*, 3 May 1997.
2. David Butler and Dennis Kavanagh, *The British General Election of 1983*, p. 336, and Butler and Kavanagh, *The British General Election of 1997*, p. 295.
3. Butler and Kavanagh, *The British General Election of 1983*, p. 296, and Butler and Kavanagh, *The British General Election of 1997*, p. 246.
4. Labour Party, *The General Election Report 1997*, p. 31.

5. Quoted in Tony Blair, speech to the Fabian Society commemoration of the 1945 General Election, 5 July 1995.
6. Tony Blair, speech to the French National Assembly, 24 March 1998.
7. NOP private poll, July 1998.
8. Stanley Greenberg, 'Popularizing Progressive Politics', in Stanley Greenberg and Theda Skocpol (eds), *The New Majority*, p. 297.

Volume II: 1997–2010
A LETTER TO THE NEXT GENERATION

Part 1. Theory: The Flow of Strategy

1. Hegel, *Encyclopedia of the Philosophical Sciences*, pp. 108–9.
2. Gladwell, *The Tipping Point*.
3. Patel, *The Master Strategist*.
4. Henry Mintzburg, 1994.

Part 2. Practice: The Long Grind of Government

The First Parliament: 1997–2001

1. Snow, *Corridors of Power*.
2. Nicolson, *Harold Nicolson, Diaries and Letters, 1939–1945*.
3. Channon, *'Chips'*.
4. Colville, *The Fringes of Power*.
5. Westen, *The Political Brain*.
6. Ibid.
7. Stanley Greenberg, Labour Party poll, July 1998.
8. Philip Gould, Labour Party focus groups, September 1998.
9. Philip Gould, Labour Party focus groups.
10. Blair, speech to the Chicago Economic Club, 22 April 1999.
11. Blair, speech to the Labour Party conference, 1999.
12. Blair, speech to the Chicago Economic Club, 22 April 1999.
13. Blair, speech to the Labour Party conference, 1999.

The Second Parliament: 2001–2005

1. Richards, *Whatever it Takes*.
2. Cooper, Gibbons, Jones and McGuire, 'Does Hospital Competition Save Lives?', *Economic Journal*, vol. 121 (2011).
3. Barber, *Instruction to Deliver*.

4. George Orwell, 'England Your England', *The Lion and the Unicorn.*
5. Dexter Filkins, *New York Times,* 7 October 2007.
6. *Twentieth Century Atlas.*
7. www.hrwreports/1992.
8. Cohen, *What's Left?*
9. Dr David Kay, Former Head of Iraq Survey Group, testimony to the Senate Armed Services Committee, US Senate, 28 January 2004.
10. Barnett, 'Media Manifesto', *Prospect,* 79 (2002).
11. Blumler and Kavanagh, 'The Third Age of Political Communication: Influences and Features', *Political Communication,* vol. 16 (1999).
12. Eurobarometer survey, November 2010.
13. Stanley Greenberg, Labour Party poll.
14. Ibid.

The Third Parliament: 2005–2010
1. Machin and Vernoit, *Changing School Autonomy.*
2. Cooper, McGuire, Jones and Le Grand, 'Equity, Waiting Times and NHS Reforms', *BMJ* (2009).

Part 3. Future

Time and its Consequences
1 Held, *Cosmopolitan Democracy: An Agenda for a New World Order.*
2 King, *Losing Control: The Emerging Threats to Western Prosperity.*
3 Ibid., p. 45.
4 Hutton, *Them and Us,* p. 89.
5 http://www.ifs.org.uk/comms/comm118.pdf
6 https://www.education.gov.uk/publications/eOrderingDownload/00357-2009.pdf
7 Polly Toynbee, 'Big society isn't new, but the Tories are purging the past', *Guardian,* 21 May 2011.
8 Internet world statistics June 2001.

BIBLIOGRAPHY

Barber, Michael, *Instruction to Deliver: Tony Blair, Public Services and the Challenge of Achieving Targets* (London: Politico's Publishing, 2007)

Barnett, Steven, 'Media Manifesto', *Prospect*, 79 (October 2002)

Beer, S. H., *Modern British Politics* (London: Faber & Faber, 1982)

Benn, Tony, *Years of Hope: Diaries, Papers and Letters 1940–1962* (London: Hutchinson, 1994)

——, *Arguments for Socialism*, edited by Chris Mullin (London: Penguin, 1980)

Blair, Tony, *New Britain* (London: Fourth Estate, 1996)

Blumler, Jay G., and Kavanagh, Dennis, 'The Third Age of Political Communication: Influences and Features', *Political Communication*, vol. 16 (1999)

Butler, David, and Kavanagh, Dennis, *The British General Election of 1983* (London: Macmillan, 1984)

——, *The British General Election of 1987* (London: Macmillan, 1988)

——, *The British General Election of 1992* (London: Macmillan, 1992)

——, *The British General Election of 1997* (London: Macmillan, 1997)

Callaghan, James, *Time and Chance* (London: Collins, 1987)

Channon, Sir Henry (ed. Robert Rhodes James), *'Chips'. The Diaries of Sir Henry Channon* (London: Weidenfeld & Nicolson, 1967)

Cocks, Michael, *Labour and the Benn Factor* (London: Macdonald, 1989)

Cohen, Nick, *What's Left? How Liberals Lost Their Way* (London: Fourth Estate, 2007)

Cole, G. D. H., *A History of the Labour Party from 1914* (London: Routledge & Kegan Paul, 1948)

Colville, John, *The Fringes of Power: 10 Downing Street Diaries 1939–1955* (New York: Norton, 1986)

Cooper, Zachary N., McGuire, Alistair, Jones, S. and Le Grand,

Julian, 'Equity, Waiting Times and NHS Reforms: Retrospective Study', *British Medical Journal*, 339 (b3264) (2009)

Cooper, Zack, Gibbons, Stephen, Jones, Simon and McGuire, Alistair, 'Does Hospital Competition Save Lives?: Evidence from the English NHS Patient Choice Reforms', *Economic Journal*, vol. 121 issue 554 (August 2011)

Crewe, Ivor, 'How to Win a Landslide Without Really Trying: Why the Conservatives Won in 1983' (Colchester: University of Essex, 1984)

——, 'Labour Force Changes, Working-Class Decline and the Labour Vote: Social and Electoral Trends in Postwar Britain' in Frances Fox Piven (ed.), *Labour Parties in Post-Industrial Societies* (Oxford: Polity Press, 1992)

——, 'The Labour Party and the Electorate' in Dennis Kavanagh (ed.), *The Politics of the Labour Party* (London: Allen & Unwin, 1982)

Crick, Bernard, 'Britain's "Democratic Party"', *The Nation*, 10 December 1960

Crosland, Anthony, *The Future of Socialism* (London: Jonathan Cape, 1964)

Davies, A. J., *To Build a New Jerusalem* (London: Abacus, 1996)

de Crespigny, Anthony, and Minogue, Kenneth (eds), *Contemporary Political Philosophers* (London: Methuen, 1976)

Desmond, Shaw, *Labour: The Giant With the Feet of Clay* (London: Collins, 1921)

Dionne, E. J., Jr., *Why Americans Hate Politics* (New York: Simon & Schuster, 1991)

——, *They Only Look Dead* (New York: Simon & Schuster, 1996)

Disraeli, Benjamin, *Sybil, or, The Two Nations* (London: Penguin, 1980)

Drucker, H. M., *Doctrine and Ethos in the Labour Party* (London: Allen & Unwin, 1979)

Fielding, Steven, *Labour: Decline and Renewal* (London: Baseline Books, 1995)

Gladwell, Malcolm, *The Tipping Point: How Little Things Can Make a Big Difference* (London: Little, Brown, 2000)

Greenberg, Stanley B., 'Reconstructing the Democratic Vision', *The American Prospect*, No. 1, Spring 1990

——, *Middle-Class Dreams* (New Haven, CT: Yale University Press, 1996)

Greenberg, Stanley B., and Skocpol, Theda (eds), *The New Majority* (New Haven, CT: Yale University Press, 1996)

Greenleaf, W. H., *The British Political Tradition, Vol. 2: The Ideological Heritage* (London: Methuen, 1983)

Heath, A., Jowell, R. and Curtice, J. (eds), *Labour's Last Chance?* (London: Dartmouth, 1994)

Hegel, G. W. F., *Elements of the Philosophy of Right* (Cambridge: CUP, 1991)

——, *Encyclopedia of the Philosophical Sciences* (1781, 2nd edition 1787)

Held, David, *Cosmopolitan Democracy: An Agenda for a New World Order* (Cambridge: Polity, 1995)

Hobhouse, L. T., *Liberalism and Other Writings* (Cambridge: CUP, 1994)

Hughes, Colin, and Wintour, Patrick, *Labour Rebuilt* (London: Fourth Estate, 1990)

Hutton, Will, *Them and Us: Politics, Greed and Inequality* (London: Little, Brown, 2010)

Jay, Douglas, *The Socialist Case* (London: Faber & Faber, 1937)

Jefferys, Kevin, *The Labour Party Since 1945* (London: Macmillan, 1993)

Jenkins, Roy, *A Life at the Centre* (London: Macmillan, 1991)

Jones, Nicholas, *Campaign 1997* (London: Indigo, 1997)

Jones, Tudor, *Remaking the Labour Party* (London: Routledge & Kegan Paul, 1996)

Kavanagh, Dennis, *Election Campaigning* (Oxford: Blackwell, 1995)

—— (ed.), *The Politics of the Labour Party* (London: Allen & Unwin, 1982)

King, Stephen D., *Losing Control: The Emerging Threats to Western Prosperity* (New Haven: Yale University Press, 2010)

Labour Party, 'Labour and Britain in the 1990s' (London, 1988)

——, 'Meet the Challenge, Make the Change' (London, 1989)

——, 'New Life for Britain' (London, 1996)

——, 'Leading Britain into the Future' (London, 1997)

Machin, Stephen and Vernoit, James, *Changing School Autonomy: Academy Schools and their Introduction to England's Education* (CEE D P 123, 2011)

Marcuse, Herbert, *Reason and Revolution* (London: Routledge & Kegan Paul, 1941)

Marquand, David, *The Progressive Dilemma* (London: Heinemann, 1991)

Matalin, Mary, and Carville, James, *All's Fair* (London: Hutchinson, 1994)

Middlemas, Keith, *The Politics of Industrial Society* (London: André Deutsch, 1979)

Miliband, Ralph, *The State in Capitalist Society* (London: Quartet, 1977)

Minkin, Lewis, *The Labour Party Conference* (Manchester: Manchester University Press, 1980)

——, *The Contentious Alliance* (Edinburgh: Edinburgh University Press, 1991)

Nicolson, Harold (ed. Nigel Nicolson), *Harold Nicolson, Diaries and Letters, 1939–1945* (London: Collins, 1967)

Oakeshott, Michael, *Rationalism in Politics and Other Essays* (London: Methuen, 1962)

Orwell, George, *The Lion and the Unicorn: Socialism and the English Genius* (London: Searchlight Press, 1941)

Owen, David, *Time to Declare* (London: Michael Joseph, 1991)

Patel, Ketan, *The Master Strategist: Power, Purpose and Principle* (London: Hutchinson, 2005)

Pimlott, Ben, 'The Labour Left', in C. Cook and I. Taylor (eds), *The Labour Party* (London: Longman, 1980)

Rentoul, John, *Tony Blair* (London: Warner Books, 1997)

Richards, Steve, *Whatever it Takes: The Real Story of Gordon Brown and New Labour* (London: Fourth Estate, 2010)

Routledge, Paul, *Gordon Brown* (London: Simon & Schuster, 1998)

Scammell, Margaret, *Designer Politics* (New York: St Martin's Press, 1995)

Seldon, Anthony (ed.), *How Tory Governments Fall* (Oxford: OUP, 1994)

——, *Major* (London: Weidenfeld & Nicolson, 1997)

Seldon, Anthony, and Ball, Stuart (eds), *The Conservative Century* (Oxford: OUP, 1994)

Snow, C. P., *Corridors of Power* (London: Macmillan, 1964).

Sopel, Jon, *Tony Blair: The Moderniser* (London: Michael Joseph, 1995)

Sykes, Patricia, *Losing from the Inside* (Oxford: Transaction Books, 1988)

Wainwright, Hilary, *Labour: A Tale of Two Parties* (London: Hogarth Press, 1987)

Wertheimer, Egon, *Portrait of the Labour Party* (London: Putnam, 1929)

Westen, Drew, *The Political Brain: The Role of Emotion in Deciding the Fate of the Nation* (New York: Public Affairs Press, 2007)

Williams, G. L., and Williams, A. L., *Labour's Decline and the Social Democrats' Fall* (London: Macmillan, 1985)

Wright, Tony, and Carter, Matt, *The People's Party* (London: Thames & Hudson, 1997)

ACKNOWLEDGEMENTS

Volume I: 1985–1997

I would like to thank:

Catherine Needham, who has been the book's principal researcher. Employed to help me with the book, she ended up as the linchpin of my office. But she also found time to get into perfect order van-loads of my notes, memos and documents, as well as providing background research for the entire period. She was indispensable to the book.

Alice Miles, who helped me write and edit the book. She has an exceptional political mind and was able to make clear many of the complex issues that were confronted in the book. Just as important were her determination and commitment over many months. She drove the book forward. Without her it would never have been completed.

David Miliband and Peter Hyman for their time and kindness. Dennis Kavanagh, Stanley Greenberg, Clive Hollick, David Lipsey, Giles Radice and Patricia Hewitt, who provided advice and counsel. Ivor Crewe, for his analysis of the 1983 election, and John Rentoul, for allowing me access to his notes of the Blair period. Deborah Mattinson, who was there at the start.

All those I interviewed, including: Simon Buckby, Colin Byrne, Liam Byrne, Charles Clarke, David Hill, Neal Lawson, Ben Lucas, Margaret McDonagh, Adrian McMenamin, Jon Mendelsohn, Fiona Millar, Sally Morgan and Chris Powell.

Tristram Hunt, who provided much of the historical

research; Benjamin Wegg-Prosser, who brought together the team that made the book possible; Gordon Corera and Tom Dibble.

Andrew Gordon, for his patience, and Philippa Harrison, for her faith; and Liz Cowen, for her help with the final draft.

Everyone who worked on the 1997 election campaign, and the two campaigns before it.

Peter Mandelson and Alastair Campbell, who are friends as well as colleagues.

Tony Blair, Gordon Brown, Neil Kinnock, John Prescott and others in the Cabinet and previous shadow Cabinets who were not involved in this book, but who ultimately made it possible.

Finally, my family, who were part of this journey too. My children Grace and Georgia, who deserve better than a father who was absent fighting an election, and then was absent writing about it. They never complained and are the best kids in the world. My wife Gail, who has been with me through the many years when victory seemed unlikely, and my part in it less likely still. It is difficult to describe what she has had to put up with, impossible to describe how well she has coped. She gave me the confidence to start the book, the advice to get it right.

Volume II: 1997–2010

Thanks to:

Georgia, without whom this book literally would not have happened; Grace, who is a constant source of support and wit; and Gail who makes everything possible, while I try to do the opposite.

Alastair Campbell, Fiona Millar and Rory, Calum and Grace, who are such a big part of this journey and contributed so much.

Ed Victor, who is the perfect agent.

Matthew Freud, who I love working with and who helped with many of the ideas in this book. And everyone at Freud Communications, who have been so great and so understanding.

Gordon Brown, who is such a formidable politician and, with Sarah, so supportive.

Peter Mandelson, there at the beginning, there at the end, and New Labour all the time.

Peter Hyman, whose comments were as always brilliant.

My publishers Ursula Mackenzie, Tim Whiting and Zoe Gullen, who could not have been more considerate.

Patrick Loughran, who drove the book forward and did so much research for it.

Sally Morgan, who was always there in the tough times.

Anji Hunter, who is like no one else in politics, and that is a compliment.

Margaret McDonagh, who simply never gives up.

Jonathan Powell, who never lost his sense of humour.

David Miliband, who I have been talking with about this kind of thing for almost twenty years.

Ed Miliband, who I have campaigned with for so many years, and to whom I wish every success.

Douglas Alexander, who enjoys elections almost as much as I do, and thinks about politics as deeply as anybody.

Tessa Jowell, who was such a big part of this and a loyal friend.

Alan Milburn, who did such groundbreaking work on the NHS.

Stephen Badger, Antonio Lucio, David Kamenetzky and John Thornton for all their kindness and ideas.

James Purnell, who is such an original thinker.

Noreena Hertz, who helped me with the concepts developed in the book.

Andrew Adonis, who understands New Labour better than almost anyone.

Dennis Kavanagh, so much advice over the years.

Marianna Trian, who was such a fantastic support to me.

Pat McFadden, who is always good and best when the pressure is on.

Liz Lloyd, Ruth Turner, Matthew Taylor, Benjamin Wegg-Prosser and Phil Collins, who did so well in the later Blair years when they were in charge.

Tristram Hunt, who is still so kind.

Carol Linforth, who kept the 2010 campaign on the road and was my picture editor for this book.

Greg Cook, who is almost always right.

Jackie Stacey, Roy and Alicia Kennedy, Peter Watt, Ray Collins and everybody else at the Labour Party Headquarters through all these years.

Steve Van Riel, Simon Jackson and Tim Horton for their research.

Melanie Jones, who was such a support.

All those who helped but I have unfairly omitted to mention because I am often forgetting things, especially these days.

Tony Blair, for being the inspired political leader that he is, and for the support he, Cherie and their family have given me, and still do.

And of course to all those doctors, nurses and medical staff who have kept me going for as long as they have. They have been fantastic. Anything I earn from this this book will go to the National Oesophago-Gastric Cancer Fund.

INDEX